UNRAVELLING MODERN CHINA

UNRAVELLING MODERN CHINA

Haico Ebbers
Nyenrode Business University, The Netherlands

World Scientific

NEW JERSEY • LONDON • SINGAPORE • BEIJING • SHANGHAI • HONG KONG • TAIPEI • CHENNAI • TOKYO

Published by

World Scientific Publishing Co. Pte. Ltd.
5 Toh Tuck Link, Singapore 596224
USA office: 27 Warren Street, Suite 401-402, Hackensack, NJ 07601
UK office: 57 Shelton Street, Covent Garden, London WC2H 9HE

Library of Congress Cataloging-in-Publication Data
Names: Ebbers, H. A. (Hendrikus Andreas), 1961– author.
Title: Unravelling modern China / Haico Ebbers (Nyenrode Business University, The Netherlands & Renmin University, China).
Description: New Jersey : World Scientific, [2018] | Includes bibliographical references.
Identifiers: LCCN 2018026886 | ISBN 9789813200272 (hc : alk. paper)
Subjects: LCSH: Economic development--China. | China--Economic policy--2000– | China--Economic conditions--2000–
Classification: LCC HC427.95 .E25 2018 | DDC 330.951--dc23
LC record available at https://lccn.loc.gov/2018026886

British Library Cataloguing-in-Publication Data
A catalogue record for this book is available from the British Library.

ISBN 978-981-12-0472-2 (pbk)

For any available supplementary material, please visit
https://www.worldscientific.com/worldscibooks/10.1142/10285#t=suppl

Desk Editors: Anthony Alexander/Lixi Dong

Typeset by Stallion Press
Email: enquiries@stallionpress.com

Preface

The idea of writing a book on China's economic development and business context first came to my mind about two years ago. It was a logical extension of my active research in China for almost 25 years — to share the knowledge I have acquired with a bigger audience other than my students. However, three factors accelerated my motivation to write this book.

Firstly, I published my book *Internationale Bedrijfskunde en Globalisering* in 2016, in which globalisation in today's world was analysed. The conclusion I made was that we witness the end of western domination of the world economy and that we are entering the Asian century, in which China is the leading country. Thus, writing this book on China was a logical follow-up.

Secondly, from my teaching about China's role in the globalised world for so many years within and outside China, I felt more and more compelled to dispel the wrongly preconceived ideas that I often came up against at conferences, round-table discussions, class-sessions and radio interviews. Ideas and views that are based on generalisations and (only) anecdotic evidence. Many of the western China-experts, as well as the media, hold extremely negative and pessimistic views about China: negative in thinking that China's growth is unfair and at the expense of western countries; and pessimistic in thinking that China's economic development must decline, on the assumption that no further development in technology and democracy can be expected. Moreover, if official data about economic growth and investments are published, people usually would question the data reliability and suspect that the information is all fake.

Thirdly, I was piqued by an old article[1] from the *Los Angeles Times* which I received from one of my former students. In it, Mr Trump stated that he had read "hundreds of books about China" and that he "knows the Chinese [...] and made a lot of money with the Chinese". Even after 25 years of working in China and reading many books and articles, I still do not understand many of the political and socio-economic choices made by China in the past decades. Furthermore, by talking to western managers and entrepreneurs in China, I do not get the feeling that making money is easy. I studied the books that Mr Trump referred to, thinking they must be important to understanding China. It became clear to me that many books on China are one-sided in perspective. They suggest a confrontation between the west (US) and China and emphasise contesting instead of cooperating with China.

A one-sided book is relatively easy to write. One just needs to select some data and evidence which fit in your argument, and a straightforward analysis is achieved. Obviously, in this case, one must leave something out. I also could downsize the complexities about China's transformations, socio-economic choices, and policies. However, my aim is to write a book that is more neutral in analysis, balancing the pros and cons. Complete neutrality can never be fully achieved since every author is forced to make choices about which facts are to be used and which elements are to be left out of the analysis. Nevertheless, I try not to leave out important facts. The consequence is more than 500 pages of information.

A most surprising learning point for myself is that I have become less black and white but greyer in my views of China. I used to think that it was essential to clearly indicate whether the Chinese government was centralised or decentralised in organisation, or that there should be a clear answer to the question if China

[1]Later, it was discovered that this article was based on fabrication by a Chinese book-seller for his marketing campaign.

can be innovative. However, the picture is blurred. China's government is centralised and decentralised; China is both an innovator and a copycat; China is opening up and closing down, and it is a threat as well as a promise at the same time. Putting it like this, China is full of contradictions.

As you will see, every chapter starts with a myth on China based on a preconceived idea about the topic discussed in that chapter. The difference between what we think is true and what is actually true about China can be large, perhaps due to misinformation and because of the many contradictions in China. The misperception is sometimes driven by a western mindset. There is an urgent need to clarify some of the myths about China, such as the view that many of the reforms initiated after 1978 were part of a larger master plan initiated and guided by the top bureaucracy. Clearly, this is not the case. Most of the reforms actually came from local initiatives. Every single chapter, hopefully, will clarify or debunk the myth that is stated at the start of the chapter.

My book aims to attract two groups of people: the specialist with vast experience working in China; and the layman who knows almost nothing about the country's economy, history and political structure. Hopefully, the specialists will gain new and interesting insights despite their knowledge, while the laymen can get an overview to understand China better despite its complexities. This book contains a broad range of topics not just about history and economics. It also refers to the business environment in which western companies must operate. In addition, it analyses the interconnections between (and within) the social and political context, and China's role in the globalised world today and in the future. The breadth and depth of this book is what differentiates it from many other books.

This book is divided into three parts and nineteen chapters. The first part explains economic success after the start of the opening up in 1978. Obviously, the success came with some negative side-effects (imbalances). As we will see, the increasing intensity of imbalances after 2010 resulted in a sense of urgency to take action on the part of the policy-makers. The second part analyses the main challenges in the medium term which goes beyond economics; it relates also to social and political issues. Continuation of economic growth today is important, but there are many aspects that need to be addressed, such as income inequality, environmental issues, migrant issues and building up a social safety net. These are topics discussed in the middle part of the book. The third part of the book takes a more business-oriented perspective. It discusses the fast-changing business environment; and related to this, the (new) environment in which international operating companies must survive. A substantial part is allocated to the question of how to connect to the Chinese middle class. Best practices will be discussed, and I will build an eclectic framework to structure the main success and failure factors of conducting business on the Chinese consumer market. Besides focusing on western companies in China, the third part of the book will also discuss China's integration into the world economy through Chinese companies going abroad. Finally, Chapter 19 is about China's future role in the globalised world.

"Noodle bowl" of reforms

This book will convey what an enormous task the Chinese policy-makers are facing: transforming the economy as well as the whole society. This task is difficult because, on the one hand, there are many transformations. On the other hand, all the required reforms are linked to each other. If the government wants to reduce income inequality, increase enrolment in the educational system, and increase the attainment of primary and secondary educational levels, it must give the 300 million urban migrant workers more rights, including social security, public housing and education, in the same way as enjoyed by full urban citizens. However, this will have dramatic consequences on the urbanisation process and housing supply. And it will certainly increase government spending, when there is already a large national debt. Reforming state-owned enterprises is needed to increase productivity, but it results in short-term unemployment and also hurts consumption. It may also affect the profitability of the state banks. And because of this, financial liberalisation is dangerous". Every element in the reform-agenda is related to each other. In that sense, it is remarkable that despite the massive changes that happened in China in the past decades, it did not result in economic and political chaos. This is what Joseph Stiglitz had in mind when he stated that if a Nobel Prize in Economics were to be given to a government, then the Chinese government would deserve it.

An optimistic view

I participated in many conferences on China in the 1990s and felt quite alone in my viewpoint: I was optimistic about China while so many of my colleagues had an opposite view. They believed that China could not continue its growth rates much longer due to the lack of fundamental reform both economically and politically. I am still visiting conferences and roundtable meetings on China today and I sense the same discussions and views on China today as 20 years ago. Again, many scholars are pessimistic on China's economic development for the same reasons as two decades ago: China's economic development will come to its end due to institutional barriers, industrial overcapacity, local government debt, risky balance sheets of banks, and the Chinese Communist Party that only wants to keep control and postponing necessary reforms.

After reading this book, it will become clear that I am quite optimistic about China's economic and non-economic transformations: my belief is that the rise of China is here to stay. Due to its size, China's development should be seen as a major factor that shapes this century. It does not mean that China will take over world economics and build a new world order. I do not agree with the view that China's development will be the end of the western world order as concluded by Martin Jacques (2012), but I am sure the impact will go much further than concluded by David Shambaugh (2013), who said that China will only be a regional power. An important assumption in the analysis throughout this book is that China needs the west and its institutions, in the same way that the west needs China.

Despite my 25 years of experience, 100 plus visits to China and my passion about China, I have failed to master Chinese. As an economist, I think in terms of opportunity cost. I am bad at learning languages, so I can either spend two hours a day reading Chinese economic and business papers or studying Mandarin. I thought it would be better to concentrate on reading and writing instead of learning a very difficult language. It means that this book is based on English publications and English newspapers available in China. However, it is supported by extensive discussions with experts, specialists, bureaucrats, consumers and Chinese students. Through this book, I hope that I have succeeded in its ultimate goal — to analyse and decouple a chaotic Picasso masterpiece into a clear and understandable picture.

My thanks go to my editors: San San Heng and Anthony Alexander for their help, accuracy, suggestions and patience, and to my students in China, Dubai, Singapore, the Netherlands and the United Kingdom for their inputs in the China-discussions in the past years. Special thanks go to Jeroen van den Brandhof for his help in designing and constructing the figures. As always, many thanks to Rinske for giving me the time and space to work on another project again.

Contents

Preface v
Overview: Five Words That Characterise China xvii

Part I: The Main Economic and Political Choices **1**

Chapter 1 Interpretation of China's Data **3**

1.1 Introduction 3
1.2 A critical assessment of China's GDP 6
1.3 Reflection on the statistical issues 13
1.4 Conclusions about reliability of Chinese data 16

Chapter 2 China's Economic Development and Political Choices Before 1978 **19**

2.1 Introduction 19
2.2 The Chinese economy before the 1949 Communist Revolution 20
2.3 1949–1978 government-led industrialisation 31
2.4 Main drivers behind the choices 37
2.5 The picture at the end of the 1970s 40

Chapter 3 China's Early Reforms (1978–1993) and the Building Up of Imbalances **43**

3.1 Introduction 43
3.2 The start of the reforms 44

3.3 The key choices in the early-reform period 47
3.4 The picture in the mid-1990s — reforms without losers 56

Chapter 4 Explaining Economic Development between 1993 and 2007 59

4.1 Introduction 59
4.2 Explaining economic development 60
4.3 Chinese characteristics in the standard growth theory 67
4.4 The business cycle between 1978 and 2007 70

Chapter 5 The Imbalanced Economy between 2007 and 2017 75

5.1 Introduction 75
5.2 The most important imbalances 76
5.3 Middle-income trap 92
5.4 Rebalancing process — today's picture 96
5.5 Latest developments in the rebalancing process 105

Chapter 6 China's Political Structure 113

6.1 Introduction 113
6.2 Governance structure in China 114
6.3 The main features of China's political system 121
6.4 The role of the local governments 126
6.5 Democracy with Chinese characteristics 128
6.6 State-owned enterprises 138

Chapter 7 The Role and Development of the Five-Year Plans 145

7.1 Introduction 145
7.2 The planned economy and the role of the five-year plan 146
7.3 The five-year plans: The process 149
7.4 The 11th, 12th and 13th five-year plans 153
7.5 The importance of the plenum sessions 158

Part II: The Main Challenges Ahead **167**

Chapter 8 Income Inequality **169**

8.1 Introduction 169
8.2 The measurement of inequality 170
8.3 China's income inequality: A historical overview 175
8.4 Rural versus urban income inequality 178
8.5 Government policy to reduce income inequality 181

Chapter 9 *Hukou* System and Urbanisation **187**

9.1 Introduction 187
9.2 A brief history of the *hukou* system 188
9.3 Urbanisation and the *hukou* system: Intertwined challenges 197
9.4 The development of China's urbanisation rate 199
9.5 Urbanisation and economic development 200
9.6 New-style urbanisation announced in 2014 205

Chapter 10 China's Export Picture **209**

10.1 Introduction 209
10.2 China's export-led growth model and the China price 211
10.3 Main features of China's international trade 214
10.4 Importance of export for China's economic development 218
10.5 Structure of Chinese export 224
10.6 The challenges ahead: From made by China to design in China 226

Chapter 11 Family Planning Policy, Ageing and Developments on the Labour Market **231**

11.1 Introduction 231
11.2 Family planning between 1950 and 1979: The period of voluntary planning 233
11.3 Family planning between 1980 and 2016 234
11.4 Ageing and the one-child policy 239
11.5 Labour shortage 244

Chapter 12 Fiscal and Monetary Policy to Fine-tune the Economy **251**

12.1 Introduction 251
12.2 Main features of China's fiscal policy 253
12.3 Fiscal policy after 2008 255
12.4 The debt picture 260
12.5 Monetary policy 263
12.6 Key issues of the financial sector and the role of banks 266
12.7 Interest rate policy and steps towards liberalisation 271

Chapter 13 The Exchange Rate: Policy and Development **275**

13.1 Introduction 275
13.2 History of the exchange rate system 277
13.3 Floating versus fixed exchange rate system 281

Chapter 14 Consumption and Savings in China **293**

14.1 Introduction 293
14.2 China's consumption and savings rate: The general picture 294
14.3 Decoupling the aggregate savings 300
14.4 Explaining China's household consumption and savings habit 305
14.5 Clustering the reasons behind China's high savings rate 307
14.6 Policies to increase consumption and rebalance the economy 311

Part III: China's Integration in the World Economy **317**

Chapter 15 Theories on FDI **319**

15.1 Introduction 319
15.2 Theories on FDI 321
15.3 China's FDI inflow 331

15.4 FDI outflow 340
15.5 The new neighbours 350
15.6 Success factors of Chinese companies 357

Chapter 16 The Business Context in China 363

16.1 Introduction 363
16.2 Confucianism and the business context 365
16.3 The Chinese middle class 373
16.4 Ease of Doing Business 380

Chapter 17 Success and Failure Factors in Conducting Business in China 385

17.1 Introduction 385
17.2 Failure factors of operating in China 387
17.3 Success factors for conducting business in China 413
17.4 The Chinese government as a success factor 435
17.5 Gradual steps and learning from experience 441

Chapter 18 China and the World 447

18.1 Introduction 447
18.2 Globalisation: A broad perspective 451
18.3 Economic globalisation 456
18.4 Political integration: Multilateralism or regionalism 462
18.5 Social and cultural integration: Hard and soft power 471

Chapter 19 The Future of Globalisation and the Role of China 477

19.1 Introduction 477
19.2 Scenarios 479
19.3 China's future 488
19.4 China's perspective on globalisation and its institutions 494
19.5 The future of globalisation and the role of China 499

References 509
Index 531

Overview

Five Words That Characterise China

China's economic growth and its accelerated integration in the world economy is one of the truly world-changing economic events of the last four decades, and the most important economic megatrend of our age. Who would have predicted that, after the dead of Mao Zedong in 1976, China would have the highest growth rate in the world over a period of almost 40 years? And that it would be an economic superpower within this time frame? Clearly, this came as a surprise. I still remember the general feeling towards China when I participated in conferences about China's development and future in the early 1990s. Most topics were related to the disadvantages of central planning, the low productivity, social chaos and poorness. The consensus was that China's development would come to an abrupt end if the political context would not change. But see what is happening today — the Chinese Communist Party (CCP) is still in power and China has witnessed its strongest growth over an exceptionally long period.

China integrated rapidly into the globalised world. One only has to look at its share in world exports or in global investment flows. For example, China's share in world exports increased from 2% in 1980 to 15% in 2017 (WB database). The development of China and the transformations that happened in other emerging markets across the world have resulted in a world in which the west is not the dominating factor anymore. The world is changing towards an "emerging markets" century (even though the century has hardly begun) and, more specifically, towards an Asian century in which China plays the leading role. One may say that we have reached the end of the era of western domination of world history. Of course, this does not mean that it is the end of the west; the west will stay the most prosperous region of the world for a long time to come, but the western countries cannot dominate the world as they did in the past 70 years after World War II.

Moreover, we see the rise (or better: the return) of Asia and the renaissance of Asian societies. It is logical to refer to "the return of Asia" instead of "the rise of Asia" because from the year 200 BC to AD 1800, China was the largest economy in the world (followed by India). So, what is happening today is a return to the norm that existed before AD 1800 (Mahbubani, 2008, based on Maddison, 2003). The importance of China is also visible in China's growing share in the turnover of international operating companies. Global companies such as Unilever, Philips, Apple and Wal-Mart are more and more dependent on the Chinese consumers. Likewise, in the past decade, the small- and medium-sized companies were able to find the Chinese middle class. The emergence of the new global middle class (of which China has an overwhelming share) is creating an enormous potential market. In many boardrooms of companies, small and big, the main question is how to connect to this new consumer.

The impact of China's development cannot be underestimated. Although extrapolation of a trend is not always accurate over a longer term, the impact of China on other countries in economic, social, technological, financial and cultural terms can potentially be enormous. It may be larger than what we saw in the United Kingdom and the United States during their takeoffs. The Industrial Revolution in England (and other parts of the UK) that started in the mid-1700s resulted in a strong increase of welfare. In the UK, real income of the 17 million people doubled between 1760 and 1840. The same happened in the US. During its economic revolution, annual growth of 2% was achieved between 1870 and 1929 (Clark, 2005). The combination of a large population (120 million in 1929) and its relatively high economic growth resulted in a massive shift of economic power. The US became the dominant economic world power in the 1920s. These are impressive figures but they are dwarfed when looking at the Chinese context.

The consensus is that China will grow at a speed of around 4% or 5% in the next thirty years or so. Coupled with a population of around one billion that is active in the market economy, imagine what the impact will be — China is experiencing roughly three times the economic acceleration of the economic revolution in the US at eight times the scale. This certainly will result in a visible and dramatic changing economic landscape that must be followed by changes in the global governance structure. Of course, the intensity of the impact depends on many factors. Technological change, innovation and productivity are the main factors that drive the changes in the longer term and we may question China's capability in these aspects. Maybe growth will be 3% or 2%, but just based on its scale, the impact will be quite staggering (as we will see throughout this book).

The first part explains the economic development of China and clarifies its economic and political choices throughout the past 40 years. In the second part, the focus is on the medium-term challenges lying ahead. The third part will focus on how to conduct businesses in China and how to compete with Chinese firms on "third markets". To give an eclectic picture is an almost impossible task because of the many facets that drive economic and business development. Think about the many non-economic factors such as institutions (e.g. *hukou*), politics (e.g. role of the local government) and social-cultural features (e.g. *guanxi*) in the Chinese context. Therefore, it is extremely difficult to draw a comprehensive picture of China's development and its economic and business context in one single book of merely 500 pages.

Naturally, I have had to simplify a great deal, making this book an easy target of dissent for specialists in the specific fields. My focus is on the bigger picture; the main structural developments and socio-economic choices. China is changing so fast that too much focus on details will blur the view on the medium- and longer-term structural trend. Consequently, the focus of my book is to deliver a "stable" thinking framework (akin to creating a sort of skeleton) that makes it possible to focus on the bigger picture instead of the many (often opposite) cyclical, pragmatic and short-term developments and decisions. I think that this longer-term focus is the only way to navigate through what I call the "troubled waters" of Chinese economic and business context.

Getting the real picture is quite complicated. We may see so many pedestrians (sometimes with animals) and vehicles of every imaginable kind in the rural areas, yet at the same time a black Audi with darkened windows and an Apple-user driver is passing by. It is 60 years of history compressed into one place in a single moment of time. Both images are real, making interpretation what is happening more difficult. When teaching about China's economy, culture, and business context, I always start with the following five words that characterise my views about China:

- Contradictions
- Speed
- Misconceptions
- Numbers
- Interpretation

Clearly, these characteristics are related and intertwined. China is full of contradictions. On the one hand, we see economic decentralisation; yet at the same time, it is a strongly centralised political structure. China's consumption is rising fast, but at the same time, we may say that China is under-consuming. These contradictions make it difficult to interpret the developments we observe and give room for misconceptions. Visiting only the cities of Beijing and Shanghai certainly will colour our views about China in general. Some western tourists and business people see China as better than it is, a misconception driven by visits to only the metropolitan cities. However, rural China is totally different from what we see in the largest cities. China's regional disparities in living standards (and associated problems) from booming Shanghai to impoverished Ningxia are enormous. The contrasts are the same as seen between developed and developing countries. We see liberalisation and market forces in certain sectors, while in other segments of the economy, the government is hesitating to implement reforms. This may blur the picture about the speed of change and again may affect preconceived ideas. China is about numbers: everything is big in China. This makes it necessary to watch out for risky ventures. The numbers make it necessary to follow a gradual, step-by-step approach because a small mistake can have enormous consequences due to the size of the country.

Contradictions

China is a country of contradictions. In general, China is at the same time both a developed country (based on its size of Gross Domestic Product) and a developing country (based on its GDP per capita in certain provinces). Part of the infrastructure in the coastal areas is first-class, while infrastructure in western parts can be labelled as "Third-country quality". Furthermore, China is centralised and decentralised at the same time. Another contradiction relates to market forces: China is clearly a private-led economy but at the same time it is state-led with a lot of government intervention in certain sectors. Below, I will introduce some of the contradictions that will be discussed in greater detail later in the book.

Firstly, China is, as we will see in Chapter 6, highly centralised in terms of political power and personal control, whereby the CCP (or party) is at the core. Yet, it is highly decentralised in terms of policy implementation and resource allocation as seen in the overwhelming role of local governments. Chapters 3 and 12 make clear that China's fiscal policy is extremely decentralised. From this perspective, we may argue that the institutional governance structure of China can be labelled as a regional decentralised bureaucratic system. For example, there is a lot of freedom for local bureaucrats to negotiate with western companies about location, taxation and preferences. In Chapter 17 where I discuss western companies in China, one key learning point is that it is preferable to negotiate with the local government instead of the central government.

An interesting side-effect of this decentralisation is that, in many cases, initiatives and micro-reforms started in certain local settings before it was taken over by the central government. The real reforms happen outside the central government and are only formalised afterwards, as we will see in Chapters 3 and 4.

Secondly, it is accurate to describe China as both a market-driven (or private-led) and government-driven (or state-led) economy. China has a large and fast-growing private sector that makes up most of the output and employment today. Private companies make up almost 90% of the total urban workforce, and more than 75% of the GDP is being produced by private companies at the start of 2017 (National Bureau of Statistics Data). In spite of the statistical difference between private companies and state-owned enterprises (SOEs), the distinction between them is not straightforward in China. For example, the Bank of Beijing is run as a SOE although only 20% of the assets are in state hands. Huawei is clearly a private company, but at the same time, the party is involved in strategic decisions. There are numerous foreign companies producing and operating in China. In 2016, around 45% of total Chinese exports was contributed by these foreign companies (often in cooperation with local partners).

The private sector's contribution is extremely large, accounting for more than 90% of Chinese exports (Eckart, 2016). However, private companies are, on average, small. Most of the largest companies in China are still state-owned and these SOEs dominate many heavy industry and several service sectors. Despite the reforms of SOEs (Chapter 6) that started in the mid-1990s, China today has a large state sector: large relative to GDP, and large compared to other major economies. Although the economic dominance of SOEs rapidly declined in the past decades, SOEs are often used as instruments of macroeconomic policy. As a result, the power and importance of SOEs are much greater than implied by economic statistics alone. The picture on China's openness is also full of contradictions. One the one hand, as we will see in Chapter 15, China is very open in the field of international trade and foreign direct investments (FDI). The economic success is partly driven by this openness and integration into the world economy. However, at the same time, China's economy can be labelled as "state capitalism", in which the government is initiating, guiding and intervening in the economy through industrial policies and interventions to help and protect the large SOEs from international competition.

Another example of contradiction relates to China's consumption. Statistically, China's consumption is extremely low compared to other countries. It stands only at 40% of China's GDP (World Bank, 2016). However, this "low" figure does not indicate that consumption is weak; in fact, it is quite strong. Chapter 14 will show that consumption spending grew by double digits in the past two decades. However, due to the enormous increase in government and private investments, total investment spending grew even faster than consumption spending, resulting in a falling share of consumption in GDP from the early 1990s onwards. These examples make clear the ambidextrous nature of China: low cost and high-cost, traditional and innovative, low value-added and high value-added products, opening up and closing down, private-led and state-led, western and local, centralised and decentralised, understandable and unclear, and logical and irrational at the same time.

Speed

When I visited Shanghai for the first time to teach international MBA students at the China Europe International Business School (CEIBS) in 1993, the eastern part of Shanghai was hardly developed. When CEIBS moved to the new campus in Pudong in 1999, farmers were looking through the windows to find out what these foreigners were doing in that new building. Even at the end of the 1990s, Pudong was partly farmland. Now after 25 years, Pudong has a Hong Kong skyline and is one of the main growth zones in the country.

Changes in rural China are also dramatic. During my first visit to the country in 1986, most people in the streets of Kunming were dressed in the blue Mao suits; they worked on the land or at SOEs, and had their social lives totally connected to the family and the company in which they worked. This picture is mostly gone and China, even in the more remote areas, has transformed into a capitalist society — "capitalist with Chinese characteristics"[2] (as we will see throughout the book).

To get a feeling about the speed of change, look at Fig. 1. The upper circle shows the total GDP from 1946 to 2016, divided into pre-reform and post-reform periods, by the year 1978, which was the start of the reforms initiated by Deng Xiaoping. It is striking that up to 2016, only 1% of total GDP was produced in the 33 years before reforms started.

In the lower circle, the period between 1979 and 2016 is split into two sub-periods; pre- and post-World Trade Organisation (WTO) entry in 2001. As shown, 68% of the total GDP between 1979 and 2016 was generated within the previous 15 years.

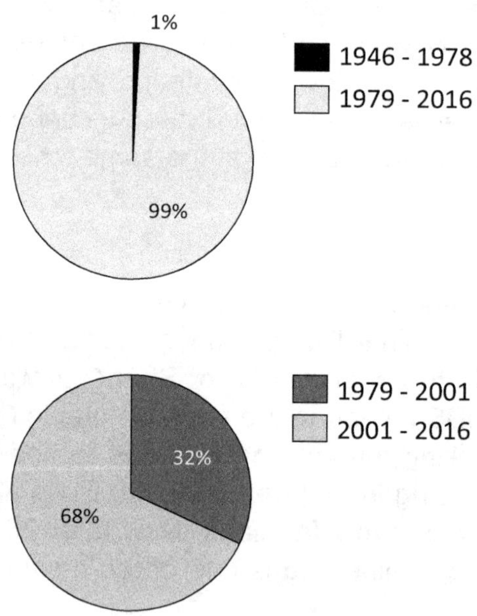

Figure 1 China's economic development (total GDP) between 1946 and 2016
Source: Based on AXA IM Research & author's calculation (IMF figures)

[2]This is the phrase used by Chinese policymakers, to indicate that China will stay Chinese despite modernisation.

Obviously, economic development in China is a very new phenomenon.

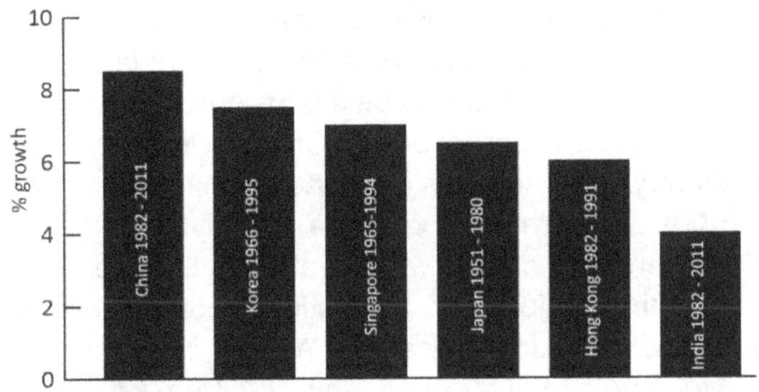

Figure 2 China's GDP growth compared to other countries

Source: Based on AXA IM Research & author's calculation (IMF figures)

Figure 2 shows that China's economic development is not unique. Economic growth in China was more than 8% between 1982 and 2011. Other Asian countries also witnessed a similar long period of high economic growth. For example, annual growth in South Korea was almost 8% between 1966 and 1995. The average annual growth in Singapore was 7% between 1965 and 1994. In this sense, China is not unique. This is an important learning point and is repeated throughout the book. Developments with respect to inequality (Chapter 8), urbanisation (Chapter 9) and imbalances in China's economy (Chapter 5) are, to some extent, in line with what happened in other Asian countries.

In the mid-1980s, China was a low-income country. Its income per capita (measured in purchasing power parity) was 30% lower than Sub-Saharan Africa's average (World Bank, 2016). However, between 1982 and 2011, the Chinese economy was doubling every eight years. Today, China is an upper-middle income country with per capita income many times higher than the average of Sub-Saharan Africa. China's GDP overtook that of the UK in 2005 and of Japan in 2010. Presently (early 2017), it is almost five times larger than the UK's and more than three times Japan's. This is based on nominal GDP. In terms of purchasing power parity, China's economy is even 10 times larger than the UK's (World Bank, 2016).

Another example of the speed of change concerns the attitude and strategy of western companies towards China. In the 1990s and early 2000s, western companies considered China as the biggest production base for exports. China was only seen as a low-cost country. This view has changed dramatically. Starting from the mid-2000s, western multinationals perceived China more and more as an interesting market with great potential. We may say that the overwhelming majority of international companies feel today that China (and its middle class) is the most important market for their surviving and global success. This shift from low-cost destination to (potential) market happened within a 15-year time span — quite a short time frame for international operating companies. It means that companies that are looking for low labour (and production) costs are moving to other countries such as Myanmar, Mexico and Vietnam.

For example, in 2001, 40% of Nike's global sports shoes output was produced in China. Due to increases in Chinese wages, Vietnam became the largest production base of Nike in 2016. In 2015, Nike closed its final production site in China. The same pattern applies to Panasonic. It stopped all its manufacturing of televisions in China in 2015. Both cases show clearly that low-value-added manufacturing activities are leaving China. Of course, increasing wages and large companies leaving the country may result in some uncertainty and unemployment, but be aware of the fact that this development is not bad per se. In fact, we will see in Chapter 7 that it is the purpose of the Chinese authorities to increase wages step by step to create a domestic market instead of depending too much on low-value-added export.

What also changed is the visibility of Chinese companies and their brands in the western world. When I asked my students to give me one or two names of Chinese companies a decade ago, I would not get an answer. Chinese companies were unknown in the west, although they already produced the products for well-known companies such as Philips, IBM, GE and Whirlpool. Today, already some names have made inroads to the west and western consumers. Names like Huawei, Lenovo and Alibaba are well-known brands in the west; and within a short time span, companies such as Xiaomi, Baidu, Zhong An Insurance and Tencent will follow. In Chapter 15, I will give an overview of Chinese companies, still unknown to the public in the west, but ready to go international with their own brands and strong enough to compete globally.

Furthermore, China's investments abroad are already much higher and more high-profile than we may think. I am driving my Volvo car which is owned by China-based Geely. Geely is also owner of the London Taxi Company. The China Investment Corporation has a 10% stake in Heathrow Airport Holdings, which owns Heathrow and Stansted, as well as regional airports in the UK. It also has a 9% stake in Thames Water Utilities, which supplies London's water. So, the message is clear: Chinese firms (state-owned and private) are more and more active abroad.

We may question how governments, companies and citizens can handle this speed of change in China. It is quite difficult for all entities in the society to change their value systems, socio-economic choices, and actions so many times in such a short span of time. The result, not surprisingly, is a highly developed pragmatism and flexibility. These terms will be used many times when discussing the Chinese government, companies and consumers. Without this attitude, it would be quite impossible to cope with such rapid change.

Misconceptions

My first visit to China was impressive. In 1986, individual travelling was hardly possible: infrastructure was inadequate, provincial borders made it difficult to move from one province to another, and an English-speaking person was, to most Chinese, an alien from a different planet. Even the visit to the Great Wall was problematic with dirty roads and walking and climbing extensively before reaching the beautiful scenery. Furthermore, travelling in the

1980s was difficult because the people working in restaurants, hotels and bus companies grew up during the Cultural Revolution (1966–1976) with heavy emphasis on ideology. Part of this ideology emphasised the bad behaviour of foreign countries in the 19th century. The result was an extremely negative attitude towards foreigners — the same attitude towards foreigners that occupied China during the century of humiliation (Chapter 2). This was the picture I had in mind when visiting Shanghai in 1993. CEIBS had asked me to teach international trade at the campus in Minhang, which was a partly rural district in Shanghai far away from the city centre at that time. It had a village atmosphere; during the weekend, the faculty moved to the city centre to stay in one of the few western hotels. My first visit to the city centre was shocking: leaving the metro station, I was amazed at how dynamic and western that part of Shanghai was. It was in such strong contradiction to my preconceived ideas. Visiting Kunming in Yunnan province can give us a very different perspective of China compared to visiting Shanghai. This comes back to the point discussed above that China is a country of contradictions. Shanghai is as much China as is the Yunnan rural region.

The perceived ideas or misconceptions about China are driven by a combination of stereotyping and ethnocentrism. Logically, journalists are also affected by this stereotyping and ethnocentrism; the further their distance (culturally, psychologically and physically) is from China, the worse the economy and society look to them, particularly when they are in China for a short period of time. The longer their stay, the less black and white, and the greyer, they see China. This is what I observed when going through western written articles on China. In many cases, they over-emphasise the negative news and downsize the positive signs. For example, this has been the case with respect to the fall in economic growth to 6.5% in 2017. Looking at China's economic growth today, obviously, there is lower growth than in the previous decade, but the fall in growth is not negative *per se*. The fall in growth is partly the result of implementing reforms that are needed to sustain economic development in the longer term.

Reducing overcapacity will reduce production in the short term but is a necessary step to rebalance the economy in the longer term. While the media, in many cases, is focusing on the negative short-term effect, the longer-term positive effect should not be forgotten. The same holds for the quarterly figures on industrial output. Undoubtedly, we can see a fall in industrial output growth in the past years, but today's economic driver in China is the service sector. The impressive growth in this sector hardly received any attention from the media during the global financial and economic crisis; the media only emphasised the problems in the manufacturing sector.

Another example of emphasising the negative side of what happened in China is the western view on the Chinese mini-stimulus program of 2014. The Chinese government announced in April 2014 that government spending was increased to stimulate the economy. There was heavy criticism because the increased spending was seen as "easy money" for local governments and SOEs, as happened in the 2008 stimulus program. In 2008, the government increased spending a lot to help local governments and SOEs even though they were unable to compete, thereby creating imbalances in the economy. Based on the 2008 experience, the media (and specialists) saw the 2014 government intervention as proof that the Chinese government deserted from the willingness to reform and continued to keep the economy afloat by government help.

However, we can also look at this stimulus package from a different point of view. For example, the package was fine-tuned to high-tech sectors with subsidies on battery cars and solar panels. Furthermore, there was the announcement of reducing overcapacity in certain heavy industry sectors. The measures, such as the elimination of 27 million tons of steel and 42 million tons of cement, were quite concrete. Listing such specific targets for a given year indicates the government's determination to eliminate this overcapacity. Furthermore, it was just a mini-stimulus package instead of a large government intervention as introduced in 2008–2009. I certainly would not label this government intervention as contradiction to medium- and longer-term reforms. It is not a step-back structural reform but can be seen as a logical step to act as crisis manager to help short-term economic development, while at the same time staying on track for the needed structural adaptation. This is an important learning point: sometimes, it is necessary to intervene in the short term to be able to continue the longer-term structural reforms.

Preconceived ideas are shaped by experiences. Western experts and journalists after 2008 were heavily influenced by what had happened in the US-housing market. Consequently, they directly linked a problem in the real estate sector to an economic slowdown. This also happened in China: in 2011, many experts forecasted a collapse of the real estate prices because of the housing bubble in 2010–2011, which would have heavy consequences for the economy as a whole. Already in 2011, I made it clear that looking at the Chinese context, this dramatic impact on the economy was not to be expected (Ebbers & Zhang, 2011) because the Chinese government would have enough power and would be capable of using different measures to fine-tune the sector if needed. This was complemented by a positive view on (private) household debt. Households are using mostly cash when buying apartments; and if loans are needed, mortgages are relatively small as a percentage of the value of the asset. Consequently, there is no need to fear that owners must sell their houses due to the fall in prices, as seen in the US in 2008 and 2009.

Ethnocentrism can also be seen with respect to issues such as corruption. One may question whether the fight against corruption is strong and systematic enough, but arguing *per se* that China must do more to fight corruption is a statement arising from a western mindset. If the authorities fight corruption too aggressively, there is a risk that government officials and SOE executives will delay decisions and approvals for fear of making a mistake or being caught in a future corruption investigation. This may hurt the society in the longer term. The anti-corruption campaign has led some officials already to take a wait-and-see attitude. The fight against corruption is a reform to the government itself and the vested interests. Such a process takes time. According to Li Keqiang: “This is not nail clipping. Instead, this is taking a knife to one's own flesh. [...] Pain is natural. However painful it may be, we are determined to keep going until our job is done." (CCTV, March 15, 2015 and published in *European Union Chamber of Commerce in China*, 2016). Clearly, fighting corruption is essential, but it should be analysed in the Chinese context.

In the west, it took many years before we changed the mentality on this. In certain European countries, corruption is still part of the institutional environment. Of course, there are real pressures to change, but the perception that corruption is bad, unethical and should be abolished in the short term once and for all is too narrow-minded. This is an important paradigm of this book: we should not always apply our western values of today to what is happening in China; it is better to analyse the development and to understand the socio-economic choices made by the authorities within the local context.

A final example in this overview about misconceptions relate to Chinese direct investments in Africa. Western media and politicians are nervous about China's investments in Africa. They see it as a new form of imperialism in Africa. Indeed, Chinese FDI from private firms and SOEs in Africa increased nine-fold between 2005 and 2015, to almost four billion dollars in early 2016 (MOFCOM Database). Anecdotic evidence can be found in Africa, such as the copper mines in Zambia, oil production in Angola, and large infrastructural investments in Ghana and Uganda. In some cases, we may question the impact on the local economy; or we may think about labour issues, environmental problems and land-ownership disputes. Furthermore, China's investments are complemented by formal aid projects and by "soft" development loans made through the Chinese EXIM bank. At the same time, we should not exaggerate Chinese investments. As we will see in Chapter 15, the total Chinese FDI to Africa constitutes less than 3% of all Chinese foreign investment globally between 2010 and 2016 (MOFCOM). Compared with total US investments in Africa, Chinese investments in Africa are extremely small. "Chinese companies (private and state-owned) are big investors in Africa if we look at the flow of FDIs in the previous years. At the same time, China is a small investor when taking the FDI stock concept into consideration. So, what is needed is to describe the development, analyse the data and compare the Chinese activities with a benchmark group; that is what we will do many times in this book, away from anecdotic evidence towards analysing with data.

Numbers

China is about numbers. The more than 1.3 billion people can be a burden but also an asset. It is a burden when multiplying any problem by China's population. Think about the ageing of the population and the need to develop and finance a nation-wide pension system. The enormous size of this future 60 or 65-plus cohort will become a substantial burden for China's future budget. Ageing of the population does not relate to 1 or 2 million such as in the Netherlands, but 200 to 300 million in the Chinese context. It is clear that a small change in legislation (e.g. an increase of pension benefits) will have dramatic repercussions with respect to government finance, income inequality and consumption (Chapter 12). The same holds for the financial and social consequences of increasing urbanisation. Chapter 9 discusses the rise of urbanisation and also emphasises the pressure of big numbers. The urban population is expected to increase from 640 million in 2015 to 950 million in 2025 (Jacques, 2012); this increase of 310 million is larger than the entire population of the US today. It means that there is a need to accommodate an urban population growing at 16 million annually; a new city with population equal in size to the Netherlands every year for the next decade. Just imagine the enormous task of catering to this additional urban population in terms of housing, healthcare, education and infrastructure. This is the scenario based on official urbanisation figures. The situation becomes even more drastic if the "illegal" migrant workers without urban *hukou* are taken into consideration. Numbers are also staggering when discussing the labour market. Rationalising and closing down companies in the heavy industry automatically will make millions of workers unemployed. What is happening in China always happens in big numbers and with potentially big problems.

On the other hand, the size of the population can also be an asset. The early economic development of China can partly be explained by the surplus of labour. The enormous supply of cheap labour, combined with a low value of China's currency, was the reason for China's export success (the topic we will discuss in Chapters 4, 10 and 13). Big numbers also relate to the explosion of China's middle class. China's middle-class population is bigger than the middle-class cohort of Germany, France, Spain and the UK combined (Credit Suisse, 2015). Of course, they earn less compared to their peers in mature economies, but much more than what we would expect in terms of purchasing power. Besides, its sheer size makes the Chinese market attractive.

Numbers also relate to how fast we may upscale activities in China. In the song *Nine Million Bicycles* by Katie Melua, this was the number of bicycles in Beijing in 2008. At that time, these bikes were owned by people. These bikes disappeared from the streets rapidly and cars took over, until Ofo introduced the rental bike in China. It became a big hit and other companies such as Mobike followed. Within a year, Beijing was congested by this new type of bicycles; shared bikes became part of a new emerging shared-economy. The number indicated in Katie Melua's song is still right but the whole ownership structure has changed from private ownership towards shared ownership. The potential speed of scaling up is enormous in China.

Another issue regarding numbers relate to reliability. Are the numbers published by Chinese authorities (and western organisations) correct? This is the main focus of Chapter 1. There are respected experts who conclude that China's economic success is just fantasy. They argue that the statistics are false. That economic growth is much lower than shown by official statistics and that we are witnessing a gigantic investment bubble, with much higher unemployment than official figures suggest, as well as much more bad debt than formally indicated in the books of the banking sector. According to this group of experts, this situation must explode. I do not agree with this negative view. No doubt, there has been a fall in economic growth that started some years ago. Certainly, there are segments in the economy that are being hit by this lower growth, including negative impact on the labour market and increasing bad loans.

However, from a macro-economic perspective, we are witnessing a "new normal" — a situation of sustainable growth of 4–5% instead of the ridiculous situation of double-digit growth in GDP. This is logical; we cannot expect a middle-income country to grow continuously by more than 10%. China today does not give us the feeling of a country in recession; the economic achievements are too obvious to be imaginary. Furthermore, whether we see 5%, 6% or 7% growth today does not matter so much; the absolute annual increase today is larger than the more than 10% growth in 2007. Too often, we lose sight of the absolute scale of China's economy in debates over a point up or down of growth.

Interpretation

An example to show that interpretation is complex is the question whether China is opening up to the outside world. In many publications, China is seen as copying the so-called "Asian Tigers": Hong Kong, Taiwan, Singapore and South Korea, who were able to generate the economic miracle because of their openness to trade in the 1980s. In the well-known report of the World Bank, *The Asian Miracle* (1994), these Asian tigers were positioned as globalisers or countries which integrated into the world economy. Because of this openness, they could achieve high economic growth. The same can be said of China: in terms of international trade and FDI, it can be labelled as being very open to the outside world. However, we know that the (local) government is intervening heavily in certain sectors. Consequently, in many aspects, China is not open at all and may be described as state capitalism with strong government intervention. Helping specific industries and companies with preferences, and creating external barriers. Hence,

China is open with respect to trade and investments; at the same time, it is closing several sectors in terms of foreign ownership and competition.

The state or central government can be very pro-active yet guide the economy from a distance and not intervene in local (and private) initiatives. Interpretation about the role of the government (and consequently, about the role of the market) is therefore difficult. This became very visible during the 2013–2017 period. On the one hand, there are signs that the policy is to give the market a more prominent role. This can be seen in the publications of the third plenum of the Party Congress in November 2013. It is clearly stated that market forces must play a "decisive" role in the economy (Communiqué of the Third Plenary Session, 2013). In former documents, market forces were labelled as "important" or even labelled as having a basic role. However, in 2015 documents, the role of the state was again emphasised; it was stressed that the state sector should have a "dominant" role in the economy. Obviously, this contradicts the decisive role of market forces and makes interpretation difficult. How do we interpret the contradicting announcements and what is the effect on future rebalancing measures?

The same interpretation problem holds for the so-called Purchasing Managers Index (PMI), a leading indicator for future growth, that is published by the Chinese Statistical Bureau. The PMI is measuring every month how optimistic or pessimistic purchasing managers are. It is based on a questionnaire and consists of two sub-indicators — the manufacturing PMI and the non-manufacturing PMI (which includes services). A PMI of more than 50 indicates economic expansion, while a PMI lower than 50 indicates contraction of the economy. Besides the official PMI, there is the PMI published by the HSBC-bank.

Looking at the past trend, the manufacturing PMI fell steadily to around 46% at the end of 2016. However, this is only half the story. Over the same period, the non-manufacturing PMI always stood above 50%. The media normally focuses on the manufacturing PMI. That was logical when the manufacturing sector was the dominating sector in the Chinese economy, but it is problematic today. Focusing on manufacturing misses the structural change in the economy towards services. Moreover, even if the PMI is under the 50-point benchmark, the link to future growth is unclear. For example, the PMI as published by HSBC is based on 430 manufacturing managers as respondents — not a very large sample and strongly skewed towards small- and medium-sized enterprises. The PMI of the Chinese Statistical Bureau covers 3000 companies, but this sample is biased towards large- and medium-sized companies, mostly from the traditional sectors. The message is clear: figures should be interpreted with care; in particular, it must be noted that quarterly figures may fluctuate due to all kind of events and circumstances that too much focus on this, makes us blind for the medium- and longer-term trends.

This problem of interpretation also relates to consumption data. Take, for example, the case of Chinese New Year. In general, the increase in consumption in the first quarter of the year is the result of the holiday period. Therefore, we should always compare the first quarter of this year with the same quarter of the previous year. Even if this is done, there are other caveats. For example, an increasing consumption share in GDP may be the result of slowing growth in export and investment. In this case, the rising consumption share is not the result of strong and dynamic consumption, but due to the weakness of the other components of demand. Another example of data interpretation relates to the export structure. China accounts for over 40% of global exports of electronics goods such as computers and smart phones; this is an increase from 5% in 2000 (WTO, 2016). Nevertheless, the majority of electronics activity in China remains final-stage assembly, where profit margins are extremely thin. In a sense, this reflects on export of Apple, LG and Samsung, not so much of China.

Difficulties in interpretation relates also to specific events such as the bankruptcy of solar cell maker Shanghai Chaori Solar Energy Science and Technology Co. Ltd. in March 2014. The company announced that it could not pay its interest anymore. The government refused to bail out the company, and the company became in default. This bankruptcy can be seen as a sign of the fundamental weakness of the corporate and financial system, and as a warning about spillovers to other companies. However, we can also interpret this from another angle: as a sign of health returning to the Chinese financial system. It is an important step to reduce the overcapacity problem and gradually move away from the soft-budget constraints (Chapters 3 and 4). It may be a message that the authorities have decided not to keep loss-making firms afloat by means of preferential treatment and subsidies.

In many cases, misinterpretations arise from the fact that we do not understand why the party, state, local government, companies and consumers react in the way they react. Therefore, history is important. Certain actions of the party and state today may be linked to the century of humiliations resulting from the Opium War, the Japanese invasion, the civil war and the foreign occupation of parts of China in the 19th century (Chapter 2). The sometimes not very logical choices by Chinese companies may also be explained by history. For example, the lack of focus may be explained by the fact that in previous decades flexibility meant surviving in a changing environment. Finally, the irrational behaviour of consumers may be explained by their experiences of living through the Great Leap Forward or Cultural Revolution. To conclude, a historical overview helps to understand present behaviour. History shows also that what is happening in China is not unique; other countries have undergone the same developments and made the same socio-economic choices.

The contradictions, speed of change, and preconceived ideas make interpretation extremely difficult. For example, is the success of the bike-sharing sector in cities such as Beijing and Shenzhen today really the beginning of the explosion of sectors in the shared-economy, or is it just a short-term hype because the business models used by these companies are not sustainable? Is the enormous success of *Sina Weibo* (the Chinese *Twitter*) as proxy for the social media sector sustainable, or will the government intervene if it becomes too big and powerful? In general, what should be considered as a short-term deviation from the structural process? To analyse what is happening in China is like attempting to hit a fast-moving target; the moving target, in this case, is the time-compression society and mixed images in China.

Part I

The Main Economic and Political Choices

In the first part of the book, we discuss the search of the Chinese policymakers for an optimal growth and modernisation strategy. China started to implement the traditional growth model in the early reform period of the late 1970s and early 1980s. The emphasis was on high savings and high investments, combined with government support to state-owned enterprises (SOEs) and keeping wages low. This was complemented by the opening up and the increasing competition after 1992, when the first special economic zones were established for foreign investors. Export was heavily stimulated, and we saw the marketisation of the SOEs.

However, there is an end-date to this type of policy. Severe imbalances became visible in the economy (and society). Think about rising income inequality and environmental degradation. There was a need to achieve "inclusive" growth: a policy that focuses on sharing the benefits of economic development with all inhabitants. Up to 2007, these imbalances could be counteracted by high economic growth, but now there is a sense of urgency.

The "new normal" of GDP growth is around 6%, China is ageing, and the efficiency is low in many parts of the economy.

Easy reforms were implemented before 2007, but more was needed. The 11th five-year plan of 2006 can be seen as the start of deepening structural reforms and modernising the economy: the process of rebalancing that focus on efficiency and innovation. This rebalancing is a search for the optimum combination of market forces and government intervention.

Chapter 1

Interpretation of China's Data

Myth 1: Chinese data is unreliable and man-made

1.1 Introduction

Generally, there are two views about the reliability of Chinese data. The first view is that Chinese data is untrustworthy. When I discuss Chinese issues with colleagues, journalists and politicians, in many cases, they indicate their reservations regarding the data. Probably because they believe China's government to be secretive, controlling, corrupt and unpredictable in many political matters, they think the (economic) data must also be unreliable. We can argue that this is a specific case of the so-called Halo-effect — the overall impression of a government influences how we feel and think about its behaviour when talking about data. From this view, the whole attitude towards the Chinese government is negative. With respect to Chinese data, we can surmmarise (to quote one of my colleagues): "Whatever the Chinese say, don't trust their data".

On the other hand, there are people and institutions that believe most of the economic data is reliable. It is clear from my time spent in China that economic data on growth, consumption and investments is authentic. China's economic success could not have happened if the government had relied on incorrect data. It also seems almost impossible to me that the party and state can steer the economy with all its transformations by relying on two sets of data — one fake and one genuine. Keeping two sets of data would have created such a complex governance structure that made this unworkable. Within this view, the problems of Chinese data are not the result of manipulating the figures, but the result of the complex way to get the statistics from such a large, fragmented and heterogeneous country. The collection becomes even more problematic if the economic structure is changing as rapidly as we have seen in China.

Despite this more optimistic view about data reliability, it is certainly the case that the Chinese authorities are secretive about the sources and methods of data collection. This makes it difficult for researchers to do independent cross-checks. The in-between view is that we need to accept a certain amount of data unreliability due to a combination of decentralised data-gathering, inconsistent methods and standards across the country, tax evasion by the private sector, and specific manipulation of data by the state, local government and SOEs. Essentially, it is a combination of deliberately publishing fake data and statistical obstacles. This was also mentioned by the International Monetary Fund (IMF).

The IMF noted in its first Financial Stability Assessment Program of China that a "full assessment of these various risks is, however, hampered by serious data gaps and access to confidential data" (IMF, 2011 & Nomura, 2011). It should be clear that many statistical problems are not only related to China, but also common for many developing countries and economies in transition. Getting correct figures "above the table" is also difficult in advanced economies with an extensive and sophisticated data-gathering process; it is particularly so with the service sector. We can argue that official statistics basically underestimate the service sector, even in a mature economy. Companies such as Lenovo, Hewlett Packard, Canon and Toyota are all classified as manufacturing companies. However, they also provide a lot of services and, in many cases, the "service part" in total revenues is even larger than from production. However, total revenues of these companies are counted as "manufacturing production", not "service production".

Most discussion is about the actual GDP level and growth, but the unreliability of data also applies to other aspects of economic and social life. Unemployment statistics is said to be underestimating the real unemployment due to problems in capturing the rural areas and the migrant workers in the cities. In addition, there are concerns about manipulating the figures. It is a puzzle how a stable official urban unemployment rate of around 4% between 2008 and 2015 is possible despite the economic crisis worldwide and fall in growth in China itself. Income distribution statistics are also questionable, based on a survey published by the National Bureau of Statistics (NBS), which sampled only 40,000 households, of which rural households were slightly under-represented. The statistics did not capture the very wealthy cohort of the population who did not participate in the survey. Moreover, the survey excluded property income and off-payroll income. In this respect, the migrant workers in the cities are difficult to capture in the statistics. Hence, the reliability of income inequality data is a significant issue.

There are also doubts about the real debt burden in China, particularly debt connected to local governments. National debt is difficult to measure due to financing vehicles (outside the books) of local governments. Moreover, the bad debt burden of the financial sector is uncertain due to "shadow" bank activities and the relationship between banks, government and SOEs. Furthermore, the bad debt is influenced heavily by the definition used. Another data issue relates to foreign direct investments (FDI). China's outward- and inward-FDI increased spectacularly over the previous decade but the question is whether these flows are "real". The statistics are heavily distorted arising from the use of Chinese tax heavens and round-tripping through Hong Kong and other tax heavens. An example makes this clear: if a Chinese company invests in the Virgin Islands, but that money is invested back in mainland China to receive preferential treatment given to foreign investors, both FDI outflow and inflow are increasing. The inflow of investments is considered as foreign, but is essentially from a Chinese entity. This round-tripping is strongly distorting the picture on capital flows, as we will see in Chapter 15.

The foregoing makes clear that we have reasons to question Chinese data. In this chapter, I will elaborate on the data issue, with specific focus on GDP. The chapter is structured as follows: Section 1.2 starts with a discussion of the arguments laid down by the cohort of people that do not trust Chinese data. They maintain that the GDP figures are "man-made". This is followed by Section 1.3 which makes clear that Chinese data on economic growth and GDP are not as bad as may be expected. The essential argument is that we should see China as a tale of two economies. Finally, in Section 1.4, we will understand why, at the end of the day, Chinese data is good enough to be used in this book.

1.2 A critical assessment of China's GDP

There are several reasons why we may distrust GDP-related data. Firstly, China's Statistical Bureau publishes official quarterly GDP data within weeks of the end of the reporting period, significantly faster than other statistics agencies. This, in itself, is not a problem, but the point is that large adjustments of the data are published afterwards (and in many cases, the adjustments are unexplained). Secondly, China is announcing its growth target beforehand. When a growth target is announced, it is logical to assume that certain man-made adjustments are done to ensure that the target is being reached. Thirdly, local or province officials may systematically exaggerate growth because reaching or overshooting the growth target will enhance their careers and result in faster promotion opportunities in the party, state or local government. Fourthly, economic growth is determined by the level of inflation; calculating inflation in China can be challenging. China's Statistical Bureau may use the wrong level of inflation and, consequently, report the wrong real economic growth. Finally, the transformation from a production-based towards an expenditure-based method to calculate economic growth takes time and is a complex process.

Fast publication and large revisions afterwards

China is one of the first countries that publishes its GDP data, often within a few weeks after the reporting period has ended. Compared with countries that are smaller and collect data more efficiently, this is very fast. As indicated above, the problem is that large revisions of GDP are implemented afterwards based on the national economic census that takes place every five years. The first national economic census was done in 2005 (over the period 1993–2004) and added 17% to total GDP. It means that China's GDP in 2004 was 17% higher than previously published. Put differently, real GDP growth in the years 1993–2004 was revised upwards by 0.5%-point per year (Holz, 2013; ECB, 2006). The argument behind this correction was that the data-gathering process was not able to take into account the fast-growing service sector. The second national census was done in early 2010 (over the period 2005–2009) and added another 4.4% to GDP over this five-year period (NBS website). To the western media, this was yet another indication of the unreliability of Chinese data.

Clearly, there is some truth in this for there was hardly any explanation as to why this revision was needed. At the same time, we can argue that there has been progress: although it is still a substantial adjustment over a five-year period, the correction is considerably lower than before. In 2015, we saw in the third national census (over the period 2010–2014) that again GDP was being corrected, now by 3.4% (NBS website). Again, the main argument of this adjustment was that the statistical authorities were not able to capture the structural changes that happened in the economy. For example, getting high-frequency data about e-commerce was a huge obstacle.

Growth target and man-made data

Distrust about the data quality is fuelled by the fact that China is one of the few countries that announces its annual GDP target beforehand. If the targets are announced beforehand, obviously some manipulation may be expected if the data is not in line with this target. That is certainly the case if the credibility of the party and state is at stake. Linked to this is the choice of the government authorities not to give quarterly GDP data. They publish annual data on a quarterly basis; so, the third-quarter performance of this year can be compared to the third-quarter performance of the previous year. We may argue that this creates more scope to "smoothen" growth rates. Another reason why experts are questioning the GDP data is the fact that the amplitude of the business cycle is so much smaller compared with other countries. Growth between 1980 and 2008 was in the range of 9–11%, which is rather remarkable for a huge country in transition. The volatility is considerably lower compared to other Asian emerging markets, and much lower than countries such as Japan and the US.

The reliability issue is also fuelled by the disconnection between GDP growth data and other economic data, such as electricity consumption and freight transport data. Indeed, it is difficult to understand why we see economic growth of 7% between 2010 and 2016 while, at the same time, electricity consumption and freight transport fell during this period. This unease about data has been intensified by the remark of then Premier Li Keqiang in 2007. He was party secretary of Liaoning province. According to him, GDP data is man-made and therefore unreliable (Reuters, 6 December 2010). To get a better picture about the state of the economy, he presented three indicators to make up the so-called *Li Keqiang index* — electricity consumption, rail cargo volume and bank lending. The *Li Keqiang index* is much more volatile than the official stable GDP development index and looks more connected to economic upturns and downturns. The Liaoning province incidence renewed scepticism in January 2017. It was obvious that the local officials deliberately inflated the production statistics for the last decade. After this incidence of faking economic data, the NBS investigated other provinces in the north of China and found that the metals and mining production data from provinces such as Hebei, Shanxi, Shaanxi and Inner Mongolia had also been inflated by local authorities.

Other indicators are also used to correct the official GDP growth, such as the floor area under construction and cargo traffic at ports. However, an important flaw when using these indicators is that they are focussing on the manufacturing sector — a sector which is falling in importance. In 2017, the share of manufacturing in GDP fell to 38% (World bank database). To take the more dynamic service sector into consideration, we should look at indicators such as retail sales, passenger car sales, tourism flows and e-commerce volume. These sectors show considerable growth which is in line with GDP growth.

Local versus national GDP figures

In 2014, Xinhua News Agency, the official press agency of the Chinese government, published *The Enigma of China's GDP Statistics*. The conclusion of that publication was clear: the translation from local growth figures into nation-GDP is problematic. To the western media, this publication presented a picture of some growth-obsessed local officials who "have cooked the books". As stated above, local officials are indeed eager to increase output in order to get promoted. Higher province or city GDP growth has been strongly correlated with promotions inside the party and state.

The Chinese media used the Xinhua-publication to explain how difficult data-gathering is in a highly fragmented environment. Many institutions are conducting their own surveys, hence coordination is missing; this may result in double-counting. Another type of double-counting relates to the value-added concept. It is very difficult to define which part of a final product belongs to which province in the case of trans-regional economic activities. For example, it is difficult to find out the value-added per subsidiary (situated in different provinces) when a big company has many subsidiaries and a fragmented production line. In this case, the added value of the subsidiaries tends to be calculated twice. If this is happening, the sum of provinces production value is definitely higher than the national production value.

During the Great Leap Forward years (1958–1960), local officials heavily overstated production. As shown in Fig. 1.1, the sum of local GDP was higher than national GDP. During this period, it was unacceptable not to achieve the agricultural production targets announced by Chairman Mao, driven by his focus on achieving an

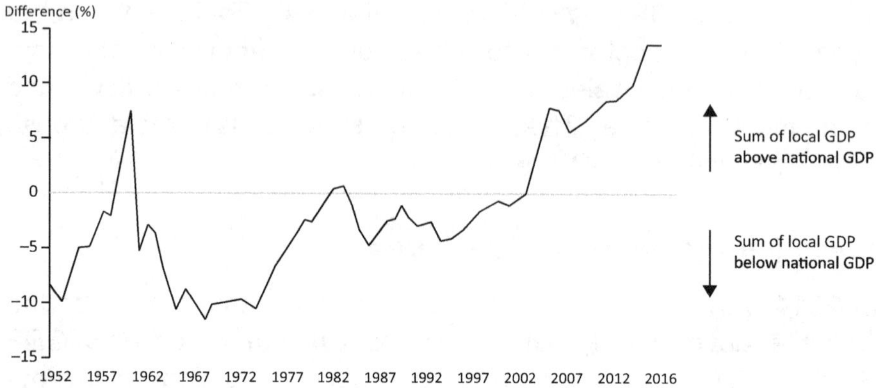

Figure 1.1 Difference between provincial and national GDP levels, 1952–2016
Source: *Goldman Sachs (2016) & NBS website*

agricultural surplus. It is interesting to observe that between 1960–2002, the sum of provincial GDP was actually lower than the national GDP. The second period in which the sum of provincial GDP exceeded national GDP was the post-2003 period. Since 2003, the sum of local production reported by the provinces has been on average 6.1% higher than the national production (Goldman Sachs, 2016). This local-national disconnection intensified after 2007. In 2016, the sum of provincial GDP was nearly 13% higher than national GDP. It is clear that we have a statistical problem.

Using the wrong inflation

Growth in GDP is always adjusted for inflation. This is logical as we want to get a picture of real growth in welfare. If inflation is eating up the increase in production (and income), this cannot be considered as a real increase in material welfare. Measuring inflation is a difficult process. In essence, several goods that are representative in the expenditures of people are selected. These goods are put together into what is referred to as a "basket". The cost of this basket is then compared over time to get the official inflation. It should be noted that we want to measure the price change in an economy by looking only at domestically produced goods and services. This is the crux: to measure the increase of prices of domestically produced products, it is necessary to correct for the changes in prices of imported products. However, this is not done in China. The Chinese National Bureau of Statistics is not taking into account the change in import prices. Consequently, inflation can be heavily overestimated or underestimated.

An example can make this clear. Let us assume that import prices of component parts are falling while the prices of the domestically produced final products made with those components are increasing by 1%. The inflation is 1% but in this case, we underestimate the inflation and overestimate real economic growth. The same happens when import prices of commodities increase, while the prices of final products on the domestic market rise by 1%. Inflation is again 1% but, in this case, we are overestimating inflation and underestimating real economic growth. In early 2015, the consensus was that inflation was about 1–2 percentage points higher than the official figure showed. In that case, real GDP growth was 1–2 percentage points lower than officially published.

GDP is production-based

Unlike most advanced economies, China's measurement of GDP is traditionally and primarily based on an output method, particularly in the agricultural sector and parts of the manufacturing sector. This approach is still a leftover of the Soviet style command economy of the 1950s and 1960s. It focuses on what the economy supplies rather than what it consumes. The measuring of GDP through the expenditure approach is focusing on consumption and other parts of total demand. This is the system mostly used by advanced economies and requires a more sophisticated data generation framework, including high-quality surveys. It is common to have some discrepancies between GDP calculations using different methods. For example, production-based GDP is overestimating true retail sales (as proxy for consumption) because it is based on output by suppliers rather than goods actually purchased by consumers. The retail sales are counted when suppliers sell the goods to retailers rather than when goods are actually sold.

The same holds with respect to investments. Investment in land to build houses or shopping malls is measured when the investor is paying for the land. To counteract speculation, developers are required to build on land they have bought within two years; otherwise, the land will be confiscated. Consequently, they will indicate to the government that the project is under construction while only a minor investment has been made in order to avoid problems with the authorities. Rising land sales, therefore, are likely to have caused an overstatement of investments. The NBS is trying to switch more and more towards the expenditure method to measure GDP, but more time is needed.

No consensus about economic growth

Due to the factors explained above and levels of freedom in interpreting data, there is no consensus on China's future economic growth by international organisations. As can be seen in Fig. 1.2, up to 2020, institutions such as the IMF, the World Bank, and the United Nations (UN) have published forecasts on real GDP growth that are within a small margin of around 6.5%. These institutions believe that the growth rate will be close to the official target of 6.5% for the period 2016–2020. However, the Economist Intelligence Unit and

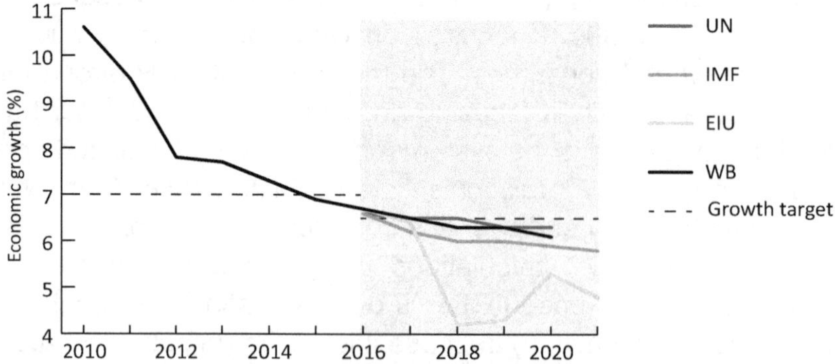

Figure 1.2 Economic growth overview by several institutions, 2010–2020

Source: Based on data summarised by Knoema Database

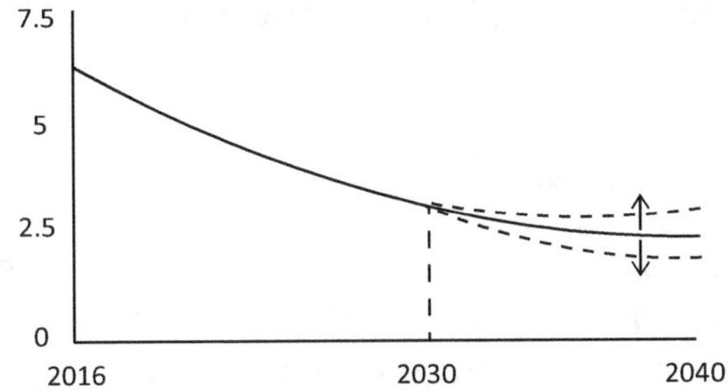

Figure 1.3 Economic growth between 2030 and 2040

Source: Based on data summarised by Knoema Database (Goldman Sachs, 2016 & PWC, 2015)

several consultancy firms are not so optimistic. For example, Marc Faber, the Hong Kong-based editor and publisher of the annual *Gloom, Bloom and Doom Report* estimates growth of only 3–4% for the next coming years.

So, there is some divergence in estimates of China's growth up to 2020. It is interesting to note greater consensus among institutions in the longer term, term, up to 2040 (Fig. 1.3). The consensus is given in the Organisation for Economic Cooperation and Development forecasts (OECD, 2016), with Goldman Sachs (2016) being slightly more positive and PricewaterhouseCoopers (PwC, 2015) being a bit less optimistic about the growth potential. All institutions predict a fall in China's growth to 2.5% in 2040. As we will see in the coming chapters, this reduction of growth is logical if a country moves into a middle-income status.

Despite significant improvements in the Chinese statistical system, China's official data still suffers from important deficiencies and lack of transparency. However, this is not unique for China; many developing and transition economies have similar problems with data collection and statistical inaccuracy.

1.3 Reflection on the statistical issues

In the previous section, I summarised the main issues regarding Chinese economic statistics. In this section, I will address the problems and discuss whether and how we can use China's official data.

A tale of two economies

China's statistical system is still biased towards the manufacturing sector that includes mining, heavy industry and industrial goods. This is problematic. We see a structural shift towards services but the statistical process is not able to capture the full dynamics of this service industry as yet. The share of the manufacturing sector in GDP reduced from 48% in 2006 to 40% in 2016 (KPMG, 2016 & NBS Website). The service sector reached 52% of GDP in 2016. Consequently, data of the manufacturing sector will not adequately reflect the growth of the whole economy. From this point of view, China is a tale of two economies: the old (traditional) investment-oriented and export-driven economy ("Old economy") which has slowed down considerably in the past years, and the new consumer-oriented economy ("New economy") — including e-commerce, tourism and personal care — which is growing strongly. Statistics within one sector (such as transportation) can even be blurred. For example, freight turnover may show a contraction while passenger turnover may grow at the same time. Electricity consumption in the industrial sector (mining, manufacturing, and construction) may decline whereas electricity consumption in the service sector (hotel, real estate, and logistics driven by e-commerce) may increase in the same period.

Therefore, only focusing on one part of the two economies is wrong. This is an important flaw in the widely used *Li Keqiang index* mentioned earlier. When Li Keqiang introduced this alternative index to measure growth in 2007, he was head of the party in Liaoning, a province in the north of China. Looking at the economic structure, the province is deeply dependent on heavy industry. The indicator may be an alternative for GDP proxy in the case of Liaoning province, but is inadequate with respect to other provinces, especially those with a large service industry.

Figure 1.4 shows specific sectors in both the old economy and new economy. Of course, the Chinese authorities understand

New China	Old China
Internet/e-commerce	Heavy machinery
Travel & tourism	Railways, shipping and other transportation
Beauty/personal care	Textiles and apparel
Healthcare	Steel/metals
Education	Chemical materials
Clean energy	Energy (coal)
Financial services/insurance	Rubber and plastics

Note: a representative sample of industries, not a full list

Figure 1.4 Sectors in New China economy versus Old China economy

Source: Mirae Asset (2015)

this, but it is difficult to change the indicators and the process of data-gathering in the short term. The conclusion is that a certain amount of decoupling between economic growth and associated indicators in the Chinese context is logical; and this may be the case for some time to come.

It should be clear that this disconnection is not only over-reporting real GDP, but also can be under-reporting GDP. The remarks earlier in the chapter that the retail sales are overstated due to the accounting system may be correct up to 2010, but I am not sure if this is still the case. The retail sales as proxy for consumption may underestimate consumption because it excludes partly some of the fastest growth types of services that are consumed outside the retail sector. For example, rents are, in many cases, not incorporated within consumption. Moreover, it is a question mark if the enormous growth of the e-commerce and its spillovers are captured in today's statistics. The growth of parcel deliveries is enormous. The number of private couriers on their bikes and electrical scooters has increased so much that they are not allowed to deliver the parcels to the doors of the student dormitories at Renmin University anymore. Instead, the couriers have to wait near the gate for their customers to pick up the parcels. Likewise for companies such as Ernst & Young, the couriers deliver packages to an allocated room near the entrance, and the employees pick them up within certain time frames.

The earlier mentioned five-year adjustment of GDP may be an indication of bad statistics. Obviously, it would be better if the data appeared to be correct. At the same time, we see progress. The adjustment by NBS of the latest GDP of 3.4% due to the census in 2014, instead of the massive 17% in 2005, can be seen as an increase in accuracy and reliability of existing GDP calculation methods. Another issue is the fact that GDP growth is given annually and not quarterly. We may question the choice of publishing the GDP data on an annual basis instead of a quarterly basis. However, this is done by many developing countries; and quarterly data can be tricky if an economy is in transition from "agriculture" to "industry" to "service". We can argue that focusing on quarterly data (as we do in the west) is questionable because it creates a short-term view. Essentially, the indicated growth target for the next five years gives a feeling that statistics are partly man-made. Since 2015, some larger cities (such as Shanghai) have announced that they will not give a growth target beforehand. This is interesting because the Shanghai party secretary is a member of the Politburo (Chapter 6). For China as a whole, it is too soon to expect an end to GDP targeting. It will remain an important policy tool for guiding and evaluating officials, but the Shanghai experience makes clear that some pilot projects are running.

1.4 Conclusions about reliability of Chinese data

What can we conclude from the discussion above? Certainly, that Chinese data is not as accurate as data from many advanced economies. It is clear that the Chinese government is missing out important sectors of the economy in its statistics and, consequently, making adjustments afterwards. This means that some correction of the official 7% growth (2016) may be needed. Even if it is 6.5% or 6.0%, this is still remarkable. Keep in mind that this 6% is actually a lot more in dollar terms than the days of 10% growth a decade ago when China's economy was much smaller. Furthermore, the data quality improved tremendously during the past decade, and there is reason to believe that the quality of data coming out of

China will improve further over time on account of the talks within the IMF. Moreover, the Chinese authorities are aware of the negative consequences of wrong figures; they know that good data is needed to monitor and fine-tune the economy in an efficient way.

Despite the progress in data quality, evidence shows that sometimes the Chinese authorities choose to use alternative facts and misleading data. In the past years, there were several examples of the government downsizing economic and social problems, such as income inequality and poor air quality in China's largest cities. For example, NBS strongly underestimated the increase in housing prices in 2014 and 2015. It was clearly misinformation. The public, social media, journalists and academia quickly spotted the distortion and the statistical agency adjusted the data afterwards. Today, there are many eyes on China and its data. Information and numbers are being checked and tested in many ways which will not give the Chinese authorities much statistical freedom. Hence, in circumstances that they are not willing to publish correct figures, they are forced to do so by the public pressure.

We must accept that the data quality issue is here to stay for the next decade or so. However, the statistics are good enough to be used for serious research, particularly if we make use of annual data and adopt a longer-term view. This is also the vision of the World Bank that scores countries on their statistical capacity to produce high-quality aggregate data. In the past, China's score was low. However, in the 2016 ranking, China was on the upper end of the ranking compared to other middle-income countries. Chinese data is good enough if we concentrate on the trends. That is precisely why, throughout this book, we must focus on overall structural development, instead of putting emphasis on quarterly or monthly data.

Chapter 2

China's Economic Development and Political Choices Before 1978

Myth 2: History is not important in today's modern China

2.1 Introduction

History can teach us a lot. In many cases, it provides lessons for the present and guidance for the future. The more we know about China's history, whether it is about politics, economics or culture, the better we are able to understand the choices China is making today, and the better equipped we are to predict how China will behave if it is a dominant player in the globalised world. For example, history can teach us why the Chinese authorities put so much focus on stability, gradualism and national sovereignty. It may also tell us why such a paternalistic role of the government is accepted by the people.

This chapter focuses on the period before opening up. We spend some words on the imperial dynasties, as well as the relatively short Communist era after 1949. Section 2.2 starts with the political and economic situation before the Chinese Communist Revolution of 1949, including important events in the 19th and 20th centuries, such as the Opium Wars, the collapse of the final Qing

Dynasty and the Communist Revolution. Section 2.3 describes the political and economic situation between 1949 and the start of the reforms in 1978. This period can be characterised as "government-led industrialisation" with heavy emphasis on the planning process. Section 2.4 follows with an overview of the main motives, drivers and objectives behind the decisions in this pre-reform period. Section 2.5 closes this chapter with the economic, social and political picture at the end of the 1970s.

2.2 The Chinese economy before the 1949 Communist Revolution

China was an economic and technological leader in the pre-modern era. There is consensus that during the Song Dynasty that began in AD 960 and continued until AD 1279, China was the economic and technological powerhouse of the world (Brand a.o., 2012). Innovations such as the compass, gunpowder, printing and paper-making emerged within this time frame. Even though China's per capita GDP growth between 1300 and 1800 flattened slightly and did not reach the growth figures of the previous centuries, Imperial China under the Qing Dynasty (1644–1912) was still a major world economic power in 1800, accounting for roughly 30% of the world's economy (Maddison, 2001). In 1800, China's share of the world GDP was almost as large as its share of world population, and China was a middle-income country by the standards of that time. The country was highly urbanised compared to other parts of the world, including Western Europe. Beijing was the largest city worldwide with also Hangzhou in the top five of largest cities in 1800.

History shows that the global order and leading countries are continuously changing. While the global economy was, in principle, Asian centric up to 1500 (driven by China and India), it changed into a more polycentric system during the 1500–1800 period, with economic power being shared between Asia and Europe, but China and India were still the world's two largest economies. Even at the end of this time frame, China was a much richer country than any parts of Europe. After 1800 when the Industrial Revolution achieved momentum, the world order shifted and became Eurocentric, dominated by

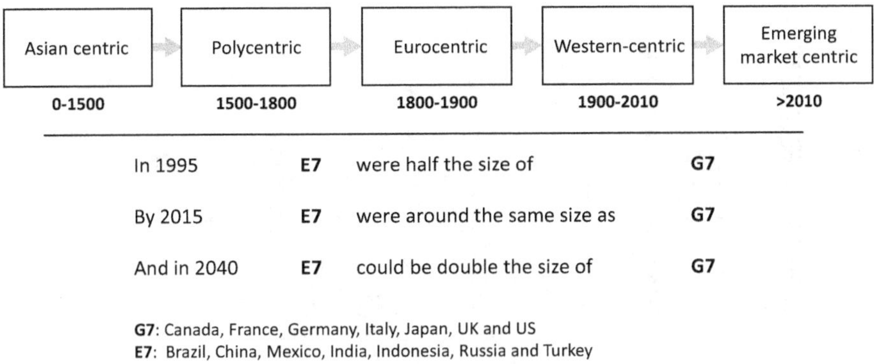

Figure 2.1 Changes in world economic power
Note: Based on PPP-GDP
Source: Based on Maddison (2001) and PWC (2015)

European countries. The 20th century is, in principle, a western-centric global order with the US as the dominating economic power-house, followed by the European countries and Japan. Today, we witness the rise of the Asian continent again, but this time driven by a broad range of fast-growing emerging markets. Although Asian emerging markets take the lead, other emerging markets from Latin America and Africa are more and more visible (and important) for the global economy. Hence, an emerging market centric world order has been building up. This development is shown in Fig. 2.1. In 2040, the largest seven emerging markets could be double the size of the seven largest economies combined in the traditional G7.

From 1800 onwards, China's economy began to stagnate (Maddison, 2001 and Lin, 1995). China had close-to-zero growth in per capita GDP from 1800 to 1950 — the period in which the European (starting in Great Britain) and North American economies took off. Although the roots of modern Europe started in the 16th century, the crucial period of change was the 19th century when Europe was transformed by the Industrial Revolution. Essentially, China missed the Industrial Revolution. However, it should be noted that the dynamism of the Chinese economy was already gone well before the Industrial Revolution occurred in Great Britain.

Britain's Industrial Revolution between 1760 and 1830 resulted in a rapid increase in welfare compared to the periods before.

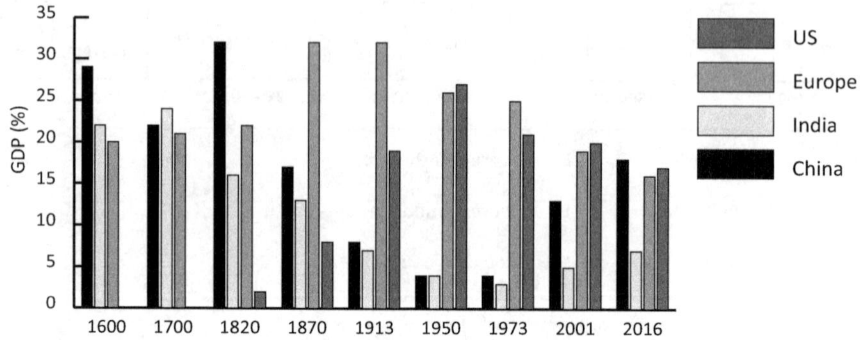

Figure 2.2 Historical share of global GDP

Source: *Based on Maddison (2001) and IMF (2017)*

It was driven by innovations, resources from colonies and institutional changes in the society. At the same time, China's development stopped and, consequently, China's share in the world economy fell. Figure 2.2 shows the fall between 1820 and 1870. While its share was above 30% in 1820, it dropped to 17% in 1870; it was still a world power but considerably smaller than the UK[1] and its colonies. By 1950, China's share of the expanding world economy had shrunk to about 3%; in 1978, at the start of the reforms, its share in world GDP was around 2%. Unmistakably, China was one of the poorest countries in the world. Of course, there were large regional differences, but the general picture was clear — in the late 1970s, China was a low-income country.

An important question is why China failed to implement the Industrial Revolution. This is the so-called Needham puzzle (Needham, 1969): why did China fail to implement technology and increase productivity when, looking at the past, they were leading in innovations? Explanations of missing the Industrial Revolution and the reasons of becoming backward (in particular, after 1800) can be divided into two views (Dimaculangan, 2014) — the

[1]The names Great Britain and United Kingdom are often used interchangeably in this book. The reason for using the two names in different parts of the book has to do with following the general rule that the UK is predominantly a political term that is being used after the early 19th century.

internal view (normally seen in western research) and the external view (mostly the conclusions of Chinese research). The western view on explaining China's economic backwardness after 1800 focuses on internal factors such as the institutional obstacles, economic problems related to the size of the country and internal chaos. The Chinese view emphasises external factors such as the occupation by European powers, Japan and the US for its backwardness after 1820.

Internal view

The main internal reason to explain backwardness is the political-institutional system during the Imperial era. According to this view, the government authorities during the Qing Dynasty were extremely conservative, traditional and strongly against modernisation. They were not willing and, in many cases, not able to fight vested interest such as intensive business structures that were built around extended families. The obstacles to change were fed by the Confucian ideology in which agricultural activities were seen as more important than commercial activities and making money. A second reason for stagnation were internal wars of, in particular, the period prior to the Revolution of 1911 and the Communist Revolution of 1949.

Other internal reasons are more economic in nature. Essentially, there was abundance of labour that did not provide incentive to increase efficiency. Furthermore, due to the natural environment, infrastructure was a bottleneck, particularly if the urban centres and the production centres (such as mines) were so far from each other. The challenges regarding infrastructure also reduced positive spillover effects — economies of scale and knowledge — from one region to another.

External view and the age of humiliation (1840–1950)

The external view of explaining China's backwardness after 1820 focuses on the two Opium Wars in the 1840s and 1850s, the occupations by Great Britain and Japan, and the conditions of the peace treaties after China's defeat. These events had a dramatic impact on the Chinese economy and resulted in a lost century, in economic sense and with respect to sovereignty — the so-called century of humiliation, which refers to the period of intervention and occupation by western powers and Japan between 1840 and 1950. It started with the First Opium War (1839–1842) and ended with the Communist Revolution of 1949. The view that the economic burden that was imposed on China by other countries in the different treaties was just too high, and resulted in an economic breakdown, has been made clear by every Chinese leader after 1840, including the Qing emperors, Sun Yat-sen, Mao Zedong, and today's leaders.

Canton system

In the 17th and 18th centuries, there were already substantial trade flows between China and Western Europe. Western traders were permitted to do business in Canton (Guangzhou) only, in particular, on or nearby Shameen Island. The Western Chinese trade relationship, concentrated in Canton after 1700 up to the early 1840s, became known as the "Canton System". Western merchants were not allowed to live or execute business in any other parts of China. Furthermore, trade was only possible through Chinese merchants who were organised in strong guilds. Although the above rules looked quite strict, the operational trade environment was relatively liberal with light regulation and low taxes.

Chinese products (particularly silk, porcelain, and tea) enjoyed high demand from the upper middle class in Europe, but the bilateral trade was unbalanced. At that time, there was not at all interest in European products from the Chinese side. The trade deficit that occurred resulted in an enormous inflow of silver in China (and outflow of silver from Great Britain). Foreign merchants had to pay in silver for their purchases of Chinese products because silver was the only accepted payment in foreign trade by China. For China, the trade surplus and influx of silver was an important part of total revenues and helped the Chinese government in their spending plans.

As stated above, the main cause of Great Britain's trade deficit was the lack of demand for western products, but that changed in the late 1700s. Merchants from the British East India Company started to sell opium, mostly grown in British-controlled India, to China. China's demand for opium was high and Great Britain could balance its international trade with China. The trade deficit disappeared and the outflow of silver stopped. Moreover, taxation of opium production increased the revenue of the British colonial government in India. China's Qing administration initially tolerated this opium import because opium trade created financial advantages in terms of more tax revenue due to import tariffs. Furthermore, the increased incomes of British merchants were used to buy Chinese products, which stimulated Chinese exports. In particular, the export of tea was lucrative for the Qing Imperial Treasury because they held the monopoly on tea exports.

First Opium War (1839–1842)

Opium exports from India to China grew dramatically between 1790 and 1830. Starting in the early 1820s, China had a trade deficit and, consequently, silver left the country. This hit government finance; essential investments in infrastructure, education, and defence could not be maintained anymore. As a result, the Qing administration decided to stop the import of opium almost instantly and justified this decision by health-related reasons. It banned the sale of opium and confiscated the opium stock waiting for distribution in Canton.

Obviously, this resulted in a trade war with Great Britain. After negotiations collapsed, the British Parliament decided to start a real war against China in 1839 — the First Opium War. We may question why this trade issue accelerated into real fights but we should not forget how important opium was for the British colonial government in India and for the geo-political stability in the colonies (Frankopan, 2015). Furthermore, this problem came in the midst of many of the risks and threats that the British Empire perceived from other parts of the world, such as France and Russia. In essence, the main reason for "playing it so hard" was to show that Great Britain could still rule the world. The more specific aims behind the decision to start the war were to reopen the Chinese market and to get compensation from the Chinese government for the confiscation of the opium. The war was short. The military power of the British was so much bigger that, at the end of the day, China had to accept these demands which were put in the Treaty of Nanjing.

The Treaty of Nanjing

The Treaty was signed on 29 August 1842 and marked the end of the First Opium War. From the western point of view, its fundamental purpose was to transform the Chinese-dominated Canton System into an open market place in which Great Britain was the leading power. The outcome was catastrophic for China. Firstly, the Treaty abolished the former monopoly of the Chinese merchants in Canton, which had a big impact on government finance. Essentially, it meant that trade could be executed with anyone. Secondly, Hong Kong became a colony of Great Britain, which gave them (and not China) an efficient harbour. Thirdly, besides Canton, China had to open several new treaty ports. Fourthly, the Qing government was obliged to pay for the damages that occurred in the opium trade and the war expenses of Great Britain. Finally, and maybe most importantly, the Treaty resulted in some extraterritorial rule or immunity from local law by westerners; China's century of humiliation had begun.

After the Treaty of Nanjing, tensions between the Qing administration and Great Britain continued, and intensified year after year. The Chinese government had problems coping with the financial problems of the Treaty, and felt extremely uncomfortable about the extraterritoriality issue that resulted from the treaty. The authorities in Great Britain felt that the Chinese government purposely violated the treaty conditions. Negotiations to save the Treaty collapsed, partly because both parties were not willing or able to understand each other. The Chinese emperor lived in a static, economically stagnated, local world, driven by an attitude of supremacy of Chinese culture, while British negotiators lived in a new, changing, dynamic, expanding and innovative world in which there was no room for conservatism and tradition. During this period and in the 1850s, other countries such as the France, Russia and the US became more and more active in China. These countries were also increasingly dissatisfied with the Qing government's failure to follow the conditions stated in the Treaty.

Second Opium War (1856–1860)

In 1856, the distrust, driven by unknowness about "the other world", resulted in the Second Opium War. Again, British military power, now combined with forces from France, Russia and the US, was too strong; China had to undergo again the humiliation of being defeated. The Treaty of Tianjin (1858) intensified the extraterritorial rule; large foreign concessions were created in major cities. In these concessions, the British, French, Russian and American laws were established; the Chinese government had no authority in these parts of the cities. In a sense, China was a semi-sovereign country by 1860. Foreigners gained full access to the interior, and were free to travel and conduct businesses anywhere in China. Furthermore, the Treaty also set a new, low tariff for imported goods, giving foreign traders an important advantage and further reducing the revenues of the Qing government.

The unequal treaties

The treaties, resulting from China's defeats in the two Opium Wars, were and still are seen as unequal by the Chinese. They granted foreigners the benefit of extraterritorial rights which made them immune to the Chinese legal system. The treaties forced importation of opium, institutionalised the freedom of foreigners to travel and operate business throughout China, forced the Chinese government to open treaty ports, and resulted in loss of autonomy to collect import duties. Therefore, the term "unequal treaties" became associated with the concept of China's century of humiliation. The status quo within the context of the Tianjin Treaty continued until the mid-1890s.

In addition, there was also the humiliation of Japanese occupations because of the Chinese–Japanese war. Tensions between Japan and China had built up in the early 1890s and resulted in the war with Japan. In 1895, Japan defeated China and gained control over a large part in the Northeast, Taiwan, and also South Korea (which Japan officially annexed in 1910). This occupation by foreign troops led to public discontent (fuelled by government rhetoric) and started the Boxer Uprising of 1899 with widespread attacks on westerners. Eventually, American, British, French and Japanese troops stepped in and Beijing was occupied by foreign troops. As stated before, although China was not colonised, in effect, it became a semi-colony with foreign troops.

During my teaching at CEIBS, I invited a manager from German-based Bayer in 1998. He started his presentation by saying with pride that Bayer-China roots could be traced back 115 years. This might be intended to generate commitment and credibility, but the first question from the audience was "What role did the company play during the period of unequal treaties?" The unequal treaties were economically a tragedy for China. The annual budgets showed large deficits due to the payments stipulated in the treaties. Solving this budget deficit was problematic because the Chinese authorities had to give away its control over revenues. The import duties were set at a very low level by the British government, and foreigners and companies living and operating in China did not pay taxation. The result was that the government had to finance its deficits by foreign loans. In 1911, the Qing government collapsed under the debt problem and the payments of interest to the foreign creditors. Between 1900 and 1910, 40% of government revenues had to be spent on servicing the foreign debt (Thomas, 2006). Furthermore, the loan conditions were quite harsh. For example, the Chinese government had to give away ownership of its railways and its new domestically-owned modern industries. The result was an even more problematic situation of how to get enough revenues to finance the foreign debt and invest in the domestic economy. It was a negative flywheel that depressed the domestic economy and created economic stagnation.

Besides the adverse economic impact, it should not be underestimated how deeply this humiliation sits in the mindset of today's Chinese; the century of humiliation has affected the Chinese psyche strongly, influencing and explaining some of today's choices. For example, borrowing money from abroad appeared to be a burden and, until very recently, the Chinese government was hesitant to incur a government deficit. The same holds for Chinese houseowners; they have the viewpoint that buying a house with savings is preferable to getting a mortgage. The century of humiliation also affects today's China's political attitude with respect to geopolitical issues. For example, non-intervention in sovereign countries is an important paradigm of China's foreign policy. In discussions in formal organisations such as the UN and the IMF, Chinese political leaders are strongly against domestic interventions in sovereign nation states.

Internal chaos

The two Opium Wars and associated treaties had a very negative impact on the Chinese economy. Furthermore, China's loss in the Sino–Japanese War of 1894–1895 and the associated war-payments had an additional negative economic effect, as did the loss of South Korea, parts of Manchuria and Taiwan. The economic stagnation continued after 1895, even up to 1949. The period 1895–1911 is characterised by internal chaos. Due to the defeat in 1895, the Qing Dynasty was under attack domestically. Several factions in the Chinese society showed their discontent. This internal fight resulted in a power vacuum in certain parts of China. Throughout this period, the country was without central authority and very fragmented. In October of 1911, a group of revolutionaries led by Sun Yat-sen started a successful revolt against the Qing Dynasty. It ended the last Imperial Dynasty and established the Republic of China. This is called the Revolution of 1911, or the Chinese Revolution.

Republic of China (1911)

Sun Yat-sen was selected as the president of the newly declared Republic of China with Nanjing as the capital city. His first focus was on getting external recognition and to make sure that the foreign nations (still present in the concessions in the big cities) would not intervene. From this point of view, he was very successful. In 1913, the US was among the first countries to establish full diplomatic relations with the new Republic. Britain, Japan, and Russia followed. Furthermore, there was the internal issue of sovereignty. Sun Yat-sen had to deal with the situation that the government did not control its revenues and expenses. It took until 1943 for China to win back its full sovereignty and autonomy over the concessions and the loss of autonomy over taxation issues. Despite some success, financial problems — together with extensive corruption and massive hyperinflation that destroyed the middle class (which had been the main supporter of the government) — resulted in domestic economic and political chaos. Not only was the urban middle class dissatisfied with the progress, but Sun Yat-sen also failed to get the support of the rural population. This shaped the context in which the Chinese Communist Party (CCP) could grow.

People's Republic of China (1949)

In the 1911–1949 period, China essentially had two political parties. Sun Yat-sen was one of the founding fathers of the Chinese Nationalist Party (Kuomintang) that was established in 1911. As mentioned above, Sun Yat-sen was not able to stabilise the domestic economic situation and enhance the credibility of the government. As a response to the bad economic situation, hyperinflation, corruption in the government, the collapse of the middle class, as well as the poverty of the rural population, the CCP was founded in 1921. During the first years, the two parties worked together to fight the common enemy — Japan. As history shows in other countries, once the common enemy is gone, the need to cooperate disappears; in many cases, the internal factions are fighting each other. This happened also in China.

The two parties stood against each other. After a decade of fights, the Communist Revolution resolved the issue of who would form the Chinese government. On 1 October 1949, Mao Zedong (the leader of the CCP) proclaimed the establishment of the People's Republic of China. Chiang Kai-shek (the leader of the Kuomintang after the death of Sun Yat-sen), a large part of the army, and about two million sympathisers left for Taiwan. After several years, the CCP was ruling the entire country and it restored the independence and unity of China, including control over government revenues and expenditures. Despite the mistakes Mao made (which we will discuss below), the unification and independency of China was clearly Mao's greatest single achievement.

2.3 1949–1978 government-led industrialisation

Most publications on China divide the almost 70 years of Communism into the pre- and post-reform period; the reform period started in 1978 when Deng Xiaoping came to power. The pre-reform period is associated with stagnation, while the post-reform period is linked to economic development and increasing welfare. As we will see, this is a logical division but be mindful of the fact that the average growth rate between 1949 and 1978 was certainly not low. Officially, growth was even higher than was seen in the west during this time frame. We may question the official statistics, but even taking this into account, growth was relatively high. The negative perception we have about the 1949–1978 period comes from the two dramatic disruptions in economic, social and human terms — The Great Leap Forward and the Cultural Revolution. I will elaborate on this later in this chapter. Here, I will start with some characteristics of the pre-reform period. In essence, it was a period of government-led industrialisation, driven by Mao's initiative of the "catch-up process" through government planning.

Planning system

The first years of the Communist Regime were focused on getting full control of the country and centralising decision-making power.

The fundamental choice was to implement a central planning or command system under the direction of the state Planning Commission. This was done using five-year plans; the first started in 1953. The first five-year plan followed the Soviet Union's economic policy ideology: a strong focus on heavy industry and having the CCP and state (or central government) allocate, direct and control production throughout the economy. The state-owned enterprises (SOEs) played a key role in this planning system. Production was mostly done in these state-controlled companies. The planning was overwhelming and the process complex. The planning process was like a puzzle: every piece of the puzzle had its own function; without every piece in place, the whole production would be disrupted. The characteristics of such a command economy can be summarised as follows:

- Private ownership is not possible. Resources such as land, houses, plants and other physical assets are owned by the (local) government, under the auspices of the party.
- Production is done by SOEs. Final products and services, as well as components and resources, are determined by state plans. Output targets are set and implemented by local governments into production plans per individual company. Obviously, the allocation of inputs needed are also set.
- Labour is allocated according to state plans. There is no freedom in profession; the command economy is allocating people into professions in line with the targets set in the plans.
- Prices are regulated entirely by the state. Prices are not reflecting costs or shortages and are absent in the production process. No cost-benefit analysis is needed. Instead of paying for goods and services, companies are allocated goods and services.

China started its industrialisation process immediately after 1949. Looking at the first five-year plans and economic choices, we may say that in the first decade, Chinese policymakers were obsessed by achieving economic growth. Therefore, the focus was on increasing investment in industries such as steel and heavy machinery. To finance these investments, the government authorities set low prices for agricultural products and allocated private savings through the state-owned banks into the heavy industry. Obviously, rural income was being depressed and, to make sure that rural residents were not flooding into the cities for work and money, rural-urban migration was restricted.

Great Leap Forward (1958–1960)

In 1958, the Great Leap Forward campaign was launched in China. It was Mao's attempt to modernise the economy and increasing growth. The catching-up aim was so strong that it did not matter what it took to increase the growth rate of the economy. In this setting, two main institutional changes took place. Firstly, there was a change in ownership in rural areas through collectivising individual household farms into large communes. Secondly, decentralising of more tasks towards the local governments (of course, within the national planning system) took place. The latter approach is the so-called "administrative decentralisation process" (Shirk, 1993). The authorities (in particular, Mao) saw the problem of central planning in a country that was so large and so diverse. Therefore, most SOEs were delegated to local governments; thus, the influence of local governments on the planning system increased strongly. The collectivisation of the private farms into large communes was motivated by economies of scale: the larger the production entity, the more efficient it is, and the lower the costs per unit of production. The ultimate aim was to become self-sufficient in agricultural products. Another argument behind the communes was to intensify the relationship between daily life and working life. The communes provided education, healthcare, dining facilities and pensions for their members. However, they turned out to be an economic disaster. They had a devastating effect on the economy and agricultural production. Agricultural output contracted by 35% and average income fell by 20% between 1958 and 1962. Due to collective ownership and lack of individual responsibility, there was no incentive to work hard and be efficient. Together with bad weather conditions, the communes led to the biggest famine in China's history, causing about 15 (official) to 40 million (academic research) deaths. To make sure that the farmers would stay in the countryside, the *hukou* or household registration system (Chapter 9) was implemented. Farmers had to stay in their rural regions, could not leave the agricultural sector, and had to follow the planning targets set by the state.

The same incentive problem was visible in the non-agricultural sector. As indicated earlier, this industrial production was dominated by SOEs. They executed the state plans and were the basic production unit of the economy during the pre-reform period. The SOEs had little economic independence; output and inputs were fully fixed and production outside the plan was not possible. The bureaucracy (party and state combined) was more or less the chief executive officer (CEO), management team and board of commissioners in these SOEs at that same time.

Cultural Revolution (1966–1976)

A second period within the pre-reform period in which living standards dramatically fell was the Cultural Revolution from 1966 to 1976. The economy and political system were greatly disrupted in this decade. In 1966, Mao initiated the Cultural Revolution in order to establish a "new world". According to him, the economic development created a privileged class of engineers, scientists and factory directors who focused too much on money instead of the Chinese culture. Furthermore, they became disconnected with the "real" (agricultural) Chinese lifestyle. He initiated a mass movement that emphasised this cultural aspect. Students were sent to the countryside; writers, economists, engineers, and anyone associated with superior knowledge and urban attitude were considered enemies of the party and the ordinary people. Many of my colleagues at Renmin University in Beijing today were sent to the rural regions for many years, away from their parents and family. Schools and universities were closed, and the atmosphere in China regarding foreigners became very negative. In 1967 and 1968, the whole society was put into chaos; GDP dropped in absolute value during this period. Poverty was high and increasing; we can say that poverty in the world in 1960s was an Asian (predomiantly Chinese) problem. More than two thirds of the Chinese people lived under one dollar per day. A central government guiding the economy was absent. There were even no annual plans in 1967 and 1968. After 1970, the ideological part of the Cultural Revolution was relaxed and more attention was given to the economy.

During the Cultural Revolution, the decentralisation process was intensified. For example, the majority of the largest SOEs were delegated to provincial and municipal governments. After this new decentralisation round, the central government only supervised 142 SOEs in 1970, down from almost 11,000 in 1965 (Qian, 1999). It should be clear that this decentralisation did not mean that SOEs received more freedom; party and government control over these enterprises remained very tight. Decentralisation mainly transferred decision power from the central to the local governments. Despite the renewed economic focus in the early 1970s, there was political, economic, and social chaos. China was in a bad economic shape and had various institutional characteristics that hindered economic development. One of these institutional barriers was the interference of the government in the SOEs.

State-owned enterprises as a government tool

SOEs were an essential tool in the hands of the party and the government. As was the case with the communes in the rural areas, daily life in the city was organised within the context of the SOEs. During the Cultural Revolution, the freedom of SOEs and their managers was constrained by the interference of the party. Mao decided that every SOE should have a Communist Party Committee. This committee was at the top of the governance structure and controlled businesses. The role of the party in the business environment was enormous. Every important managerial decision had to be approved by the Communist Party Committee.

Furthermore, the committee also guided and supervised the employees on how they should behave. One key characteristic of this interference in SOEs was the fact that there was always a bail-out by the government and the state-owned banks; in other words, there was a soft-budget constraint.

Soft-budget constraint

In China's planned economy during the 1949–1978 period, SOEs could not go bankrupt. This is the so-called soft-budget constraint (Kornai, 1980 & 1992). The soft-budget constraint was in essence the guarantee of a bail-out by the government (or the state-owned banks) if a company was in trouble, even if the poor outcome was the result of bad behaviour. This explains why loss-making SOEs could continue to operate. This bail-out could have different forms, such as soft loans, government subsidies and cheap credits through the state-owned banks. The banks had enough liquidity because of the high saving rate of the Chinese people, driven by the fact that there were hardly any consumer products for people to spend their money on. So, due to this soft-budget constraint, SOEs and their managers were protected. This insurance led to a moral hazard: whatever was done and whatever risks taken, if anything went wrong, there was always the government to help directly or indirectly. The same moral hazard worked in the banking sector because the bank manager knew that there was always a government that would help. This soft-budget constraint was the result of the powerful triangle relationship that existed between the government, SOEs and state-owned banks, visualised in Fig. 2.3.

Clearly, the system did not create incentives for firms, workers, bank employees and farmers to become more productive or become more concerned with quality. It is remarkable that there was still relatively high economic growth in this context. As indicated earlier in this chapter, the annual growth rate between 1949 and 1978 was about 4%, slightly higher than in the western advanced economies. I will elaborate on this issue in the next chapter.

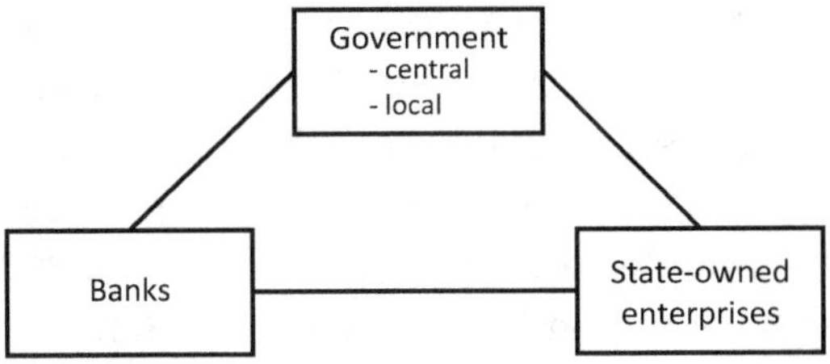

Figure 2.3 China's triangle of soft-budget constraint
Source: Based on Fan He (2006) & NG Beoy Kui and Thorud (2006)

2.4 Main drivers behind the choices

In the perception of many China observers, the pre-reform period is a sequence of policy mistakes, wrong choices and chaos. This may be correct but be aware of the fact that this period also shaped the preconditions for economic success after 1978. Throughout this book, I will elaborate on this more in depth, but I present some introductory notes below about the cultural, institutional and economic context in the mid-1970s, the final days of the Cultural Revolution and its impact on today's choices and affairs. I will introduce the decentralisation process (in combination with the cultural supremacy), the eagerness to create harmony and stability, the overreaction on sovereign issues, and the search for the market-state balance in economics.

Decentralisation, cultural supremacy and civilisation state

When the Chinese use the term "China", they are not usually referring to the country or nation so much as focusing on Chinese civilisation: its history, the dynasties, Confucian culture, the way of thinking, the role of the government and the role of relationships. Even after the period of economic chaos in the 1970s, China believed that it was culturally the centre of the world, in the same way as what we saw in Imperial China. The emperors had an ethnocentristic view on the world — a world in which Chinese civilisation was considered the be superior. This was clearly the case during the Dynasty era when foreign diplomats had to touch the ground nine times or *kowtow* before the emperor. This ethnocentric view is the result of seeing the country as a civilisation. Of course, there had been many civilisations within the borders of China but what is remarkable is that in the Chinese case, civilisation and state largely coincide. China has existed within roughly its present borders for 2000 years (major exception being Western China) and the emperors (together with the bureaucracy) were able to keep a common nation-wide culture.

Because of this, China can be seen as a civilisation-state and only became a nation-state during the century of humiliation (Jacques, 2012). During the Imperial period, the emperor and bureaucrats enjoyed unchallenged authority, backed by Confucian culture and the Confucian system of governance; this was the case, even during times of foreign occupation. China is too big to centralise; consequently, local bureaucrats enjoyed great autonomy, a characteristic of a civilisation-state. Governing was done by bureaucrats. The key mechanism for the selection of the bureaucratic elite was the imperial examination system which had been institutionalised during the time of the Tang Dynasty (AD 618–907). As indicated earlier, the provinces (and cities) accepted the rules from the central authority, but had freedom to make their own choices (and sometimes ignored the central rules). Emphasising the civilisation-state issue is important because in the mindset of many Chinese today, China's civilisation is seen as far more advanced and superior than other cultures. That may explain the racist element in China's civilisation today.

Stability is the main goal

After the chaos of the Great Leap Forward (1958–1960) and the Cultural Revolution (1966–1976), the main objective of the authorities was to restore the party's legitimacy and create political stability. The best way to achieve this was through economic growth. The chaotic situation also explains why in the 1970s, risky reforms were avoided. It may even give us the reason why we see a relatively gradual approach towards reforms today. Avoiding chaos is the key. Achieving harmony is essential, but be aware that within this harmony, as Confucius emphasised in his writings, differences are possible and needed. This is what we see today. This acceptance of differences is a guiding principle when looking at China's decentralisation of power to local governments. The same holds with respect to today's "one country, two systems" related to Hong Kong. Moreover, the same holds with respect to Taiwan. The Chinese have accepted that the issue cannot be resolved and, consequently, put this issue on hold more or less indefinitely (provided that Taiwan does not seek to declare independence). We also see this acceptance of differences during the Hu Jintao period with the focus on building a harmonious society. It also explains the power of the party and state. In the Chinese mind, stability and social order rank higher than civil and political freedoms.

As stated before, achieving stability and gradualism are related. This gradualism is visible in many aspects. Experiments were rolled out step by step through pilot projects and learning by doing was (and still is) a key element in implementing new policies or structural changes. Of course, gradualism is a relative concept. I wonder, when looking at statistics in 1986 (my first visit to China) and today, if we can label the changes as gradual. A once completely state-owned economy is now driven largely by private (and small) firms. The restructuring of SOEs resulted in approximately 40 to 44 million lay-offs between 1995 and 2001 (Rawski, 2002 & Jefferson, 2005). Mao's "iron rice bowl" of cradle-to-grave social welfare (pension, healthcare, employment and education) has been dismantled. One of the most egalitarian societies in the world has become one of the most unequal, and that all within this time frame of 30 years.

Market and government

It is always dangerous to have a black and white view. This is clearly the case when we examine the role of the market and the government in China's economic success. On the one hand, we see that the success of Chinese modernisation (even before 1978) has come about because the party has guided (and reacted on) certain reforms and taken over the role of the market. On the other hand, success has been the result of markets and local initiatives outside the official governance structure. History shows us that the truth is somewhere in the middle. During certain periods of time, there was clearly a government-led growth. In other periods, the economic development was driven by the fact that the government retreated from the economy and left it to the market. This retreat is, however, relative. The party and government are always visible and sensible. Note that the legitimacy of the government in China goes so much further than in western countries. In the Chinese culture, the group (family) is more important than the individual. This is seen in the fact that the family name always comes before the given name. The Confucian culture stresses loyalty to the family and respect to authority in the family. As the state is modelled on the family, the role of government has less boundaries in China compared to the west. In line with a father that makes decisions for the family, there are less limits to the government's authority. The government had, and still has, an essentially paternalistic role; in the same way as we see this in Japan and Singapore.

2.5 The picture at the end of the 1970s

The years after 1911 (the Chinese Revolution) were an economic and political chaos; only after 1949, when the CCP took over, was there a credible central authority. During the 1949–1978 period, there were adaptations and several modernisations in the economic structure, but these did not change the core of the command economy and the growth model that focused on SOEs and heavy industry. Certain reforms were implemented, but the main economic-institutional problem — the soft-budget constraint and the lack of incentives by workers, managers of SOEs, farmers and local governments — was not tackled.

By 1978, 75% of industrial production was produced by SOEs, according to centrally planned output targets. The rest came from the collective sector. 80% of the total urban employment was dominated by the state sector. In the 1960s, the country recovered from economic chaos and human development indicators increased step by step. After the Great Leap Forward, life expectancy at birth was 36, the lowest in Asia. In the early 1970s life expectancy increased to almost 60 years. The positive development in economics and human development indicators came to an end during the Cultural Revolution.

In 1978, China was one of the poorest countries in the world. The real per capita GDP in China was only one-tenth the Brazilian level. In 1978, China was primarily an agrarian economy and urbanisation was low. From an international point of view, the country was isolated from the world economy. China's share of world trade was less than 2% in 1978 (World Bank database) and China was also almost absent on the world capital market; it had rarely any foreign direct investments (FDI). At the end of the Cultural Revolution, the top leaders of the party and state (as well as the public) realised that the command economy (and its focus on heavy industry and capital accumulation) was not an optimal strategy anymore and that more focus should be given to market forces. Looking back, the economic chaos at the end of the 1970s can be considered as the perfect circumstances to discuss different opinions and allow open policy debate. The crisis provided the reformers with a window of opportunity to push for a new reform-agenda.

Within the planning process, decentralisation was a key feature of the pre-reform period. Local governments executed but also interpreted central policy. From this point of view, China was much less centrally planned than the Soviet Union at the end of the 1970s. This decentralisation was a logical choice due to the enormous size and regional differences in the country. Furthermore, the bad infrastructural conditions made autonomy of supply by provinces a rational choice. Also, the decentralisation of production ensured that strategic production in, for example, Tianjin could continue in Chengdu (far away from the Japanese) if Japan were to attack the industrial base in Northeast China. But clearly this decentralisation also had disadvantages. It created doublures and inefficient production.

Some important events occurred in the 1976–1977 period. First, then Premier Zhou Enlai died in January 1976. He was in favour of reforms. Already in the 1960s, he had introduced the idea of the "Four Modernisations" — modernising agriculture, industry, national defence, and education. In September 1976, Mao died. This happened in the midst of political and economic chaos that the Cultural Revolution created. Within the party, two factions battled for power. On the one hand, there was the political elite inside the party that wanted to continue the Cultural Revolution. On the other hand, there was the faction informally led by Deng Xiaoping that wanted to reform the economy and institutional structure. In 1976, the Deng Xiaoping faction came to lead and that ended the Cultural Revolution. Deng played an important role in China's politics in the 1960s. He supported Mao's choices in the early reform period, but his economic ideas became more and more different from Mao's political ideologies. As a result, during the Cultural Revolution, in October 1969, he was sent to work in a factory in rural Jiangxi province.

In 1976–1977, Deng made his political comeback and became Chairman of the party in the post-Mao period. He started his reforms in the educational system. He stressed the importance of education for future economic development. Step by step, his reform philosophy generated momentum and, finally, was accepted at the Third Plenary Session of the Communist Party held in December 1978. This session proved to be a turning point in China's reform strategy. Deng announced the official launch of the Four Modernisations propounded by Zhou Enlai, formally marking the beginning of the reform era: a more efficient agricultural sector; building up a strong, modern and efficient diversified industrial sector that could compete internationally; modernisation of the military apparatus; and modernisation of the educational system with more emphasis on science and technology. Hence, the early-reform period started; driven by the learning points from history.

Chapter 3

China's Early Reforms (1978–1993) and the Building Up of Imbalances

---

Myth 3: The reforms that have been initiated after 1978 are part of a broad masterplan to restructure the economy and society

---

3.1 Introduction

The previous chapter discussed the pre-reform period of 1949–1978. During that period, the main objective of the Chinese Communist Party (CCP) was to increase production through industrialisation, in particular, capital-intensive heavy industry. Furthermore, all industries were dominated by state-owned enterprises (SOEs) with few incentives to improve efficiency. Another feature of the pre-reform period was the very inward-driven policy with hardly any economic connection to the outside world. Obviously, these characteristics were covered under the umbrella of an overwhelming central planning system, particularly during the 1950s and 1960s. In the late 1970s, when Deng Xiaoping came into power, the growth strategy changed dramatically. Deng's focus was to concentrate on China's comparative advantages. With China's abundance of labour, it was logical to concentrate on labour-intensive light manufacturing. He also emphasised the need to increase efficiency and to achieve this, sectors were opened up, the power of SOEs was reduced, and more money was invested into the university system.

Deng also observed that the command system itself created too many inefficiencies, economic problems, fiscal (finance) burdens and imbalances in the economy. The choices were clear: economic reforms and opening up, while closing the political doors. His focus was on economics and increasing welfare, turning away from the Maoist focus on ideological and political debate, and building up the country from its economic chaos. Few, if anyone, could have imagined in 1978 how much economic and social progress China would make because of these economic reforms and the open-door policy. Indeed, economic growth exploded from the late 1970s onwards.

The period studied in this chapter begins with the start of reform when Deng came into power and ends with the year of Deng's famous southern tour in January 1992, in which he called for an acceleration of economic reforms. This chapter starts by analysing the starting position of China's reforms in Section 3.2. It is followed by Section 3.3 that concentrates on the three basic pillars (i.e. unbalanced development, gradualism in executing reforms and pragmatism) and the main fundamental choices during this early-reform period. An important choice was to adjust to local initiatives. Section 3.4 summarises the reforms up to 1992 as "reforms without losers" and draws the economic, political and social picture of the early 1990s.

3.2 The start of the reforms

The timing of the reforms was logical. Because of the disruptive Cultural Revolution, China was in economic chaos. In 1978, there was an economic urge to start reforms as soon as possible and in such a way that these reforms were part of an unstoppable process. The timing was also logical because of the political vacuum that occurred in 1977–1978. This created opportunities for the reformers. Furthermore, the public was in favour of change. As indicated before, Deng Xiaoping started with opening up the universities and millions of students who had to leave the cities for the country side returned. This greatly increased the legitimacy of the party and government.

Besides the relative good position with respect to infrastructure and education, there were also some lucky external circumstances to explain the success in the early-reform period. For example, successful export-driven neighbouring countries (such as Japan and the Asian Tigers) gave an easy-to-follow template for economic development. Moreover, export was relatively easy due to fast-growing export markets. This export strategy occurred within the context of an efficient nearby Hong Kong harbor and trading hub. In addition, the shipping container that was invented in the 1950s created the precondition for global production chains and boosted export flows. The focus on export resulted in the need to adapt to the international competitive market. The need to compete internationally stimulated productivity and created technological spillovers.

Successful neighbours

At the end of the 1970s, China witnessed the economic success of Japan and the Asian Tigers. These countries served as the model for China's economic process. Their success rested on three development principles:

- Reforming the agricultural sector towards private ownership — This created incentives to increase efficiency and resulted in a large agricultural surplus, freeing up the resources for state-led investment in basic industry and infrastructure.
- International competition in the export-oriented manufacturing sector — Consequently, there was a need for the process of technological catch-up and increasing productivity. (This is not the case when the economy is isolated from abroad; in that case, companies often have less incentive to invest in technology. For example, because they can use their relationships with governments).
- Financial repression — Control over banks and financial markets gave the government the opportunity and power to direct

capital to strategic sectors. Financial repression included a regulated low interest rate, an undervalued currency and capital controls.

Despite differences between countries, these principles formed the basis of the so-called East Asian development model (mostly clustered around Hong Kong, South Korea, Singapore and Taiwan). This model has been embraced by the Chinese authorities and formed the basis of the early reforms. Mao-era communes were broken up into small, partly private owners; light manufacturing and export was stimulated; and a financial system was set up to finance large-scale investments in infrastructure and basic industries (partly to accommodate the export industries).

Choice for export

After some decades of isolation and economic chaos from time to time, China's capital stock and technology were outdated and substantially lower in quality than that of its East Asian neighbours in the late 1970s. To modernise its capital stock and technology, China urgently needed foreign exchange to pay for imports of modern machines and equipment. Therefore, an export-driven strategy (and trade reforms) was needed to earn foreign exchange. This focus on export started immediately after the opening up of the economy in 1978, but it was considerably intensified after the Tiananmen Square protests in 1989. In the years after the event, GDP growth slowed down significantly due to the collapse of investments and the low growth of consumption. To counteract the fall in domestic spending, the focus was directed toward export. This policy-driven jump in exports that started in 1990 resulted in a strong increase in net export (export minus import) and China's integration into international trade flows. To be able to export, there is a need for a broad and competitive manufacturing sector. From this point, it is logical that China's authorities put heavy emphasis on the manufacturing sector. Building up a large and broad industrial base was an important aim of policies in the early-reform period. For example, in terms of share of GDP, China's manufacturing sector in 1980s and early 1990s stood around 45%, whereas the figure was only 15–20% in India (World Bank database). The industrial base was able to increase competitiveness vastly. The opening up and the link to international competition helped with this. In that sense, the Chinese experience fits into Gerschenkron's (1962) theory of economic backwardness in which China could skip some development stages by adopting western advanced technologies and practices.

Good human development indicators

During the pre-reform period, the CCP and government invested substantially in primary education, health and transport infrastructure. China was a very poor country in 1978. However, in terms of human development indicators such as literacy rate, life expectancy, and education enrolment, China did a much better job than many less developed countries. This created a good starting position for the take-off. Also, the strong family ties in general and the family farming system in particular resulted in a strong social cohesion in which people were helping each other. Another favourable condition at the start of the opening up was equality, in the rural areas as well as in the cities. China was one of the most equalised countries in terms of income distribution in 1978.

3.3 The key choices in the early-reform period

The transformation to a "market-based economy" started in the late 1970s with deregulation (or decollectivation) of the agricultural sector and the "opening up" of the Chinese economy towards the world. Part of this opening up refers to the creation of special economic zones (SEZs) in which foreign companies could operate outside the planned domestic economy. The early 1980s also saw more "enterprise autonomy". The above terms are within quotation marks because these are western terms but with Chinese characteristics. For example, a market-based economy does not mean

Year	Reforms
1978	Opening-up policy initiated
1979	Changing collective farming into household responsibility system
1980	Explosion of Township and Village Enterprises (stimulated by government)
1980	Creation of the first Special Economic Zones
1984	Announcement of the manager responsibility system in SOEs
1985	Dual track system (abolishment of the planned economy)
1989	Strong export-led growth (after Tianamen Square event)
1990	Stock exchange started in Shenzhen
1991	Focus on urban reforms
1993	Acceleration of reforms through "Socialist market system"

Figure 3.1 Overview of economic reforms, 1978–1993

Source: Adjusted from BBVA Research

that the government is absent. Market-based means more market and at the same time more state involvement. Opening up does not mean full opening up. Opening up implies economic freedom but also directives and government involvement. Autonomy relates to more responsibility of the manager and bottom-up communication, but at the same time we see top-down directives and state intervention. An overview of some important keystones in the early reform process is shown in Fig. 3.1. The reform process started in 1978 with the government-led opening up strategy and ended with the need to accelerate reforms.

We can distinguish three fundamental features of the early reforms. They were unbalanced, gradual and pragmatic.

Unbalanced

The early-reform growth strategy can be labelled as unbalanced. It was heavily focused on manufacturing, investments and economic growth instead of services, consumption and sustainability issues. As stated before, China followed the choices made by countries such as Japan and South Korea. In principle, a period of unbalanced growth is not illogically (despite what many experts say) and there is no reason to believe that an unbalanced growth strategy would hinder economic development. Countries such as Japan and South Korea have grown rich, thanks to a long period of unbalanced growth that focused on industrialisation. Only after some decades did the countries transform towards services.

Gradual

The Chinese early reform process has been gradual in nature. Many reforms were first introduced on an experimental basis in some regions, often in SEZs, and, if successful, extended to the rest of the country. This is in strong contrast with previously Communist countries such as Poland and the Baltic states where the reforms were implemented in one Big-Bang. According to the Chinese authorities, a step-by-step approach was, and still is, needed because of the enormous size of the population. One small mistake may have dramatic effects when multiplied by 1.3 billion people. Furthermore, the Big-Bang approach is in contradiction to the *Yin–Yang* concept of Chinese culture that focuses on harmony. Another explanation for the gradual route was to reduce opposition from groups with vested interests. The central authorities needed the support of the local bureaucrats and SOEs in executing the reforms.

Pragmatic

Looking backward, one can say that there was no single master plan to guide the reforms. The authorities tried out many approaches to achieve economic growth; some failed while others were successful. It is interesting to note that most of the successful reforms came from local initiatives. These initiatives started at grassroots levels or through local governments before being taken over by national legislation; the party and central government only adapted these local reforms afterwards. Local initiatives are logical due to the large regional differences. For example, there are significant differences between the family businesses that drive China's coastal provinces and the much greater influence of SOEs in the industrial northeast. Both may need a different local reform approach.

An example of a local initiative that was taken over and successfully rolled out nationwide was the household responsibility system, introduced at the beginning of the early reform period. As we will see later, this was an initiative that came spontaneously. The government accepted this initiative as being in line with socialist farming and stimulated the development further. Another example to show that the bureaucracy is reacting instead of guiding through a well-conceived masterplan was the government's strategy of private car ownership. In 1985, the government suddenly decided to allow private spending on cars. Consequently, more than 350,000 cars were imported from Japan within one year, which made China one of the largest export markets for Japanese cars almost overnight. The Chinese government was totally surprised that so much money was available and that people were willing to spend money on imported cars. Consequently in 1986, they imposed a moratorium on car imports and started to think about a strategy of domestic production, hence starting the joint venture strategy in automotive. Such adaptation and pragmatism is still visible today.

The four fundamental choices

The early phase of the reform period up to 1993 was based on four fundamental policy choices. Firstly, the reforms started in the agricultural sector. Secondly, the focus on industrialisation was not only based on large SOEs but, in particular, on the development of smaller private companies known as township and village enterprises (TVEs). This was again an initiative that came from local authorities. The third fundamental choice was to keep the triangle between banks, government and SOEs intact and, consequently, not solving the soft-budget constraint. Fourthly, continuation of fiscal decentralisation was a key element of the early reforms.

1. *Agriculture first*

The economic reforms started in the agricultural sector. Rural attention was needed because of the chaos and stagnation due to the Cultural Revolution. Getting agriculture right was seen as the essential first step for successful industrialisation. The Chinese agricultural sector at the end of the 1970s was very important with a share of 37% of GDP and 65% of total employment (NSB). The focus was to improve the production and living standard of the farmers (and thus increase the legitimacy of the party). It was clear that the command economy had to be adjusted. Therefore, the household responsibility system was introduced in rural areas. Individual households, after fulfilling the production quota set by the government, were free to sell their excess production of agricultural goods on the market at flexible market prices which were normally relatively high. This possibility to earn money after contributing to the government resulted in a strong increase of agricultural production.

Because of this incentive, within just several years, agricultural production (and productivity) nearly doubled. The result was that fewer and fewer farmers were needed and became available to the fast growing industrial (export-driven) sector. Many farmers started to work part-time outside the farm. Between 1978 and 1984, almost 49 million workers partially left the agricultural sector without reducing the agricultural production (Xiaodong Zhu, 2012). Consequently, the farm income was complemented by off-farm wage, creating higher income and increasing spending on consumption goods. Because labour productivity was generally higher in the industrial sector than in the agricultural sector, the reallocation of workers to the industry contributed positively to aggregate productivity growth — a topic dealt with in the next chapter. Despite some obstacles after the farms were decollectivised in the mid-1980s, the household responsibility system can be labelled as a big success.

2. *The emergence of the township and village enterprises*

The early reforms after 1978 started in the countryside with the dismantling of collective farming and the introduction of the household responsibility system. The unexpected consequence of the relaxation of planned production was the growth of small, labour intensive and rural industrial firms, mostly set up by township and village-level governments — the TVEs. The growth was unexpected in the sense that it was not centrally planned; these non-state enterprises were the product of markets. The TVEs were mostly producing labour-intensive consumer goods such as fans, bicycles and kitchen appliances. The first step was to focus on the domestic market but, more and more, the attention shifted to export activities. It was the start of the modern private enterprise in China.

The focus of these TVEs on labour-intensive products was in line with China's comparative advantage. Focusing on industries which used a lot of cheap labour was logical but in strong contradiction to the emphasis on heavy industries through SOEs as the government had implemented before. In this period of growth of TVEs, the legal basis of (individual) enterprises was unclear. For example, the companies could only have a maximum of seven employees by law. However, the reality on the ground was totally different. Many of these TVEs had more than hundreds of employees. The central authorities reacted in a pragmatic way and new legislation came into place. After the new legislation, the TVEs could grow further; now within a formal legal framework. And they became the driving force behind China's industrialisation and growth.

An important feature of these TVEs was their hard-budget constraints. They only could survive in the market if they were competitive enough. Their employees did not have an "iron rice bowl" and could be fired. Therefore, they were more productive than the SOEs. From the mid-1980s onwards, by far the majority of the basic products outside the agricultural sector were being produced by these TVEs. Their success was a combination of entrepreneurial energy, competition and a certain amount of local government support. Due to the increased competition from TVEs, the SOEs had to adjust to be able to survive the competitive battle. As a result, there was an increase in productivity over a broad range of sectors.

3. *Triangle relationship continued*

As we saw with the household responsibility system and the growth of TVEs, incentives matter. If incentives and a hard-budget constraint are absent, we will witness the free-rider problem. This was the case with respect to rural communes because the reward after a day of hard work had to be shared with everyone. Likewise, SOEs had a motivation problem. Competing with the efficient TVEs was hardly possible. Furthermore, the SOEs were forced to implement the "iron rice bowl", which included taking care of employees by providing housing, healthcare and pension. This burden was an additional obstacle in competing with the lower-cost TVEs. An important characteristic of the early reform was the continuation of soft-budget constraint in the state sector and therefore the continuation of the strong triangle relationship between the government (budget), SOEs and state-owned banks. The policy was aimed at allocating the increased income of households towards SOEs through the state-owned banks; even SOEs that were not able to compete received credits from the banks. The soft-budget constraint was being reinforced because of the decentralisation process. Local governments and local banks had an even stronger incentive to protect local enterprises.

Keeping SOEs afloat was also driven by the government's aim to have provincial self-sufficiency. Therefore, fragmentation of production continued during the period of the early reforms. However, it also reduced the opportunity to generate economies of scale and efficiency.

Consequently, the SOEs continued to receive loans. For example, at the end of 1993, 87% of all loans from the state-owned commercial banks went to SOEs (Chiu and Lewis, 2006). Due to such a relationship, a crisis in one sector of the triangle of soft-budget constraint (Fig. 2.3) easily leads to crisis in the others. If the SOEs were not able to repay their debts, banks would be confronted by an increase in bad debts. At the end of the day, the government must step in through its fiscal policy and legislation.

Furthermore, labour market considerations led the government to protect SOEs. Due to population growth and the increase of labour supply, it was more and more difficult to provide jobs for everyone. Hence, SOEs had to be kept afloat and protected, yet at the same time, there was a need to increase their efficiency and competitiveness.

Immediately after 1978, we saw the first government approach to increase competitiveness of SOEs. For example, the introduction of a manager-responsibility-system gave the SOE-managers more discretionary power. This was later complemented by permitting SOEs to produce outside the compulsory production targets: the so-called dual-track price system, established in 1985. We can say that China began to attack an important pillar of the command economy, namely its price controls, relatively early in the transition process. The dual-track regime functioned in the form of controlled prices of key inputs such as coal, oil, and steel within a plan system. However, prices were liberalised for production (and purchases) of these key inputs outside the plan, after the company fulfilled its quota. A producer of the key inputs could only sell its products in the market after it had produced its quota. In the same token, an enterprise using those inputs had to purchase them from the market at market prices once they reached the quota stated in the plan.

Price liberalisation was needed to solve shortages in the economy, which were a structural problem in China. At the same time, liberalising prices too quickly would result in hyperinflation. In that sense, the dual-track price system dealt with these two potential problems. Liberalisation of prices of consumer goods directly attacked shortage and, by controlling the prices of key inputs, reduced the risk of hyperinflation. By the early 1990s, the two tracks of prices converged, and finally the dual-track price system was abolished in 1994 (Xiaojing Zhang & Xin Chang, 2016). One may ask the question why the central authorities did not choose privatisation as a solution for the problem of inefficient SOEs in this period. But privatisation was a step too far. The goal for the state sector was, and has always been, to make itself more efficient, not to dismantle itself.

4. *Decentralisation*

As indicated earlier, decentralisation of administrative and economic power to local governments was a main feature of China's pre-reform choices and this continued after 1978. The local government's role in total expenditures and revenues increased strongly. China had always a strong administrative capacity, especially at the provincial level. Thus, when the central authorities decided that further decentralisation was needed to stimulate local reforms, provincial governments were able to take on the new responsibilities.

The reforms discussed above gave more freedom and incentives to enterprises, local governments, and individuals, but only step by step. A local pilot project had the advantage that identification of good or bad policies was possible. If the outcome of a specific reform was favourable, it could be implemented in other parts of the country, a process Deng Xiaoping referred to as "crossing the river by touching the stones". The dual-track system is an example of this gradualism. Also, the SEZs are an example of the step-by-step approach. When these SEZs appeared to be successful, they were scaled up to other regions and other sectors. This idea of feeling the stones when crossing the river resulted in pilot projects in isolated (not so important) regions or sectors. For example, the household responsibility system as a pilot reform started in several remote provinces.

The development of TVEs started in the Wenzhou area, which (in the 1980s) was an isolated region in Zhejiang Province. That was why the region received special permission to be a pilot region for rural industrialisation. One of my colleagues told me that the only reason Shanghai was not being selected as one of the first SEZs in the late 1970s was that it was just too big and too important for such an experiment. It was safer to select a small village like Shenzhen in the south of China, nearby Hong Kong and far away from Beijing, as an experimental zone. Using pilot projects and the choice for gradualism is logical. One should keep in mind that in many cases, Chinese authorities did not have a precedent; there was big uncertainty about the impact of all these reforms and, therefore, it was risky to make radical choices.

The discussion above is summarised in Fig. 3.2 in which the three pillars of the early reforms are combined with the fundamental

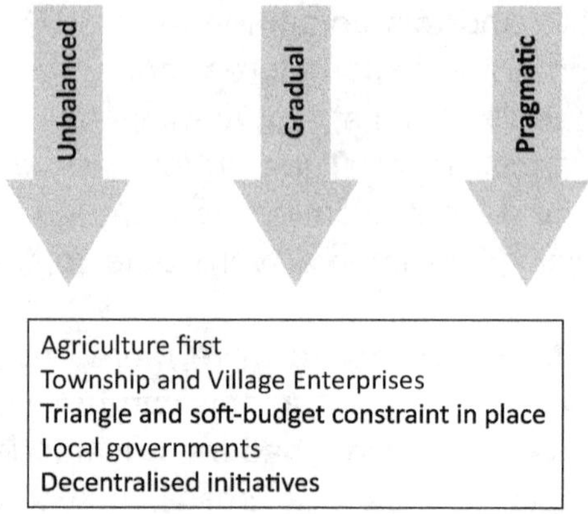

Figure 3.2 The basic pillars and key choices during the 1978–1993 period
Source: Adjusted from World Bank (2013)

choices. One of the key outcomes of the early-reform period was the protection of vested interests — "reforms without losers".

3.4 The picture in the mid-1990s — reforms without losers

Essentially, the early reforms did not harm the vested groups, including the local government and high officials at SOEs. They could be a significant barrier to market-oriented reform. Therefore, the party and state chose reform strategies that involved minimised political opposition. Gradualism was also needed because an ideological mindset shift of the people who lived in an ideology-driven, single-party command governance structure was hardly possible at short notice. This applied also to local officials, managers, as well as the public.

The outcome of all these choices in the early-reform period was that the non-state sector grew without downsizing the state sector. This was the only way to minimise social instability and reduce resistance to reform. An example was the continuation of the economic and financial triangle of government, banks and SOEs. It is interesting to note that between 1979 and 1993, employment in the state-owned sector remained constant at about 17% of the workforce (adjusted from Xiaodong Zhu, 2012). The government intervened strongly in the economy. It helped SOEs in difficulty and stood behind the banks if the firms were not able to repay their debts. This strong intervention is not visible in official statistics. The official fiscal deficit was around 1% of GDP, which is healthy and sustainable by international standards. However, if the policy loans were regarded as implicit budget expenditures in the 1990s, the implied fiscal deficit would be as high as 25% of GDP (Bartel & Huang, 2000). Furthermore, one may argue that the fundamental roots of the problem, namely, distortions in the price system, were not being tackled. The artificial low interest rates created an imbalance between investments and savings on the one hand, and consumption on the other hand. The artificial low exchange rate resulted in large trade surpluses and high profitability in export-related industries. In addition, the artificial low prices of coal (and thereby electricity) acted as an implicit subsidy to China's capital-intensive industrial sector.

In the 1980s, the economy was growing at a healthy rate and the absolute welfare levels of the population increased strongly. This reduced the sense of urgency to reform. In particular, the rural population witnessed a strong increase in income and purchasing power (helped by government support). Looking back, one may argue that not enough emphasis was given towards the urban population in the early-reform period. For example, the result of the higher agricultural prices was high inflation in the urban centres in 1986–1988. Discontent about high urban inflation, complemented by more and more dissatisfaction about corruption, resulted in social instability, with the Tiananmen Square demonstrations of 1989 as the dramatic result.

The choice of the party to intervene with the help of the People's Liberation Army (PLA) had a dramatic impact on the Chinese economy. Total spending declined and inflow of FDI stopped. The first years of the 1990s were weak in economic terms for the urban as well as the rural population, and urgency for structural changes intensified. In the 1990s, there was a need to shift from rural-focused reforms towards urban-focused reforms. It became clear that the greatest threat to the party came from the cities. The focus on urban development was translated into new party leaders with an urban history. For example, Jiang Zemin and Zhu Rongji were both party generals of Shanghai and had mainly dealt with urban issues. Another adjustment in the reform policy related to exports. In his South China speech in early 1992, Deng Xiaoping stressed the need to invest in new machines to increase productivity and to increase exports. This focus on export-driven development was an important new feature of China's new growth model.

One may say that the Chinese governance system was very effective in the early-reform period. The party's control over the state media, universities, and larger companies (in addition to the tradition of hierarchical governance) made it possible to inform and guide the citizens effectively in the direction of reform. But the chapter makes clear that the reforms were not packed into a consistent, logical master plan. In many case, the party and government reacted (in a pragmatic way) to local initiatives.

Chapter 4

Explaining Economic Development between 1993 and 2007

Myth 4: In 2007, China's economic development reached its ceiling due to the growing imbalances in the society

4.1 Introduction

The year 1993 was the start of accelerated reforms after the easy ones were implemented. Features of this acceleration were the opening up of formerly closed sectors and the restructuring of state-owned enterprises (SOEs). In that year, the Chinese Communist Party (CCP) defined the role of the market as "basic" in allocating resources. This was an important step in adopting a socialist market economy. The year 2007 was the start of the worldwide financial and economic crisis. It was also the year in which China started its rebalancing process, changing from growth based on investments and export towards growth driven by consumption and efficiency.

Already in the 1990s, China's political leaders stated again and again that a change of the growth model was needed. However, before 2007, China's policy initiatives in this field had been relatively modest, and economic growth remained disproportionally dependent on investments and export. One may say that before 2007, the focus was still on picking the "low hanging fruit" in terms of reforms and untackled fundamental imbalances. Structural reforms would hurt economic growth and this had to be avoided. The paradigm was clear: high economic growth above other objectives. From this point of view, the policy was a success. The 1993–2007 period witnessed extremely high growth, and increased substantially the absolute welfare of the Chinese people. At the same time, it became clear that this growth strategy also created severe imbalances in the economy such as overcapacity in certain sectors, rising inequality and environmental issues. These imbalances were first addressed in the 11th five-year plan of 2006, which can be seen as the start of deepening structural reforms. The focus on growth at all cost was changed to one that balanced economic growth with several social goals in order to develop a "socialist harmonious society" and to further modernise the economy.

This chapter is structured as follows. Section 4.2 explains China's longer-term development and economic growth up to 2007 with a focus on the supply side of the economy. This will be complemented in Section 4.3 with some typically Chinese features within the standard growth model. Section 4.4 focuses on the short-term explanation of economic growth, emphasising the demand side of the economy. Throughout the chapter, we will learn how China's growth pattern resulted in extreme imbalances in all fields, and it will become clear that there was an increasing sense of urgency to counteract these imbalances.

4.2 Explaining economic development

When discussing economic growth, we need to distinguish between the short-term and long-term development. Of course, governments, households and companies are concerned with the short-term ups and downs of the business cycle: What is the economic growth this quarter compared to a year ago? What is the impact on unemployment? To answer questions like these, we must focus on the demand side of the economy, which is about spending. Developments in the expenditures in the economy result in high or low growth of the Gross Domestic Product (GDP). Although the expenditure approach is logical for short-term fluctuations, in many cases, these short-term fluctuations are of less significance in the longer span of history.

In the longer term, we may ask ourselves the question why China was growing over the past 15 years and how much richer the average Chinese worker today is compared to 25 years ago. To answer such questions, we must seek explanation from the supply side of the economy. Supply determines the capacity of the economy and the growth potential of an economy. From the supply point of view, there are three factors of GDP growth per capita in the longer term:

- Size and growth of the working population, and associated to this, the size and growth of the labour force;
- Size and growth in the physical stock, referred to as capital accumulation; and
- Increase in the productivity of physical capital (i.e. better machines), human capital (i.e. skills of workers) and more efficient institutions. This relates to technological progress, which has the effect of increasing output from a given amount of resources.

The Chinese strategy to increase GDP in the period 1993–2007 was mainly based on a growing labour force, in combination with capital accumulation (World Bank, 2012). Excess supply of rural labour migrated to the urban centres to work in SOEs. This influx of migrant workers kept wages low and helped China's manufacturing-export sector. High investments were a central feature in this growth strategy. It was clear that more investments in machines per worker would increase output. High investments were financed by high national savings. These savings went into the banking sector and were translated into cheap credits to the SOEs, mostly in the heavy industry. The credit expansion (and the associated problems of bad loans) was backed by government support and the fact that the government would bail out SOEs and banks in default. Also, the third factor behind long-term development, being the increase in productivity, can explain part of the economic success in the 1990s and early 2000s. In particular, the shift of workers from the agricultural sector (with its low productivity) to the manufacturing sector (with a much higher average level of productivity) contributed to production growth in this period. It should be clear that this increase in productivity was driven more by mobilisation of resources and less by technological advancement and innovations.

Throughout this period, government intervention in the economy was intensive and visible, and many distortions existed. The capital market was distorted due to the highly regulated interest rates. The labour market was also distorted due to the relatively low wages compared to productivity. Distortions also occurred on the product market with government interventions in many sectors. Companies were subsidised through low prices for land use and energy. Starting in the mid-1990s, the first steps were taken to increase market forces in the economy and increase productivity. It was logical to start with the SOEs.

Protect the large, release the small

The SOE reforms started in 1995 with the slogan above. On the one hand, the focus was on making a small number of large, strategically important SOEs more efficient and profitable, through government protection and help if necessary. These big state-controlled conglomerates were seen as the new flagships being able to compete also on foreign markets. On the other hand, the choice was to privatise smaller SOEs in sectors such as electronics and other consumer goods. These privatised companies did not receive government support anymore. The 15th Congress of the CCP held in 1997 officially confirmed this approach. The product market became more liberalised with lower barriers to operate, lower tariffs and a new regime to attract foreign direct investments (FDI). Part of this policy mix of opening up was driven (and forced) by the process of becoming a member of the World Trade Organisation (WTO) in 2001.

Between 1993 and 2007, private enterprises grew rapidly at the expense of the TVEs that also became privatised one by one. By 2007, domestic private enterprises (comprising local companies, foreign companies and joint ventures) accounted for 60% of total urban employment in the manufacturing sector (NBS, 2009). The combination of privatisation and trade liberalisation had strong effects on productivity growth in both the state- and non-state sectors. The productivity growth in the manufacturing sector was high with 14% a year between 1998 and 2007 (NBS database). The picture was different with respect to the service sector. The service sector saw less competition, significant barriers to exit and, consequently, had a low productivity growth in this period. In 2007, the state sector still accounted for 77% of total urban employment in services, in contrast to 15–20% in manufacturing (Xiaodong Zhu, 2012).

As stated before, all three growth factors were important between 1993 and 2007, although their importance shifted from period to period. Capital accumulation financed by high savings and increase of the labour force were both important during the entire period. With respect to productivity, the picture was a bit blurred. With reference to Fig. 4.1, there was strong productivity growth due to the reallocation of resources from agriculture to manufacturing, and from the state to the private sector, in the mobilisation phase of growth (between 1993 and 2007). It should be stressed that this increase of productivity due to reallocation of resources is relatively easy. A person moving from agriculture to manufacturing automatically result in a productivity gain. However, productivity increase because of technological progress

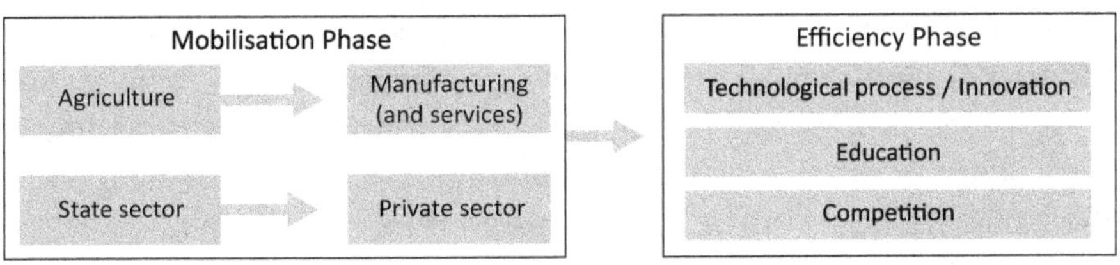

Figure 4.1 Sources of productivity growth

Source: Based on IMF (2006)

was still lagging. Essentially, China did not entered the efficiency phase. Already in the mid-2000s, it became clear that more in-depth reforms were needed to ensure that the efficiency phase of growth could begin (Kroeber, 2016). Hence, the focus shifted to increasing competition, innovation and investing in education to increase skilled labour.

To summarise, throughout 1993–2007, the focus was on mobilising resources, mainly combining more machines with more labour. Maximising the efficiency with which those resources were used received less attention. Visitors in China could (and still can) see the waste and inefficiencies everywhere. Of course, this may create a problem, but such waste can be irrelevant so long as it is a by-product of an effective process of meeting basic needs. By focusing on creating a massive number of houses, schools, hospitals, and roads, it is understandable and hardly surprising that in this process, useless jobs were created and low-quality products produced. Definitely, this waste cannot continue forever even though it was an acceptable by-product of fast economic growth and improvement of living standards. Hence, a transition towards the efficiency phase is needed.

Reaching the ceiling

Continuation of the early-reform focus on mobilising resources was a logical choice by looking at the resources available and the starting position of the country at the end of the 1970s. However, in the 1990s, this mobilisation stage reached its ceiling. The surplus of labour disappeared and a further increase in capital stock could not achieve the same results as before. Obviously, new capital projects had to meet some basic productivity standards. For example, building a bridge that was not connected to a road on either end was a pure waste of money, as was building an export-beer bottling plant 3000 miles away from a port. Besides these basic requirements, the emphasis was still on investments and increasing the capital stock.

If a country is developing, as did China in the 1990s, this efficiency of capital is becoming more important. At the end of the day, simply throwing more capital in the system achieves fewer and fewer benefits. The roads are there, the equipment is there and new investments hardly create more production. When this happens, growth must come from increasing the amount of output that a given unit of capital can produce, that is, by increasing the efficiency of resources use through technological progress.

The short analysis above makes clear that without technological progress, long-term growth cannot sustain; there is a need to move into the efficiency phase of reforms. A sense of urgency to change the growth strategy developed between 1993 and 2007 but it was not strong enough to make decisive choices. I can understand why the Chinese authorities' attitude was that postponements of structural reforms were still possible. This relates to some of China's unique features: the sheer size of its population and labour force, and the differences between regions and sectors. These features, in combination with being economically backward, extended the mobilisation phase or the period of "easy" productivity growth.

China's success can be attributed to its backwardness in terms of productivity at the start of the reforms. For example, China's productivity level was much lower than in countries such as Brazil, Malaysia and South Africa. Because of this backwardness, productivity growth grew relatively easy and fast from year to year. The relationship between productivity level and productivity growth is summarised in Fig. 4.2. The lower the productivity level (compared to the more productive countries), the higher the annual average growth in productivity. Hence, China had the advantage of being backward (Gerschenkron, 1952). It could achieve high annual productivity growth over a longer period of time because of the large distance to the most innovative and productive countries.

This is also what we saw in the Asian Tiger economies. These countries witnessed strong productivity growth when they started their reforms and during their early catching up process; but as soon as they approached 60–70% of the US productivity level, annual productivity growth declined (OECD, 2012). The same can be expected of China. This is partly why longer-term forecasts (up to 2040 or 2050) are so much lower than the 6.5% growth we see today. For the medium-term future, "easy" productivity growth

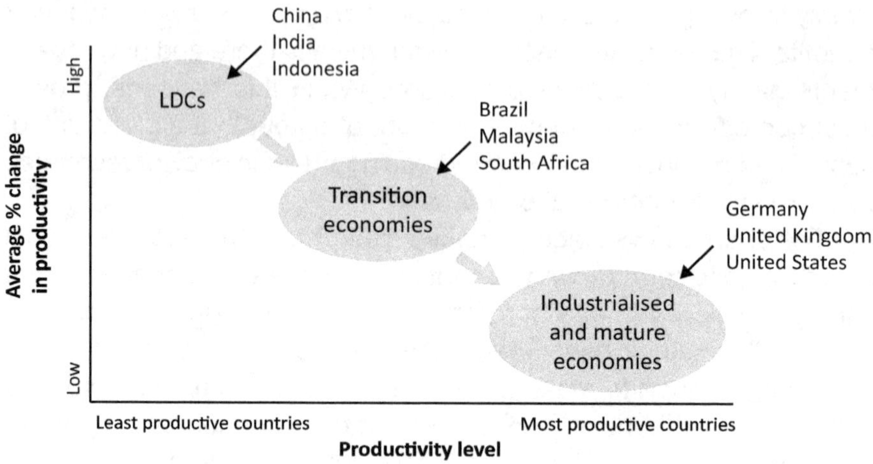

Figure 4.2 Productivity level versus annual average productivity growth
Source: *Based on OECD (2012)*

can still play an important role. Even after 30 years of reforms, the Chinese productivity level of the whole economy compared to the US is still low (around 25%) and relatively "easy" productivity gains may be expected in the years to come. Moreover, even if the average productivity level reaches the 60–70% benchmark, there are large sectoral differences between the outward export-oriented industry and the domestic-focused service sector, which also create room to continue the mobilisation phase. Another argument why the old growth model based on the mobilisation phase would still be possible relates to the availability of labour. The figures differ from source to source, but essentially can be summarised as follows: in 2007, there were 480 million working age population in rural China. On paper, each had a rural *hukou*, but around 200 million had already migrated into the non-agricultural sectors in the cities. It means that 280 million people were still available for work outside agriculture. According to the productivity level in agriculture, the sector needed about 150 million people. As a result, the surplus labour was 130 million. Obviously, not all of these 130 million people could be easily absorbed in manufacturing (or services). For example,

50% of the farmers were over 40 years old and part of this group had below primary education. As a result, the real surplus was 75–85 million people in 2007, less compared to past decades but still a lot of people. In this sense, the migration flow, and growth model based on the mobilisation phase associated with it, may not be exhausted. The same holds with capital accumulation.

The third idea behind the continuation of the easy productivity growth phase is related to the large differences within China. The efficiency of new investments declined but do not forget that the west and north of China are completely different from the coastal areas. In many parts of the country, there was still a shortage of capital and a need for airports, highways, universities and housing.

4.3 Chinese characteristics in the standard growth theory

Despite postponement of structural reforms, the period 1993–2007 witnessed important market-oriented reforms and choices. Key elements included the strong emphasis on the industrial sector, continued decentralisation and macro-economic policy that could counteract the negative effects of the SOE-reforms.

Emphasising the industrial sector

Industrialisation was the main objective of the authorities and was seen as synonymous to modernisation. In this sense, China's economy followed the pattern of development in the west, which started with industrialisation; only when per capita income rose did the service sector take-off. However, China's development path differs from that in other emerging markets, where services play an important role very early in the reform period. In Brazil, India and Russia, the service sector dominated the economy throughout the reform process. In contrast, China opted for a strong industrial sector by being the factory of the world in the 1990s and early 2000s. This emphasis on the industrial sector changed in the mid-2000s.

The reform of the SOEs created problems for the labour market and the fall of employment in the manufacturing sector had to be absorbed. The service sector was seen as important because of its labour-intensive nature and its absorption capacity when economic growth declined, or changes in economic structure occurred.

Creating local initiatives

China's strategy of "crossing the river by feeling the stones" resulted in gradualism and small-scale pilot projects. These initiatives often started spontaneously and were driven by local initiatives; only later did formal institutions, laws and regulations catch up with reality on the ground. In many ways, the local governments can be considered as the real entrepreneurs (behind the corporate entrepreneurs) in China. The institutional system between 1993–2007 intensified the administrative decentralisation, continued to stimulate local initiatives and transformed local governments into real owners of the pro-market reform process. Local initiatives and the overlap between government and business were made possible by institutional changes that further legalised the decentralisation.

Maintaining macroeconomic, social and political-stability

Macroeconomic stability is a precondition of economic growth. That is the reason why John Williamson put macroeconomic stability as the first of the ten policy recommendations that he summarised as the Washington Consensus for the restructuring of the Latin American economies after the dramatic sovereign debt crisis in the 1980s (Williamson, 1990). China has done a good job in maintaining a stable macroeconomic environment. This is quite an achievement if one considers the different transformations in the 1993–2007 period. The transition from a planned economy to a market-driven economy went smoothly. Furthermore, the authorities were able to change the economic structure quite substantially without disrupting the economy, and in such a way that that it could absorb redundant workers from SOEs. The policies introduced in this period were also able to tackle the problems caused by the influx of migrant workers in the big cities. It solved the issue of the state banks which were burdened with large and increasing non-performing loans mainly from indebted SOEs. The authorities also had to work out how the central government's role in fiscal policy could be strengthened. Many of these transformations would cause hyperinflation and economic downturns, but economic development between 1993 and 2007 was relatively smooth. There were several recessions and also periods of high inflation, but most of them were mild compared with other developing and developed countries.

Figure 4.3 presents China's inflation rate between 1980 and 2016. Two periods of very high inflation rates are evident: 1988–1989 and 1993–1995. The price hike in 1989, which caused widespread discontent among the urban population, was one of the driving forces behind the Tiananmen Square protests in 1989. In essence, inflation in the 1993–1995 period was driven by the attempt to reform prices. Furthermore, a severe flood increased food prices and wages increased quite dramatically in the early 1990s. In 1994, the inflation rate reached 24%, the highest in China's history. After 1994, inflation declined very fast and, after the Asian Financial Crisis (1997), even became negative. This deflation

Figure 4.3 China's consumer price index, 1980–2016

Source: *National Bureau of Statistics*

continued until 2003 when China entered a new round of moderate inflation up to 2007. The inflation in 2007 was mainly caused by China's large current account surpluses, credit expansion and strong investment growth. It can be seen that inflation declined in 2008 but increased again in 2010 after the large stimulus package was implemented in 2008 and 2009; however, this price spike was very short-lived. Overall, despite these spikes in inflation, it is remarkable that the Chinese authorities were able to achieve reasonable price stability in the 1993–2007 period.

4.4 The business cycle between 1978 and 2007

Although the period of interest in this chapter is 1993–2007 (grey areas in Fig. 4.4), I will discuss the business cycle from 1978 onwards. The period after 2007 will be dealt with in Chapter 5. The analysis of the business cycle is done through the expenditure approach. Expansion of yearly GDP is driven by the growth of expenditures associated with consumption (both private and government), investments (again private and government), and net export of goods and services.

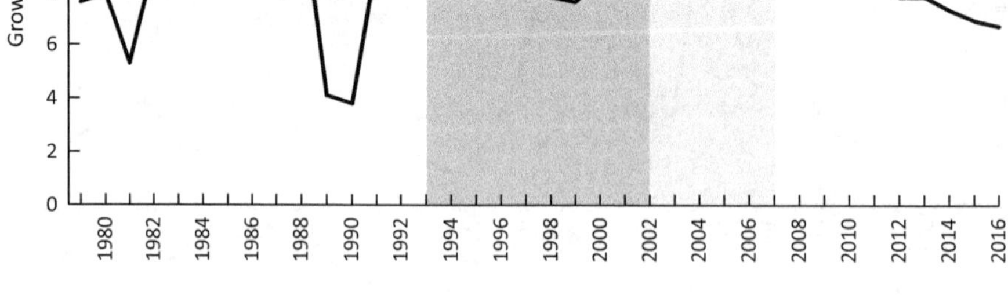

Figure 4.4 The business cycle, 1978–2016

Source: National Bureau of Statistics

By focusing on these demand factors, we can divide the period up to 2007 into four phases. The overview below is partly based on Xiaodong Zhu (2012).

1978–1988 consumption and domestic market-led growth

From the start of the early reforms up to 1988, household consumption was rising fast; much faster than the other determinants of total demand. To gain political support for the reforms, the government carried out policies to increase the income of ordinary people. Wages increased in SOEs and heavy emphasis was given to increase the income of farmers. The strong growth in income stimulated household consumption (although with high urban inflation in certain periods as a negative side-effect). Net export in the first decade of reforms was rising fast. However, the growth originated from a low basis and, as a result, export did not have much impact on the growth rate of the economy. Investments (mostly government-initiated) were growing but in line with the growth in GDP. In essence, the period 1978–1988 can be characterised as a domestic-market led growth.

1989–1991 rapid increase in export

The Tiananmen Square event resulted in an economic recession. During this short period of three years, GDP growth slowed down significantly, mostly due to a strong reduction of growth in investments and consumption. As a result, the government focus shifted towards export. This period is considered as the start of the policy-driven export strategy with an increasing role for exports in China's growth model. The export share of GDP rose from 12% in 1990 to 18% of GDP in 1992 (MOFCOM). The government stimulated export through supportive measures to export-driven SOEs, cheap credits and an artificial low value of the Renminbi (RMB). For example, exports rose by almost 40% in 1990 alone; in that same year, the Renminbi devaluated more than 20% compared to the US dollar.

1992–2001 investment-led growth

The period 1992–2001 can be described as investment-led growth period. The period started after Deng Xiaoping's famous southern tour in 1992, in which he called for an acceleration of economic reform, and ended with China's accession to the WTO on 11 December 2001. In this period, fixed investment played the leading role, growing almost three percentage points faster than GDP on an annual basis and contributing 40% of GDP growth over this decade (BBVA Research). Household consumption and government consumption grew in line with GDP. Unlike in the preceding period, exports played a relatively small role in economic growth between 1992 and 2002. It does not mean that export stagnated; it was still growing at 7–8% every year, but GDP (in particular, investments) was growing even faster.

2002–2007 export- and investment-led growth

The period 2002–2007 can be described as export- and investment-led growth. Fixed investments and exports became the main factors accounting for growth in the early 2000s. Estimations vary, but the consensus is that around 75% of GDP growth in the 2002–2007 period was driven by these two factors. After 2001, the export share began a rapid and consistent rise. Over this period, the export share rose from 22% to a remarkable 39% of GDP. In Chapter 10, we will discuss more in-depth the role of export because the focus on export as percentage of GDP is not taking into account the fact that a lot of the exported products needed imported components; so, in essence, we should focus on the domestic value-added created by this export. However, export (without making this adjustment) was the largest driving force behind China's economic growth in this period. Fixed investments also grew rapidly in this period, driven by government investments in housing, infrastructure and manufacturing, largely linked to building capacity in the export sectors. The share of fixed investments rose to an extremely high average of

41% of GDP over this period. Although, investments were a key ingredient in explaining growth, the enormous size of investments created fewer results than what one would expect. To put it in the words of Martin Wolf: "the surprising thing about the Chinese economy in recent years is not, as so frequently emphasised, how fast it is growing but rather, given the astonishing share of output devoted to investment, how slowly it is growing" (quoted by Lardy, 2007). This point was precisely considered when the authorities announced the need to rebalance the economy away from investments and exports.

The need to rebalance

China's economic growth peaked at 14% in 2007, and with an average growth of more than 10% in the 1993–2007 period, economic policy can be labelled as successful. Despite the success in terms of growth, China's development process had some negative side-effects. It became more and more visible that urban income did not hold track with GDP growth. Furthermore, as indicated above, the growth strategy based on capital-intensive manufacturing did not create enough jobs. Both factors had a negative impact on consumer spending and, consequently, consumption was low compared to GDP. The focus on manufacturing led to environmental issues, while the labour-intensive and environment- friendly service sector was underdeveloped. Moreover, income inequality (associated with corruption) became a big issue. In the early 2000s, China's export strategy was under attack due to the enormous trade surplus that resulted in some protectionist tensions.

Investments created more and more overcapacity issues in specific markets. In many speeches after 2004, the needed change in the growth model and the need to rebalance the economy was stressed; but before 2007, China's policy initiatives had been relatively modest in this field of rebalancing, and economic development remained disproportionally dependent on investments and export. One may say that on paper, China already started its rebalancing process but implementation of the reforms was postponed. Growth was achievable within the context of the traditional growth model linked to the mobilisation phase.

Chapter 5

The Imbalanced Economy between 2007 and 2017

Myth 5: China's imbalanced growth pattern is unique

5.1 Introduction

The traditional growth model implemented between 1978 and 2007 focused on high savings and high investments. Despite the low interest rates, Chinese households saved a lot and, via cheap credits, these savings were transferred to the industrial state-owned enterprises (SOEs). The government's role was visible in supporting national and local champions through industrial policy. Furthermore, excess supply of agricultural labour and the migration to more productive sectors kept wages below productivity level (and growth), which helped export and attracted foreign direct investment (FDI). Because of the low wages and the uncertainty felt by the people, consumption was low. To compensate for the low private spending, the government increased its investments and stimulated export. Consequently, the exchange rate was kept at a low (and undervalued) value, leading to easy export. In 2007, it became clear that after three decades of opening up and spectacular economic growth, the problem was no longer how to achieve growth but how to manage the consequences of growth. Severe imbalances became visible in the economy as a negative by-product of fast economic development. Consequently, rebalancing the economy was needed.

In March 2007, then-premier Wen Jiabao highlighted the need to rebalance the Chinese economy away from an investment-led, export-driven economy towards a consumption-oriented economy when he told reporters at the National People's Congress: "The biggest problem in China's economy is that the growth is unstable, unbalanced, uncoordinated and unsustainable [...] These are all pressing issues that need to be addressed as soon as possible or they will threaten China's economic growth". (Xinhua news). After 2007, the focus changed towards social goals in order to develop a "socialist harmonious society" and to further modernise the economy. This was clearly stated in the 11th (2006–2010) five-year plan. The plan made clear that promoting consumer demand, addressing income inequality, reducing pollution and deepening structural reforms were essential to achieve the combined aim of economic growth and increasing quality of life. However, the start was slow because of the global financial and economic crisis (2008), as well as the need for the government to act as crisis manager to stabilise the economy.

The structure of this chapter is as follows: Section 5.2 discusses the main imbalances in the Chinese economy. The choices in the 1993–2007 period resulted in an overreliance on investments and export. In addition, it resulted in underdevelopment of the service sector. The industrial-driven growth also had adverse impact on the environment. This is followed in Section 5.3 by a discussion on the middle-income trap and the introduction of the so-called Lewis turning point. Section 5.4 gives an interpretation of the data regarding rebalancing. This interpretation of the progress is rather difficult; certain signals point to a more balanced economy while not so much progress has been made in other parts of the society. In Section 5.5, the focus shifts towards the latest developments and steps taken to rebalance the economy. It should be taken into account that most of the reform policies and the imbalances itself will be elaborated in the second part of the book (Chapters 8–14).

5.2 The most important imbalances

Figure 5.1 shows again the business cycle between 1979 and 2016. Economic growth between 2007 and 2016, highlighted by

Figure 5.1 Economic growth, 1979–2016

Source: *National Bureau of Statistics*

the bold line, was impressive, although the growth rate reduced, in particular, after 2009. In 2016, economic growth was 6.7%, substantially lower than 14% achieved in 2007, but still high compared with other countries.

The fundamental shift towards another growth strategy was unmistakably noticeable in the 12th five-year plan (2011–2015). This five-year plan can be considered as the country's rebalancing blueprint. A key term used in this 12th five-year plan is "inclusive growth" — a more people-oriented growth. The plan indicated many social-related targets and there was a strong emphasis on increasing quality of life and living standards of ordinary people. With respect to the role of markets in the economy, the party clearly indicated a more robust role of market forces in setting prices and allocating resources. This was being emphasised by the Central Committee of the 18th Communist Party during the third plenary session in November 2013. At this meeting, it was stated that the market was set to play a "decisive" role ahead. This was quite different from the "basic" role to which the market was limited thus far. This change from basic to decisive did not mean that the market was taking over the role of the government, but it was clear that more market-driven incentives were implemented. An important step in achieving this was the opening up of more previously closed sectors in the economy.

The rebalancing is also visible in the newest (13th) five-year plan that runs from 2016 to 2020. The plan emphasises the sustainability issue a lot and, once again, there are concrete targets for social spending in healthcare, education and pensions. On paper, the reform agenda and the statements are undoubtedly impressive. The need for reforms has also been emphasised verbally. For example, in the keynote speech at the opening of the 2013 World Economic Forum annual meeting of the new champions (the Summer Davos), then-premier Li Keqiang said that "without structural transformation and upgrading, we will not be able to sustain economic growth in the long term". However, the actual implementation of the announced decisions varies greatly across areas and gradualism is key; the starting point is always to achieve stability and avoid chaos.

The growth strategy up to 2007 resulted in economic success but also many imbalances at the same time. The strategy of cheap labour helped export, but also created an unsustainable trade surplus. The cheap money strategy resulted in over-investments. Cheap energy prices reduced the costs of SOEs, but created big environmental problems. Easy access to credit by SOEs resulted in large debts. Thus, structural transformation was needed. Figure 5.2 shows four interrelated problems that need to be tackled: external, internal, environmental-distributional and financial distortions.

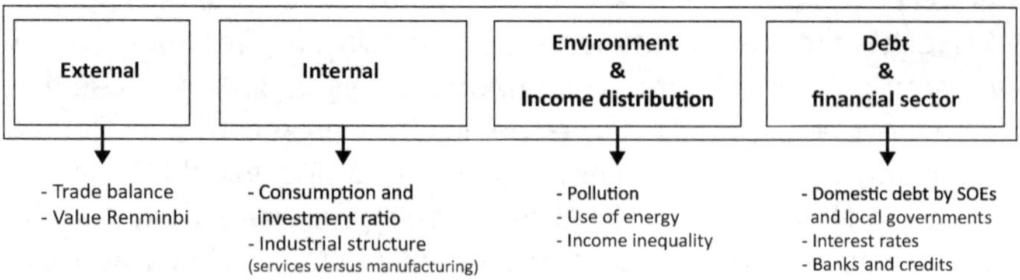

Figure 5.2 Problems of rebalancing

Source: Based on ECB (2013) & IMF (2016)

I will elaborate below on the main imbalances in an introductory way because many of the issues will be dealt with later in the book.

Over-dependence on investment

A high and rising investment share in GDP in itself might not be a problem, as investment is a necessary driver of economic growth. However, a very high investment share increases the risk of excess capacity and low returns with negative spill-overs to the banking sector and labour market. Furthermore, the investments are financed by savings and, as a result of high investments, consumption is low. As Fig. 5.3 shows, the rising share of investment in GDP was enormous between 2004 and 2008, increasing from 37% to 47% in just five years. After 2008, a first sign of rebalancing is visible with a declining investment share (although it increased again in 2015).

As stated before, a high investment share is not in itself a problem and is relatively common in transition economies in the take-off stage. Singapore had investment shares above 40% in certain periods in its development. Likewise, Malaysia and Thailand (1990s), South Korea (1970s), and Japan (1960s) reached their investment peaks around

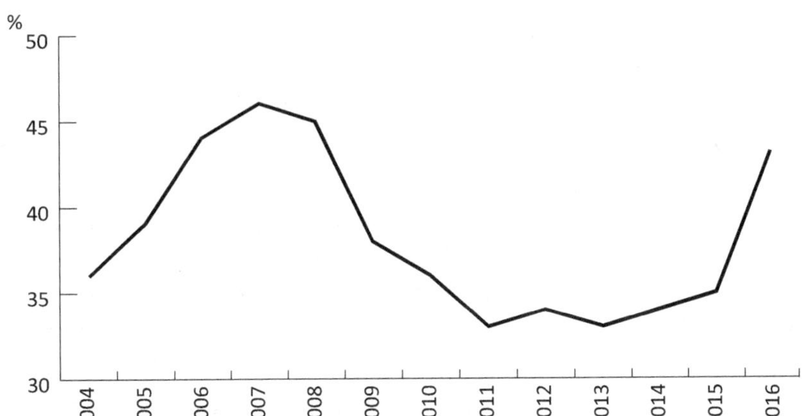

Figure 5.3 Investments as percentage of GDP, 2004–2016

Source: National Bureau of Statistics & IMF (2016)

40% (Lardy, 2007 & ECB, 2013). It is difficult to conclude when an investment rate is too high. It depends on specific conditions in countries, but according to the Chenery Standard (Chenery and Syrquin, 1975), China's investment share of GDP in 2007 was 15–20 percentage points higher than may be expected. Based on this, China should move towards an investment ratio of around the mid-30% of GDP. The main problem of investments as driver behind growth is that it automatically will lead to declining efficiency of resource use. This lower efficiency of investments can be seen by looking to the debt accumulation in the economy. The level of debt compared to the size of the economy (debt-to-GDP ratio) increased dramatically in the previous decade to reach 250% of GDP early 2017 (Lombard Odier, 2016 and IMF, 2017). It is clear: SOEs (but also entrepreneurs) are taking on more and more debts to finance projects with lower and lower returns. Obviously, this cannot continue and payment problems may start a contagious effect on the financial markets.

Suppressed consumption

In contrast to the investment share going up, the household consumption rate decreased from 60% in the pre-reform period to 36% in 2010. As shown in Fig. 5.4, the consumption share fluctuated around 50% in the 1980s before it dropped substantially in the early 1990s. SOE-reforms, abolishing of the "iron rice bowl" and uncertainty were the main drivers behind this fall. After 2010, we see a moderate increase as a result of specific government policies to increase purchasing power.

This consumption share is extraordinarily low compared to the 1970s and 1980s, and is also very low compared with many developing and industrialised countries. The consumption data shows that Chinese households have not benefited as much from China's economic growth as other cohorts in the economy. Nevertheless, the falling consumption share does not mean that consumption is stagnant; it is not. Consumption was quite dynamic with growth of more than 8% per year between 1990 and 2016 (NBS Database). One only has to look at the growth in sales in the

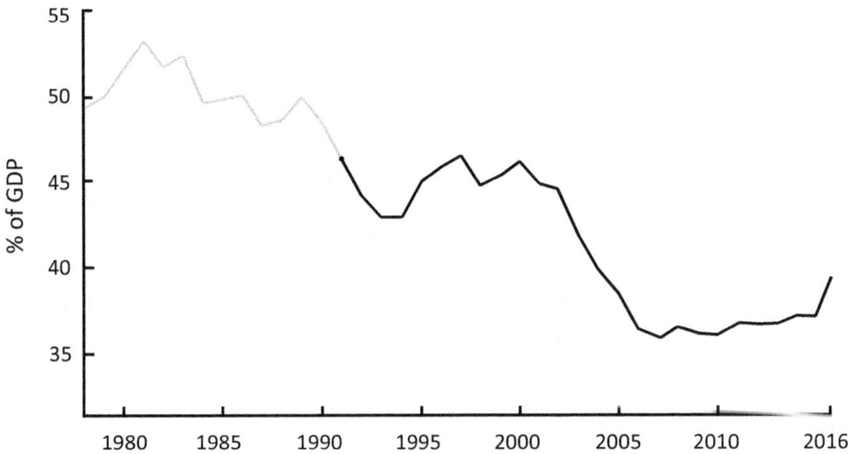

Figure 5.4 Consumption as percentage of GDP, 1980–2016
Source: National Bureau of Statistics

retail, automotive and electronics sectors. The imbalance exists due to an abnormally high contribution of investment to growth. Hence, consumption is lagging overall growth. As a consequence, its share in total GDP fell to low levels. Be aware of the fact that the low consumption to GDP ratio is virtually the only number that points to a weak consumption performance.

Excess reliance on the manufacturing sector; service sector is underrepresented

The third (internal) imbalance relates to the structure of the economy. The industrial sector is still relatively large in China. China is much more industrialised than other emerging markets at the same development stage and mature economies in past decades. The large industrial basis is the result of explicit government intervention.

Industrial policy that focused on specific industrial sectors created a relatively capital-intensive growth model and weak employment growth. Despite GDP growth of 8%, employment increased by only 1% per annum in the 2001–2012 period. The underdevelopment of the service sector is the root cause of weak employment growth.

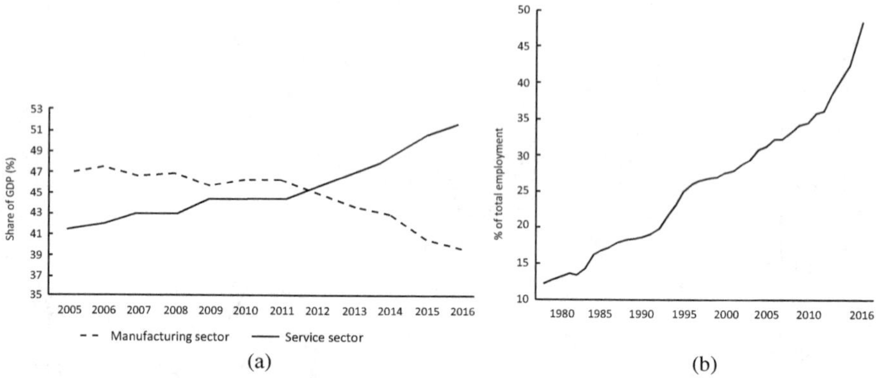

Figure 5.5 Share of the service sector in (a) GDP and employment (b)
Source: *National Bureau of Statistics*

Obviously, the service sector is more labour-intensive than manufacturing and an output shift from the manufacturing to the service sector would help spur employment growth. In Japan (1970s) and South Korea (1980s), the service sector as percentage of GDP and in total employment increased dramatically during the take-off. The same can be seen in China today.

As shown on the left graph in Fig. 5.5, in 2012, the share of the service sector in GDP became bigger than that of the manufacturing sector. Furthermore, as the right graph shows, in 2016, almost 50% of total employment was in the service sector, compared with only 12% in the early 1980s. Despite the growing importance of the service sector in China, it is still underdeveloped today and its share in the economy is relatively low compared to other countries such as Brazil, Indonesia and South Africa.

Export-led growth

China's current account (and trade) balance showed a surplus in every year after 1994, but until 2001, the current account surplus was not extraordinarily large. The surplus as percentage of GDP fluctuated around 3%. There were countries such as Germany and Japan with much higher current account surpluses as percentage of GDP. In that sense, one may question the term "export-led growth" which is being used in many publications. After 2001, the year that China became a member of the WTO, China's current account surplus exploded. Between 2001 and 2007, the surplus rose from 1.3% to 10.1%. The sharpest rise occurred after 2004 (MOFCOM), so the large current account and trade surpluses are a relatively recent phenomenon. Fig. 5.6 shows a first sign of external rebalancing. After 2007, the current account surplus as percentage of GDP fell sharply, reaching 2% in 2016. Much of the decline was caused by the global crisis that hit Chinese export. Part of the decline can also be explained as the result of increased Chinese private consumption (and imports). The falling current account surplus is also attributable to growing imports of steel, machinery and chemicals as a consequence of the government stimulus package of 2008 and 2009.

The current account surplus is closely tied to the Renminbi exchange rate policy. It is logical to expect that the current account surplus (and the incoming flow of FDI) would increase the value of the Renminbi. But, that was not the case. Obviously, the monetary authorities intervened on the currency market to keep the value of the Renminbi stable towards the US dollar. The rapid accumulation of China's foreign exchange reserves after 2001 shows the large (and

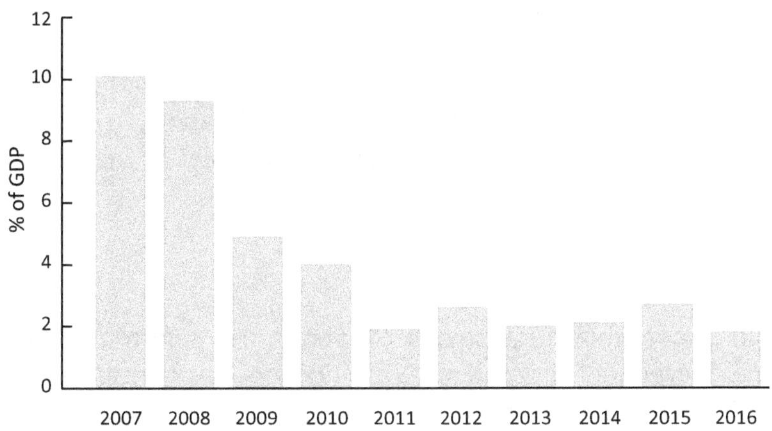

Figure 5.6 Current account as percentage of GDP, 2007–2016
Source: *National Bureau of Statistics*

one-sided) exchange rate interventions aiming to prevent an appreciation. The result was an undervalued currency (according to several western experts) which made export easy, but also created discontent amongst western policymakers. For example, Mr Trump emphasised in his election campaign again and again this unfair practice by China and implemented protectionist measures in his early presidency period.

Rebalancing from the public to the private sector

Although the share of the private sector steadily increased over the years, the state sector (including hybrid markets in which the government intervenes strongly) is still very large compared to other emerging markets in transition. A consequence of this is the domination of SOEs in certain sectors. They are protected and receive easy finance, while private small- and medium-sized enterprises (SMEs) face difficulties in getting loans from the banks. Banks are also protected from competition. Until recently, deposit rates were set artificially low (relative to economic growth). At the same time, the lending rate was set relatively high, which resulted in a large interest spread for banks. The savings available for investments were allocated to SOEs due to the lower risks, and the guarantee that the government would step in if SOEs had difficulties repaying their loans. This system is only changing very gradually. Essentially, on many consumer markets, the entry and exit barriers are gone and the market can be considered as open, but liberalisation of financial markets and business-to-business markets is only done step by step and with minor adjustments.

Income inequality

As the most important result of economic reform, household income increased dramatically during the past three decades. Rapid income growth lifted hundreds of millions of people out of poverty and the living standards of rural and urban residents improved significantly. At the same time, however, income inequality increased spectacularly, not only between rural and urban areas or between provinces, but also between residents in each city (Li Gan, 2013). One can argue that today's income inequality is mainly a city-issue. Income inequality in China today is one of the highest in Asia. Institutional elements in the Chinese society are fuelling this inequality. Think about the *hukou* system and the fact that private land ownership is not allowed in agriculture. Because of this, land cannot be used as collateral for a house mortgage or investment-loan. This is in strong contradiction to the privatisation of the housing programme in the urban centres, a topic which will be dealt with in Chapter 8. Explicit policies to solve inequality is needed to counteract potential social unrest.

Environmental challenges

The focus on heavy industry and the attitude of "growth above everything" resulted in an environmental nightmare. If we multiply a problem by the population, it becomes a major problem. Based on the analysis of Energy Information Administration (EIA, 2016), on a per capita basis, China does not look so bad. It consumed the equivalent of 22 barrels of oil per person in 2016, much less than the 57 barrels consumed by the average American in that year. But when we look at the ratio between domestic energy consumption and GDP, the picture is totally different. China is by far the most energy-intensive major economy; it uses much more energy per unit of GDP than other major countries. There are several reasons behind China's high-energy intensity:

- The heavy industry, in particular, has a relatively large share in total GDP. This industry (steel, refining petrochemicals, cement, etc.) is very energy-intensive.
- Coal is abundant and relatively cheap. Consequently, China's reliance on coal for its energy consumption is high. More than 55% of its energy demand is fulfilled by coal while the world average is around 25% (EIA, 2015). However, coal is less

efficient fuel for power production than natural gas or oil, and is a major source of air pollution and emissions of carbon dioxide (CO_2). It should be noted that in many cases, these coal-fired power plants are quite new and efficient, often more efficient in their conversion of coal into electricity than are the outdated US coal-powered plants. The low price of coal also affects the oil consumption. Oil is important and increasing its share in energy consumption year on year, but China is an oil-importer. The decision to buy relatively expensive oil abroad or using cheap domestic coal is uncomfortable; it is tempting to use cheap coal. Despite having shale gas, it is very difficult unlocking it because of the geology of China's shale formations and, therefore, too expensive.

- Little attention has been paid to building in a sustainable way. Houses are hardly isolated. It is obvious that there has been so much pressure in building more houses for the growing urban citizens that quality issues were of secondary importance.
- Essential legislation is in place, but the central government has found it difficult to force SOEs and local governments to comply with environmental laws, especially when it will come at the expense of economic growth and increased unemployment. Furthermore, local governments continue to support unprofitable local industries that use a lot of energy for relatively little contribution to the economy.

The situation today is dramatic and moving out of coal is needed. According to a report of the Asian Development Bank (Zhang and Crooks, 2012), less than 1% of the 500 largest cities in China met the air quality standards recommended by the WHO in 2011, and seven of these cities were ranked among the ten most polluted cities in the world in 2017. The emerging Chinese middle class demands clean air and water, and farming needs water for irrigation and the authorities reacted on this. The focus on the environment can be seen in the latest five-year plan. China has also ratified the

Paris Treaty on global warming. But implementation measures are complicated and China feels discontent on three issues.

Firstly, Europe and the US should shoulder a much larger share of the burden of reducing carbon emissions because of their long history of pumping CO_2 into the atmosphere. I still remember discussions, based on the Club of Rome,[1] about pollution problems in large cities in Europe, Japan and the US (such as Pittsburgh and Los Angeles) in the 1960s and 1970s.

Secondly, part of China's emissions is, in reality, the responsibility of western companies producing in China. As stated before, almost half of China's export is produced by western companies operating in China. This also includes steel and chemical products. Thirdly, China wants to have more time to roll out the environmental policies. As stated earlier, economic growth is still needed and a hard landing should be avoided. It is clear that China's attitude about the environment is changing and the authorities are eager to handle this issue, by legislation as well as enforcement. However, whatever the steps taken, China needs economic growth and adjustments are made only within this context.

There is a correlation between a country's income level and its environmental performance. This relationship is visualised as the so-called Environmental Kuznets Curve, shown in Fig. 5.7. The idea behind the curve is very straightforward: when people and governments are too busy to escape poverty, they don't particularly care about air and water pollution. As wealth increases, other needs such as housing quality and fresh air become more important. In that sense, environmental issues can be considered as luxury products.

---

[1] Established in 1968, the Club of Rome — an informal international gathering of experts from the fields of academia, civil society, diplomacy and industry — studied the implications of continued worldwide growth and concluded that the world resources could not support economic and population growth in the longer term, even with advanced technology.

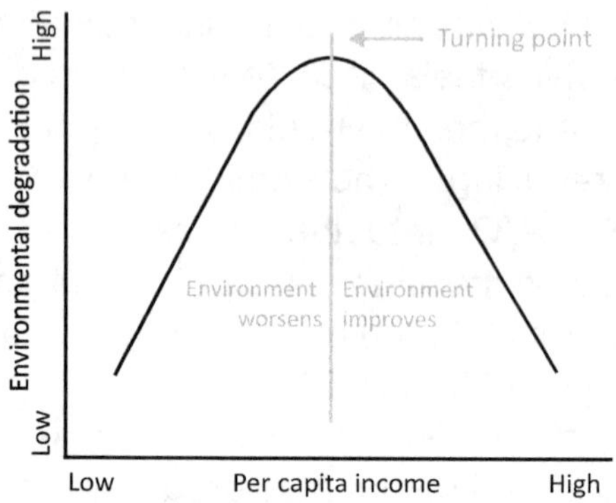

Figure 5.7 Environmental Kuznets Curve
Source: Based on Yi Jiang, Tun Lin & Juzhong Zhuang (2008)

The environmental deprivation in the first stage of the Environmental Kuznets Curve is driven by the need to escape poverty. At this stage, the focus is on achieving economic growth. Moreover, changes in the economic structure during this first stage makes the environment worse. In the early take-off period, the economic structure shifts from a clean agrarian economy to a polluting industrial economy (based on heavy industries). The second stage of the Environmental Kuznets Curve shows an improvement of the environment, driven by the tendency of the emerging middle class to have greater preference for environmental quality. Not only are richer consumers more willing to pay for "green" products, they also ask for better institutions to protect the environment. Furthermore, at this second stage, the economy shifts from manufacturing, being energy-intensive, to a more service economy with a more knowledge- and technology-intensive production process. The technological improvement plays a key role in improving the environment. In general, one may say that the turning point occurs when countries are entering middle-income status. In addition, political choices may help the environment: for example, the government may raise the price of energy. In terms of political choices, China has a long way to go; energy (electricity) prices are still artificially low due to government intervention.

Like other theoretical concepts, one may also criticise the Environmental Kuznets Curve. For instance, it is not clear when the turning point is reached. Furthermore, the environment is a broad concept: air pollution did receive some attention in China but progress on water and soil pollution has been much slower. Cleaning up contaminated rivers, lakes and soil has barely begun. The need to rebalance with respect to environmental issues is unquestionable. There are some signs that China is close to the peak of coal consumption and, if that is the case, its share will fall step by step. However, it is difficult to conclude whether this is the result of government policy or just the result of weaker coal demand as part of economic slowdown.

Large domestic debt

As shown in Fig. 5.8, China's debt burden (CH) was very high relative to its GDP in 2014. The correlation between the two axis is given by the upward sloping in line in the figure below. The debt-to-GDP ratio of 220% was much higher compared with other

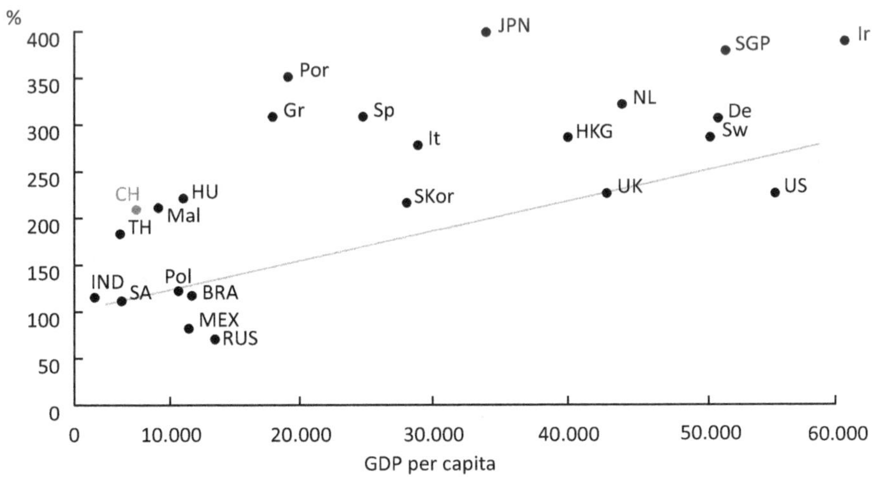

Figure 5.8 GDP per capita versus debt-to-GDP ratio, 2014

Source: Based on Goldman Sachs (2016)

countries in transition such as India (IND), South Africa (SA) and Brazil (BRA). It is on par with the US and the UK, where GDP per capita was about seven times higher.

Uneasiness about the debt burden does not only relate to its size but also is driven by the fact that the growth of debt is rising extremely fast, primarily of SOEs and local governments. As we will learn in Chapter 12, due to the implicit guarantee, both types of debt can be considered as government debt. The largest rise of debt occurred due to the enormous fiscal stimulus plan that the government executed in 2008–2009 to fight the negative impact of the worldwide economic crisis.

The debt as percentage of GDP rose from 150% in 2008 to 280% in 2016 (Fig. 5.9). The fiscal stimulus was 4-trillion-Renminbi ($570 billion) which was, at the time of the announcement, equivalent to almost 13% of China's GDP, much higher than

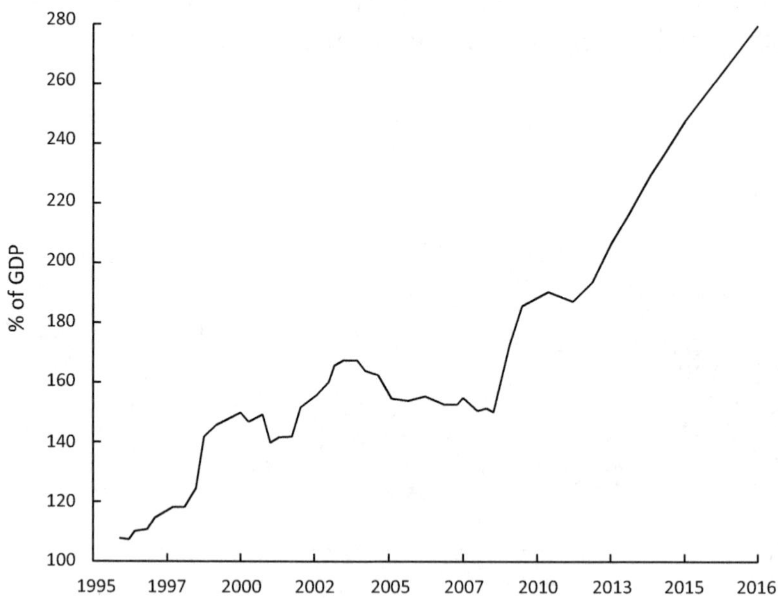

Figure 5.9 Development of total debt to GDP, 1995–2016

Source: Based on Centre d'Etudes Prospectives et d'Informations Internationales (CEPII) Policy Brief (2016)

witnessed in the US and in Europe. Although the effect of this stimulus was spread over time, it created a liquidity surplus; there was just too much money in the system. The fiscal stimulus itself (executed through state banks) resulted in strong increase in credits to SOEs. At the same time, it also generated overcapacity in many sectors which made it difficult to repay the debt, with an increase of bad loans as the outcome.

The debt problem is seen as one of the major risks of the Chinese economy in the short- and medium-term. The Chinese authorities are aware of this debt problem and (as we will discuss in Chapter 12) some first steps have been taken to solve this debt problem.

Lower economic growth

Structural imbalances are visible in many parts of China's economy and society. It is logical to see imbalances emerging when a country is going through many types of transition: moving from a planned to a market economy, changing the economic structure from manufacturing to service, and shifting from a rural towards an urban society. And it is logical to witness lower economic growth during these transitions. The same happened in countries such as Japan and South Korea. These countries which relied on an export- and industrial-led growth model driven by a cheap currency, low interest and cheap labour experienced rapid growth rates in the early years of development, but inevitably at some point in their development, they began to experience much slower growth. In this sense, China is not unique.

As countries move into a middle-income status, their growth begin to slow down from double digits to about 4% or 5% of GDP growth. This is caused by the fact that the original drivers behind growth are reaching their ceilings and that growth should be taken over by other drivers such as productivity, technology and innovation. But these drivers are constrained when the economy is unbalanced. This transition to another growth model appears to be very difficult and, in many cases, countries are not able to make the final jump to sustainable growth and high-income status. This phenomenon is known as the middle-income trap (World Bank, 2013).

5.3 Middle-income trap

In the past decades, many developing (or low income) countries were able to make the transition to a middle-income country,[2] but they were unable to move further into the high-income status. They stayed in the middle-income level for many decades without substantial progress in welfare: the middle-income trap. The concept was made popular by a World Bank Report (2013) which was based on *An East Asian Renaissance: Ideas for Economic Growth* (Gill and Kharas, 2008). Low-income countries can achieve economic growth by combining more labour and more machines. Because of surplus of labour (in combination with being backward), they can compete in international markets by producing labour-intensive, low-cost products using technologies developed abroad.

However, this "easy" growth has its limits. As countries reach middle-income levels, the surplus of labour will disappear, wages will increase, and productivity gains will be smaller. This will erode competitiveness and, consequently, the export-led growth strategy is not working anymore. To grow further, these countries have to find new sources of growth. In essence, growth beyond middle-income level is not possible without improvement of productivity. It means that focus must shift towards the supply side of the economy such as better education, investing in R&D, competition to stimulate innovative behaviour, and a shift to high-value services. The switch towards this new growth model is difficult and, consequently, countries may be stuck in the middle-income trap.

According to the World Bank, of the 101 countries that had obtained middle-income status by 1960, only 13 became high-income

---

[2] Definitions differ, but in general, middle income relates to US$1,300 to US$13,000 annually per capita. Middle income countries are divided into lower-middle (US$1,300–4,500) and upper-middle (US$4,500–13,000) income countries; all in current US$ (World Bank, 2018).

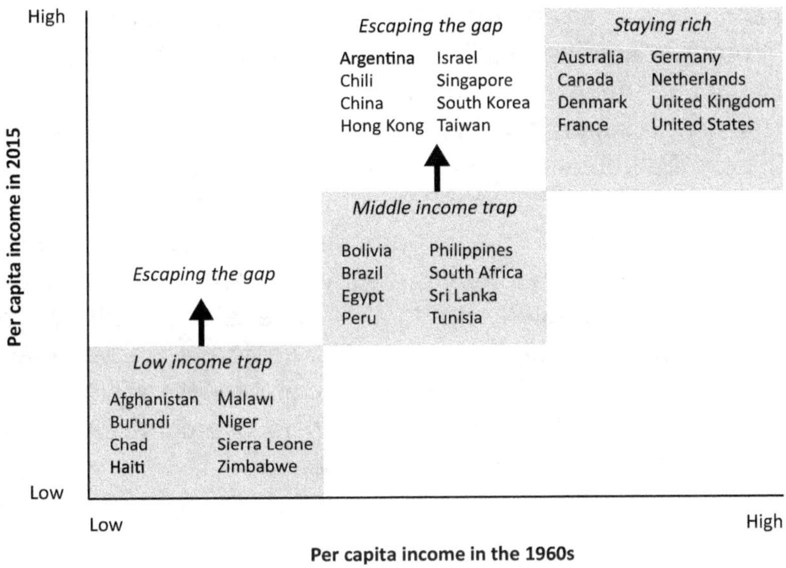

Figure 5.10 Middle-income trap

Note: Vertical axis indicates the income in 2015, instead of 2008 as was done in the World Bank (2013) publication

Source: Based on *Asian Development Bank (2012)* and *World Bank (2013)*

economies by 2008 (World Bank, 2013). In particular, countries in Latin America show characteristics of the trap hypothesis. Most economies in this region reached middle-income status as early as the 1960s and 1970s, but have remained there ever since. This is visualised in Fig. 5.10. Be aware that this is only an indicative list with example-countries.

Promising countries in the 1960s, such as Brazil, Peru and the Philippines were not able to escape the middle-income trap. The same holds for several African countries (e.g. South Africa, Egypt). At the same time, countries such as South Korea and Singapore were able to make the jump to high-income level. We also implemented Argentina and Chile in this overview. They are on the edge of making the jump. The learning point is clear: countries must implement structural reforms robustly enough, in the correct sequence, and on time to escape the trap. In Fig. 5.10, China is put in the cohort of countries that escaped the middle-income trap. At the moment, China is an upper-middle income country, but forecasts are that it may escape the middle-income status within a decade.

Escaping the middle-income trap requires robust structural reforms on the supply side of the economy. This is also the analysis of Kishore Mahbubani. In his book *The New Asian Hemisphere: The Irresistible Shift of Global Power to the East* (2008), he explains why we see the rise of Asia (in particular, China) today. His answer is that the Asians have finally discovered and implemented the "seven pillars of western wisdom". These are the pillars which brought development and welfare to the western countries after the Industrial Revolution. His seven pillars of western wisdom are in line with the World Bank view on how to overcome the middle-income trap and are summarised below.

- Free-market economics
  Markets are essential because they generate incentives to increase productivity. Markets and opening up the economy were essential elements in achieving economic development in the west. We see the same happening now in China. The Chinese believe in free market economics (sometimes complemented by government intervention). This was the main reason to join the WTO. The Chinese are not afraid to compete, which is in contrast to many other countries that fear international competition. Before Russia became a WTO member in 2012, a Russian colleague articulated to me that Russia should not join because he felt the WTO rules were an imposition on the country. The Chinese believe instead that the WTO rules benefit China.

- Science and technology
  Europe became dominant for centuries because it surged ahead in its mastery of science and technology. Now, this focus on science and technology is shifting to Asia. At PhD and post-doctoral graduations all over the world today, the graduates are mostly Asian (in particular, Chinese). If we extrapolate from what we see on campuses and colleges today, soon 80–90% of all new PhDs in science and engineering will be held by Asians; or

maybe it will be 70% or 60% but it is still a remarkable shift from the past.

- Meritocracy
  Why is Brazil a soccer superpower but economically a medium power? This is because when it comes to soccer, Brazil looks everywhere, searching for the best players in cities as well as in the favelas. However, when the country looks for economic and political talent, it only looks to the upper class or middle class. Asians have discovered that the millions of brains that are not used for centuries can generate huge benefits. Social mobility is one of the many silent revolutions that are happening in China (and other Asian countries) today.

- Pragmatism
  The opposite of pragmatism is idealism and dogmatic thinking. Both are not helpful in achieving economic development. As Deng Xiaoping said: "It doesn't matter if a cat is white or black as long as it catches mice". In most of Asia, the ideological debates are left behind or, as is the case with respect to mainland China and Taiwan, are set away for an infinite period of time. Today, the focus is on (inclusive) economic development.

- Culture of peace
  In the 1950, 1960s and early 1970s, the Asian continent was a war-zone. Think about the South Korean War, Vietnam War, Indo–Pakistani War, China–Burma conflict, China–India conflicts and also Civil Wars such as the Cambodian Civil War. However, that changed dramatically; since the 1970s, the region has been stable despite geopolitical disagreements. Due to this stability, foreign investments came and international trade increased.

- Rule of law
  A rule-based economic system is essential for longer term economic development. Some work must be done in this aspect but most Asian countries are moving towards this aim. For example, China is

implementing a rule-based governance structure, but this is a system with Chinese characteristics, as we will see later in the book. It is interesting to note that Mahbubani only referred to the rule of law and did not mention democracy and political openness in his list.

- Education
  The hunger for education in Asia is phenomenal. Research by Nyenrode Business University (Ebbers and Zhang, 2015) shows that educational expenses are in the top-3 of saving-motives. This is supported by government investments in education. For example, China provides free primary education for everyone. After the six years of primary school, the government also pays the first three years of compulsory secondary education. Moreover, it heavily subsidises studying at the university.

China today is a middle-income country, but to escape the middle-income trap, structural (supply side) reforms are needed, hence the need for rebalancing.

5.4 Rebalancing process — today's picture

It is interesting to observe that important publications by the State Council that are published in the 2013–2016 period are readable as being World Bank or IMF publications. They are full of measures that should be implemented to make the supply side of the economy more efficient and productive. For example, the third plenary session of the Chinese Communist Party in November 2013 indicated clearly the "decisive" role of the market. At the same time, it emphasised that both private and state-owned enterprises would be the foundations of China's economic development in the future. Because of these contradictory remarks, it is difficult to get a clear picture about the choices within and the speed of the rebalancing process.

Speed of the reforms

I am sure that there are intense debates in the most important party and state bodies (behind closed doors) about the speed of implementing the reforms. Clearly, this is a key question for the next decade. With so many challenges, there are arguments for both sides. If reforms are introduced too quickly, the party and the government may lose control over the economy. For example, if China opens the capital account too quickly, it might face significant outflow of capital that would weaken the currency and destabilise the economy. If it fully opens its markets to foreign competition too early, SOEs might suffer, which would affect the labour market. If China fights corruption too aggressively, there is a risk that government officials and SOE executives will delay decisions and approvals for fear of making a mistake or being caught in a future corruption scandal.

On the other hand, gradualism also has its price. If the central government stands behind the local governments and SOEs, and continues to guarantee their debts, it will have a negative impact on efficiency and longer-term development. The same holds if SOEs are being protected by domestic and foreign competition. Finally, waiting too long to fight corruption will certainly create social tensions and may erode the credibility of the party.

The Chinese authorities are looking for the optimum balance between gradualism and speed. The search for an optimum transition is a long and complicated endeavour; fighting one imbalance can make another element of the rebalancing process worse. As stated before, the whole transition and reform agenda is like a "noodle bowl". It is very difficult to get one strand of noodle out of the bowl without disrupting the others. Until now, China is using a unique asymmetrical market liberalisation approach in which the product market is liberalised almost completely, but work is still needed to liberalise production factor markets.

While continued gradualism in implementing the necessary reforms has its advantages, accelerated transition in certain markets may be needed, even if it comes with higher short-term volatility. One of the drivers behind the need for speeding up the reforms is the demographic situation. There were many reasons for China's rapid growth, but a major one was the country's favourable demographic structure. Population was growing and, as a result, the labour force was on the rise, while the dependency ratio (ratio of the non-working population to the working population) was falling. Clearly, China had a demographic dividend in which the population (and labour force) was a key driver behind economic success.

However, this positive demographic picture is changing fast and China is losing its demographic dividend. The change from surplus of labour to shortage of labour refers to the Lewis turning point (Lewis, 1954). According to the Lewis development model, an economy at the starting point of economic development is characterised by a dual economy: the unproductive and stagnant traditional agricultural sector on one hand and the highly productive and dynamic (modern) industrial (export-driven) sector on the other. The agricultural sector is assumed to have surplus of labour and, consequently, labour productivity is low (or even zero). Due to higher productivity, wages are higher in the industrial sector, which attracts migrants to leave the rural areas and move into the urban centres looking for work. A continuation of migration flow will keep wages low compared to productivity in the industrial sector. Furthermore, because the marginal productivity in agriculture is so low, labour can leave this sector easily without reducing total output. This will continue in the early years of transformation, but it cannot continue; at the end of the day, the surplus of labour is exhausted. Hence, we reach the Lewis turning point. Be aware that the Lewis turning point is a period of time rather than a point in time, which may extend over a number of years. This Lewis turning point will be further discussed in Chapter 11.

Approaching the Lewis turning point clearly creates a sense of urgency in speeding up the reforms. For example, the proportion of young workers available to migrate from rural areas is already decreasing. At the same time, there are Chinese social and institutional features that may block the movement to the Lewis turning point for a while. The recent reforms of the *hukou* registration system which give broader coverage of public services for migrant workers will likely increase the willingness of rural families to move to the cities, and will stimulate the move from the agricultural sector into the industrial (and service) sector. Whether the Lewis turning point will be reached in 2020 or 2025 does not make so much difference: speeding up reforms is needed.

Short- versus long-term growth

An important act of the government is to create a balance between the short-term need for economic growth and the long-term need for structural reforms. This is complicated because, in many cases, structural reforms may have an adverse impact on the short-term growth. China needs millions of jobs every year to keep unemployment below the 5%-target (Koleski, 2017). Therefore, in the short term, the focus is on growth that creates enough jobs and the way to do this is through own investments, helping SOEs and cheap credits. However, to achieve long-term growth, structural reforms are needed; reforms to stimulate consumption and increase the share of the service sector in the economy. This may have a negative impact on banks and SOEs but should be considered as negative-by-product of rebalancing. Fig. 5.11 summarises the new growth strategy.

Creating more certainty in the field of healthcare, pensions and education will decrease savings while stimulating spending. This is complemented by increasing wages. The result is more private consumption and this will stimulate investments in the service industry. At the end of the day, more value-added jobs for the

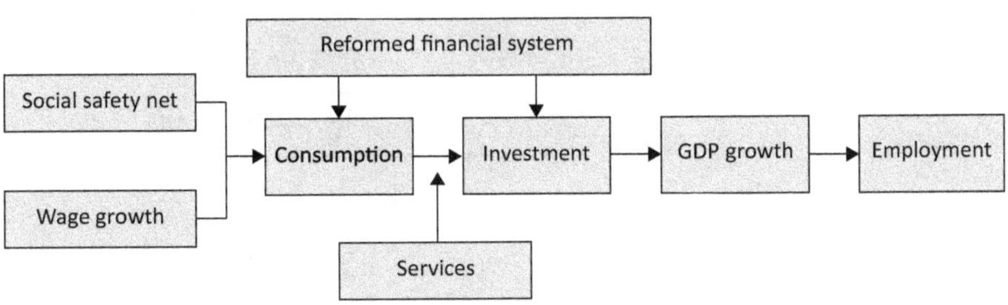

Figure 5.11 The rebalancing growth strategy

Source: Adapted from Bertoldi & Melander (2015)

higher-educated population have been created. To achieve this rebalancing, reforms in the financial system are also needed.

Although the long-term growth model is clear, there are circumstances in which the government should act as crisis manager. It must step in if there is risk of a hard landing of the economy with total demand declining. Private consumption may fall due to uncertainty. Investments can fall due to less availability of credit, combined with increasing risks. Exports may decline because of economic problems with China's main trading partners. If the government does not react, the drop in total spending results in a hard landing. Government policy through expenditure and via monetary policy may help to stimulate demand. This short-term, cyclical policy clearly deviates from what is needed in the longer term, but is required under certain circumstances, such as the financial-economic crisis after 2008. The situation between 2008 and 2011 is visualised in Fig. 5.12.

Easy credit helps investments, and keeping the value of the currency artificially low may stimulate exports. This is the classic growth pattern which we saw in the early 2000s. This investment- and export-led strategy stimulates growth and generates jobs. The additional demand for labour will increase the wage level in specific sectors. Obviously, this is a step backward from rebalancing, but driven by cyclical moves of the economy.

The cases above make clear that it is difficult to interpret the government actions as being in line or against rebalancing and

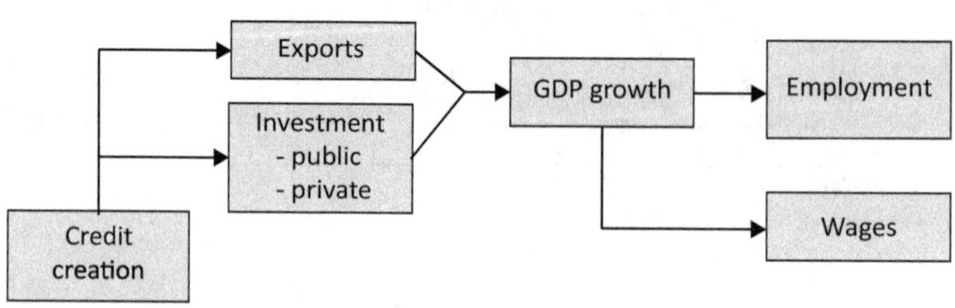

Figure 5.12 Short-term growth strategy to fight an economic crisis

Source: Adapted from Bertoldi & Melander (2015)

structural reforms. The increase of credit to SOEs to overcome the crisis can be labelled as a step backward from rebalancing, but it can also be seen as a crisis tool for a short period of time that is complementing the steps taken by the government to rebalance the economy. Having said this, the large stimulus package of 2008 clearly worsened the imbalance problem and postponed needed reforms for some years.

A related issue is the interpretation of macroeconomic data. For example, is the increase in consumption-share in GDP in 2015 and 2016 a sign of rebalancing? Maybe the slow growth in export and investment was the main reason why the consumption-share went up. If we define rebalancing as a radical shift in government policy to downplay investment and boost household consumption, such a shift may not be labelled as rebalancing. Moreover, the interpretation of government spending is complicated within the rebalancing-discussion. Increasing government expenditure (and investments) is not necessarily wrong. It can help the rebalancing if it is targeted towards healthcare and housing. Therefore, to find out if rebalancing, driven by government actions, is really happening is complex.

How much rebalancing is needed?

When answering the question above, one should be certain that the key indicators in official statistics are correct. Undoubtedly, statistics are improving, but Chapter 1 made clear that extra steps are needed. For example, household income and private consumption in China are maybe underestimated and, consequently, the domestic imbalance is overstated. Housing income is underreported due to grey income sources such as gifts and land transactions. Household consumption may be understated because capturing the e-commerce, driven by the three Chinese corporate champions known as BAT (Baidu, Alibaba and Tencent) is statistically difficult.

Another issue related to how much rebalancing is needed is how to interpret the investment share in GDP. The general conclusion is that the Chinese economy needs less investment than before and that investment as a share of GDP is too high, but is this really a problem? Yes, according to many specialists (based on the discussion earlier in the book), but as easily one may argue that the high investment share in GDP is not problematic. Firstly, China's high investment rate is the consequence of an extremely low initial capital stock at the start of the reform period. Secondly, despite strong growth in investments, China's capital stock is still small relative to its population and economic development. For example, in 2016, China's capital stock per capita was only 10% of the US level at market exchange rates (or 19% at purchasing power parity). Furthermore, China's capital stock per worker was about 40% less than other middle-income East Asian countries in 2014 (PWC, 2015). From this angle, we can argue that carefully selected investment projects will continue to generate respectable returns. The high-quality infrastructure in Beijing and Shanghai masks the still sub-standard living conditions in many of China's smaller cities, not to mention the underdeveloped infrastructure in the rural areas. With 43% (2017) of population still living in rural areas, China's investment-driven growth may continue for the next decade.

The same holds when urbanisation continues for the next several decades. Investments are needed to build the houses and infrastructure in the new and expanding cities. To find out if China really needs to lower the investment share substantially, the allocation of the investment flows is crucial. The investment-driven growth strategy can continue if the investments go into infrastructure and housing. However, it is another matter if a lot of these investments are used for helping SOEs which are unable to compete, or if funds are being used for unnecessary projects that only pump up GDP and advance local official careers. In these cases, continuation of investment-driven growth will automatically (and within short notice) result in lower economic growth.

Consumption growth is key in avoiding a hard landing in the rebalancing process, but can consumption grow fast enough to offset declining investment in the future? Some economists argue that it will be near impossible for consumption to grow more quickly than the rates seen over the past decade and, as a consequence, low investment growth will result in lower GDP growth. Hence, rebalancing can only be achieved at much lower economic growth. However, the example of Taiwan shows that it is possible for consumption growth to outpace GDP even when GDP is growing rapidly (Lardy & Borst, 2013). Although no other economy is a perfect economic analogy for China given its size and the magnitude of its economic imbalances, the experience of Taiwan's rebalancing suggests that it should be possible to compensate a sharp fall in investments with rising consumption. Taiwan had a relatively unbalanced growth model during the early stages of its development, with the household consumption share of GDP steadily declining from 75% in the early 1950s to 47% in 1960s. Rebalancing in Taiwan began in the early 1970s with heavy emphasis on stimulating consumption. Between 1987 and 1996, real growth in private consumption expenditure averaged 9.1% annually, while real GDP grew at a rate of 7.5%.

It will take a long time for household consumption to play the major role in the Chinese economy. If there is a continuation of 8% growth of consumption and China witnesses GDP growth of around 6%, the rebalancing is a natural but slow process. Even if we assume 10% consumption growth, it would take China 18 years to reach the level of Taiwan and South Korea in terms of consumption as a share of GDP, and 30 years to reach the level of the US. Thus, to expect household consumption to replace investment (and export) to become a bigger driver of the economy in the near future is unrealistic. To conclude, consumption is already the most important driver behind economic growth but in the decade to come, it cannot overtake the combined role of investments and export. Hence, putting too much focus on short-term rebalancing with substantially lower investments is not wise: government initiated and financed investments are still needed in the decades to come.

Economic growth is still needed

The above discussion makes clear that rebalancing will hurt economic growth because consumption cannot take over the role of investments in the short term. We may see very strong consumption growth (even more dynamic than in the previous 10 years), driven by pro-consumption policies by the government, e-commerce development and increasing real wages. Despite this optimistic view on consumption growth, it may not counteract the fall in investments. It is wrong to believe that China no longer needs government initiated investments to grow. Essentially, the government needs to generate jobs and increase welfare to prevent social unrest and keep the party's credibility. Thus, it cannot sacrifice growth in a very significant way. The government will tolerate a slower growth (expressed as the "new normal") but it will not accept a hard landing.

Thus far, the Chinese government has emphasised that a stable economic and social environment is a necessary condition for reform. That is logical; it is much easier to launch a reform plan when the economy is growing fast. A boom period generates more revenue and part of the new revenue can be used to compensate the losers of reform. Growth also increases the credibility of the party and government, which is very important for the success of policy implementation.

Competition is key

I hear many times in discussions that to create a productive society, it is essential to privatise the SOEs. I do not agree with this view. The crucial feature of a market economy is not private ownership but competition. It means that privatisation is not needed as long as SOEs are competing with the private sector, of course within the context of a level playing field. Competition (and not privatisation) forms the basis of China's restructuring of SOEs. The opening up of sectors and the freedom of private companies to operate in these sectors go hand in hand with state interference. The private sector can develop freely and it should compete against the state sector but not replace it. Obviously, competition only works if the loss-making firms exit the market through bankruptcy or acquisition by stronger players. However, until now, this is not always happening due to local government support, preferred access to bank credit and informal relationships. In short, SOEs may not be monopolies any more, but are in many ways still protected from competitive pressure. Further steps need to be taken to initiate and stimulate competition in a broad range of sectors. Opening up towards international trade and FDI is part of this approach. Foreign companies may create many spillovers, forcing Chinese companies to compete and pushing them to achieve quality as demanded by international standards. It is, therefore, logical to place openness and competition at the heart of the newest development strategy.

5.5 Latest developments in the rebalancing process

To realise the goal of increasing productivity and technological advancement, the government has put a range of policies in place. The focus on rebalancing can be seen by looking at the choices made in the two latest five-year plans.

From made in China to design in China

A key priority in the 12th (2011–2015) and 13th (2016–2020) plans is to transition the country from *Made in China* to *Design in China*. These five-year plans also state repeatedly that a more sophisticated and innovative manufacturing sector is essential, and stress new features of higher-value added industrial development. This is in line with the supply-driven, innovation-based strategy that is needed to avoid the middle-income trap. A typical example of the *Made in China* policy is the iPhone case which will be discussed in Chapter 10. The iPhone is manufactured in and exported from China. Statistically, it is seen as Chinese production and export. However, to be able to produce the iPhone, almost all components are being imported. Only the assembly is done in China and as a result, slightly more than 3% of the iPhone value is Chinese value-added. Essentially, the production and export of the iPhone hardly increases GDP. This would change dramatically if the iPhone were created by a Chinese firm and if all components were developed and produced in China.

The policy change from *Made in China* to *Design in China* is visible. For example, the State Council's Science and Technology Development Plan stated in 2011 that by 2020, 2.5% of GDP should be spent on research and development (R&D). At that time, the ratio stood at 1.8%, which was considerably lower than in mature economies (but relatively high compared to developing countries). Stimulating R&D and new technologies will boost productivity and help China to move up in the global value chains. In addition, the government selected seven strategic emerging industries as key growth engines in the medium term in its 12th five-year plan. The total size of these seven industries is expected to account for 15% of GDP in 2020, while its share was only 4% in 2010. The key growth engines were extended in the 13th five-year plan whereby ten priority strategic sectors were indicated to boost innovation and productivity.

Figure 5.13 shows the newly selected emerging industries, all more or less related to new technologies. The list includes new materials, aerospace and railway equipment, new-generation IT, and alternative-fuel automobiles, among others. The C919 produced by Commercial Aircraft Corporation of China Limited (COMAC) and officially launched in November 2015 is an example of the *Design*

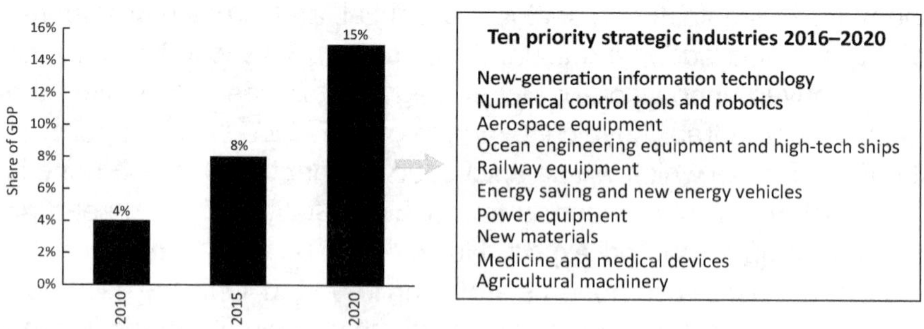

Figure 5.13 Share in GDP of strategic sectors, 2010–2020

Source: *State Council (Adapted from The Economist, 2016)*

in China policy. It is the first homemade, large passenger aircraft that took its test flight in May 2017. The C919 is not just an homegrown Chinese passenger jet, but also the nation's first large plane with intellectual property rights.

Service sector

The rebalancing process is at the heart of the 13th five year-plan. For example, strong emphasis is placed on social spending, boosting consumption and tackling environmental issues. A lot of attention is also given to the importance of a mature service sector, and concrete measures have been announced to stimulate the service sector.

The service sector (such as banking, insurance, telecommunications, transportation, retail, hospitality, tourism, healthcare and real estate agencies) is extremely important in China's development process because it is labour-intensive; it can absorb a large part of the employment that is not needed anymore in the manufacturing sector. In addition, the sector is better for the environment compared to the heavy industry, and it needs skilled labour and give opportunities for graduate students to find decent jobs. The year 2012 was a turning point in China when the service sector exceeded the manufacturing sector in its contribution to GDP for the first time in modern history. Even so, the authorities are eager to increase the share of the service sector in the economy further. China's service sector is still underdeveloped compared to an average developed economy where the service industry makes up about 70% of GDP (World Bank, 2017). The same can be said with respect to emerging markets such as Brazil and Indonesia.

Despite the growth of the service sector, a large part is still closed for new entrants and dominated by a few inefficient large SOEs. Examples are the banking sector, medical care sector and heavy industry. Steps are taken to open these sectors to allow domestic and foreign companies to enter the market, but there is fear that these dominating SOEs are not ready for competition and that opening up will affect the labour market negatively. Finding out the optimum speed of opening up the service sector is complicated because of the uncertainty about market developments and company reactions. I still remember the discussion in the Netherlands about opening up the telecom sector in the late 1990s. According to experts, there would be room for two or three companies. Today, less than twenty years on, there are numerous mobile operators in the Netherlands, and the telecom market has grown to be 10 times larger than anyone could have imagined in the late 1990s. The example makes clear that opening up specific sectors may create unexpected results; uncertainty that should be avoided.

Overcapacity problem and further restructuring of the SOEs

Overcapacity is seen as one of the key problems of the Chinese economy after 2013, particularly within the heavy industry. Overcapacity is defined as the difference between production capacity and actual production. Overcapacity in the industry intensifies the need to rebalance the economy towards services. It also accelerates the discussion about intensifying competition and allowing companies, including SOEs, to go bankrupt. Solving overcapacity is not only needed for domestic reasons but certainly also for external reasons, in particular, the discontent in the west about cheap Chinese products that are sold on foreign markets.

One of many dramatic examples of overcapacity is the aluminum sector. In just over a decade (2006–2016), China's share in global aluminum production went from 10% to over 50%. Over the same period, one third of European aluminum smelters shut down. Despite the enormous growth of Chinese production, in 2015, only 76% of the Chinese capacity was being used. China's overcapacity alone is now five times greater than the primary aluminum production in the European Union (EU). The same holds with respect to steel, bicycles and solar panels. China's steel industry now accounts for more than half of global output, or more than twice the combined output of the next four biggest steel makers: India, Japan, Russia and the US. And, at the same time, we see an overcapacity of around 30%. The overcapacity is caused by the desire on the part of the Chinese provinces to be self-sufficient. This created capacity duplication at the national level. Furthermore, the Chinese stimulus package in 2008–2009 stimulated extra production and capacity. There are some overlapping causes, but sector-specific factors are important in explaining overcapacity. In sectors such as cement and chemicals, inadequate enforcements of regulations are the reasons behind overcapacity. Overcapacity of flat glass is associated with the heavy investments in real estate to accompany rising urbanisation. In shipbuilding, the overcapacity has been caused by easy access to finance to keep companies afloat.

Overcapacity is not new in China. It relates to industrial fragmentation, which has its origins in the 1950s and 1960s, when planners encouraged regional self-sufficiency. This old industrial pattern with low industry concentration has, in many regards, remained with local governments favouring local firms. Overcapacity was also a problem in the late 1990s. High investments and the focus on GDP resulted in a situation whereby many smaller companies with poor performance were only able to survive through government support; like zombies, these companies just would not die.

Due to this fragmentation and duplication of industries, capacity utilisation in China is not very high despite the fast-growing economy. For example, the average utilisation degree in manufacturing was around 65% in the late 1990s and only around 80% during the boom period of 2003–2007 with double-digit growth figures. This is low compared to countries such as Brazil, Japan and South Korea. These countries had utilisation degrees of 80–85% with growth figures substantially lower than China. It shows the intensity of competition in the Chinese market and the enormous growth of government-led production capacity. Sectoral overcapacity became again problematic in 2013–2014. China's capacity utilisation in this period was 79% in manufacturing as a whole, not dramatically low and certainly not a serious problem. However, there was high and rising excess capacity in economically important subsectors such as cement, steel, refining and automotive.

Industry	Utilisation Degree
Paper & paperboard	84
Flat glass	79
Aluminium	76
Shipbuilding	75
Cement	73
Steel	71
Refining	66
Automotive	63

Figure 5.14 Sectors with overcapacity in 2015

Source: Based on DBS (2016) and adapted from Xinhua-net

Figure 5.14 shows the utilisation degree of these industries in 2015. In particular overcapacity existed in the automotive sector (63%) and in refining crude oil (66%). The heavy industry sectors such as steel and cement production witnessed high excess capacity and low utilisation degree in 2015. It should be noted that when disaggregating the sectors further, we will see even lower utilisation degrees. Because regions are specialising in certain industries, sectoral problems automatically are also regional problems.

Rationalisation is needed (as was done in the late 1990s) in these sectors and, as a consequence, production capacity must be reduced (and companies closed). This is a difficult choice: closing down a large refining or steel company will certainly create unemployment for many thousand employees. Furthermore, large SOEs are an important instrument to execute government policy. Therefore, capacity reduction may be seen in smaller (often local-government) enterprises, but it is not to be expected that large-scale rationalisation is happening in large SOEs in the short-and medium-term. Before 2008, the Chinese producers could get away with their overcapacities, exporting goods when domestic consumption was not enough. Exports acted as a safety valve, but in 2008, Chinese export collapsed and overcapacity became a visible problem. As companies in overcapacity industries suffered from low profits, they had problems repaying back their debts, with negative spillovers to banks that financed the investment projects. Overcapacity also has a longer-term impact. Because of the low profits, there is not sufficient cash for new R&D projects, which leads to less innovation and is bad for longer-term competitiveness. Finally, overcapacity may result in trade tensions if part of this overcapacity is sold on foreign markets at low prices or even below costs of production.

The choices ahead

China today is totally different from China twenty years ago, in economic as well as in social terms. The economy doubled every eight years between 1978 and 2016. We see an emerging middle class with its own views on environmental and social issues. We saw the start of a transformation in economic structure towards the service sector and we see much more inequality today compared to the early-reform period. At the same time, we can argue that not so much has been changed fundamentally: investments are still extremely important in the economy; SOEs are being protected and they receive preferential treatment from the government; the banks are still executing the policies of the party and government; the party is leading in economic and social issues; and the government-banks-SOEs triangle is still functioning. The steps to rebalance and the outcomes are confusing and often contradictory.

Furthermore, the outcome of the choices ahead is uncertain. For example, to solve overcapacity and restructure inefficient SOEs, real competition in formerly protected sectors is needed. To open up sectors and achieve competition, the authorities have announced the move towards mixed ownership. Private investors can invest and become shareholders in SOEs; in these formerly closed sectors. This may help, but like always, there is uncertainty. Are private investors keen to invest in SOEs when the party (and government) has an important say in managerial issues? Moreover, vested interests may block needed reforms because they benefit from the status quo. If the reforms are implemented too quickly, the authorities risk a confrontation with the people who are needed to execute the reforms. If the reforms are implemented too slowly, China might not be able to tackle the root causes of some structural weaknesses of its economy and these distortions might result in a continuation of income inequality, environmental problems and unsustainable increase in its debt-to-GDP ratio. This can also cause political instability.

This is the explanation of the ambiguous nature of China. On the one hand, the reforms are speeding up; on the other hand, changes are implemented only step by step. For example, it is highly unlikely that the central government will let several major SOEs default on their debts; consequently, the debt problem is here to stay for the next decade or so. What is clear is the strong emphasis (in legislation on paper) of a greener aspect of growth and the human side of the reforms. This focus on "people first" (and associated with this, an increase in social spending by the government) is clearly visible in the newest five-year plan. Political choices and the content of the newest five-year plan are towards rebalancing but the main issue is how to execute this in an optimal way.

This chapter makes clear that many of the imbalances in the Chinese economy and society are not unique. Experiences in other fast-growing Asian countries have shown that imbalances are a logical side-product of structural transformations during the take-off stage and the journey towards escaping the middle-income trap. Experiences of other countries also show that specific government policy is needed and that timing is important. Market forces cannot do the work alone and a strong government is essential to guide the necessary reforms. Therefore, in the next chapter, the focus is on China's governance and political structure.

Chapter 6

China's Political Structure

Myth 6: China's governance structure is extremely centralised

6.1 Introduction

The political structure of China comprises two main interconnected entities: the Chinese Communist Party (CCP) and the government (central and local). During the 1950–1978 period, the CCP and the government operated as one entity with the party having absolute leadership. In the late 1970s, the party and government functions were slightly separated. Today, the government (at all levels) manages the policy-execution and day-to-day administration of the country, leaving personnel, ideology and security to the party.

To ensure its control over the government, the party maintains a robust presence inside the government. Almost without exception, the leadership of the CCP wears multiple hats, holding positions simultaneously in the party, the government, and the military. The leadership of the party is unquestionable, as seen in its power over the military. The People's Liberation Army (PLA) is not a national army belonging to the government but headed by the party and serving the party. The power of the CCP also relates to personal appointments. Key government persons, CEO of SOEs, key persons in courts of justice and chief editors of the main newspapers are all appointed by the party. It controls the bureaucracy at all levels of government.

As stated above, we see a division in the policy-making process. The party makes the major strategic decisions (published in the five-year plans), while the government implements and executes policies. Within this execution process, the different levels of government have some freedom to adjust the basic decisions of the party to local settings; there is interpretation freedom. This does not mean that there is division of power between the central and local governments; only room to manoeuvre and interpretation. The political structure is a complicated mix of centralism and decentralisation.

In this chapter, we will concentrate on the Chinese governance structure, in particular, the roles of and relationship between the party and the government. Logically, Section 6.2 starts with a discussion of the essential entities of China's governance structure. This is followed in Section 6.3 by an overview of the main features, including collective leadership and decentralisation among others. The decentralisation aspect is being elaborated further in Section 6.4 that analyses the role of the local governments. Section 6.5 discusses democracy in China with its focus on economic human rights. Finally, Section 6.6 focuses again on SOEs. However, in this chapter, the focus is on the main reforms of the SOEs that started in the mid-1990s.

6.2 Governance structure in China

In this section, we will concentrate on the two entities — party and government — of China's political system and not discuss other organisations such as the PLA and other parties aside from the CCP. In Fig. 6.1, the party is distinguished from the central or national government, which consists of the State Council (or cabinet) and the

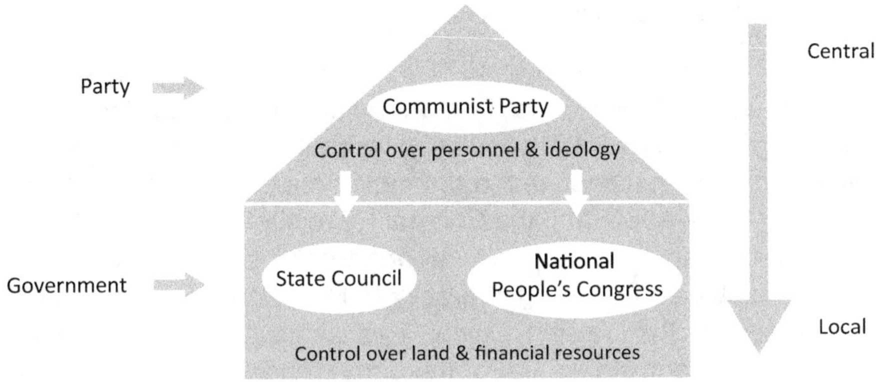

Figure 6.1 China's governance structure
Source: *Based on Chenggang Xu (2015)*

National People's Congress. However, both are integrated into one concept of party-state bureaucracy in policy-making.

Figure 6.1 illustrates the four institutional features of Chinese governance. Firstly, the party is higher in rank than the government at every level and has full control over personnel. It exerts control over the political system through educating, monitoring and managing officials, a system which more or less resembled the governance structure during the different dynasties. The party appoints and monitors the high officials, and delegates similar powers to the party secretaries at the local or provincial level. Secondly, the party sets the ideology in policy-making, while the central government (state) has control over land ownership and financial resources. Thirdly, the party–state bureaucracy is responsible for top-down policy-making. Its centralised control over personnel, ideology, land ownership and financial resources allows a high degree of decentralisation. Fourthly, the implementation of policies is done in a very decentralised way, executed by local officials (in consultation with local party members). Control over lower officials is complemented by an incentive structure to ensure that the local officials are executing what is needed.

The Chinese Communist Party

The CCP was established in 1921. Prior to 1949, the party's main base of support were the farmers, who constituted the overwhelming majority of the population at that time. I always find it rather amazing that despite the dramatic periods of the Great Leap Forward (1958–1960) and the Cultural Revolution (1966–1976), the CCP enjoyed so much support throughout the years. This support may be explained by linking it directly to Mao Zedong, who is seen as the person that unified China. This achievement is so much greater than the mistakes he (or the party) made during his life that his hero-status has not been under attack. In addition, the continuous support was driven by increasing material welfare, more or less spreading around the country. China was a poor country in the 1950s but also an equal society. A final reason why support stayed was that the CCP was able to change itself after the 1970s. The party was capable of renewing itself again and again; the party today is quite different from the one in the pre- and early-reform periods.

When discussing the CCP with my western students, it is clear that many of the students have the perception that the CCP consists mainly of farmers, grey officials and senior citizens. However, this picture is not correct anymore. The almost 90 million party members (2017) are relatively young. 50% are younger than 45 years. Moreover, 20% are females. Membership in the party is open to any Chinese citizen over the age of 18 who is willing to accept the basic ideas and statute. Membership involves quite a few obligations, such as studying the main publications of Confucianism and participating in regular activities organised by the party. Joining the party is still based on ideological motives but the opportunity to make personal connections is also an important motive, as party connections may accelerate one's professional career. In the 1990s, membership became possible for people working in the private sector. This policy was Introduced by President Jiang Zemin (1993–2003) and clearly had the aim to make sure that all segments of an increasingly diverse society were represented in the CCP. In this period, membership grew strongly by more than 2 million members

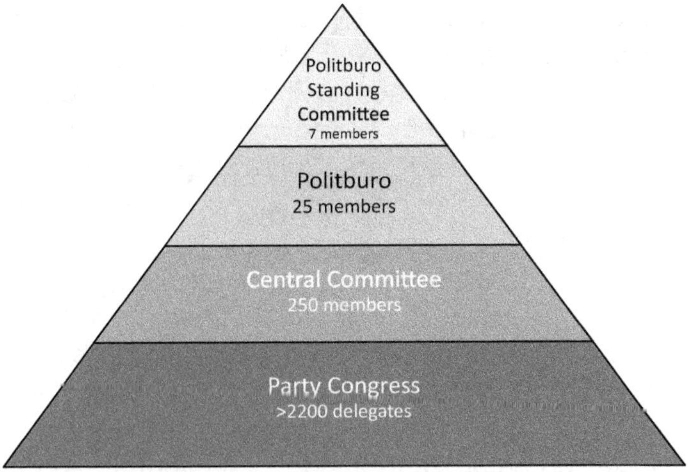

Figure 6.2 CCP hierarchy
Source: *Lawrence & Martin (2013)*

per year. However, growth in membership slowed down after 2013 due to higher entry levels to increase the quality of membership. Today, 6% of CCP members have a non-public background.

Although execution of policies is very decentralised, a lot of power in policy-making is formally concentrated in the hands of the Politburo Standing Committee shown in Fig. 6.2. In 2017, the Politburo Standing Committee had seven members. The full Politburo, including its member of the Standing Committee is involved in decision-making only in the case of important policy shifts and with matters of immediate urgency. The official head of the Politburo and its Standing Committee is the party's general secretary. The size or membership of the Politburo and its Standing Committee changes with each Party Congress.

Selection of the Politburo members and its Standing Committee is a complex and non-transparent process. For example, in 2012, even China-experts were unsure who would be selected. Despite having a single party, the political environment in China has several factions ("populists" versus "elitists") with different views on the needed strategy (market versus government). The composition of the Politburo Standing Committee should be such that both factions and viewpoints are balanced. With Xi Jinping and Li Keqiang in power, there is again an equal split between the two camps: the populist group represented by Li Keqiang and the elitist group represented by Xi Jinping, a so-called "princeling", meaning a child of one of the early senior party officials and thus someone with elite personal connections.

At the bottom of the party hierarchy is the Party Congress with more than 2200 delegates. It is difficult to find out what type of discussions are made during the annual sessions. Apart from the opening and closing addresses (normally in October), everything takes place behind closed doors. It is clear that most decisions are already discussed beforehand and are only formalised during the sessions of the Party Congress. Around 70% of the Party Congress members have a high position in the party, while the other 30% are "grassroots" delegates, mostly not working in the CCP.

The government

The second major entity of the Chinese political system is the government. The highest government administrative body is the State Council comprising ministers at the top of departments. While most senior government officials are party members, party membership is not a requirement for higher government positions. In 2007, the newly appointed Minister of Science and Technology Wan Gang became the first person to rise to ministerial rank without being a member of the CCP. He was chairman of the Zhigong Party, the party that represents Chinese who have returned to China after living overseas or who have relatives living overseas. The State Council is in essence the cabinet and is headed by the premier. Given the size of the State Council (about 50 people), the daily operations are generally handled by the State Council's Standing Committee or the core-cabinet.

Besides the State Council, the National People's Congress (NPC) is also indicated in Fig. 6.1. According to China's constitution, The NPC is the highest organ of state power. On paper, it has a lot of legislative power and responsibilities (such as to approve the budget and elect the members of the State Council), but in reality, its position is rather weak. In essence, it is following the guidelines from the party and State Council. The NPC has around 3,000 deputies and meet in March every year. During the two weeks of sessions, they formally agree with the choices made by the State Council (as directed by the party). The NPC's members are not elected, but are selected instead for five-year terms by the next lower tier of "people's congresses" — deputies at the provincial and municipal level, as well as by members of the armed forces. The list of candidates must be approved by the party, which is involved in the whole selection process.

Other entities in China's political system are think tanks and the several official minor political parties outside the CCP. China's think tanks such as Chinese Academy of Social Sciences (CASS) provide analysis and recommendations on potential new policies, laws and regulations. They are often seen as unofficial "messengers" for the government to start a public discussion or inform the public about a certain policy choice. In addition to the CCP, China has eight other minor political parties, established before the CCP came into power. Therefore, officially, China has a multi-party system and is not strictly a one-party state. However, in reality it is; the combined members of the minor parties number fewer than one million, compared with the CCP's 90 million members. In addition, these parties must accept leadership of the CCP and must follow its policies and choices.

Levels of formal administration

In line with the party structure, the government (and, consequently, the ministries) are also organised into hierarchical levels with offices at the provincial, prefectural (or municipal), county, and township level, as shown in Fig. 6.3. It should be stated that officially, villages are not considered as part of the formal administrative structure. They are considered "mass organisations of self-engagement at the grass-roots level". Their status outside the official government hierarchy gives village authorities the freedom to implement and

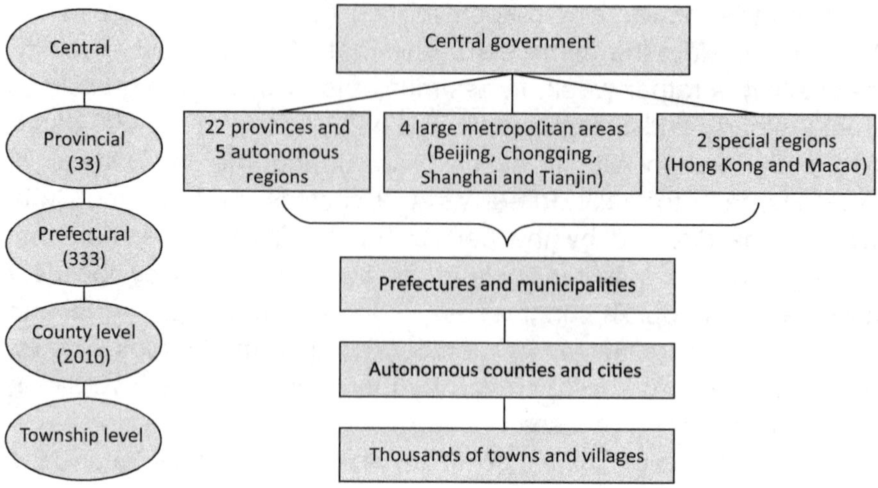

Figure 6.3 Central and local governments
Source: Rongxing Guo (2013)

execute specific government policies without setting a precedent for the formal administrative entities. For example, China introduced direct elections at the village level in the 1980s, but because of the disconnection to the official structure, there was no reason to broaden this to other levels in the governance structure until now.

We already discussed the State Council and the NPC which form the central government of China. Below the central government are 22 provinces, five autonomous geographical regions which have large ethnic minority populations (Guangxi, Ningxia, Inner Mongolia, Tibet and Xinjiang), four large metropolitan cities (i.e. Beijing, Chongqing, Shanghai, and Tianjin) that report directly to the central government, and the two special administrative regions of Hong Kong and Macau. This is the overview normally adopted in international publications. In China, the official number of entities at the provincial level is 34 because it includes Taiwan. Below the provincial level are the prefectures and municipalities. The fourth level of administration includes more than 2000 counties and cities. The lowest level of the official administration is made up of approximately 45,000 smaller towns and villages. A parallel in governance by both the party and government is found at all the lower levels of administration. Furthermore, there is overlap between the levels. For example, some party secretaries of provinces are also members of the Party's Politburo.

Officially, China's political system remains highly centralised and hierarchical, with lower levels of government reporting to higher level officials and following the directives of the central authorities. However, in reality there is a lot of freedom for the local officials. In many cases, this freedom is a consequence of the many contradictory directives received from the central authorities (although self-interest may be an important driver). For example, directives from the Ministry of Transportation may contradict with directives from the Ministry of Environment. In this case, local officials choose to comply with one directive and ignore the other.

6.3 The main features of China's political system

The formal Chinese political system has a number of distinctive features. The most important features are discussed below. The analysis is partly based on Chenggang Xu, 2015.

Collective leadership

The CCP subscribes to collective leadership. Clearly, there will be heavy discussions and debate, and different members and factions may have different opinions, but at the end of the day, the outcome is a compromise that every member can live with. Once the decision of the party is made, all members are expected to uphold that decision. This idea of collective leadership was introduced and implemented by Deng Xiaoping. He saw what happened if one person was in full power. Mao Zedong's decisions that resulted in the Great Leap Forward and the Cultural Revolution had catastrophic economic and social consequences. The collective leadership feature of the Chinese political system should guard against this situation. From this angle, we can argue that the economic policy of opening up was not only the choice of Deng but a collective decision, despite different opinions. Collective leadership is still a main feature of China's political system today, although certain steps taken by President Xi Jinping point to a more centralised leadership and concentration of power in one person, more than what we saw in the past decades. For example, Xi is heading the structural reforms published in the latest 13th five-year plan, while this was done previously by the premier. Whether this is a temporary step or should be seen as trend breach from the past remains to be seen. Another sign of centralising leadership was the rumour early 2017 that Xi will be allowed to remain President after his second term.

Decentralised administrative system

China has a very decentralised governance structure. The central authorities in Beijing face the problem of having to deal with issues typical of both developed and developing countries. The complex and diverse economic and social environment makes centralisation difficult and decentralisation needed. Decentralisation resulted in local initiatives. Many of the reforms started at local government level; only when local experimentation was successful did the central authorities step in and adjusted legislation. Obviously, decentralisation also has disadvantages. Local initiatives may frustrate national directives. They may also create regional barriers for trade and foster corruption. To counteract these potential problems, the party and central government kept control over personnel through appointments and promotions. This control has proven quite effective. For example, after the central government decided (in late 2013) not to evaluate performances of local governments based on GDP growth anymore, about half of the provinces cut their 2014 GDP growth targets substantially.

Adjustment and flexibility inside the political structure

Ideology matters more in China than in many other political systems. However, revision of ideology was needed throughout the years. This balancing act was, and still is, extremely complex. How much revision or adaptation is necessary for the CCP's survival and keeping its monopoly on power? In the late-1970s, the party had a legitimacy crisis. China's economic performance between 1950 and 1978 was bad compared with its Asian neighbours, including Taiwan. The Great Leap Forward and the Cultural Revolution were economic and social disasters, and because of centralisation of power, one could only blame the party for this. The choice to regain legitimacy was through tangible benefits for the population, hence the focus on economic growth whatever it takes.

To avoid chaos, a gradual approach was adopted. Gradualism was the only way to avoid the resistance of the social and political groups whose interests were tied to the old system. Within this gradualism, flexibility became a main feature of governing the country. Formal and informal institutions were created if needed and disappeared if they did not work. In some cases, informal institutional frameworks worked in conjunction with (and sometimes in contradiction to) the formal institutional structure. These institutions were not perfect but were optimal for that specific period of time. The dual-track price system introduced in 1985 and discussed in Chapter 3 is an example of such a flexible institution. It was certainly not optimal, but it avoided hyperinflation. It also managed to evade the backlash of the groups with strong vested interests in the planned economy. In essence, it was a pragmatic solution for that time.

In general, many reforms (and institutional changes) have not followed any blueprints. China's governance structure (including formal and informal institutions) today is the result of flexibility and pragmatism. The belief in pragmatism fits in with China's culture; there is no ultimate truth (as we will see later in the book when discussing Confucianism and Taoism). Flexibility and pragmatism have helped China go through the turbulent phase of economic reform. These characteristics also relate to political power; on several occasions, the party has accepted some erosion of power in order to keep the economy growing. The one instance when economic growth was sacrificed for political control was the Tiananmen crisis of 1989.

Meritocracy

Meritocracy means that political power should be vested in individuals almost exclusively based on ability and talent. No one is likely to oppose this philosophy, but the crux is that, in many cases, meritocracy results in a system that is run by a ruling class. The Chinese bureaucracy has a strong flavour of meritocracy. The party — which manages personnel appointments across the political system, the military and all public institutions — argues that meritocracy helps to make China's political system superior to the political systems of countries that elect their leaders in competitive, multi-party elections.

In China, meritocracy has two significant characteristics. Firstly, government officials are selected after a long process in which they have to show that they are both capable and willing to serve the people and the party. If they show their capabilities, promotion within the system is possible. Promotion within China's government (and Army) is generally based on performance indicators set and evaluated by the central authorities. As stated earlier, due to this evaluation of personnel, the central authorities can execute their control at lower levels. China's governance structure with its loyalty to the central authorities and performance assessments can be dated back to 1500 years ago when a civil examination system was established (Yang Yao, 2014). The exam was mainly on the Confucian classics, hence the bureaucracy had been deeply influenced by the Confucian doctrines. Although the civil exam for officials was abolished in the early 1900s, its core ideas have been preserved.

Secondly, instead of holding government officials accountable to the law, the Chinese regime emphasises the responsibility that government officials should hold towards the people. Obviously, there is a legal framework, but its role is supplementary; the Chinese regime was (and for a considerable part is still) dominated by the bureaucracy. Corruption is a logical consequence of this meritocractic system, and at the same time, attacks the fundamentals of the meritocracy philosophy. This makes fighting corruption so difficult and complex. To reduce the risk of corruption, the central authorities appoint provincial leaders who are not from the provinces, and they usually rotate with some regularity. This is done to prevent any person from creating a strong local power basis. Officials below the provincial level, by contrast, are generally from the local areas and less likely to be removed from their local offices (unless they are promoted or dismissed). Because local government officials are generally from the local areas, in many cases, they stay on their posts for a long period of time. Therefore, the potential for abusing power is reasonably high. Many of the complaints about government corruption in China are allegations against county and prefectural or municipal officials, rather than provincial and central officials.

Meritocracy should create a situation whereby the most capable people (based on transparent performance indicators) should be promoted to the highest posts. In a sense, looking at their educational background and experience, many Chinese leaders are certainly capable and highly skilled. However, there are cases in which promotions are not based on capabilities but are based on family names. The children of high-level officials (the so-called princelings) are particularly prominent at the highest levels of the Chinese political system.

"Rule by law" instead of "rule of law"

"Rule of law" is the legal principle that the law is used to govern a country, as opposed to being governed by decisions of individual government officials (based on arbitrary viewpoints). Put differently, in *rule of law*, the law is something the government serves; in *rule by law*, the government uses law as the most convenient way to govern. In the Chinese case, *rule of law* is not very strong. Regulations on paper may be clear and in many cases, up to "western" standards, but following the rules is another issue. For example, the law on intellectual property rights is in line with international standards. The same holds for the present labour law. However, there is some inability and unwillingness of Chinese authorities to enforce these laws. This low execution level resulted in much discontent in the US with increasing protectionism as a result in the early 2017. Another dimension in the discussion on this topic is the fundamental choice to keep the party outside the legislative framework. The party stands above the law. In essence, the party supports *rule by law* in which the law is seen as a tool for governance, instead of *rule of law* in which the society is driven by legislation. This is indicated earlier in the chapter by the fact that the Army is headed by the party and not by the government. There are many examples showing that the party is above the law. For example, judicial authorities cannot investigate party members without the party's permission. In the case of former Chongqing party secretary Bo Xilai, the party conducted its own investigation and then chose to hand the accused over to the state judiciary in 2012.

6.4 The role of the local governments

China's governance structure is highly decentralised. This was, and still is, the only way to govern such a large country with immense differences per region. As a consequence, local governments have taken the freedom to interpret central directives and regulations and have become important initiators of local reforms. There is another advantage to having this highly decentralised system. As the central government domination is reduced and responsibilities are transferred to lower levels or to the private sector, the central government can no longer be blamed by the population for the various frustrations of daily life. It is now the private employer, the school head, or a local official who is perceived as blameworthy.

In line with the role of the local governments, China has one of the most decentralised fiscal policies in the world. This fiscal (and related to that, institutional) decentralisation started during the Cultural Revolution but is still a characteristic of today's fiscal policy. For example, governments at the provincial level (and below) are largely responsible for public spending on education, healthcare, unemployment insurance and social security. Figure 6.4 presents the shares of the central and local governments in total government revenue and expenditure between 1976 and 2016. The share of

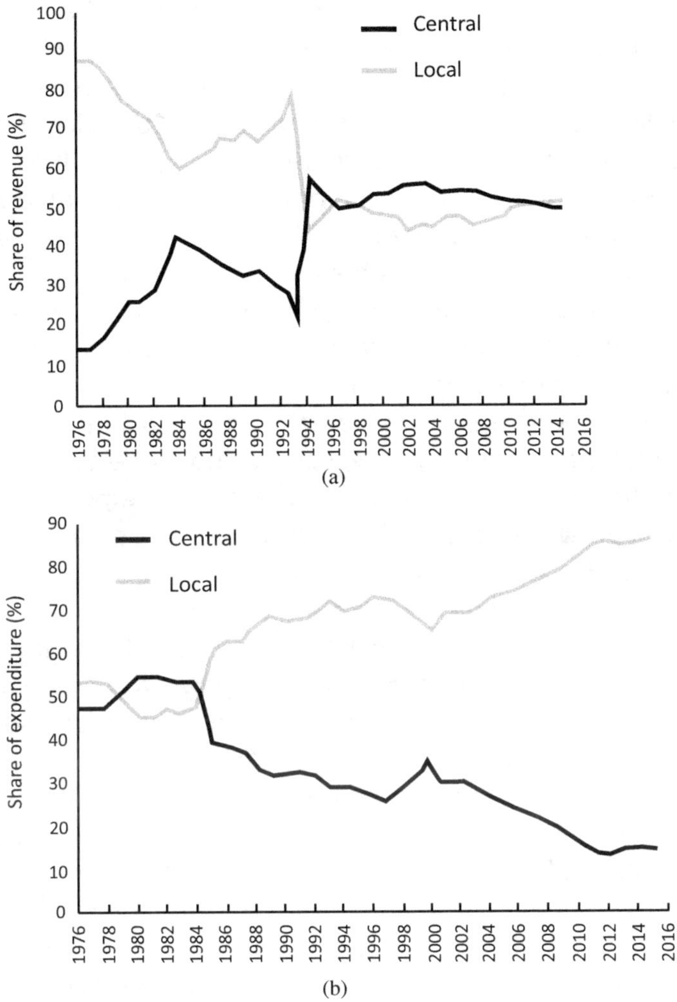

Figure 6.4 Shares of central and local governments in total government revenue (a) and expenditure (b)

Source: *Based on Lin Shuanglin (2009) & National Bureau of Statistics*

local governments in total government expenditure increased strongly in the 1980s to around 70% in 1990. It had been increasing ever since to above 80% by 2016. The picture regarding government revenues shows high volatility between 1976 and the mid 1990s. By the end of the Cultural Revolution (1976), the local government's share of revenue was a staggering 88%. It dropped to 60% in 1984, but then began to rise again. It declined strongly to 45% in the first year of the tax reform (1994) and has since more or less stabilised around 50%. The tax reform of 1994 had the aim to increase central government revenues and to ensure that the central government directly controlled half or more of the revenues.

Decentralisation may result in a system which is very fragmented. If a local firm has problems, local officials have both the incentive and the power to keep the business running. This creates excess capacity and explains why utilisation degrees in many sectors are relatively low despite periods of high economic growth. For example, there were still 100 automobile manufacturers in China in 2016 (Xinhua-net), many obviously producing far below their capacities. The same problem holds with respect to cement, consumer products, steel and solar panels, as we saw in the previous chapter. Another negative side-effect of decentralisation is the building up of local debt, an issue which will be tackled in Chapter 12. The tax reform of 1994 created a financial gap between local government expenditures (that continued) and revenues from Beijing (that dropped substantially). There is a saying in China that "the central government invites the guests, but the local government pays the bill". Although local governments know that they will eventually receive the money from the ministries, there is a lot of uncertainty and discontent about how much and when they can receive the finance. Therefore, local authorities feel great pressure to raise extra revenues to cover their expenses. As a result they look for other sources of income (such as extra-budgetary income through selling land), which result in the building up of local debt.

6.5 Democracy with Chinese characteristics

There is no consensus on how to define democracy; as a result, measuring (the level of) democracy is difficult. Although definitions are different, in most cases, we can agree on a minimum set of fundamental features of democracy. These include broad concepts such as freedom, citizen involvement and accountability of the leaders. We may translate these broad concepts into key-features of a democratic system: a government based on majority rule, the existence of free and fair elections, the protection of minorities, respect for basic human rights and equality before the law. There is often the view that democracy is necessarily a dichotomous concept: a country cannot be democratic and non-democratic at the same time. However, one may question this sharp division line as there can be varying degrees of democracy.

Notwithstanding differences in defining the term, a well-known measure of democracy is published by the US-based Freedom House organisation. It calculates political freedom (based on 10 indicators) and civil liberties (based on 15 indicators). Both values are combined to establish a 1–7 rank to measure the level of democracy. Of the 195 countries assessed in 2016, 87 (45%) were rated *Free*, 59 (30%) *Partly Free*, and 49 (25%) *Not Free*. China was labelled as *Not Free* (Freedom House, 2017). In a discussion with some colleagues at CEIBS, it was stated that emphasis on stability and deprioritising political freedom is essential in China's transitions. The viewpoint is that political stability and a long-term perspective will bring economic development. Within the Confucian culture, good governance means governing by good people rather than governing through good laws. However, while there is little pressure in China for this western-style democracy, there is a strong and growing demand for accountability of government at central and local levels. Most of the adjustments in the governance structure relates to increasing accountability and transparency instead of achieving western democracy.

Democracy and economic growth

There are many publications concluding that economic development needs a democratic environment. The supporting argument is linked to innovative behaviour and efficiency, the key drivers behind longer-term development. Innovative behaviour and efficiency are constrained by a non-democratic environment and a "free mind" is needed for creativity. Hence, modernisation and sustainable development need

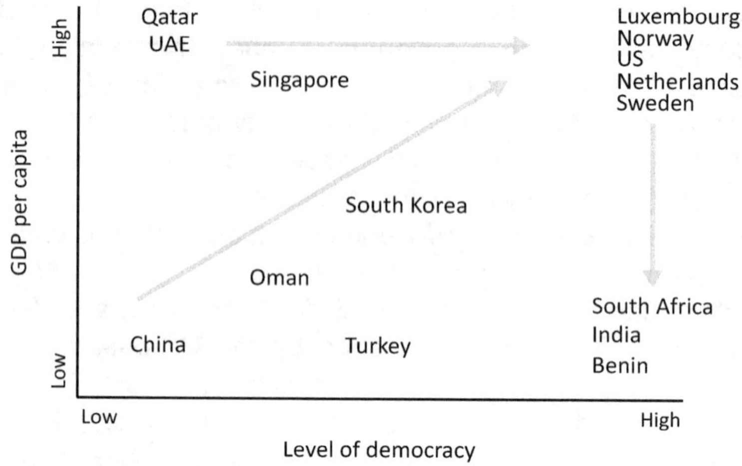

Figure 6.5 Relationship between level of democracy and GDP per capita
Source: Based on Holmberg & Rothstein (2014) and Freedom House (2017)

democracy. This was also pointed out by former president Hu Jintao during his visit to the US in April 2006: "If there is no democracy, there will be no modernisation [...] Important steps in this field are needed". At the same time, there are as many publications suggesting that this relationship between development and democracy is absent or very indirect. Moreover, the overview of the seven pillars of western wisdom in Chapter 5, introduced by Kishore Mahbubani (2008), made clear that democracy is not a necessary condition for economic progress (according to him). In Fig. 6.5, the relationship between the level of democracy and level of development (GDP per capita, as proxy for economic development) is given. The conclusion is clear: there is not a strong relation between the two concepts.

The level of democracy is the same in countries such as Benin, South Africa, the US and Norway, but there are large differences in GDP per capita between these countries. The welfare of Qatar equals the income level of Luxembourg and Norway, but clearly, there are large differences in their levels of democracy. Furthermore, when looking at specific countries over a period of time, we may question the argument that democracy is a precondition for economic development. During the take-off and the period thereafter, the Asian Tigers certainly did not have democratic systems but were able to increase welfare for their populations substantially at the same time.

The low rank of China in the latest Freedom House publication does not imply that the political system is not changing. In one way or another, the CCP was able to reinvent itself throughout the past decades to hold public support. The basic idea that the economy changed dramatically while its political system had been static is not really true. The governance system of 2017 bore little similarity to that of the early 1980s. At that time, China was a country without laws. Now, it has established a comprehensive body of laws and regulations. This is a significant improvement in the system of governance, even if it falls short of the western ideal of representative democracy. Today, if needed, minor adjustments in the political system are implemented, although the emphasis is on economics: to generate economic growth and increase living standards of the people. The Chinese leadership sees democracy as a means to an end, and certainly not as a goal. This way of thinking is visible by looking at specific reforms. For example, the Chinese government began experimenting with limited village elections in the 1980s and has continued to allow some form of local elections to this day. It means that local officials must compete with candidates who may or may not be party members. Nonetheless, in many cases, local party officials and higher level government officials have the authority to disallow candidates from being listed. It is clear that the party secretaries are to remain in overall command. The same holds with respect to democratic reforms in factory management, already implemented in the 1950s and continued up to the 1980s. It allowed the top management to be elected in some factories. Clearly, the aim of this workplace democratic process was not to install democracy but to be a means of improving efficiency.

Democracy and the Chinese middle class

In many publications, a growing middle class is associated with democracy. Defining the middle class (in income cohorts and life styles) will be done in Chapters 14 and 16. The focus in this section is whether the Chinese middle class is, or will be, an important driver behind establishing a western-style democracy. Of course, ideally everyone want to pick its leaders, but in the case of China economics goes above prioritising political rights. In essence, the Chinese middle class wants success, not western-style democracy. I will build this argument on three distinctive features of the Chinese middle class.

Firstly, China's urban middle class is the main beneficiary of the last four decades of economic growth and have benefited disproportionally from economic reforms. After 1978, their standard of living increased spectacularly and, consequently, they have much to lose. Understandably, the middle class tends to be risk-averse and wants to avoid chaos. This fear of chaos tends to limit their willingness to risk political change. Changes in the political system and institutions to establish a democratic environment may affect their living standards negatively. This holds for all segments of the middle class. The young generation focuses on material welfare and compares today with the stories they heard from their parents. The older generation is also risk-averse, particularly those who directly and personally experienced the Cultural Revolution (the generation of 60 years and above).

Secondly, a key characteristic of the Chinese middle class is its high degree of connection with the CCP. The middle class in China (mostly urban, being entrepreneurs, middle and high officials, and people working in state-related organisations such as universities) did not emerge against or outside the party, but with and within the CCP. The high degree of connection between entrepreneurs and the party is explainable by the fact that many entrepreneurial initiatives emerged from within the party ranks, with officials making use of their positions in the new market-driven society. Political connectivity was important, in particular, during the early phase of reforms and such political connection remains very useful today when running a business. Consequently, a large part of the middle class is eager to join the party to advance their careers and break a political glass ceiling.

Thirdly, the educated middle class in China is elitist and stands behind the CCP. Many of them do not want China's peasant majority to play a decisive hand in determining who rules the country. They believe that the rural population is not yet ready to participate in decision-making. The argument above that the Chinese middle class is not prioritising political rights may be against the perception of the western media. In the western media the Tiananmen protests of 1989 were used to highlight the demand for more democracy and political freedom. However, the protesters did not demand multi-party democratic elections. They wanted political relaxation in ways that concerned themselves. They wanted to be able to play a role in organising their own clubs and associations. They wanted the government not to interfere in their personal daily lives. They wanted access to more interesting magazines and films, and the freedom to have public intellectual discussions. Naturally, they admired Gorbachev and the political reforms he was carrying out, but the focus was much more on taking control over their personal freedoms. Furthermore, the collapse of the Soviet Union in the early 1990s and the corruption and dramatic decline of living standards in the former Soviet Union changed the idea of China's educated middle class. Many of the urban educated who had demonstrated in 1989 began to feel relieved that China had followed Deng Xiaoping's policy of economic rather than political reforms.

The image of the CCP in China's society is still at a high-level. Despite frequent public protests in the countryside as well as in the cities, the central leadership of the party and the state enjoys a considerable degree of support. Most of the discontent relates to the local officials; in particular, the government becomes increasingly unpopular further down the hierarchy. Discontent is largely directed at the abuse of local officials, not at the system as a whole.

Although the direct relationship between democracy and welfare is not strong, changes in the political system to become more open and representative may be needed. Experiences in Western Europe, Eastern Europe (Czech Republic, Baltic states and Poland), Japan and South Korea suggest that a certain degree of democratic process is needed for sustainable growth after the take-off stage. This may be expected also in China, but democracy may have different features in China compared to the west. Most significantly, state sovereignty over the people is and will be much stronger because the people believe it should do so. But this democracy with Chinese characteristics is far from cost-free. In particular, creativity and innovation may be depressed due to a lack of full democracy. It is difficult to imagine creativity blossoming if the government places heavy restrictions on the rights of people to express their views and share information, as well as censors news. In the medium term, this lack of innovation can be counteracted by industrial efficiency and service sector deregulation (as we see today), but at the end of the day, creativity and innovation are needed. An important question then is how the authorities are able to find a way to combine specific features of Chinese democracy with the need to increase creativity and innovation.

While demand for changes in the current political system rarely emerges from the middle class, the middle class is critical on specific issues from time to time. Social unrest is not only originating from migrant workers (protesting against their work conditions or their limited access to social welfare in cities), farmers (protesting against land purchase or corrupt local authorities), but also increasingly from the urban middle class. In particular, China's urban middle class is active in fighting the environmental problems and worries about corruption. The same holds for discontent related to food-safety and labour issues. Overall, the middle class wants better governance and a legal system that protects them instead of full western-style democracy.

Democracy does not say too much about the quality of a country's governance. This topic was heavily discussed after the election of Mr Trump as president of the US and the political situation related to the UK referendum of Brexit. It is indeed a big question whether a democratic process would result in a good, prudent and wise government that makes good decisions, whether it is a proportional representation (based on majority vote as is the case of Brexit) or a winner-takes-it-all system (as in the US). The discussion about democracy and quality of the government is not new. The same discussion was heard in the 1990s and 2000s when Greece, Italy and Poland had a high turnover in their governments. Because of the democratic process, political power games and short-term views, the result may be weak governments and governance.

China's culture and democracy

I have held many discussions with my western students about the role of the government in China. Mostly, they cannot understand how Chinese people are willing to accept that the government intervenes in daily life so intensely. Many times, the one-child policy is given as example. For them, it is unbelievable that a government can say that a couple may have only one child and that one must follow that rule. This different perspective narrows down to the way the citizens view the government. In the west, the government is an outsider and, consequently, its power should be limited. In China, in contrast, the party, government and the citizens are seen as an integrated entity. Chinese citizens see the bureaucratic system as the guardian of Chinese civilisation. Within the Confucian tradition, the party and state are seen not just as a member of the family but the head of the family. And of course, we should listen to our fathers because they know what is best for us. In this sense, choices of the party and government are in essence not being questioned. Surprising as it may seem to many westerners, the Chinese governance system enjoys great legitimacy, even more so than in many western countries.

Unlike in the west, the legitimacy of Chinese governance does not rest on democracy. It should be clear that, in general, democracy is not the only source of legitimacy; it has a range of different sources. The legitimacy source in China relates to the Chinese civilisation. China's sense of what it is and who the Chinese are have been overwhelmingly shaped not by China's experience as a nation state but by its civilisation history. Therefore, the most important political value for the Chinese is the unity of the country, which is intimately linked to the priority attached to order and stability above western democracy and its potential instability.

Progress on democracy

The Chinese authorities indicate again and again that democracy (with Chinese characteristics) is important, but that time is needed. Western experience makes clear that the way to democracy is indeed a long one. The modern society in Britain started with the Industrial Revolution in the late 18th and early 19th centuries. However, it was not until 1880s that most men gained the right to vote, and not until 1918 (so over 130 years after the beginning of the Industrial Revolution) that women (over thirty years) won the same right (Jacques, 2009). In the more modern history, the experience in Asia makes clear that none of the Asian Tigers achieved take-off under democratic conditions. In this light, it seems misconceived to argue that China is now ready for, and should become, a multi-party democracy based on universal ideas. The country is only halfway through its industrial revolution with so many people still living and working in the countryside and a new round of transformations on its way.

Another Chinese perspective on democracy relates to China's discontent about the democratic process in global institutions. The global governance structure is hardly democratic. The voting power within the International Monetary Fund (IMF) is still in the hands of the US, Europe and other OECD countries, while the world in economic terms changed dramatically towards new economic powers in the past decades. It is clear that most emerging markets, including China, are underrepresented in the IMF decision-making process. The same holds (although more informally) with respect to the WTO. Another argument why China is critical about western style democratic institutions relates to the democratic deficit in the EU. The EU is hardly democratic with only the European Parliament being directly elected. The European Commission has much more power but the European commissioners are not elected; they are selected by national governments. In general, there are no international institutions that can be described as democratic. While the west is focusing on internal democracy (within the nation state), the Chinese are focusing more on the external democracy issue.

Of course, these arguments are finetuned to fit the main aim of keeping power at the party and to continue with a highly centralised political structure, but there is some truth in the arguments.

Changes towards more democracy are expected in China, but the steps will be focused on continuation of stability. Fighting corruption and strengthening its legal system are important issues, as well as to find ways to protect human rights, although maybe differently defined as in the west. The Chinese prefer to talk about economic human rights instead of human rights as the west defines it. In this context, China will change, but it will remain a one-party system for a long time to come. This is the reality we have to recognise. Clearly, internet and social media will change the dynamics of discussion, expression and debate. The internet landscape facilitates involvement in public debates and occasional complaints by a population that previously did not necessarily express such personal opinions openly. Platforms as Weibo and WeChat make this happen. Online expression has been possible despite the fact that not all information is accessible due to censorship. It is interesting to see how intense the debate can be on social media, also regarding unfair practices by officials. In that sense, people may express their discontent. However, this freedom of expression has its limit. Discussions about the legitimacy of the party, the *Falun Gong*[1] or Tibet are hardly possible and sharing of information through platforms such as Weibo are under attack due to government intervention. Of course, the authorities are unable to stop the development of the social media, but are trying to guide it as much as possible.

---

[1] *Falun Gong* is a modern Chinese spiritual (or religious) movement that combines meditation with moral values that centres around Buddhist and Taoist beliefs. It received enormous attention in the late 1980s and early 1990s in China. The CCP was not able to control this movement, which was growing outside the state-run organisations. Their growing size and independence from the state, and the large number of higher-ranking party officials among their followers, created discomfort in the CCP and in 1999, membership of the movement was forbidden because it would threatened social stability.

6.6 State-owned enterprises

In a chapter about China's political structure, some words about SOEs are needed because they are an important tool in the hands of China's bureaucracy. As part of the triangle, the SOEs face a soft-budget constraint: an implicit guarantee that they cannot go bankrupt, even if this is the consequence of risky and bad behaviour. Banks and governments bail out loss-making firms, usually to preserve employment. This soft-budget constraint has some disadvantages and that is why more market forces are implemented to harden the budget constraints. In the west, this has been done through privatisation. In China, another route has been chosen. Only partial privatisation occurred in which the government keeps a majority of the shares. The aim is not to substitute public for private ownership but to have market and government operating together.

The SOE reforms (after 1978) can be divided into five phases (Fig. 6.6). During the first phase (1978–1984), the SOEs were fully integrated in the planning system. Although some market incentives were implemented (such as the dual-price system), the SOEs followed essentially the commands from the planning committee within the context of the soft-budget constraint. The second phase (1984–1992) can be labelled as institutionalising the experiments of the early-reform period. Successful pilot projects resulted in legislation in regard to private ownership and freedom to operate. Furthermore, the market was partly opening up for domestic private firms as well as foreign companies through joint venture constructions. In 1992, at the end of phase two, the role of SOEs was still relatively large. They employed 70% of all urban employment and accounted for 60% of the total gross investments. In terms of industrial output, step by step, the SOE share fell from 65% in 1985 to 40% in 1992.

In the third phase of SOE reform (1993–2002), the number of smaller SOEs fell strongly and rationalisation occurred that had a big impact on the labour market. In this period, between 30 and 40 million SOE-workers lost their jobs. Although growing sectors (in particular, the service sector) were able to absorb these people,

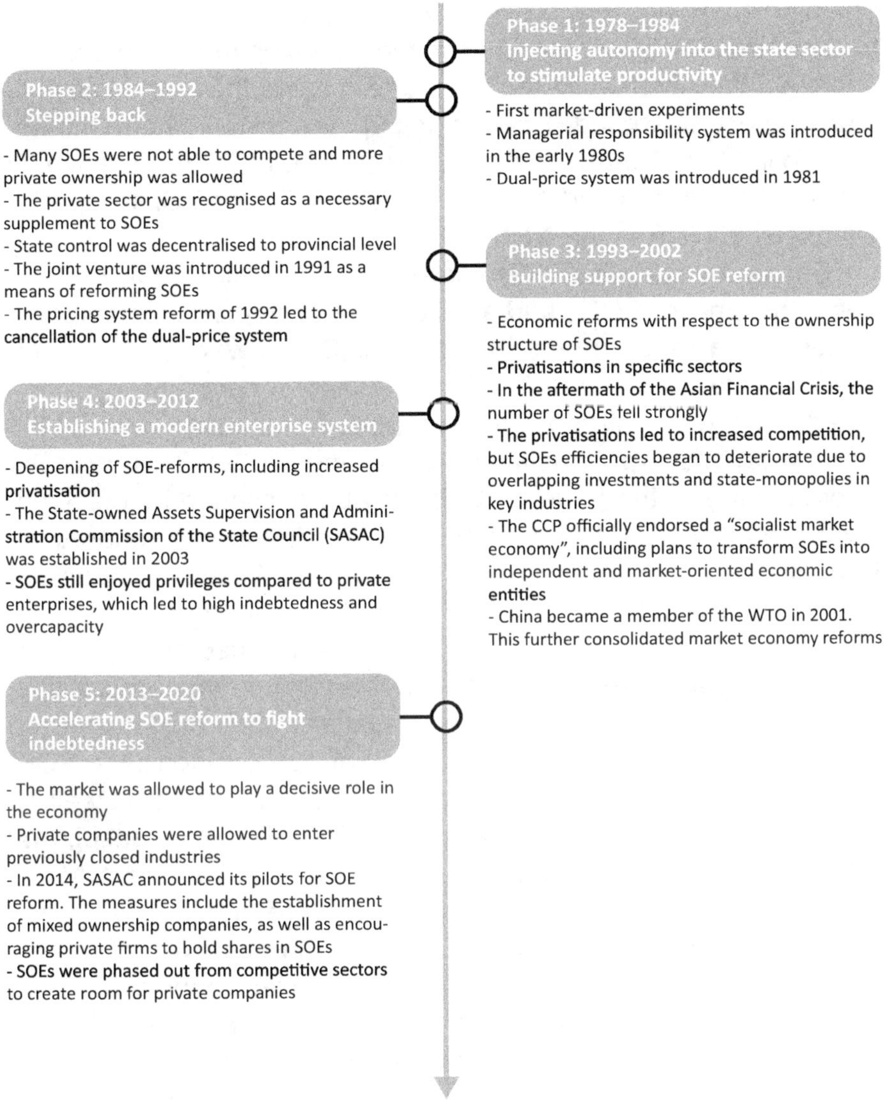

Figure 6.6 SOE reform timeline, 1978–2016

Source: *Adjusted from BBVA, China Economic Watch, 27 November 2015 (based on National Bureau of Statistics)*

unemployment became a big issue. At the same time, the restructuring of the SOEs, combined with implementing more competition, improved their profitability strongly and created the precondition to start operations abroad. The opening up was driven by WTO membership in 2001. Domestically, the importance of SOEs declined. In 2002, SOEs accounted for less than one third of GDP, against almost all of GDP in the early 1980s.

Phase four (2003–2012) shows a mixed picture. On the one hand, the smaller SOEs had a difficult time and many experienced losses. As a result, numerous smaller SOEs were partly privatised. On the other hand, profits in the largest centrally controlled enterprises grew strongly in this period (although due to the world-wide crisis, profitability declined after 2009). This increase of profitability of the largest SOEs may be explained by the lower involvement of central government in day-to-day operations through the emergence of the State-owned Assets Supervision and Administration Commission (SASAC), which can be considered as a buffer between government and enterprise management. SASAC played a key role in the SOE-reform. It was, and still is, responsible for the supervision and administration of state-owned assets. It has a say in the management composition in a SOE, and is responsible for the restructuring plans of SOEs as well as international mergers and acquisitions. There is a consensus that SASAC is important in strategic decisions. For example, SASAC required the companies under its umbrella to increase overseas business income to 50% of total revenue in 2014 (up from less than 40% in 2013). However, it remains unclear how far SASAC has managed to penetrate the day-to-day activities of SOEs.

Phase five (2013–2020) pertains to steps to reform SOEs in the near future. Essentially, more market-incentives, combined with opening up formerly closed sectors to private capital, drive these reforms. Today (2017), China has about 150,000 SOEs which employ over 27 million people. They account for 25% of the country's total corporate assets but at the same time receive 75% of total bank loans. This dominance in banking loans is a heritage of the triangle system. SOEs contribute to 15% of total employment in the country. Obviously, they are still important, not only in economic size but also as the tool to finetune the economy if needed. Consequently, structural problems in these SOEs may spillover to other parts of the economy. Below are the most important problems relating to SOEs today.

- China's corporate debt, mostly taken by SOEs, has soared since the beginning of the financial crisis in 2007 and increased to around 180% of GDP in 2016.
- Efficiency and profitability are relatively low in SOEs with a high proportion of public ownership and low proportion of foreign investment. In general, profits grew strongly between 2004 and 2008, but after the start of the world economic crisis, the SOEs have difficulties in surviving without direct or indirect government support.
- Overcapacity (defined as the actual output as a proportion of total installed production capacity) is a feature amongst large SOEs (and sectors with large shares of public capital). The biggest overcapacity problem is in sectors related to the construction boom after 2008.

As can be seen in Fig. 6.6 (Phase 5), the market will play a more important role in the economy in the future. The role of the market was upgraded to "decisive" in 2013. An example is to open formerly closed sectors in the economy to private firms and foreign companies. Other announced reforms include the reduction of administrative interference in the operations of SOEs, and attracting private sector participation in SOEs (the so-called public–private partnerships). In addition, as the authorities indicated, further consolidation by reducing the number of SOEs is needed. It means that the government will stop subsidising loss-making SOEs or zombie enterprises. This will take time. Protected sectors such as banking, automobiles, telecommunication, construction and mining must still undergo sophisticated restructuring before they can be fully exposed to private and foreign capital. The promotion of mixed-ownership model as a basic principle of these sectors is logical from an efficiency point of view, but implementation is difficult, particularly if it relates to job losses. From this point of view, it

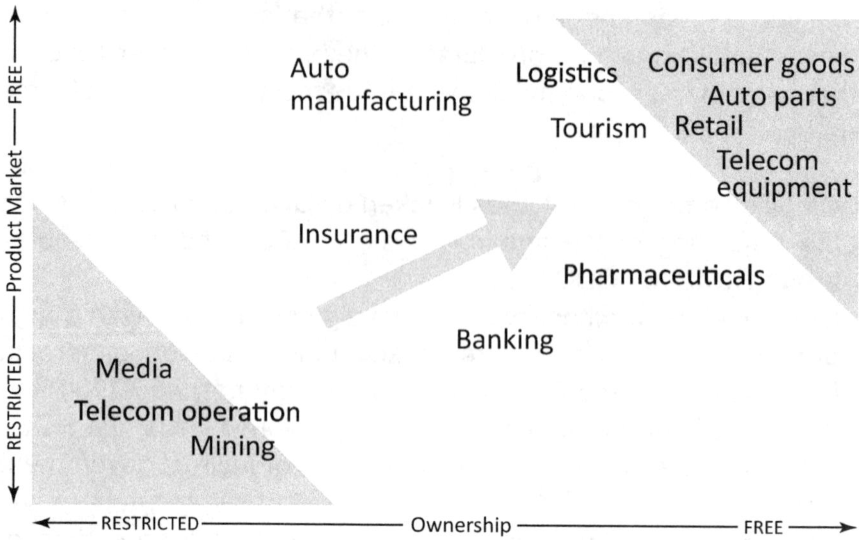

Figure 6.7 Freedom in ownership and product market in specific sectors
Source: China Monitor Nyenrode (2013)

is not strange that the process of providing support for private capital in traditional state-dominated sectors slowed in recent years; time is needed.

Figure 6.7 shows the difference between sectors in regard to restrictions on ownership and operations. The consumer goods sector experiences high ownership freedom and high product market freedom because Beijing does not see this industry as strategic. Also, Chinese companies in these sectors are ready to compete domestically as well as internationally. Telecom by contrast is labelled as a strategic sector; hence, ownership and product market freedom are still restricted. The same holds for mining and media. The arrow in the figure indicates that most industries are moving in the direction of market freedom and liberalisation of ownership restrictions, but some industries are liberalising further and faster than others, depending on whether the government has labelled the industry as strategic or not. Moreover, with respect to these more restricted sectors, some opening up steps are in the pipeline. Opening up sectors for private investors also relates to foreign investors. New energy and environment-friendly products are highly encouraged through concrete policy measures to attract foreign companies. Recently issued regulations related to FDI show that only investment projects that help to improve the environment and contribute to sustainable development will receive favourable treatment by China's investment authorities whereas foreign investment in resource-intensive and highly-polluting industries are discouraged.

The general view is that SOEs operate specifically in the sectors with restricted ownership. Indeed, many of the largest SOEs are in sectors such as banking, mining and telecom. However, it should be noted that this observation should not be black or white. The line between SOEs and private companies has blurred considerably in recent years. In a sense, the ownership structure matters less and less.

Undoubtedly, we see more government intervention in China compared with what we see in the west. At the same time, keep in mind that twenty years ago, the CCP and government controlled almost every aspect of doing business and citizens' lives. The economic and social environment changed dramatically; so did the political system, within the borders of stability. What has not change is the strong decentralisation and the freedom of interpretation to the lower levels of the bureaucracy. What also has not changed is the use of the five-year plans in guiding the economy and the society, which is the topic of the next chapter.

Chapter 7

The Role and Development of the Five-Year Plans

Myth 7: The five-year plan will be abandoned soon because it does not fit in the move towards markets

7.1 Introduction

To understand the role of the party, the government and economic planning in China, it is necessary to review the history of the five-year plans briefly. Five-year plans are social and economic development blueprints of the CCP that were adopted in 1953 and modelled in line with the Soviet central planning process. China practised a rigid central planning up to 1978. During the pre-reform period, the main function of planning through the five-year plans was to direct the production of major products by state-owned enterprises (SOEs). After the reforms started in 1978, the status of the five-year plan changed. Rather than strict targets and aims, they have become more like rough guides on how the party wants to guide the country; it is the party programme and its priorities for the next five years. Furthermore, the five-year plans are no longer just economic in focus. Much attention is also given to environmental protection, social safety issues and innovation. Despite the changing role, it is still important to see how the party is looking at (and taking steps related to) a range of social, economic, educational, cultural and environmental issues. From this point of view, the five-year plans are a logical part of the centralised governance system.

Section 7.2 points out some key features of the planning system and explains why China chose the five-year plans as a tool to guide the economy. It also shows how the plans evolved over the years. Today's five-year plan is considerably different from the five-year plans that were developed within the command economy. In Section 7.3, we describe the planning process and the role of the party and state in this process. In Section 7.4, the focus is on the latest five-year plans. We start with the 11th five-year plan with its focus on rebalancing and fighting disequilibria in the economy. This is followed by the 12th five-year plan with its focus on consumption. The latest (13th) five-year plan (2016–2020) has the focus on social spending and emphasises the role of the service sector in the economy. The annual sessions of the party and state are important as integrated part of the planning process. That is why we dedicate Section 7.5 to these annual plenums.

7.2 The planned economy and the role of the five-year plan

In general, we can distinguish three types of economic systems: a planned economy, a market economy and mixed systems. Every economic system must answer the basic questions in economics. These questions relate to what to produce, how to produce and for whom to produce. In a planned or command economy, it is very straightforward. The government determines what, how and who is going to get those goods and services that have been produced. Planned economies have the ability to adjust rapidly to changing circumstances because the authorities have the ability to shift resources away from one industry to another, if needed in a short time frame. However, a planned economy has some important shortcomings. Firstly, it is extremely difficult for central planners to find out and understand what a society needs. Consequently, planning mistakes result in surpluses and shortages of products and services. Secondly, in a planned economy, efficiency is of secondary importance; products have to be produced and in many cases, it does not matter how the companies are doing that as long as they stick to the plan. Thirdly, the system does not give people the incentive to work hard or to take the opportunities. There is clearly a motivation problem which negatively affect production and productivity.

In a market economy, private companies and individuals decide what to produce and what to buy. An "invisible hand" (market) coordinates economic activity and the government does not intervene in demand and supply. A market economy is based on economic freedom, financial incentives and, in general, tend to be relatively efficient. The disadvantage is that the market can overreact, creating bubbles and economic crises. A mixed system combines the role of the government and the market. In a mixed system, the market will do its work, but if needed, the government may intervene in order to stabilise (sectors in) the economy and to achieve social aims. Market failures, such as the sub-prime mortgage-induced financial crisis in the United States that reached a climax in 2008 and the sovereign debt crisis in Europe in 2010, demonstrated that government intervention is helpful (and sometimes needed) to stabilise irrational behaviour of the market. It is clear that finding the optimum mix of market forces and government intervention is difficult. We can translate the planned and market economy into Communism and Capitalism. This is done in Fig. 7.1. The figure shows also the main characteristics of the mixed economy.

It may be a bit provocative, but you could argue that China's combination of market and state is in line with countries such as Denmark, Sweden and Finland. That is why we also indicate China as a mixed economy in Fig. 7.1. In certain parts of the economy, the government is absent, while intervention is visible when the markets overreact or when markets does not bring the desired results.

	Communism	Mixed economy	Capitalism
Basic philosophy	Command and directives by the government	Market forces but if needed (crisis, welfare level, healthcare) the government steps in	Free markets and no government interference
Ownership of resources	Productive resources are owned by the government	Markets are functioning but certain resources in State-hands; e.g. strategic industries and banks	All productive resources are privately owned
Allocation of resources	Centralised and planned by the government	Key industries and industrial policy if need; otherwise: market forces	Capital, labour and land is allocated by the market
Role of government	Government is a key player in the economy and takes over the role of the market	Government is needed for public goods, promoting competition and creating a stable business context	Market forces, driven by competition on the market

China
Denmark
Finland
Netherlands
New Zealand
Sweden

Figure 7.1 The spectrum of economic systems
Source: *Adapted from Clayton (2003)*

The changing role of the five-year plans

During the period from 1953 when the first five-year plan was published until the end of the 1970s, China practised central planning under the direction of the State Planning Commission (SPC). During this era of Mao Zedong, China's five-year plans put down very specifically how much of which item should be produced and consequently it planned precisely how much input (labour and machines) was needed to be able to produce a certain product. The production of major products was done by SOEs. In agriculture, it specifically stated how much livestock was allowed to achieve the planned production targets. Economic life (in terms of production and consumption) was driven by the government decisions and set by the planners. The market was absent. If the society is not too complicated, an intensive command system may be possible, but the more complex a society becomes, the more mistakes are made with misdirection of resources and with negative impact on the economy as a result.

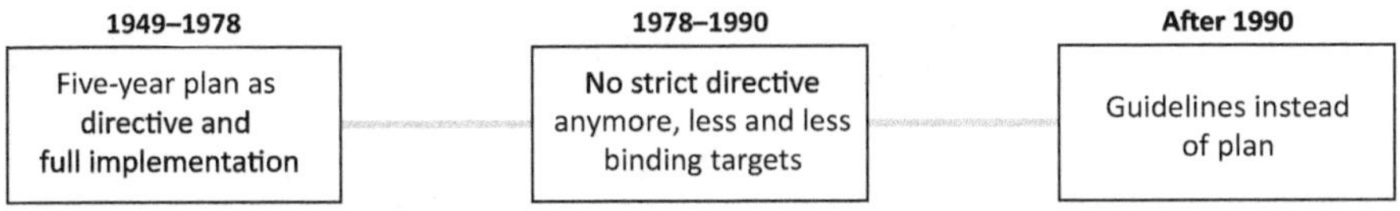

Figure 7.2 The changing role of the five-year plan
Source: Based on BBVA Research

Figure 7.2 shows that from 1978 onwards, the Chinese government changed the economic system gradually towards a combined command-market economy, allowing non-state enterprises to produce and compete with SOEs. In the 1980s, as the government loosened its grip on the economy, it also became a bit more relaxed about the five-year plans. Rather than strict agendas, they have been transformed into a list of priorities set by the party for the next five years and may serve as evaluation tool. It is interesting to note that, starting with the 11th five-year plan, the name changed from plan to guidelines programme. Although the role of the five-year plan changed from directives towards guidelines, the plan is still there and important to guide the economy and society and shows the strong interference of the government in certain aspects of daily life. In the spring of 2016, China's National People's Congress (NPC) approved the 13th five-year plan, which will guide economic and social policy through 2020. The document set dozens of policy goals, and included many quantitative and qualitative targets related to the economic, social and environmental context. The goals are set in a broad way and in many cases, it gives enough room for local officials, companies, banks and citizens to implement it in a flexible way. A colleague told me to look at the five-year plan as large neon signs in a shopping street to show where the CCP wants to take the country.

7.3 The five-year plans: The process

It should be clear that there is a considerable overlap between the different five-year plans; the new plan is in many cases a continuation of the strategy set out in the earlier plan. Only in exceptional cases we see a big difference between two five-year plans. This is

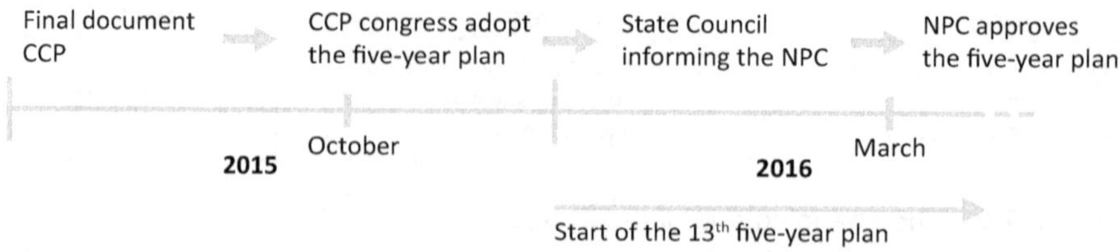

Figure 7.3 The process towards the new (13th) five-year plan
Source: Author's overview

logical; five years is not a long period and implementing reforms may take a large time span. It means that in many cases, part of the implementation of a five-year plan may overlap with the formulation of the next five-year plan. Harmonisation and coordination of the two plans is therefore needed. In this sense, the newest 13th five-year plan must be viewed as part of an evolutionary planning and policymaking process. Figure 7.3 shows the five-year plan process by referring to the latest plan that started in 2016.

The 13th five-year plan process began in early 2015. The first official document in the process was the Communist Party's Brief, which is normally introduced in February or March. The document was the result of months of closed-door meetings among high party officials who represent competing interests. Next, the party document was discussed and fine-tuned for approval in October 2015 when the 250 members of the Central Committee of the Communist Party came together in Beijing for the party's fifth plenum (the term which will be discussed later). One may say that after the approval, the five-year plan was ready. The confirmation and ratification of the Party Congress in October was a ceremonial act. After October, the government stepped in. The National Commission for Development and Reform, in coordination with the State Council, then wrote the 100-page document which is the published five-year plan. It is interesting that the commission that wrote down the five-year plan does not have the words "plan" or "planning" in its name. The official formal approval was done by the National People's Congress (NPC). The NPC annual meeting is always in March. The

NPC discussed the document, without making many changes to it, and approved the 13th five-year plan in March 2016. The session ended with a press conference hosted by Premier Li Keqiang, during which details on China's 13th five-year plan were unveiled.

The preparation and discussion of the 13th five-year plan overlaps with the 12th five-year plan period. Due to its relatively short time frame of five years, implementation of all the measures on time is difficult and in many cases, local officials may have to improvise because the plans are not detailed or clear enough. In general, the large, national thematic sub-plans are released in the first year of the plan, and the follow-on implementation documents in the following second and third years. Fiscal support measures and evaluation procedures often lag even further, meaning that the full web of national and local policies is generally only complete in the latter half of the plan period. The consequence is that implementation of measures will roll over to the next planning period.

The five-year plans and their priorities

As stated before, from the 2000s onwards the government substituted the term "plan" to "programme" or "guidelines", emphasising that the five-year plan is an overview of the main priorities and requires a high degree of institutional freedom and local autonomy to implement the needed policy measures. At the same time, the five-year plan is Beijing's core mechanism for coordinating and implementing policies across national ministries and local governments, and plays a central role in the reform programme. It is also a political tool that strengthens the role of the party because promotions are often based on the level of achievement of the goals mentioned in the plan. Every five-year plan has a key focus, which is the overwhelming objective for that period of time. This is shown in Fig. 7.4. In the first years, five-year plans were centred around industrialisation and economic growth. The essential reforms of the SOEs started in the 8th five-year plan, while the start of the rebalancing process can be seen in the 11th five-year plan. The 12th five-year plan was a pro-consumption plan, while productivity

Plan	Dates	Key feature
First	1953–1957	Industrial development and growth through centralised planning
Second	1958–1962	Industry focus and Great Leap Forward
Third	1966–1970	Agricultural focus and defence
Fourth	1971–1975	Cultural revolution
Fifth	1976–1980	Modernization and reform
Sixth	1981–1985	Adjustment and pilot projects with respect to reforms
Seventh	1986–1990	Market implementations
Eighth	1991–1995	Opening up and SOE reforms
Ninth	1996–2000	SOE reform and urban development
Tenth	2001–2005	Strategic restructuring and reducing inequality
Eleventh	2006–2010	Start of the rebalancing process
Twelfth	2011–2015	Fighting inequality and stimulating consumption
Thirteenth	2016–2020	Domestic rebalancing and innovation

Figure 7.4 Key features of the five-year plans, 1953–2020

Source: *Ebbers and Zhang (China Monitor)*

and innovation are the key elements in the latest five-year plan. It is interesting to observe that the focus of the 13th five-year plan is on domestic rebalancing. It shows that external rebalancing (fighting distortions with respect to the Renminbi and the capital account) is not the key objective and is postponed to 2020 or later.

Besides general statements about increasing welfare of the population, protecting the environment and fighting inequality, the five-year plan also lays out specific (quantitative) economic targets. For example, it indicates the annual growth target over the five-year period. It also gives specific (growth) targets with respect to reducing rural poverty, education enrollment, pension coverage and environmental protection. Some targets are more important than others. Specific quantitative targets are divided into "binding" and "indicative". Binding targets are part of the evaluation and promotion process. By contrast, "indicative" targets are not given the same weight and are not included in the formal bureaucracy evaluation criteria.

Figure 7.5 shows the GDP growth target from the 8th five-year plan onwards in combination with the real growth. The current 13th five-year plan aims for average annual growth of 6.5% between 2016 and 2020. In most cases, real economic growth was (much) higher than the targets indicated in the plan. For much of the last 25 years, the economy had overshot government target growth by

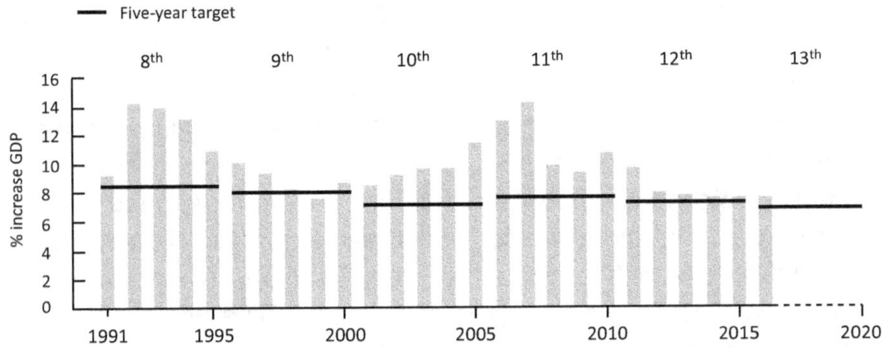

Figure 7.5 GDP growth and the five-year targets

Source: Based on Economist and NBS

large margins. It was only since 2010 that Chinese GDP growth numbers came to be very close to the targets set in the plan. In this sense, the growth targets should be seen as a floor. The growth target is set in such a way that it can be achieved relatively easy without forced government intervention. But, if actual growth forecast will be lower than the growth target, the government will step in with inflationary monetary and fiscal policy.

According to one of my colleagues at Renmin University, slower growth target (and consequently slower actual growth) is tolerable as long as enough jobs are created. This may explain the large differences between the growth target and actual growth up to 2010. If the government is uncertain about the actual number of people unemployed it will make sure that economic growth is high enough to counteract a possible negative impact on the labour market. Now better data are available and consequently there is no need to have much higher actual growth compared to the growth target. They know that with 6.5% growth, the labour market is stable.

7.4 The 11th, 12th and 13th five-year plans

There are many similarities between the 11th, 12th, and 13th five-year plans. The "harmonious society" in the 11th five-year plan has been changed into "inclusive growth" in the 13th five-year plan (although the same term was already used in the 7th plan), The "transformation to domestic demand" in the 12th plan has been changed into "shift away from export to consumption" in the latest 13th five-year plan. Changes in China take time and there is a step by step approach. It means that strategic choices take more time than one five-year period to be fully implemented. Therefore, we concluded earlier that the newest plan is a logical follow-up based on the previous plan. There were two exceptions. The 5th five-year plan of the late 1970s and the 9th five-year plan (1996–2000) showed clearly a significant shift in China's economic strategy. The 5th five-year plan focused on opening up and market reforms. The 9th five-year plan set the stage for ownership transition and it gave private initiative a legal basis. Today, there is intensive discussion whether the newest 13th five-year plan should also be considered as a significant shift of strategy. Unmistakably, it shifts the focus away from export and investment-driven growth towards domestic consumption. However, this was already set in motion some years ago and from that perspective it can be considered as a gradual continuation of the strategy set in with the 12th five-year plan.

In Fig. 7.6, we made a comparison between the 11th and 12th five-year plans with respect to targets (and steps taken) that focus on the rebalancing process. Some interesting observations can be made from the overview below. Firstly, there is a clear emphasis on increasing the growth in income (relative to GDP

	11th five-year plan	12th five-year plan
Real economic growth	7.5% p.a.	7.0% p.a.
Per capita disposable income	5% p.a.	>7.0% p.a.
Population covered by basic urban pension	5.1% p.a.	7.5% p.a.
Construction of housing	10 million*	36 million
Increase service sector in GDP	3 pps	4 pps

(*) According to budget; no binding target

Figure 7.6 Comparison of the 11th and 12th five-year plan; specific targets
Source: *ECB (2013)*

growth). In the 12th five-year plan, the target was to increase per capita disposable income by more than 7% annually. Secondly, there are ambitious targets set to increase coverage of a nation-wide urban pension system. Thirdly, for the first time there were concrete targets with respect to social government spending. For example, there was the binding target in the 12th five-year plan to build 36 million (social) houses. Finally, one can see an acceleration of the share of services in GDP. In the 12th five-year plan, the service sector should increase by 4 percentage points over the five-year period.

The 12th five-year plan focused specifically on stimulating consumption. The way the policymakers planned to stimulate consumption is summarised in Fig. 7.7. The plan formalised three (intermediate) goals to achieve the consumer-led growth: boosting employment, rising wages and increasing the marginal propensity to consume. Obviously, policy measures should be implemented to achieve these goals. For example, building up the (labour intensive) service sector would generate extra jobs. Furthermore, developing a nationwide social safety net would reduce precautionary savings and stimulate consumption. This is complemented by an increase of minimum wages and stimulating rural incomes.

Another key element in the 12th five-year plan was the focus on science and technology. The term "innovation" was mentioned 46 times, followed by "sustainability" (9 times). It is clear that the focus

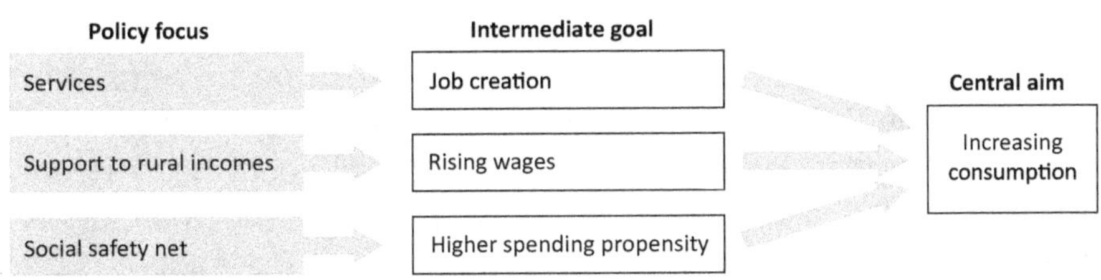

Figure 7.7 Achieving a consumer-led growth

Source: *Based on BBVA*

on sustainability and high-tech industries (away from environmental unfriendly industries such as cement and mining) was a key priority. Almost all binding targets in the 12th five-year plan relate to the environment or social welfare.

These priorities are fully in line with the (needed) rebalancing process that started in the 11th five-year plan. On the demand side, rebalancing requires reducing reliance on exports and fixed investment and boosting domestic consumption. On the supply side, it requires greater reliance on services and less on manufacturing, and greater focus on productivity and innovation. All these reforms are needed to tackle problems in the field of inequality and the environment. These strategic choices continued in the 13th five-year plan.

The newest (13th) five-year plan

In March 2016, at the annual session of the NPC, the 13th five-year plan was approved and published. The plan shows the priorities of the main economic and social goals during the period of 2016–2020. Some of these goals (targets) are binding while the rest are indicative (and in a sense forecasts). Although summarising a complex document into one short paragraph is a challenge, the main choices are given as follows.

Firstly, the authorities set the annual growth target on 6.5% over the next five years and holding to their long-term goal, stated in the 12th five-year plan, of doubling the country's GDP size in the decade of 2010–2020. Within this 6.5% growth target, the strategy is to accelerate the rebalancing process. The plan reaffirmed the authorities' intention to push forward structural reforms and facilitate this economic rebalancing. Secondly, at its heart, the 13th five-year plan is about innovation (and productivity). There is a strong focus on addressing legal, financial and institutional obstacles to innovation. The plan clearly shows the eagerness to achieve higher levels of endogenous innovation in order to move up global value chains. This is in line with the "Made in China 2025" plan, announced in 2015. The aim of this plan is to transform

China from being a manufacturer of quantity to one of quality. Thirdly, the newest plan emphasised strongly the need to solve the domestic imbalances. More consumption and less investments, more services and less manufacturing, and more social spending to solve part of the income inequality. The plan does not mention capital account convertibility and Renminbi internationalisation at all, signalling that the authorities no longer give priority to them.

Fourthly, there is a focus on SOE reforms and related to this the start to solve China's (corporate) debt problem. China's corporate debt has increased dramatically since the global financial crisis and reached its peak in 2016 at 180% of GDP (The World Bank). The rising debt level is concentrated in the SOEs because they were used by the government as instruments to stimulate the economy after 2008. At the same time, the SOEs are operating in sectors with overcapacity. The 13th five-year plan emphasises the need to reduce the overcapacity problem and introduced some measures to restructure large SOEs in sectors such as steel, cement, coal and shipbuilding. For example, it is stated that the policies to facilitate investment projects along the One Belt, One Road route, thereby solving part of the excess capacity. In addition, overcapacity is attacked through boosting urbanisation. The plan forecasts that some 100 million Chinese will be urbanised in the next five years. It goes without saying that such process will bring additional demand for urban infrastructure, which relates to the sectors with excess capacity. Fifth, the 13th five-year plan (again) emphasised China's ageing population and its consequences. It will not only lead to a tighter labour market but also add pressure on the country's welfare and pension systems. Therefore, the authorities relaxed the one-child policy and its *hukou* system. We will discuss this in the upcoming chapters.

Figure 7.8 shows the targets (binding and indicative) of the 13th five-year plan over the 2016–2020 period. Most binding targets are in the field of social and environment protection. For example, there are binding targets for decrease in energy intensity and water consumption. Reduction of rural poverty with a minimum of 56 million people is also a binding target.

Resource and environment protection	Target	Status
Average GDP growth	6.5%	Indicative
Share service sector in GDP	56%	Indicative
R&D as percentage of GDP	2.5%	Indicative
Internet penetration; fixed	70%	Indicative
Internet penetration; mobile	85%	Indicative
Cultivated land area	0%	Binding
Decrease in energy intensity	15%	Binding
Decrease in water consumption	23%	Binding
Increase new energy in energy consumption	3%	Binding
Decrease chemical emissions	10–15%	Binding
Decrease in carbon intensity	18%	Binding
Average increase household income	6.5%	Indicative
Average education of labour force	10.8 year	Binding
New job creation	50 million people	Indicative
Reduce rural poverty	56 million people	Binding
Increase coverage basic healthcare	8%	Indicative

Figure 7.8 Targets of economic and social development, 2016–2020
Source: BBVA (2016)

There is much discussion in the media and among experts about the role of the CCP in implementing economic and social measures. In general (up to 2015), the division of power was clear: the party drafted the five-year plan and prioritised the strategy and targets, while the government (under auspices of the State Council) implemented and translated these priorities into concrete implementation measures. However, it looks like that the role of the party in implementing the reforms is increasing. In the final chapter of the 13th five-year plan, the role of the party in carrying out the plan is explicitly and repeatedly emphasised. This may indicate that the balance of power shifts (further) to the party, in particular in the hands of Xi Jinping. It was interesting to see that he broke the protocol in October 2016 when he unveiled the plan's guidelines himself instead of China's Premier, Li Keqiang, as has always been done.

7.5 The importance of the plenum sessions

Because flexibility is needed and implementation of the measures announced in the five-year plan takes time and may have its impact only with a time lag, the annual meetings (or plenums) of the party and the National People Congress are important. The first or second plenums refer to the first and second time the (new) leaders lead the plenary session. Consequently, within the cycle of the five-year plan, there are five plenums. This not only refers to the big plenary sessions but also to the plenums in smaller settings such as the annual meeting of the Party's Central Committee with its 250 members. In general, the plenums are following a fixed format. During the first plenary meeting, the top members of the CCP are being selected. The second plenum focuses on the top positions in the government. Third plenum generally takes place a year after new leaders take office and when they have established their power base. Therefore traditionally, reforms are expected at the third plenum. The fourth and, in particular, fifth plenums are (partly) designated to discuss and draft the proposals that should be implemented in the next five-year plan.

As stated above, third plenums of the Party's Central Committee are important to announce and start important reforms. Figure 7.9 shows a summary of the third plenums up to 2008. For example, during the third plenum of December 1978, Deng Xiaoping announced the opening up of China's economy and the establishment of free trade zones. At this meeting, the market received attention (including the statement that being rich is glorious) and it was decided at this meeting to depart from China's previous "iron bowl" policy which emphasised egalitarianism. All these issues were in line with the fifth five-year plan but were stated in much more concrete terms during the third plenum. Also, the third plenum in November 1993, is seen as a pivotal event. During this plenum, Jiang Zemin announced the "socialist market economy" and the dismantling of a large part of China's state-owned sector. This opened the door to discussing China's membership of the World Trade Organisation. Despite these examples, it should be noted that even the plenums of 1978 and 1993 implemented reforms in a step by step approach. The well-known phrase "crossing the river by feeling the stones" came from the 1978 third plenum communiqué; Chinese policymakers are not keen on surprises.

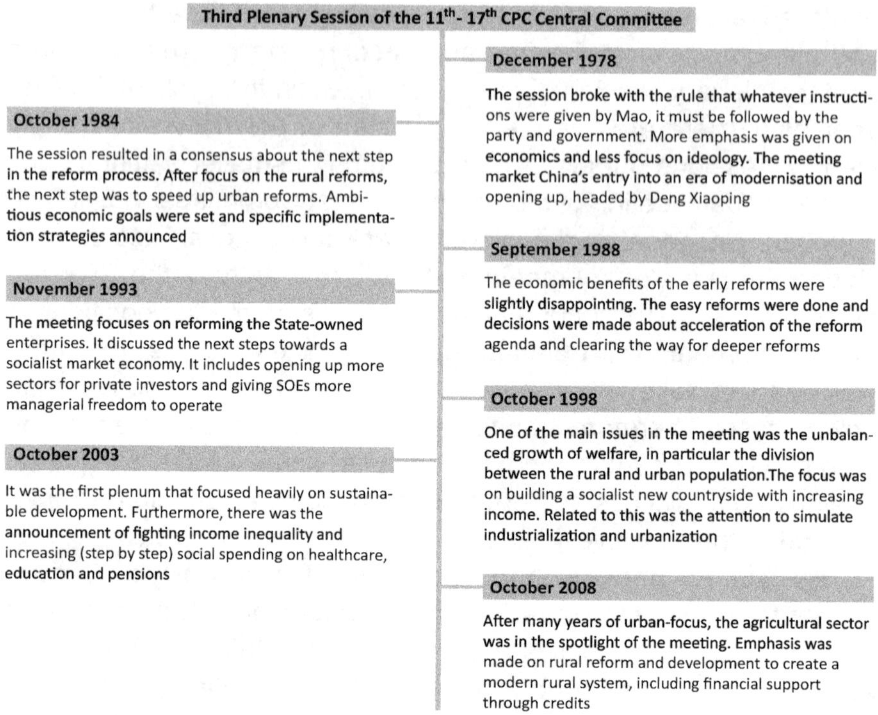

Figure 7.9 Importance of the third plenums, 1978–2008
Source: *Xinhua news*

Not all third plenums are as important and successful as the examples above. During the third plenum in 2003, Hu Jintao announced the need to tackle China's unbalanced growth. However, driven by economic crisis, he left office with the economy even more unbalanced than ever before.

The third plenum of 2013

The third plenum of the 18th Party Congress that took place in November 2013 is seen by several experts as just as significant as the ones in 1978 and 1993. This is logical; on paper, the third plenum came up with the biggest package of market economic reforms since the early 1990s. One of my Chinese colleagues told me that the documents that were used as the basis for the meeting can be read as a wish list from the International Monetary Fund, including the need to break up state-owned monopolies, easing controls in the financial sector, implementing more market forces and speeding up the opening up process for private and foreign companies. Steps on paper were robust but implementation difficult. The sense of urgency to speed up the reforms was emphasised by using (and discussing) the concept of the middle-income trap. However, the third plenum was in the period of worldwide financial and economic crisis. The worldwide crisis made it difficult to speed up the reforms in short notice. Some crisis management was (still) needed and consequently the government intervened in the economic process (helping SOEs, reducing the role of the market and de-accelerated the opening up of specific sectors). The outcome of the third plenum was the so-called 3-8-3 plan that aimed to transform the Chinese economy by 2020 and served as the basis of the 13th five-year plan. In essence, the 3-8-3 plan involves a reform trinity (market, government and corporations), eight key areas of reform and three necessary breakthroughs (increase competition, social security for all citizens and agricultural reforms). The eight key areas to tackle include: cutting administrative approvals, promoting competition, land reform, opening up banking including the liberalisation of interest rates and the exchange rate, reforming the fiscal system including setting up basic social security, reforming SOEs, promoting innovation including green technology, and opening up the services sector. The summary is given in Fig. 7.10.

Whether the outcome of the third plenum in 2013 should be seen as a turning point in China's growth strategy remains to be seen. Interpretation of documents is complex within the Chinese context. For example, in the communiqué of the third plenum, we see the statement that in the future, market forces would play a decisive role in resource allocation. Prior party documents had assigned market forces a merely important role. However, the same document also reaffirmed the principle that the state sector should have a dominant role in the economy. Western observers have difficulties with this: how to interpret the leading role of the

Reform trinity

Market	Deepen the reform and allow more market forces as driver in the economy
Government	Reduce government interventions, increase governance transparency, accelerate fiscal reforms, increase the quality of public service and emphasis the rule of law
Corporate	Expand market entrance, encourage competition and stimulate innovation and productivity

↓

Key sectors

1. Administrative reform to improve markets and reduce government interference
2. Reform basic industries such as railway, oil and gas, and power by opening the sectors for private companies
3. Land reforms aimed at giving both rural and urban land equal rights
4. Reforming the financial sector by further liberalisation of interest rates and exchange rates
5. Fiscal reform with emphasis on social spending and building up a nationwide basic social security system
6. Reforming SOEs by redefining the role of the government in strategic and daily operations
7. Promoting innovative and green development by opening up sectors for private investors and increasing competition
8. Opening up the economy further, in particular the service sector

↓

Breakthrough

Lowering market entrance to invite investors and increase competition
Setting up a basic social security package nationwide
Allowing collective lands to be traded on the market

Figure 7.10 The reform agenda

Note: It is interesting that the environment is very prominently visible in the publications of the third plenum 2013, but at the same time, the Ministry of Commerce stated in a press release on 24 November 2013 (Xinhua) that "FDI in manufacturing, including iron and steel, chemicals and vehicles, will be further relaxed"
Source: Based and adjusted from BBVA

market and of the government at the same time. This transmits to many aspects of the reform agenda such as transforming SOEs and fighting corruption.

Sources of corruption

In the 1980s, one of the biggest sources of corruption was the dual-track price system, under which factories committed to sell a certain amount of their output at relatively low-planned prices, but they could sell any excess production on the free market, at higher prices. This created the incentive for officials to use their influence to purchase goods at low-plan prices and then resell them at higher market prices. The price reforms which eliminated the two-track system also eliminated this source of corruption. In the 1990s, international trade (possible by opening up the economy) took over the dual-track system as a main source of corruption. The relatively high tariffs and non-tariff barriers made many goods more expensive in China than on the global market and this resulted in an enormous amount of smuggling. Because of lower tariffs in the late 1990s and early 2000s and much more border checks and control in the south of China, smuggling as a source of corruption disappeared. Starting in the 2000s, the two single biggest sources of corruption came from intransparancies in government financed infrastructure investments and profits from land extracted from farmers at far below its true market value. In the previous decades conversion of suburban farmland to other uses was especially rapid in the larger cities. The crux is that villages own rural land, not the farmers, who only contract land from villages. This is a source of corruption; local (village) officials often get side payments or bonuses in secret deals for industrial projects. At the same time, the compensation to the farmers is (too) low.

In the Corruption Perception Index, published by Transparency International, China ranked 79 out of 176 countries and regions in 2016. To give a broader picture of China's political and social environment, Fig. 7.11 summarises China's rank in international publications and reports about democracy, the rule of law and freedom. The conclusion is clear; there are additional steps needed.

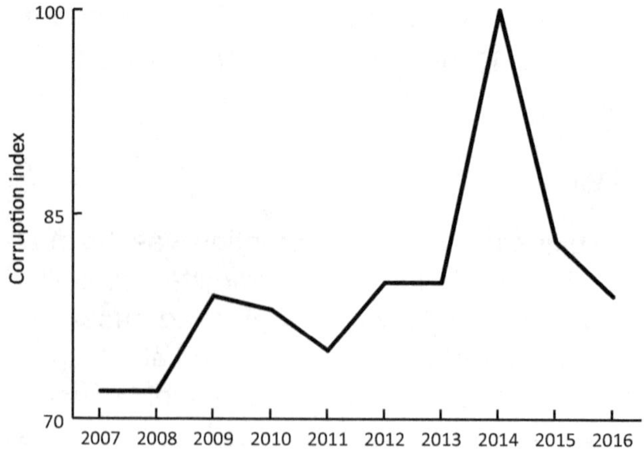

Ranking (2016) in other related indices

Corruption perception index (Transparency International)	79 (out of 176)
Democracy index (Economist Intelligence Unit)	136 (out of 167)
Rule of law index (World Justice Project)	80 (out of 113)
World press freedom index (Reporters without borders)	176 (out of 180)
Index of economic freedom (Heritage Foundation)	111 (out of 180)

Figure 7.11 Corruption Perception Index, 2000–2016
Source: *Transparency international and the other sources mentioned in figure*

Corruption in China is relatively high while at the same time the country was able to sustain economic growth rate of around 10% for almost four decades. The pessimistic view is that it is just a matter of time. Uncontrollable corruption will eventually force the system into either political collapse or economic sclerosis. However, you may question this view. Sometimes corruption must be accepted as a side product of good policies. Corruption in China was a side effect of reforms that also brought powerful economic benefits. The benefits of restructuring outweighed the negative impact of corruption. For example, the dual price system was an important source of corruption, but there was no alternative. If the government would dismantle the planned system at once, it would create shortages, high inflation and social disorder. You could even argue that this type of corruption gave information to the planners about the market because illegal activities reacted on market signals. From this point of view, you may argue that corruption helped to implement the needed reforms. If the vested interests would not profit from important changes, it would blockade necessary reforms. Undoubtedly, corruption is bad and is reducing the credibility of the party (and government). Consequently, legislation to counteract this is needed. This is indeed what we see in China. Maybe not fast enough, but in line with China's tradition of gradualism.

In the medium term, many of China's problems are so severe that concrete targets and government-led guidance is needed. The market cannot solve all the transformations through its invisible hand. Government intervention is needed. The five-year plan serves as a beacon in the medium term. So, the five-year plan will stay for many years to come. But it is clear that it must adjust to the changing economy and society. Further adaptation is needed to make sure that the plan is responsive to preferences and demands from people, including the new and rising middle class, as well as the new generation of migrant workers.

Part II

The Main Challenges Ahead

The second part builds further upon the conclusions of the first section of the book.

In the first part of the book, we mainly discussed China's economic policy and choices in the post-reform period that started in 1978. The growth strategy, guided by the party and governments, can be labelled as extremely successful in economic terms. More than 400 million people were able to escape the official poverty criteria and material welfare increased throughout the 1978–2017 period. At the same time, the growth pattern resulted in more and more imbalances in the economy. These imbalances could be set away partly because GDP continued to rise at a high level, but now there is a sense of urgency. China is ageing and the efficiency of investments is under attack. The old and traditional growth strategy of putting more (and cheap) labour and machines in the production process has arrived at its expiration date. A new growth model is needed: a model that focusses on efficiency, innovation, and one that is counteracting the most important imbalances such as the income inequality, the relatively low consumption and environmental problems.

In the second part of the book, the focus shifts towards these medium-term challenges. Essential choices by the CCP and government must be made concerning the income inequality problem. The same holds with respect to urbanisation, the *hukou* system, the labour-market shortages and the consumption-issues. This is a complex process; a choice on one aspect may have a negative impact on other (also important) subjects. Discussing these topics in a consistent way is complicated because of the many spillover effects we see. For example, in Chapter 8, we discuss the income inequality problem. Obviously, the discussion about inequality touches upon issues such as the privatisation of the urban housing market, urbanisation and the *hukou* system; they are all related. A full discussion with all the needed side steps would make the picture too complex. This is why we choose to discuss the interrelated topics one by one in separate chapters. We are building Chinese Walls around them. Only later in the book, step by step, we can draw the full picture.

Chapter 8

Income Inequality

Myth 8: China's spending on social welfare is high as it fits in a socialist-market economy

8.1 Introduction

Fast economic growth has caused several unwanted side effects, one being the widening income disparities within the country. In the pre-reform period, China was poor but had a relatively equal income distribution. China today is growing rich, but at the same time, it is one of the more unequal societies in the world. As we will see, an increase in inequality can be in parallel with an absolute increase in real income of the (poorest) people in the country. In the period that income inequality increased dramatically, hundreds of millions of people were lifted out of poverty. In early 2017, the number of people below the poverty line of US$1.90 per day (converted at purchasing power parities) had fallen to less than 2% of the total population (World Bank, 2017).

The key sources of inequality in China are the same as in other emerging economies. It includes geographical factors (between provinces and rural–urban division), a large informal sector, gaps in access to education, barriers regarding access to basic services such as social benefits, and barriers to employment and career progression for specific groups. Although the sources are in line with what we observe in other countries, there are some specific institutional factors in China that intensify income disequilibrium. For example, the *hukou* system (discussed in Chapter 9), in combination with the enormous number of migrant workers, is an important source of inequality. The same holds with respect to the housing privatisation scheme in the cities that started in the 1990s. This increased the inequality between the urban and rural centres dramatically. We will see in this chapter that up to the mid-2000s, the rural–urban differences dominated economic inequality in China. In the mid-2000s, inequality became an urban problem. Solving income (or asset) inequality is part of the discretionary policies of the government. But, we will see that despite some important steps, the government does not have a good track record in reducing inequality over the years.

Section 8.2 discusses the Lorenz curve and the Gini coefficient, the main indicators to measure the income inequality in an economy. The development of inequality relates to economic advancement and the transition from a low-developed economy towards an industrial and high-growth economy. This transformation affects the Gini index as we will see. In Section 8.3, we focus on the Chinese determinants behind income inequality. We follow a historical perspective that starts in 1978, i.e. the start of the reforms. In Section 8.4, the spotlight is on the differences between rural and urban income inequality. Finally, in Section 8.5, the emphasis is on the government social policy to fight income inequality.

8.2 The measurement of inequality

The indicator mostly used for measuring inequality is the Lorenz curve and, related to this, the Gini coefficient. The Lorenz curve shows the percentage of income earned by a given percentage of the population. This is shown in Fig. 8.1, where the cumulative percentage of the income is plotted against the cumulative percentage of the population. The 45-degree line in the diagram represents

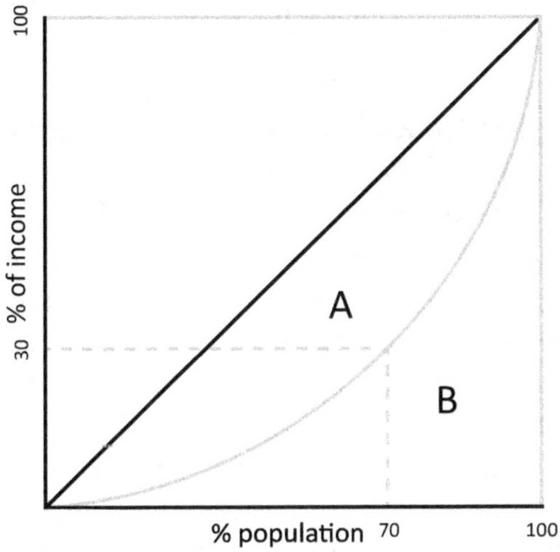

Figure 8.1 The Lorenz curve

Source: Based on Ying Liang et al. (2015)

complete equal distribution in a society. If each income group had the same income, then the Lorenz curve would follow the 45-degree line. If the highest income group earned all the income, the Lorenz curve would be flat, following the bottom edge of the figure, and then jump to the top of the figure at the very right-hand edge. But of course, both extremes are not seen in reality. In Fig. 8.1, we indicate the situation in which 70% of the people earn 30% of income. Greater inequality means that the Lorenz curve will be more "bowed" away from the 45-degree line.

The Gini coefficient (named after the Italian statistician Corrado Gini) is an economic indicator measuring (household) income distribution. Once a Lorenz curve is known, calculating the Gini coefficient is straightforward. Look at Fig. 8.1 in which we indicated areas A and B. The Gini coefficient is equal to A/(A+B). The more bowed the Lorenz curve is, the higher is the Gini coefficient (reaching maximum of 1), and the greater the income gap in a society. If the Lorenz curve is following the 45-degree line, the Gini index approaches 0, which represents perfect equality.

Limitations of the Gini coefficient

Because the Gini coefficient summarises the overall distribution of income to a single number, it also loses some detail. Some reflections are needed while using the Gini coefficient when talking about China. Firstly, as stated before, it is possible for the Gini coefficient to rise (due to increasing inequality of income) even when the number of poor people, living in absolute poverty, decreases. This is because the Gini coefficient measures relative, not absolute, wealth. It also explains why many Chinese do not feel discontent with the increasing inequality. For example, between 1988 and 2008, average per capita income grew by more than 200% (National Bureau of Statistics, NBS). This huge improvement in material welfare is considered much more important than the general rise in inequality.

Secondly, the Gini coefficient does not reflect inequality data between population segments. For example, if the Gini coefficient has risen, one cannot conclude if this was the result of an increasing share of the top 20%, or the top 10%, or top 1%. Thirdly, the Gini coefficient may change due to structural transitions in the society, such as ageing and urbanisation. In this case, the change in inequality is the result of external factors instead of concrete policy measures. Fourthly, income distribution is also affected by (social) benefits that are not captured in statistics or are difficult to value. For example, subsidised housing, free medical care and education for the poorest section of the population. Finally, we are measuring what is indicated on the vertical axis. In Fig. 8.1, we indicate the income of the people, but other indicators can be used. For example, we may measure inequality of disposable income (after paying taxes). When plotting the income after taxation on the vertical axis, the Lorenz curve may become less bowed and consequently, the Gini coefficient falls. Besides income, we can also put asset ownership on the vertical axis. Inequality of asset ownership is harder to measure but appears to be more extreme in China.

Data about the income inequality in China are gathered through surveys and published by the NBS. There are data available from the early 1980s onwards. We are not certain about the accuracy of the data. In particular, the period 2000–2013 is blurred because the NBS did not fully indicate how they did the sample and calculation. Besides the figures of the NBS, there are several other organisations (e.g. World Bank) that publish income distribution data. The Gini differs substantially from source to source. In general, the WB publishes higher Gini coefficients than the officially published data by the NBS. A problem is the quality of the NBS-sample. During a round table meeting at Renmin University in June 2016, one presenter stated four reasons for this sample issue. Firstly, the sample of the NBS (which is based on 40,000 households) does not cover the very high-income people because they often refuse to participate in the survey. Secondly, in the sample of the NBS, the rural households are slightly underrepresented. Thirdly, property income and off-payroll income are not included in the NBS research. A final statistical flaw is the underrepresentation of migrant workers in the survey. In general, the migrant workers in the cities without local *hukou* are difficult to catch in the data, but are among the poorest of the urban population. Furthermore, the earnings from migrant workers have become an important source of income in rural areas, contributing to rural income growth and moderating the urban–rural income gap. The official statistics treat migrant workers who stay in the city for more than 180 days in a year as urban resident. This may underestimate the income brought back home by migrant workers. Despite the statistical flaws, the analysis in this chapter is based on NBS figures. For periods in which NBS figures substantially deviate from (western) statistics, we will make some adjustments.

Economic development and income inequality

Research on the relationship between economic development and income inequality comes with mixed results. The traditional textbook economic argument suggests that inequality should promote growth by creating incentives for people to work harder and be more efficient. This is what we have seen in China since the beginning of the economic reform in 1978. Increasing inequality within the context of strong economic growth can also be observed in the early transition process in other countries. In the 1990s, Malaysia's GDP growth rate was around 6% annually and its Gini coefficient increased to 0.49 at the end of that decade. The same pattern can be seen in Argentina. The country had high economic growth of around 7% up to 2003 and saw an increasing Gini coefficient which peaked at 0.55 in 2003 (IMF, 2015). But if a country reaches maturity (leaving open how to define that), a further increase in welfare will reduce inequality due to specific government policies of income redistribution; mostly forced by public-demand. This increase in inequality in the early stages of development, followed by a decline in the later stages, is the essence of the so-called Kuznets curve (see Fig. 8.2). After the Kuznets turning point, discretionary government policy will fight inequality with fiscal measures and legislation. Obviously, this turning point may differ from country to country. In the case of China, the Gini coefficient reached a peak of 0.49 (at a GDP per capita level of around US$8000 in purchasing power parity) before the government was willing and able to step in.

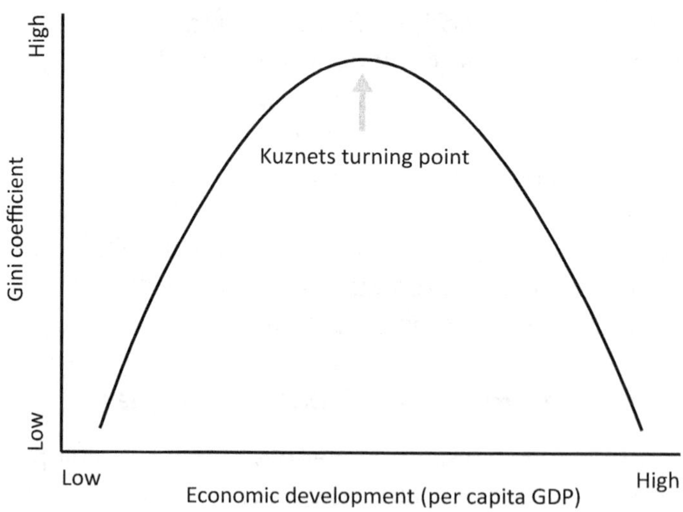

Figure 8.2 Kuznets curve

Source: Simon Kuznets (1955)

Inequality as a necessary price for economic growth sounds plausible but, in many cases, we do not observe it. When looking at countries today, there appears to be little relation between the level of economic development and the extent of inequality. Countries may have identical income inequality, but at the same time differ greatly in wealth, e.g. United States and China or Switzerland and Poland. The disconnection between inequality and economic growth bears an important lesson regarding government policy: policymakers should not rely on any automatic tendency for inequality to decline as their economy develops. Specific policies regarding inequality are needed. This is why we see so much more social spending in the latest five-year plans.

8.3 China's income inequality: A historical overview

Inequality in China relates to inequality within urban areas, within rural areas and between urban and rural areas. Although the drivers underlying inequality are difficult to disentangle and often overlap, it is important to examine income inequality in rural and urban areas separately to be able to understand income inequality in China as a whole. But we start this session with the total, nationwide picture.

In 1978, at the start of the reforms, the nationwide Gini coefficient stood at 0.30. By 2009, the Gini coefficient of the whole country reached 0.49. The number then declined marginally to 0.46 in 2016. Figure 8.3 shows two periods in which nationwide income inequality drastically increased. The first period is 1987–1994 and the second period of increasing inequality runs from 1997 to 2007 in which China's nationwide Gini coefficient increased by nearly 10 percentage point. Looking at the two periods separately, one can conclude that in the first period, income inequality was mainly driven by widening inequality within both urban and rural areas, while the growing income gap between urban and rural areas was the main driver behind inequality in the second period. Again, as stated before, this increase in inequality did not mean that welfare level dropped. Quite

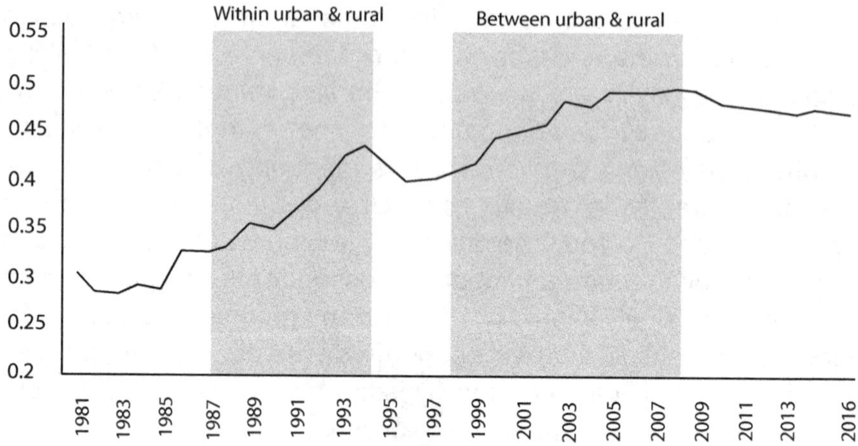

Figure 8.3 Income inequality in China, 1978–2016

Note: For the period 2000–2013, the official NBS figures are slightly adjusted based on WB-data.
Source: NBS

the opposite, the increase was in parallel with robust income growth of the poor. But China's track record on inequality is bad. It is high both from the perspective of China's past and high in comparison with other countries at similar stages of economic development.

Beginning in 2009, the Gini coefficient falls slightly. This is the result of a combined set of factors. Incomes were growing faster for low-income people than for high-income people, due to an acceleration of the minimum wage level. Moreover, the supply of young migrant workers started to decline and created shortages of labour in specific sectors, resulting in higher market wages. Specific government (taxation) policies reduced income inequality as well. In the 1997–2007 period, inequality was mostly attributed to the housing privatisation process.

Housing privatisation

The years between 1949 and 1978 was the period of China's welfare housing system. The government provided housing for free or at very low rents. The government financed this solely through its budget. The social housing system, combined with the increase of urbanisation and the growing population, placed an enormous financial burden on the government finance. As part of the economic reforms (and in order to keep expenses under control), the government launched a market-oriented housing reform in the early 1990s. This complemented the SOE reform. In 1994, SOEs (and government work units) were ordered to sell the houses they controlled to tenants at prices that represented a big discount to market value (normally at construction costs). The government vigorously encouraged residents to buy their houses from the SOEs before the end of 1998, the year that the welfare housing system was officially abolished. Specific government measures were implemented to make the transition to private ownership possible. Examples were a new housing finance system to help individuals with (almost interest free) mortgages and increasing rents to make renting less attractive. Consequently, within two years (1995–1997), more than 60% of urban public housing was being sold to individuals. Due to potential speculation, buyers were often prevented from selling their newly acquired houses for a certain period of time, i.e. typically five years. This trend of increasing private ownership continued; in 2005, 82% of the urban housing stock was in private hands (Xiao-Xi Hui, 2009) and it stabilised around 88% up to early 2017. This privatisation is one of the greatest wealth transfers from public to private in China's history.

The benefits of housing privatisation are clear — economically as well as politically. In economic terms, a new property-owning middle class emerged. They could use the house as collateral for credit that could be invested (often in extra houses) to make additional money. This helped boosting urban consumption. From a political point of view, it increased the credibility of the party. There emerged a middle class that does not see the benefit to overthrow the party. The new middle class wanted better governance and a legal system that protects private ownership. However, at the same time, the benefits came with large costs in the form of increased inequality and unfairness. Only the households that had urban *hukou* could buy the houses. Almost 90% of the families in the larger cities live in homes they own. In contrast, less than 10% of migrants own their house or apartment (NBS, 2017). In addition, this urban wealth creation was not happening in the rural areas; rural land was (and still is) owned by the government and village collectives. As a result, individual farmers were not able to use the land as collateral. This is why we label the period 1997–2007 in the figure above as urban–rural inequality; inequality that is strongly linked to urban–rural differences. Urban pensions and social benefits have also increased, while building up a rural pension system started only after 2010. It is rather strange that until recently the rapid rise in income inequality can be associated with specific government policies that effectively favour urban residents over rural residents, and favour coastal, more developed regions over inland and less developed regions. Only in the previous years, starting in the 12th five-year plan, this has been changed.

8.4 Rural versus urban income inequality

Although the development of income inequality shows the same pattern in rural and urban China, it is important to distinguish the two patterns because the causes of inequality are different. By concentrating on the rural sector, it should be kept in mind that during the 1980s, the rural sector consisted of two activities. On one hand, there were farmer activities to produce agricultural products. On the other hand, we saw the development of manufacturing activities in Township and Village Enterprises (TVEs), discussed in the first part of the book.

Rural inequality

During the first few years of (rural) reform between 1979 and 1982, the Gini coefficient declined while household income per capita increased by 61% in real terms (NBS). This short period in the early 1980s can be considered as the golden years of rural development in China. Privatisation of the user right of land led to a significant increase in farming production (at higher prices), which had an equalising effect on income distribution. In general, agricultural prices determine the rural income inequality heavily; the fall of the Gini coefficient is strongly associated with rising prices of agricultural products in the early 1980s. It resulted in narrowing of the income gap between the agricultural households and others that were mainly doing non-agricultural activities in the TVEs.

As can be seen in Fig. 8.4, rural income inequality has risen since the early 1980s. The Gini coefficient rose from 0.23 in 1982 to 0.34 in 1995: an increase by 1 percentage point per year during this period. The rising rural income inequality was largely due to the unbalanced development of the rural non-agricultural sector (TVEs) across regions and provinces.

After the mid-1990s, the Gini index increased slightly up to its peak in 2009 provinces (0.40) as a consequence of more market-driven reforms and hardly any specific government measures to reduce inequality in the agricultural sector. Only after 2010, specific government policies were implemented to solve the growing rural inequality and the Gini coefficient somewhat fell to 0.35 in 2016. The government measures were focused on building a socialist

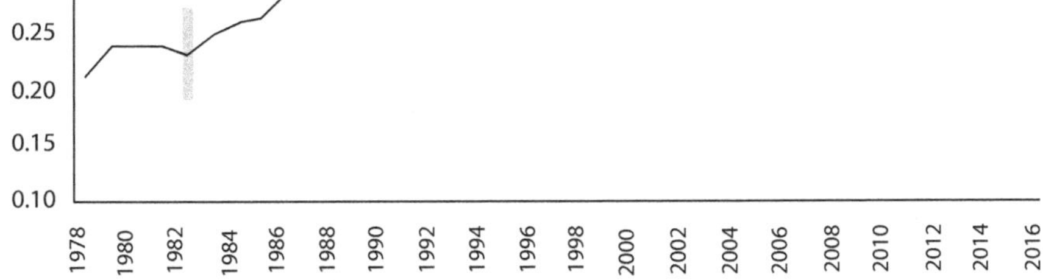

Figure 8.4 Development of the Gini in the rural areas

Source: NBS

countryside, including social welfare and basic education for the rural population.

Urban inequality

Before the economic reform, the urban economy was under full control of the party and government. Wages were fixed and the SOEs were responsible for housing, pension, education and healthcare. These factors contributed to a very low income inequality in urban China. According to the NSB, the urban Gini coefficient was 0.16 in 1978.

The development of urban inequality is quite similar to that of rural China (Fig. 8.5), but the specific drivers are different. If we focus on the 1984–1994 period, we can distinguish several factors that increased urban inequality. The first driver relates to the reforms (and growth) of private firms in the 1980s and early 1990s. Their fast growth in turnover and profit resulted in the rapid rise of income inequality within the cities. Also, SOEs that operated in monopolised industries witnessed a sudden expansion of income (including the people working in these sectors). Secondly, we saw a dramatic

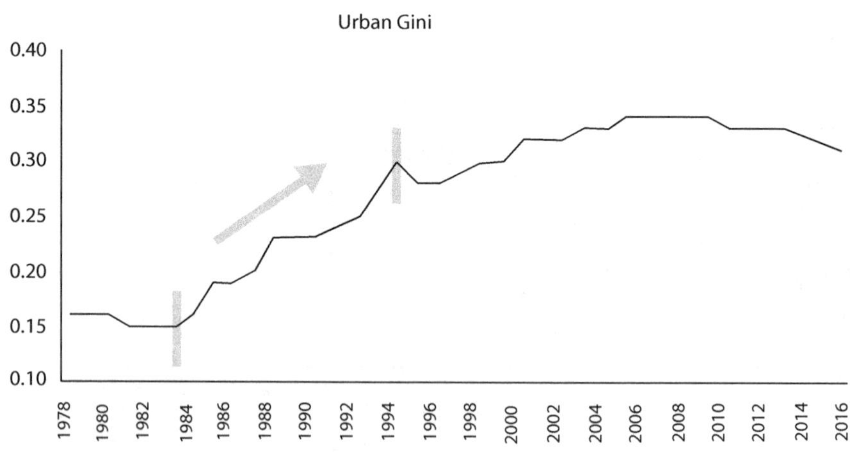

Figure 8.5 Development of the Gini in urban clusters
Source: NBS

transformation from a uniform wage structure towards a wage distribution which was based on market forces. Thirdly, the restructuring of the SOEs (that started in the late 1980s) increased urban unemployment. The cohort of unemployed people did not receive any social benefits because the social security system was abolished. All these factors resulted in a significant rise in urban income inequality in the period 1984–1994 in which the Gini coefficient increased from 0.15 to 0.30, an almost two percentage point increase per year in this decade. WTO entry resulted in many (new) opportunities and market incentives, but not everyone was able to profit, resulting in a further rising Gini coefficient in urban areas after 2001. Only after 2010, we see a downward trend in the Gini coefficient.

Part of this picture about inequality relates to the migrant workers and the associated *hukou* system. Within urban areas, inequalities between migrant workers and the population with urban *hukou* remain. Even though migrant wages have been catching up and migrants are increasingly paid wages comparable to those of urban residents doing similar work, migrants often lack the skills and educational background for higher-wage jobs. Hence, the migrants (and the *hukou* system) are big obstacles to solve urban inequality.

8.5 Government policy to reduce income inequality

China's government track record in the field of equalising incomes is poor and only from the previous decade, policy is more focused on social spending and helping the poor. Starting in the 11th five-year plan, there has been more emphasis on reducing inequality. When President Hu Jintao and Premier Wen Jiabao took over office in 2003, they introduced the "harmonious society" concept as the key priority in the 11th five-year plan (2006–2010). The objective was to achieve social stability in a fast-growing economy. It emphasised actions in the field of rural development, broader enrolment in education, an accessible healthcare system and a nationwide social security system, all measures linked to reducing inequality.

Despite this (new) orientation, implementation appeared to be difficult and income inequality in China remained persistently high.

Experiences in other emerging markets show that government policy to fight inequality can be effective if they are robust enough, as was seen in the case of Brazil in the early 1990s. In 1989, Brazil's Gini coefficient reached provinces 0.60, extremely high and a basis for social unrest. To narrow the income gap, the Brazilian government implemented transfer payment policies that increased disposable income of the poor substantially. Among these programmes, the project "Bolsa Familia"(introduced at the end of 2002) was the largest policy package. It aimed at increasing financial help for the poor, improving children's education and assure basic medical help. The total package covered about 1.1 million households, accounting for 50% of the nation's poor families. Due to this programme, the Brazilian Gini coefficient gradually decreased from 0.60 in 2001 to 0.51 in 2016 (based on WB 2017; Loman 2014). This example relates to government spending, but helping the poor can also be done through taxation measures. Clearly, these measures must be done with care because it may adversely impact efficiency, which is essential for longer-term development.

Figure 8.6(a) shows conceptually the positive impact of reducing taxation for the (poor) people. Due to a taxation structure that focusses on the poor and taxes the rich cohort, the Lorenz curve becomes less bowed because of a more progressive tax system. In China, the government implemented substantial tax cuts for lower income groups some years ago. Part of the taxation package was to increase the income level before starting to pay taxes. The new benchmark for tax payments was increased to 3,500 Renminbi. As can be seen in Fig. 8.6(b), this measure created a more progressive tax structure and as a result is shifting the Lorenz curve to the left.

Apart from taxation measures, other steps are taken to fight inequality, for example, the adjustment of the *hukou* system. The migrants who moved to the cities were not eligible to receive socials benefits through China's social welfare programme. The beneficiaries of the system had to have a local *hukou* (and a

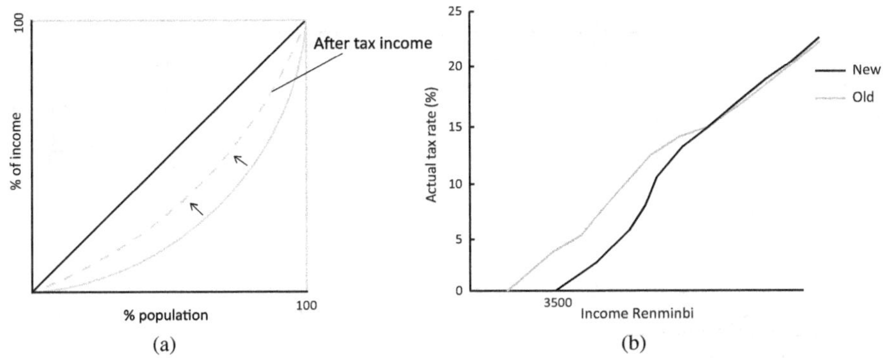

Figure 8.6 Lorenz curve before and after public transfers

Source: Based on BBVA Research; Juzhong Zhuang and Li Shi, 2016

household per capita income that is lower than the local minimum standard). In the previous years, the system has been adjusted and step by step, it may help migrant workers to become real urban citizens, but more time is needed to reduce inequality substantially. Another policy target that appeared to be difficult to implement has been the building up of a nationwide social security and healthcare coverage in the countryside. While pension and healthcare coverage increased significantly in the city, rural pensions and healthcare system have been slow. All these factors resulted in a society with more visible and invisible social tensions. According to CASS, there were 100,000 mass group incidents in China in 2016. Western sources indicate a much larger number of mass protests ranging from 150,000 to 200,000 in 2016 (Human Rights Watch).

From many angles, it became clear that the government should react. Indeed, the 2010–2016 period saw a strong increase in social spending as can be seen in Fig. 8.7. Be aware of the fact that an increase in social spending as percentage of GDP means that the growth in social spending is higher than the growth in GDP. With growth of around 8%, social spending should increase with the same 8% to keep the share in GDP the same. Although statistics on social spending by the government is difficult to harmonise (e.g. social housing in China is not part of the government consumption

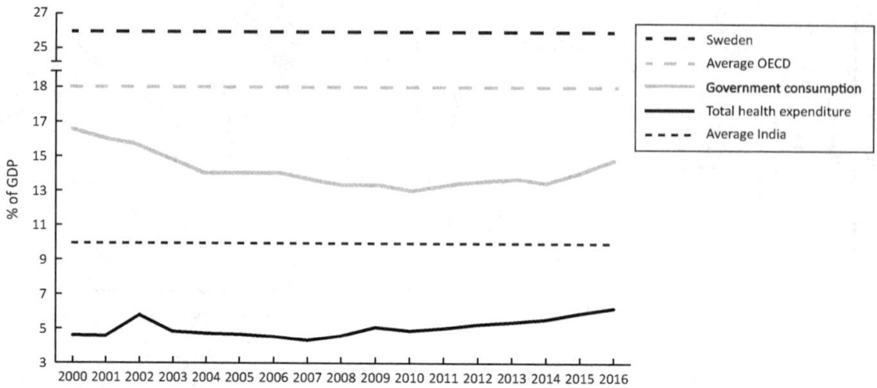

Figure 8.7 Public social spending as percentage of GDP

Note: China's government consumption is used as a proxy for social expenditures. Part of the social spending relates to healthcare expenses
Source: NBS, OECD-Database and WB-Website

which is the indicator for social expenditure), the figure makes clear that starting in 2010, social expenditure in China has been increased and accelerated after 2014. Figure 8.7 also indicates the average share of social spending of the OECD, Sweden and India over the 2000–2016 period.

China's policy makers did not gave a lot of attention to cohorts in the society (rural, as well as urban) that were unable to connect to the growing economy. In this sense, you could argue that there was high economic growth without a human face. Government social spending became very low between 1990 and 2010; quite remarkable for a socialist country. Only after 2010 steps were taken to include the poor in the welfare creation, but a lot of work must be done. In 2016, less than 15% of migrant workers were affiliated to the unemployment insurance system and only 65% had a labour contract despite the new labour law. Of course, the Chinese government recognises the importance of reducing income inequality and steps are taken such as increasing the minimum wage level and increasing tax rates for rich households. But there is always another side. Increasing wages may distort the labour market and may affect market efficiency. Policies designed to protect one group in the labour market should not have a marked adverse impact on other groups. And as stated before, a small mistake in regulation may have an extremely large impact due to the size of the country and its population. The next wave of social spending relates to education. Reducing educational inequality can reduce income inequality. By comparing the household income gap among different education levels, the income gap is smaller within the higher education group. The focus on education is an example of policies designed to reduce inequality that at the same time also boost growth.

Analysis of the set of policies suggests that there is no one general solution for the income inequality problem. Some policies that work in the short term may have undesirable consequences in the long term. China currently has an extensive set of social and poverty-alleviation programmes in place, many of which were implemented as part of the "harmonious society" agenda. Yet, there is room for improvement in the implementation, target and design of these programmes. Redistributive policies, however, can only do so much in reducing inequality if there are still forces that exacerbate or create new sources of inequality. Two of these forces are the *hukou* system and related to this is the increase in urbanisation.

Chapter 9

Hukou System and Urbanisation

Myth 9: As can be seen from the many megacities, China is highly urbanised

9.1 Introduction

The *hukou* (or household registration system) can be seen as an internal passport. Until recently, it divided the population as urban versus rural and as local versus non-local. The Chinese household registration system has had a significant impact on many aspects of life. Only with local *hukou,* you get (local) benefits or services, ranging from small benefits like being able to buy a city bus pass to much more important matters such as free public education beyond elementary school, public medical insurance and low rent housing. Migrant workers living in cities without local *hukou* are called the floating population; they live in cities but are not yet able to get permanent residency rights and associated social benefits. In essence, these migrant workers cannot integrate into the urban society, and incomplete urbanisation is thus the result. The *hukou* system is a significant barrier to social mobility within cities, and consequently an important source of injustice and inequality. Despite the *hukou* system, around 200–250 million rural residents have migrated to Chinese cities for work since the 1970s (Kam Wing Chan, 2013).

China's internal passport system is closely intertwined with topics such as the (privatisation of the) housing market, urbanisation, the labour market, fiscal policy, economic growth, consumption and income inequality issues. In this chapter, only the *hukou* system and urbanisation are combined; leaving to other connected issues to the following chapters. Urbanisation is a key element of China's development process. It stimulates the development of services and may increase productivity — two key items of the newest five-year plan. Furthermore, it will boost consumption and provide employment. An urban dweller consumes as much as three times that of a person in a rural area. Therefore, urbanisation is a relatively easy way to boost consumption, which has been a key aim from 2010 onwards. Undoubtedly, helping migrant workers to merge into city life will be one of the most vital goals of urbanisation. Therefore, the success of urbanisation is strongly related to solving the migrant issue and changing the *hukou* system.

The chapter is organised as follows. In Section 9.2, we start with a brief historical overview of the *hukou* system. It will become clear which aims were being targeted during its introduction. We discuss how the *hukou* system has been adjusted throughout the previous 50 years. Of course, we will focus on the latest reforms, and the inter-linkages to other *hukou*-related issues will also be highlighted. In Section 9.3, we link the *hukou* system with urbanisation. This is followed (Section 9.4) by a discussion of the urbanisation timeline. It will become clear how fast China changed from a rural to an urban society. This is followed by Section 9.5 with a discussion about the pros and cons of urbanisation, and finally, in Section 9.6, a brief note will be given on the latest reforms and the challenges to come.

9.2 A brief history of the *hukou* system

Like so many institutional arrangements, the *hukou* system also dates back to previous Imperial Dynasties. The Han Dynasty (206 BC–220 AD) used it as a way to collect taxes and to determine who should serve in the army. The Song Dynasty in the 11th century also implemented the residence registration system as a tool to collect taxes. China is not unique as the other Asian countries had also implemented a sort of *hukou* system for all kind of reasons. The "modern" *hukou* system in China was implemented in 1958, in the early Maoist era, and can be described as being much more restrictive than the traditional one.

The household registration system of the 1950s divided the population into two cohorts: agricultural (rural) and non-agricultural (urban). Furthermore, it classified people into local versus non-local *hukou*. Therefore, until recently, in a city like Shanghai there were the following four types of citizens:

- Local Shanghai and non-agricultural *hukou* (Shanghai urban residents)
- Local Shanghai and agricultural *hukou* (Shanghai outlying districts)
- Non-local and non-agricultural *hukou* (migrants from other cities)
- Non-local and agricultural *hukou* (migrants from the countryside outside Shanghai)

The aim of the *hukou* system in the 1950s was to restrict labour mobility, i.e. to make sure that poor rural farmers were not moving into the cities. This restriction was needed to reduce urban unemployment and to ensure that enough agricultural production was being produced (creating an agricultural surplus that could be used for industrialisation). From this point of view, the *hukou* system fitted logically in the planned economy during the 1950s and 1960s. Informal movements were difficult to handle in a planning system and were capable of disrupting the whole planning process. The restriction to leave the countryside had dramatic effects during the Great Leap Forward when farmers were locked in their villages and were unable to find work and food outside the rural areas.

As stated above, there are 200–250 million migrant workers (without local *hukou*) working and living in China's cities, in particular in the big cities. Among today's (2016) population of

Shanghai (25 million), nearly 11 million are migrant workers. Furthermore, 30% of the population in Beijing (22 million) do not have a Beijing *hukou*. Shenzhen, the tier 1 city in the southeast of China, has more migrant workers than official residents. This pattern is not only visible in the big cities but also increasingly evident in second- and third-tier cities.

Not having a local *hukou* is problematic in many aspects. For example, the problem of participating in the national university entrance exam. During one of my teaching periods in Shanghai, I had a meeting with a family not having a local *hukou* (they had a Chengdu *hukou*). They indicated how much disturbance this created and they explained the situation with respect to the national university entrance exam. The child of the couple had to travel to Chengdu to take the national university entrance exam. A lot of time, energy and money was spent to make sure that their kid arrived on time (and was well prepared). Moreover, the parents had to negotiate with their employers to get some free days (by working extra days in the weekend). This national college entrance exam (*gaokao*), in the second week of June, is an enormous event. Almost 10 million young people take the test every year in 300,000 large exam halls across the country, and many of them travel a long distance from their hometowns to take the exam. This causes a lot of discontent. This was clearly the case when talking to the Chengdu couple. I'm sure the government is aware of this discontent, but not so much is changing yet. It is interesting to observe that the editorial in the *China Daily* on 31 May 2011 focused on the positive impact of the national exam on the (regional) economy. It has been calculated that the local economy profits substantially from the increase in high-tech electronic cheating equipment, a rise in hotel reservations near the exam halls, money spent on teachers to help students prepare and a strong rise in holiday bookings after the exams. Also, the taxi sector makes additional money due to the national exams. Taxi companies set up a reservation system for students, and many additional (temporary) taxis are being used to meet the growing demand in the second week of June. Although this may help the local economy, it is clear that these kinds of effects due to the *hukou* system create dissatisfaction.

Changes in the hukou *system from the 1960 to early 1990s period*

The *hukou* system was very strict and enforced firmly in the 1960s and 1970s. Changing the *hukou* status was a difficult process because both central and local governments were involved and hesitated to help. After 1978, the role of the central government has been reduced substantially. In line with the increasing decentralisation in the early 1980s, the power to change the *hukou* was more and more in the hands of the local government. The local authorities had some freedom of interpretation, and consequently differences between provinces (and even cities) were the result.

Although, officially the *hukou* system did not change throughout the 1980s and early 1990s, enforcement became less strict as factories in coastal regions needed a lot of labour which they could not find nearby. The mass migration accelerated in the early 1990s, mostly to the (southwestern) coastal areas. Migration had a double-sided advantage; it kept wages down, stimulating the export sector, and at the same time, it transformed China from a rural-based economy to an urban-based one. Local officials, eager to promote economic growth, allowed a free inflow of migrant labour. City authorities were permitted to grant local *hukou* to investors and professionals who had a stable job and place of residence in the city (Kam Wing Chan, 2013; Buckingham, 2008), but the numbers were low. Most of the new urban cohort did not receive local *hukou*.

In the mid-1990s, the government simplified the *hukou* system. The new policy of 1995 only related to local versus non-local and did not include the non-agricultural and agricultural *hukou* classification anymore. However, it took a couple of years before this was put into legislation. Even today, agricultural versus non-agricultural status is still reported in official publications. The increasing power of local authorities to grant local *hukou* continued in the 1990s and in 1995, the power to admit local status to the migrants was totally delegated to the cities. They also developed their own (localised) "entry conditions". As a consequence, the entry conditions to receive local *hukou* were different from city to city. For example, migrant workers had a preference for large cities where there are more government-provided benefits (including better public schools). To protect the city from an influx of migrants, the local authorities of these larger cities tend to put up the most stringent entry conditions which made it almost impossible to obtain *hukou*.

Changes after the mid-1990s

In the mid-1990s, local governments had full power and discretion to set their admission criteria and limit the annual number of new local *hukou*. Obviously, there was (and still is) a preference of granting local permanent *hukou* to those who are very rich, able to buy high profile real estate or invest in the economy, highly educated and those who are immediate family members of urban residents.

Despite reforms in the *hukou* system, restrictions continue to affect the lives of Chinese migrants, and full citizenship was heavily constrained. Good education, social housing and stable employment was hardly possible for migrants and their children. That is why, step by step, legislation was being implemented to reduce the distance between local and non-local *hukou*. For example, the State Council announced that local governments must take up the responsibility of providing nine-year compulsory education for migrant children through the public-school system in 2001. One more reform in the same year was the policy encouraging small cities and towns to grant unconditional urban *hukou* to migrants. The aim was that within five years (2001–2006) migrant workers would be divided more or less evenly to cities of all sizes throughout the country, rather than moving to a small number of attractive (large) cities. Another example of relaxation was the legislation to abolish the *hukou* requirement while hiring new civil servants in 2006. New positions were open to all citizens, including rural residents, regardless of their *hukou* status. However, implementation appeared to be difficult and the restrictions continued. Another wave of legislation can be seen after 2010 with the aim to increase integration of rural migrant workers in cities. As with (almost) all the main changes in China, new policy and legislation was first introduced as a pilot project. In 2011, Chengdu became the first city that provided equal access to urban social benefits and gradually reduced the privileges previously attached to urban *hukou*.

China's working age population peaked in 2010, the labour force declined and the dependency ratio has been showing a rising trend. This created a sense of urgency in accelerating the changes in the *hukou* system. Allowing more migrant workers to become true urban residents would lengthen their labour supply period. Currently, it is common for migrant workers to return home after several years due to the absence of free medical care and pensions. With the reforms of the *hukou*, they would integrate much more in urban life, participate in healthcare and pension schemes, and would be able to give their children adequate education. The reform of *hukou* would also attract more surplus labour from the agricultural sector and they would bring their children. This may help to reduce inequality and increase productivity. A final positive effect of reforming the *hukou* system is that it would encourage consumption. Only with decent wages and enough social security will we see an increase in the marginal propensity to consume among the migrant workers. In a major speech at the opening of National People's Congress in March 2010, Chinese Prime Minister Wen Jiabao promised to ease rules denying public welfare services to migrant workers and do more to meet the social security needs of China's poor.

The *hukou* system was also used in an illegal way. In the *China Daily* edition of 3 June 2011, there was an interesting article with the title "The *Hukou* Hunt". The article focused on Beijing. The Beijing *hukou* is the most valuable in China. One reason is the presence of highly regarded universities and, of course, the job opportunities after graduation. Graduates from Beijing universities do not get a Beijing *hukou* automatically; a Master's degree helps, but in most cases companies are not able to provide Beijing *hukou* for their new employees. The Beijing government offers annually between 5,000 and 7,000 *hukous* to non-native college graduates; a large part is allocated for overseas returnees. The government also gives a certain number of *hukous* to SOE and high-tech companies to attract talented graduates. If SOEs are not using the *hukou*, they can sell it on the market. We see advertisements in which companies are selling allocated Beijing *hukou* for 150,000–180,000 Renminbi. Of course this is illegal, but hard to control.

Besides economic reasons to relax the *hukou* system, majority of the public opinion is also in favour of reforms; in particular, attention towards the children of the migrant workers is growing. This is also visible in legislation. For example, the central government required local governments to include migrant children in the local education systems, accommodating them mainly in local public schools. The implementation of the policy was supported by fiscal resources from both central and local governments. Yet, migrants still face difficulties in enrolling their children in urban public schools. There are still specific migrant schools which typically have poor teaching facilities, insufficient funding and less qualified teachers. Barriers that keep migrant children out of the mainstream education system include capacity constraints in urban schools, which were planned for the official (and legal) citizens.

Public discontent on this issue is growing. In the fall 2011, there were many articles in the Chinese media on this topic. The cause of this media attention was the closing down of a number of migrant schools in cities such as Shanghai and Beijing. The local Beijing government closed 24 (out of 230) migrant schools just before the beginning of the new school year because the schools did not meet safety and hygiene standards. More than 14,000 migrant children were affected by the closure. The local authorities were forced to take back the decision, but the case makes clear that *hukou* reforms are not easy. With equal rights, the vested interests in the cities foresee that services must be shared with a large group of new people and they also anticipate a strong increase in taxation to finance the additional social spending. This also relates to housing. Selling houses to migrant workers, most of whom are poorly paid, would likely require huge subsidies as housing prices in many urban areas are so high that migrants would have little hope of affording homes without assistance. Another problem of equal rights is that although the migrant workers suffer from various discriminations in the urban areas, most of them are unwilling to give up their rural *hukou*. The main reason is that when accepting a local *hukou* the migrants are required to give up their land entitlement in their home village. The rural *hukou* guarantees the right to use farmland. If they encounter difficulties in the cities, they can always choose to go back and become a farmer. Another reason for not willing to give up rural *hukou* is that a rural *hukou* gives the opportunity to have more than one child. However, this restriction has been relaxed in the previous years, as we will see in Chapter 11.

Newest adaptations of the **hukou** *system*

Starting in 2013, the reforms of the *hukou* system accelerated. The reforms fit within the concept of inclusive growth, which is the "human centric approach" of economic development. The aim is clear, i.e. providing the country's 200–250 million migrant workers equal social security, public housing and education, the same as enjoyed by full urban citizens. The plan is that by 2020, China (under auspices of the Ministry of Public Security) will establish a new social benefit system based on the place of residence rather than on a person's place of origin. If this is the case, you may say that the household registration system has ended. Citizens will be classified simply as "residents" rather than as "agricultural" or "non-agricultural" or as "local" or "non-local". The new residence cards have been introduced from 2014 onwards. It gives people access to education, housing and social benefits; privileges that are now disconnected from *hukou*.

It is local government discretionary power to come up with their own design to implement the residence card system. Several cities have piloted this residence permit programme (Guangzhou, Shenzhen, Chongqing, Shanghai and Tianjin). Most use a points system under which migrants earn credits for years of employment, taxes paid, educational qualifications and other criteria. For example, Shanghai relaxed the rules so that professionals who have lived in the city for seven years as tax-paying temporary residents can qualify for permanent resident status. Relaxation is a key priority of the central government, but at the same time the government is afraid to implement measures too fast because of the fear that relaxation of the *hukou* system would encourage more rural people to migrate to the already overcrowded cities. Despite the reforms in the *hukou* system and the introduction of the residence card, the problem of inequality will not be solved in short notice. The latest step taken to reform the *hukou* system is the policy measure that actively encourage people to move into smaller cities (less than 1 million inhabitants). Migration into cities with a population above 5 million is still tightly controlled.

Reforms of the *hukou* system have been implemented, visible and accelerated in the previous years. This is in line with the views of President Xi Jinping. While serving as the Governor of Fujian province, he had urged to stop the *hukou* system in his doctoral thesis. Reforms of the *hukou* system are motivated by social as well as economic advantages. Removing barriers to build a decent urban life will continue to attract more surplus labour from the agriculture sector. The migrant workers will bring their children who will receive better education and fill the needs of employers as most industries will move up the value chain. Furthermore, today's generation of migrants who were brought up in cities by their migrant worker parents graduated from middle school and have different skills and capabilities. They are connected to urban life and urban work. Productivity will increase if they stay in the cities: the essential new growth driver of China. Until now, one may say that China has done a good job of urbanising employment, but a poor job of urbanising people. Now it is time to urbanise the migrant worker. The change of the *hukou* system relates to the new urbanisation plan announced in 2014 and summarised as "human-centred urbanisation".

9.3 Urbanisation and the *hukou* system: Intertwined challenges

Urbanisation is a key element of China's development process. But there was (until the new urbanisation plan of 2014) no master plan for urbanisation on the table. Mostly, the government reacted with new legislation if migrants moved to the cities. Since the onset of the economic reforms in 1978, the urban population increased by about 500 million people. Currently, 52% of the Chinese live in urban municipalities, compared to 18% at the start of the reforms in 1978. At the same time, the share of urban residents with urban *hukou* has decreased. In several of the largest cities, only half of the population enjoyed urban *hukou* in 2016 (NBS). The ratio fell to less than 20% in Shenzhen (2016). These figures make it clear why we see differences between publications with respect to the urbanisation degree in China. If calculations are based on the *hukou* system, instead of residency, the urbanisation degree would drop substantially to around 39% in early 2016 (Mizuho Bank, 2016). However, if we incorporate the 200–250 million migrant workers that live in cities without *hukou*, the figure increases dramatically.

Another constraint to get harmonised urbanisation figures is the arbitrary choice of where to make the division line between rural and urban. Look at a city such as Chongqing, which is labelled as the largest city worldwide by western media. Chongqing is a territory as big as Austria with a population of 32 million people, but 70% of them are rural inhabitants. The urban core is "just" 9 million (Fig. 9.1). The Chongqing case also makes clear that an increase in urbanisation is not always the result of migrant inflow. Partly, the increase relates to the move from people in rural Chongqing to urban Chongqing. This counts also for China as a whole. Approximately 40% of the rise in urbanisation between 2000 and 2017 can be explained by this move. Around 45% of the increase has been driven by migration. These migrant workers are not well integrated in urban life. This is a real challenge today, let alone if the urban population will grow, as projected, to 930 million in 2025 (UN, 2017). This increase of 300 million urban dwellers is larger than the entire population of the US today, and the main question is how to increase urbanisation without creating (too much) social tension and financial shortage. We already see megacities which can hardly handle additional influx of 20 million migrant workers every year. To give a feeling of the magnitude, look at Fig. 9.1 which shows the comparison between the largest cities in China and Europe. For example, Beijing saw its population skyrocket from 10 million in 1990 to 22 million in 2016. According to NBS (2016), there were 102 cities in China with more than 1 million people, many of who are not known outside the country, or even by Chinese.

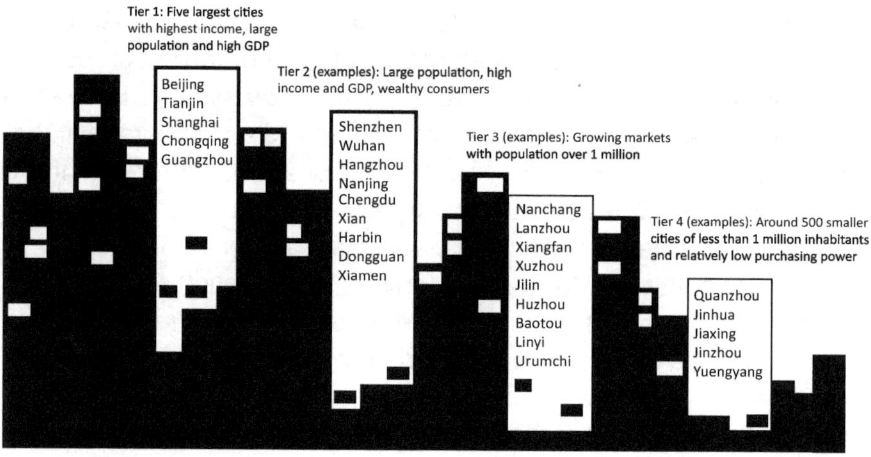

Largest cities China	Mln	Largest cities Europe	Mln
Shanghai	25.3	Istanbul	14.8
Beijing	22.1	Moscow	12.3
Tianjin	16.1	London	8.6
Ghangzhou	14.1	Saint Petersburg	5.2
Shenzhen	11.3	Berlin	3.5
Wuhan	10.2	Madrid	3.1
Dongguan	9.3	Kiev	2.9
Chongqing	9.1	Rome	2.8
Nanjing	8.3	Paris	2.8
Chengdu	8.1	Bucharest	2.2

Figure 9.1 Largest cities in China, 2016

Source: *Xinhua-net*

As stated so many times, China is full of contradictions, and this holds also with respect to urbanisation. On one hand, we see these megacities and the more than hundred cities with 1 million people or more. And at the same time, one may conclude that China is not very urbanised at all. You may even argue that China is underurbanised when looking at other countries. The urbanisation degree in countries such as Brazil, Mexico and South Africa is considerably higher than China (World Bank, 2017). Crucial for a successful urbanisation and retaining social stability is solving the migrant issue and making sure that migrant workers can find a job in nearby (smaller) cities instead of moving to the megacities. The new urbanisation plan of 2014 (Section 9.6) gives priority to the development of townships and smaller cities near rural areas. In addition, the plan emphasises the need to build satellite cities around big cities. Through legislation, the government tries to allocate the new migrants into these smaller cities, and many of them have already relaxed their household registration system.

9.4 The development of China's urbanisation rate

Figure 9.2 shows the rise of China's urbanisation. Between 1950 and 1979, urbanisation increased only marginally from 12% to

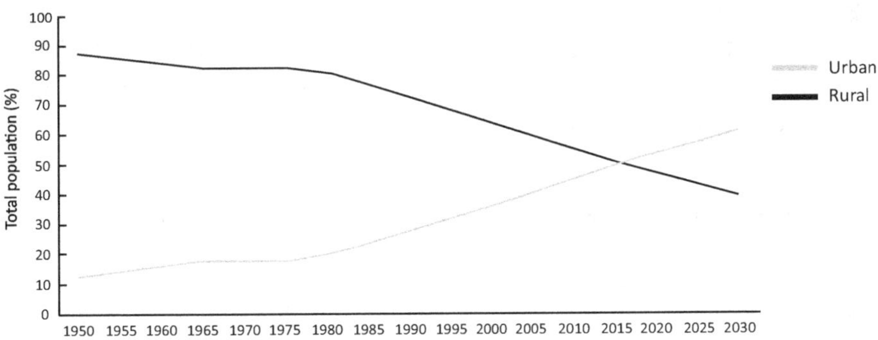

Figure 9.2 China's urban and rural population; percentage of total, 1950–2030

Note: *The NBS statistics are slightly lower than Data from UN, World Bank and CIA-World Fact Book*

Source: *NBS*

18%. However, after 1979 we witness a strong acceleration. In 2016, the urban population increased to 52% of the total (NBS), and growth will continue. The aim is to reach an urbanisation ratio above 60% after 2020, which is an enormous increase from the 18% it was at the beginning of the reforms in 1979. It means that urbanisation will continue at a speed of 1–1.5% point per year. Until now, the increase of urbanisation has been absorbed relatively smoothly, despite the problems faced by the big cities in terms of environment, traffic and diseconomies of scale. This is quite an achievement as we are talking about the accommodation of an urban population growing at 16–17 million annually, a new city, equal in size as the Netherlands, every year for the last 35 years.

Although China's urbanisation is without precedent in absolute numbers, the increase in its urbanisation rate has not been exceptional when compared to other countries. The Soviet Union urbanised at about the same rate as China since 1978. Between 1917 and 1982, urbanisation rate increased from 18% to 64% (Yanitsky, 1986). Urbanisation was also rapid in countries such as South Korea, Japan and Malaysia at comparable stages of development. In Japan, urbanisation rate increased from 37% in 1950 to 65% in 1960, an increase of 25% point in just one decade. In South Korea, urbanisation rate increased from 42% in 1966 to 66% in 1980 (Chengri Ding and Xingshuo Zhao, 2011). Urbanisation in Asia was considerably more rapid than the urbanisation we saw in the United States and the EU in the past. And as stated before, despite China's impressive urbanisation and migration record, the country is still less urbanised than expected from its industrialisation and income level.

9.5 Urbanisation and economic development

Cities are important for economic development. Cities have been the major drivers of China's GDP from the 1980s onwards, and they will become even more so over the next 20 years. The proportion of China's GDP generated by cities will rise from 75% today to 95% by 2030 (McKinsey, 2016). Urbanisation interacts with economic growth in four (integrated) ways, corresponding roughly with China's stages of economic development.

1. In the first period of development, transfer of people from agriculture to manufacturing in the cities contributed to economic development. The flow of migrant workers to China's cities has led to large gains in efficiency through this reallocation of labour from rural to urban (manufacturing) activities. Productivity of the industrial worker is much higher in a modern factory than in traditional agriculture.
2. After a certain point, urbanisation in itself contributes to growth. The workers need housing, infrastructure, telephone and hospitals. Building urban infrastructure creates new employment and increases demand for basic materials like steel and cement. Obviously, the growth impact of this second stage is of lower quality than the first because it does not create by itself large productivity gains.
3. After a certain period, the explosion of the middle class and urban lifestyle generates growth in private consumption.
4. Urban density allows frequent face to face contact among employees, entrepreneurs, suppliers and financiers, contact that in turn promotes innovation and productivity. Proximity also stimulates the growth of specialised services such as legal, software, data processing, advertising and management consulting firms. The results are so-called agglomeration effects.

Agglomeration effects

Agglomeration effects are benefits that firms obtain by locating close to each other. International experience suggests that, if done well, urbanisation can be an important driver of productivity increase and growth due to positive agglomeration effects such as innovative behaviour and easier knowledge spillovers. Agglomeration effects can also occur in smaller cities but in general, you need a certain size.

The framework that is often being used to discuss agglomeration effects in a concentrated geographical area is the diamond approach of Michael Porter. The model was used in his book, *The Competitive Advantage of Nations* (1989), which was the first attempt to explain competitive advantage based on the productivity of companies situated in a country instead of the comparative advantage that is focusing on countries. It is considered as the start of research on (innovative) clusters. The four points of the diamond represent four interrelated determinants that create competitiveness on domestic as well as on international markets. Figure 9.3 shows these four factors, which are firm strategy, structure and rivalry, related supporting industries, demand conditions and factor conditions.

Firm strategy, structure and rivalry refer to the fact that intensity of competition leads to businesses being forced to increase efficiency and innovative behaviour. Related supporting industries refer to upstream and downstream industries that facilitate innovation through cooperation and exchanging ideas. It means that vertical cooperation, e.g. between supplier and buyer, may increase efficiency and innovation and lower costs of production. Demand conditions refer to the size and nature of the market. Of course, customers who are willing and able to buy the (new) products are needed. When Porter wrote his book, he emphasised the home market, but more and more markets are becoming global and we

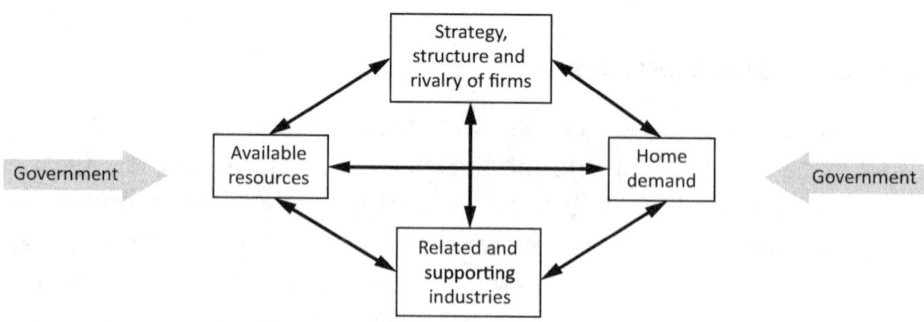

Figure 9.3 The diamond framework

Source: Based on Porter (1989)

see companies that go abroad instantly, the so-called "born globals". It means that the market can be everywhere. The final determinant to achieve innovative behaviour and competitiveness is the factor conditions. Factor conditions (or available resources) are those elements that Porter believes a country can create through smart investments in education and physical infrastructure. For example, a large cohort of skilled labour, high quality infrastructure and efficient physical capital goods. Porter argues that these factor conditions which are created are more important in determining a country's comparative advantage than naturally inherited factors such as land and natural resources. As indicated in Fig. 9.3, there is an important role of the government to create a highly innovative and sustainable cluster. Through direct or indirect measures, the government can stimulate all the four factors. For example, through regulation regarding competition, it can stimulate the intensity of competition between companies. And via subsidies, it may boost demand for green and environment-friendly products.

The emphasis on urbanisation as a key element of China's development process is clear; it assumes that competitive clusters and agglomeration effects can be achieved in urban settings. However, rapid urbanisation since 1980 also generated serious problems.

Negative side effects of China's fast urbanisation

When discussing the agglomeration effects, one should keep in mind that these positive spillover effects can be easily outweighed by congestion costs such as pollution, traffic jams, waste and air pollution, and higher costs of living. Housing prices may rise fast and, in many cases, urban dwellers are not able to live in the city anymore. There are also social costs. Rural migrants must adapt to urban life and must find work in urban centres. And when finding a job, income revenues are uncertain and there is always a risk of unemployment; this is quite different from the stable rural life. Another challenge of fast urbanisation is how to find sufficient skilled jobs for the university graduates in the cities. In addition, the announcement of equalising public services for urban and rural *hukou* make the middle class a bit uneasy. They have to share their "civilised space" with a large group of migrant workers. There is clearly a conflict of interest between the new and old urban citizens. The migrant population may rise as access to urban services increase. If at the same time, the migrant workers are not able to find a job, it will create a large additional demand on services, and this may undermine service quality for existing urban residents, which could aggravate social tension.

Another challenge regarding fast urbanisation is the problem of how to get enough land for cultivation. Today, we already see a lot of discontent on this issue. Nationalisation of land and houses is needed to make urbanisation happen. But there is a lot of discussion and anger about the compensation people receive for the farm land and rural houses. In the 13th five-year plan, there is a binding target that the cultivated land area should not be enlarged. A final challenge is that urbanisation increases government spending and places strain on the entire public-funding system in providing urban services.

Financing urbanisation

A big issue of China's urbanisation (and the change in the *hukou* system) is who will pay for this. Implementing the new urbanisation plan will result in an enormous financial burden, such as the cost of the physical infrastructure and spending on providing millions of new urbanites with healthcare, welfare and education services. HSBC (mentioned in EY, 2014) estimated that the total fiscal cost for local and central governments on public housing, education and other infrastructural investments would be more than 6-trillion-Renminbi for the approximately 250 million migrant workers in cities, equivalent to 53% of China's national fiscal revenue in 2012.

Until recently, the central government was absent in designing and financing urbanisation. The central government has provided only very limited financial support to local governments, leaving the job mostly to the local party and government officials. Because of the lack of central finance, most funding for urbanisation at the local level has come from two sources: loans from banks and land sales. Land sales were common in the 1990s, but today we have the binding target about growth of cultivated land area in the 13th five-year plan which was set at zero. Local authorities are not allowed to increase the cultivated land area. The second finance option of the local government was (and still is) debt, primarily through bank loans (and new methods such as local bonds). Technically, Chinese local governments are not able to borrow directly from banks. Despite this limitation, many have found ways to access bank funding by using municipal investment entities, known as Urban Development Investment Corporations. They accounted for between 80% and 90% of debt-funded urban infrastructure spending in the previous decade (BBVA, 2016). Today, local debt really becomes a problem, and new initiatives are emerging to finance the urban infrastructural investments and social spending in another way. For example, we see more and more public–private projects. The government grants a private company the right to build a project and allows it to operate the project for a profit over an agreed period. After the period expires, the private company transfers the project to the government. As with most reforms, we will see a period of experimentation, pilot programmes and incremental expansion before nationwide legislation will be in place.

9.6 New-style urbanisation announced in 2014

In 2014, the State Council published a "new-style urbanisation" model (2014–2020) on the Xinhua-news website. The aim is to reach an urbanisation ratio of 60% by 2020 and 70% by 2030 — quite an ambitious target knowing that urbanisation was around 50% in 2014 (Cheshmehzangi, 2016). The new urbanisation model gives priority to the development of townships, small cities and satellites around big cities. Importantly, the term used for this new form of urbanisation was "townification", to emphasise the development of smaller cities. China is moving away from megacities (avoiding the Latin Americanisation of cities with an overwhelming number of new and informal migrants) to smaller, more sustainable "eco-cities". Another goal of new-style urbanisation is to reduce the size of the agricultural labour force further (to 12% by 2030) and at the same time, to increase agricultural productivity through mechanisation and economies of scale. The more productive farmers will be linked to fully commercialised, modern urban chains of production. So, linking the urban centres to the rural areas is a key feature of the plan. Hence, the importance of an efficient transportation network.

Another aim of the 2014 urbanisation plan is to narrow the urban–rural income trap. The plan involves attention for the rights of migrant workers and is therefore called "inclusive urbanisation". It means that the provision of local public services will be (further) disconnected from local *hukou*. Turning migrants into permanent urban residents removes a critical source of uncertainty that restrains consumption. Inclusive urbanisation will increase consumer spending which is essential in China's rebalancing process. Another aspect of the urbanisation plan is to stimulate service-related activities. The service sector is important because of its labour-intensive nature. Furthermore, it is relatively green compared to (heavy) industry.

Urbanisation, historically, has been a process that carries great potential for instability. It has frequently given rise to political protest, demand for democracy and social movements. To counteract the risks involved with fast urbanisation, the Chinese government indicated in the new urbanisation plan the need to achieve orderly urbanisation. This is partly why we see some ghost cities today. Building urban infrastructure and housing before the inhabitants arrive is one part of this strategy to create this orderly urbanisation. What look like ghost cities today could be thriving urban centres in a few years.

The projected scale of urbanisation is unprecedented. The 2014–2020 urbanisation plan calls for the absorption of 100 million new urban residents and the integration of around 250 million current migrants within a seven years period. However, it is not clear how to do this: the plan is heavy on goals but it is light on specific policy measures. That mode of policymaking is nothing new in China, where Beijing leaves policy details to be worked out by local authorities. The finance of the new urbanisation plan is a big question mark and there is fear that it may increase the local debt burden even further. Local governments had built up a very worrisome amount of debt in the years before 2014 and now, the central government actually wants local governments to start borrowing again to co-finance the new urban infrastructure. In addition, banks are allowed to lend directly to qualified local government financing vehicles for building public housing projects. This is needed and worrisome at the same time. Finding the balance between the supply of affordable housing on one hand and manageable (increasing) debt on the other will be a challenge.

Housing market issues

The aim to increase urbanisation and the objective to solve the negative consequences of the *hukou* system at the same time will have a big impact on the housing market. Urbanisation will drive the demand for houses and is the main structural factor behind future increase in property prices in the (larger) cities. This is already a problem for the (lower) middle class and migrants that are not able to buy a house or apartment. Trying to solve this issue started after 2010. For example, in the 12th five-year plan (2012–2016), there has been dramatically more social spending than in the previous five years and partly this relates to the mass affordable housing programme, i.e. building 36 million units of affordable housing during the 2012–2020 period, mostly made available to migrant workers. But prices continued to rise. Part of the price increase in real estate is driven by (destabilising) speculation. After 2010, the Chinese government has introduced some cooling measures to crack down on speculators, but with hardly any effect. For example, the square metre price of an apartment near Renmin university (in Beihing's Haidian district) was around US$10.000 in 2017. This is even too expensive for a professor of international economics! The Chinese government is aware of the negative effects of runaway housing prices and took the following (stricter) measures to cool

China's housing market between 2011 and 2013 (Ebbers & Zhang 2010–2015):

- Higher down payments for second homes (from 50% to 60%)
- Local residents owning one property can only purchase one more property; not more
- Non-local residents with one property already, will not be allowed to purchase any additional property
- Property taxes were introduced in Shanghai and Chongqing as a pilot

Over the next decade, a growing share of housing is likely to be either directly subsidised social housing or housing that is indirectly supported by the government through mortgage guarantee programmes. This is indeed what is needed: more specific central government action. Since the mounting problems regarding affordable houses cannot be solved by the market, there is need for government interventions. Government-led urbanisation will continue in the medium term future. Despite the numerous cities with more than 1 million inhabitants, China needs higher urbanisation degree as part of the rebalancing process.

Chapter 10

China's Export Picture

Myth 10: China's economic growth in the previous years is based on export

10.1 Introduction

The perception is that China is an export-oriented economy and highly dependent on foreign demand. This view is driven by "Made in China" products that are visible all over the world. It looks like most products we see in the shelves of retail chains are produced in and exported from China. Statistics are in line with this observation. In 2000, China's exports, measured in dollars, were a third of those of the US and around half of those of Japan and Germany. By 2009, China had become the largest exporter in the world, and its share in global merchandise exports increased strongly between 1990 and 2016, from less than 2% in 1990 to 14% in 2016 (Fig. 10.1). When visiting the coastal regions with all the export-oriented companies, you may have the same feeling: China is the manufacturing plant (and export power house) of the world.

There is also the perception that the export success of Chinese firms is unfair in the sense that many of these exporters receive government support in one way or another that makes it possible for them to compete in foreign markets. This refers to the "China

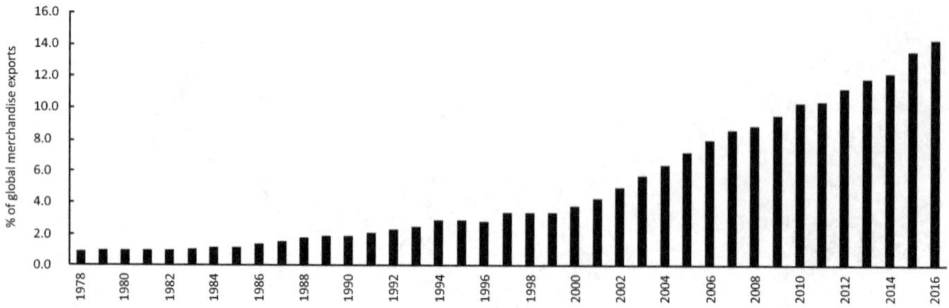

Figure 10.1 China's share of global merchandise exports, 1978–2016
Source: *NBS*

price" discussion: the price of stereotypical Chinese products such as clothing and shoes in the west (in particular, in the US) fell by 30–40% between 2000 and 2010, and to many observers, this is only possible through government support. Hence, the China price is the result of unfair competition. Along with the Chinese exporters, the major gainers from this China price have been the consumers in the developed world. The low price increased their purchasing power. The main losers have been the developing countries like Mexico, Indonesia and the Philippines whose comparative advantages are similar to China. Also, the blue-collar workers in the US who found their jobs being outsourced to China and the plant employees in Mexico who lost their jobs because of Chinese competition are the losers of this China price. The China price was a key issue in the US during the latest presidential elective campaign in 2016. President Trump stated during the election campaign (and also after his election) that he will fight this unfair competition from China and protect American jobs, and even bring jobs back to the US.

These two viewpoints (high export dependency and unfair competition) are widely accepted, but we will argue in this chapter that they are not fully correct. Export may be of less importance for China than expected. To see all these "Made in China" goods spreading around the world, it is easy to conclude that this must be the bulk of what China produces. However, the numbers tell a different story. The export share in the economy is lower than in most other Asian countries, and despite the rapid growth of export, the actual contribution to GDP is barely rising over time. The other view that China is stealing jobs from the west through unfair competition may miss the point that most of the export from China is done by western companies in China.

The chapter has been built as follows. In Section 10.2, we discuss the export-led growth strategy. Part of the section relates to this China price discussion. In Section 10.3, we introduce the main features of China's international trade. The conclusion is that official statistics is not showing us the real picture of the impact of international trade on the Chinese economy. We will elaborate on this issue in Section 10.4 that includes the famous iPhone case. In Section 10.5, the focus shifts towards the structure of China's export. The final Section 10.6 is about the main challenge to rebalance export orientation to more value-added products.

10.2 China's export-led growth model and the China price

The term "export-led growth" refers to the strategy of promoting export. The term has a negative association because export promotion goes hand in hand with an undervalued currency, government support to exporting companies and protecting domestic companies. From this point of view, an export-led growth model is seen as unfair: Chinese manufactures can considerably undercut competitor prices over a wide range of products because of unfair competition. Because of this China price, China produces more than 90% of the world's personal computers, 70% of the worldwide energy saving lamps, 60% of the world's solar panels, and 50% of the world production of smartphones, electronics, steel and shoes (2016). Based on the work of Harney (2008) and Navarro (2006), we discuss the following eight factors contributing to the China price:

- Low wages
- Government support

- Lack of environmental regulations
- Currency manipulation
- Protectionism by the Chinese government
- Copyright and counterfeits
- Industrial network clustering
- Foreign companies

Discussion about the China price is complex. On the one hand, one may say that this China price is the result of bad working conditions in combination with no attention given to the environment and safety issues. This is complemented by government support in the field of subsidies, not paying for energy use and tax breaks. On the other hand, the low price may be legitimate as the result of innovation and efficiency in the production process, in combination with low wages. Low wages that are connected to the low productivity of Chinese workers, and the result of the massive influx of migrants.

Unfair competition

Low wages are logical due to the abundance of labour. It means that China has a comparative advantage in labour-intensive products. The reason why low wages are being seen as unfair is that wages are much lower than expected because of the absence of safety standards and not paying social benefit premiums by Chinese firms. The second element of the China price is government support. Government support is essentially unfair. Within the WTO framework, some government support is allowed, but only if it relates in helping new (infant) industries. However, in China we (also) see government support to mature (senile) sectors such as heavy industry. The third factor relates to the lack of environmental standards. This will clearly reduce the costs of production for Chinese firms. This is perceived as unfair because western competitors must put a lot of energy and costs in aligning to environmental legislation. An artificial low value of the currency (the fourth factor of the China price) clearly makes export relatively cheap and easy. How much the Chinese currency is undervalued is part of a heavy discussion

(Chapter 13). Factor number five of the China price relates to protectionism. Chinese companies are protected, and because of this profitability on the domestic market is high, which creates a financial buffer for international expansion. Not paying for patents, and copying products and processes, (factor 6) is also unfair. Furthermore, due to industrial networks, Chinese companies may increase competitiveness by generating external economies of scale. They have lower (external) cost of production because they are participating in specific clusters. These clusters are often being helped by government in terms of taxation benefits. Finally, foreign companies are also part of the China price. They bring technology to China, and this technology transfer is helping the Chinese competitors. The point is that in many cases, this technology transfer is forced by the Chinese government. Entering China is, in many cases, only possible if technology is being shared. This is particular an important issue for the US government and generate tensions in China–US trade relationship.

Is it unfair competition?

You may argue that there is some common sense in the view that the China price is an artificial low price that is the result of unfair practices, and therefore the demand for protectionism from western leaders is logical and fair. However, certain elements of the overview above do not really relate to unfair competition. We already stated that wages are low because of the abundance of labour in the Chinese economy but the time of low wages is over. Looking at the previous decade, wages went up by around 10% annually, much more than productivity increased. Furthermore, you may question the statement that the Chinese Renminbi is strongly undervalued. Research generates mixed results (as we will see in Chapter 13). Moreover, it is clear that some sectors are (still) protected and not open for foreign companies. This can be considered as state capitalism, the strategy where the state is protecting some sectors and specific (large) companies. Within the WTO, this is not allowed if it does not relate to new, infant industries. At the same time, one should be aware that a certain degree of protectionism is sometimes needed to counteract large transitional imbalances. For example, opening up the banking sector instantly will certainly result in bank defaults, financial crises and increase in unemployment. As member of the WTO, China is in the process of further opening up the service sector. But some additional time (protectionism) is needed to adjust. And looking back, China has a relatively good track record in opening up its economy. Within a reasonable short period of time, most consumer industries are fairly open.

The Chinese clusters (factor 7 of the China price) will certainly increase productivity and reduce costs, but this has nothing to do with unfair competition. The same holds, to a great extent, about the impact of foreign companies. Of course, there are cases in which we see forced technology sharing, but in many sectors foreign companies can operate via a wholly foreign-owned company and a joint venture (or joint adventure) is not needed anymore. This overview should not give the impression that the China price is a completely legitimate competitive advantage. Clearly, this is not the case either. The answer about the China price lies in the middle and is again supporting the general view of this book that it is both. There is unfair competition and there is real competitiveness.

10.3 Main features of China's international trade

An important turning point in China's trade was its WTO membership in 2001. When analysing China's trade development, the year 2001, in many cases, is the dividing point. As shown in Fig. 10.2(a), there were noticeably two periods in China's trade growth: one before and one after 2001. In the 10 years between 1991 and 2001, China's export (and import) grew by an average rate of 13–15% per annum. Between 2002 and 2008, the export increased 27%, while import grew by 24% per annum (MOFCOM database). The exponential growth cumulated in a 10 times larger trade between 2000–2016. The upper half of the figure makes clear (and it is a

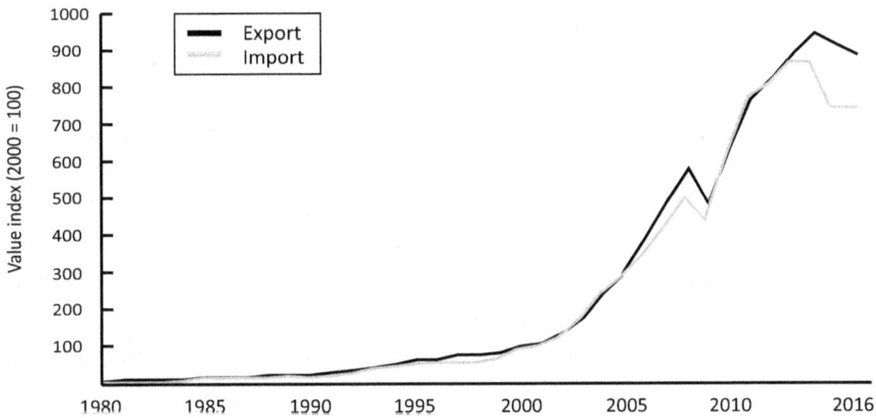

(a)

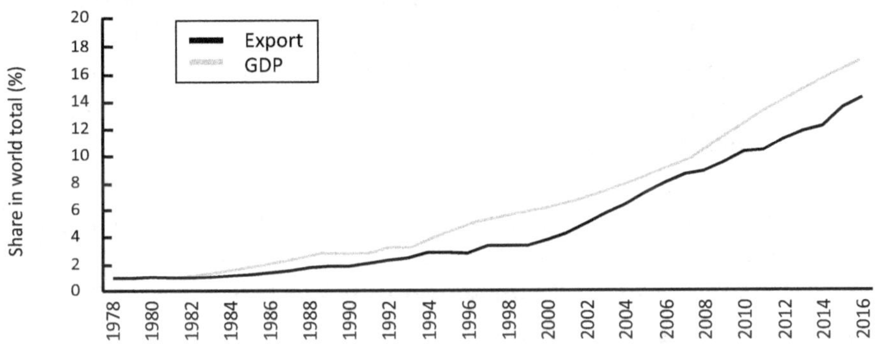

(b)

Figure 10.2 China's trade value (a) and shares in world GDP and export (b), 1978–2016

Source: Based on Yang Yao (2014) and World Bank Database

factor that is often overlooked) that, since 1998, China's import growth has generally kept pace with its rate of export growth. Figure 10.2 also shows the large drop of export and import in 2009, and the recovery in the next year. Also, the fall in import is visible after 2014, driven by government policy measures; to be discussed later in this chapter. Another feature of China's trade is that it relies heavily on processing trade. In general, China imports intermediate goods from Asia, and assembles them to consumer goods that are shipped to the US and EU. An indication of a high share of processing trade is the parallel development of exports and imports.

The share of processing export in total export reached 60% in the early 2000s, but has since dropped, and by 2016 it was around 35% (Joong Shim Kang and Wei Liao, 2016). One of the main features of processing trade is that, by definition, it creates a trade surplus. As a matter of fact, China's entire trade surplus since the early 1990s was the result of processing trade. As we will see later, China's processing export has a very small per-unit value-added. The huge trade surplus created by processing export is mainly due to its large quantity. With low value-added, and consequently, low impact on GDP growth, it has often been questioned whether processing export is a sound strategy for China to hold on to. And the answer given in Chapter 5 was that it is not — hence the need to rebalance the economy towards higher value-added production. Another (incorrect) notion is that China export is relatively high compared to its economy. It is not. China's export share in the world total has been kept in line with its GDP share in world total, as is shown in Fig. 10.2(b).

The final feature of China's international trade is that China's trade surplus is a relatively new phenomenon. During 1990–2004, China's trade surplus was modest, except for two large surpluses of 4.0% and 4.4% of GDP in 1997 and 1998 (Fig. 10.3(a)). China's large (and accelerated) export surpluses in the 2005–2008 period have drawn much attention and resulted in warnings from western leaders that protectionism may be needed. We saw an explosion of the trade surplus up to US$400 billion in 2008 (Fig.10.3(b)). In 2007–2008, China's trade surplus was above 8% of the GDP. Again, while such an enormous export surplus appears unsustainable, not least for political reasons, it is a relatively recent (and short term) situation; in 2016, trade surplus was "only" 2% of GDP.

From this angle, it does not look as if China is so much different from other export-oriented countries with trade surpluses. Indicated in Fig. 10.3 are the countries with the highest trade

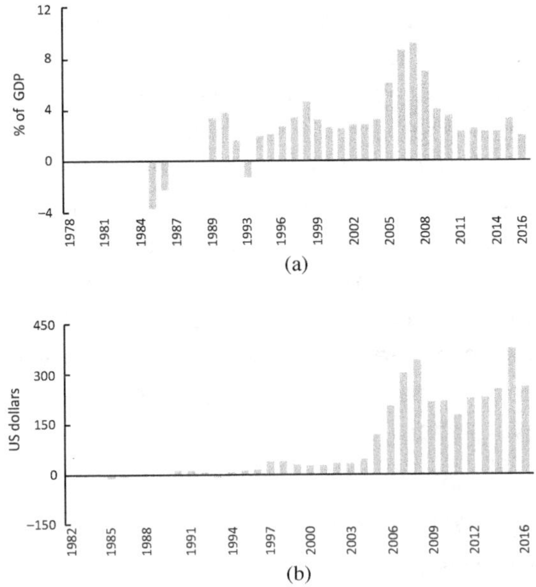

Trade disequilibrium 2013–2016

Surplus countries	Deficit countries
China	United States
Germany	United Kingdom
Japan	Brazil
South Korea	Australia
Netherlands	Canada
Taiwan	Turkey
	India

Figure 10.3 China trade balance, percentage of GDP (a) and in US dollars (b), 1980–2016

Source: Based on World Bank Database

surplus. China had the highest trade surplus over this period: higher than countries such as Germany, Japan, South Korea and the Netherlands. But, one must keep in mind that this trade surplus in dollars strongly relates to the size of the country. As percentage of GDP, the trade surplus of China is substantially lower than Germany, Japan or South Korea. After 2008, China's trade surplus declined, driven by the global economic crisis. Exports fell strongly because most of the final products were exported to the mature economies in Europe and North America, economies hardest hit by the crisis. It also was the result of the large stimulus package which was implemented in 2008–2009. The enormous stimulus programme (of more than 12% of 2008 GDP) resulted in domestic investments and production, which automatically reduced its trade surplus.

The single most important trade imbalance relates to the bilateral trade between the US and China. In 2016, the US goods trade deficit with China was US$350 billion. Part of this disequilibrium may originate from the China price, but China's export to the US is not so much different from China's export to other countries. In essence, the problem is not so much the high Chinese export growth to the US, but the fact that Chinese imports from the US are dropping. The US is losing market share in China. There are two main reasons for this. Firstly, the growth in Chinese imports has been driven by growth in demand for commodities and raw materials. These are not sectors in which the US has a comparative advantage. Related to this are legislative barriers to buy high-tech products from the US. Secondly, the US is losing market share everywhere and not just in China.

10.4 Importance of export for China's economic development

When I ask my students the question which determinant of total spending is the most important one in explaining China's business cycle in the previous decade, mostly the consensus answer is export. According to them, export is the main contributor to China's economic development; more important than consumption or investments by governments and the private sector. However, the answer is slightly different. This is because there is a difference between real Chinese export and China's processing export. Due to its heavy reliance on processing export (between 1990 and 2005), China's exports contribution to overall GDP (and growth) is much lower than what you would expect. Not only is China an enormous exporter, at the same time China is an exceptionally big importer. We are building up this argument in three steps. First, we discuss China's export to GDP. This is followed by the iPhone example before moving into the discussion of the net exports/GDP ratio. At the end of the analysis, it becomes clear why China is less dependent on export than normally is indicated by students, as well as the media.

China's openness, measured in terms of trade (export and import) relative to its economy, is far greater than ever achieved by the US in the post-war period and even higher than the levels of openness reached by the UK at the peak of its power during the British Empire. The ratio of trade to GDP for the US rarely exceeded 15% in the period after 1995, compared with China's current ratio of 57% (2016). Even in Japan, which is well known for its export competitiveness, the trade/GDP ratio is less than 20% (2016). China is integrated in the world through trade in a way that the US, Japan and Germany never were.

Export/GDP ratio

Earlier in the book, we labelled the period 2001–2007 as the export- and investment-led growth period. This period began with China's entry into the WTO in December 2001. Figure 10.4 presents the share of export in GDP for the period 1960–2016. The two periods (pre- and post-WTO membership in 2001) are observable in the graph. In this latter period, China's pattern of growth was much more based on export. After years of exports growing faster than GDP, the export to GDP ratio in China had reached 38% by 2006.

This export/GDP ratio is somewhat difficult to interpret. You could say that exports now make up more than a third of the Chinese

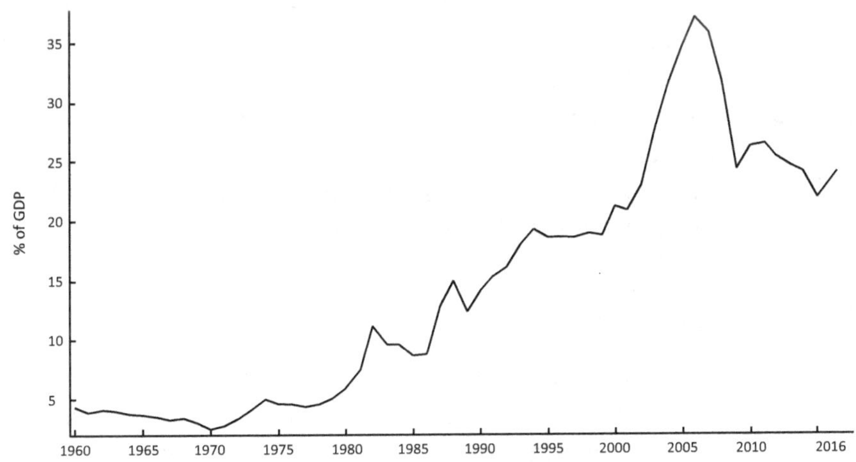

Figure 10.4 Share of export in GDP, 1960–2016

Source: *World Bank Database*

economy. However, the export/GDP ratio is very misleading. Malaysia, Hong Kong and Singapore have ratios around 200%. It clearly does not mean that the export sector is larger than the economy itself. This figure above 100% can be explained by the fact that exports are defined as gross export, while GDP is measured in value-added terms. You may compare it with the difference between revenue and profit for a specific company. Assume that the total GDP of a small country is US$30 billion. The country hosts several very large companies which are exporting most of their production, for example, US$40 billion. In this case, GDP rises to US$70 billion. However, part of the revenues earned by the factories is used to import products (components needed in the production process, but also finished products imported by consumers and other entities in the society); assume that US$40 billion is being imported. In this case GDP falls back to 30, while exports are 40, resulting in an export/GDP ratio of 133%. If all inputs of the economy's exports were produced domestically, the ratio could be used as a direct measurement on the contribution of external demand to GDP. However, modern international (processing) trade in manufacturing products is accomplished through global supply chains in which companies located in various countries contribute to produce (and assemble) a single product. This is especially true in the case of China because of its central role in the East Asian production network. To be able to export, China needs a lot of imports. Hence, the high share of processing trade makes the export to GDP ratio a poor indicator to measure export dependency (and its impact on economic growth). The example above makes clear that we may question the traditional way of looking at trade flows, trade surpluses and deficits. We can make it more concrete by using the iPhone case.

The iPhone example

The discussion below is based on the ADBI (2010) paper, but we adjusted the analysis by showing the newest information regarding the iPhone 6S. Manufacturing the iPhone 6S in China involves many companies that produce the needed components such as the display, camera and battery.

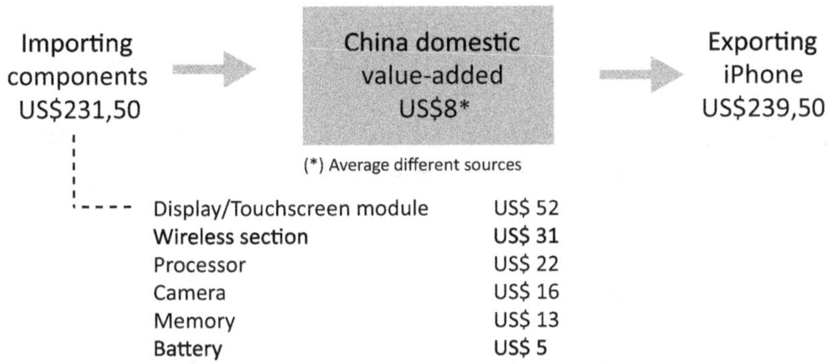

Figure 10.5 China domestic value-added when producing the iPhone 6S
Source: Adjusted from ADBI (2010)

These components are produced outside China and are shipped to China, where Taiwan-based Foxconn (located in Shenzhen and Chengdu) assembles the iPhone. Since the iPhones are assembled in and exported from China, the shipments to, for example, the US are recorded as China's exports, thus becoming part of the US trade deficit with China. As can be seen in Fig. 10.5, most of the export value per iPhone is attributed to imported parts and components from third countries and has nothing to do with China's domestic production and export. The figure above shows that the production cost (and presumably the export value) per iPhone is US$239,50. These costs are a combination of importing components (with a value of US$231,50) and the costs to assemble the iPhone in China; being US$8). The domestic value-added is US$8, which is only 3.4% of the total manufacturing costs per iPhone. The traditional way of thinking is that the US$239 per iPhone is Chinese export, but looking at the domestic value-added, only the assembling costs should be considered. The "real" Chinese export is only US$8. Chinese workers simply put all these parts and components together. When calculating bilateral trade flows by looking at the value-added created by export, the bilateral trade deficit of the US with China would almost disappear. We can draw two conclusions from this iPhone case. Firstly, only domestic value-added is increasing GDP, not total export. Secondly, conventional trade statistics do not give the picture of today's fragmented supply chains and related trade flows, and statistics provide a distorted picture about bilateral trade imbalances. We should be aware of this when referring to trade disequilibria. Therefore, the focus on net export (export minus import) is needed.

Net exports/GDP ratio

This net export to GDP ratio is a better indicator for export dependency. As can be seen above, it adjusts the gross export to GDP ratio by stripping out the import content. After adjustment, the actual (true) export share of most Asian countries is far less than what the export/GDP ratio would suggest. It is single digit for most (larger) Asian countries, and for Hong Kong and Singapore it moves around 20–25%. The figure of China is fluctuating around 3% over the last decade (coming from 8% in 2006), slightly more exposed to exports than Japan or India, but far below export-driven economies like Taiwan and Thailand. Other figures point in the same direction. For example, 45 million workers earn their living in export-oriented sectors (2016). This is less than 30% of the total employed in all industrial manufacturing. It is only 6% of the actively mainland workforce (750 million in 2016). So, the export share of the labour market is rather small. Combining these two observations and it becomes clear that China's trade dependency is less than what you would expect.

Using the net export to GDP ratio is a more accurate indicator for trade dependency, but the contribution of net export (as well as other expenditure components of GDP) can vary greatly from quarter to quarter and from year to year. Such variation does not have any relationship with the (longer term) structure of the economy such as openness of the economy. A longer term view, therefore, is needed. The relatively low net export as percentage of GDP also has consequences when analysing economic growth. As shown in Fig. 10.6, the relative contribution of net export to GDP growth in China between 2012 and 2017 was very low.

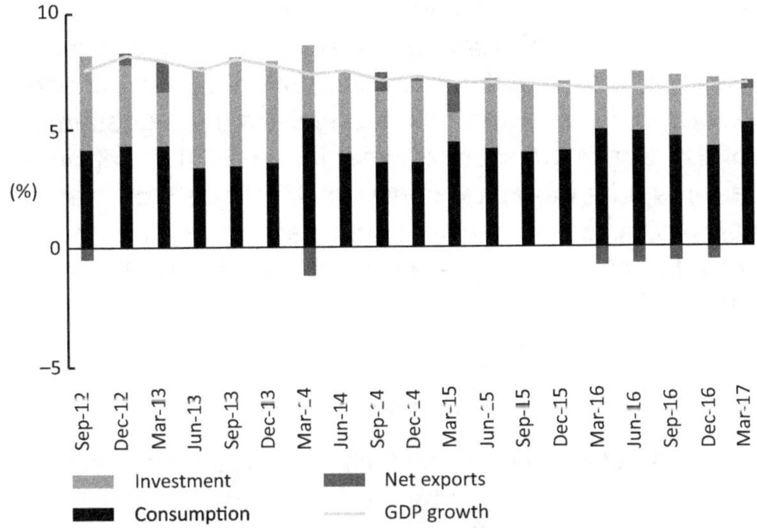

Figure 10.6 Determinants of economic growth, 2012–2017
Source: BBVA Research; China Economic Outlook (2017)

It is interesting to note that private consumption (and not net export or investments) is, by far, the most important determinant of quarterly economic growth in the previous years, a subject which will be dealt with in Chapter 14.

Decline in imports

China's rising trade surplus in the period 2004–2008 was not due to an acceleration in export growth; growth in exports actually slowed over this period of time. The reason behind the rising trade surplus was the sharp decline in import growth since 2004. This decline was the result of a strong rise in domestic production that substituted imports. In other words, net exports may be contributing strongly to overall growth between 2004 and 2008 but this had nothing to do with growing export or growing external dependence. Instead, it is all about rising domestic supply and displacing import: it is about reducing exposure to the global economy. As Fig. 10.6 demonstrates,

China's economic growth, in fact, comes predominately from domestic sources, not from net exports. Looking at the previous five years, the net export is not important in explaining economic fluctuations in the economy. China remains the biggest manufacturer of the world, but most of what it makes stays at home and the clear majority of what it consumes is made there too. This is the macro-picture. Obviously, some sectors still rely heavily on foreign demand, including electronics, textiles and apparel, but most don't.

10.5 Structure of Chinese export

The structure of China's export has changed dramatically over the past three decades. China's top 10 export products in 1990 are totally different from the exports in 2016 (Table 10.1). In the 1980s, the majority of Chinese exports were resources and agricultural goods. In the 1990s, garments became China's top export product, and today, electronic products are, by far, the largest

Table 10.1 China's top 10 exports; percentage of total, 1990 and 2016

1990	% share in total	2016	% share in total
Clothing	9.9	Electronic equipment	26.3
Miscellaneous manuf. art.	9.2	Machines, engines, pumps	16.0
Leather	8.2	Furniture, lighting, signs	4.3
Non-edible agricultural prod.	7.4	Knit or crochet clothing	3.7
Crude oil	6.8	Clothing (not knit or crochet)	3.4
Carpets	5.4	Medical, technical equipment	3.2
Knitwear	5.3	Plastics	2.9
Yarns fabrics	3.3	Vehicles	2.7
Consumer electronics	3.2	Iron or steel products	2.7
Plastic articles	2.5	Footwear	2.3

Note: *The role of western companies in China's trade (and structure) is enormous*
Source: *Based on MOFCOM database and worldstopexports.com*

category of China's exports. Looking at the top 10 export products in 2016, there are only a few products which fit in the stereotype products based on comparative advantage (see Table 10.1). Furniture, clothing and plastic products are sub-sectors with a labour-intensive production process that fit China's comparative advantage based on the abundance of labour. China has made substantial progress in upgrading its exports, and export of most of the products in 2016 must be explained through other (modern) trade theories instead of the law of comparative advantage. The structural change does not mean that the traditional concept of comparative advantage is useless in analysing today's trade structure. But, it should be complemented by other trade theories. For example, electronic products and vehicles exports are driven by activities of foreign companies in China. The medical and technical equipment sector and certain mining companies were able to become competitive through protectionism and government subsidies. Rodrik (2006) and the WTO (2016) show that exports from China have been more sophisticated than exports from countries with similar income levels. China is exporting statistically high-tech products such as iPhones and medical equipment, but the export of these products is based on processing trade in which China is doing the assembly. China's assembly role is consistent with its underlying comparative advantage. But the traditional theory cannot explain the whole picture and other factors, such as the role of foreign companies in China and the role of the government, should be taken into account.

A substantial share of medium- and high-tech products are assembled (and exported) not by Chinese-owned firms but by foreign firms that are using China as an export platform. Think about Foxconn that assembles the iPhone. Figure 10.7 shows the share of foreign companies in the Chinese export and import. During the mid-2000s, almost 60% of Chinese export and import was done by foreign companies in China (including joint ventures). Partly this connects to processing trade, but it also relates to western companies that use China only as an export platform of relatively low-tech products that does not include imports.

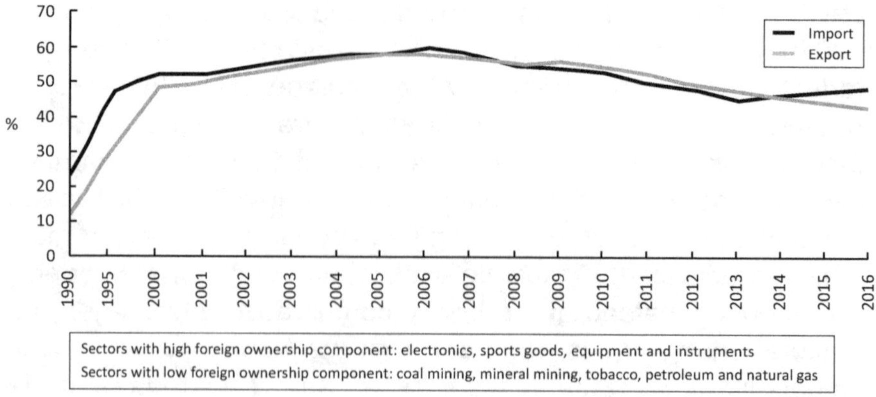

Figure 10.7 Share of foreign companies in China's import and export, 1990–2016

Source: *Morrison (2013) and MOFCOM database*

For example, US-based Walmart produces a large share of its products in China, and these products are being exported from China. Looking at the value of Walmart products shipped to the US consumer, between 2004 and 2006, Walmart attributed around 10% to the US trade deficit with China in that period. If Walmart were a country, it would rank in the top 10 of China's biggest trading partners. And this is just one of the largest US-based companies in which China is playing an important role in its value chain. Figure 10.7 makes clear that the share of foreign companies in China's international trade is slightly dropping, reaching 40–45% in 2016.

10.6 The challenges ahead: From made by China to design in China

Investigating the exact contribution of external demand to Chinese GDP growth is crucial for understanding the urgency of rebalancing and the challenges of structural reform. Traditionally, net exports over GDP and exports over GDP have been used as a quantitative measure for the contribution of external demand to the economy.

Both of these measures are biased. Net exports underestimate the contribution of external demand to economic growth as it assumes all imports are for export, while, in fact, some imports might be for consumption and investment. The gross export to GDP ratio overestimates the contribution of external demand by assuming the entire value-added of exports is produced domestically. This leads to an overestimation of the contribution of external demand to GDP. Despite the statistical issues, it looks like that China is less dependent on trade than normally assumed.

In spite of the fact that China as a whole is not extremely sensitive to external demand, some of its regions are very sensitive to external shocks, in particular the southeast with its dominance in manufacturing production and high export dependency. Guangdong, for example, has both the highest ratio of export to GDP and the highest concentration of manufacturing employment. Table 10.2 makes clear that provinces such as Jiangsu and Zhejiang are also vulnerable to a fall in foreign demand. The problem with relying so much on exports is that if your trading partners run into trouble, so do you.

Rebalancing the economy means to reduce its dependency on low value-added export in favour of domestic consumption and related to this, increasing the domestic value-added component in China's production and export. It also means the transition from made by China (assembly) to design in China (R&D). We start the discussion with the so-called smiling curve shown in Fig. 10.8. The vertical axis shows the value-added of important functions of the

Table 10.2 Regional variation

High export dependency	Middle export dependency	Low export dependency
Guangdong	Fujian	Anhui
Jiangsu	Beijing-region	Henan
Zhejiang	Shandong	Hunan
Shanghai-region	Liaoning	Qinghai
Tianjin-region	Xinjiang	Shaanxi

Source: Wang Dewen (2010)

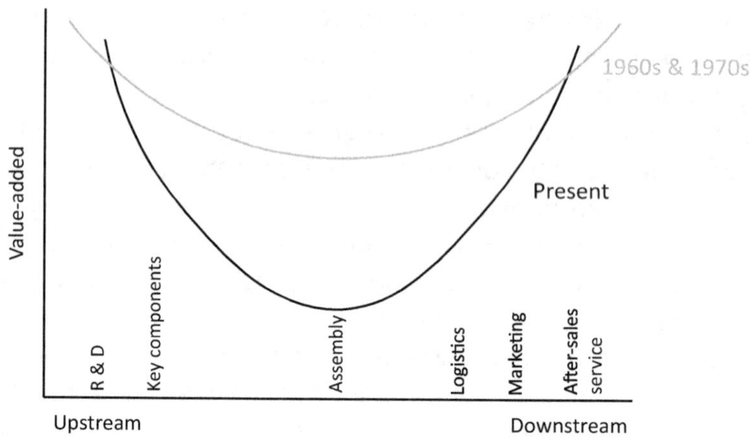

Figure 10.8 The smiling curve
Source: *Based on Shih (1996) and Ming YE et al. (2015)*

supply chain, ranging from R&D, and components towards marketing and after-sales service. In essence, it shows that, focussing on assembly activities in the global supply chain does not give much value-added (and profitability).

Rebalancing and profitability can be reached by moving left (upstream) or right (downstream), away from assembly activities. Upstream activities such as R&D, design and production of key components give a relatively high value-added. The "Made in China 2025" programme, published in May 2015 aims to raise the domestic content of core components to 40% by 2020 and 70% by 2025. The plan indicates the need to transform "Made in China" to "Made by China", moving along the smiling curve. The same holds when focussing on downstream activities such as logistics, marketing and after-sales services.

Figure 10.8 shows that the smiling curve is becoming deeper compared to the 1960s and 1970s. This is the result of more competition between countries to attract foreign companies. It means competition on wages that attract companies and production processes with low value-added. Competition become intensive because more and more countries are opening up and are integrating in the world economy (such as Central and Eastern Europe in the 1990s, African countries in the 2000s and new Asian markets such as Myanmar after 2010).

Besides the transformation from "Made in China" to "Made by China", there is a second transformation visible: changing "Made in China" to "Design in China". This relates to innovation; again a movement away from being an assembly platform as part of the global supply chain. The innovation-driven goal started with the Scientific and Technological Development Plan for the 2006–2020 period, published in 2006 and was complemented by measures in the 11th (2006–2010) and 12th (2011–2015) five-year plans. The Scientific and Technological Development Plan stated that China wants to become an "innovation-oriented society" by 2020 and a "world leader in science and technology" by 2050 (Bichler and Schmidkonz, 2012). The term "indigenous innovation" was introduced and elaborated on in the 11th five-year plan. Essentially, it focus on technology-led economic transformation; guided by the government and executed by domestic firms. Innovation should be done by domestic companies. Furthermore, it meant that there should be more domestic ownership of intellectual property rights.

What innovation precisely means was not defined. It could be a leap in technology compared to existing products or processes, but incremental innovation is also possible. Clearly, game-changing products such as the iPhone are not coming from Chinese companies, but they are brilliant at introducing products that fit the purpose. The companies are masters at incremental innovation. The indigenous innovation concept is also visible in the newest, 13th five-year plan. Innovation is set within the context of the "new normal" with respect to economic growth. The "new normal" is the sticker China's leaders use to describe the growth they are aiming for. Growth will decelerate to an average of 5% in the decade of the 2020s. And to achieve this innovation is essential.

This rebalancing will clearly change the structure of GDP and type of exports. It will also reduce the trade dependency even further. However, the move to a different type of economy is a slow process and for the next decades to come, China will be the most important exporter, trade disequilibria will continue and trade tensions (between China and the US) will remain. Therefore, it is important to have a correct perspective on trade flows. Most of the trade statistics (and policy choices based on that) are using the concept of country of origin, using customs statistics that register the volume and value of goods leaving or entering the country. As we see in the case of the iPhone and with respect to processing trade in general, a new method is needed that focus on trade volume and value in value-added terms. This approach is slowly gaining ground. This is logical; there is hardly any product that is actually made in a single country today. Products are generally "made in the world". Looking at trade flows in this way makes China's export (and trade surplus) much lower and its export dependency much smaller that you might expect.

Chapter 11

Family Planning Policy, Ageing and Developments on the Labour Market

Myth 11: Due to the enormous population, the labour force will continue to grow in the medium term

11.1 Introduction

There are not many other issues that have received as much attention and uneasiness in western media as China's family planning policy, in particular its one-child policy. The western mindset is not ready for so much government interference in private life. From an economic point of view, it may be a good thing that China has a big population. A large population means production and relatively easy longer-term economic development. At the same time, however, the production (and income) must be shared with a large population, which sometimes creates a Malthusian catastrophe. Malthus (1798), warned that without any checks, population would theoretically grow at an exponential rate, rapidly exceeding its ability to produce resources to support itself. The result is famine and social disaster, a situation we saw during the Great Leap Forward (1958–1960; with overlap towards 1962). Family planning and the one-child policy, introduced in 1980, were motivated by the aim to reduce the population pressure and increase welfare per head of the population.

In line with the other chapters and topics, the family planning policy touches upon several other elements of the broad reform agenda. It can be linked to urbanisation, labour market, ageing, government budget and social issues. In this chapter, we complement the discussion on the one-child policy with two other (related) issues: the labour market and ageing. The one-child policy affected the labour supply dramatically. China used to have a large labour surplus on which its growth policy was based. But the falling fertility rate that occurred after the 1980s resulted in labour shortages in several segments of the economy and in various regions from the mid-2000s onwards. The one-child policy also had a dramatic impact on ageing. The share of seniors is already high, with more than 230 million citizens aged 60 or above in 2016. This is 16% of the total population, and it will increase further if at the bottom of the demographic pyramid the growth is low. China is on the edge of becoming an ageing society. Ageing will lower labour supply further and create more intense shortages on the labour markets. The ageing population, in combination with the one-child policy between 1980 and 2016, also resulted in a (potential) social time bomb. The social cohesion between generations is under pressure due to the 4-2-1 phenomenon: one child will be obliged to look after two parents and four grandparents during his working age life. From this point of view, it is therefore not surprising that the one-child policy was under attack in the previous decade and has been changed radically in 2015 and 2016.

The chapter is structured as follows. In Section 11.2, the emphasis is on the family-planning policy during the pre-reform process (1950–1979). This period can be characterised as (forced) voluntary planning. We continue, in Section 11.3, with discussing the one-child policy that started in 1980. As we will see, between 1980 and 2016, the policy has been adjusted and relaxed step by step. But only in October 2015, was the one-child policy officially abandoned. The linkage of the one-child policy and ageing is explained in Section 11.4, in which we also discuss the Lewis turning point. In Section 11.5, we relate the one-child policy to the labour market and discuss the problem of labour shortage.

11.2 Family planning between 1950 and 1979: The period of voluntary planning

The approach towards family planning after 1949 was more economic than ideological. The aim was to increase welfare of the people, and this appeared to be difficult to reach with total fertility rate (total number of children per woman in her lifetime) approaching six in the 1950s and 1960s. The demographic "burden" became extremely visible during the Great Leap Forward (1958–1960) when agricultural production was just too low to feed the people. The government stepped in with a voluntary family-planning policy, wherein people were educated and asked to reduce family size.

The China birth planning commission (under the auspices of the State Council) was set up in 1964, and it monitored and guided birth control. Local governments executed the policy by using grassroot birth planning workers. In the late 1960s, government interference increased, and after 1970, the family-planning policy can be labelled as "forced voluntary planning". The 4th and 5th five-year plans during the 1970s set specific (and binding) targets of population growth. The slogan used in the early 1970s was: "later, longer and fewer"; later marriage, longer birth intervals and fewer births. Fewer meant no more than two children for urban families and three for rural families, with penalties for those who did not comply. So, birth planning enforcement was already a normal practise during the 1970s in both rural and urban areas, preceding the launching of the official one-child policy in 1980.

Figure 11.1 shows that the "voluntary" approach remarkably brought down China's total fertility rate from 5.7 in the early 1970s to 2.5 in the early 1980s. The fall in the number of children

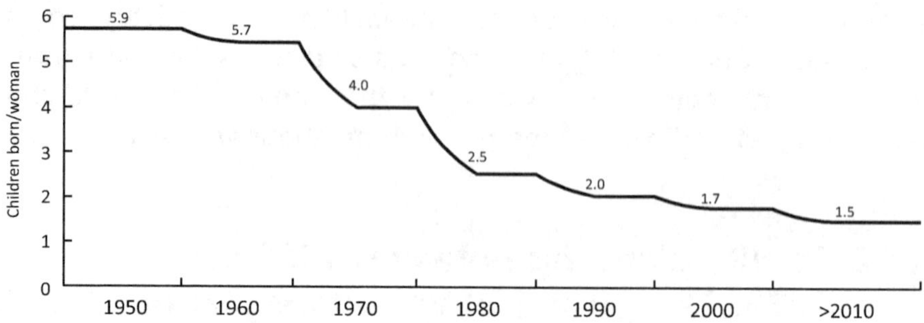

Figure 11.1 Total fertility rate, 1950–2016

Note: Total number of children per woman; averages are used per decade
Source: Based on NBS and Yi Zeng and Heskett (2016)

per woman started already in the late 1960s, before the launch of the one-child policy. After 1980, the fertility rate declined further to 1.5 today.

11.3 Family planning between 1980 and 2016

The formal and mandatory one-child policy started in 1980. From the beginning, it was understood as a policy to be implemented for one generation, just to make sure that population would not become a burden. Be aware that the experiences of the excessive death in the famine years were in the minds of the policymakers. Although population growth was already sharply reduced in the 1970s, the strict one-child policy was seen as a way to increase the per capita economic growth. While it was a nationwide policy, in particular in urban areas the one-child policy was enforced strictly. Several sources are indicating that 400 million births have been prevented (for an overview, look at King Whyte, Wang Feng and Yong Cai, 2015). If the policy had never been adopted, China today might have had a population of 1.7–1.8 billion, and per capita income, arable land, grain, forests, drinking water and energy would have been substantially less than what it is today. Indeed, many children are not born because of the one-child policy, but this 400 million may be an overestimation. The calculation was done by China's birth planning commission in the late 1990s and was taken over by western media.

Basically, the report used a straight line to portray the overall fertility trend between 1950 and 1970, and then simply extrapolated this line forward into later years based on the (wrong) assumption that this extrapolation provided an accurate projection of what China's fertility would have been in the absence of birth planning campaigns. However, looking at experiences in other (Asian) countries, fertility declines as economies grow. The fertility rate would have fallen even without the one-child policy due to economic development and rising income. Whether 400 or 300 or 250 million births have been prevented, it is still an enormous number, and it helped to achieve the ambition to increase welfare per capita (as part of the Chinese Dream to double the 2010 GDP per capita in 2020) substantially.

As we can see in Table 11.1, the Chinese population will fall after 2017 due to the low fertility rate and the imbalanced demographic pyramid as a consequence of the one-child policy. Chinese families' average of 1.5 children per woman is well below the 2.1 level that is considered the replacement rate or what is necessary to avoid a shrinking population.

China's bureaucratic system in which the party and state keep control over the local authorities and at the same time grant them

Table 11.1 Most populated countries; 2000, 2017 and 2050

	Country	2000 Population	2017 Population	2050 Expected Population
1	China	1,268,301,605	1,388,232,693	1,301,627,048
2	India	1,006,300,297	1,342,512,706	1,656,553,632
3	United States	282,162,411	326,474,013	398,328,349
4	Indonesia	214,090,575	263,510,146	300,183,166
5	Brazil	174,315,386	211,243,220	232,304,177
6	Pakistan	152,429,036	196,744,376	290,847,790
7	Nigeria	123,945,672	191,835,936	391,296,754
8	Bangladesh	128,734,672	164,827,718	193,092,763
9	Russia	147,053,966	143,375,006	129,908,086
10	Mexico	99,775,434	130,222,815	150,567,503

Note: Ranking is based on 2017 population
Source: UN database and Internet World Stats website

autonomy, can also be seen with respect to family-planning policy. Starting in 1984, provincial governments were allowed to fine-tune the birth control policy, paving the way for local variations. For example, certain ethnic groups were allowed to have two children and also residents of some agricultural rural–urban clusters in Gansu, Hubei, Shanxi and Hebei could have two children. Other exceptions followed in the 1990s: for example, allowing a rural couple to have a second child if the first is a girl. By the end of the 1990s, this "two-child" policy had been extended to couples, who were the only child in their respective families. So, there were exceptions and some regional differentiation. At the same time the central authorities stayed in control. Keeping the number of births down became one of the key criteria used in the annual performance ratings (and promotion indicators) of local officials. Couples who ignored the rules could face heavy fines. After 2001, the Chinese government recognised that the low fertility rate was a problem rather than an achievement. The rapidly ageing population and decline of birth rates negatively impacted the labour supply and the longer-term development of the economy. Therefore, the stringent enforcement was relaxed. But the penalties remained.

The penalty of having too many children was calculated as the social cost of raising children. I remember heavy discussions in the media on how large these costs are. In general, the major criteria for calculating the social cost (and the penalty) of bringing up children is the per capita income of the parents (relative to the average in that area) and the circumstances involved in violating the one-child policy. Clearly, the outcome can be different from case to case. For example, in Beijing the penalty violating the policy is 3 to 10 times the average disposable income of residents. In Chaoyang, the richest district of Beijing, the penalty is much higher than in other districts. Yet, it is hard to say that a child born in Chaoyang would consume more resources and be a heavier burden on society than the child in another Beijing-district. The differences in calculations and the freedom of local authorities to set the penalties was and still is a potential source of discomfort to the public.

Need for action

The economic and social context of the early 1980s when the one-child policy started is so much different from today. Today, fertility rates are extremely low, income per capita has reached middle-income level, rapid urbanisation is seen, and there is dramatic rise in education enrolment and new attitudes towards lifestyle (like singlehood or late marriage). These trends make the one-child policy obsolete, and even damaging to economic and social life. More specifically, it has saddled the country with several unintended problems, including an ageing population, a shrinking workforce and a distorted sex ratio. In the early 2030s, about 400 million people (30% of the population) will be older than 60 years (NBS). The working-age population will fall by an average of 8 million people annually from 2023 onwards, as the ageing problem continues to grow. Another undesirable outcome of the one-child policy is the gender imbalance. China's gender imbalance is one of the highest in the world, together with Vietnam and India (WEF Gender Report, 2016). By 2020, China will have 25–30 million "leftover men" (CASS), who will not be able to find a wife. The nationwide gender imbalance reached its peak in 2004 (121 boys born for every 100 girls) but fell to a nationwide average of 114 in 2016. The normal gender ratio would range between 103 and 107. The goal set in the 12th five-year plan for the gender ratio (below 115) has been reached, but it is to be expected that a further fall of the imbalance is difficult (WEF, 2016). Furthermore, there are large regional differences. Provinces such as Anhui and Fujian are among the regions with the highest (above 120) gender ratio (*China Daily*, 17 September 2015).

Abolishing the one-child policy, 2013–2020

Relaxation of the one-child policy accelerated after 2013. In November 2013, the government announced that urban couples could have a second child if either the husband or the wife was an only child. In October 2015, the party decided to extend the "two-child" policy nationwide to all couples, to allow all couples to have two children regardless of their residence, ethnicity or their status of being an only child or not. The penalty for a third child is still there because the many controllers and authorities must keep their work and the money received through these penalties is a substantial source of revenue.

The speeding up of the reforms to increase fertility rate may be too late. Much like in other countries that have seen incomes rise, the majority of Chinese prefer smaller families, as evidenced by a recent study in Jiangsu province (*Bloomberg*, 12 November 2013). Already 70% of rural families in this province favour having just one child. Experiences in Singapore, Taiwan, Hong Kong and South Korea have shown that when fertility rates have reached low levels (1.8 or lower), lifting birth control cannot return it to the replacement level. The impact of specific measures may be modest. It means that the 4-2-1 problem will not been solved, not even in the medium or longer term. Most of the elderly in China are still cared for by relatives, in particular the children. In that sense, every little emperor and empress has a burden on his or her shoulder. Despite research by CASS in 2016 which concludes that due to the abolishment of the one-child policy one million extra children have been born, we do not expect a substantial structural effect.

Figure 11.2 summarises the development of China's one-child policy. It started with voluntary family planning in the 1960s and changed into a nationwide one-child policy in 1980. Step by step, local variations (and exceptions) were accepted and we saw relaxation of the strict enforcement. In 2015, the one-child policy was

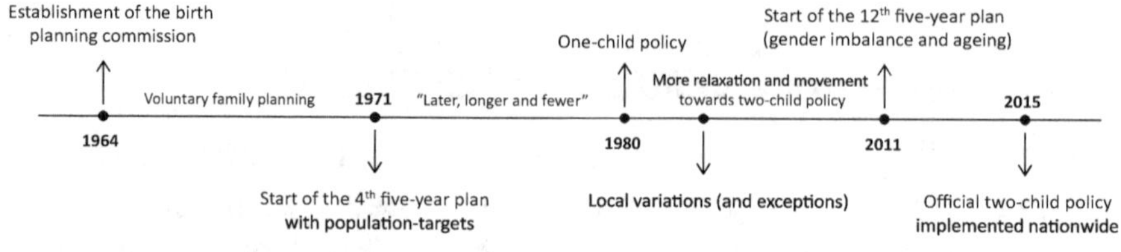

Figure 11.2 The chronology of family planning in China

Source: *Based on China Daily*

officially abolished. Chinese authorities are hoping that the new policy may absorb part of the problems related to ageing.

11.4 Ageing and the one-child policy

China, today, is in the middle of a demographic transition. This transition has three typical features. Firstly, an enormous increase of the work-age population in the 1990s and 2000s, and the dramatic fall it will witness after 2020. Secondly, the number of older people is becoming extremely high for a country that is classified as middle-income. Thirdly, the speed of the demographic transition is enormous. These features (and challenges) are partly the results of China's one-child policy.

Working-age cohort is large and rising

One of the consequences of the one-child policy has been the drastic increase in the working-age population (and its share in total population) between 1990 and 2010. Because the birth rate has declined sharply, the cohort of young people has dropped quickly. On the other hand, the old age group was still relatively small. The dependency ratio (the number of young and old people for every 100 working-age people) fell from 80 to 36 between 1975 and 2010 (Kroeber, 2016). It was clearly an important favourable condition; economic growth is relatively easy because of the large proportion of working-age group in the total population. Moreover, China's demographic dividend was unusually large and long lasting; driven by its unique context. Firstly, the excessive deaths in the famine years (1958–1960) reduced the number of people entering retirement age. Secondly, after the Great Leap Forward, China had a tremendous baby boom. This can be seen in Fig. 11.3. The cohorts aged 5–14 in 1978 is the effect of this baby boom. Thirdly, due to the family planning policy, China's fertility rate declined strongly, a process that had already started before the introduction of the one-child policy in 1980. Fourthly, we saw improvements in healthcare and sanitation that strongly decreased infant, childhood and mater-

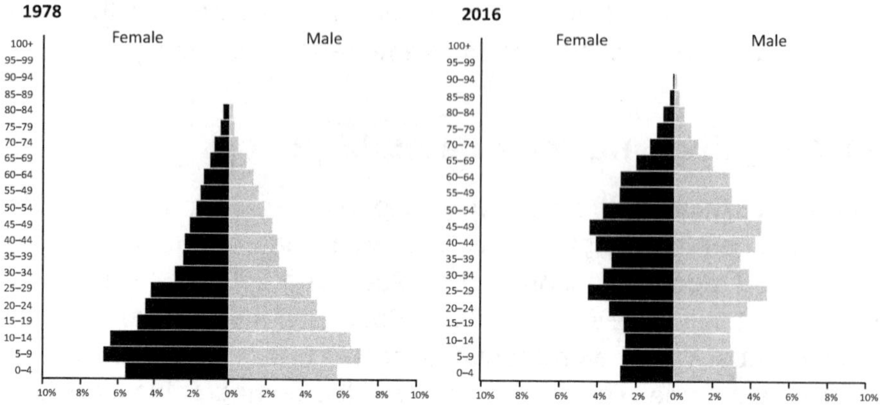

Figure 11.3 China's demographic pyramid, 1978 and 2016
Source: *NBS*

nal mortality. Starting at 41 years in the 1950s, Chinese life expectancy continuously increased from an average of 67 years in the 1980s to 75 years in 2016.

The dependency ratio fell substantially, but unfortunately, after a few decades this process started to move in reverse. The baby boomers of the 1960s are now approaching retirement age. The right-side of Fig. 11.3 shows that the 40–54 age range is the largest cohort in 2016. And with retirement age of 60 years, these people will leave the labour market shortly. The phase when the population ages rapidly is called the demographic transition and tends to be associated with slower economic growth and larger government budget challenges. At the end of the day, the demographic dividend becomes a demographic burden and the country passes its so-called Lewis turning point, the concept we introduced in Chapter 5.

The modern manufacturing sector takes advantage of the excess supply of labour (migrated from the agricultural sector) until the surplus labour is exhausted. This Lewis turning point with respect to China is indicated in Fig. 11.4 and has been put at the year 2025 (although some experts conclude that it has been reached already). The reason to put the Lewis turning point at 2025 is that the growth of the dependency ratio will steadily rise from

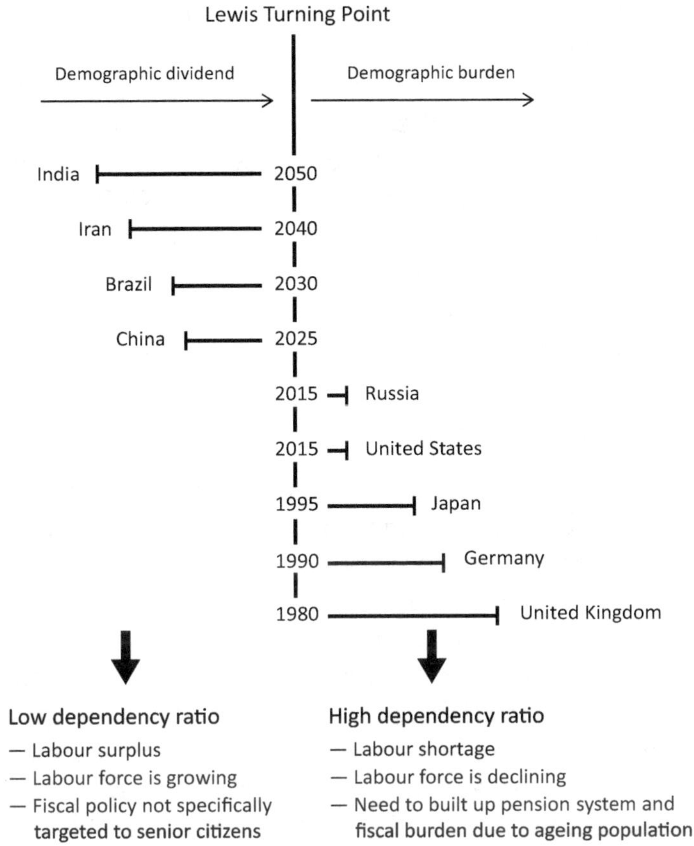

Figure 11.4 Lewis turning point, several countries

Note: Although the turning point is given as a specific time point, it should be seen as a period which may extend over several years

Source: Adjusted from Cai and Du (2009) and BBVA Research (2010–2016)

0.39 in 2015 to 0.43 in 2025 but will accelerate thereafter, reaching 0.65 in 2050 (NBS). Another reason to plot the Lewis point at 2025 is because after this year China's working-age population (and labour force) will decline in absolute numbers. Further signals that indicate that we are approaching the turning point relate to structural labour shortages and more problems to finance the growing social spending on senior citizens. This is a big issue: China is getting old before it gets rich.

Figure 11.4 makes clear that countries such as India, Iran and Brazil have a young population, and a large cohort in the working age. This results in labour surplus, low dependency ratio and growing labour supply. It gives them a relatively easy growth pattern in which labour is not an obstacle but is seen as dividend. India will reach the Lewis turning point only around 2050. Countries such as the UK, Germany and Japan already passed the turning point. They have a demographic burden and do not, any more, have the window of opportunity to make use of relatively abundant (and cheap) labour.

Size of ageing and speed

There are many reasons for the Chinese miracle in the previous decades, but a major one was the country's favourable demographic structure. The growing working-age population (15–59) increased while the dependency ratio (ratio of non-working population to working population) was falling. The abundance of labour offset many negative elements such as the diminishing returns of investments and the low level (and growth) of productivity. The analysis above made clear that this is changing. It is not only changing, but is changing fast. Before giving some figures on ageing, some statistical remarks are needed. In several Chinese reports (CASS and NBS), the benchmark of becoming a senior is set at 60 years. This is logical from the Chinese point of view. Today, the retirement age for men is 60 years. In western reports (World Bank and UN), ageing relates to 65 years because that is the retirement age in most western countries. The UN defines a society as ageing when the proportion of people older than 60 is more than 10% of the population, or the number of people older than 65 exceeds 7%. The Chinese numbers are staggering. In early 2016, nationally, 9.7% of China's population was 65 years or older. In 2015, the number of older (65 plus) people in China (136 million) exceeds Japan's total population (126 million). In 2030, the total projected population of Japan plus Egypt (231 million) will be smaller than China's projected 65-and-older population (238 million). By 2050, it will take the combined total population of Japan, Egypt, Germany and

Australia (345 million) to match the older population in China (348 million). China will thus face the largest ageing-society challenge in the world (UN-WHO, 2015).

As can be seen in Fig. 11.5, the ageing of the population is not only a Chinese problem, but also a problem in most Asian countries. The growth of the 65-plus share between 2000 (7%) and 2050 (24%) will be 350% in China. Countries such as Brunei and Malaysia may even witness a 400% growth. All countries that are becoming grey before becoming rich are urgently looking for a solution to solve the ageing problem and financial burden related to this. The speed of ageing in China is fast. Although the share of the older population in Europe passed 10% in the 1930s, it will not exceed 30% until the 2030s, a century later. The same development of an increase of 20 percentage points is happening in China in just two generations. Obviously, the one-child policy intensified this ageing process of the Chinese society. The speed of ageing will also affect labour markets, in particular it will result in labour shortages.

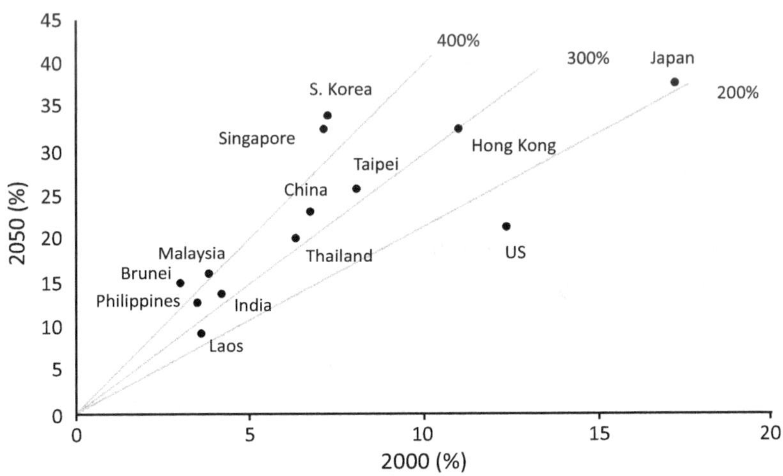

Figure 11.5 Share of 65 years and older; specific countries

Source: World Bank Database

11.5 Labour shortage

As the ageing problem continues to grow, it will have a big impact on the working-age population. Ageing will lower the working-age population and, linked to this, we will see a fall in the labour force. According to NBS-statistics, it will fall by an average of 8 million people annually from the mid-2020s onwards.

China's labour shortages first came into focus in 2004, when reports of migrant labour shortages in the export-oriented coastal regions began to emerge. Today, there is the view that anecdotal evidence of shortages of labour in some areas and large increases in (real) wages indicate that the Lewis turning point has been approached. As we stated earlier, we think that some time is still available before China reaches this point in which labour surplus change into a labour shortage. It is interesting to note that the discussion about labour shortages peaks every year at the end of January/early February. Many migrant workers who return to their hometowns for the spring festival holiday decide to stay there for a variety of reasons, including the lower cost of living, new prospects closer to home and wanting to be with children they had not seen for months or even years. This period is normally a period of labour shortage and a battle for hiring migrant workers, in particular in regions such as the Pearl River Delta. The consequences are that wages are increasing, migrant workers are not accepting poor housing conditions anymore and additional payments are becoming a normal phenomenon. This may give the impression of structural labour shortage.

But there is also a counteracting view. Evidence shows that labour shortage is very specific and should not be seen as a structural trend. For example, rising food prices and government measures improved the living conditions of farmers a lot, and consequently, there was no need for the migrants to leave the rural areas. But as soon as agricultural prices fall, migrant flows will start again. Furthermore, regional shortages (mostly in the southern coastal areas) are not the same as nationwide shortage of labour. In addition, not all workers are in strong demand; there may be shortage of female workers in the 18–25 age segment, but still surplus in

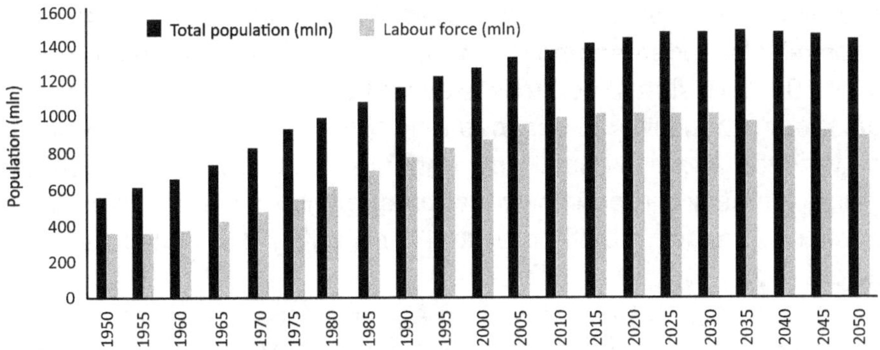

Figure 11.6 Population and labour force between 1950 and 2050

Note: *Despite the long term of the data, demographic statistics are relatively accurate over a long period of time*

Source: *NBS*

other cohorts. Specifically, after 2008, the shortage of labour was attributed to the enormous stimulus package that resulted in strong demand for low-skilled labour in the construction sector. But that has changed in the previous years with more and more industries fighting against overcapacity. To sum up all these arguments, we conclude that there is still (hidden) labour surplus available up to mid-2020s. This is a paradox: migrant labour shortage and at the same time still considerable volume of unskilled labour available.

Figure 11.6 gives information about the total population development and the growth of the labour force. Total population will grow up to the 2030s and will drop afterward. The development of the labour force is following the same pattern, but already in 2025, the labour force is falling. And this continues up to 2050.

Whether the Lewis turning point has been approached or not, the labour market issue demands action from the government. Some solutions are on the table and (first) discussions have started. To increase its labour force, even though the working-age population has started to decline, the Chinese authorities must increase the participation rate. This can be done through increasing the statutory retirement ages. Another measure to counteract the fall in the labour force is to improve access to education so that people can join the labour force more easily (and longer). Also, the shift towards services may help. Services create a larger number of physically undemanding jobs that people can keep doing through their 60s. This shift to services is essential. Even though the growth of labour productivity in services tend to be relatively low, the good news is that there is a lot of low hanging fruit to unlock productivity gains: increasing productivity just by opening up service industries (logistics, finance, healthcare) that are heavily dominated by inefficient SOEs.

By focusing on China's working-age population (aged 15–64), we see the decline in absolute numbers. Between 2010 and 2050, China's potential labour force will decline from 1 billion to 850 million people, a drop of 150 million people (Fig. 11.7(a)). The figure also shows the development of the working-age population in India. Because of a relatively young population, Indian's potential labour force will grow from 780 million in 2010 to 1.1 billion in 2050. Consequently, India will reach the Lewis turning point only around 2050. Also, the age group 15–64 years in Nigeria is growing, while this segment is falling in absolute numbers in countries such as Germany and South Korea (Fig. 11.7(b)). As can be seen, the UN expect that the age cohort 15–64 will rise in

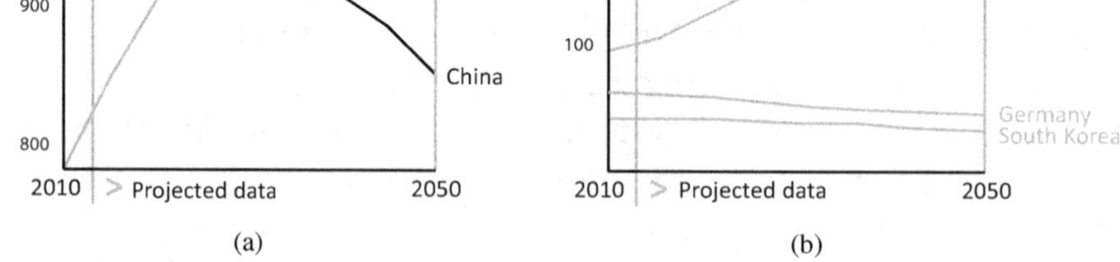

Figure 11.7 Development of working-age population between 2010 and 2055, specific countries and in millions

Note: The population age 15–64 is referred to as the potential labour force
Source: Based on UN database

the US up to 2050. It should be noted that this is based on migration laws and regulation during the Barack Obama presidency. There are indicators that the new president Mr Trump will implement stricter migration laws and as a consequence, the rise of the working-age population may be less than expected.

Obviously, labour shortage will have its impact on wages. Market wages will automatically rise because of the mismatch between high demand and low supply of labour. Wages are also determined by specific government policies. As part of the rebalancing process, the Chinese government aims to build-up a strong domestic market and stimulate consumption, hence increasing wages, including minimum wages. It should be noted that to achieve rebalancing, an increase of nominal wages above nominal GDP growth is required. It looks like this has started to happen.

In Fig. 11.8(a), the development of China's wages is given. While the annual wage in 2006 was 24,932 Renminbi (US$3,300), it moved up to 67,569 Renminbi (US$9,200) in 2016. There are large differences between cities. In Beijing, the average wage level in 2016 was 110,000 Renminbi, compared to a second-tier city like Harbin with an average wage-level of 72,000 Renminbi in 2016. The differences between the average national wage level and the wages in some of the largest cities makes clear that there exist a large gap between the urban and the rural regions. In Fig. 11.8(b), the legal minimum wages per month are shown. The minimum wage level for China is calculated as a weighted average of China's provinces and 40 largest cities as China's minimum wage varies both on a provincial and an urban level. The minimum wage should be seen as the floor; in reality, most salaries will be higher. It is obvious that since the introduction of the revised labour law in 2008, China's workers are now much better off than before and are amongst some of the best paid in Asia. China's average labour cost is second only to Malaysia but significantly higher compared to countries such as Vietnam, Indonesia, India and Philippines.

The one-child policy prevented many births (although the estimation of 400 million may be overstated). After 1981 it was seen

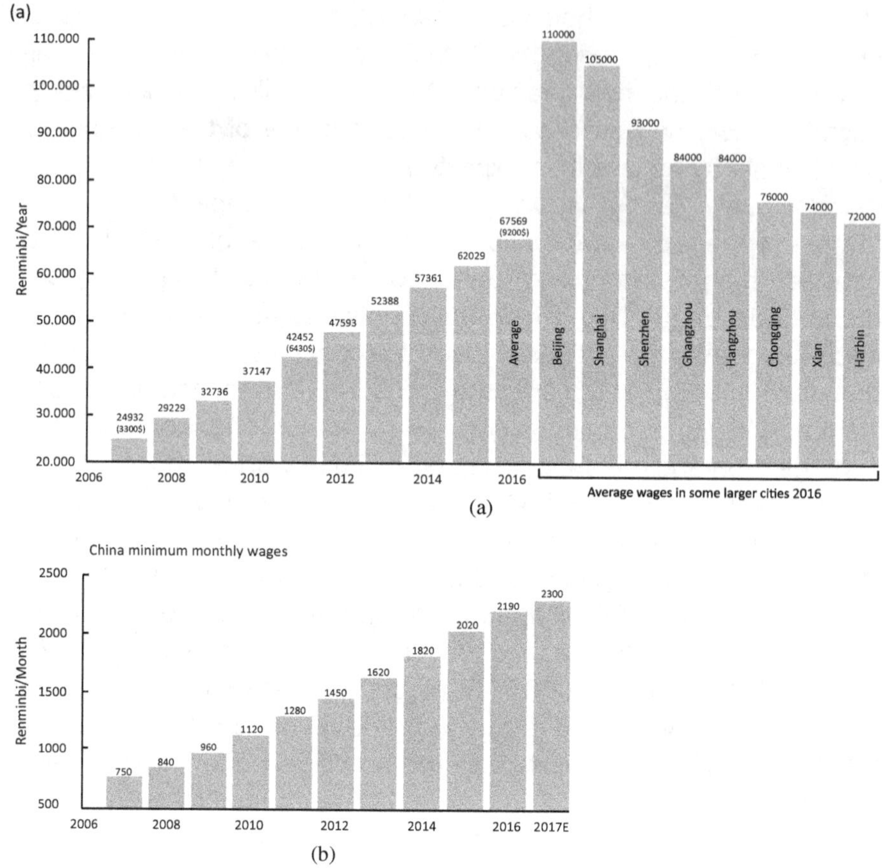

Figure 11.8 China's wage development, 2006–2017

Note: *The minimum monthly wages are the net wages without mandatory welfare payments which could reach 50–60% of the net wage. 2017E is the expected minimum monthly wage*
Source: *NBS-statistics, December 2016*

as a good and logical policy to increase welfare per head of the population. China, today, and perhaps the world, in general, are better off in multiple ways as a result of the success in controlling population size. In a special report, *The Economist* (20 September 2014) on global efforts to curb greenhouse gas emissions, ranks China's one-child policy as the fourth most important policy or action contributing towards this goal in recent decades. The one-child policy was logical considering the low dependency ratio, the labour surplus and the growing labour force. But this environment changed dramatically. Developments in the 1990s and 2000s reduced the fertility rate significantly to 1.5 on average, but in cities it dropped to 0.7, not even one-child per woman. We see an increasing dependency ratio, a decline in the labour force, first indications of labour shortage and increasing wages. Hence, the family planning policy changed and in 2015 the one-child policy was officially abandoned.

Whether this policy change is enough and on time should be seen. The two-child policy that was implemented in early-2016 may help. As stated earlier, there were 1 million more births in 2016 compared to 2015 which had 16 million births. However, this increase may not be the result of the new policy. 2015 was the year of the sheep, and this was widely perceived to be a not-so-good year to having children. Many couples may have postponed having children in 2015 to wait for 2016, the year of the monkey. Furthermore, as countries develop and educational and employment opportunities for women grow, childbearing tends to be postponed. So, it clearly depends on additional measures such as social welfare, costs of living, housing and kindergarten access. You may question the effectiveness of these measures in the present context. More is needed. In the *China Daily* of 27 July 2014, there was an item about a Japanese local official who suggested a bizarre solution to overcome the demographic crisis in Japan. He suggested that deliberately punctured condoms must be distributed to married couples to increase the birth rate. If a problem becomes so intense, all kind of solutions are put on the table. The editorial strongly stated that this specific action should not be done by the Chinese authorities but that out of the box measures may be needed.

For the first time in Chinese history the Chinese authorities are confronted with shortage of labour. This gives some discomfort and a strong believe that structural reforms are needed. These structural reforms will take a large part out of the government budget; the topic of the next chapter.

Chapter 12

Fiscal and Monetary Policy to Fine-tune the Economy

Myth 12: China's fiscal and monetary policy cannot prevent a collapse of the financial system

12.1 Introduction

In principle, there are three instruments that can be used to boost or deflate the economy in the short run; you may label these instruments as crisis tools. These instruments are fiscal policy, monetary policy and the policy regarding the value of the currency (the topic of Chapter 13). Fiscal policy involves the government changing the levels of taxation and government spending in order to influence the level of aggregate demand in the economy and, therefore, growth of GDP. If the government (central and local combined) is spending more than it receives through taxation (and some non-taxation items), resulting in a budget deficit, it stimulates the economy through an expansionary fiscal policy. Clearly, this policy is not a free lunch; spending more than received means a budget deficit. Cumulation of previous budget deficits creates a public debt which, at the end of the day, must be paid back. If the debt becomes too high, it will be a burden for the economy due to the interest payments and the impact on credibility of the country. This is why textbooks are indicating that in a boom period, the government must execute a deflationary fiscal policy, cutting government expenditures and/or raising taxes and creating a government surplus. In this way, earning money to repay the public debt. As stated in the previous chapters, China is among the most decentralised countries in the world as far as fiscal policy is concerned. Seeking the optimum balance between decentralising and centralising fiscal policy is a continues quest.

Monetary policy, involving setting the interest rate, is done by the People's Bank of China (PBC), the central bank. An increase in the interest rate will deflate demand in the economy, while a fall in interest will stimulate spending through higher consumption and domestic investments. Until recently, the PBC fixed the benchmark saving (deposit) and lending rates, and banks were only allowed to deviate from this interest rate within a very narrow margin. On the surface, the financial sector looks very much like any other developed economy's financial sector with banking and non-banking institutions, domestic and foreign banks, private and state-owned banks, stock and bond markets, and central bank and financial regulators. However, if you look beneath the surface, you will find a series of characteristics that distinguish the Chinese financial sector from any modern financial sector in the developed world. For example, China has an extreme bank-dominated financial system. This emphasis on bank loans instead of the capital market is not unique; you can also see it in other Asian countries, as well in countries such as Germany, but the size of the banking sector in China is overwhelming.

With respect to monetary policy, we will see that banks are subject to much political influence from the central government. Consequently, the government is able to use monetary policy relatively easily; this is very helpful in periods of economic crisis.

The chapter is organised as follows. Section 12.2 gives a historical overview and the main features regarding China's fiscal policy. This is followed (in Section 12.3) by the choices on fiscal policy after 2008 up to today, including the different stimulus packages. Section 12.4 focusses on the debt picture, local government debt specifically. After discussing the fiscal policy, we move to monetary policy by first discussing the role of the central bank and the state banks in China (Sections 12.5 and 12.6) and followed by a discussion of the latest developments in monetary policy, in particular related to interest rate policy (Section 12.7).

12.2 Main features of China's fiscal policy

Fiscal policy is influencing total demand in the economy through the government expenditures and the taxation revenues. For a long time during China's development, the government decided not to use active fiscal policy. For example, in the pre-reform period, between 1958 and 1978, there were basically no government deficits and China did not issue either foreign or domestic debt (Kuijs and Gao Xu, 2008). A debt was seen as an "owing issue", which gives an uncomfortable feeling. Of course, this discontent with debt (and the burden to pay it back) was the result of the massive debt burden associated with the century of humiliation (Chapter 2). As can be seen in Fig. 12.1, between 1979 and 2016, limited government deficits occurred. Government borrowing became a normal pattern due to government deficits associated with the Asian financial crisis and the effect of the stimulus package that was

Figure 12.1 Budget deficit and surplus over the years 1978–2016

Note: Not including policy loans and NPLs and between 1979 and 1993, adjusted according international practice

Source: China Statistical Bureau-Yearbook, various years

implemented in 2008–2009 to fight the world financial and economic crisis. Also, the smaller stimulus packages of 2012 and 2014 resulted in larger budget deficits.

Data on China's budget deficits differ substantially between organisations. This makes interpretation of the data not very easy. A significant part of government spending and revenues is not included in the official budget. These are the so-called extra or off-budget expenditures. For example, social security funds (pensions, medical expenses and unemployment benefits) are not included in the government budget. It also does not include the activities of the state-owned enterprises (SOEs). This makes the analysis complicated because we know that these SOEs (and banks) appear to play a large role in infrastructure investment that exploded after 2008. Not only do we see off-budget expenditures at the central level, but, in particular, the off-budget expenditures of local government are high, vastly rising and difficult to find accurate figures.

Building up local debt

One of the typical features of China's fiscal policy is its strong decentralisation. In previous chapters, this economic decentralisation has been discussed. Now the focus is specifically on the debt issue which resulted from this decentralisation process.

In the early 1990s, the regional governments collected about 80% of the total tax revenues and accounted for 70% of the total expenditure (Lin Shuanglin, 2009). Before 1994, the Chinese tax system was decentralised to local governments, but it should be noted that despite this high share of localisation, in principle, the local government had little or no formal ability to set its own tax policies or tax rates. That was set at the central level. In 1994, the large fiscal centralisation process was implemented and the central government share of revenues jumped from 22% in 1993 to 60% in 1994 (and stayed around 50% through 2016). With respect to expenditures, the share of the local governments increased dramatically after 1994 to around 90% in 2016 (NBS). Local governments suddenly found that they continued to carry most of the responsibilities for spending on local public goods but that there was a large gap between what they had to spend and what the central government gave them. And this situation stayed (and even intensified) during the late 1990s and 2000s.

Fiscal policy in China imposed a structural operating deficit on local governments. Local governments were still forced to execute the centralised strategy but with less and less "own" money. Although local governments knew that they would receive money for their tasks, in practise, the transfer system worked poorly and it created uncertainty. This shortage of finance came in the period of the large SOE reforms. Due to the massive layoff of SOE workers, urbanisation plans and houses in urban centres, large sums of money were needed. Waiting to receive it from the central government was not an option. The lack of money allocated from the central government encouraged local governments to look for their own resources to fund projects, which would help them to accelerate growth (and gain recognition and promotion). So, one important outcome of the 1994 tax reform was that the local government had expenditure responsibilities far in excess of their direct revenue resources. As we will see later in this chapter, the local governments found solutions for this shortage of money, in particular through confiscating land. The government owns all land and farmers are merely granted land use rights and are forbidden to sell or use this land as collateral for loans. Consequently, land as well as farmers are an easy target for local government. They used the land as their own collateral. Since the price of urban land had been artificially suppressed, the difference between the actual land price and its expected value after redevelopment was enormous. Local governments recognised this and began to borrow based on the expected increase in land values.

12.3 Fiscal policy after 2008

The 10-year period between 2008 and 2017 can be divided into three periods. The first period of fiscal policy between 2008–2009, focused on stabilising the economy from the dramatic collapse in export due to the global economic crisis. The government acted as a crisis manager. Between 2010 and 2015, fiscal policy was navigating through cyclical ups and downs but the focus shifted more towards rebalancing and the longer term. In the latest 13th five-year plan that was published in 2016, some new elements with respect to fiscal policy have been introduced.

The stimulus package of 2008

In November 2008, the Chinese government announced and directly implemented a 4-trillion-Renminbi stimulus package to counteract the fall in export and to stimulate the economy. This stimulus package was equivalent to 13% of China's 2008 GDP, which was considerably larger in size than countries such as the US, Germany and Brazil (Fig. 12.2(a)). It resulted in an enormous investment boom; the investment contribution to GDP increased from 47% in 2008 to 88% in 2009. The fiscal stimulus was harmonised by monetary measures to make credits available and cheaper. The investment focus can be seen in Fig. 12.2(b). Most of the additional money was allocated to infrastructural investments and housing.

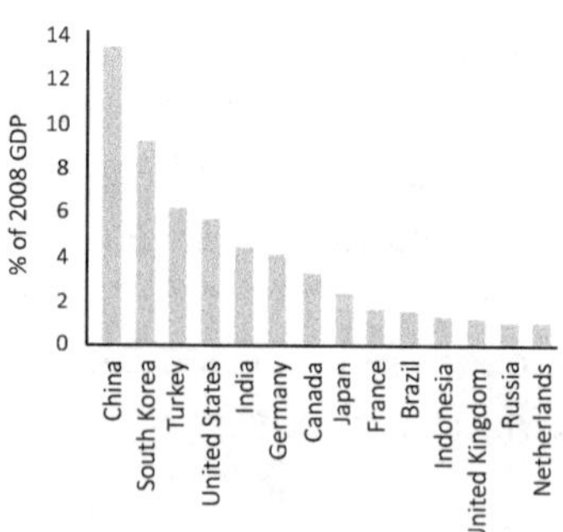

(a)

4-trillion-Renminbi stimulus package	(10-billion-Renminbi)	%
Transport & Power infrastructure	170	42.4
Post-earthquake reconstruction	100	25
Rural infrastructure	37	9.3
Environmental investments	35	8.8
Public housing	28	7
Innovation and economic restructuring	16	4
Healthcare & Education	14	3.5

Note: part of the increased expenditures in infrastructure relate to education and culture
Large differences in using additional expenditures (e.g. China, France) or declining taxation (e.g. Netherlands)

(b)

Figure 12.2 Fiscal stimulus in response to the 2008–2009 crisis; percentage of 2008 GDP (a) and allocation of money within the stimulus package (b)

Source: ILO (2011) and China National Development and Reform Commission (Xinhuanet-website)

This large fiscal stimulus package of 2008 was one-sidedly focused on stimulating the economy. Arguments regarding the need to rebalance were not important. Stimulation was needed even though it would increase the imbalances further. The result was that China witnessed only a soft landing. The negative side-product of the large stimulus package was that it created some sectoral overcapacity, bubbles and inflationary pressure.

The period 2010–2015: Finding the balance

After the first crisis was counteracted, the aim and measures of fiscal policy shifted more to the rebalancing process. Fiscal policy shifted from (infrastructural) investments (and helping SOEs) to social spending that includes social protection, healthcare and education. Finance was also allocated to environmental problems with less spending on heavy industry and more spending on green initiatives and fighting distortions on the energy market, essentially by making industrial inputs such as energy and water more expensive. Social spending received a lot of attention, but this was not new. Strong growth in social spending as part of the fiscal policy to rebalance the economy started with the 11th five-year plan that set the following objectives to be accomplished by 2010:

- Setting up a basic healthcare system for both urban and rural people, including a national basic (and free) drug system
- Implementing a standardised medical insurance scheme
- Developing a community health service system in the urban areas to provide public health as well as basic medical services to the urban residents

In August 2012, China presented a new 8-trillion-Renminbi stimulus package to boost economic development again. This was necessary because the economy appears to be cooling faster than expected. New stimulus was possible because inflationary pressure went down in 2011 and 2012. Part of this stimulation (that already started before the official launch of the stimulus package) was the faster approval process of investments. Only in April 2012, the National Development and Reform Commission approved 4 new airports and 100 clean energy projects. Besides speeding up investments via faster approval procedures, the stimulus package consisted of building subsidised houses. An important learning point from the previous stimulus package of 2008 was that a lack of worthwhile investment opportunities inevitably drive private capital into a few narrow-defined industries. This was partly responsible for bubbles such as in the urban real estate. Therefore, the new stimulus package also involved measures to open some formerly closed sectors for private investments. This opening up may make those sectors more competitive while helping the economy to develop in a more balanced way.

Also, the 2014 stimulus package which was referred to as a "fresh round of mini-stimulus" was focused to counter growth headwinds. The total stimulus package of almost 2-trillion-Renminbi focused again on the environment and on increasing social spending. It should be noted that the stimulus packages of 2012 and 2014 were quite different from the massive 4-trillion-Renminbi stimulating plan at the end of 2008. The 2008–2009 plan was designed to primary bail out large SOEs. In contrast, the mini-stimuli of 2012 and 2014 contain no favours to SOEs and no new money for local governments. It was mostly spent on new houses, social benefits and targeted infrastructure such as high-speed trains.

From the surface, it looks like the expansionary fiscal policy in the previous years was only focused on maintaining economic growth and, therefore, should be seen as a step back in the process of rebalancing. Experts were extremely negative about this additional spending in 2012–2014 after the large stimulus package of 2008 and 2009. They criticised the additional spending as easy money for local governments and SOEs, and as abandoning of the commitment to reform. However, as stated before, the picture is slightly different. The stimulus packages after 2010 were not a repetition of the 2008–2009 stimulus. Instead of throwing money at the problem, as was done in 2008, the government aimed for a more managed and selective stimulus. In addition, the stimulus package was substantially smaller in size and most of the measures fit in the rebalancing agenda. For example, several of the measures related to strengthening domestic demand of energy saving and environmental-friendly consumer products; subsidies worth of 26-billion-Renminbi became available for home refrigerators, washing machines and heaters. Billions of Renminbi were made available for LED and other energy efficient lighting, cars with engine capacity below 1.6 litres and hybrid buses. Another example of fiscal policy in line with the rebalancing process is the affordable housing programme which started in 2010. The overview of measures clearly indicates that the (mini) stimulus packages were targeted to social spending, consumer durables and "green" product"; all in line with the rebalancing process.

Fiscal policy after 2016

The focus in the newest 13th five-year plan (2016–2020) with respect to public finance is on reducing expenditures by local government, increasing social spending and controlling the large local debt. In one of the paragraphs in the report of the State Council associated with the 13th five-year plan, the following section on reducing government expenditures and increasing supervision on local government policy and expenses is given: "We will be stricter on spending on official overseas trips, vehicles for official use, and official hospitality. We will reduce meetings, reform the system for the use of official cars and further reduce administrative costs. Furthermore, building large gymnasiums and stadiums is subject to central approval [...] We will strengthen supervision of local government debt and guard against risks. We will continue to deal with outstanding debts properly by classifying them into different categories and managing them accordingly. [...] We will further investigate and standardise financing companies run by local governments" (Xinhua). This quotation gives a feeling of the enormous task in the field of fiscal policy; so many intertwined issues and so many changes are needed, and all need prompt action.

The quotation also makes clear that the local government (and SOEs) debt is a big concern. Despite some bankruptcies, the central government made it clear that they do not intend to permit large defaults, not from local governments and not from big SOEs. Consequently, the Chinese government will remain to face the inconvenient trade-off between accommodative policies and fast growth versus reforming the structure of its economy in the upcoming years. Having said this, the government seems to be less focused on cyclical growth and more on structural reforms. Until now, this choice was relatively easy because the labour market is stable. But soon, as unemployment is moving up, the government may use the break on the reform agenda. Therefore, we expect that a considerable part of the (future) subsidies will still be linked to SOEs because opening up previously monopolised industries will hurt SOEs and some protection is needed.

12.4 The debt picture

Total debt consist of borrowed money from the local government, central government, companies (in particular SOEs) and households. We start with the analysis of local government debt. The tax reform of 1994 in combination with the incentive to invest in infrastructure and housing, and the shortage of money received from central government resulted in a tendency of the local officials to find other sources of finance. Local governments began to borrow against expected increase in land values. However, there was a formal prohibition on local government borrowing. Therefore, cities usually transferred land assets into a special-purpose company, later termed as Local Government Financing Vehicles (LGFVs). In 2011, China had more than 10,000 LGFVs created by local governments to fund the building of roads and other infrastructure as part of the 4-trillion-Renminbi stimulus package. And in early 2011, net revenues from land sales and leases accounted for 20% of local government revenues and peaked to 27% in 2015, before falling to

25% in 2016 (NBS). The loans came directly and indirectly from the banking sector.

The central authorities encouraged the use of these LGFVs and building up debt. The idea was that spending on infrastructural investments will generate revenues (and growth of GDP), enough to pay back the debt. However, the rate of return on many of these projects is much lower than the interest rate promised when these debts were raised. Furthermore, there was a maturity mismatch; local government normally borrowed for 3–5 years to finance their infrastructure whose benefits (and revenue streams) would only materialise over two or three decades. It means that payment will come before they have enough revenue to repay them. According to some investment banks and rating agencies, this will certainly lead to financing problems and defaults in the next coming years.

The speed of building up local debt has been extremely fast. The local public debt was around 24% of GDP in 2013 but had reached 40% in 2016 (NBS). The officially reported numbers may even understate true magnitudes. Local governments can borrow in a variety of non-transparent ways, including through a shadow banking system that has expanded significantly in recent years. According to BBVA Research, shadow banking assets amount to 83% of GDP and 27% of total banking assets as of end-2016.

In 2016, China's central government debt stood at 18% of GDP. This means that the official gross public debt stands at 58%, which is still low by international standards. But be aware that certain expenditures (such as bank restructuring costs due to cleaning up the non-performing loans) are not included in the official figures, and we miss the shadow bank activities. A positive point is that the majority of public debt-financed infrastructure is likely to have a positive impact on economic growth eventually. The consensus view is that as long GDP growing at 6% annually, government debt is not the key problem in China.

The main debt problem in China is the debt of inefficient SOEs that borrowed money to finance their (unprofitable) investments, partly because they had to obey the government directives. The level (and growth) of this corporate debt deserves the most attention, logical with almost 160% of GDP in 2016. As with the local debt, the acceleration in corporate over-borrowing can be traced back to the 2008 stimulus package. Easy money in combination with implicit guarantees to SOEs have led to misallocation of resources, helping a low productive industrial sector. It also had another negative side-effect: no credits were left over for the dynamic, growing and job-generating small and medium-sized enterprises (SMEs), hence the growth of the shadow bank system.

Besides the government and corporate debt, we also have the household debts. The debt of households as percentage of GDP is relatively low with 45% in 2016 (BBVA and Nomura Research). So, we have low central government debt, high local government debt, low household debt and extremely high corporate debt.

Until 2008, the gross debt (of households, corporations and governments) was around 140%. By the end of 2014, this figure had risen to 230%, and today (early 2017) it has increased to 280% of GDP. The level of debt is not itself worrisome. With its economic growth, China will have more income to service its debt. It also has a lot of assets available that could be sold to pay down debt. The problem of this debt is not its absolute size, but its rapid expansion. Between 2010 and 2016, government debt increased at an annual rate of more than 20%, much higher than the nominal expansion of GDP during the same period. We should be worried by the rapidly rising leverage, but we don't believe China is on the brink of a debt crisis. The central government ratio of debt to GDP is still low. Furthermore, as almost all government debt is denominated in China's own currency and held domestically, the central bank can prevent a crisis with its unlimited access to liquidity, driven by national savings. The classic trigger for an emerging market debt crisis is an inability to pay back foreign lenders. This is obviously not the case in China. Its foreign borrowings are small (10% of GDP) and its gigantic foreign reserves give it plenty of ammunition to fight a speculative attack and preserve the value of its currency. Furthermore, China runs an annual current account surplus of 2% or 3% of GDP. But having said this, solving the local government and corporate debt is needed to make sure that a major debt problem in the banking sector is not happening. Problems in repaying debt will have an impact on the banking sector, and the same holds for the LGFVs. Corporate debt is becoming increasingly hard to service by the SOEs. Many SOEs have operated in an environment of protectionism, government support, low efficiency and excess capacity for a long time. This is something that needs to change, meaning that some of these companies will have to close. Banks will be negatively affected, in particular now that their interest earnings are under attack. Non-performing loans (NPLs) increased during the 2008–2016 period. It is difficult to get a precise picture of the proportion of NPLs within Chinese banks. It ranges from 1.8% (NBS, based on Chinese Central Bank Data) to 5% of total bank loans (Credit Suisse, 2015).

Despite uncertainty about the figures, the general conclusion is that the local debt problem is large but manageable. However, in the longer term, discipline is needed and, consequently, default is also needed. The first steps to solve the local government debt were the ban of the LGFVs in 2015 and debt-restructuring into long-term bonds. In the first issues of local bonds in 2015, all carried virtually the same interest rate and were very close to the rate on central government treasury bonds. This showed that investors saw these bonds as central-government-guaranteed securities. Hence, investors expect a bail out by the central government if that is needed. A relative new step is to have more and more public–private partnerships within infrastructural investments.

12.5 Monetary policy

Monetary policy can stimulate or deflate total spending through the interest rate transmission mechanism. This works as follows: the fall of the lending interest rate encourage firms to invest, since it is cheaper to borrow money. It also encourages consumers to spend, since borrowing through personal loans and credit cards is now cheaper. At the same time, it discourages savings. This net effect can be seen in total spending. The same holds when increasing the

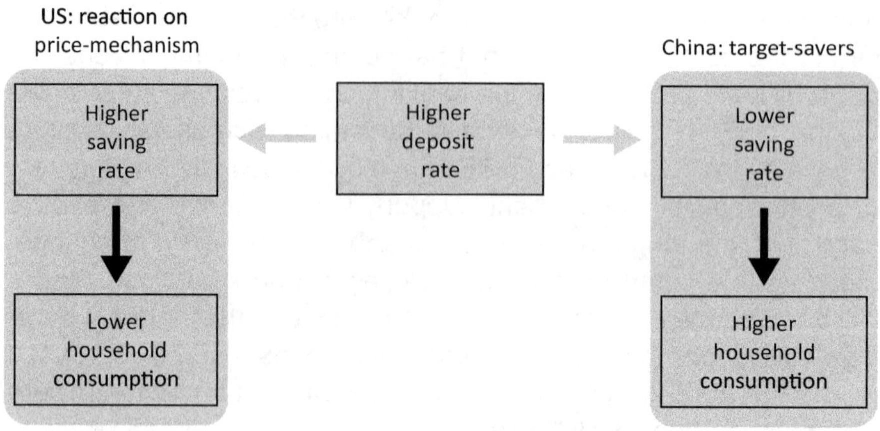

Figure 12.3 Reaction on monetary policy
Source: Adjusted from Lardy (2013)

interest rate. This will increase savings and reduce consumption, as shown on the left side of Fig. 12.3. Although monetary policy is broadly working in the same way as we see in the west, there are certain Chinese features that make the outcome of monetary policy a bit uncertain. There were some periods in time when higher deposit rates actually lowered the saving rate. This looks paradoxical but can be explained by the fact that many Chinese households are target savers. They save for a certain specific goal. If you need to save 100,000 Renminbi for the education of your child within six years, the interest rate will affect your saving behaviour. This is shown on the right side of Fig. 12.3. The target-saver context is a Chinese characteristic but it is an exceptional situation, where, in many cases, we see that monetary policy is being used in the same way and with the same assumptions as in the west.

Before 2015, the PBC was able to set the interest rate by directive. This is different from the reality of market economies, where setting this interest rate is done through intervening in the money market to ensure that the interest rate that has been announced is also the equilibrium interest rate on the market. After 2015, a more market-oriented interest rate has been established, that gives more freedom to the banks.

Historical overview

During the pre-reform period (1949–1978), China effectively had one bank, the PBC, which was both the central bank and the only commercial bank that accepted deposits and granted loans. The government (under auspices of the party) fully controlled the PBC. In fact, it was organised as a department of the Ministry of Finance and headed by the State Council. In the planned economy of the 1950s and 1960s, the interest and allocation of credits was done by the government.

The first step in building up a more mature financial sector occurred in 1979. In that year, two banks (Bank of China (BOC) and China Construction Bank (CCB)) were separated from the PBC and the Ministry of Finance. They specialised in foreign exchange transactions (BOC) and large investment projects (CCB), respectively. In the same year, the Agriculture Bank of China (ABC) was established to handle agriculture-related commercial bank activities. In 1983, the transfer of commercial activities from the PBC was completed when the fourth state-owned commercial bank, Industrial and Commercial Bank of China (ICBC), was established. These four banks dominated the financial system from mid-1980s to mid-2000s in terms of branches, employment, deposits and credits. For example, in 2007, 70–75% of total bank credit was done by these banks. Anno 2017, the Big Four share of total bank loans shrank to around 50%, but even today they dominate many aspects of the banking sector.

From mid-1980s onwards, the government allowed some competition in the banking sector. Several regional banks started operations (both rural and urban), such as Merchants Bank and the Shanghai Pudong Development Bank. The first private bank, Minsheng Bank, was established in 1995. In the mid-1990s, the government established three policy banks to ease the burden of lending for the Big Four. The three policy banks are China Development Bank, The Export–Import Bank and the Development Bank. The aim was to finance government-directed projects that would likely not generate a commercial rate of return. Also, foreign banks were permitted to operate in China, although in a gradual way.

Prior to 1991, foreign banks were only allowed to conduct business in special economic zones, later new areas were opened up, starting with coastal cities. The initial scope of business for foreign banks was limited to foreign currency and export-finance activities. After China's entry into the WTO in 2001, it became easier for foreign banks to conduct business in China. By 2016, there were around 130 foreign banks present in China (KPMG 2016 and CEIC 2016). However, foreign banks' share of total banking assets and liabilities remain marginal. Only 1.4% of the commercial banking assets were held by foreign banks in 2016 (CEIC Data). A final step in the banking sector history was the international public offerings. In the autumn of 2005, CCB raised more than US$8 billion on its initial public offering in Hong Kong. The other banks followed, first the BOC, then the ICBC. Finally, in 2010, the Agricultural Bank of China was the latest of the Big Four to get (partly) listed on the stock market. Although, their market share fell considerably in the previous year, they are extremely big entities. In 2016, these banks occupied the top four places of the largest banks worldwide in terms of assets (S&P Global Market Intelligence).

12.6 Key issues of the financial sector and the role of banks

Key challenges of the Chinese financial sector are the structural problem of bad loans in the banking system, the independency (and credibility) of the central bank, the dominance of banks within the financial sector, the shortage of capital for small and medium-sized companies, and the emergence of the shadow banking sector.

Building up bad debt

From the start of the reforms in 1978 to the late 1990s, the state-owned banks financed the investments of the SOEs. The central government reduced direct financing more and more, and the banks took over the responsibility by increasing credit. Bank loans to GDP increased from 50% to 120% in this period. By the mid-1990s, over one-half of the SOEs were making losses and non-performing loans increased substantially. In 1998, the NPLs exceeded 40% of the total outstanding loans (Bonin, 2002). The government reacted by establishing four asset management companies in 1999, one for each of the four large state-owned banks. Bad loans were extracted from the banks and placed in these specialised asset management companies. This process was finished in 2000 when the banks were relived from the troubling loans. In addition, steps were taken to increase profitability of the banks. The sequence in the steps taken to solve the bad loan issue can be summarised as follows:

- Separate out the NPLs from the state banks
- Once the bad NPLs were separated, the banks could then lend on a commercial basis, meaning they can refuse loans
- The government worked on rationalising the small and large SOEs. This means a combination of restructuring and bankruptcies
- The central bank fixed the interest rate floors and ceilings so that the banks were guaranteed a large interest margin. The profit made it possible to write down any remaining bad loans on their books
- The banks were open for strategic shareholders to put new money in the banking system

The measures helped and China escaped from its financial crisis in the 1990s and was able to keep the bad loan problem manageable in the 2000s. However, an important learning point is that it escaped mainly through fast economic growth. Looking back, one can say that the quality of bank lending has gradually improved, with more of it going to the dynamic private sector. But, after 2008, loans to SOEs grew fast with all the potential risks associated with it. Despite a low percentage of bad debt compared to 1999, it is still a concern, in particular because fast economic growth with double digits is not helping anymore. What is needed is a growth rate of credit that is substantially lower than GDP growth. Only then the debt to GDP ratio can fall. Looking at the previous decade, it appears to be very difficult to cut back credit growth.

Independency

The PBC is not independent. Article 2 of the Law on PBC states, "The People's Bank of China shall, under leadership of the State Council, formulate and implement monetary policies" (PBC website). Hence, the PBC is under the leadership of the State Council or more accurately under auspices of the Party's Politburo. This means that the PBC cannot freely set its final or intermediate targets. Its policy is severely constrained by its obligation to follow the central government targets and execute the government choices. The State Council sets annual inflation and growth targets, and decides the state of monetary policy (interest rate and growth of the money supply): being expansionary or restrictive. Government interference is also visible when looking at credit quotas. Until the late-1990s, the State Council, through the central bank decided on credit quotas to specific sectors which had to be followed by the general banks. And even though official credit quotas were abolished in 1998, the PBC still holds monthly meetings with the banks to discuss and advise about the credit conditions across sectors. The period 2008–2009 made clear that this guidance (or direct instructions) from the PBC on the commercial banks' lending decisions is still happening.

Dominance of banks

In China, the banks are the financial system. In 2010, more than 80% of all corporate capital raised came from the banking sector. The share fell to 60% in 2016 because the securities market has since gained additional market share (CEIC). The relative weight of banks in finance is roughly comparable to that of Germany in the 1980s or South Korea in the 1990s, and is higher than in other emerging market today. In 2016, the banking sector employed about 2.5 million workers. Almost half were employed by the Big-Four with 310,000 employees working at BOC (CEIC Data).

As stated before, Chinese banks are among the largest companies worldwide, in terms of assets, sales and profits. Before 2015, by far, the largest driver behind their profits was their net interest margin, the difference between lending and deposit rate. Banks such as the Industrial and Commercial Bank of China and the Agricultural Bank of China made more than 70% of their profits due to this net interest income between 2009 and 2015 (Xinhua). In 2016, we saw a shrinking net interest margin as a result of a series of rate cuts driven by the government's policy to liberalise interest rates. Their massive size and their important role in the economy (system banks) make it necessary to protect them by an implicit guarantee of the central bank and government.

SMEs and banking loans

One should keep in mind that, until the 1980s, the main job of the banks was to collect deposits from individuals and companies, and to extend working-capital loans to SOEs. They made virtually no loans to private firms or households. Despite the increased competition and commercialising of the banking sector, the main role of the large banks remained feeding the large SOEs with capital according to the wishes of the government.

In 2015, China's capital market was still heavily segmented. On one hand, there are large and cash-rich SOEs that have easy access to (cheap) credit, in many cases, backed by the government. On the other hand, we see smaller private firms that are struggling to get finance. This financial constraint faced by the private sector in accessing the capital market was an important driver behind the growth of shadow banks.

Shadow bank system

Shadow banking is the credit intermediation involving entities and activities outside the regular banking system. It does not mean that banks are not involved in shadow bank activities; they are heavily involved through wealth management products and other off-balance sheet activities. Off-balance activities are outside the books of the banks and not subject to banking-legislation. The growth of shadow bank activities after 2008 can be explained by several drivers:

- The stimulus package following the financial crisis led to a rapid increase in local government lending: most of the extra spending was carried out by local governments. Part of the funding was done through the earlier-mentioned LGFVs. Shadow banks acted as an alternative source of funding these LGFVs, besides the regular bank loans.
- Wealth management products emerged because depositors only received around 3% return on their money. This is low when inflation rose to around 5% in 2010. The real one-year interest rate on deposits was negative during most of the 2006–2010 period (Elliott and Yan, 2013).
- PBC operated a strict control on interest rates in this period. These factors led investors, enterprises and wealthy individuals to seek the shadow market for higher returns.
- Small and medium-sized firms found it hard to raise capital from the large state-owned banks and then looked for other sources in the informal market, including the shadow banks.
- Shortage of finance occurred because the authorities tried to control money supply. To limit the growth in loans, the authorities increased the banks' required reserves ratios several times during 2010 and 2011, and less money was available from the formal banking sector.

Shadow banking grew to play a role that the banks and government could not fulfil: providing loans to new sources of demand in the economy. Between 2010 and 2014, annual growth in bank lending stayed fairly stable at around 14%, but there was a massive increase in shadow lending. It drove total credit growth to a peak of 23% in 2013 (NBS). Shadow banking is not a problem in itself and, considering the narrow financial market in China, it is rather a good thing that extra financing takes place outside of the banking sector. Sheng *et al.* (2015), for example, pointed out that China's formal banking sector does not provide sufficient credit to the SMEs and retail sectors, creating a vacuum that fosters shadow banking activities. Similarly, Elliott and Qiao (2015) argued that the societal benefits associated with China's shadow banking sector appear to outweigh the risks since they benefit small and private firms which are disadvantaged by the formal banking sector. But the problem of this shadow banking is the close link to the regular banking sector (either via trust companies that rely on bank funding or the Wealth Management Products developed by the banks themselves). A crisis in the non-regulated activities of the banks can easily transferred to the formal banking sector. After 2015, the shadow banking and shadow bank loans have been falling in importance. A more liberalised operating environment for banks helps to move shadow bank activities into the regular banking system. The complete deregulation of lending and deposit interest rates that took place in late-2015 reduced the role of shadow banks further and this may continue in the next coming years.

12.7 Interest rate policy and steps towards liberalisation

Until recently, the PBC set the benchmark interest rate of the one-year lending rate and the one-year deposit rate. Before 1997, interest rates offered by the commercial banks were not allowed to differ from the benchmark interest rates at all in either direction (Lardy, 2012). Besides the interest rate, the PBC also used a set of administrative guidelines and quantitative-based instruments to regulate lending. From 1997 to early 2003, the inflation-adjusted interest rate for one-year deposits was almost 3%. The real interest rate was quite high, driven by the low inflation in this period, with even years of deflation. But this changed after Hu Jintao adopted a classic financial repression strategy in 2004 and set the deposit rate (2%) below the rate of inflation (3.7%) in 2004. The deposit rates were below inflation in most of the period between 2004 and 2015. So, Xi Jinping followed this policy during the first years of his presidency. Financial repression refers to a set of policies designed to channel funds away from households towards the government to finance investments. This low interest rate is a hidden tax on depositors, but it helped SOEs. By subsidising polluting and capital intensive industries with cheap money, it made the environmental issue worse and increased the imbalances in the economy.

A first step in financial liberalisation was the abolishment of the lending rate ceiling in 2004, followed one decade later by the removal of the lending rate floor. However, the more important control on deposit rates continues up to 2015. Finally, on 23 October, the authorities announced the official abolishment of the caps on deposit rates nationwide, and one may say that, today, we have full interest rate liberalisation. This interest rate liberalisation was introduced as a pilot in the Shanghai free trade zone (SFTZ) that started in 2013. In the SFTZ, banks could set their own interest rates and compete for deposits instead of them being centrally set by the PBC. After experimenting with this interest regime, the pilot was implemented for the whole country.

Figure 12.4 summarises China's monetary policy between 2003 and 2017. To ensure sustainable and steady development of the economy and maintain a stable price level, the PBC has adjusted its monetary policy several times after 2006. To protect the economy

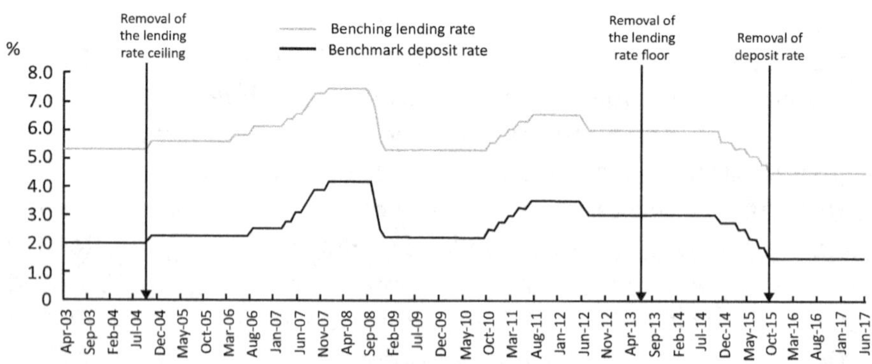

Figure 12.4 Monetary policy and the process of interest rate liberalisation; 1-year lending and deposit rate, 2003–2017

Source: *BBVA Research*

from overheating, it increased the interest rates in several steps in 2007. In the second half of 2008, the PBC strengthened its support for the stimulus package by lowering the benchmark deposit and lending rates. In the face of upward inflationary pressure, the PBC shifted its monetary policy stance from moderately loose to prudent at the end of 2010 and changed its monetary policy goal from fighting against the crisis to combating inflation. From 2010 to the third quarter of 2011, the PBC lifted its benchmark deposit and lending rates (while, at the same time, increasing the reserve requirement ratio in several steps to 21.5%). In 2014, economic growth slowed considerably and inflation rate dropped. Accordingly, the PBC has gradually changed its monetary policy stance, lowering its reserve requirement ratio and reducing its interest rates from the late 2014s onwards.

The goal (on paper) of full interest rate liberalisation was achieved in October 2015 as the PBC gave banks full liberty of determining interest rates they offer to their borrowers and depositors.

The main discussion today is how sensitive the banks are to the policy of the central bank. As stated before, besides the benchmark interest rate, the PBC has other measures to influence the behaviour of banks. Intervention by the authorities is also done through (changes in) reserve requirement ratios. We assume that of the big state-owned banks are far less sensitive because of the large basis of retail deposits that tend to be weak interest-elastic. However, small banks may follow the interest rate policy set by the central bank. All in all, interpretation of how big the pressure is of the central bank (and the party) on the behaviour of the commercial banks is complex. We expect to see occasionally politically driven lending to SOEs and local governments. But the general picture will be that fiscal and monetary policy will serve the rebalancing process. Fiscal policy must focus on increasing social spending on healthcare, pensions and housing. Monetary policy must solve the asymmetry in credit allocation between SOEs and private firms.

Despite dangerous "Chinese characteristics" in executing fiscal and monetary policy, the fear of a financial and debt crisis are not justified. Important steps are taken to align fiscal and monetary policy to the rebalancing process. Obviously, we will see the next coming years expansionary fiscal policy. The economic world (including trade tensions) is and will stay risky and to offset this, government spending may rise. The same holds for monetary policy: we may see inflationary monetary policy in the next coming years. However, these short-term measures will not reverse the rebalancing process; there is just too much urgency to implement structural reforms. We may expect a step-by-step removal of restrictions on foreign shareholdings in banks and other financial institutions. Also there is discussion on giving more freedom to operate foreign banks.

Chapter 13

The Exchange Rate: Policy and Development

Myth 13: The undervalued Renminbi created the large trade surplus and consequently, a rise in the value of the currency will solve the trade disequilibrium with the US and EU

13.1 Introduction

China's export growth has been impressive in the previous decades. Besides low wages, government subsidies and cheap credits, a low value of the currency also helped. A low value of the currency compared to main trading partners makes export easy. The large trade surplus after 2004 and the feeling that the Chinese authorities are keeping the value of the Renminbi artificially low as part of the export-led strategy results in big discontent among western policymakers. Discussions about China's currency and exchange rate policy are intense and, in many cases, politicised.

This debate (and discontent) about China's currency policy could be seen in the previous US presidency campaign in 2016. According to Mr Trump (and in this case, he does not stand alone), China keeps the value of the Renminbi artificially low to the dollar boosting its exports and trade surplus at the expense of trading partners, thus allowing Chinese firms to steal jobs from the US companies. If the Chinese had maintained a floating exchange rate, appreciation would likely have occurred but this has not happened because the Chinese authorities chose to manipulate the currency level through intervention to keep its value low; too low according to the American president. Consequently, the US has consistently pressurised China to allow the Renminbi to appreciate at a faster pace and to let the currency fluctuate more freely in line with market forces. The International Monetary Fund, the World Bank and many economists have also concluded that the value of the Renminbi is too low and argued for faster appreciation and a more flexible exchange rate policy.

The Chinese view is different. According to them, the large trade surplus of China with the US is driven by lower import from the US, not because of an increase in export. Furthermore, you may question the trade statistics as we saw in the discussion of the iPhone case in Chapter 10. Export from China is often not real Chinese export but done by foreign companies in China that first import before being able to export. When only taking the "real" (value-added) Chinese export into account, the trade surplus with the US would disappear. Furthermore, Chinese officials argue that its currency policy is not meant to manipulate trade but is implemented to foster economic stability and investor confidence, a policy that is practised by a variety of developing countries.

The structure of this chapter is as follows. Section 13.2 starts with a historical overview of China's exchange rate system. This section focusses on the development of the Renminbi over the years and some strategic choices by the policymakers. Discussion about the two exchange rate systems, i.e. the floating and the fixed exchange rate systems is given in Section 13.3. Within this context of the two extreme systems, China made its choices. One of these choices is the amount of flexibility in the system. This flexibility relates to the discussion about the Renminbi undervaluation and the China–US trade disequilibrium.

13.2 History of the exchange rate system

When China was a planned economy before 1978, the official exchange rate was not connected to international transactions and played no significant role in foreign trade. There was state monopoly in foreign trade and exporting and importing were not driven by commercial considerations. However, the role of the exchange rate changed after economic reform began in 1978. Foreign trade, in particular export, became important as the export sector created jobs and earned foreign currency which was important to import needed equipment. We can divide the post-reform foreign exchange rate policy in two phases. During the first stage (1979–1993), China adopted a dual exchange rate system. During the second stage (since 1994), it unified the foreign exchange market and made its current account convertible. In line with Chinese tradition, the whole process of reform was gradual and implemented step by step.

Figure 13.1 shows the exchange rate development. On the vertical axis, the amount of Chinese Renminbi per US dollar is given.

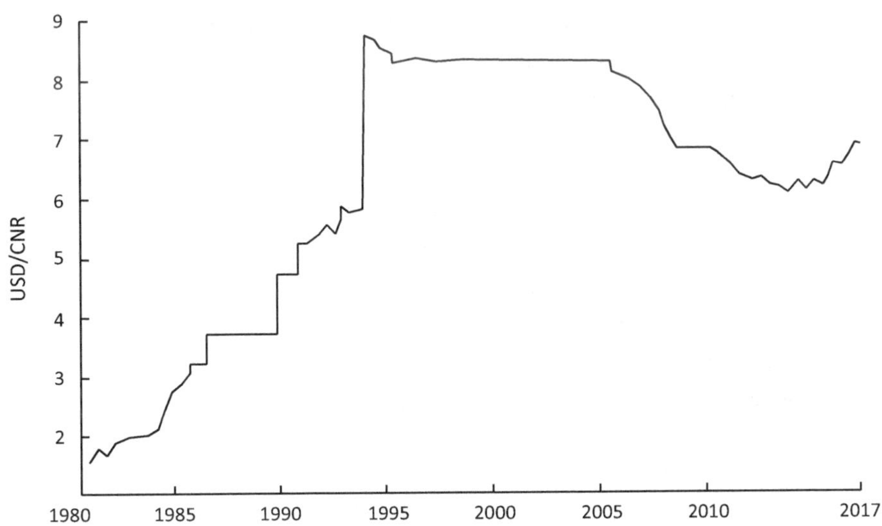

Figure 13.1 Development of the Renminbi–US$ exchange rate, 1980–2017

Source: *NBS*

An increase in the number of Renminbi per dollar means depreciation, while a fall in the number per US dollar means appreciation. It should be noted that the Renminbi–dollar rate prior to 1994 is the exchange rate published by the Chinese statistical agency. This was the official rate. China maintained a dual exchange rate system up to 1994 which consisted of an official fixed exchange rate system (used by the government) and a market-based exchange rate (used by importers and exporters). The two rates differed a lot from time to time. But despite the large gap, China's dual exchange rate system was abolished in 1994 and the official exchange rate became the market exchange rate.

As can be seen in Fig. 13.1, the Renminbi devaluated dramatically between 1980 and 1994. In the eight years before pegging the currency in 1994, the Renminbi devaluated by 55%. China's currency policy after 1994 can be divided in four periods based on the types of exchange rate regime the Chinese government used.

A pegged system, 1994–2005

As part of a comprehensive reform package to stimulate trade and increase economic growth, the authorities decided to introduce a pegged exchange rate system. The choice for the peg to the US dollar was aimed to create certainty for international trade and foreign investments, but certainly also to protect the currency from appreciating too much (which hurts export). In the months after the integration of the dual exchange rate system, the authorities let the exchange rate float (in a managed way), to figure out the Renminbi's true international market value. It reached 8.3 to the dollar in May 1995, and this was adopted as the fixed rate for the next nine years, with only a small daily trading range permitted.

The Asian crisis of 1997–1998 challenged this fixed system. Most of the Asian currencies were heavily depreciating against the US dollar, while China had its pegged exchange rate to the dollar. China's competitiveness was falling, but despite some domestic pressure from local authorities and corporations, China did not devalue its currency and the peg to the dollar continued. This enhanced the credibility of China's system a lot. The authorities chose long-run stability for investors over the easy and short-term support for exporters. Foreign investors were happy with Beijing's commitment to a stable rate, and FDI inflow accelerated even further. At the same time, exporters had some difficult years.

Intensive discussion on China's exchange rate started in the summer of 2003. Two (intertwined) events happened in 2003–2004. Firstly, the dollar started to decline on the global currency market after spring 2002, and this continued in 2003 and 2004. Automatically, the Chinese Renminbi also declined due to the pegged system. Secondly, we saw in this period (starting in 2004) an explosion of China's trade surplus. Policymakers made the link between the low value of the Chinese currency and the trade surplus. Trade specialists (mainly from the US, but also from the EU and Japan) claimed that the Renminbi was seriously undervalued and that China's exporters were taking unfair advantage. Whether the Renminbi was heavily undervalued in this period is hard to say. It should be noted that the Renminbi in 2004 had the same value against the dollar as in 1994, but obviously, it depreciated against other currencies in 2003–2004. Looking at China's enormous growth of its trade surplus, the assumed linkage to undervaluation is logical, as was the intense political debate on this issue.

Managed floating, 2005–2008

In 2005, the Chinese government replaced the fixed exchange rate regime. In July of that year, it announced a switch to a managed floating system. It was a combination of an official revaluation by 2.1%, allowing the currency to float more freely based on market demand and supply, and switching from the dollar peg to a "basket" of currencies. The Renminbi was theoretically managed against the dollar, euro, yen and South Korean won. Because the basket was overwhelmingly weighted to the dollar, in practice, the Renminbi was still managed against the dollar. In this managed floating exchange rate regime, the Renminbi exchange rate was allowed to fluctuate by up to 0.3% daily against the basket (later adjusted to 0.5%). From July 2005 to July 2008, the exchange rate went from 8.11 to 6.83, which is an appreciation of almost 20%. Despite this increase in value, the discussion about manipulating its exchange rate did not disappear in the US and Europe; driven by the continuous large trade surplus. This view was counteracted by the Chinese authorities. An interview with vice premier Wu Yi in the *China Daily* on 23 May 2007 makes this clear: "My advice to the US would be to seek measures to address the problems at home first [... low savings ratio and government deficit] rather than blaming or pressuring the other side, which is of no help at all and will make the situation more complicated".

Pegged revisited, 2008–2010

The continuous appreciation between 2005 and early 2008 of the Renminbi was a millstone around the neck of exporters and policymakers. In July 2008, the Chinese monetary authorities stopped its managed floating exchange rate regime in order to secure its economy from the global financial crisis and fall in exports. In 2009, Chinese exports fell by 15.9% over the previous year and over 20 million migrant workers lost their jobs in that year (Ebbers & Zhang 2010–2015). The new exchange rate needed to meet two conditions. Firstly, it had to be low enough to ensure that China's exports would remain competitive. Secondly, the rate also had to be close enough to the true market value so that it could sustain for a long time with little variation. To keep the peg, one-sided currency-intervention was needed. Intervening in the currency market to stabilise the Renminbi against the dollar meant that the Chinese monetary authorities had to purchase more and more US dollar based government debt to maintain the value of its currency against the dollar. China became an important creditor of the US trade (and government) deficit. It created a bilateral inflexibility: the US could not survive without Chinese money, while China could not survive without US government securities.

Floating exchange rate ... with some interventions, 2010–2016

On 19 June 2010, the PBC announced that it would stop the pegged system and enhance the Renminbi exchange rate flexibility. The Renminbi started to rise. On 4 August 2011, the exchange rate was 6.44 to the dollar, an appreciation of 6.1% compared to mid-June 2010. In April 2012, the government allowed the trading band to widen. The Renminbi was now allowed to fluctuate by up to 1% on a daily basis against the basket of currencies. This trading band was again widened in March 2014 when the daily fluctuation that was allowed for the Chinese currency changed to 2%.

Although market forces are determining the exchange rate, if needed, the monetary authorities will step in. For example, in August 2015, the Renminbi dropped substantially. At that point, the monetary authorities intervened on the currency market to control the rapid fall, keeping the Renminbi within a narrow margin. Since then, the Renminbi has continued to fall gradually. In early 2017, the Renminbi fluctuated around 6.80. We expect continuation of a downward pressure during the rest of 2017 and early 2018. Some depreciation of the Renminbi is expected due to trade tensions, higher interest rates in the US and (marginal) slower economic growth in China. At the same time, the Chinese authorities will ensure that depreciation will be relatively small because a sharp currency depreciation could threat financial stability.

13.3 Floating versus fixed exchange rate system

China chose for a fixed exchange rate system to the dollar between 1994 and 2005 and during the early years of the worldwide economic crisis that started in 2008. There are certain advantages of having a fixed currency system. Firstly, it avoids currency fluctuations with the pegged currency. If the value of currencies fluctuates significantly, this can cause problems for firms engaged in trade. For example, a rapid appreciation of the Renminbi would make China's exports uncompetitive. In addition, if a Chinese firm relied on imported raw materials, a depreciation would increase the costs of imports, reduce profitability and generates higher inflation. With a pegged system, this can be avoided. Secondly, stability encourages investment; investors like stability and certainty. China's focus on attracting FDI made it necessary to stabilise the value of the Renminbi as much as possible.

A pegged system requires large amounts of reserves as the monetary authorities are constantly buying or selling foreign and domestic currencies. In the case of China, to protect the currency from appreciating against the US dollar, it must increase its foreign reserves by buying dollars (in particular, US treasury securities) by selling Renminbi. As long as the Chinese are willing to accumulate dollar reserves, they can continue to maintain the peg.

During the fixed exchange rate periods, Chinese foreign exchange reserves grew significantly each year to maintain the US dollar peg rate. The pace of growth in reserves was so rapid that it took China only a couple of years to become the country with the largest foreign exchange reserves (2011). As of January 2017, it was announced that Beijing owned US$3.1 trillion in reserves, lower than 2015 but an astronomical number (*Reuters*). The problem with large currency reserves is that it can create unwanted economic side effects such as inflation. The currency reserves are widening the money supply and if there is (too) much liquidity, the result is higher prices. This indeed happened in the 2010–2011 period when inflation increased to 5%. The large international reserves of China are a proof that intervention in the currency market was necessary to reduce the appreciation of the Renminbi. Obviously, large international reserve is needed to finance international trade (in the presence of capital controls), and it is logical to see a country to increase its foreign reserves for these purposes as its economy and trade grew. However, in the Chinese case, the international reserves are disconnected from trade finance. The increase in foreign exchange reserves in China has significantly outpaced the growth of GDP or imports in the last few years. Clearly as a result of currency intervention.

Capital account liberalisation: Step by step

Capital account convertibility remain a long-term goal of the Chinese policymakers. You may argue that further acceleration of the Renminbi's internationalisation requires further progress on liberalising the capital account. At the same time, China is not in a hurry to open-up the capital account. Currency crises in the past were (partly) attributed to opening up the capital account too early in the transformation process. Furthermore, the emphasis within the rebalancing process is on the domestic side, less on solving external disquilibria. There is a big disadvantage of having a fixed exchange rate within the context of capital liberalisation: the monetary authorities are losing their main instrument because the interest rate must be used to fine-tune capital flows and to keep the currency pegged. Consequently, monetary policy cannot be used to stimulate (or deflate) domestic demand and economic growth. For example, a peg would prevent a country from lowering its interest rates to offset an economic downturn. If it reduces interest, capital would flow out of the country to assets with higher interest rates in the rest of the world and the country would find its currency peg under pressure. The alternative to the pegged currency system is a floating exchange rate in which supply and demand of the currency market determines the bilateral exchange rate. If the demand for Chinese goods (export) or assets (capital inflow) increased, more Renminbi would be demanded to purchase those goods and assets, and the Renminbi would rise in value. The big advantage is that monetary policy can be fully used to fine-tune the domestic economy. The interest can be used freely despite the fact that it may reduce the value of the currency. Also, there is no need to keep large international reserves (which generate low profitability) and the country is more flexible to absorb external shocks. However, there is another side. The main disadvantage of such a floating system is the volatility of the exchange rate and the negative impact on trade and investments. There is little consensus among economists and policymakers whether floating or fixed exchange rates are preferable. Both systems and the many hybrid systems in between have their advantages and disadvantages. Furthermore, since countries differ significantly in their economic and demographic conditions, an exchange rate regime that suits one country may be unsuitable for another. The same holds if the economic structure is changing fast; in this case also an exchange rate (system) must adapt.

The impossible trinity

The choice of the optimum exchange rate system is essentially driven by three preferences. In general, countries would prefer stable exchange rates (thus a fixed currency), independent monetary policy (free in using interest rate) and free movement of capital (because capital surpluses and deficits can be counteracted). The problem is that these three preferences cannot be reached at the same time, hence the so-called impossible trinity (Mundell, 1963) as indicated in Fig. 13.2. In practice, a country can only manipulate two of the three constituents of the trinity. For example, the yen–euro exchange rate is floating, and consequently freedom of capital and autonomy of monetary policy are both possible. In this case, it would not be possible to have a fixed exchange rate system. The combination of interest rate differences between countries and freedom of capital flows, by definition create volatility of the

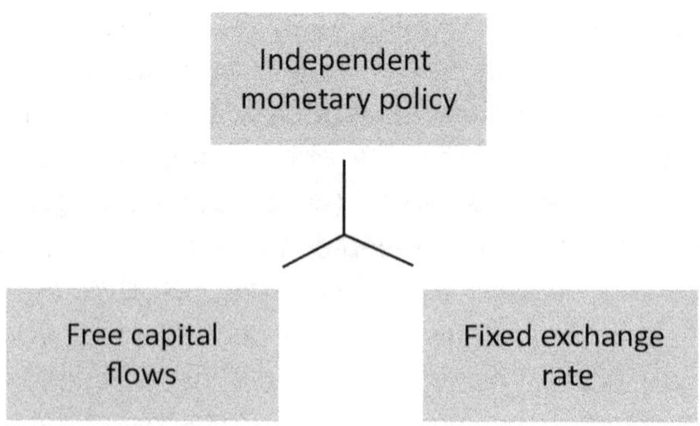

Figure 13.2 The impossible trinity

Source: Based on Aizenman and Hiro Ito (2011)

exchange rate. The same principle holds if the choice is a pegged system. For example, the choice of the peg between the Hungarian forint and the euro makes it impossible to have free capital movement and monetary autonomy at the same time. Within the context of freedom of capital, the central bank of Hungary is not able (and willing) to execute its own monetary policy. This is done by the ECB (and followed by the Hungarian central bank). The third choice (in Fig. 13.2) is to have an independent monetary policy and a fixed exchange rate, but this is only possible if capital flows are restricted. This is the choice by the Chinese authorities.

The Chinese monetary authorities can peg its exchange rate and maintain an independent monetary policy as long as it maintains control over capital flows. And this is (still) happening today. The currency is convertible (free exchangeable) on a current account basis (such as for trade transactions), but not on a capital account basis. For various types of financial flows, such as portfolio investments, there remain strict and complex regulations. Because capital cannot easily leave China when interest rates are lowered, China retains some flexibility over its monetary (and fiscal) policy despite the fixed exchange rate. Although China officially has abandoned the fixed exchange rate regime and now allows the exchange rate to fluctuate more freely, the capital controls in China are still in place. It does not only generate monetary autonomy, but the capital controls also decrease the likelihood of speculative attacks, which have been a major cause of economic crisis in developing countries, including Thailand, Argentina and Turkey in recent years.

Undervaluation of the Renminbi

The theory of explaining undervaluation can be quite technical and goes beyond the focus of the book. In essence, it means that the value of the currency is too low, lower than it ought to be and lower than the value based on economic fundamentals such as productivity and export. The value of the undervalued currency is not sustainable. If you would give freedom to the market (demand and supply), the undervalued currency would increase in value, but this is not happening only because of the intervention of the monetary authorities. This is also the discussion with respect to the Renminbi. Only because the Chinese authorities are buying large amounts of US treasury bills and other US dollar assets, the Renminbi is not increasing in value, resulting in easy export; not based on competitive strengths but unfair competition. An interesting remark was given by an expert at a strategic China session at the Dutch Ministry of Foreign Affairs in February 2017. According to him, undervaluation was and still is needed because China is disciplined as member of WTO. Before WTO membership, China was able to use industrial policies, but as member of the WTO (after 2001), this is no longer permitted and as a result, an undervalued currency is more or less the only one of the few protectionist measures left over for stimulating trade and protecting exporting sectors.

Over the years, there have been multiple studies examining the degree of misalignment (mostly undervaluation) of the Renminbi against the US dollar. Surprisingly, results of those studies varied enormously, even when looking at the same time frame. For example, undervaluation in 2008–2009 ranges from 12% (Reisen, 2009) to 50% (Ferguson and Schularick, 2009). Two studies over the 2008–2014 period are concluding that the Renminbi was overvalued, both from Chinese researches.

The US–China disequilibrium

Because China's central bank is the single biggest foreign holder of US government debt, it is often said that China is "America's banker". This gives some discomfort in the US; the Chinese authorities could undermine the US economy by selling all its dollar holdings, thereby causing a collapse of the US dollar and perhaps the US economy. It is correct that China is the largest foreign owner of US debt, but these fears are slightly misguided from different perspectives. Firstly, the Chinese authorities are just too dependent on the dollar and selling its dollar holdings (resulting in a dollar-depreciation) would reduce their assets. The Chinese authorities will not take this risk. But it is to be expected that they will very gradually change the composition of its international reserves away from the dollar into other international currencies. Secondly, China is not, in any practical sense, "America's banker". China holds just 5% of outstanding US treasury debt (January 2017); American individuals and domestic institutions hold 65%. In addition, China holds just 1% of all US financial assets (including corporate bonds and equities); US investors hold 87%. Moreover, Chinese commercial banks lend almost nothing to American firms and consumers; the large majority of that finance comes from American banks.

Also, the view that an appreciation of the Renminbi will solve the US trade deficit with China is not fully correct. The example of the iPhone, in Chapter 10, makes clear that we may question this viewpoint. Conventional trade statistics are not giving the real picture in today's fragmented supply chains and related trade flows. By using the same data as Fig. 10.5, you may question the impact of a Renminbi depreciation on US–Chinese trade disequilibrium. The appreciation can only affect a small proportion of the export-value, namely the assembly costs in China. Assume that the Renminbi appreciates by 20% and assume no productivity growth. In this case, the 20% will raise the iPhone assembly cost to US$9.6 per unit from US$8 and add US$1.6 to the total manufacturing costs. It is not be expected that this will change bilateral trade flows because Apple will not pass this additional US$1.6 to the US consumer. Even a 50% appreciation of Renminbi against the dollar would not bring a significant change in total manufacturing costs. The expected pass-through effect of the Renminbi appreciation on the price of the iPhone would be insignificant and the demand in the US would not be affected. In most cases, economies of scale, and related productivity gains, can offset the appreciation easily. It cost US$265 to produce the iPhone when it was introduced in 2007. Within one year, the unit cost of the iPhone dropped to US$178. Furthermore, the profit margin of more than 50% leaves Apple with enough room to absorb increased manufacturing costs. So, a direct effect on trade flows due to an appreciation (and price change) is not to be expected. Of course, this relates to a very specific product in the premium segment. The story will be different when talking about a low value-added final product that is competing on price. However, the argument is the same: do not expect too much from currency movements in today's global supply chains. In addition to the small direct impact, there can be another, more important impact on trade flows. The appreciation against the dollar is increasing the purchasing power of China's consumers for goods from the US. This may increase import and consequently reduce the trade surplus.

International currency

An international (reserve) currency is a currency that is held in considerable quantities by governments and institutions as part of their foreign exchange reserves. In addition, it is a currency which is used for international trade transactions. More and more, the Renminbi is seen as an international currency, but this is quite a new phenomenon. Only after the financial crisis broke out did we see a strong rise in the Renminbi's international presence. Internationalisation of the Renminbi is logical. It was quite odd for the currency of a trading nation of China's size not to be internationally traded. After the crisis of 2008, the Chinese authorities emphasised the need to accelerate the internationalisation of the Renminbi.

The freezing up of letters of credit, the most important instrument of trade finance was an important factor behind the dramatic fall in exports in 2008; there was no finance available for trade. Most letters of credit were denominated in dollars. If trade would be financed with Renminbi denominated financial products, it would protect itself against international financial storms. Another factor behind the eagerness to increase internationalisation was the desire of the Chinese central bank to accelerate domestic financial liberalisation. The financial sector had to become more competitive and efficient, and some competition would be helpful to initiate this development of higher efficiency and a more liberal interest rate. Furthermore, as discussed earlier, there was the aim of interest rate liberalisation, driven more by market forces and less by government planners. Based on these arguments, Internationalisation of the Renminbi took off after 2008. That said, the Renminbi is still very far from being a major international currency. It was involved in 4% of global currency trade by value in 2016 (Bloomberg database). The dollar and euro are dominating with 85% and 39%, respectively (because every trade involves two currencies, the total for all currencies is 200%). The position of the dollar is overwhelming. The dollar accounts for about 64% of the reserve holdings of the world's central banks, followed by the euro (20%) in 2016. Furthermore, 39% of the world's debt is issued in dollars (Bloomberg database).

Besides international currencies, there is another international reserve asset created by the IMF at the end of the 1960s: the Special Drawing Right (SDR). It was created to supplement its member countries' official reserves. Countries receive SDRs in proportion to the IMF quotas they pay. Before 2016, the value of the SDR was based on a basket of four currencies: US dollar, euro, yen and British pound. In October 2016, the IMF added the Chinese Renminbi to the basket of currencies. There are two main criteria for a currency to be included in the SDR basket. First, the currencies in the basket are related to the top exporters of the world. Second, the currency must be widely used for international transactions and widely traded on the exchange markets. This second criterion is clearly not being reached yet; there is still no full capital convertibility. But the IMF recognises the progress made in reforms to China's monetary, foreign exchange and financial system. Besides, China's trade and capital flows are just too big to ignore. There are certainly some advantages (besides political prestige) for China for being a part of the SDR basket.

1. As a reserve currency, borrowing can be done in Renminbi. China would be able to issue most of their debt in Renminbi, removing the potential exchange rate risk and lowering transaction costs. Additionally, there is no need to keep only dollars as international reserve.

2. In general, we may expect that being a reserve currency would be accompanied by a rise in its value over the long term. If correct, this would help to boost Chinese consumption by lowering import costs.
3. It could also increase China's influence, particularly in Asia, as trading partners may choose to align their currencies to the Renminbi. Moreover, reserve status promotes regional economic integration and enhances China's ability to provide financial support. This is very helpful if the One Belt One Road project is getting momentum.

Reserve currency status will lead to (further) internationalisation of the Renminbi. The inclusion of the Renminbi in the SDR basket enhances the attractiveness of the Renminbi as an international reserve asset. But be aware that this increase in international use does not go automatically. The reserve currency status is, at the end of the day, determined by the willingness of foreign central banks to hold the currency. Look at what happened in Japan. The yen accounted for 9% of global central bank reserves in 1990, but its share dropped to less than 4% in 2016 (Bank of Japan). Furthermore, the share of the yen in forex trading was in 2016 not much higher than its share in 1990. This stagnant market share is not only because of slow economic growth but also because the Japanese authorities refused to open up the financial system (Bank for International Settlements, 2017). In line with this, there are some potential costs related to the increased international status of the Renminbi. A potential risk is that the monetary authorities lose control over the value of the currency. By definition, a reserve currency is one that both public and private agents wants to hold; sometimes based on sentiment or speculative objectives. Therefore, speculation is always lurking. In particular, this can be the case if a currency serves as a "safe haven" currency. In that case, overshooting is possible which means that due to speculation, the currency increases strongly in value in such a way that it is not connected to economic fundamentals. This overshooting can also work the other way round. In this case we will see a strong drop of the value that spurs inflation.

As the Renminbi becomes more and more used internationally, the impact of domestic monetary (and fiscal) policy decisions increasingly influence the rest of the world. More international coordination and cooperation is needed. That will be a balancing act between behave as a responsible monetary authority and at the same time keeping domestic issues in mind when implementing currency and monetary policies. The new status and its associated responsibilities may intervene with the timing in the minds of the monetary authorities in China; domestic reasons are always predominant. Although the Renminbi will maintain a weak trend in 2017 and early 2018, international political pressure could be so high that some appreciation may occur in certain periods of time. But this appreciation will not solve the trade disequilibrium with the US and the EU. What may help to reduce the disequilibrium is the emphasis the authorities give on building up a strong domestic market through increasing domestic consumption. This is the topic of the next chapter.

Chapter 14

Consumption and Savings in China

Myth 14: Wages and consumption are both low in China, compared to other countries in transition

14.1 Introduction

The size of China's private consumption is gigantic. The new Chinese middle class spends a lot and annual retail sales increased by almost double digits in the previous decades. The explosion of e-commerce and the growing urbanisation are important drivers behind the level and growth of China's consumption. Given its prominent size, China's consumption is becoming globally relevant and has a significant impact on global sales of international operating companies, the topic which will be dealt with in the final part of this book. Although its absolute value is enormous and consumption per capita increased strongly, China's private consumption to GDP ratio has been below the international average for many years, representing only 38% of China's GDP in 2016. This makes the discussion about consumption complicated. Between 1990 and 2016, average per capita consumer spending rose six-fold in terms of inflation-adjusted US dollars and at the same time this was dwarfed by the growth of GDP (and, in particular, investments). Hence, explosive growth in consumer spending occurred in the context of falling consumption to GDP ratio.

According to the World Bank, private consumption represented 60% of world GDP in 2016. For countries categorised as the middle-income group, to which China belongs, the average consumption ratio was 55% of GDP, which is about 20 percentage points higher than that of China. Consumption as percentage of GDP is not only low but also has been falling in the previous decade. The low and declining share of consumption in GDP has another side of the coin: a high (and rising) aggregate savings ratio. High savings are a central feature of the Chinese economy. Since 2000, there has been a rise in the savings rate, reaching a peak at 53% of GDP in 2007. Although the household savings received most attention in the media, it should be emphasised that China's total savings consists of three sources: corporate, household and government savings. A breakdown of aggregate savings into these three components is needed because their developments (and drivers) differ.

The chapter is structured as follows. In Section 14.2, we discuss the general trend of consumption and savings with a focus on the nationwide savings and consumption rate. This is followed, in Section 14.3, by decoupling the savings rate into household, government and company savings. Section 14.4 continues specifically on the household savings and consumption, and we will make some linkages with theoretical models. In Section 14.5, we cluster the main reasons for the high savings rate, while in Section 14.6, we discuss the measures taken by the government to increase the share of consumption in the economy.

14.2 China's consumption and savings rate: The general picture

We start our analysis with the nationwide savings and consumption development after 1978. The discussion starts with the savings rate development.

Development of China's savings rate

China has seen four distinct phases in its savings rate in the post-reform period. The first phase is the period between 1980 and 1994 in which total savings showed a steady increase from 35% to 43% of GDP (Fig. 14.1). The second stage starts in 1994 during which the savings rate declined to 37% by 2000. In the third phase (2000–2007), the savings rate increased dramatically to 52%. As we will see later in the chapter, income growth and uncertainty are two important drivers behind savings in the early 2000s. This period brought prosperity and uncertainty at the same time. After 2008, the fourth stage of China's savings rate development, China's high savings rate dropped and reached 47% in 2016, which is still high by international standards.

The increase in the savings rate after 2000 is very strong but not unique. Fast-growing Asian economies in their transition phases also experienced large and sustained rises in their savings rates. For example, Japan's aggregate savings/GDP ratio rose by 15 percentage points during 1955–1970, and South Korea's savings rate increased from 16% to 40% between 1983 and 2000. During the period 1998–2007, India's savings rate also registered

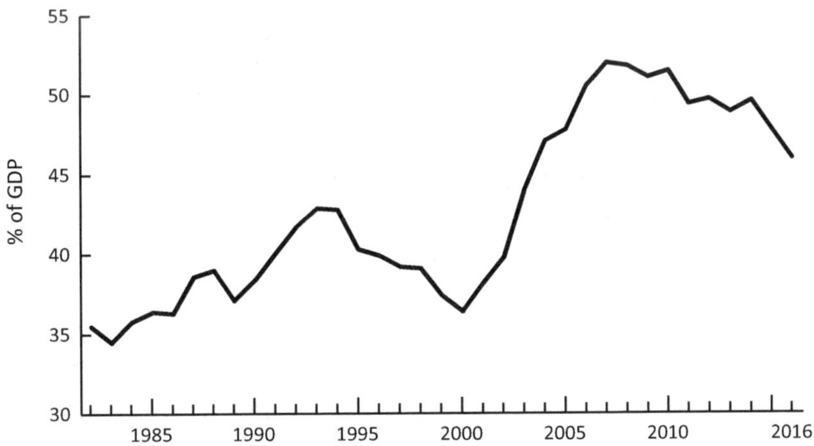

Figure 14.1 Nationwide savings as percentage of GDP, 1982–2016

Source: *NBS*

a rise of 10 percentage points of GDP, reaching 35% in 2007 (Guonan Ma and Wang Yi, 2010). Although, not unique in terms of change, one can conclude that China's savings rate was high by international standards in 2007.

The national savings rate of China was 27 percentage points higher than that of Japan, 38 percentage points higher than that of the US and 29 percentage points higher compared to France. A key feature of the Chinese savings rate after 2000 is that households, corporate, as well as the government each have contributed to the rise in gross national savings.

- Household savings increased due to higher income and more uncertainty.
- Corporate savings increased through its monopolistic position and relatively low wages.
- Government savings increased through fiscal decentralisation, increased taxation revenues and low social spending by the central government.

In terms of each component, China's savings is high but not exceptional. As a share of GDP, China's corporate savings are in line with Japan. China's household savings are in line with countries such as India and China's government savings is for example, lower than South Korea's. However, what really distinguishes China from other countries is that all three savings components are high (Tao Yang, 2011).

Most of the discussion about China's savings rate focusses on households. Therefore, we will introduce some key features of the household savings ratio in this section. Household savings accounted for 12% of GDP in the early 1980s but grew to about 27% in 2007 before it slightly dropped to 25% in 2016 (Tao Yang, 2011 and NBS Statistics, 2017). In Fig. 14.2, we use a different approach (although, we see the same trend). In this figure, we put disposable income (instead of GDP) on the vertical axis. Household savings is then calculated as the difference between disposable income and consumption of food, clothing, housing services, education, medical care and other miscellaneous items.

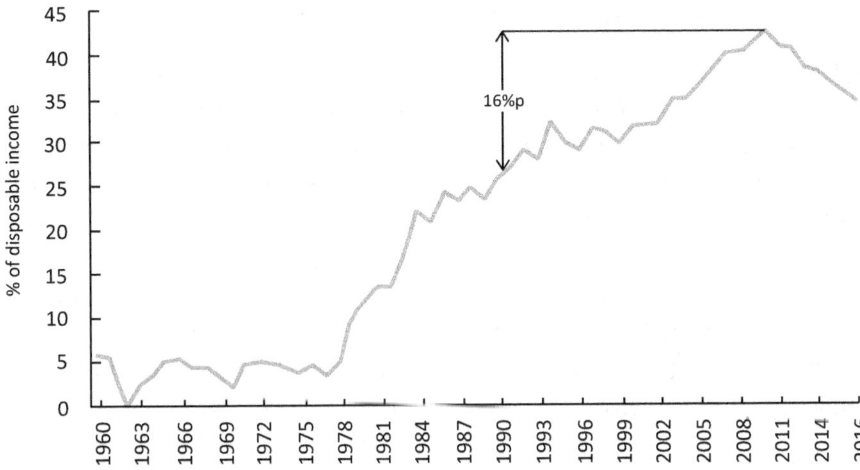

Figure 14.2 Household savings rate: Development between 1960 and 2016

Note: Based on wage earners (excluding self-employed families)

Source: IMF Working Paper 16/183 (2016) and NBS

The household savings started to grow immediately after the reform period started in 1978, and this continued up to 2007. Figure 14.2 makes clear that between 1990 and 2007, the household savings rate increased by 16 percentage points from 26% in 1990 to 42% in 2007. Besides the growth in per capita income, we can distinguish two factors behind the growth in household savings. Firstly, in the early 1990s, the government implemented reforms to commercialise state-owned enterprises (SOEs). It meant that the SOEs were not delivering social benefits such as housing, healthcare and pensions to their employees (and families) anymore. People had to cope with this by themselves. Uncertainty about healthcare expenses and education resulted in higher savings. In addition, the absence of a national pension system intensified the need to save. Secondly, underdeveloped financial markets and limits on household borrowings also stimulated savings. It was difficult to borrow money for large expenses such as housing and cars, and consequently savings were needed. Clearly, this rising share in savings means a reduction in the consumption rate.

Development of the consumption rate

Domestic consumption comprises household consumption and government consumption. We will elaborate on the role of the government in China's gross consumption in later sections but focus now on the household consumption pattern. Although the government can be an important driver behind the fall in the national consumption ratio in specific years, households have an overwhelming impact on the gross consumption rate, and in most discussions on China, the focus is on household (private) consumption.

In general, the household consumption to GDP ratio shows a declining trend between the late 1970s and 2007 before it stabilised around 37% until today. As stated in the introduction, China's low consumption-GDP figure does not indicate that household expenditure is weak; in fact, it is quite strong. Compared to other countries, household consumption expenditure in China has grown at a strong pace for an extended period. Figure 14.3(b) shows the annual growth of consumer spending by households. The consumption growth was double-digit in many years. Nonetheless, the share of household consumption in total expenditure in the Chinese economy has declined (Fig. 14.3(a)) as the growth in investment spending has been even more rapid than that of consumption; especially in the 2000s decade. Consumer spending grew very fast over the previous 25 years, but investment spending (and GDP) grew even faster.

A decreasing share of consumption is not something which is unique to China. Countries that are going through a rapid industrialisation process as part of the economic take-off generally witness this. Countries where a similar decline was observed are Japan (1955–1987) and South Korea (1964–1988). The same can be said with respect to countries in transition such as India, Vietnam and Indonesia. Also, countries such as the US went through a period of falling consumption share in GDP (Barnett *et al.*, 2012). But the case of China is different due to its extremely low value. Figure 14.4 shows the fall in household consumption rate in China compared to South Korea. The same development can be seen during the take-off stage. Figure 14.4 indicates that at the end of the 1964–1988 period in South Korea, the household consumption

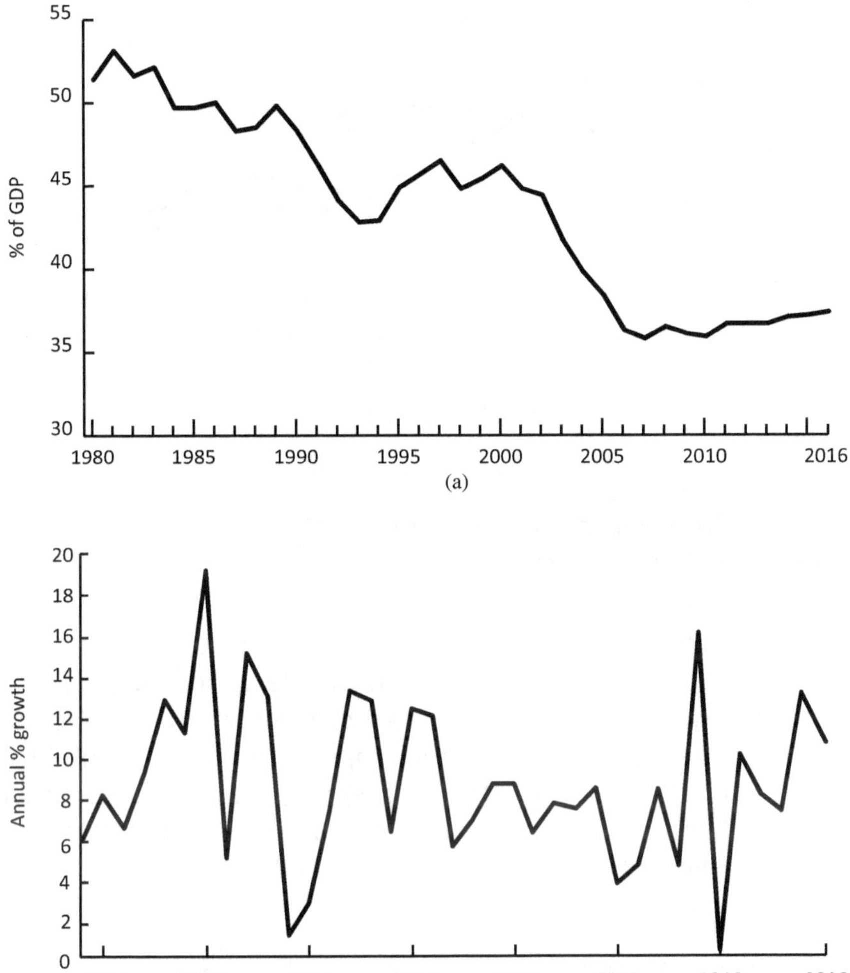

Figure 14.3 Household consumption as percentage of GDP (a); and annual growth (b), 1980–2016

Note: *Housing services are excluded*
Source: *NBS*

rate was still above 50%, considerably higher than in China. Other countries in transition such as India, Vietnam, Thailand and Indonesia also show much higher household consumption rates at the end of their take-off stages.

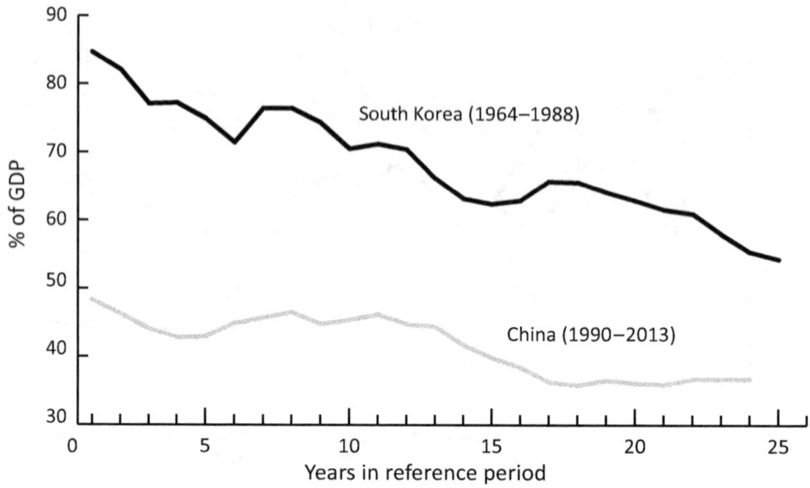

Figure 14.4 Household consumption rate development, China and South Korea
Source: Adjusted from Barnett (2012)

Part of the explanation of today's low consumption ratio in China is its unusually low consumption rate at the beginning of economic reforms. When Japan started the investment-intensive stage of growth in 1955, household spending was 66% of GDP. The same holds for Taiwan and South Korea; both countries started the take-off phase with a consumption rate of 65%. But in 1980, the Chinese consumption ratio was only around 50%.

14.3 Decoupling the aggregate savings

As indicated in the introduction, the total savings consist of corporate, government and household savings. Decoupling the analysis is needed. For example, between 1978 and 1984, the household savings continued to rise, while in the same period, the government savings fell dramatically. The result was a stable aggregate savings rate. If one only concentrates on total savings, one may miss the point what precisely is behind this development. The focus of the analysis below is on the early 1990–2017 period.

Corporate savings

Corporate savings equal the value-added of companies minus labour compensation, taxes and other (needed) payments. By not making it too technical, we assume that these corporate savings equal the profits made by the companies after paying all stakeholders. China's corporate savings doubled from 12% of GDP in 1992 to a peak of 24% in 2004, but, has since declined to around 18% in the 2008–2016 period. This is still remarkably high by international standards. Between 1992 and 2008, it has been the most important contributor to the increase in China's aggregate savings (Guonan Ma and Wang Yi, 2010). This improved profitability was mostly associated with the SOEs. Government policy was clearly designed to help SOEs in order to promote industrial growth and exports. Protectionism through closing down certain sectors for private (and foreign) competition created monopolistic SOEs. The profits of these monopolists exploded. Other drivers behind the growing profits of SOEs are the suppression of wages (relative to productivity), cheap credits, subsidies for energy inputs and low land rentals.

Another explanation of the high corporate savings rate was the limited access to finance. This forced the companies to save to get around uncertainties and to use internal funds to finance expansion. Although this may relate to SOE, small and medium-sized private firms are in particular confronted with shortage of external finance. They rely, in many cases, on their own savings to finance investments. Therefore, the high savings of enterprises, including SMEs, can be interpreted as reflecting the difficulties in obtaining financing from state banks. A final cause of the high retained earnings is the low dividend payments by Chinese firms. The Chinese government did not ask SOEs to pay dividends until 2008, even though they had enjoyed improved profits. The latest drivers are today less important than before. While China's financial system remains underdeveloped, it certainly has advanced in the previous decade and loans are more easily available for investments. Today, SOEs need to pay dividend to their shareholders (including the government). Together with a more challenging external environment, corporate savings sees a slightly downward trend in recent years.

Government savings

The government has been the smallest saver in China but a major contributor to the rise in national savings after the mid-1990s. As a share of GDP, its savings increased from less than 5% in 1992 to 11% in 2008 and then stabilised around 10% up to 2016. The marked increase in government savings largely reflects higher government income since the mid-1990s. This has been the combined result of high economic growth (which increased revenues automatically), the 1994 tax reform that resulted in broadening the tax base, increased land sales and relatively low spending on social welfare.

The 1994 tax reform aimed to lift both the share of government revenues in GDP as well as increasing the share of the central government in the overall fiscal revenues. Looking at the figures after 1994, both goals have been met. In the 2000s, the rise in tax revenues on production was the largest contributor to the growth in government income. At the same time, we saw reduced social spending. The government played an important role in the economy, but mostly through government investment rather than consumption. In other words, much of the government income gain has been invested and saved rather than consumed in the 2000s.

Whether this was a good choice, is difficult to answer. The emphasis on savings and investments made the imbalances in the economy bigger. But you could also argue that under the given circumstances, emphasis on investments instead of consumption was (and still is) is logical. For example, it may be needed by taking the ageing problem into account. The anticipation of rapid population ageing and the 1997 pension reform prompted increased pension contributions by the corporate and household sectors. These contributions are parked under various pension funds administered by the government. These funds have been invested, directly or indirectly, in financial and physical assets at home or abroad. So, part of the government savings relate to the build-up of pension assets. Furthermore, government investments will achieve economic growth in the medium and longer term. And, consequently generate a greater stream of money that can be used for future government consumption.

Household savings and some theoretical observations

Figure 14.2 showed the strong increase of household savings between 1990 and 2007. In this period, the household savings rate rose to 42% of disposable income in 2007. In that year, the average family puts away about six times the savings rate of US households and three times the rate of Japanese households. The rising share of savings in GDP (or disposable income) automatically reduces the consumption share. Therefore, theories on consumption and savings are intertwined.

Most empirical studies conclude that income is, by far, the most important variable driving private consumption. For example, Keynes (1936) indicated that consumption is based on the current (disposable) income, the so-called current-income hypothesis (or absolute income theory). The theory holds that consumption in any one period depends on income during that period. It seems reasonable to expect that consumption spending by households will be closely related to their disposable income. However, it is not so obvious that consumers base their consumption in any one period on the income they receive during that period. While buying a new car or house, for example, consumers might look not only to their current income but also on the income they expect to receive during the next three or four years. It seems likely that virtually all consumption choices are affected by expectations of income over a (sometimes very) long period. The cumulation of all expected annual income people expect to receive for the rest of their lives is called permanent income, and the theory built around it is the life-cycle hypothesis (Modigliani and Brumberg, 1954). An important implication of the permanent income hypothesis is that a change in income regarded as temporary will not affect consumption much, since it will have little effect on average lifetime income. A change regarded as permanent will have a significant consumption effect.

The consumption theory and associated patterns can be translated into the savings habit. Personal savings in any one year are also influenced by permanent income. People who have the same current income but different permanent incomes might reach very different savings decisions. Someone with a relatively low current income but a high permanent income (a medical university student) might save little or nothing now, expecting to be able to save for retirement and for large expenses later. A person with the same low income but no expectation of higher income later might try to save some money now to provide for retirement or other high expenses later. Furthermore, when consumers are young, they borrow to finance education, housing and the first car. When approaching middle age, they repay these loans and accumulate savings for retirement, while there is no need for the senior citizens to save anymore. The consequence is clear, demographic patterns have a large impact on household savings and consumption pattern.

Chinese case is not in line with theory

That savings would grow in a country emerging from poverty is not surprising, but the magnitude of the rise in China is not easy to bring this practice together with economic theory. Theory predicts that people smooth out consumption over time by saving when their incomes are high and dissaving when their incomes are low. The direct implication is that consumers with rising incomes should start spending more and save less because of future income growth. Clearly, this is not happening in China. In fact, rapid income growth led to high and growing savings rates. This is surprising given the fact that the country still has low per capita income and good future growth prospects both of which should lead to lower savings. Another disconnection with the theory relates to the saving pattern between generations. You would expect the following "hump shaped" pattern: Young workers save little (in anticipation of rising income); savings rates tend to peak when earnings are high (middle age) and fall as workers approach the retirement phase. However, in China, the highest savings rate is observed among the younger and the older households. Obviously, other specific Chinese features are working.

14.4 Explaining China's household consumption and savings habit

In Fig. 14.5, we explain China's low consumption as percentage of GDP. Consumption is driven by income level and its development (upper half of Fig. 14.5), and the percentage of income spent on consumption (driven by marginal propensity to save and the availability of finance), indicated in the lower half of the figure.

Two main factors account for the large fall in the share of household consumption in total expenditure during the 2000s. Firstly, relatively low wage growth drives the share of household

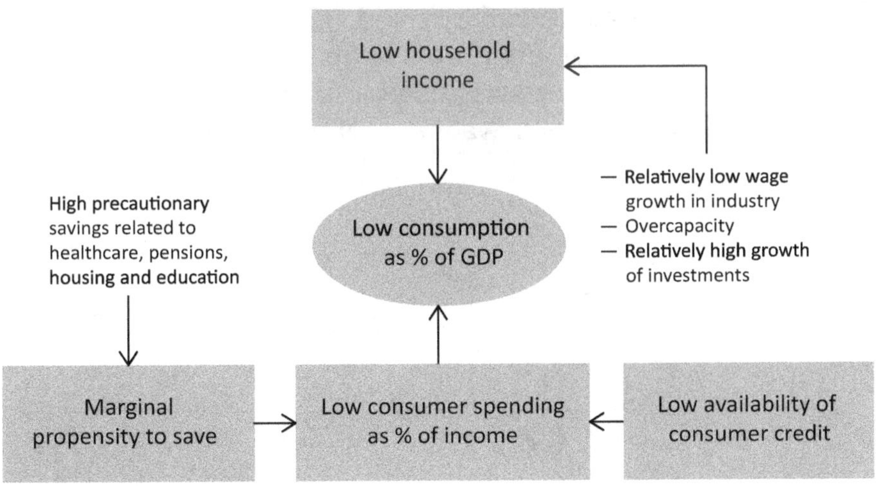

Figure 14.5 Explaining the low consumption rate

Note: The consumption rate refers to the consumption as % of GDP
Source: Adjusted from BBVA Research

income in the total economy down. Secondly, the increase in household savings driven by uncertainty.

Share of household income is falling

Household income relative to total national income (or GDP) has declined strongly. At the same time, the shares of total national income accruing to the corporate and the government sectors have risen. The increase in the corporate income share mainly reflects lower costs following the termination of the requirement that enterprises provide social services to their workers (in the late 1990s), while the increase in the government income share is due to higher tax receipts after the mid-1990s.

Wages constitute 75–80% of the Chinese household disposable income over the previous decades, and therefore serve as a proxy for household income. Figure 14.6 shows that the wage share in the economy declined to only 47% in 2011.

The continuous influx of migrant workers and unemployment in certain cohorts of the labour market has prevented wages from rising as fast as productivity and GDP, leading to this continued decline in the share of wage income between the mid-1990s and 2011. Be aware that it is not about an absolute decline in wages; in fact, wages strongly increased, but less

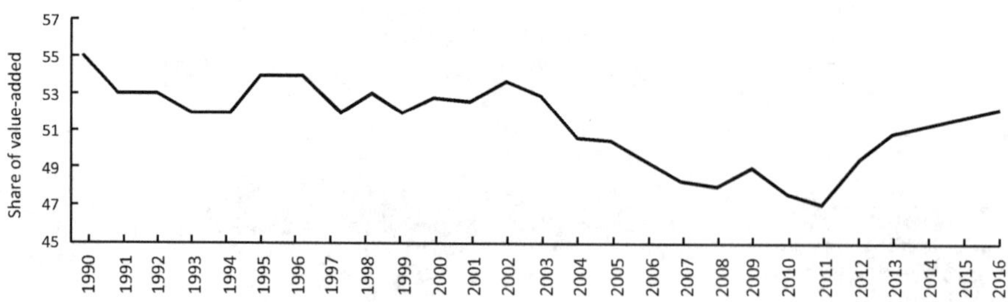

Figure 14.6 Wage share in China's GDP

Note: In official statistics, income from self-employed individuals is allocated to capital and consequently, data underestimates the labour share in the Chinese economy

Source: National Bureau of Statistics of China, OECD Data (2016)

compared to the growth of GDP. This falling share of household income is the main cause behind the decline in consumption as a share of GDP in the 2000s.

Increase in savings

The second factor behind the low consumption rate has been the increase in household savings (marginal propensity to save) in the 2000s. The household savings ratio has increased steadily, to reach 42% in 2007. Although, it dropped slightly after 2007, we see an extremely high savings propensity. Many factors contributed to this household savings behaviour.

14.5 Clustering the reasons behind China's high savings rate

Below, we cluster the main factors in explaining and understanding the high savings rate of Chinese households. We rank the factors in importance, starting with the most important factor.

1. *Precautionary savings due to institutional reforms*

Several major institutional reforms since the 1990s significantly influenced the Chinese savings trends. Between 1995 and 2005, China executed a tough corporate restructuring process. Part of the restructuring was the abolishment of the enterprise-based cradle-to-grave social safety net. Commercialising the SOEs was the final step in abolishing the "iron rice bowl" welfare system. This resulted in big uncertainties by employees (and consumers) regarding healthcare and pensions. Facing uncertainty of these potential expenditures and the situation that borrowing money was not very easy, most households tend to save more under precautionary motives. Besides healthcare and pensions, they also witnessed increasing cost of (higher) education. This is particular the case with respect to urban savings.

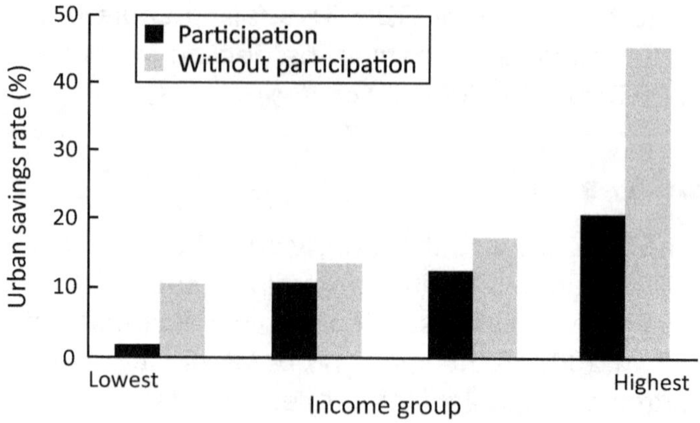

Figure 14.7 Urban household savings rates with and without participation in social security schemes

Source: *Wang Dewen (2010)*

In Fig. 14.7, one can see a significant difference in the marginal propensity to save between urban households with social security coverage and those without. The outcome is based on research on households in the largest cities in 2009. For example, the urban households with social security coverage in the highest income group save 21% of their gross income, while those without social security coverage save 46% of their total household income in 2009. As discussed before, the provision of social security services (which started to accelerate after 2010) can make individuals and households feel more secure in their spending, which is helpful in reducing savings and boosting consumption.

Another important institutional change that influenced (urban) precautionary savings was the introduction of private home ownership. Housing prices have increased dramatically in most Chinese cities between 2000 and 2016. Although mortgages are available, Chinese home buyers often pay a high down payment (higher than required by law). They have to save quite a lot in order to buy a home.

Private house ownership is a relatively new phenomenon and also the (thin) stock market is relatively new. Hence, until recently (and even today), there were not so many options as to what to do with the savings, and consequently the supply of savings was and stayed high (the so-called "forced savings"). An interesting observation earlier in the book was that in China you see that people may save more even in the context of a low or falling interest rate. This looks like a paradox, but it is logical in the Chinese setting. Households save to meet multiple needs such as insurance, retirement, meeting the down payment to purchase a home and appear to behave as though they have a target level of savings in mind; they are target savers. When the return to savings falls, households have a tougher time meeting their target savings and react by increasing the share of their disposable income that they save. So, the low level of social security, rising housing prices and credit constraints, all resulted in high (and growing) precautionary savings.

2. Hukou *system and consumption*

Until recently, the *hukou* system served as an obstacle to stronger consumption and stimulated savings. Obviously, the savings of migrant workers are relatively low due their lower wage level, but their marginal propensity to save is relatively high; they save a large part of their income. Migrants from rural to urban areas are often restricted to access public services. Hence, they have to save more of their income to assure against risks. In addition, they work in the cities but are hardly spending; they send as much salary back to the family that stay in the rural sector. As long as these migrant workers are not integrated in a decent welfare system, they will save instead of spending the money.

3. *Cultural and historical factors*

Since so many high-savings economies are in Asia, a tempting explanation for China's high savings rate is culture. In particular, the argument is that China's culture has a tradition of emphasising the long term, and that this tradition is a driver behind the savings habit. It is indeed the case that several Asian countries have the highest savings in the world, together with oil- and resource-rich countries. The problem with this argument is that it does not explain why savings rates have fallen substantially in Japan and Taiwan since growth rates slowed down in the previous decade. Another explanation in which the past plays a role is the fact that a large part of the Chinese population, rich or poor, experienced the disastrous periods of the Great Leap Forward and the Cultural Revolution. They experienced hardship and as a result they are passionate savers and cautious spenders. From this perspective, however, you would expect that the rural savings rates would be relatively high because rural residents have suffered disproportionately. However, this is not the case. Urban savings does not differentiate from rural savings. As a result, only a small part of the savings habit may be explained by cultural and historical factors.

4. *Liquidity constraints*

China's consumers make limited use of credit. In particular, younger consumers have difficulties to get a loan from the banking sector. Therefore, they have to accumulate savings for buying a house or paying for education. As a result, young people are substantial savers which is in contradiction with theoretical models discussed before. Although we still see a borrowing constraint that stimulate personal savings, bank loans to the Chinese household sector have expanded substantially after 2010, reaching 15% of the total outstanding bank loans in 2017 (Xinhua). In other words, the availability of consumer credit does not appear to be a major constraint to consumption anymore.

5. *Demographics and urbanisation*

Demographic changes stimulated by China's one-child policy affected savings and consumption. Theoretically, the higher the share of young and old people in total population, the lower household savings will be. This is not being observed in China. Within the Chinese context, institutional features are more important than the demographic impact on savings and consumption behaviour. Furthermore, cities provide a more favourable climate to consume than rural areas. Low urbanisation is, therefore, regarded as another factor that contributes to low aggregate household consumption rate in China. Higher rates of urbanisation mean that rural, agricultural workers are moving to cities to take advantage of higher-wage labour markets. This raises households income. And as we know, urban consumption growth is considerably higher than the rural growth in consumption.

6. *Other explanations*

In the media, more (indirect) causes are given to explain the low consumption and high savings rate in China. For example, the intensified competition among men for potential wives stimulates households with a son to spend less and save more to be able to buy an (additional) apartment. In this way, gaining a competitive edge in the marriage market. So, there could be an effect of sex ratio imbalance on household savings. By looking at the overview above, it is to be expected that the savings rate will drop and that the consumption ratio may rise. But more is needed; hence, specific government measures to stimulate consumption.

14.6 Policies to increase consumption and rebalance the economy

Rebalancing towards consumption will require, among other policies, measures to raise household income and induce people to save less and consume more. This is indeed what we see in choosing the measures taken by the government in the previous years. We will focus on three policy instruments: increasing disposable income, enabling the consumer to spend its money and reducing precautionary savings.

Boost disposable income

Higher income encourages households to spend more. Therefore, to increase consumption, household disposable income should be boosted through increasing the wage and the non-wage part of the income. We see government action in this field. For example, starting with the 11th five-year plan, the government increased its minimum wage quite dramatically from 2010 onwards. This has been complemented by taxation measures and spending on public financed education. Also, stimulating the service sector fits in this approach. An expanding service sector (and a move to higher value-added manufacturing) will require a more skilled labour force, which also implies that wages will rise. As a result, market wages have climbed quickly since 2010. Government policies have increasingly favoured workers and their rights. For example, the Labour Contract Law of 2008 improved the wage standards as well as provided more protection for workers. Through various subsidy schemes and agricultural reforms, rural incomes have also increased rapidly.

Besides specific government policy, the increase in wages have been driven by two market forces. Firstly, there is a shortage of skilled workers in coastal China, where the majority of manufacturing takes place. The shortage stems, in part, from the rising cost of living in megacities like Shanghai and Beijing. Secondly, ageing of the workforce and increasing education levels among younger workers have made it more difficult for companies to get workers to agree to the same terms earlier generations had accepted.

Figure 14.8(a) shows the manufacturing wages per hour for several countries in 2015 and projections for 2019. It is clear that wages in China are not extremely low anymore. Obviously, it is much lower than wages paid in the US or Japan, but higher compared to countries such as Vietnam and Indonesia. A remarkable development is the China wage growth relative to a country such as Mexico. In 2003, China's wage level was 60% lower than the Mexican wage level, but this changed dramatically within a decade. In 2016, Chinese wages were 40% higher compared to the wages in Mexico (Fig. 14.8 (b)).

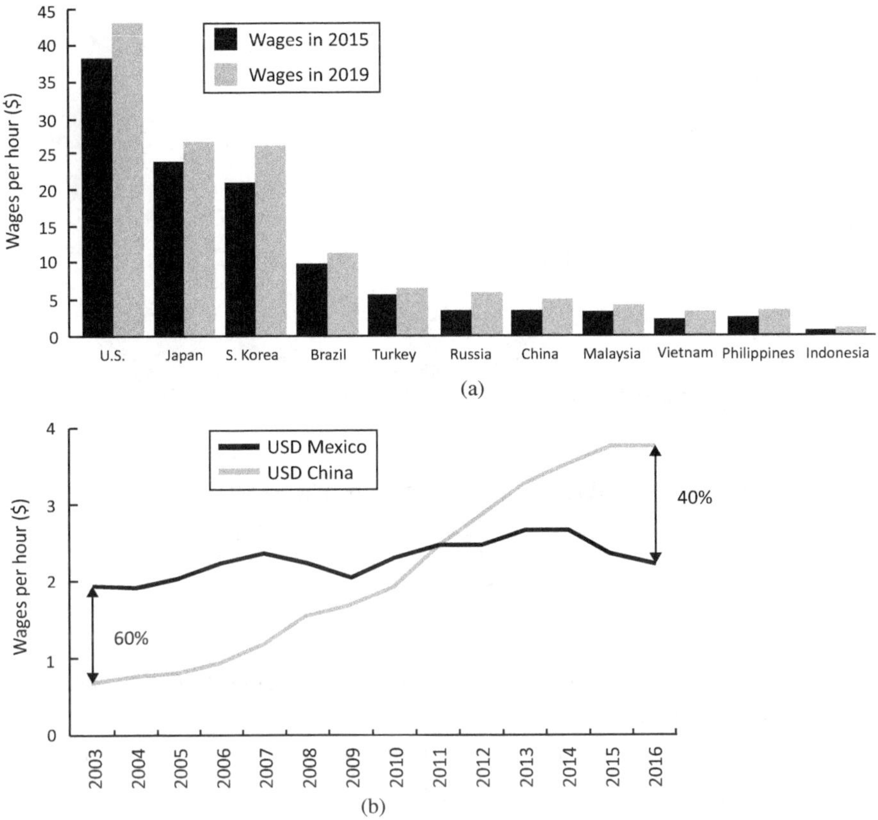

Figure 14.8 Manufacturing wages per hour (US$); specific countries

Source: *Adjusted from FT (14 January 2016) and Economist Intelligence Unit Database*

Enable consumer spending

At the end of the day, people decide what to spend and how much they save. Having said this, the government can stimulate household spending. For example, to make credit and finance more available. Figure 14.9 shows the development of retail sales. Most of the retail sales are done in the urban areas. And until 2012, also the growth of urban retail spending (15%) was higher than in the rural areas (10%). An interesting observation is that between 2012 and 2016, the growth of rural retail sales is

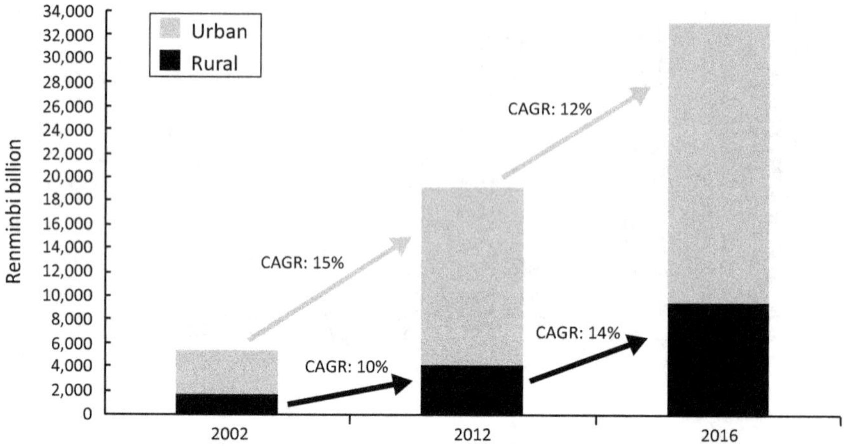

Figure 14.9 Urban and rural retail spending, specific years

Note: *The compound annual growth rate (CAGR) is the year-over-year growth*
Source: *Adjusted (and extended) from McKinsey insights China — Macroeconomic Model update (March 2011) and BBVA Research*

higher, indicating the growing role of the rural middle class in total consumption.

Increasing access to consumer credit helps spending. The rising popularity of new products such as credit cards, mortgages and auto loans all signal the growth of a consumer culture, and hence will reduce savings rates. Furthermore, the modern retail sector is introducing concepts such as consumer loyalty cards linked to credit cards. From this perspective, you would expect a fall in savings rates and an increase in consumption in the next coming decade.

Reducing precautionary savings

As insurance markets develop, the need for precautionary savings will fall. For instance, improved medical insurance and guaranteed pension benefits will reduce the need to save for potential medical expenses. From 2010 onwards, the Chinese government implemented regulations that provide basic pension and insurance

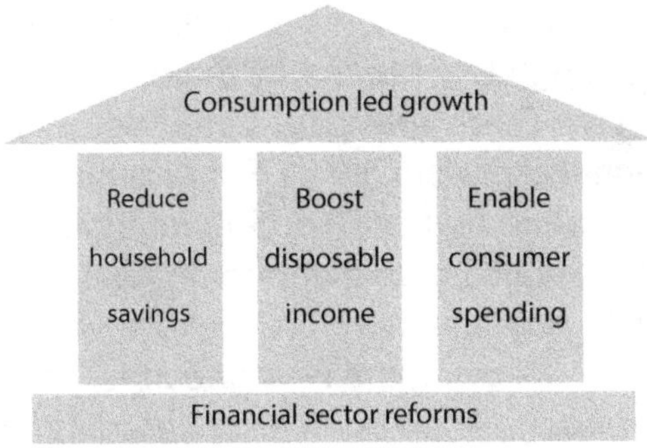

Figure 14.10 Steps to increase household consumption
Source: Based on Xinhua and adjusted from BBVA

coverage for all citizens. All these measures will reduce the precautionary motives for saving. Clearly, the Chinese social security system has been improved, but it is still at a primary stage. The Chinese middle class acknowledged the improvement, but it will take some time before we see a significant drop in precautionary savings.

The above steps taken to boost consumption, is summarised in Fig. 14.10. The main drivers are increasing the disposable income so that people can spend. Furthermore, steps are taken to reduce household savings so that people are willing to spend. The final step in boosting consumption is to enable consumer spending through opening sectors for private companies and to make credit more available.

Financial reforms will lay the foundation over which other reforms can be successfully executed. That is why there is additional (and easier) credit available for SMEs. This is important because they provide employment and extra household income over time. Important steps are taken to reduce savings and increase the marginal propensity to consume. These policies involve institutional changes, such as social security or healthcare reforms. Other reforms that are needed involve the position of the migrant worker in China's society.

These structural changes will be implemented step by step. It may not be fast enough to drive the development of consumption in the upcoming years. There are quite a number of barriers that hinders the full potential of consumption. For example, banking reforms to ease access to credit by SMEs and households will be relatively slow. Consequently, building up a strong domestic market, driven by a robust household consumption, may take a while. Therefore, the outside world is and will be, in the next decades, essential in China's development. The result is an even stronger integration of China in the world economy, the focus of the final part of this book.

Part III

China's Integration in the World Economy

The following Chapters (15–19) focus on China's integration in the world economy through foreign direct investments (FDIs) and international trade. We start with explaining FDI inflow and outflow. The next step is to analyse the strengths and weaknesses of Chinese firms entering western markets, followed by the success and failures of western companies doing business in China. We will close this part by providing a glimpse about the future of integration and China's role in it.

In line with the previous parts of the book, the analysis is heavily influenced by the five words introduced in the Overview. Discussing China's integration today and the future means inherently toughing on the keywords that are characterising China: contradictions, speed, misconceptions, numbers and interpretation.

Chapter 15

Theories on FDI

Myth 15: China is an important host of foreign direct investments, but it will take a while before we see a substantial increase of Chinese outward investments

15.1 Introduction

Foreign direct investment (FDI) is defined as a cross-border investment made by a company in one country in order to obtain a long-term interest in a foreign company that is situated in another economy. The investment should result in direct management control by the investor. This is why an FDI is also termed as a direct investment. Investing abroad and putting the foreign subsidiary under the umbrella of the mother company result in a multinational enterprise (MNE). This management control distinguishes FDI from a portfolio investment. For statistical purposes, a transaction is considered to be an FDI when the company in question obtains, at minimum, a 10% stake in a foreign company (UNCTAD). In that case, it is assumed that this voting power of more than 10% creates management control.

FDI relates to inflow as well as outflow. Chinese inward FDI already accelerated in the early 1990s, while outward FDI only started after the mid-2000s. Measuring and reporting FDIs can be done by using the flow and stock concept. FDI flows (inward and outward) record the value during a given period of time, usually a quarter or a year. The stock of FDI (inward and outward) measures the total level of direct investments at a given point in time by summing up all the previous flows. Because Chinese companies started relatively late with investing abroad, its stock of outward FDI is still small compared to other countries, while at the same time China was the second largest investor in terms of outward FDI flow in 2016. It should be noted that FDI flows can fluctuate considerably due to one or two large transactions in a specific year. The stock of FDI is more stable and gives a more structural picture. FDI stocks are measured in US dollars and as a share of gross domestic product (GDP). This may complicate the discussion. For example, we see in absolute terms enormous Chinese outward FDI in the previous years, but at the same time China's outward FDI as a percentage of GDP is much lower than what we see in more mature economies such as the US and the UK.

Although the MOFCOM Statistical Bulletin of outward investments is in accordance with international standards, and despite considerable improvements in its transparency and registration process in the previous decade, real FDI data may be quite different from statistics. For example, most (smaller) private firms do not apply for their investments projects abroad. Consequently, the MOFCOM data that is based on its registration record is underestimating FDI outflow. Another complicated factor in the discussion on FDI relates to the so-called round-tripping issue. Round-tripping of FDI refers to Chinese capital that first goes to Hong Kong (and other destinations) and then re-enters China in the form of FDI. Besides Hong Kong, also well-known tax havens such as the Virgin and Cayman Islands are in the top five Chinese outward FDI destinations and inward FDI investors over the period 2005–2016. The round-trip of investment capital is done to make use of tax and regulatory benefits made available to foreign investors in China.

The chapter is structured as follows. In Section 15.2, we discuss the most important theories that explain FDI flows. In

Section 15.3, we analyse the main characteristics of China's inward FDI and explain the enormous increase in foreign investments towards China that started in the early 1990s. Then, in Section 15.4, the focus shifts to China's outward FDI: the emergence of Chinese companies in the west. Again, we will concentrate on the main determinants explaining the pattern of outward FDI. Section 15.5 continues with Chinese companies going abroad by discussing what type of companies we may expect to take the firsts steps. In Section 15.6, the focus is on the main success factors of Chinese firms abroad.

15.2 Theories on FDI

The study of FDI has its roots in the transaction costs approach originally developed by Coase (1937) and extended by Williamson (1975). Firms choose to keep all activities within the boundaries of the firm because this is cheaper compared to using the market. For example, there are costs involved in negotiating, monitoring and resolving disputes with an external supplier. There are circumstances in which these costs are much lower if that supplier is integrated (internalised) in the company. Of course, you may have coordination costs inside the company, but they may be lower than all those costs that involve finding, checking and monitoring external entities. From this perspective, internalisation (keeping the transactions inside the hierarchy of the company and therefore establishing an MNE) is driven by transaction costs in the broadest sense. Dunning (1980) used this internalisation aspect in his famous OLI framework. Dunning also borrowed some elements from Hymer (1976) and Penrose (1956). According to them, companies have some specific resources and competences which are so strong that they can also use it on foreign markets. These resources or competences are, in many cases, intangible assets such as knowledge, patents, technology and brands. Dunning combined the main elements of the partial explanations of internationalisation into one broad (eclectic) framework.

The eclectic (OLI) theory of Dunning

According to Dunning (1980), companies will undertake FDI if the company possesses certain ownership advantages, the host country holds certain location advantages, and the internalisation in itself holds advantages for the company.

1. Ownership-specific advantages (*why to invest abroad*)
2. Location-specific variables (*where to invest abroad*)
3. Internalisation incentive advantages (*how to invest abroad*)

Ownership (O-) advantages enable the company to compete with local companies and answer the question why the investment is done. According to Dunning, the ability to compete follows from brands, technology, know-how about the market, sufficient budgets and business contacts. Chinese firms have, in many cases, very specific ownership advantages. For example, flexibility and familiarity of operating within an emerging market context. This type of O-advantage is called a relational asset or networking skills, sometimes linked to the Chinese diaspora. Chinese firms can exploit this O-advantage successfully in difficult emerging economies with a large resident population of ethnic Chinese. Related to this is the O-advantage of being flexible. Many Chinese companies have survived tough conditions in their home markets, such as infrastructural constraints, policy changes, local protectionism and unclear legislation. And this gave them the O-advantage on other difficult and vastly changing markets: their capability to adapt to local circumstances. These are quite different O-advantages compared to western companies. Their O-advantages include proprietary technology, powerful brands, marketing power and other managerial capabilities. The O-advantages of Chinese firms are more towards their ability to adapt technology to develop products suited to the special needs of local customers, and making the products cheaper and more affordable. This ability to design products without unnecessary bells and whistles is being exploited internationally.

Location (L-) advantages of the host country is answering the question where to invest. It is answering the question why, for example, Philips is investing in and producing medical equipment in China or why China-based China Minmetals is investing in Peru.Location advantages are heterogeneous but are associated with the political and institutional environment. This includes political stability, level of corruption, bureaucracy, public service quality, laws and regulations, and FDI incentives. These are factors that make a location attractive to foreign investors. Laws and regulations that influence the FDI location choice relate to government attitude towards foreign capital and companies. Chinese FDI in Peru increased dramatically in the mid-1990s, driven by the new government that stimulated inflow of foreign investors in the mining sector. This was a big change from the prevailing policies during much of the post-war period. Up to 1990, Peru had heavy government intervention. But after 1990, when President Fujimori was elected, private sector involvement was actively encouraged and many of the mining companies were privatised. The Fujimori administration was in need of hard currency and, as part of the IMF stabilisation plan, declared promotion of FDI. This clearly increased Peru's L-advantage and Chinese investments in Peru (Sanborn and Chonn, 2015).

Another important L-advantage is the market. Investing is done because of the large and increasing purchasing power in the country. This may be the domestic market but can also be related to neighbouring countries if the host country is part of a larger trading block. In that case, the foreign company may not be forced to set up full operations or supporting offices in each country in which it wants to be active. China's integration in Asia through its association with the ASEAN Free Trade Agreement or the newest One Belt, One Road initiative, increases its L-advantage considerably. The same holds with respect to countries in the EU or the NAFTA. A final L-advantage relates to our discussion in Chapter 9 about Porter's diamond (1990) and its agglomeration effects. This agglomeration effect (clustering of firms within the same geographical area and creating positive externalities) has a significant and positive impact on inward and outward FDI. Clustering of companies (for example, within a special economic zone) can lead to many spillover effects. These spillover effects can make an investment location attractive to companies seeking cost advantages.

Finally, Internalisation (I-) advantages refers to the how question. It relates to the mode of entry choice. In Chapter 17, we will discuss the entry strategy issue, but it is clear that the company has several choices on how to enter a foreign market. Only if there is control over strategic choices, such as in the case of a takeover or greenfield investment, is an MNE established. In this case, the company is internalising its activities. Lower transaction costs, effective management and good quality control are examples of Internalisation (I-) advantages that result in choosing an investment with management control and having the activities internalised within the framework of the MNE. Obviously, the OLI framework is closely related to the motives of going abroad.

Motives

Based on the OLI paradigm, Dunning (1998) separated four types of FDI motives: market seeking, resource seeking, efficiency seeking, and strategic asset seeking (Table 15.1). Companies that are looking for new markets (market seeking) will mainly focus on L-factors such as market size, market growth, income-level, and urbanisation rate of the country or region. The urbanisation rate is an important factor since cities provide large consumer markets in a relatively small geographic area which makes logistics and marketing relatively easy (think about the development of e-commerce). In the case of resource-seeking FDI, the company seeks to secure scarce resources like raw minerals at lower costs. A distinctive feature of this resource-seeking FDI in the Chinese context is that it is dominated by SOEs, mostly helped by (local) governments. The process in which the Chinese government helps SOEs abroad with aid and financial assistance is part of what is called "infrastructure diplomacy". The Chinese SOE is taking over a company abroad,

Table 15.1 Motives of foreign direct investments

FDI type	Description
Resource seeking	Investing abroad to acquire (part of) natural resources and raw materials. Foreign resources can be interesting due to lower costs of production
Market seeking	Investing abroad to take advantage of the current (or potential) market. The various reasons relate to follow suppliers or customers, to adapt products to local needs and avoiding transportation (and serving) costs
Efficiency seeking	Investing abroad to take advantage of differences in availability and costs with respect to labour and capital. It includes the possibility to achieve economies of scale and scope
Strategic asset seeking	Investing abroad to acquire (part of) new technology, knowledge and building up brand image

Source: Based on Dunning (1998)

while government-associated organisations are taking care of soft loans and making funds available for infrastructural investments to make sure that the products can be efficiently transported to the home country.

Efficiency-seeking FDIs will occur if companies are searching for opportunities to lower their costs of operations, for instance, by lowering the costs of labour. This used to be a main motive for western companies investing in China up to the mid-2000s, i.e. to make use of lower production costs. Finally, strategic assets are resources and capabilities of a company with which the company has a competitive advantage compared to its rivals. Strategic asset-seeking FDIs occur when a company wants to have access to unique capabilities, for instance, knowledge, technological skills or brands. This can be seen today with many Chinese companies taking over high-tech and knowledge-intensive companies abroad.

Besides the four motives, there are more (firm and sector specific) motives mentioned in the literature to explain FDI. For example, companies decide to undertake FDI due to heavy domestic competition, to avoid high tax rates or as reaction on moves from competitors. According to the oligopolistic reaction theory (Knickerbocker, 1973), companies tend to follow their (major) competitors when it comes to investments in foreign markets. If a leading company in a specific industry invests in a foreign market, other companies within the same industry tend to react by investing in the same market, i.e. follow the leader theory. The same can be said with respect to clients. In this case, companies are investing abroad because they are following their main clients. For example, this was the main motive of German-based Leoni AG, a large provider of cables and wiring systems to the automotive industry. It built a new plant in Langfang, just outside Beijing in Hebei province. At the opening of the plant, it was stated that the company is in China because it followed German automakers.

Adjusting theory due to emerging market companies

Dunning's ownership advantage within the OLI theory is the notion that the company investing abroad should have a specific competitive advantage, being tangible or intangible assets. Of course, Chinese companies do have competitive advantages but of a very different nature from that possessed by developed market MNEs. Chinese companies may have weaker technology, marketing knowledge and management skills. But they have developed organisational and strategic innovations that (more than) compensate for their lack of technical and managerial capabilities. They have their own unique competences. For example, they obtained international competitiveness because of their experience in working in an unclear, fast changing and weak legislative context. Precisely working in this context gave them the flexibility, entrepreneurship and higher tolerance for risk needed to operate in other difficult markets.

Rugman (1981) developed a framework in which he elaborates on these O-advantages. He divides the competitive advantage of a firm into firm-specific advantages (FSAs) and country specific advantages (CSAs). In most cases, the success of Chinese firms abroad relies on their home country advantages: cheap labour, cheap resources and cheap money. They are based on resource endowments (minerals, energy), labour force (low wages) and government support. So, Chinese companies may have a competitive advantage, but this is based on the country. According to Rugman, at the end of the day, to be able to compete on third markets, the Chinese companies must switch towards FSAs. This can be done in several ways. For example, through collaboration with foreign firms. This cooperation is sometimes mandatory within a joint venture (JV) construction or a contracted strategic alliance. In many cases, it involves sharing of technology, which was a big issue in the US, early 2017. A second way to improve FSA is through competition and allowing private and international firms to compete on the domestic market. This will create more incentives to develop own firm specific advantages. An important motive of Chinese companies for international expansion through an FDI is to buy (and build up) this FSA. This is the essence of the Linkage-Leverage-Learning (LLL) model of Mathews (2006), also referred to as the "springboard perspective" (Luo and Tung, 2007). The LLL-model is based on the notion that Chinese companies are internationalising despite their weak O-advantages, precisely to build these FSAs. The above analysis is done from a company's point of view, but we can also analyse FDI flows from a country's point of view.

Investment development path model

According to Dunning and Narula (1996), the economic development of a country determines the outward and inward direct investments. This is the essence of the investment development path (IDP) model. The IDP theory differentiates five main stages in the development of a country. Each stage corresponds to a specific outward and inward direct investment picture. Outward FDI is driven by firm-specific O-advantages, while inward FDI is attracted by country's L-advantages. Figure 15.1 shows the five stages of the IDP.

The net outward investment position (NOI) is indicated on the vertical axis of Fig. 15.1. It is defined as total outward minus total

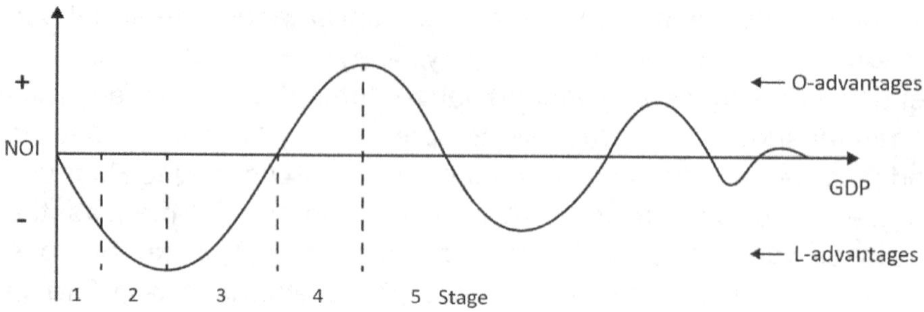

Figure 15.1 Investment development path
Source: *Dunning and Narula (1996)*

inward direct investments. A positive NOI means that outward FDI is larger than inward FDI. In the case of a negative NOI, the inflow of FDI is larger than the outflow of FDI. The figure shows the relationship between the state of economic development ranging from a less developed country (stage 1) via a middle-income country (stage 3) to an industrialised and mature high-income country (stage 5), and the net outward investment position. In the first three stages, the FDI inflow outpaces the outflow, in stage four, country's FDI outflow is higher than inflow, while in stage five a balance between inflow and outflow develops. As we will see later, from this analysis, one may expect a continuation of the Chinese FDI outward as China is (still) in stage three of the Dunning and Narula model.

Stage 1

In the first stage, as the country's development level is low, the location-specific advantages of the country are insufficient to attract large FDI flows. As there is a low per capita income, the local market generates little demand. Also, the low quality of infrastructure and shortage of skilled labour limit the inflow. However, we will see some inflow related to natural assets. The role of the government is important to attract resource seeking FDI in this stage. It may give foreign companies substantial preferences and this increase the L-advantage. At the same time, the O-advantages of the domestic companies are low. They cannot compete on foreign markets and may lack knowledge to manage international operations, and consequently outward direct investment is very small at this stage.

Stage 2

As a result of economic development, the inward investments start to increase in stage 2. Step by step, the domestic market grows and is the main driver behind the increase of the L-advantages of the country. The structure of inward FDI is not changing too much; it still concentrates on natural resources, primary commodities and low-tech manufacturing. The government's role in attracting FDI is important, although it may change slightly from stage 1. Now, government policy shifts towards creating a stable and transparent business environment and is less focused on giving subsidies and preferences to specific foreign companies. In addition, O-advantages of domestic firms start to emerge as a result of learning how to cooperate and compete with foreign companies. The government supports the outflow by (export and technology) subsidies.

Stage 3

In stage 3, the NOI increases as outward direct investment becomes higher than inward FDI. Rising incomes and growing competitiveness of local firms characterise this stage of a country. The initial low O-advantages of firms will rise; technology is being absorbed and there are important learning effects related to management and marketing. L-advantages also change as a result of the growing local market and its middle class. The (potential) market is taking over the low production costs as the main L-advantage. The function of the government at this stage will be more indirect than in stage two; achieving a transparent and stable business climate in which innovative behaviour is being stimulated and where foreign companies feel comfortable.

Stage 4

In stage 4, the level of FDI outflow equals or exceeds the level of inflow. In this stage, local firms are capable of competing with foreign firms both on their domestic market, as well as abroad. The L-advantage of the country will be based on a high-skilled labour force, efficient infrastructure and a mature market. Inward investments at this stage will be mostly market seeking. Higher wages are reducing the original L-advantage, but it is taken over by skilled labour (that is still relatively cheap). Outward direct investment will grow significantly as domestic firms further increase their competitiveness and are learning fast from their international experience. The role of the government is at the backstage, concentrating on its regulatory function and less and less on executing specific industrial policy.

Stage 5

In stage 5, the NOI position of a country converges to the zero level, although we see temporary surpluses and deficits. In this stage, the level of inward and outward direct investment continues to increase. It is possible that a country emerges as net outward investor in a specific industry and at the same time, in other sectors, attracts a lot of investments.

The development of China's inward and outward FDI between 2000 and 2016 is given in Fig. 15.2. Before 2005, China can be labelled as a stage 2 country in the Dunning–Narula framework: growing inflow of FDI but hardly any outward FDI, creating a large negative outward investment position. The FDI inflow was associated with low production costs in this period. China had an L-advantage with respect to labour costs.

After 2005, we see a strong catching up of outward FDI, driven by rising O-advantages of Chinese firms and building up these O-advantages through international takeovers. In 2008, even as global outward FDI fell by 15%, Chinese outward FDI more than doubled. In 2009, when global outward FDI plummeted by 43%, Chinese outward FDI (helped by the government) stabilised. In

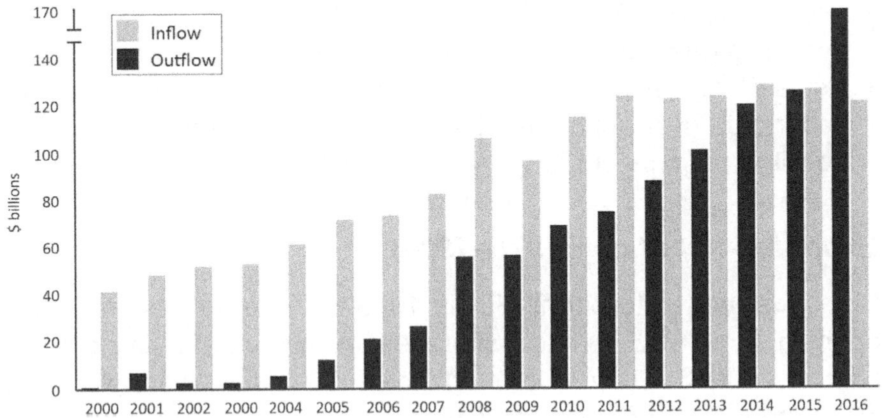

Figure 15.2 Development of China's inflow and outflow of FDI, 2000–2016, US dollars

Note: *Due to Round-tripping we may overemphasise the FDI inflow and outflow figures*
Source: *National Bureau of Statistics and MOFCOM*

2016, outward FDI exceeded inflow of direct investments, and it looks like China is approaching the end of the third stage in the Dunning–Narula model. If China is following the IDP, we may expect much more Chinese investments abroad in the near future.

15.3 China's FDI inflow

A feature that set China apart from other East Asian countries is its openness to FDI early in its transformation process. The central government has allowed foreign companies into China at a much earlier stage of its development compared to South Korea and Japan. It does not mean that the doors were set open from the beginning; as always, China followed a gradualist policy. Its policy regarding FDI between 1979 and 2016 can be divided into three stages.

- Experimental stage (1979–1991). The legal basis was set up and four special economic zones (SEZs) were opened for foreign companies. Furthermore, from the mid-1980s, there was an improvement in the law and regulations to facilitate and stimulate FDI.

- Growth stage (1992–2002). Strong growth of FDI inflow due to specific measures, combined with a robust worldwide rise in FDI.
- Adjustment stage (2003–2016). Shortage of capital is not an important driver anymore. The focus is not to attract as many as possible projects but to attract high-quality investments.

Experimental stage (1979–1991)

China first began to permit FDI in 1979 with the JV law, including opening some SEZ. In this first stage, China wanted to avoid competition for its SOEs from foreign firms. The result was that only a small amount of FDI entered China and this was concentrated in sectors in which either domestic Chinese firms did not participate (export and some service sectors such as hotels) or ones where China urgently needed capital and access to foreign (advanced) technology such as oil exploration and heavy industry. Essentially, the shortage of capital motivated Chinese policymakers to allow FDI in the export sector. Because the Chinese export sector was not able to sell abroad, there was shortage of foreign exchange to buy foreign technology. China needed foreign companies to be able to export and to earn foreign exchange. The authorities saw the advantages of opening up. Foreign companies would introduce competition and achieve learning effects of domestic companies. The need to cooperate and to compete would give incentives to increase productivity and quality. The JV construction would help to accelerate this learning effect.

Up to the mid-1980s, FDI inflows remained modest, constrained by uncertainty about legislation and the need to cooperate with a local partner. For many western companies, this was perceived as problematic because you had to share your skills, competences, knowledge and innovations with the Chinese partner (which was an SOE). The 1979 JV-law required the chairman of the board to be a Chinese, regardless of the Chinese share of equity contribution. Foreign partners in JVs have been pressed to build commitments into their agreements such as to maximising exports (which was a priority of the authorities), increase local sourcing and share technology; clearly, commitments which were not in the interest of western firms.

Full foreign ownership was explicitly allowed after 1986 when China introduced the wholly foreign-owned enterprise law. In several sectors, western companies could have full ownership and full control over management. This reduced risks and FDI inflow increased after the mid-1980s. The first wave of FDI was concentrated on the eastern coast, largely owing to the proximity to capital from Hong Kong and Taiwan. As stated before, be aware that much of this foreign investment was not actual foreign. A substantial amount of FDI was the result of round-tripping; investments by Chinese firms are done in Hong Kong and this money is reinvested back in Mainland China as a foreign investment, in order to capture tax breaks and other benefits reserved for foreign firms.

Growth stage (1992–2002)

Beginning in 1992, significant market reforms were implemented and new sectors were opened for foreign investments. In addition, the approval process became very liberal and more and more decision making was transferred to local governments. In several cases, what was not possible on paper (published by the central government) was possible when talking with local authorities. Local governments had (and still have) the authority to offer incentives in excess of centrally stipulated rules. You could say that in the 1990s, local governments have clearly taken the lead in stimulating inflow of FDI. One of my colleagues at CEIBS told me in 1996 that local governments had such a degree of operational autonomy that the central government hardly knew how many local development zones were created by local governments to attract FDI.

Step by step, restrictions on FDI were eased and access to the domestic market enlarged with new sectors gradually opening up for foreign companies. Besides institutional changes, the strong growth of the domestic economy also helped in attracting FDI. Growth of FDI inflow was enormous, in particular in the 1992–1997 period. FDI explosions could be seen around the world, but China was an extraordinary case. In this stage, the overwhelming share of FDI was flowing into industrial sector activities that were highly export intensive. The regional distribution of FDI inflow was still very uneven in the 1990s. Obviously, this was logical in the time of the SEZs during the experimental stage, which were located in coastal areas. But despite opening inland cities and legislation to encourage to invest in the inner areas, the regional imbalances stayed. Coastal provinces received between 70% and 80% of FDI between 1992 and 2002 (NBS). This unequal division of FDI is plausible: the highest purchasing power was in the east and the coastal regions had endowments which gave them comparative advantages over inland provinces. Think about geographic proximity to international markets, better transport infrastructure and more skilled labour.

In 1995, the authorities issued the catalogue for the guidance of foreign-invested enterprises. The overview identified sectors in which investment was encouraged, restricted or prohibited depending on its position within China's economic development. It was clearly a tool of industrial policy to attract investments in specific sectors and blocked FDI in other (more sensitive) sectors. Foreign investments were encouraged in manufacturing and export-related industries. At the same time, a large part of the economy was still closed for foreigners, for example, the service sector.

Adjustment stage (2003–2016)

Starting after the Asian crisis of 1997, it became clear to the Chinese authorities that dependency on foreign markets (export) is not by definition good and that building up a domestic market is essential. China's domestic policy was shifting more and more towards higher wages, higher value-added production, innovation and building-up the domestic market instead of being dependent on the outside world. This had big consequences for the policy on and the type of FDI inflow in the period after 2003. FDI started to shift from traditional manufacturing to industries with higher technology-intensity. The example of Nike's investments and production in China make this transition clear. In 2002, the Chinese factories of Nike accounted for 40% of the company's global sports shoe output, compared to just 13% for Vietnam (Nike annual reports). In 2010, Vietnam took the lead with a 37% stake, while Chinese stake fell to around 30%. The same pattern can be seen in other labour-intensive manufacturing. Dutch-based Philips built a new factory in a small Dutch town Drachten (2012) instead of extending its operation in China. In the same year, General Electric moved production from China to its appliance park in Louisville (Kentucky). Other US-based companies, such as Sleek Audio LLC and Scovill Fasteners Inc., made the same choice. China is no longer the top low-cost manufacturing destination, and consequently FDI inflow changed from low-skilled manufacturing companies towards firms that invest to capture part of the growing mass market often associated with the service sector.

The continuation of the uneven distribution of FDI inflows across China was seen as problematic. It contributed to regional economic disparity between the coastal regions and other parts of China. Therefore, the central government announced the "Western Development Strategy" in 2000. The goal of this strategy was to reduce the regional differences by promoting infrastructural projects, improving the investment environment and encouraging FDI in the western regions. Industries and specific companies received government support if they moved production towards central and western areas. Besides the regional perspective, we can also witness a new focus: away from attracting FDI in manufacturing and towards investments in services. This became very visible after 2007 when the central authorities issued a revised catalogue in which the prior bias towards manufacturing for export was reversed. FDI into businesses solely to export was being limited. Underlying this shift was the government's desire to reduce the economy's dependency on volatile export markets and at the same time, the opening up of the service sector for foreign investments. For example, China opened up its retail sector, significantly reducing JV restrictions with respect to retail chains; not only in the retail sector, but also in other service sectors such as tourism and insurance.

In 2013, we saw the latest steps to stimulate specific FDI inflow. In early 2013, the Shanghai free trade zone (SFTZ) was established. This was the first pilot project that used a negative list for foreign investment. A negative list specifies the circumstances and areas where foreign investors are blocked or limited. Those sectors not listed are fully open to foreign investors. Until 2013, China used a positive list in regulating foreign investment. After the SFTZ, more cities and regions used the negative list for foreign investment to test the effects of this new approach. It is interesting to observe that the new initiatives after the 2013 Shanghai zone are more liberal. The negative list is smaller and there are less special regulatory measures that ban or limit overseas investment. Also, the limitations in stakeholder limits have been abolished.

Inflow of FDI stabilised after 2011 at a very high level. The figures are impressive. In 2012, for the first time in recent history, China became the largest recipient of global FDI. In 2014, China's inflow of FDI was US$129 billion compared to US$107 billion direct investments towards the US (Fig. 15.3). And this is only Mainland China, not including the inflow of FDI in Hong Kong. The US attracted a lot of FDI in 2015 and 2016, influenced by several megadeals. In 2016, China's FDI inflow stood at US$139 billion. The forecast of 2017 shows a further increase of FDI inflow, driven by simplified procedures. These are impressive figures. One should keep in mind that in 1979, China's inward FDI was almost zero.

Uneven distribution until 2010

The first wave of FDI was concentrated on the eastern coast, largely owing to capital from Hong Kong and Taiwan. Obviously, this was the result of the SEZs in the coastal regions in the east and south and the explosion of the middle class that occurred in the coastal regions. After 2000, the government stimulated FDI flow into the western areas, but the regional imbalances stayed until 2010. In the previous years, we see a new situation. Between 2010 and 2016, much more FDI went into Central and Western China, driven by substantially lower wages and the

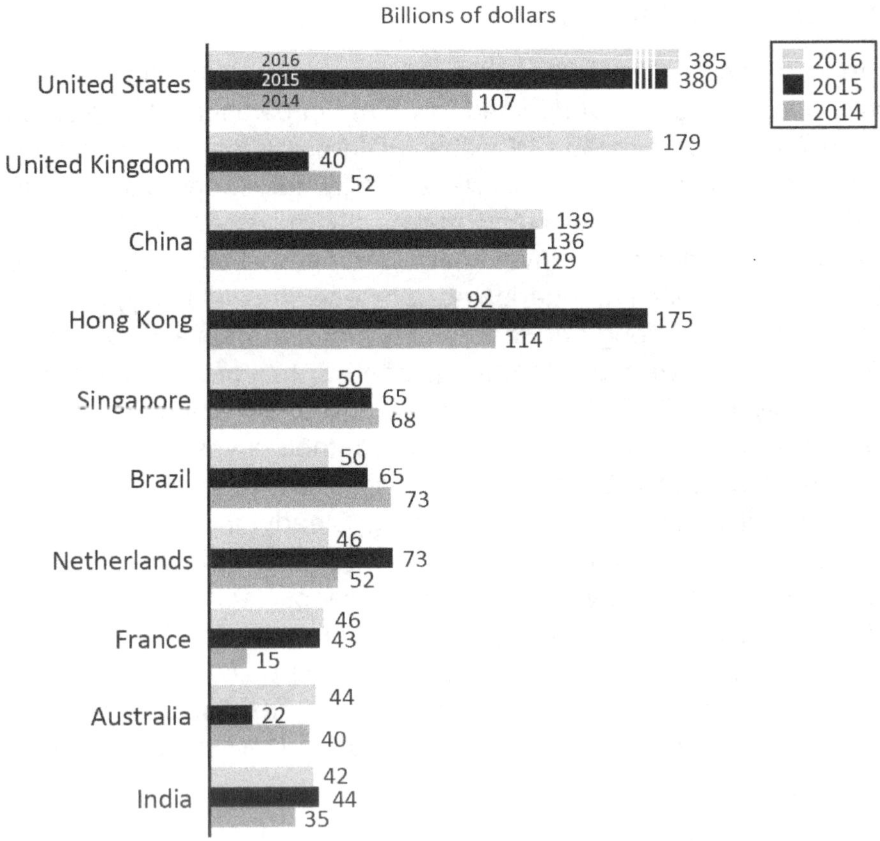

Figure 15.3 Countries with the highest FDI inflow, 2014–2016

Source: Based on National Bureau of Statistics and MOFCOM

growing middle class in these regions (Chapter 14). Government support (subsidies and tax exemptions) helped companies to make the decision to move production to inland. For example, Intel has moved its chip testing and packaging facility from Shanghai to Chengdu after it received substantial (local) preferences. The same holds for companies such as Volvo, DSM, Siemens and IBM. These investments in Chengdu are showcases of the combined "Made in China 2025" policy and the "Go-west strategy" of the Chinese government.

Mostly Asian investors

Up to the end of the 1990s, Asian countries accounted for an overwhelming share of FDI directed to China; in particular, Hong Kong (and Taiwan) dominated FDI inflow. FDI from these regions can be considered as specific in two ways. Firstly, the strong cultural and family links with the mainland makes this flow of FDI almost an "internal" (or domestic) investment. Secondly, FDI inflow relates heavily to so-called round-tripping. Chinese firms (illegally) transfer money to Hong Kong and then invest it in the mainland to benefit from the preferential treatment offered to foreign investors. Obviously, not all FDI from Hong Kong is round-tripping. For example, if US and Japanese firms place their investment on the mainland via subsidiaries in Hong Kong, this investment shows up as direct investment from Hong Kong. Clearly, this investment is not connected to round-tripping. It is difficult to find out how large this round-tripping is. We will discuss this topic later in this chapter. It looks like that round-tripping is becoming less of a distortion factor than in the previous years because China unified the corporate tax rate for foreign investors and domestic firms at 25% in 2008 and stopped preferential treatment for foreign investors in 2010.

Impact on economy

There are several and opposing views about the impact of FDI on the Chinese economy. The views range from extremely positive to at most neutral. The positive view concludes that the recent economic development of China is almost entirely due to FDI. Foreign companies have introduced competition, created learning effects and increased efficiency compared to a previously command economy. FDI created important spillover effects such as transfer of technology and management expertise. The capital intensity (level of fixed assets per employee) of foreign companies in China is, on average, much higher than domestic firms. Foreign enterprises[1] also have a greater technology content in their production. You may expect that

[1]Foreign enterprises also include the JV

this spills over to local companies. Furthermore, the investments from Volkswagen, Philips, Carrefour and Unilever, among others, created employment, both directly and indirectly, and increased purchasing power of the Chinese people. The indirect employment effects, e.g. via backward and forward linkages, are difficult to measure but are, in many cases, higher than the direct employment impact. Quite a few Chinese SMEs have affiliated to the foreign companies in China, creating learning effects and increasing productivity. In addition, FDI is believed to promote exports which in turn will stimulate economic development. There is indeed evidence that FDI has a positive influence on China's foreign trade (Zhang, 2006). The role of foreign companies is particularly noticeable in China's export, and even more in China's high-tech exports. The share of foreign companies in high-tech exports was around 80% in 2010 and then fell slightly to just below 70% in 2016 (BBVA Research).

On the other hand, there is the view that foreign companies hardly affected the Chinese economy. Within this view, the inflow of FDI is seen as activities with no or only a few domestic linkages; mostly related to low-skilled labour and low value-added products, not helping the Chinese economy much. An important part of China's exported products is carrying the foreign brand name, produced with foreign materials and controlled by foreign owners. In this case, China serves as an assembly base and export does not give a lot of additional welfare (an issue we discussed earlier in Chapter 10). Furthermore, you may question the positive impact of western companies on China's trade balance. There were periods in which foreign firms increased China's trade deficit or offset its trade surplus. This negative contribution was mainly due to foreign firm imports of equipment goods. The two opposing views boil down to the question on how intensive the linkages are between foreign firms' activities and the domestic economy. Foreign investments in manufacturing and assembly can help transform the host economy through the introduction of newest technology, production processes and management practices that are learned by local partners and imitated by domestic rivals. But the question is if this happened on a large scale. It looks like much of the FDI in the 1980s and 1990s did not transfer technology to China, at least not at the level the Chinese government hoped for (Miesing and Tang, 2016). But there are large sectoral differences. For example, technology transfer looks relatively high in automotive and high-speed trains. To make the discussion more complex, it could be the case that spillover was low with respect to technology, but high with respect to organisational dynamics and managerial skills.

Despite all the uncertainties (and maybe some disappointing results because expectations were high), there is little doubt that FDI has contributed significantly to Chinese economic development after 2000, mostly via the growth of China's exports where foreign companies are dominating. Also by looking at the growth in per capita income in these regions where FDIs are clustered, one can see the relationship between FDI inflow and domestic welfare. This beneficial impact is on the short term (employment, higher income and consumption) and on the longer term (increasing competition, efficiency and innovative behaviour). This is also the view of the Chinese authorities, and future (high quality) FDI inflow will continue to be stimulated.

15.4 FDI outflow

Statistically, a stake of more than 10% of the investment in a foreign company is seen as FDI and management control is being assumed. That is logical when we consider greenfield investments (setting up new facilities) and M&A, but that is not always the reality in a JV construction. In that case, it depends on the contract and the resources both parties will bring in. While discussing outward FDI, we may think about SOEs and some private companies. But, because minority stakes are also seen as FDI (if they are higher than 10%), part of the Chinese investments relate to sovereign wealth funds (SWF), such as the China Investment Corporation. In fact, these SWFs are the largest investors in the previous years, and they also created the biggest discomfort in the west. We divide the development of China's outward direct investments between 1979 and 2016 into four phases.

- 1979–1991 Cautious internationalisation
- 1992–2000 Learning from mistakes
- 2001–2015 Take-off
- After 2015 Regional initiatives

Cautious internationalisation (1979–1991)

During the 1980s, most Chinese firms did not have enough knowledge and competitiveness to invest (and compete) abroad. In line with Dunnings' eclectic approach, they lacked O-advantages. Furthermore, capital outflow was restricted by the government, given the scarcity of foreign exchange. Up to 1985, only selected SOEs could invest abroad. After the mid-1980s, we see some gradual liberalisation of investment procedures and private companies were able to invest. But, due to the low O-advantage and the legal constraints, outward FDI was negligible.

Learning from mistakes (1992–2000)

President Jiang Zemin declared in 1992 that Chinese companies should spread their wings. This was taken over by the State Council and in the early 1990s, more than 100 large SOEs were selected that were ready for internationalisation. They received government support and procedures to get approval became easier. In this stage, outward FDI increased but the success record of Chinese companies abroad was low. Who has heard about Zhurong (telecom), Yuchai (diesel engines), Kunming Machine Tool and D'Long, the latter being a conglomerate from food to financial services? They were among the first Chinese companies being active abroad. Despite their size and government support, they were not able to survive (international) competition. Partly, this was the result of having no experience at all with doing business abroad. In some cases, there was an underestimation of the cultural differences and risks. Consequently, the government tightened approval procedures, and set up a screening and monitoring process. In the mid-1990s, to get government approval to invest abroad became more difficult. This was a remarkable shift from the previous "wait and see" period.

In 1999, the government announced a new strategy to stimulate outward investments with the slogan "grasping the large and letting go the small". Its aim was to create strong and competitive large SOEs (that are operating on a protected domestic market) and develop them into global champions. And, at the same time to allow the small- and medium-sized firms to face market forces. The larger companies should be able to compete abroad and received government support in their internationalisation process. The start of this Go Global policy was announced in the 10th five-year plan (2001–2005).

Take-off phase (2001–2015)

The period after 2001 can be considered as the take-off of outward FDI. This happened in parallel with China's accession to the WTO (2001) and the Go Global strategy of 2001. In 2004, private companies also could (legally) invest abroad, and they did so in large numbers. The Go Global strategy was further stressed again in the 11th five-year plan (2006–2010). To facilitate outward FDI, the government signed numerous bilateral investment and taxation treaties. Furthermore, we saw substantial relaxation of regulations. For example, in 2006, the State Administration of Foreign Exchange (SAFE) abolished quotas on the purchase of foreign exchange for overseas investment. Another factor that accelerated outward investments was the harmonisation of procedures. Before 2014, China's regulations on foreign investments were quite fragmented. In addition to the State Council, three government bodies (NDRC, MOFCOM, SAFE) had their role in the procedures on outward investments. SAFE was in charge for regulating the use of foreign exchange in foreign projects. All projects had to be registered with SAFE to obtain a foreign exchange registration certificate, which was a prerequisite to sending any currency overseas. The NDRC and MOFCOM shared the power to test and inspect the legitimacy and usefulness of foreign investments. Streamlining the administrative procedures started in 2014 when the Chinese government substantially relaxed the administrative measures for foreign investments. Outward FDI projects no longer required approval, only registration of large transactions is needed. Strategic industries (and specific countries) are excluded. It will take time before the streamlining of procedures is fully executed, but important steps are taken. This harmonisation of regulation and specific government support stimulated FDI outflow strongly after 2014.

Regional initiatives (after 2015)

In early 2016, we saw a renewed emphasis by the Chinese government on stimulating outward investments, driven by domestic economic circumstances. Overcapacity on the domestic market became a burden that stimulated companies to find markets abroad. Also, the large international reserves became more and more a worry due to their low yield. Investing abroad is one way to diversify into higher yielding assets. In addition, the Chinese government was pushing internationalisation not only at the level of individual companies, but also with regional initiatives such as the One Belt, One Road (OBOR) initiative. Under the OBOR initiative, investments in countries along the new silk route accelerated. The investments in countries such as Pakistan, Singapore, Russia, Indonesia, the United Arab Emirates and India have contributed more than proportionally to the rapid growth of China's outward FDI in the previous years. Today most of the outward FDI projects are done under the umbrella of the OBOR initiative.

Fast growth

Chinese outward FDI has grown very rapidly after 2004, and China is now the second largest foreign direct investor in the world, after the US (Fig. 15.4). Chinese companies are globalising at an exceptional rate. However, as a latecomer, China's stock of outward FDI globally is small compared to other major economies even after such a dramatic growth in the previous years. Also, by using indicators such as outward FDI as percentage of GDP or in terms of per capita value, China is lagging far behind the US and western countries. According to UN data, China's FDI outward stock as percentage of GDP was

11% in 2016. The average of the EU was 60%, while the percentage of the US was 34% in 2016 (UN database). It is interesting to note the extreme high figure of Hong Kong, where outward FDI as percentage of GDP stands at 476% in 2016.

Despite the relatively small stock of foreign investments, a great deal of publicity has been generated by the actions of Chinese companies, particularly through the takeover of several high-profile targets. China's outward investment totalled US$175 billion in 2016 (Fig. 15.4), which accounts for around 10% of global FDI outflow of that year. Late 2016, there was the consensus view that outward FDI would drop in 2017 due to stricter rules and a more careful decision process.

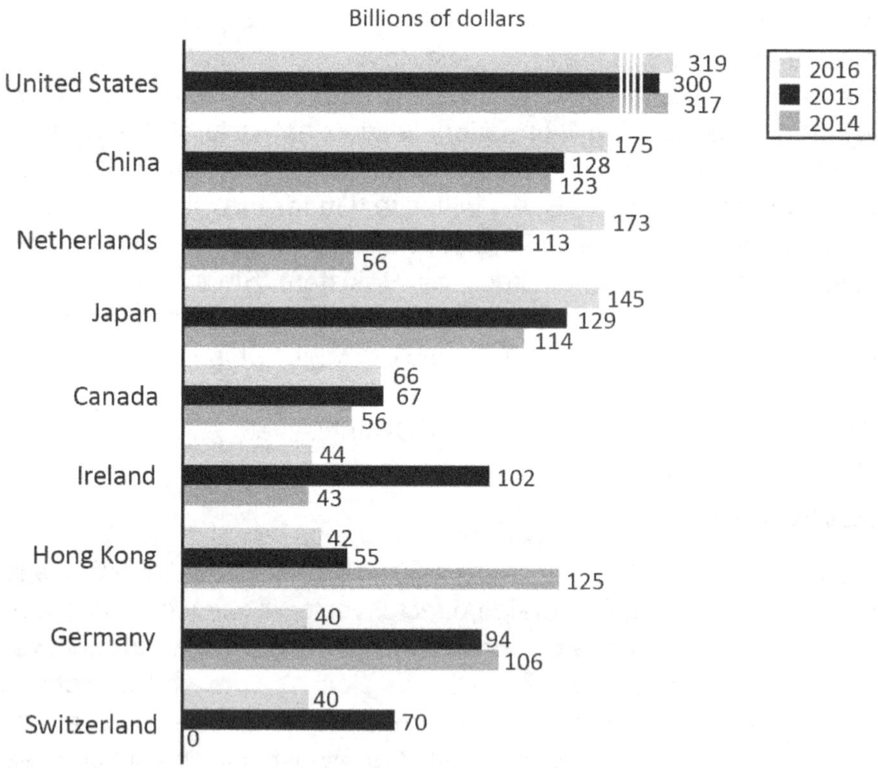

Figure 15.4 Countries with largest FDI outflow, 2014–2016

Source: Based on National Bureau of Statistics and MOFCOM

This difference between flows and stock of FDI is important while discussing China's investment in Africa. China has become a leading source of FDI in Africa, and the absolute flows in the previous years are very high. Although perception may be different, China's investment stock in Africa is relatively very low. Far from matching those of traditional investor countries, it accounts for less than 3% of total FDI stock in Africa in 2016 (UNCTAD, 2017). This does not say that China's influence in Africa is low. It is not. The reason is that FDI is not the only source of capital into Africa. We must link Chinese investments with other government support measures such as China's Official Development Aid (ODA). The size of China's ODA flows to Africa was more than twice as large as that of China's total FDI flows to Africa between 2010 and 2016. Furthermore, ODA is only part of total project finance in Africa. In line with the development of ODA, project finance dominated China's investment flows in Africa in the previous decade. So, to analyse China's influence in regions such as Africa, we should look at the total capital flows instead by using FDI statistics only. The picture is complex. For example, soft loans to finance (infrastructural) projects does not look as market driven since involvement of Chinese private companies is minimal. At the same time, more private companies are involved in FDI transactions.

With respect to outward FDI, one may expect a further rise in the medium to longer-term. Chinese companies are generating important O-advantages. Combined with the gradual move to capital liberalisation, this will further accelerate the trend of outward FDI. Despite the longer-term trend of rising Chinese outward FDI, we may see some short-term hick-ups in the next years to come due to restrictions set on capital outflow. The enormous outflow of capital gives some discomfort and there are signs that larger SOEs find it more difficult to get approval from central authorities to invest abroad.

Role of SOEs

Centrally controlled SOEs are dominating outward FDI in terms of value, while smaller (private) firms are dominating in number of projects. In 2016, the share of SOEs in total value was 80% but only 15% with respect to number of projects (OECD, 2017). SOEs' dominance is in particular visible in the natural resource sector due to their monopolistic power, government support and their preferential access to financial resources. The difference between number of projects and value is also relevant with respect to the type of FDI. More than 75% of all FDI projects are related to greenfield investments between 2000 and 2017. In terms of value, however, the bulk of the investments is attributed to acquisitions, i.e. around 85% over the same period. This is the result of the fact that M&A deals are generally much larger. Having said this, we see some changes in the previous years. Megadeals still account for a big share of total Chinese investments, but small and medium-sized M&A deals have grown particularly strong since 2011, driven by private (often family-owned) companies.

An interesting observation is that Chinese investors are increasingly willing to buy smaller stakes in foreign companies instead of taking full control of their target. Before 2010, most Chinese investors wanted to have full ownership and control. But in the previous years, we see more and more non-controlling stakes. This is not only the result of new investors, such as CIC that normally focus on small minority holdings, it also relates to the realisation of Chinese firms that equal (cooperative) partnership can help to be successful on a foreign market.

A significant proportion of China's multinationals are partially or fully owned by national or regional governments. However, it is difficult to find out how much party or government intervention happens in these companies. In March 2003, the State-owned Assets Supervision and Administration Commission (SASAC) was established. SASAC became an instrument to address the problems of indebted SOEs that undertook risky projects domestically as well as internationally. It monitors around 100 largest SOEs and also invests in these companies if needed. Besides, it is responsible for the restructuring plans of SOE and it has a say in strategic choices such as internationalisation, M&A choices and exit strategies. You may argue that SASAC is reducing the power of the party and government in specific companies, but at the same time, it may be seen as a new instrument in the hands of the authorities. It is unclear how far SASAC has penetrated the day-to-day activities of SOEs, but our impression is, by discussing this topic with colleagues, that the influence of SASAC is in fact indirect concerning commercial and strategic choices.

Regional diversification

The annual regional spreading of Chinese outward FDI is quite volatile and driven by one or two large transactions. For example, the takeover of Swiss-based Syngenta by ChemChina in 2016 heavily influenced that year's picture. The last column of Table 15.2 presents the share of Chinese FDI outflow by geographical destinations in 2016. Because Hong Kong is disturbing the picture, we decided to give the figures without Hong Kong. In 2016, 60% of the mainland's outbound investment flows went to Hong Kong.

The table also shows the regional spreading of outward FDI stock. The annual flows over the previous years totally changed the regional diversification. While Asian countries (besides Hong Kong) were dominating in 2013, the allocation of FDI stock moved towards the US and Europe. In 2016, 26% of China's outward FDI stock and 42% of its flow was in Europe. The top recipient between 2013 and

Table 15.2 China's FDI outflow by destination

Region	Stock 2013 (%)	Stock 2016 (%)	Flow 2016 (%)
Asia	68	30	14
Europe	8	26	42
North America	4	20	33
Oceania	3	8	2
Africa	4	11	2
Latin America	13	5	7

Note: Percentages are based on total outward FDI, excluding Hong Kong
Source: Based on NBS and MOFCOM

2016 was the UK, followed by Germany (OECD, 2017). The UK takes the number one spot due to a mix of factors, including the unique role of London as a financial centre and its attractiveness to commercial real-estate investments. A relevant factor that sets Germany apart is the high number of privately owned small- and medium-sized businesses, which are interesting targets for Chinese companies in search of the newest technology.

Round-tripping

China's outward FDI flows have been highly concentrated in a few host countries. The top destinations in the previous years include Hong Kong, British Virgin Islands and Cayman Islands. Between 2013 and 2016, 70% of all outward investments went to these countries. As indicated earlier, a large part of the investments to Hong Kong are ending up as FDI inflow in China's Mainland. This round-tripping creates, on the one hand, foreign investment status (guarantee of property rights, lower tax rates, and less regulatory uncertainty), and on the other hand financial freedom. Private firms do not have access to the same credit channels as SOE and they move offshore with the specific purpose of raising capital. By establishing a holding company, Chinese firms can raise equity capital from investors outside China. The distortive role that offshore tax havens may play on global FDI statistics is a phenomenon which is not limited to China. A large share of global FDI flows are intermediated through tax havens. Part of this connects to round-tripping (with respect to China), but another part relates to onward journeying. Onward journeying is the strategy to make the investment in third countries via the vehicle in these tax havens. As we saw earlier in this chapter, since early 2008 the new enterprise income tax law has harmonised tax rates for foreign investors and Chinese business. This means that offshore holding companies are being treated as a domestic enterprise for China's taxation purposes and being subjected to the Chinese income tax at the rate of 25% for their global income. You would expect a reduction of the share of round-tripping (and therefore in the dominance of Hong Kong) in the upcoming years, but up to 2016, Hong Kong dominated the picture.

The views on Chinese companies abroad

There are different views about the impact of Chinese investments abroad. On one hand, Chinese investors are seen as stealing technology and there are fears about the continuity of companies after they have been acquired by a Chinese owner. The idea is that Chinese headquarters may have decision power that can hurt the foreign subsidiary. In the case of Africa or Latin America, the view is that Chinese companies (and consequently the government) is taking over important resources. In Africa, Chinese investments are sometimes considered as a form of neo-colonialism. Also in the US and Western Europe, there is discomfort about Chinese investments.

There is a lot of hesitation to accept the new Chinese owner, particularly in the US. For example, the bid for US-based Maytag by Haier in 2005 failed. The takeover coincided with the attempt by another Chinese company, CNOOC, to buy US oil producer, Unocal. This deal, which did not materialise eventually in the face of strong political resistance, created an environment in which even the purchase of an American company in a mature and hardly high-tech sector such as appliances was seen as worth the attention of security agencies. Maytag was in the end acquired by Whirlpool. Other takeovers that resulted in some discomfort are the takeover of MoneyGram by Ant (part of the Alibaba consortium), the Dalian Wanda takeover of Legendary Entertainment Group, Haier that acquired the GE-appliance division and Anbang Insurance that tookover Starwood hotels. It should be noted that, in the US, there exists the committee on Foreign Investment that is actively screening corporate takeovers to find out if there is a national risk involved. This is not the case in most European countries. But, there is also an increasing unease in Europe if Chinese companies are investing in strategic sectors such as utilities. For example, there was heavy discussion in the UK when in November 2012 the China Investment Corporation (CIC) invested 450 million pounds for a

10% stake in Heathrow airport holdings. It also invested, in the same year, 276 million pounds for an 8.7% stake in Thames Water Utilities Ltd., a London-based private utility company responsible for public water supply and waste water treatment. According to CIC, the investment stake is not to control the company, but UK policymakers felt unease that a sovereign state fund such as CIC is taking over some strategic assets. The same discussion happened in Germany in 2016 and early 2017 when China-based Midea took over robotics maker Kuka.

On the other hand, there is the view that the Chinese investment is a welcome source of foreign capital and that the western companies can only survive with this capital injection and the access to the (new) Chinese market through the linkage with the new owner. The takeover of western companies by Chinese companies may rescue a company in crisis. Indeed, there are cases where the Chinese injection helped a lot. You may think about Volvo, MG and the London taxi company. Geely restarted full production of the London black cabs at London taxi company's old factory in Coventry. Another example is MG. In 2005, China-based SAIC bought MG (Rover) after the company went into liquidation. With the help of SAIC, MG cars are now produced in China for the local market. A well-known example of a very successful Chinese investment is the harbor of Piraeus, just outside Athens in Greece. COSCO, the Chinese shipping, logistics and shipbuilding SOE started its operation in 2009. In the first five years, the container terminal increased its monthly handling ability to 200 cargo vessels, up from 40 in 2009. It also created 1,200 direct jobs in that period, apart from the many indirect job opportunities it created as a part of the shipping chain.

15.5 The new neighbours

It is interesting to find out what type of Chinese companies are to be expected when referring to future foreign investments. In this section, we will introduce a way of thinking to determine which type of companies are favourably positioned to become globally

Figure 15.5 The main factors influencing the step to invest abroad
Source: Based on IBM (2006)

active. This is a difficult task. There are many firm-specific reasons why companies move abroad. Also, unexpected circumstances and events may result in opportunities of moving to foreign markets. At the same time, we think it is possible to cluster the main preconditions of a Chinese firm to go international. We use four "filters" for this exercise (based on IBM-Research in 2006). The four filters to identify which type of Chinese companies are ready to go abroad are company size, industry characteristics, company features and timing. The four filters are indicated in Fig. 15.5.

The first filter is the company size. You may expect that companies need to have a minimum size before going international. Although in today's globalised world, born globals are moving abroad right from the start of their existence, in the majority of cases, the firms need size and resources. Also, size relates to experience; important for going abroad. That is what we see in China, the larger companies moved abroad first. The second filter to identify potentially internationalising Chinese companies connects to specific industry features, such as industry size as a percentage of GDP, level of industry concentration, export intensity and government support. You would expect that companies operating in these large, competitive and open industries are going abroad. Experiences with export make investments abroad "easier". The same holds for government support. The government support to the Chinese solar panel industry clearly was a precondition for many companies to move international. The third filter identifies the company characteristics, such as a strong global vision of management, leading position in domestic market and government support. Clearly, these are company-specific factors expected to be seen in companies that are ready to go abroad. The government support plays an important role in both the second and third filter. Various government agencies, such as the National Development and Reform Commission (NDRC), SAFE, the Ministry of Finance and the Ministry of Commerce (MOFCOM), have established policies to support Chinese companies to make overseas investments. The government uses various incentives to encourage outward FDI projects, including access to below market rate loans, direct capital contribution, soft loans from China Development Bank (CDB) and China Export and Import Bank (EXIM bank). Also, the earlier-mentioned official aid programs indirectly support Chinese firms overseas.

Companies that have scale, operate in industries that are open to competition, that receive government support (whether to the sector or to the individual company) and have the ambition to become international players are to be expected on foreign markets. But they may still decide to focus on the domestic market for various reasons. Therefore, the fourth filter relates to timing: When to invest abroad? The following factors determine the timing of going abroad:

- The life cycle of the product: The shorter the product life cycle, the sooner Chinese companies may go abroad. Since a laptop is replaced about every three years, a new Chinese entrant gets around three chances to sell a laptop to a given customer in a 10-year period. However, selling heavy equipment for infrastructure is different. The equipment will certainly be used for the next 10 years, so new entrants have only one chance over this decade to sell a machine, which reduces the speed of going global.
- Intensity of segmentation: The more markets are segmented by quality and price, the "easier" it is for Chinese entrants to challenge the incumbents in the low and middle segments where customers are more willing to compromise on quality or brand name. This can be seen in sectors such as electronics. The lesser the branding issues are influencing the buying process, the easier it is for Chinese companies to enter international markets. The same holds for services. For example, Chinese firms that

make products that require little after-sales will move quicker to foreign markets.
- Margins: If the domestic margins are robust, there is no need to go abroad. If overcapacity, lower margins and intense competition are features on the Chinese market, companies will move abroad faster.

There are numerous examples of Chinese companies that took over foreign companies (along with their technology and brands) in the previous decade, and we may expect much more. While most Chinese companies remain anonymous contract manufactures with little or no global consumer branding power, some companies became global players with well-known brands. Think about Lenovo, Huawei or Xiaomi. These examples relate to consumer markets. At the same time, we see Chinese firms building up their industrial status, mostly through process innovation to keep costs (and prices) low.

The new global challengers

The Boston Consultancy Group report "Global leaders, challengers and champions" gives an overview of the main emerging market companies that can become a worldclass competitor in the not too distant future (BCG, 2016). The BCG-report is an annual publication to find out which emerging market companies are on the edge to challenge the western companies on international markets. The selection of the companies is based on the following criteria. Firstly, the companies in the list are "real" emerging market companies, therefore leaving out JVs and subsidiaries of western MNEs. Secondly, BCG only look at large companies by setting the benchmark at US$1 billion revenue. Thirdly, it eliminates companies whose international turnover share is less than 10% of total. The fourth and final step in the analysis is giving the companies a scoring. This scoring is a subjective analysis by experts and based on criteria such as the international presence (as indicated by number of foreign subsidiaries), major international investments over the

Table 15.3 Chinese companies in the top 100 of global challengers

The 27 challengers from China	
China communications Construction Co.	ChemChina
China International Marine Containers	Sinochem
Aviation Industry Corp. of China	Sinohydro
China National Offshore Oil Co.	Goldwind
China Railway Construction Corp.	Trina Solar
Fuyao Glass Industry Group	Unionpay
China Eastern Airlines	Zoomlion
China Shipbuilding	Sinoma
Shanghai Electric	Alibaba
China Minmetals	Mindray
Dalian Wanda	Tencent
PetroChina	Xiaomi
CITIC Group	Geely
Wanziang	

Source: *BCG (2016)*

past five years, the depth of its technologies and its intellectual property portfolio, and the international appeal of its products. When focusing on Chinese companies, the BCG report selected 27 Chinese companies on the list of the top 100 global challengers. These future global players are presented in Table 15.3. Chinese companies such as Haier, Lenovo and Huawei gained international brand recognition and are on their way to becoming a global leader. That is why they are not on the list of BCG anymore — they graduated.

The impressive list of companies (certainly if you compare it with the overview of a decade ago) can be attributed to factors which we already discussed earlier, factors such as strong government support, increased economic liberalisation and openness (in China as well as internationally), creating economies of scale on the home market, pressure from the middle class that is demanding more quality at reasonable prices, and cheap sources of capital. For example, when

ChemChina agreed to buy Italian tire-maker Pirelli for almost US$8 billion, it received funding from the government through some state funds. Furthermore, a government investment vehicle (under the umbrella of OBOR) took a 25% stake in ChemChina to increase its financial power. The final part of the payment was financed through a loan below market rate by one of the larger banks.

Strategies of Chinese firms abroad

With respect to strategic choices, Chinese companies are facing the same challenges as western companies. They must answer the same type of questions regarding internationalisation; questions like how, when and why they are going international. Furthermore, they should also find the optimum balance between costs and revenues.

Because these internationalisation choices are based on firm, sector and market-specific characteristics, we see a variety of internationalisation strategies. For example, Xiaomi, the online-sales-only smartphone company, chooses an international cost leadership strategy (combined with a trendy marketing campaign) . By creating economies of scale and through standardisation, they can lower costs substantially which gives the opportunity to set relatively low prices. There are other Chinese companies that have a slightly different approach. For example, Lenovo is trying to attack the growing premium segments of the global laptop market. It also stepped in the business to business segment. Through the takeover of IBM, it became owner of the ThinkPad brand which gives them a stake in the business (premium) segment of the laptop market.

In many cases, international Chinese firms started as an original equipment manufacturer (OEM) by producing products for well-known brands. For example, Galanz (based in Guangdong) started by producing for other foreign brands. The same holds for Good Baby. It also began as an OEM for other brands. Today, the retail company is the largest seller of baby strollers in China under its own brand name. Another example of a company that made the move from OEM to a consumer brand is TCL. It manufactured for companies such as Philips and Panasonic. The same holds for automotive company BYD (Build Your Dreams). In 2008, it became the world's second-largest battery producer, quite impressive for a company that was only established in 1997. It manufactured the batteries for products such as the Barbie dolls of Mattel. BYD developed a new production process of lithium-ion batteries based on the fact that the process can be performed at room temperature. The saving in costs has resulted in lithium-ion batteries gradually replacing nickel–cadmium batteries. In early 2003, it started with the production of green hybrid cars under the BYD brand name and within 10 years, it became the world's biggest electric-vehicle maker. Despite these examples, it is clear that this switch from OEM to a consumer brand is quite difficult, particularly in building up recognition in foreign markets. ZTE, BYD and Galanz have established brand names in China but still lack brand recognition in markets abroad.

Another interesting feature of the largest Chinese companies acting abroad is that, at home, they operate across a broader range of industries compared to their activities in foreign markets. They are, in many cases, large conglomerates at home, while on international markets, they focus only on one or two sectors. There are several reasons for this diversification strategy on the domestic market. Due to the fast-changing economic environment at home, flexibility to switch to other markets was (and still is) needed. The same holds with respect to legislation. If rules are suddenly changing, switching to other markets is helpful. Another reason for this broad range of activities is that they can exploit the brand name into other markets. Shenzhen-based Mindray produces medical equipment for hospitals and at the same time is making use of its brand name by producing consumer gadgets to check your health. It also has an in-house bank. In many cases, Chinese conglomerates have their own financing sources because a bank is part of the consortium. This is a big advantage if external financing is problematic. These reasons for a diversification strategy is related to the Chinese context; there is no need to diversify abroad.

A final feature of the Chinese companies in their strategy regarding internationalisation is that they start in other emerging markets before venturing into developed economies, if at all. For example, Xiaomi started internationalisation in India and is active in most Asian countries. Together with Samsung, they are the market leaders (early 2017), but the company is very careful to take next steps to move further to more developed economies. Another example of cautious and step by step internationalisation is Tencent. They invested first in Internet and online gaming companies in markets that were culturally close to China such as Vietnam and Indonesia, countries that they understand. This careful and regional internationalisation is not always visible. A slightly different approach was taken by Haier. The start of its internationalisation process was towards countries such as Indonesia, Philippines and Malaysia, but already in 1999 (early in the internationalisation process) they made the step to the US, followed by other OECD countries.

15.6 Success factors of Chinese companies

Chinese companies became very active internationally in the previous decade. But active does not necessary means successful. With respect to international takeovers, the results from the Chinese point of view are mixed. A many cross-border M&As executed by Chinese companies were successful, as for instance the acquisitions performed by Lenovo. Lenovo successfully integrated the PC Business of IBM into the company structure and was able to mix the Chinese and US cultures. However, many cross-border M&As done by Chinese companies failed dramatically; for instance, as it was the case with SAIC investing in SsangYong automotive. SAIC was not able to cope with the aggressive labour unions in South Korea. The company underestimated the effects of cultural differences, which eventually led to the failure and the disinvestment (2010). In the Chinese context, labour unions are essentially state controlled. Labour organisations must be affiliated with the State controlled All-China Federation of Trade Unions, that mostly side with management. So, SAIC was not used to working together with independent trade unions. Today, the role of trade unions is changing. Independent trade unions started in Guangdong in 2015 and there are pilot projects in which trade unions are discussing salaries and other work-related advances instead of organising only leisure activities. Consequently, they are seen more and more as one of the stakeholders of the company. This development is also taken abroad. Chinese firms are becoming more sensitive to labour demands and are more adjustable to the western standards on this issue.

It is interesting to see how western companies are looking at the strengths and weaknesses of their Chinese competitors. Obviously, we see differences, depending on who execute the research, the composition of the sample and the methodology used. In Fig. 15.6, we summarise the conclusions of the main publications on this issue between 2015 and early 2017 which were executed through questionnaires by western embassies and consulates in China. It gives the strengths and weaknesses of Chinese competitors in China. We may extend the outcome to other emerging markets and even to more mature economies because it is logical to assume that the strengths and weaknesses in the Chinese market can be exploited in foreign markets as well. Figure 15.6 shows that the advantages of Chinese companies on the Chinese market relates to factors such as quicker to capture

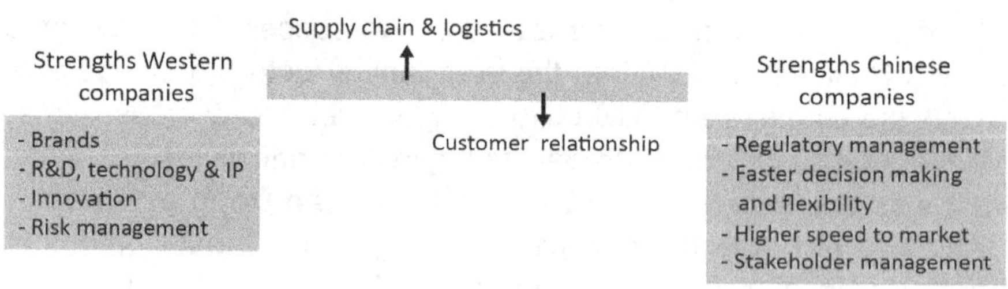

Figure 15.6 Strengths and weaknesses of Chinese firms

Note: *Combined results (2015–2016) on the question "what are the strengths and weaknesses of Chinese companies compared to your own [...] Western company"?*

Source: *Based on questionnaire research executed by EU embassies in 2016 and 2017*

market opportunities, faster speed to market, more flexibility to connect with the customer, and better government (or regulatory) relationships. It is remarkable to see that, according to western companies, the Chinese competitors are (slightly) better in customer relationship. According to the MNE-managers of western companies, their own strengths are in the field of branding, technology and innovation.

The challenges of operating in emerging markets include selling profitably to price-sensitive customers, dealing with immature logistics and distribution environments, navigating through ambiguous legal environments, handling rapid change of consumer habits and tastes, and managing operations despite shortages of management talent. In particular, on these difficult markets, Chinese firms have some advantages. A company that is capable of surviving these constraints at home will have an advantage when seeking to grow in similar markets abroad. A difficult Chinese business environment is helping them survive in other difficult markets. If we translate the specific advantages indicated by previous research into the main (clustered) success factors of Chinese firms in other (emerging) markets, we come to four distinct success factors: the good enough strategy, localising, low price and flexibility.

The good enough strategy

One of the key strengths of the Chinese companies is their ability to tailor products and services to their local customer bases, which, in many cases, is at the bottom of the economic pyramid. Chinese firms can reduce costs and adapt in such a way that the (lower) middle class are able to buy the product. Xiaomi exemplifies this business model which can be described as "80% of the quality for 60% of the price". These are reliable goods with functionality that is behind the leading edge, but still good enough for most buyers in China and other emerging markets. This ability to design products without unnecessary bells and whistles is a key competitive advantage. Innovation extends to processes and operations as part of the search for cheaper, simpler and more flexible business models, is what Chinese companies are good at. Chinese companies have demonstrated their strength in development (D), instead of (fundamental) research (R). The move from development to research is difficult, but a select number of Chinese companies are moving rapidly up the value chain, as was shown in the BCG reports.

Localising and mass market

Connected to the above point is the capability to adjust to local circumstances. Many large Chinese companies create new markets by adapting an existing product so that it taps into the preferences and needs of a new lower middle-class consumer segment. Understanding these customer needs and considering cost constraints is the crux. An example is Haier. The company was leading China's white goods market because of its knowledge about the Chinese customers and it had the skills to develop products tailored to those needs. For example, Haier introduced washing machines that can clean vegetables such as sweet potatoes for its rural consumers. The company's repairmen discovered that customers in rural areas used their washing machines not only to launder clothes but also to clean vegetables. They informed the product manager of Haier and the engineers installed wider drain pipes that would not clog with vegetable peels. Haier even put large stickers on the modified washers, with instructions on how to wash vegetables safely using the machine. It did the same in India and other developing Asian countries.

Low price

We indicated before that many Chinese companies started as OEMs. These companies learned how to reduce costs in their operations because that was their only competitive advantage. I always say to my students that even if you think it is not possible anymore, Chinese companies are always able to reduce costs further. Obviously, a low price is not always an advantage in mature markets, but, in many cases, it is in less developed countries and economies in transition; in particular, if it is complemented by increasing brand reputation. China-based Galanz is an example of an OEM that started to build a consumer brand name in the 1990s. It started to produce and sell on the domestic lower-end market at a low price. It introduced a simple, energy-efficient microwave at an affordable price for the (lower) middle class and small enough to fit in their kitchens. There was no competition by global brands on this low-end market; foreign brands only served the high-end market in China. Therefore, Galanz could easily increase its market share. In 1995, it had 25% of the Chinese market, and in 1998, its market share increased to 62%. In early 2000, it began to disrupt the microwave market in developing countries. Today (early 2017), Galanz is the largest microwave producer in the world. Another example of the transformation from OEM to the consumer market with own brands is TCL. Until the mid-2000s, most of its products were manufactured on a contract basis for other companies. As a contract manufacturer, TCL learned how to keep costs low and meet demanding international quality standards at the same time. This learning was applied to foreign markets. This strategy used by Galanz and TCL is called "disruptive innovation from the base of the pyramid" (Hart and Christiansen, 2002).

Flexibility and taking risk

Chinese companies tend to be more comfortable with a higher level of risk because of their own challenging environment in which they have developed. One of their major strengths is their political connectivity; also in foreign countries. This is the result of long experience in dealing with an interventionist (local) government in their own country. This experience can be quite useful when entering other countries. In an environment of weak laws or poor governance, greater tolerance of ambiguity can be an asset if it leads to grasping opportunities that a more rules-driven manager would ignore. For example, tolerating the notion that contracts may not be enforceable in emerging nations can be a competitive advantage to a Chinese manager who is willing to accept the uncertainty, while a western manager wants to have a detailed contract.

Chinese companies are extremely flexible, as are their managers. Because Chinese do not evaluate, re-evaluate and reflect much on what they do, they are free to act quickly and to move on. It also relates to the organisational design. As stated before, we see greater frequency of very diversified conglomerate structures. In many cases, this may be a disadvantage, but in emerging markets characterised by poorly developed institutional settings, the benefit of group affiliation may outweighs their disadvantages. To make the analysis more complex, flexibility and speed occur sometimes with slowness. In some situations, Chinese firms will be tremendously cooperative and straightforward, while in others they act like war-strategists, waiting, postponing and manoeuvring. Again, this is the ambiguous nature of China and China's businesses.

The growth of Chinese FDI outflow is the result of Chinese companies building up specific O-advantages. We see progressively successful international expansions and we expect that this will continue in the upcoming decade. Chinese firms (and their) managers are learning fast and it is to be expected that building up firm-specific O-advantages will continue. The assumption behind the growth of Chinese investments is that regulators and governments in the US and Europe are not blocking the inflow of FDI motivated by national interests. There is a tendency to limit Chinese investments through a strict screening process. But we have to be ready to see more and more Chinese brands and companies; we have to be ready to meet our new neighbours. In the following chapters, we shift our attention to the Chinese business context: How does this business context look like, how is it changing and how can western companies be successful on the Chinese market.

Chapter 16

The Business Context in China

Myth 16: China is westernising

16.1 Introduction

When organising a global immersion program for Dutch students, I hear remarks such as "McDonald's and KFC are so successful in China". Indeed, they are very visible in the streets of the tier 1 and 2 cities. And according to the *China Daily* of 20 February 2017, Yum! (the US-based mother company of KFC and Pizza Hut) will accelerate its presence in China with 600 new restaurants in 2017. In early 2017, Yum! already had 7,500 restaurants in China. Also, McDonald's and Disco's are very visible in the streets of Beijing and Shanghai. Both also announced plans to open around 150 restaurants every year between 2017 and 2025. Unquestionably, the foreign fast food chains are successful in Beijing and Shanghai, but be aware of two facts. Firstly, they are visible and operating in the largest cities in China but in many tier 3 and tier 4 cities, it is difficult to find a western fast food chain, not to mention in the rural areas. Secondly, the combined number of outlets and revenue of all western fast food stores in China are substantial and growing, but they are still a minority in the Chinese fast food sector and represent a minuscule fraction of all the restaurants and eating places in China. Chinese fast food restaurants take up more than 75% of the fast food industry in China.

However, there is no single enterprise or chain that dominates the domestic market. For example, Kungfu, a leading Chinese fast food chain operated "only" 450 restaurants in 2016.

KFC and McDonald's may attract a great deal of attention, but they paint a distorted picture of eating habits in China. An overwhelming share of the Chinese eat in Chinese restaurants and Chinese fast food chains. In a sense, rather than westernisation of China's eating habits, it would be more appropriate to emphasise that despite the enormous investments made by western (US) fast food chains, we still see a continuation of Chinese eating habits, and if western chains are successful, they are successful because of the Chinesification (or Asianisation) of their menu. Also, the middle class, keen to experiment with western food, still focuses on Chinese (local) dishes. This is logical. Many cultural habits, in particular, with respect to Chinese food, rooted in history that covers thousands of years, are not changing fast. Obviously, at the same time we see some changes. Economic growth and urbanisation led to changes in the diet with more meat and dairy products.

The culture and its features, whether we talk about guanxi, Feng shui or the way people are thinking and interacting, are heavily influenced by Confucianism (and Taoism) and are important to understand when conducting business in China. It is true that the traditional Chinese methods of doing business are gradually changing, but the role of culture on today's business should not be overlooked. Besides the cultural obstacles of conducting business, we also have the challenging legislative and bureaucratic business environment. Notwithstanding some improvements in the previous years, China ranks relatively low in the Ease of Doing Business ranking of the World Bank and in many surveys that are used to find out the main obstacles of doing business. This combination of the regulatory business context and the large cultural distance between the home and host countries makes China a difficult place to be successful. These obstacles for success should be set against the enormous potential of the Chinese market. The middle class is exploding and is able and willing to buy western (branded) products. In Chapter 17, we will discuss the success and failure factors in China intensively, while in this chapter some of the aspects of the non-controllable environment are being discussed.

Section 16.2 gives a general overview of the Chinese culture, central theme being Confucianism. We dive into Chinese cultural features such as Face and guanxi, combined with some cultural aspects that influence doing business today. The link between culture and business is made through Hofstede's 6D-model. In Section 16.3, we continue with defining and discussing China's middle class. The chapter closes with Section 16.4 in which we elaborate on the Ease of Doing Business.

16.2 Confucianism and the business context

Of course, we know that cultural differences can be visualised as the iceberg; at the surface, it looks not so big, but be aware that most of the cultural differences are below the water; not visible and very subtle (but important). On the outside, when visiting urban China, the country looks, in many cases, quite similar to any western country. But inside, it is very different; China is outwardly western but inwardly Chinese. The country is changing fast, but the values and beliefs in the mindset of its people do not change easily. In this sense, cultural differences will have a far-reaching impact on the nature of modernity as we will see when China develops further (the topic of the final chapter). China remains, notwithstanding the fact that it is developing fast, very different from its Western counterparts. It comes from entirely different cultural coordinates and despite some harmonising processes, cultural differences are there to stay.

Chinese people are extremely connected to their (long ago) past and they feel that the past is relevant and meaningful in today's life. The cultural and social roots of the Chinese society are more than 2,500 years old and are fundamentally based on Confucianism (551 BC). Many books are written about the works of Confucius and its impact on the Chinese society. Summarising this in a short paragraph is clearly undoable. We only introduce some subjects that will come back in the chapters that follow.

Confucian ordering of the society was based on quite strict hierarchical layers. The society was governed by "men of wisdom" helped by civil servants (mandarins), selected based on meritocracy. They were responsible for the administration of the empire. Below the mandarins were the peasant classes, followed by artisans. Traders were seen as a lower class, although making money was not forbidden. This hierarchical society embraced respecting ranks and order, showing respect towards the emperor, father, older brother and the boss. This also includes respect for age (which is helpful for a grey professor like me). Confucianism provides an intrinsic respect for and acceptance of authority. Paternalism is an important feature within Confucianism (and the Chinese society) and it may explain why, in China, we have the rule by law (or rule of men), rather than the rule of law (Chapter 6). Laws, within Confucianism, are relatively useless, since even good laws administered by bad men would have negative outcomes. The rule of law is an instrument, not a principle. The authorities know, driven by their moral compass, what is best for the people; and the people accept this. Confucius believed that the emperor (state) should be immune to popular pressure. It should govern according to ethical principles rather than popular demands. Working in the bureaucracy was seen as the most prestigious form of employment. Even today, many of the brightest students choose a career within the bureaucracy. Within Confucianism, the family is the template for the state, in which the emperor's role is akin to that of the father. The Chinese view the state as the head of the family. Confucius also emphasised the dominance of society over individual.

Another feature of Confucianism is the obligation to seek harmony. The world consists of contradictions and inequalities. This is not problematic as long as balance and stability are guaranteed, i.e. *Yin* and *Yang* should be kept balanced. Therefore, we see a strong avoidance of conflict — conflict disrupts harmony. The Confucianist culture makes China quite different from other countries. This can be seen in Fig. 16.1, which shows the 6D model of Hofstede for China, the Netherlands and the US. Hofstede (1980)

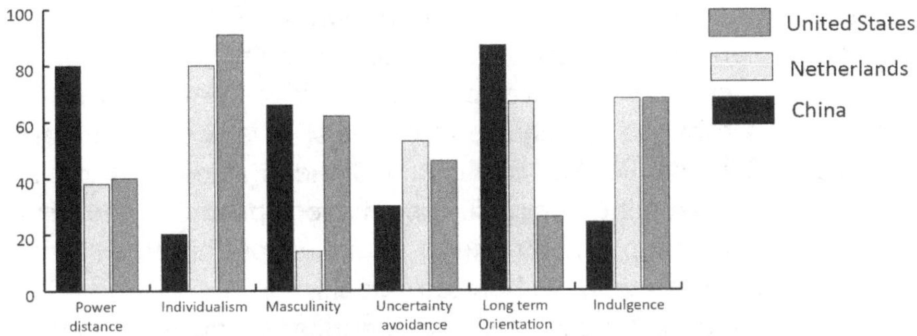

Figure 16.1 Hofstede's 6D model of China, the Netherlands and the United States

Source: Website Geert Hofstede (www.hofstede-insights.com)

investigated the differences in thinking and social action that existed among people in over 50 countries within subsidiaries of one large multinational business organisation (IBM). From the initial results. Hofstede developed a model that distinguishes cultures on four dimensions: power distance, individualism, masculinity, and uncertainty avoidance. The fifth dimension (long-term orientation) was added after Hofstede focused specifically on China. This long-term orientation obviously is based on Confucianism. In 2010, he added a final cultural dimension in his framework, indulgence (Hofstede, 2011).

As can be seen in Fig. 16.1, China's score on individualism is very low. The individualism dimension refers to whether people think with the mentality of "I" or "We". The American (and the Dutch) culture is very "I" focused, meaning that the emphasis is more on own careers instead of focusing on the company, club or another group. The low score of China means that they are highly collectivistic and think as a group instead of individually. Power distance is the extent to which less powerful people (in an organisation or society) will accept and expect power to be distributed differently. Driven by the Confucionist culture, China ranks high on power distance. This means there is a lot of hierarchical distance between subordinates and superiors, and that it is accepted as normal. The Chinese rank extremely high on long-term orientation, meaning they focus on persistence and perseverance, and that they will devote however much time is required to achieve their goals. This is seen in many aspects of Chinese life. You see it with Chinese students and also in the time-consuming Chinese negotiation process, the time required to build trust and long-term relationships, and their focus on long-term results versus short-term goals.

With respect to masculinity, the Americans and the Chinese are quite similar, while the Netherlands's score is extremely low. It means that Chinese and Americans are very much driven by success, competition, and achievements. For example, the Chinese will often put work before leisurely activities. The uncertainty avoidance dimension expresses the degree to which the members of a society feel uncomfortable with uncertainty and ambiguity. China scores relatively low on this dimension. This weak uncertainty avoidance means a more relaxed attitude about the future and a society in which practice counts more than principles. Indulgence is defined as a society that allows relatively free gratification of basic and natural human desires related to enjoying life and having fun. This dimension is essentially a measure of happiness, whether or not simple joys are fulfilled. Obviously, there is a connection between individualism and indulgence. Indulgent cultures will tend to focus more on individual happiness and well-being, leisure time is more important and there is greater freedom and personal control. This is in contrast with restrained cultures, such as China, where positive emotions are less freely expressed and happiness, freedom and leisure are not given the same importance.

The business implications are clear. For example, the high-power distance in the case of China results in the tendency towards top-down management and autocratic leadership. The long-term orientation makes the negotiation process extremely difficult and time consuming. The low score on individualism may explain the difficulty of Chinese firms to execute successful innovations. The high score on masculinity results in the focus on success and achievement. This also relates to the Chinese approach to parenting and raising children. This was highlighted in Amy Chua's book: Battle Hymn of the Tiger Mother (2011), in which she sums up Chinese parenting in seven views:

- Schoolwork always comes first
- An A-minus is a bad grade
- Your children must be two years ahead of their classmates in mathematics
- You must never compliment your children in public
- If your child ever disagrees with a teacher or coach, you must always take the side of the teacher and coach
- The only activities your children should be permitted to do are those in which they can eventually win a medal
- That medal must be gold

This obsession for success begins at birth as parents are looking for "improving" products such as baby formula that claimed to stimulate brain development. This fixation on success continues during the growing-up period. To get into the best universities, it is essential to have a high grade in the college entrance exam, known as the gaokao. This test, which hung over children throughout their childhood and adolescence, decides where they go to study.

The low score on uncertainty avoidance within Hofstede's research is interesting. The Chinese are comfortable with uncertainty and vagueness. This is again a part of Confucianism (complemented by essentials of Taoism). The Chinese way of looking at the future can be seen in the story about the old man and his horse. The essence is that nothing is absolute and it is hard to say what is good or bad, another example of the Yin and Yang balance. "A man named Sei Weng owned a beautiful mare which was praised far and wide. One day this beautiful horse disappeared. The people of his village offered sympathy to Sei Weng for his great misfortune. Sei Weng said simply, "That's the way it is". A few days later the lost mare returned, followed by a beautiful wild stallion.

The village congratulated Sei Weng for his good fortune. He said, "That's the way it is". Sometime later, Sei Weng's only son, while riding the stallion, fell off and broke his leg. The village people once again expressed their sympathy at Sei Weng's misfortune. Sei Weng again said, "That's the way it is". Soon thereafter, war broke out and all the young men of the village except Sei Weng's lame son were drafted and were killed in battle. The village people were amazed as Sei Weng's good luck. His son was the only young man left alive in the village. But Sei Weng kept his same attitude. Despite all the turmoil, gains and losses, he gave the same reply, "That's the way it is" (Chin-Ning Chu, 1991).

Other Chinese cultural features

Communism (or more specifically Maoism) explicitly rejected Confucianism, but one may say that 30 years of Maoism did not change the Chinese DNA that has developed for more than 2,500 years. The Communist era did not change the Confucianist culture and its superstitious beliefs. The Communist governments (and the Nationalist authorities even before them) tried to eradicate superstitious practices in China in an attempt to modernise the country, but in many cases this was unsuccessful. Even today, people still go to fortune tellers to find a good date to get married, they still believe in lucky and unlucky numbers, pregnant women are still obsessed with "cold" food during their pregnancy and asking a Feng Shui expert for advice when building a house or an office is part of the routine.

Feng Shui is the Chinese practice of creating harmony to improve the balance of *Yin* and *Yang*. One of my young, western and open-minded MBA students at CEIBS in Shanghai indicated to me that he visited a Feng Shui expert to make sure that the house he wanted to buy would bring good luck. Superstitious beliefs have large economic effects. For example, a house that faces north represents darkness and bad luck. Houses or apartments facing north have lower rents or prices than their counterparts facing south. The same holds for houses with numbers 4 and 8. The number 4 is considered as unlucky because it sounds similar to the word death. The Beijing No 4-hospital located in Dongcheng district changed its name to the Beijing Puren Hospital in 2000 because many patients were reluctant to go there. The number of patients witnessed a great increase a month after the name change (*China Daily*, 22 June 2012). On the other hand, the Chinese believe that number 8 is lucky because the pronunciation of the word is close to "prosperity or wealth". Houses with this lucky number have a higher rent or selling price due to its relatively large demand.

At Nyenrode, I worked with a Chinese who was born in the Netherlands. Her parents immigrated to the Netherlands in the 1970s. I still remember her motivation when buying a second-hand car. Her choice of the car was strongly based on the license plate; She was looking for a car with a good number, including the number 8 and avoiding the number 4. This made clear to me how deep cultural beliefs are integrated into Chinese people, even when they are born in the Netherlands. This lucky number 8 also determined the precise starting date of the Beijing Olympic Games on 8 August 2008 precisely at 8 PM. The authorities obviously chose the date and time to respect the Chinese superstitious beliefs. China is undergoing dramatic shifts in social, economic and cultural contexts. And superstitious beliefs may be less visible and less a driver behind specific choices made by the younger generation, but it is good to understand that there is also a large part of the iceberg below the water, still there but hidden. This also holds for the concept of Face.

The concept of "Face" (Mianzi) in Chinese culture is very complex. It may be defined as "prestige or status", but be aware that this does not cover the nuances. Face is the most important foundation of the relationship between people. Keeping a respected Face to each other is a precondition for a friendly connection. Everything is concentrated on earning (and saving) Face; to look good in front of others. Losing Face is extremely humiliating. I witnessed this with one of the students during my stay at Renmin University in Beijing. A student presented her paper in front of her classmates and a jury of three professors: One Chinese and two foreigners. After the presentation, the American professor in the jury was extremely critical about the way the student presented and even used words as "disagree" and "big mistakes". You could see how the Face of the student changed physically. This was a dramatic Face-losing situation. This was not only Face Losing for the student, clearly, the professor also lost face (although he was not aware of that). Besides Losing Face and earning Face, one can leave Face for others. There is an important learning point here: in China, failure is bad. There is less scope for failure in China compared to the Netherlands or the US. For example, if you think of Silicon Valley, it is almost a badge of pride in how many companies you were involved in that went bankrupt. This is different in China. This is what the American professor could have done but did not do so. Finally, there is the concept of offering Face to others, meaning helping the other.

Guanxi

Guanxi is a concept which describes personal relationships that may result in the exchanges of favours or connections that are beneficial for the parties involved. In a sense, it's not *what* you know, but *who* you know that is important. And not only knowing the person is important, but there should also be an informal contract that you help each other. Chinese business operates through a web of personal relationships, and access to these networks requires connections which is based around trust and friendship and, in many cases, based on family relationships. There is strongest loyalty towards the family, friends and school mates. Also, some relations are being built with business colleagues and associates. But in general, loyalty to a company would be outside the guanxi circle. Loyalty to the manager is high and more prominent than loyalty to the company. If a key person decides to leave the company, he may be followed by employees who are loyal to him, not to the company. Guanxi is, for example, important if a western company is looking for a Chinese firm to be an agent, supplier or partner. The role of the intermediary which has guanxi will help you establish the contact. The function of this intermediate is not only to make the connection, but also, to some degree, guarantee for the integrity of the person being introduced.

Guanxi has certain characteristics. First, it is transferable. This can be seen by the role of the intermediate person in making the connection. The mediator transfers his guanxi to the person looking for a supplier or business partner. Second, it is reciprocal. A person who does not return a favour loses Face and as a result its guanxi. Third, it is intangible. It is done in a silent and subtle way. Fourth, it is more utilitarian than emotional. If it is not on mutual interest, the relationship can be broken. Fifth, it is personal. Organisations do not have a group identity; it is the guanxi between individuals that bind the firms. As we stated earlier in the book, guanxi can also be considered as the cause for institutional corruption. In China, many transactions are based on personal relationships with giving and taking. In that sense, it is as difficult for a Chinese to get a transaction done as is in the west. In terms of institutions, there is no (additional) barrier, but the main obstacle is the (lack of) personal relations that makes it difficult.

These cultural factors should be taken into consideration if a company decides to be active in China. Despite the cultural obstacles, the Chinese market cannot be ignored. The explosion of the middle class is happening and, in many cases, the Chinese market can counteract the flat market developments in more mature economies. We elaborated earlier in the book on the Chinese middle class and its attitude towards democracy. In the next paragraph, the focus is on defining the middle class and to show its development.

16.3 The Chinese middle class

Up to the mid-2000s, China attracted essentially two types of investments. The first one related to China's cheap labour and building up export platforms. The second type of investment was motivated by the current (and potential) domestic market. Both motives were logical; there was a rising domestic urban market and at the same time, labour costs were relatively low. After the mid-2000s, the picture changed; wages went up quite dramatically and associated with this, we witnessed a fast growth in purchasing power of a broad middle class. As a result, most western companies invested in China to make use of the large and growing market driven by this middle-class. At the same time, low value-added activities that used China as an export platform started to move to other low wage countries. For example, Adidas closed its fully owned factory in Suzhou, Jiangsu province in 2012 due to the pressure of higher labour costs and the difficulty to get enough labour.

There is no international agreement on how the middle class should be defined (World Bank, 2011 & Euromonitor, 2010). Households making US$25,000–75,000 are normally considered as middle class in the US. But undoubtedly, these benchmarks cannot be used for defining the middle class in China. In China, it is even more complicated because of the large regional differences. An annual income of US$7,000 may give you a reasonably pleasant stay (and middle-income status) in a third-tier city, but certainly, it is not enough to live a middle-income life in Beijing or Shanghai. In the above examples, the focus is on income, and that is mostly done in statistics: the segmentation of the population (and within this the middle-class cohort) is based on income. However, there is also a broader definition of the middle class, a definition that goes beyond income and considering lifestyle, occupation and education. In this broad definition, middle class people should have at least a tertiary education, possibly a professional or white-collar job, own a house and a car, enjoy modern lifestyle and consumption patterns, and some status in society. In this broad concept, the focus is on both economic and social significance. Although there are many factors that determine one's place in the system, the financial status is still the predominant factor in defining the middle class. But be aware of the fact that this income focus may be far from sufficient for marketers of consumer goods in China. Income is just one of the determinants in purchasing decisions. Other factors are also important; sometimes playing an even greater role than (disposable) income, as we will see in the next chapter.

Middle class as an engine of growth

The Chinese middle class plays an important role in China's development, as an impetus for long-term growth (productivity) and as a leading force in consumption. The middle class tends to spend a relatively large share of its disposable income. This is important to rebalance the economy towards a domestic market economy. Another role of the growing middle class is its connection to the rise of the service sector. They become increasingly willing to spend money on services such as entertainment, travel, leisure, care services and security services. Besides being a market, the urban middle class is creating increasing numbers of skilled workers who are contributing to higher productivity. Skills are the basis for innovation and technological advancement, enabling industries to upgrade and climb the value chain. In this sense, an increasingly prosperous and productive middle class will (continue to) be the key to China's sustainable growth in the long term.

We discussed some features of the Chinese middle class earlier in the book. Our observation was that the Chinese middle class can be considered as a stabilising force and a keeper of the status quo. Satisfied with their wealth and status, the middle class tends to be proponents of social order and stability and opponents of social unrest. The Chinese middle class is and remains supportive of and cooperative with the party and government.

In many publications about the Chinese middle class, a division is made between the middle class inside the establishment of the bureaucracy (party and government) and the middle class outside the bureaucracy. The inside middle class consists of civil servants and people working in hospitals, education, and middle management in SOEs. The outside middle class consists of private business owners and self-made entrepreneurs. Unlike other countries, a considerable proportion of the Chinese middle class is from inside the establishment. A large number of officials have seen their living standard upgraded to middle class level and it is unlikely that they will challenge something that they depend on for a living. Also, the outside middle class is not eager to change the system.

They are all direct beneficiaries of the government pro-market and pro-business policies, and still keep a close connection with the establishment in one way or another.

Middle class will grow specifically in lower tier cities

China is vastly becoming a middle-class nation, and this is mainly happening in cities. The Chinese statistics on urbanisation are dividing the cities from tier 1 to tier 5. Tier 1 cities being the largest megacities such as Beijing and Shanghai. Tier 5 cities are municipalities near the rural areas. In western publications, the division of cities run up to tier 4 (excluding the municipalities and villages). In 2002, 40% of China's urban middle class lived in four tier 1 cities: Shenzhen, Beijing, Shanghai and Guangzhou. But as Fig. 16.2 shows, the geographic centre of middle class growth is shifting towards tier 2 and 3 cities. In 2022, 45% of China's urban middle class will live in tier 2 cities. The fastest growth can be seen in tier 3 cities; 15% of the Chinese urban middle class lived there in 2002 and this will increase to 31% in 2022 (Figure 16.2 right-side). The share of the tier 1 cities in the total middle class will decline substantially from 40% in 2002 to 16% in 2022 (Barton, Chen, and Jin, 2013).

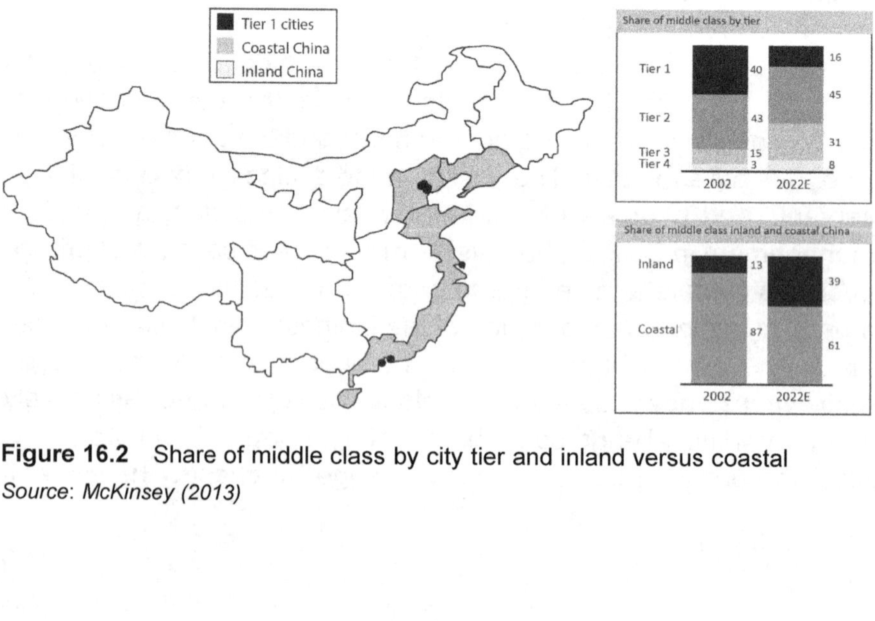

Figure 16.2 Share of middle class by city tier and inland versus coastal
Source: McKinsey (2013)

Because most of the largest cities are situated in the coastal areas, there is a strong connection with the division of the middle class between inland versus coastal as is shown in Fig. 16.2. In 2002, 87% of the middle class was situated in the coastal areas around Beijing, Tianjin, Shanghai, Guangzhou and Shenzhen. This will change dramatically; in 2022, almost 40% of the Chinese middle class will be working and living in the inland areas of China. The development of the middle class is a challenge for western companies; now, they have to operate in more difficult lower tier cities, often away from the coastal areas with their high quality infrastructure and skilled labour.

Another challenge for western companies is that China is so immense and its regions so diverse that it should be treated almost as a collection of separate countries. At the broadest level, China consists of three economies: the eastern area, which accounts for 58% of national GDP and consists of eleven provinces (Beijing, Tianjin, Hebei, Liaoning, Shanghai, Jiangsu, Zhejiang, Fujian, Shandong, Guangdong and Hainan). The Central area, 24% of the national economy and eight provinces (Shanxi, Jilin, Heilongjiang, Anhui, Jiangxi, Henan, Hubei and Hunan). And the western area, 18% of national GDP and twelve provinces (Inner Mongolia, Guangxi, Chongqing, Sichuan, Guizhou, Yunnan, Tibet, Shaanxi, Gansu, Qinghai, Ningxia and Xinjiang). The three regions have a large difference in the average income per capita, and this geographical disparity in income levels becomes more pronounced when the comparison is made at the provincial level. The highest level of nominal GDP per capita (Shanghai) is almost 10 times the lowest (Guizhou).

It is logical to see this unequal development. The openness to external trade tends to be much higher in the eastern region than in central and western areas. These provinces have benefited the most from the growing demand of Chinese goods abroad, the special economic zones, and the earlier discussed agglomeration effects. In Fig. 16.3, we indicate the richest provinces (income per capita) according to the newest overview published by the National Bureau of Statistics (April 2017). As can be seen, except Inner Mongolia, they are all in the coastal area. For companies, these developments are important.

Figure 16.3 Richest provinces in China, 2016
Source: *Based on Eurasia Group (2011) and NBS Database*

Understanding the variations in the rate of development is important because they will affect which categories of goods and services are in high demand. Furthermore, the increasing share of the lower-tier cities in China's middle class must have its impact on a company's strategic choices. In the previous decade, many MNEs have invested heavily in expanding into tier 2 and 3 cities. For example, KFC is opening more restaurants in tier 3 cities compared to tier 1 and 2 cities in the previous years. When it entered Nanchang, a lower tier city in Jiangxi province, it put up signs saying, "we are sorry for being late here".

Middle-class segment

Prior to the reforms of the 1980s, China was a highly egalitarian, but also a highly impoverished country. In 1985, Deng Xiaoping remarked that some people would need to get rich first in order to pave the way for the mass to follow. And this is what has happened; China today is a far richer, but a less egalitarian society than it was in the past. We can divide the society into different segments based on income level: affluent, middle class and poor. It is interesting for companies when people start to leave poverty and enter the (lower or mass) middle class. People are buying branded and higher quality products only after reaching a certain income benchmark. Organisations and research institutes use different income brackets to define the middle class. For example, Euromonitor, by using World Bank definitions, focusses on disposable income when defining the middle class. Households with over US$3,000 annual disposable income are part of the Chinese middle class. According to them, the middle class makes up more than 40% of China's population (2016). In the publications of the McKinsey group, gross income is used instead of disposable income. They also focus on household income. Other organisations such as the Asian Development Bank is using the income per capita to define the middle class.

The McKinsey research on the Chinese middle class divides the middle class into two segments: the mass middle class (60,000–106,000 Renminbi) and the upper middle class (106,000–229,000 Renminbi). This translates into US$9,000–16,000 range for the mass middle class and US$16,000–34,000 for the upper middle class, based on nominal exchange rate. Figure 16.4 makes clear

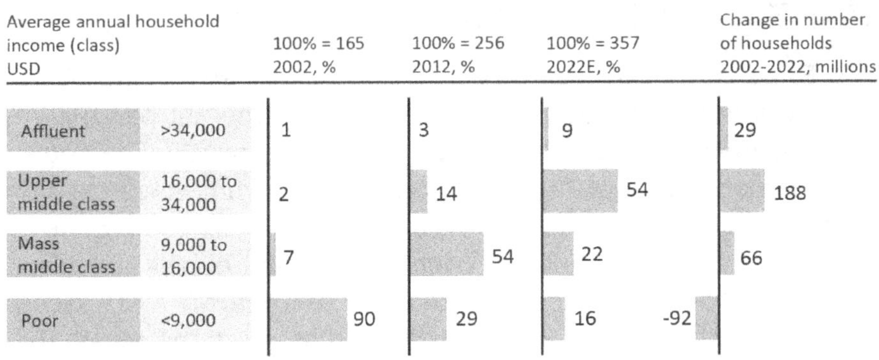

Figure 16.4 The upper and mass urban middle-class development; 2002–2022

Source: Based on McKinsey insights China, 2010–2016

how fast the middle class cohort grows. As recently as 2002, only 9% of urban households in China were middle class. That share had soared to 68% by 2012. Expectations are that, by 2022, 76% of the urban households can be considered as middle class. It means that, in 20 years (from 2002 to 2022), the number of households in the middle-class segment increased by 254 million. Be aware that Fig. 16.4 only refers to the urban middle class. In line with the analysis in Chapter 9, the figure shows the strong increase in urbanisation; growing from 165 million households in 2002 to expected 357 million households in 2022.

As we will see in the next chapter, although the middle class are willing to pay more for higher quality and brands, they are still price sensitive. And consequently, the business model that western companies are using in China must be adapted to the Chinese market. This was, for example, done by Ikea. It entered China in 1998 with a premium price strategy, but that was not working. Middle class customers filled Ikea stores to look around but bought less than expected. Thanks to adaptation of the business model, including more local sourcing and localisation of processes and products, Ikea was able to cut prices by an average of 50% in more than 1000 categories between 2005 and 2010 and is very successful today.

16.4 Ease of Doing Business

The Ease of Doing Business report, is published by the World Bank. It is an aggregate index that includes different parameters which define how easy it is to do business in a country. The aggregated rank consists of 11 sub-factors, ranging from how easy it is to start a company, how long it takes to get a business license to the time and costs to enforce contracts and the quality of judicial processes. New Zealand is ranked number one on the Ease of Doing Business ranking 2017. It is the country with the most business-friendly regulation. And while there was some reordering of countries in the ranking, the top of the list remains very similar to previous years, including countries such as Singapore and Denmark.

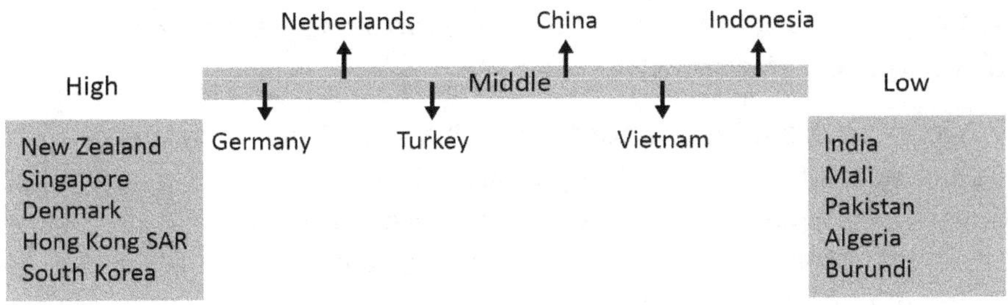

Figure 16.5 Ease of Doing Business ranking; specific countries; 2017
Source: *World Bank, Ease of Doing Business, 2017*

However, be aware that a high rank does not say that doing business is easy. South Korea is ranked high (number 5 in 2017), but due to cultural differences, doing business (and being successful on the South Korean market) appears to be difficult. Figure 16.5 shows some specific countries in the ranking. As expected, the legislative frameworks of conducting business in countries such as Burundi, Pakistan and Mali are extremely difficult.

China ranked 78 (out of 157) in the 2017-ranking. The ranking is the picture today, but it should be noted that there was a big improvement in the overall score of China over the past decade. The business tax reform in the previous decade contributed a great deal to the rise. In 2008, China made paying taxes easier and less costly for companies by unifying the criteria and accounting methods for tax deductions and by reducing the corporate income tax rate. And, in 2009, a new corporate income tax law unified the tax regimes for domestic and foreign enterprises and clarified the calculation of taxable income for corporate income tax purposes. But this is just the regulatory environment of doing business in China. Besides this legal framework on paper, companies have the practical experience on the floor and they still have to deal with cultural challenges. In line which what we did in the previous chapter, namely, summarising the views of the western companies and managers towards the strengths and weaknesses of their Chinese competitors, in the upcoming section, we are giving an overview of the main challenges in the Chinese market according to Western companies and managers.

What are western managers in China saying about the main challenges?

While there are a number of factors that are of major concern, such as the economic situation, legislative matters, and currency risks, human resource management issues are always high in the list of business challenges for foreign companies doing business in China according to recent studies conducted by different Chambers of Commerce in China. This is logical if we take one look at the annual turnover of labour in specific companies. It is not uncommon that 30% of the staff are leaving the company in a year. Not only is there a need to find new work staff, but also there is a need to recruit even more people if the business is growing. Consequently, it is not unusual to renew total workforce in two or three years. During one of the interviews in China, a manager of a production site told me (informally) that if he would be a customer, he would never buy products from his plant in the two months after the new year holiday, normally end of January or early February. So many employees do not show up after the holiday period that it is a challenge to keep high quality standards because new employees must be trained (partly on the job). There are plenty of motives for employees to leave the company. Payment may be higher somewhere else or migrant workers may stay in their hometown to help the family.

The above issue relates not only to unskilled labour. The war on talent is even more intense in the segment of skilled labour. It is interesting to see that, in the previous years, the talent war between foreign and Chinese private-owned companies is beginning to turn in favor of Chinese private firms. More and more of my Chinese students indicate that they prefer to work for a Chinese company. Factors that are mentioned are better payment and benefit packages and long-term career development. This was quite an eye-opener for me. I'm sure that some years ago, most students would have preferred a foreign company, precisely for the same reasons.

The European Chamber of Commerce executes an annual research on the main challenges of conducting business in China.

2012	2013	2014	2015	2016
Shortage of qualified management	Labor costs	Labor costs	Labor costs	Incosistent regulatory interpretation and unclear laws
Incosistent regulatory interpretation and unclear laws	Incosistent regulatory interpretation and unclear laws	Incosistent regulatory interpretation and unclear laws	Incosistent regulatory interpretation and unclear laws	Labor costs
Shortage of qualified employees	Shortage of qualified employees	Shortage of qualified employees	Shortage of qualified employees	Obtaining required licenses
Obtaining required licenses	Corruption	Shortage of qualified management	Shortage of qualified management	Shortage of qualified employees
Corruption	Shortage of qualified management	Obtaining required licenses	Increasing Chinese protectionism	Industry overcapacity

2016 Top Ten
Incosistent regulatory interpretation and unclear laws 57%
Labor costs 54%
Obtaining required licenses 29%
Shortage of qualified employees 29%
Industry overcapacity 29%
Shortage of qualified management 29%
Increasing Chinese protectionism 29%
Corruption 26%
Tax 26%
Intellectual property rights infringement 23%

Figure 16.6 Top five business challenges in China, 2012–2016
Source: *EU Chamber of Commerce in China, Business Confidence Survey 2012–2017*

The 2017 results (based on 2016 survey) are translated into the top 10 challenges. In Fig. 16.6, we show the top 5 challenges in the previous five years (left) and the top 10 challenges in 2016 (right). In 2016, inconsistent regulatory interpretation and unclear laws ranked top, followed by high and increasing labour costs. Also, human resource-related challenges, such as shortage of qualified employees and management, are visible in this overview. It is interesting to note that the top challenges are more or less stable over the previous five years; only overcapacity (and related to this price pressure) is a new factor that gives discomfort to managers of European companies in China. In the discussions I had with western managers in China in

2017, I guess that the outcomes of the 2018 results are not so much different. Despite the development of the Chinese market and its middle class, western companies still have problems with the changes in the regulatory framework and they will continue to feel the pressure on prices due to overcapacity in several industries.

On paper, this regulatory context looks transparent, rule-based and reasonably "easy", but the surveys make clear that working on the ground is difficult. It should be noted that in many cases, the (transparency of) legislation itself is not the problem, but that the local interpretation and local rules that fill-in (central) legislation is often unclear and intransparent. Inconsistent regulations, obtaining licenses, government protectionism and corruption are among the top 10 challenges in 2016. Besides these factors of the ease of doing business, we also have the challenges due to specific Chinese cultural features; as we will see in the next chapter. A final aspect of doing business in China is that you must compete with fast-learning and highly competitive Chinese companies. Competition is not only driven by lower costs anymore, but is becoming increasingly dependent on innovation. In many surveys executed over the previous two years, managers from western multinational enterprises indicated that some of their Chinese competitors were equally or more innovative than themselves. This innovativeness (being products or processes), together with having key advantages with respect to government support and their speed to market, makes them difficult to fight on Chinese grounds. Cultural differences make doing business even more challenging. The chapter makes clear that in many aspects the Chinese business context is heavily influenced by Chinese culture. And that deep cultural differences are there to stay: China is modernising but is not westernising.

Chapter 17

Success and Failure Factors in Conducting Business in China

Myth 17: The main obstacles for being successful are the institutional and cultural differences

17.1 Introduction

Every company that fails, fails in its own way. This happens with small and medium-sized enterprises as well as large and powerful corporations. They entered China with high hopes and expectations but, at the end of the day, left China battered, confused and defeated. It's not because the companies and their managers were incompetent. Many of the biggest failures relate to well-known and globally successful companies such as eBay, Home Depot and Media Markt. All of these companies are successful on foreign markets, but not in China. Some suffered from a lack of flexibility or a failure to localise. Others fell because of bad timing or a superior local competitor. Despite the heterogeneous causes of failure, we will try to cluster the most important failures in this chapter.

There are also many western companies that have seen success in China. This is important because if companies want to become global, they have to be successful in China. No company in the world, going forward, can say they are global and successful unless they have a successful business and a growth model in China. In a way, the battle in China between western and Chinese companies will result in winning or losing global power. Multinational enterprises (MNEs) that cannot compete successfully in China will probably not acquire the capabilities needed to compete against Chinese companies in their traditional markets. The title of the last chapter of Hexter and Woetzel (2007) book, *Win in China or Lose Everywhere*, says it all.

The complexity to organise the failure and success factors can be seen if one looks at Walmart, the American-based retailer. On one hand, we saw the failure of Walmart in countries such as Germany and South Korea. On the other hand, the company was very successful in Japan and the UK. In Germany, Walmart exported its American business model, but underestimated the local context. Walmart found it difficult to compete when Germany's strict laws governed its opening hours; it had to close at 6.30 pm on week-nights and remain shut on Sunday. Walmart entered South Korea in the late 1990s and clearly failed. It left the country in 2005. South Korean consumers were more quality conscious and more brand loyal than their American counterparts. South Korean consumers perceived Walmart as a cheap marketplace. But the same strategy worked in other countries, even in countries within the "same" cultural context: Germany versus UK and South Korea versus Japan. The Every Day Low Price strategy was a success in Japan and the UK. It also prompted Walmart to move the strategy to China. However, in the first 10 years after its entry in China, sales stayed (far) below expectations. Only in the recent years do we see the start of a successful business operation in China.

Nearly every company understands the need to adapt to the local culture and to put emphasis on the relationship with governments if it moves abroad. This is no different in China. At the same time, they underestimate how much adaptation is needed. The cases of Walmart and Disney make this clear. Walmart became (more) successful after it changed its strategy towards local adaptation and reducing costs through local sourcing. Also, the Disney amusement park in Hong Kong that opened in 2005 was not successful during the initial years. Disney management made the mistake of assuming it would be successful without any adaptations because consumers wanted an "American" atmosphere. After some years, Disney made some necessary changes. The company learned fast. When it opened Disneyland in Shanghai (in 2016), it was successful from the start due to typical Chinese elements that are not found in other parks. This adaptation is not only needed because of specific cultural features, but is also needed because, by definition, one addresses low-income consumers (also known as the base of the pyramid). Companies such as Walmart and Disney are beginning to realise that the mass market (instead of focusing on the affluent elite) is needed and, consequently, strategy and operations should be fine tuned to this mass market (and not any-more on the affluent niche). This mass-market approach automatically means the need to lower costs, adapt products, and increase operational excellence. Doing business in China is the same as in many emerging markets. However, China has some very specific features. The chapter will focus on these specific Chinese characteristics that make the Chinese market so difficult for western companies and managers.

The chapter is organised as follows. We start in Section 17.2 with the failure factors of conducting business in China. Although the overview is a bit anecdotal, we go one step further by grouping the failure factors in six clusters that give a general picture of failures across sectors. This is followed, in Section 17.3, by the overview of the success factors. The success factors are divided into two segments: localisation in association with the role of the head office on one hand and focusing on cost reductions on the other hand. Because the role of the Chinese government is, in many cases, an important success factor, we discuss this separately in Section 17.4. We finish the chapter with Section 17.5 and some final words on the need to execute a step-by-step Chinese strategy.

17.2 Failure factors of operating in China

Sometimes, mistakes are relatively easy to solve. For example, Nike sold white sneakers with special Chinese characters printed on both heels to celebrate the year of the monkey. The character on the left shoe, *Fa*, means good fortune. The character is associated with the traditional spring festival. The character on the right shoe, *Fu*, symbolised wealth. However, when the two characters are combined and shoes are kept next to each other, the meaning alters completely. Instead of wealth and good fortune, it means "to become fat". In line with this, there are numerous examples of western companies struggling with the correct translation of its brand name into Chinese characters. Mercedes Benz originally went for the name Ben Si. Although phonetically it sounds a lot like Benz, the meaning of the characters does not fit anywhere near the message they wanted to convey. Combined, it meant "rushing to die", which is kind of unfortunate for a company building cars travelling at dangerous speeds. After realising the error, they immediately changed the name to Ben Chi which means dashing speed, and is a significantly more positive message to potential consumers. Correcting this "mistake" is relatively easy. In other cases, mistakes are more difficult to solve. For example, US-based Home Depot made a fundamental mistake by underestimating how the Chinese culture of the Do-It-Yourself (DIY) concept differs from the American way. They entered the Chinese market with their DIY concept. However, in the Chinese context, do-it-yourself is a sign of poverty. It appeared just too difficult to change this mindset.

To make the discussion about success and failure more complicated, a company can be a failure in certain point of time but can be a success story in other periods of time. This is, for example, the case with Walmart. They faced big problems in China in order to survive the intensity of competition and to connect to the new middle class. After some changes and restructuring, it looks like the company has found its way in the Chinese jungle and appears to be relatively successful.

Despite the many company-specific failures, the following overview clusters the main failures into six factors:

1. *Not knowing the consumer.* This may connect to underestimation of the price sensitivity of Chinese customers. But it may also relate to not knowing the buying habit of the different segments

in the market, in particular when moving to second- or third-tier cities; away from the coastal areas.

2. *Problems dealing with the bureaucracy and non-transparent regulations.* This not only includes the elements of the ease of doing business (Chapter 16), but also goes much further. It also refers to the fact that, in many cases, companies are just not able to understand why certain legislation is implemented or changed.
3. *Underestimating the need for local help and consequently, choosing the wrong mode of entry.* These two elements are connected. If a company chooses to conduct business with full ownership in China, you must do it by yourself. Being a western company can be complicated in the Chinese context. Therefore, local help through a joint venture (JV) may be advisable.
4. *Underestimating the intensity of competition, in particular from local players.* The Chinese competitive environment consists of numerous small local players, large state-owned enterprises (SOEs) and western competitors. Consequently, the intensity of competition is heavy. Associated with this is the fact that in many markets, the competition pressure increased in a very short time frame.
5. *The wrong mindset of the head office.* The attitude of the head office may result in a bad timing, a centralistic approach with respect to products, processes and R&D, and not giving enough freedom and flexibility to the Chinese outlet. It is essential to change the mindset because the economic and business environment is changing very fast and flexibility in the organisation is essential.
6. *Underestimating external factors.* Uncontrollable factors, such as geopolitical issues, currency policies and economic crisis in other markets, may affect business in China. Part of this external environment also connects to domestic issues such as the quality of infrastructure and distribution system.

Of course, these factors are intertwined. For example, not knowing your customer is partly blamed by the fact that the head office is not listing to the people "on the floor". In this case, the ethnocentric attitude of the head office means standardised rules which does not fit with the way the Chinese operate. The centralistic view of the head office also affects the mode of entry choice. To operate by yourself is sometimes not a good choice, for example, if connections to the government are important. This was the reason why Uber chose to cooperate with Baidu. It was driven by the hope that Baidu could open the Chinese market for Uber due to its connection with the government. Despite these linkages between the failure factors, in the discussion below, we will handle these factors separately.

A final remark is about how to define a failure. The case of Uber makes clear that failure is a bit ambiguous; one can have success and failure at the same time. In 2016, Uber had about 20% of the Chinese ride-hailing market, which is much lower that its Chinese competitors and much lower than what we see in other markets. From this perspective, Uber failed in China. At the same time, however, 4 out of Uber's top 10 cities by the number of rides hailed per day are in China, the largest cities being Guangzhou and Chengdu. Looking at its name recognition and the fact that China is Uber's largest market globally, the entry into China was successful. However, if one cannot make money and the market share is far below its main competitors, you may question this success.

1. *Not knowing the customer*

You cannot target China as one big market; it is a collection of individual sub-markets. The coastal regions and cities, such as Shanghai, Hangzhou, Shenzhen and Guangzhou, are mostly highly developed and their population has a much higher per capita income compared to China's poorer western regions. There are also considerable differences in cultures, food, dialects, climate and buying habits between China's regions and cities. Of course, this is known; in that sense, doing business is not so much different from other large (emerging) markets. But it makes segmenting the market difficult, in particular if one combines the large regional differences with the speed of change of the Chinese consumers (and their preferences). Because China is changing so fast, generations only a decade apart have grown up in quite different circumstances, which has created some striking cross-generational disparities. I remember the picture of a young guy around 35 who drives an Audi. He stops at his apartment and the two kids are walking to the house, looking and playing on their smartphone. The man had been shopping and I saw the plastic bag of City market, a high-priced supermarket chain in Shanghai. Also, an older woman stepped out of the car with some fresh vegetables from the daily market and before going into the (large) house, she checked the garbage and took something out of it. This was clearly one family, three generations totally different from each other including their (buying) behaviour. This is a huge challenge to marketers. In such situations, using the average household income as proxy for buying habits is not enough due to the enormous difference between the members of the (extended) family. Obviously, there is a need to de-average general trends concerning the middle class.

Overestimating demand

Home Depot entered China in 2006 by acquiring China-based home improvement retailer Home Way. Home Depot is an example of an MNE that overestimated the (potential) demand for its products. China was seen as an interesting market due to the growth of home sales, in particular, in tier 1 and 2 cities. However, the rising demand of houses in these larger cities came from speculators who purchased homes to sell them later. Due to this, homes did not have any residents and there were no buyers for home-improvement products. In addition, more and more furnished homes were sold in the urban areas. This left very little things for the people to do on their own. Finally, and most importantly, China is not the land of DIY. In China, labour is easily available and cheap. Everything is being outsourced by hiring a handyman, from cleaning the house to repairing the door and other home improvement-related work. It is just not considered appropriate to do it yourself. Most customers in China associated DIY with poor people. The problem of Home Depot was that it replicated its US model by selling only the hardware products and advising customers on how to lay their own tiles and install lighting. Although the problem was the DIY concept, Chinese are not totally averse to a DIY model; look at the success of IKEA which also sells DIY furniture. But IKEA provided its buyers the option of assembly services. Home Depot did not have such installation services.

Another element associated with under-expected sales was the retail format. While Home Depot specialised in big-box retailing, in China, the trend was towards specialised retailing. The Chinese are not used to buying all the products under the same roof. They prefer to buy from different speciality shops after comparing the prices. Also, the product portfolio was not tailored to the Chinese customer. Selling (standardised) products like garden houses, picnic tables and outdoor furniture is not very logical because most Chinese people live in small apartments without a garden or a balcony.

Product portfolio disconnected from consumer

The product portfolio of Home Depot was clearly disconnected from the Chinese (potential) consumer. The same can be said with respect to M&S. M&S's problems in the Chinese market are explained by its failure to understand the needs of its consumers. Certain mistakes, for example, too much focus (and oversupply) on oversized clothing or no promotional material adapted to fit the Chinese market, (using models and mannequins that were western) could have been easily avoided. But certain failures were difficult to solve. For example, it fully underestimated the importance, the purchasing power and the preferences of the city's young female shoppers. Another company that had difficulties in fine tuning its product to meet the needs of the Chinese consumer was Uber.

Uber has been designed for American users, and it entered China without adjusting the core product. For example, it started with only credit cards. This presented a major obstacle for many potential Chinese users because only a minority of the urban elite possessed a credit card and could use the Uber app. Later, Uber added the option of payment through Alipay, a mobile wallet system developed by Alibaba. Another adjustment was needed due to

Google Map's extremely limited (and inaccurate) coverage of China. Instead, Chinese users preferred the mapping technology of Baidu. Consequently, Uber-China entered into a strategic partnership with Baidu.

Price setting

For (marketing) managers, the Chinese consumer is very complicated. For example, if the product or service does little or nothing to boost its status, the Chinese consumer becomes extremely price conscious. But the same person is willing to pay a big amount of money for a product which he can show off to his friends. For example, the man who bought and proudly wore a genuine Rolex watch might bargain over a US$50 microwave. Most of the western companies are struggling with their price strategy. In many cases, they underestimate the price sensitivity of the Chinese consumer and the price reduction strategies of Chinese firms. Low prices are essential. One of my colleagues at Renmin University stated that his job at the university is to make money, and that his second job at home is to shop in ways that will save money, i.e. spending a lot of time to find the best bargains. Also, the price strategies of Chinese firms can hurt MNEs. Competition is enormous; reducing prices or giving discount will be followed almost instantly by Chinese competitors. For example, Carrefour faced big challenges while competing with the local retailers in the 1990s. In the early days, the French company had discounts on Coca Cola or Sprite, while local chains offered a discount on soy sauce or other typical Chinese products. Overall, the prices offered by the local retailers are not *per se* lower, but they are cheaper in categories where the Chinese consumers tend to pay more attention.

The failure of Media Markt is also attributed to this price sensitivity of the consumer. Media Markt entered China in 2010. It differentiated itself from competitors by putting a lot of emphasis on showcasing the products and giving the customers the possibility to test and try the products. But, at the end of the day, the customers made their buying decision about electronics mainly based on price.

They were loyal to Lenovo, Haier, Philips or LG, but they were not loyal to retailers such as Media Markt. Media Markt closed all its seven stores in China along with its Chinese head office in Shanghai in March 2013.

Similar problems can be seen for Home Depot. The main determinant to compete was the price and Home Depot was not able to compete on price against the Chinese competitors (such as the mom and pop shops). The same happened with IKEA and Toyota. They also entered China with a price level that was too high for the local market and both underestimated the price sensitivity of the Chinese consumers. Both companies adapted their prices successfully. IKEA reduced costs mainly by local sourcing. It built a number of factories in China and increased local sourcing of materials. While globally, 30% of IKEA's products comes from China, about 65% of the volume sales in China come from local sourcing (IKEA website). In addition to low production costs, these local factories resolved the problem of high import taxes. All these measures resulted in significant cost reductions, and consequently prices were lowered. In 1998, it opened the first store in China and, at that time, the price of its "LACK" table was 120 Renminbi. Today, the price has dropped to around 40 Renminbi. Toyota also had problems with its price strategy, in particular with respect to Chinese carmaker BYD. BYD car models were not only copies of Toyota cars, but were substantially cheaper. Toyota reduced the prices of its Vios and Corolla models in China, step by step, in the mid-2000s.

2. *Not able to deal with the bureaucracy and legislation*

Although we discuss bureaucracy and red-tapism from a western company's point of view, it should be noted that Chinese people and companies also face red-tapism in their daily activities. There was a lot of (social) media attention when Premier Li Keqiang referred to a typical example of "ridiculous bureaucracy" (*China Daily*, 8 May 2015). A Beijing resident had to fill in a form before going for a family trip abroad. He wanted to name his mother as the emergency contact during the trip, but an official asked him to provide paperwork to confirm his relationship with her. It took him several visits and considerable amount of energy to get the papers in order. Li used this case as an example to demonstrate that red tape must be cut; excessive bureaucracy is not helping the public. So, bureaucracy is annoying for western as well as Chinese people and companies. Most common complaints are clustered around obtaining the required licenses and permits. For example, to get the permission for a shop in Shanghai Pudong area, the UK-based retailer B&Q had to negotiate with the Ministry of Commerce in Beijing, the Shanghai municipal government, the Pudong government and officials from Huamu Township where the B&Q store was located. With the latter, they also agreed on the number of hired locals. In one of the meetings with B&Q officials, they told me that they regret not using a local partner to take care of these procedures.

Connectivity to the (local) government is important. This is an important reason why many companies choose to enter China through a collaboration with a local partner who may help to connect easily with the government. For example, Uber's cooperation with Baidu allowed Uber to use Baidu Maps for its China services, but more importantly brought the politically connected and economically powerful Baidu into its inner circle of investors. The Uber case makes clear that connectivity to the government, although important, is not always generating success. Despite its cooperation with Baidu, local competitors (such as Didi and Kuaidi) won the competition battle; partly through preferences given by the government. There is another important learning point from the Uber case. The aggressive move of Uber to disrupt the traditional taxi sector was not in line with the (local) government's policy. The Ministry of Transportation published a document in which it was stated that the transition to a new taxi environment should be gradual and that municipal governments should not abandon their traditional taxi firms. Looking back, Uber was too aggressive. By cooperating with local governments and the incumbent taxi industry, China-based Didi and Kuaidi avoided most regulatory controversies. Only after developing these government and consumer relations did both companies begin to add private car products. Both companies continued to promote official taxis as an important component of their service. Uber, on the other hand, made aggressive moves without considering the impact on the powerful regular taxi sector and without making the connection with the government.

When cooperating with the Chinese government, companies need to be flexible. Boeing had difficulties in dealing with the Chinese government. Collaborating with and adapting to the Chinese government was not exactly what an American military giant expected it would have to do. Boeing had to accept that some supply activities had to be moved to China to please the Chinese government. Another interesting case on dealing with the government relates to the Disney movie *Pirates of the Caribbean: At World's End* (2007). In the movie, Captain Sao Feng recited a Tang Dynasty poem in Cantonese. However, the Chinese government made it clear that Disney had to edit the poem (as well as other parts) before the movie could be released in China. Disney agreed but needed some time to adjust the movie for the Chinese market. At the end of the day, DVD pirates were faster and made the copies from the international version of the movie. In June 2007, the movie was available in China on screen but DVDs were already available and you could download it from unauthorised websites. The two weeks delay had a big impact on revenues. The M&S case clearly shows how important a good preparation is to reduce government interference. It launched a flagship store on West Nanjing Road in the heart of Shanghai's shopping district in 2008. However, M&S food shipments had been blocked at Shanghai customs due to certain clearing procedures, which meant that the food section of the store was empty for the first three months. There are many other examples of companies that failed in China because they could not cope with the bureaucratic and legislative rules of the government. Occasionally, it is indeed difficult to adjust. For example, how to adjust to a sharp increase in the local content rules? It is difficult for many MNEs to increase the local content in short term; specifically, in the high-tech sector because not so many domestic suppliers were and are able to guarantee the quality standards used by western MNEs.

In many cases, MNEs will adjust, but sometimes there is no other option than to leave China. The lesson from Google's China failure is clear; in the end, large and important foreign companies who want to flourish in China must abide by the rules set by the central and local governments. That means either compromising with policies you may find unpleasant, as Google did at first, or leaving China which was the case in 2010.

Websites targeting the Chinese market face a choice: establish a server presence in China or maintain an offshore server and force users to endure significant delays caused by the acting Firewall. With a lot of hesitation, and despite concerns about censorship and putting users at risk, Google decided to launch Google.cn in 2006. The searches on Google were monitored by the Chinese government and certain search results were blocked. In December 2009, Google detected an extensive cyber-attack that targeted some specific organisations, companies and people. This, complemented by critical notes from NGOs and politicians in the US and Europe, made Google announce in 2010 that it would stop with Google.cn. Google users were now redirected to a new service on Google.com.hk. The Hong Kong site, however, was outside the Great Firewall (and therefore slow) and censoring by the Chinese government was replaced by Google's self-censoring tools. Early 2017, Google's market share was neglectable, while the Chinese search engine Baidu had a market share of 75%. Also, Facebook, Twitter and YouTube are blocked and replaced by Chinese substitutes, such as Renren for Facebook, Youku and Tudou for YouTube, and Tencent's QQ as answer to MSN Messenger. Furthermore, Sina Weibo is the Chinese Twitter.

China's local players were quick to reap the benefits of the government's policy to block the western social media brands and they developed their own versions of these popular sites. Weibo was introduced in August 2009. It was accepted by the Chinese authorities as long it executed self-censoring of the tweets. It was a great success from the start with more than 500 million registered accounts as of 2013. After 2013, it has been used slightly less due to government intervention. Users sensed more and more monitoring by the government. In April 2012, Tencent introduced WeChat, which was available on all major smartphone app stores. In 2013, Tencent introduced various additional features in WeChat such as payment services and an extensive games centre. These are examples of the government supporting domestic companies in the social media sector. But you see it in many (strategic) sectors. For example, the C919, developed by Commercial Aircraft Corporation of China (COMAC) is now a competitor of the Boeing 737 and Airbus A320 due to government support. The examples above make clear that connectivity to the bureaucracy is essential. This is summarised by my collegue: "you need to play nice with the government".

3. *The wrong mode of entry*

There are many options available when going international, ranging from exporting to a greenfield investment (Fig. 17.1). It comes back to the question how much control is needed and how much control are you willing to give away? Wholly owned subsidiaries through greenfield investments and M&As are high control modes. Building a new plant from scratch or taking over another company will give the investor full management control and the freedom regarding

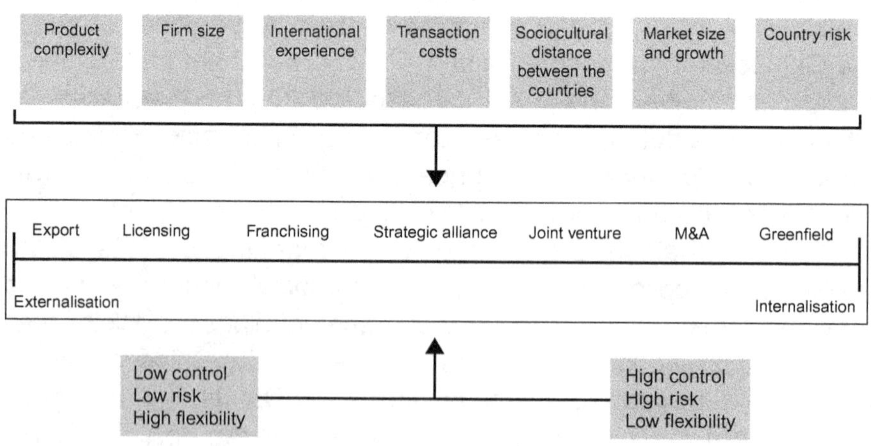

Figure 17.1 Entry mode and drivers behind the mode of entry choice

Source: *Based and adjusted from Hollenson (2010)*

strategic choices. In Chapter 15, we explained the choice to have full control within the OLI-framework of Dunning (1980). In essence, a company is internalising its activities to keep control over technology, image and prices. As can be seen in Fig. 17.1, greenfield investments and M&As are high control, high-risk modes of entry.

Joint ventures (JVs) are intermediate control strategies; both parties invest in a new company. The control is shared between the two parties based on the amount of equity invested (equity joint venture) or based on a contract (contractual joint venture). There are also entry modes without involving equity. Think about strategic alliances where the companies are helping each other in terms of R&D, logistics or sales. Finally, the easiest way to sell the product in China is through export as the risk is low and it generates more flexibility compared to equity stakes. However, this choice for externalisation means that you do not have control over your product as soon as it enters China. Whether we talk about a JV, export or M&A, selecting the right partner is always a key factor in success or failure.

Obviously, the choice of the entry mode depends on numerous factors. In Fig. 17.1, we only indicate some of the main determinants. For example, the larger the sociocultural distance between the home and host country, the more you may need a local partner. Consequently, a JV as an entry strategy is logical. If a company already has a lot of international experience, it learns how to approach a new foreign market and may have economies of skills which can be transferred to other international markets. In this case, you might do it by yourself via a greenfield or takeover. If operating in a country is risky, you may prefer a non-equity entry mode before investing money. Also, product characteristics will influence the mode of entry choice. For example, the more complex a product is, the sooner the company will decide to produce it in-house because of higher transaction costs when using the market.

Until the early 2000s, a JV was the common entry mode in China. In some cases, working with a local partner was needed by law, and even if other alternatives were possible the JV construction was being chosen because the local partner could help in dealing with the (local) governments or it may have an efficient logistical

Advantages	Disadvantages
- Certain sectors are only open through a joint venture - Chinese partner has experience conducting business in China - Ability to leverage Chinese partner's guanxi with (local) government, party, suppliers, and (potential) clients - Chinese partner can help with bureaucratic procedures - Access to sales and distribution network of Chinese partner - Shared risk of failure	- Cultural differences makes management complicated - One bed, two dreams - The joint venture is self-managed which creates distance to head office - Finding a good Chinese partner can be lengthy and costly - Potential problems related to sharing technology and knowledge - Joint venture partner is partnering with more western companies and may appear as a new competitor

Figure 17.2 The advantages and disadvantages of JV entry mode
Source: Constructed by author

network. In general, the foreign company can make use of the guanxi that the Chinese company has. Today, most (non-strategic) sectors in China are open for foreign companies and there is no need to form a joint venture anymore. The most important pros and cons of the JV construction are given in Fig. 17.2.

When looking at the disadvantages shown in Fig. 17.2, it is not illogical that the joint venture sometimes is called a joint adventure. Different motives and goals of the alliance (one bed, two dreams) are important sources of failure. In some cases, the JV partner appears to be a new competitor. In the mid-1990s, Danone, the French food giant, acquired 51% in China's Wahaha beverages. However, Wahaha was operating (secretly) a parallel firm in markets and with products that were similar to Danone. The problem that the domestic partner might create an alternative production facility and compete against the JV was also the case with Japan-based Honda (the motorcycle business unit). Honda formed a JV with a Chinese motorcycle firm and created its own enemy; the Chinese partner produced clones and even exported its low-end motorcycles to Japan. When the management team of Honda saw these products, they were impressed by the local firm's low-cost production capability and relatively high quality, and after some talks, Honda even intensified the cooperation, but now including the production line of the cheap clones.

Another example of a JV in which partners had different objectives, was the GM-Chery case. GM produced the Chinese Chevrolet Spark at US$7,500 at the end of 2003. However, before it could sell the first few cars, Chery began to sell almost identical cars at US$6,000. GM was unable to fight Chery because it was 20% owned by GM's main JV partner in China, SAIC.

The choice of doing it by yourself (through a greenfield or takeover) is appealing if we look at the governance problems related to a JV. Full control means that you have the freedom to take the decisions by yourself. However, to do it by yourself is complicated in the Chinese market. British retailer Tesco entered China by itself and after some loss-making years they decided in August 2013 to merge its unprofitable operation with an SOE (China Resources Enterprise Limited) as a minority partner of 20%. Negotiation problems with suppliers and regulators were cited as one of the main reasons behind Tesco's failure. We saw similar problems with B&Q, Marks and Spencer, and Home Depot. They also initially sought to transplant their British business model in China but needed local help at the end of the day. As stated earlier in this chapter, Home Depot entered China acquiring a local home-improvement retail chain (Home Way) in late 2006. Home Depot decided the acquisition route instead of the greenfield approach. It hoped to benefit from the experience and local knowledge of Home Way executives and its 3,000 strong sales force. However, the head office decided that the Home Depot brand and the standardised store format should be used. The head office changed the outlets instantly, and the rebranded shops opened in August 2007. But as indicated earlier, it was not a success due to the structure of the market and the buying habit of the consumers.

Foreign firms typically come to China with superiority in skills and capabilities that relate to marketing, advertising, logistics, distribution management and brand management. But these specific superior skills cannot always be translated into competitive advantages. For example, it has been difficult for foreign firms to replicate and execute their home-based networks and to make use of their superior logistic capabilities. Companies such as Walmart and Home Depot had problems with the fragmented distribution system in China. Establishing nationwide distribution channels is crucial in industries where economies of scale are significant, such as home appliances, PCs, mobile phones and household products. There was no national freight carrier, which meant that Walmart and Home Depot could not replicate the efficient logistics system that it operates in other markets. The only way to solve this competitive obstacle is to connect to local firms through JVs or strategic alliances. In this case, the MNE can make use of the already established networks.

4. *Underestimating the intensity of competition*

Under the planned economy before 1979, many industries were replicated in parallel in each province and even within provinces. This was driven by the objective of spreading out the risks and creating self-sufficient regions. It also reduced the complexity of the planning process. Although the business landscape in China changed dramatically, the fragmentation that resulted is still visible today. This fragmentation has been intensified further by certain institutional features, such as the discretionary power of local governments and the role of the banks. They made it possible for unprofitable firms to stay afloat. This results in overcapacity and intense competition. In 2004, there were more than 200 carmakers, most of them were relatively small Chinese firms owned by (local) governments. In 2016, there were 140 car production plants in China (including JVs with foreign firms). Obviously, some consolidation happened, but that did not solved the overcapacity issue. The capacity of manufactured cars is much more than what can be sold on the market. We see evidence everywhere. For example, Chery today has the capacity to make 900,000 vehicles annually, while sales in 2016 reached around 510,000.

One of the main problems for foreign companies in China in the 1990s was that everyone entered China awaiting the consumption explosion to come but nobody was leaving. MNEs were not leaving the market because they saw the growth of the middle class and so many opportunities that leaving was not an option. Chinese firms were also not leaving the market despite low margins or losses. SOEs did not leave because there was a government that helped if needed. Smaller private firms were not leaving because they were capable of reducing costs, even if you think that it may not be possible anymore. There is also a more cultural element: an entrepreneur would not leave a market easily, admitting incompetence to cope with the competition, saving their own face. The result was a dramatic overcapacity in many markets, ranging from electronics to automotive and the beer market. A colleague of mine, during one of his lectures, stated that China in the 1990s and early 2000s can be seen as "corporate Vietnam" with respect to competition. Also today, this intensity of competition is extremely high in China.

The competition from local Chinese firms was based on costs and prices, but the competition is now shifting towards design, innovation and branding. This development of competing from price towards design and innovation can be seen in the case of China-based Galanz. Galanz started to produce and sell in the domestic lower-end market. It introduced a simple, energy-efficient microwave at an affordable price for the lower middle class. The microwave was small enough to fit in their kitchens. There was no competition from global brands on this low-end market. Because of the absence of western MNEs in this segment, the company was able to increase market share relatively easily (and achieved economies of scale). The next step of Galanz was to move up in the market, and it began to disrupt the microwave market in China and abroad. This strategy to produce good quality (and in many cases, quite innovative) products for the lower middle class is called "disruptive innovation from the base of the pyramid" (Hart and Christiansen, 2002). The same can be seen in other industries. Media Markt is seen as a low-price shop in its home market but was not able to compete on prices with local players like Gome and Sunning. I still remember the opening of its first store on Huai Hai road in Shanghai in November 2010. Incidentally, I was in Shanghai during the opening ceremony and saw the enormous number of people showing interest in the shop. In 2012, Media Markt had seven stores, all in Shanghai. The company had big plans; to have 100 stores across the country in 5–7 years. However, at the end of the day, competition was just too intensive. In the case of Media Markt, not only competition resulted in the faliure, other mistakes made it impossible to fight the local competitors. For example, the sales personnel in the shop were employees of Media Markt. On the contrary, the Chinese competitors leased out the retail space in their stores to suppliers and received either rent or a commission on sales from the suppliers. Most of the sales personnel were employed by the suppliers. While Media Markt had to buy items from the suppliers, pay the wages to its personnel and also incur the rising rent costs. The Chinese retailers earned rent, and did not had personnel costs.

Competition is strong in all consumer sectors, ranging from cars and electronics to cosmetics and fast food. Competition for western fast food chains like KFC, McDonald's and Pizza Hut is enormous. On one hand, we see domestic food chains like Malan Noodle and Ronghua chicken that compete by focusing on Chinese dishes and competitive pricing. Ronghua claimed "American style fried chicken with Chinese characteristics". On the other hand, we see many domestic restaurants copying the western style of operation and food to attract customers. Yong He King, Shanghai-based fast food chain with 80 outlets used Colonel Sanders's look alike in its logo and the red-and-white colour scheme of KFC. Fast food chain HiPi (run by Shanghai Liantai Food Company) served food with a store layout and menu format similar to McDonald's. Earlier in the chapter, we stated that Uber had difficulty in connecting with the (local) government, but another factor that led to its failure in China is the intensity of competition. By the time Uber entered the Chinese market in 2014, there were two domestic companies that dominated the Chinese taxi-hailing app market: Didi Dache and Kuaidi Dache. Didi Dache started in early 2013 with financial help from Tencent. Kuaidi Dache was helped by a financial injection from Alibaba. In late 2014, both captured about half the market. Uber was not able to compete against the two large domestic players.

Domestic firms are used to fighting the intense competition battle; not only on lower prices but also on design and quality. Esprit and Mango, two western high-end brands, felt this competition in the previous years. An example of a typical domestic fashion brand that competed against Esprit and Mango was Me&City. It works with international designers and, at the same time, is offering the products at considerably lower prices. It was interesting to see that both Esprit and Mango had completely underestimated the progress and learning process that had been made by Me&City and other Chinese firms. Another company that underestimated the Chinese competitors was US-based eBay. eBay entered the Chinese market in 2002 with the partial acquisition of EachNet. At that time, EachNet was China's largest player which held 90% of the Internet C2C market. In the early 2000s, the practice was that many customers used the website to negotiate deals; later, they met the seller at a public place to examine the goods and made their payment. The majority of the trade, therefore, was between people in the same city and was heavily concentrated in the large cities. Step by step, EachNet facilitated online transactions. Starting in October 2010, it worked as an intermediary collecting agent between the buyer and the seller. It delayed the payment to the seller until the delivery of goods was confirmed by the buyer. It charged 3% of the transaction amount. Like eBay, EachNet charged sellers a fee to list items and a separate fee once the transaction was completed. In 2003, the Chinese online shopping website Taobao (founded by Alibaba) started. Taoboa offered free services which fit the price sensitivity of Chinese consumers. In a famous remark by Ma, founder of Alibaba, it becomes clear that fighting Chinese competitors is difficult: "eBay may be a shark in the ocean, but we are the crocodile in the Yangtze River. If we fight in the ocean we lose, but if we fight in the river, we win".

The examples above are about real competition between western and Chinese firms. Of course, we also see competition from fake products; this gives the competitive battle a specific Chinese dimension. According to industry reports, in 2016, between 50% and 70% of the counterfeit items anywhere in the world came from China (Bloomberg). We already discussed Disney's *Pirates of the Caribbean*. DVDs of the film were available well before its release in

China. Also, LEGO had difficulties in fighting counterfeit products. There was an interesting case that even the main production manager of LEGO, when confronted with imitated pieces, could not differentiate between the fake and original products since they were identical in quality. One should keep in mind that not just western companies are being hit. In January 2017, Chinese authorities visited (and closed) nearly 50 small-scale factories that manufactured fake versions of widely used food seasonings and sauces sold under names such as Knorr and Nestle, as well as China-based companies such as Totole (owned by Nestlé) and Donggu.

5. *The wrong attitude of the head office*

The head office may underestimate the challenges of conducting business in China. They may choose a top-down communication structure in which centralisation and standardisation are the key words. For example, in one of the interviews I had with the management team of FedEx-China, it was stated that the rule of the head office was to visit a main account in China every quarter as was the procedure internationally. However, in China this was not working. Visiting a main account should be done more often as trust, which is essential in the Chinese business context, can be built only gradually. Another example relates to the issue of after-sales in China. In general, Chinese customers are not used to paying for after-sales. It is, therefore, quite common in China to incorporate the after-sales activities in the selling price. However, this does not fit in the administrative system of the head office, i.e. how to deal with after-sales activities (including costs) throughout the years without specific revenues? I know of some European companies where the head office demanded to change this and to sell after-sales activities separately to the Chinese clients. As a consequence, the selling process was heavily interrupted and clients dropped out. These examples make it clear that the attitude of the head office can be a failure factor. Too much centralisation and standardisation as well as low flexibility on the "Chinese floor" are preconditions for failure. There are many examples of this head office mismatch when conducting business in China. In 2011, Whirlpool China developed a new energy-efficient refrigerator. They started a process to find suitable Chinese component suppliers for the new and innovative product. Of course, suppliers had to match some important criteria such as minimum quality audit score and innovative capabilities. In addition, the head office also indicated how the payment had to be put in the contract. This standardised payment contract was similar to the ones used in other markets, but in the Chinese case, there were no suppliers willing to accept these payment terms. Consequently, the company had to postpone the production of the new fridge and lost its first mover advantage in China.

Decision-making at eBay was extremely centralised. The subsidiary, eBay China, had to follow the rules and directives from eBay headquarters in the US. For example, China's pricing was changed to conform to that of the parent company and the head office decided not to follow the advice of a local manager to incorporate Chinese features such as a chat function in its platform. While Taobao allowed buyers and sellers to chat over instant-messaging and voice mail, giving them a chance to establish a personal connection, eBay did not. This interaction is typically the Chinese way of buying products, not waiting for an e-mail from the seller you are unfamiliar with. Furthermore, Taoboa designed its categories in accordance with the typical structure of a Chinese department store, with separate sections for men and women. In contrast, eBay China used the category structure set by eBay's global platform. Centralisation also harmed eBay China's technical performance. The regular server maintenance at eBay head office happens on Thursday nights to prepare for the peak traffic on Fridays in the US, but in China, this coincided with Friday afternoons, eBay's heaviest traffic of the week in China, resulting in performance problems and customer complaint.

The attitude of the head office regarding centralisation and standardisation is closely linked to the number and positions of expatriates. A large number of expats may signal an ethnocentric head office. In the early 2000s, large MNEs used a lot of expats. In

2002, two-thirds of key position holders in Dutch-based Philips were expatriates and only one-third were local, which was clearly not a desirable ratio. A specific issue relates to the use of Japanese managers in the Chinese context. For example, Toyota made the mistake of employing Japanese managers during the early days of its operations in China. This resulted in tensions because of the complicated bilateral relationship between the two countries and the attitude of Chinese towards the Japanese. After some years, Toyota used American managers as they were considered "culture-neutral". Having an ethnocentric attitude and using expats to manage the China operations, is dangerous. The role of the head office is sometimes disconnected from the Chinese practice of conducting business. Because Chinese (managers) do not evaluate, re-evaluate and reflect much on what they do, they are mentally free to act quickly. This is a very intense, practical way of getting things done that is difficult to understand and be handled by the expats and the managers in the head office. Expats may also result in a glass ceiling for high potential local employees. One of the most challenging aspects of doing business in China is finding the right people for the job and ensuring that they don't leave within a year. Therefore, career development in the company is important.

The head office decides about the timing and speed issues. In general, it sees the opportunities and is eager to enter the market as soon as possible. Waiting is seen as losing the opportunity and momentum. Although there are several examples of successful early entries, in many cases early market entry is difficult and risky because the market and the company both are not ready to take this step.

Timing and speed

Early timing can have its advantages. First movers such as Volkswagen, Motorola and Kodak aggressively went to China, gaining a first-mover advantage. They captured strong positions on specific markets, making it possible to create economies of scale and earning oligopolistic profits. Also, name recognition was relatively easy because there were no (western) competitors. However, a first mover advantage does not come easy. A lot of

Advantages	Disadvantages
- Competitive edge gained by being the first to introduce a product or service	- Cost of pioneering can be high such as establishing distribution network and connecting to customers
- Opportunity to capture easy market share	- No experience on this market and consequently greatest risk of failure
- Chance to build brand loyalty	
- Enhances reputation	- Loyalty of first time buyers is often weak
- Create entry barriers for potential competitors	- Experiences of the early entrants are easily imitated

Figure 17.3 Pros and cons of early entrance
Source: Constructed by author

investments and commitment is needed in building up distribution networks and an efficient sales department. There is a great risk of failure because of the lack of experience on the Chinese market. As Fig. 17.3 indicates, a first mover is also confronted with low consumer loyalty. Entering too late is also problematic. Renault started production in China through a JV with Donfeng in 2013, many years later than its competitors. It is a question whether this late entrance is a wise decision or not.

In general, it takes time for MNEs to become profitable in the early period. In particular, building up a distribution network is problematic. The logistics industry is extremely fragmented with numerous small companies, delays, red-tapism and administrative costs. Therefore, several companies choose to build their own network. For example, Yum! has built more than 20 distribution warehouses in China and has its own fleet of trucks. For many companies, this is not possible and they rely on outside logistics providers.

The first movers are confronted with a market and customers that often are not ready yet. One of the largest revolving door companies in the world is Dutch-based Boon-Edam. The family business is very successful on the Chinese market and many of the iconic buildings have a Boon-Edam revolving door. But in the 1990s, selling these doors in South China was problematic because the market only saw the revolving door as a means to keep the cold air outside. This is not really a problem in the south. The sales team of Boon-Edam discussed a lot with potential customers about the advantages for the environment and reducing energy costs, but only from the previous decade have the revolving doors started to sell in South China. Looking back, one may say that Porsche started its operations too early in China. During its first year in China (2001), they only sold 27 cars and less than 100 cars during the next three years. The Chinese consumers were clearly not ready for Porsche and its sports car culture. LEGO started to operate in China in the 1990s, but the Chinese consumers were not ready at that time for LEGO toys. Only in 2014 was the market more open to the idea of educational toys, which gave LEGO a boost. Timing issues also relate to different business units and products within the same company. The Proctor & Gamble (P&G) case makes this clear. On one hand, we see a first-mover advantage of P&G Head & Shoulders shampoo that was successfully introduced in the late 1980s. On the other hand, we have Pampers baby diapers that were introduced only in 1997. It is interesting to note that the initial idea of P&G was to start selling laundry detergent in China, but research indicated that Chinese consumers were not ready and would not value the superior performance of this P&G product. At the end of the day, the decision was made to start with shampoos. But even at that time, the market was not ready yet. The Head & Shoulders brand shampoo was introduced in 1988. It was introduced in a large variety of product sizes; even single-use sachets costing 0.5 Renminbi. It was new to sell shampoo as a packaged product; normally, soap was used or customers took their own containers to a local store to fill shampoo from a bulk container. P&G had to invest heavily in marketing and advertising to explain the product to the consumer. The company underestimated the size of the market, the price sensitivity of the customer and some preconceived ideas. Pampers was introduced in a context in which people thought that it caused infertility and bowed legs. Only after several years of fighting preconceived ideas and other obstacles, the sales grew rapidly. As stated earlier with the Boon-Edam case, companies need to educate the (potential) consumer about their products. Please note that P&G began advertising in China even though it was not selling any product there. The same holds for Coca Cola; it started a media campaign to make the potential consumer ready for its product.

Timing is important, and there are examples of first-mover's advantages. But in general, one may say that being second is perhaps the best. In that case, there is no need to educate the (potential) customer about the product. Furthermore, there are learning points from the mistakes made by the first mover and in many instances, the market is large enough that being a bit late does not create a problem. That was one of the reasons why Renault was so late in China. According to the management team, the Chinese market is still large enough to host an additional company. The management of Renault made it clear that, for them, the main issue is if the company is ready for it. The need for an internal health check to find out if the company is ready to operate in China is sometimes not done because of emotions and opportunities. Rushing is not always good and waiting is not always bad.

6. *Uncontrollable external factors*

External factors are, in many cases, unexpected events. An example is the SARS outbreak in 2003 and the bird flu outbreak in 2004. This was heavily felt by fast food chains such as KFC and McDonald's. The sales of KFC collapsed by 30% (2004) because of this. Another example of an unexpected event was the explosion of demand for foreign branded baby infant formula in the previous years. This was driven by the baby boom in the year of the Dragon (2012) and the melamine scandal that started in 2008. Another unexpected event was the economic crisis that started in 2008. Companies such as Unilever, Nestlé and Hershey felt this strongly. In the press release of Hershey (published together with the second quarter results of 2015), it was stated that macroeconomic challenges are heavily affecting the shopping behaviour of Chinese consumers. Hershey announced that it would cut down 300 jobs worldwide due to undesired results in China. At the same time, due to the stimulus package that the Chinese government executed in 2008 and 2009, companies such as Caterpillar and Komatsu witnessed a strong growth in sales.

Geopolitical events and tension are other uncontrollable factors. In particular, Japanese firms operating in China are vulnerable due to geopolitical tensions. This was visible in 2005 when the then Japanese Prime Minister (Koizumi) visited a sensitive Tokyo shrine. In 2010, there was tension over eight uninhabited islands in the South China sea. The political tension resulted in government action, targeted towards Japanese firms. For example, in August 2010, the Chinese government warned the Japanese companies operating in China not to raise prices and the state-connected trade unions organised strikes in Japanese firms. In 2012, agitations over a group of islands (called Diaoyu in China and Senkaku in Japan) again resulted in heavy tensions and a negative attitude towards Japanese firms. Due to the territorial dispute between Japan and China, large protests were seen in China. The anti-Japanese backlash was the strongest in the coastal and north eastern provinces which had been occupied by Japan during the late 1930s. In September and October 2012, Toyota's sales almost halved, while those of other Japanese car makers such as Nissan fell by 30–40%.

Another geopolitical issue that disrupted business in China relates to the Carrefour case. In 2008, LVMH, one of the largest shareholders of Carrefour had financed the Dalai Lama's government in exile in India. Together with Dalai Lama's visit to President Sarkozy of France, Carrefour became a target of a protest which grew stronger every day. Carrefour suddenly received visits from government officials to check if everything in the shops were in order. Of course, they found a stick to hit Carrefour. The same happened with KFC. KFC became the target of attack in the wake of NATO-led bombing of the Chinese embassy in Belgrade in May 1999. Suddenly, KFC received several audit visits in the summer of 1999. According to many western companies, the Chinese governments (local and central) are a part of the unforeseeable and uncontrollable external environment. For example, Apple had problems when the Chinese government devaluated the currency in August 2015. A weaker Renminbi meant less revenue when the currency was converted back into dollars. Furthermore, many contracts with suppliers were made in dollars instead of Renminbi. It was good for companies such as Foxconn because they paid their workers in Renminbi and earned much of their income in dollars, but it was a financial burden for Apple (although they could handle that with such a high profit). A final example of an uncontrollable external factor is the emphasis on reducing corruption. The fight on corruption and the directive given by the party that the officials must lower their expenditures resulted in a dramatic fall in sales of certain luxury products. For example, the sales of high-end Swiss watches, luxury bags and expensive wines declined strongly as the bulk of the purchases were done by high-ranked bureaucrats and SOE managers. Austerity measures implemented in 2010 to curb gift giving and spending at official banquets have reduced large orders of wine. Since western MNEs were operating in these markets, they felt the impact more than proportionally.

As stated before, there is a close relationship between the six failure factors and, in many cases, it is a combination of factors that creates the disappointment. The next step in the analysis of conducting business successfully in China is to find out how we can learn from these mistakes. A warning beforehand, there is not one simple path that leads to success, but we can generalise some success factors.

17.3 Success factors for conducting business in China

Every firm failed in its own way. The same can be said with respect to success. Finding a format of how to cluster the success factors into one consistent, logical framework is quite challenging. Obviously, some of the success factors are more important in certain industries and are more applicable for specific companies. To make it more complicated, the same company can have success and failure at the same time. The Apple iPhone was a great success in China, while iTunes received less response and, by some experts, can be seen as a failure because Chinese consumers were reluctant to pay for intellectual property rights. Despite these observations, the overview below is arranged in such a way that the success factors can be generalised across sectors and companies.

The first cluster of success factor deals with the need to localise and the attitude of the head office on localisation. There are two opposite views on this. On one hand, the perception that China is unique; hence, what works in France will not work in China and adaptation is needed. Product, price, marketing and processes should be adapted according to the Chinese context. On the other hand, the opposite view is that China has changed. The Chinese market is like other (emerging) markets and adjustment is not really needed anymore. In this view, placing emphasis on adaptation is based on outdated views on China's market; China has changed, while many western MNEs have not.

Clearly, the truth is somewhere in the middle. Maybe consumer differences are exaggerated, but the problem of segmentation in combination with today's move to lower-tier cities undoubtedly must have its impact on the level of adaptation. Success in China cannot be achieved (anymore) by selling to a small cohort of affluent consumers in large coastal cities without adjusting the product. Our starting point is that western MNEs will have to move into China's mass market and adapt their products and processes to connect with these new consumers and to adjust their business models, including their operations. This is shown in Fig. 17.4.

The business model is based on the value proposition (upper half) and the operations (lower half). The value proposition is about the products or services and customers. The operating model cap-

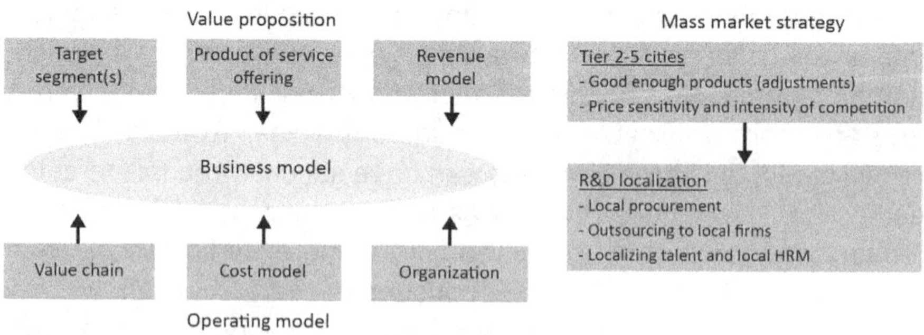

Figure 17.4 The business model; value proposition and operating model

Source: *BCG Research (2009)*

tures choices in the field of value chain, cost model and organisation. The connection is obvious: if the target segment is the affluent consumer in cities, such as Shanghai or Beijing, the operations, including the cost model can stay within the global framework. In that case, there is no need for local sourcing or reducing costs of production. But this changes when the target segment becomes the new mass middle class in lower-tier cities. It is clear that serving the mass markets potentially impacts how companies do business across the entire value chain, from R&D to sourcing, after-sales service and support. Serving the mass market means that localisation is needed because the (new) market is mostly in the lower-tier cities. Here, the consumer has, lower purchasing power which may lead to different buying habits. Moreover, on this market, we see a lot of (local) competition.

In the late 1990s, localisation, including local sourcing was already a key success factor. Ericsson's success up to 2003 was related to its adaptation and localisation strategy. It produced locally, procurement was done locally and research was done locally as well. Two of the company's mobile phone models (T18 and A1018) had more than 60% of their components from domestic suppliers and all its batteries were being made in China.

The second cluster of success relates to creating operational excellence, reducing costs and finding a mass market. The examples earlier in the chapter make it clear that reducing costs (and prices) are essential to attract the extremely price-sensitive Chinese consumer. This focus on reducing costs is a relatively new phenomenon for many western companies in China. In the early 2000s, it was not needed to prioritise cost reduction. If China was used as an export platform, manufacturing costs were so low that many multinationals have been running plants in China less efficiently than at home. Productivity issues and reducing waste were not on the agenda in western boardrooms in China. Keeping costs under control became more important when approaching the Chinese market, but most companies targeted the affluent and upper middle-class cohort and could sell their (global) products, despite the higher costs and prices because these consumers were eager to find out what a western company had to offer. However, these times are over. "Good enough" execution is not sufficient anymore to survive competition in China; operational excellence is the key.

1. *The localisation issue and the role of the head office*

In principle, MNEs have the capabilities to make in-depth analysis of the market and based on this, they can segment the market. However, when it comes to the Chinese market, they often cannot exploit its advantages. Fundamentally, historical data form the basis of segmentation, but in China, market data are not always complete or available. Applying traditional market research techniques are difficult since Chinese consumers often tend to provide misleading information to questions in surveys. Hence, companies had to adopt other ways of studying Chinese consumers such as close observations. For example, some of my students were being asked by a large MNE to visit middle-class families (in their home) to see how they lived, how large the kitchen was and to check if some branded equipment was visible in the kitchen.

In general, consumer behaviour in China is hard to predict and assumptions are difficult to make. For example, when cities are located close to each other, one may assume that there is some cross-contamination between these cities which lead to similarities in consumer behaviour on the grounds of values, taste and beliefs. However, in China, this is not necessarily the case. For example, two adjacent cities, both located in the province Guangdong, are Shenzhen and Guangzhou. The citizens of the neighbouring cities show opposite behaviours. In Shenzhen, the citizens are characterised as migrants, being single young men/women without families. They are hard workers, mainly focused on saving money for their families in their home village and, obviously, they are constrained spenders. Guangzhou residents, on the contrary, showcase a totally different behaviour. This local market is characterised by consumers who are more open and internationally focused. It is one of the cities in China with the highest consumer ratio. This illustrates the importance and complexity of market segmentation in China. Segmentation is needed in many ways: related

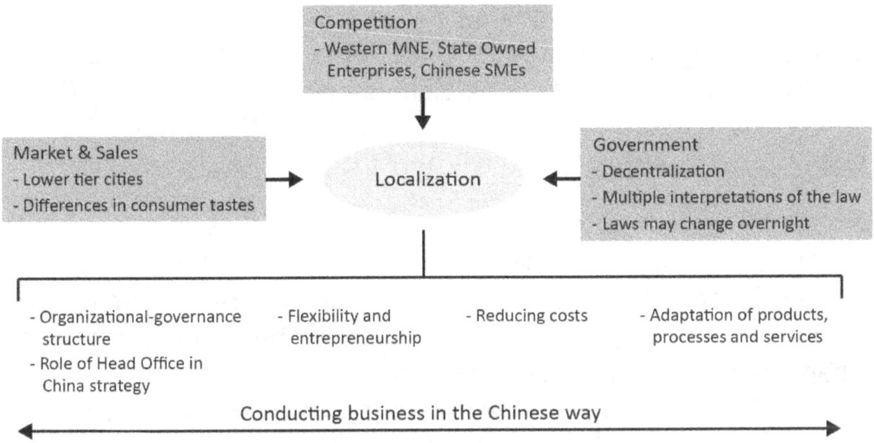

Figure 17.5 The main drivers behind the need to localise and how to execute the localisation strategy

Note: In many cases, the laws are not changing overnight, but the interpretation by local officials may change overnight
Source: Based on Cheung and Ebbers (2010)

to the consumers (poor-affluent) as well as in geography (east versus west) and distribution channels (modern versus traditional retailers).

Figure 17.5 makes it clear that there are three main drivers behind the need for localisation: the market (and sales), competition and the government. These factors of the business environment have urged the MNEs to localise and will continue to drive (and even accelerate) localisation. For example, the future battlefield to fight for the Chinese consumers will be in second- and third-tier cities, away from the "easy" markets in Shanghai and Beijing. In these lower-tier cities, the multinationals are confronted with different types of middle classes and their differences in consumer behaviour. This results in a need for more segmentation, and consequently a need for intensifying local adaptation. The choice to localise must have a large impact on the value propositions and operations of the company. As Fig. 17.5 shows, flexibility is needed to be able to adjust, and reducing costs is essential when moving into the mass market along with product and process adaptation. Finally, the organisational structure (including the role of the head office) should be such that localisation strategy can really be executed on the ground. Essentially, the foreign subsidiary should be able to conduct business in the Chinese way.

Tier 2- and 3-cities

China's expansion of the middle class and rising purchasing power started from the Pearl River Delta (including Guangzhou), the Yangtze River delta (including Shanghai) and the Bohai Rim (including Beijing and Tianjin). But the explosion of the middle class today is happening in smaller cities. The race is now on to sell in places like Yantai, Shaoxing and Wuxi, where middle-class income is rising the same way they rose in tier 1 cities less than a decade ago. These customers are trading up from the lower-end products they previously purchased. KFC took full advantage of the rapidly expanding middle class in lower-tier cities. The same holds for P&G that started a strategy to enter these markets in the late 1990s. Obviously, consumer tastes are different from tier 1 cities. When starting to sell in lower-tier cities, P&G found out that in the smaller cities in the west of China, a person used only three cups of water to wash his/her hair and consequently, it had to develop a different type of shampoo. These new markets in lower-tier cities were the reason why Hershey (chocolate) bought an 80% stake in Shanghai Golden Monkey Food company in 2014, which had an extensive logistics and sales network in smaller cities and rural areas. The same holds for Caterpillar. In 2008, Caterpillar acquired a local wheel loader maker, Shangdon SEM Machinery, to enter the second, lower priced line segment in wheel loaders. So, China consists of many Chinas, and success in China requires a multi-country strategy.

Consumer taste

KFC opened its first outlet in 1987, becoming the first western restaurant chain in China. It targeted the middle-class consumers and put a lot of emphasis on adaptation. Compared to around 35 items on the US menu, the menu in China includes 50 items or more. Over the years, KFC introduced very specific Chinese items such as the Dragon Twist, incorporating the flavours of a famous Beijing dish. It customised products to suit the Chinese taste such as Beijing duck, congee (rice porridge) and bamboo-shoot soup. The same dish is far spicier in Sichuan province then it is in Shanghai. KFC outlets in China were built to accommodate large groups of friends and family who wanted to dine in, whereas, in America, restaurants were smaller to accommodate more takeout business. Local adaptations by western companies can be seen everywhere. Lay's introduced potato chips with fish-head soup flavouring. Adaptation can also be seen in marketing. L'Oréal used Chinese actress Zhang Ziyi in the commercials of Maybelline lipstick. For its men's segment, it used Hong Kong actor Daniel Wu. Product offerings were also localised. For example, P&G made different shampoos and hair colours in China compared to other parts of the world. Nestlé adapted its coffee taste because Chinese find western coffee (too) bitter. So, it developed a cold milk-based coffee called Smoovlatte that tasted less bitter. It is really a different product; the product can hardly be labelled as coffee.

Many companies are struggling to find a way to connect with the Chinese middle class. Sometimes, small adjustments in a product or format can be enough. But, in many cases, designing for the local market is needed. An example of a format change was Walmart's introduction of (an unsuccessful format store) SmartChoice (Hui Xuan) in December 2008. It was a fraction of the size of the traditional Walmart supercenter. Only two years later, in March 2012, Walmart China closed all SmartChoice shops claiming it was just a test and denying the format was a failure. Examples of designing a new product for the Chinese market can be seen in the automotive industry. Car manufacturers such as BMW and GM adapted to the Chinese preference of having more comfortable back seats. GM customised its Buick LaCrosse extensively to the Chinese market. BMW launched localised versions of the 3 and 5 series. The BMW 5 sedan with a long wheelbase was only produced for the Chinese market. Such a strategy requires high sales volumes to outweigh the considerable cost of adaptation. Also the marketing campaigns were adapted. The promotional activities of

BMW in China were different from its global advertisements. While globally, BMW advertised about the driving pleasure that it provided, in China, it concentrated on showing BMW as a mark of success.

The success of Carrefour, KFC and P&G are based on designing the right products for the emerging Chinese consumers in the fast expanding middle market or "good enough market". The emphasis on "good enough products" can also be seen in the case of Coca Cola when it introduced its juice and dairy drinks. Minute Maid Pulpy (2005) was very successful because of its low price. Target consumers could not afford to buy 100% juice. Consequently, the formula was 10% juice along with a considerable amount of orange pulp. This should give the consumer the 100% juice drink feeling. Also, its new drink "Pulpy Super Milky" was a huge success. It was low priced, but profit was still possible because the juice content was low so the production costs could be kept low. This low price is needed due to the intensity of competition in the Chinese market.

Competition

If products are localising along with services and operations, automatically, the need to localise research and development (R&D) will also increase. Competition will spur MNEs to seek more low-cost innovation. Controlling costs become highly important, including designing products for the local market. This "low-end innovation" in China, for the domestic market, will become more prevalent for two reasons. First, the mass market does not fit with the globally designed products in terms of price and functionality. Second, the Chinese government will create an impetus for local R&D. In many cases, the government policy is favourable for sectors and companies that are focusing on innovation, research and design. Due to these drivers, local R&D must increase. For this, a new mindset by western companies is needed. They must create products for the Chinese markets which are good enough and where the R&D costs stay within financial limits. An interesting case is P&G R&D centre that was established in Beijing in 1998. It became a centre of excellence worldwide within P&G detergents and toothpastes. Many of the new (tailormade) products are designed from the outset to meet certain costs. For innovation, the best product is not always good: the "good enough" (at lower costs) may become the norm. The need to localise R&D and to develop products that are "good enough" is mostly initiated by strong local competition. For example, China-based Mindray sold medical devices to many community hospitals and clinics. These devices were not really using the newest technology but they were good enough. This had a big impact on the type of R&D executed in Shanghai by GE. The company started to develop technologies that targeted the mid-range market. The first step needed was to understand customer needs. GE employees regularly visited community hospitals and clinics, talking with administrators and doctors as well as observing their workflow. It became clear that certain features such as increasing picture resolution and improving ergonomics were not relevant to these institutions. Consequently, they focused R&D and product engineering towards medium-range equipment fine-tuned to Chinese needs. An example was the Brivo CT 315/325 scanners which were 30% less expensive than imported products. They also established a local R&D centre in Chengdu (2012) to develop healthcare products for rural areas.

Government

Although the government will be discussed as a separate success factor later in this chapter, in Fig. 17.5, the role of the local governments has been mentioned as a driver behind localisation. The essential point here is that, in many cases, the (local) government has freedom to operate and interpret legislation and therefore, connecting to the local government is essential. This local freedom to interpret (central) rules can be summarised with my experience when I booked a non-smoking room in a hotel in Chengdu. Despite being a non-smoking room, there was a badge on the table that stated, "This is a non-smoking room but if you want to smoke, use this ashtray". As one of my colleagues stated: "everything is possible as long as it is not stopped". When Carrefour entered China in 1995, foreign retailers were only allowed to operate in a few cities. And foreign ownership was also limited to no more than 49% of the shares in any Chinese JV. However, within this legal environment, Carrefour could open numerous outlets without any problem. The company's connection to the local governments was important. Local governments were eager to attract Carrefour in the city because it showed modernisation and could create agglomeration effects. Looking backwards, you may argue that they hold the key in Carrefour's' expansion. Another example that shows the entrepreneurial government relates to Komatsu. In the 1990s, Japan-based Komatsu set up a wholly owned dealer network in China. People who became dealers were former government employees who had been in charge of procuring machineries for the local government agencies and who would always be helpful to connect with the local government.

Finding the balance between global and local

The conclusion is clear, there is a tendency (and need) to localise activities in China; the pressure for local responsiveness (driven by markets, competition and government) is just too high to ignore. The starting point of the discussion about how much localisation is needed is the so-called Integration-Responsiveness Grid by Prahalad and Doz (1987), shown in Fig. 17.6.

Figure 17.6 shows the cost pressure on the vertical axis, while the local responsiveness pressure is indicated on the horizontal axis. Based on these two axes, four possible strategies are given: global, multidomestic, transnational and international. There are two extreme strategies: On one extreme, the MNE is adopting a global strategy, by using uniform standards, products and procedures. The pressure for local responsiveness is low and at the same time, due to the intensity of competition, the pressure to lower costs is high. This could be seen in the 1990s when most MNEs entered China through the premium segment and the affluent and upper middle-class cohorts. They sold existing products at

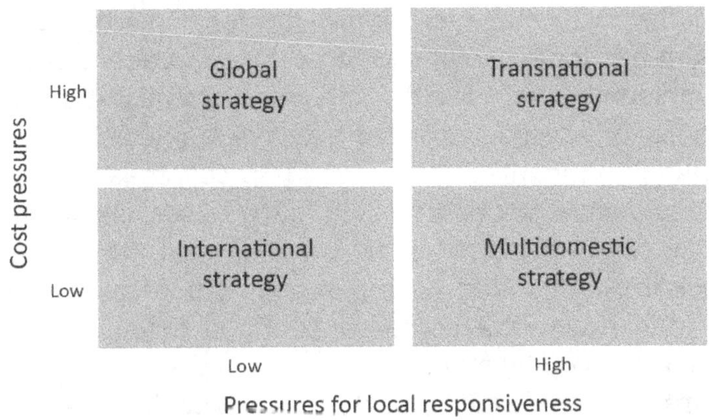

Figure 17.6 Integration-Responsiveness grid

Note: *The basic idea is from Prahalad and Doz (1987). Later Bartlett and Ghoshal (1989) came up with a somewhat overlapping typology and that resulted in this figure*
Source: *Adapted from Dörrenbächer and Geppert (2016)*

premium prices with no adaptation. Corporations pursuing this strategy do not customise their products or marketing strategy for local markets. It should be noted that, in many ways, this global strategy is not fully global. Global MNEs adapt their products if needed to fit the local consumer tastes. Think about the menu adaptations of KFC and McDonald's in China.

The other extreme is the multidomestic strategy which focuses totally on local adaptation. The most difficult type of adaptation relates to designing and selling products targeting the Chinese customers specifically. Products in the automotive that were especially produced for the Chinese market are the long-wheelbase Audi A4 and A6, the Mercedes-Benz C-class (2015), and the BMW X1 in 2016. The congestion in the larger cities means that executives spend hours in traffic, and therefore, they prefer to use that time working or stretching their legs. Obviously, this product adaptation will increase the production costs and within the context of high cost pressure due to intensive competition, this strategy can be complicated. A multidomestic strategy is often associated with substantial strategic decision-making at the subsidiary level because the local managers know the local market. Obviously, localisation has the disadvantage that it may not generate integration advantages. That was the reason why Dutch-based Philips changed its organisation structure in the early 2000s. In 2001, Philips had 160 manufacturing sites in 35 countries and hundreds of business units. They operated, in many cases, like independent companies, lacking intercompany coordination. The absence of such coordination created an impending barrier for capturing synergies. That is why the company changed towards centralising more functions step by step.

The transnational strategy is the "in-between" strategy of global standards and norms on one hand, and enough local responsiveness on the other hand. This strategy is used where the pressures for cost reductions and local responsiveness are both high. These competing demands make this a difficult strategy to pursue. There is often a mixture of decentralised decision-making at the subsidiary level and centralised decision-making at the parent corporation level when following this strategy. As stated earlier, this is the new reality of the Chinese markets. Even a company such as Coca Cola has followed a transnational strategy in many aspects of its operations, including marketing, product-portfolio and distribution. About 99% of Coca Cola's products are procured domestically.

The international strategy combines low local responsiveness with low cost pressure. Corporations are using this strategy to centralise their core competencies such as R&D and core marketing but leave other decision-making to subsidiary operations. The role of overseas subsidiaries is to adapt and leverage parent company competencies. Knowledge is developed at the centre and transferred to overseas units. In many cases, we see this strategy in B2B companies.

Prahalad and Doz (1987) listed several conditions that work in the direction of cost pressure and global integration and circumstances that work in the direction of local responsiveness. This list has been expanded over time by various authors and is summarised in Fig. 17.7. Pressures for local responsiveness are driven by a high need for adaptive operations and strategies tailored towards the local market. The most important factors behind local adaptation are differences in consumer tastes, culture and the specific

Pressures for global integration	Pressure for local responsiveness
- Opportunities to reduce costs through economies of scale - Converging consumer trends; no need to adjust - Opportunities for global sourcing - Achieving economies of skills - No barriers in entering countries - Control over brand, image and reputation	- Differences in customer needs - Differences in conducting business, including distribution, marketing and sales - Cultural differences - Local government regulations and legal requirements - Strong local stakeholders such as trade unions, NGOs and consumer groups

Figure 17.7 Arguments for global integration and local responsiveness
Source: Adjusted from Prahalad and Doz (1987)

(and different) local business context. The primary benefit of a local responsive strategy is that it ensures strategic fit between the strategy of MNEs and the local demand. In addition, it enables local managers to create a more solid relationship with suppliers, customers, competitors, authorities and distributors, leading to sustainable competitive advantages. However, adopting a locally responsive strategy sacrifices achieving the benefits of global integration and reducing costs. The pressures for global integration involve the presence of economies of scale and scope, standardised consumer demands as well as control over brand name.

As stated before, we see a clear shift towards more localisation, and consequently a transnational or multidomestic strategy. From a market perspective, this is logical; the new markets in lower-tier cities, local government regulations and the intensity of competition make it necessary to shift towards more local responsiveness. A difficult issue is how the head office is reacting to this.

Role of head office

The strategies discussed above must match with the role and attitude of the head office. In the case of the multidomestic strategy which focuses on local adaptation, the head office must give subsidiaries abroad a large degree of independence. In that case, the head office should govern from a distance, give freedom and flexibility to the international subsidiary. The work should be done by local managers who know and understand the market. This type of head office is called a polycentric head office (Perlmutter, 1969). At the other extreme, a global strategy must have a head office that is in full charge. The head office makes the decision and is controlling all aspects of the company. Products are global, services are globalised and processes are standardised. In this case, the corporate culture of the head office is translated to all subsidiaries and communication is top-down. This type of head office makes use of many expats. This refers to an ethnocentric head office. Executing a transnational strategy means that we need a balance between global and local activities. In this case, we see a geocentric head office. This type of head office is combining local managers with expats and is combining global standards with local adaptations. It is an internationally recognised company but with national interests. The connection between the strategy chosen and the attitude of the head office is shown in Fig. 17.8.

Strategy	Global	Transnational	Multidomestic
	↓	↓	↓
Attitude of head office	Ethnocentric	Geocentric	Polycentric
Type of governance	Top-down	Mutual negotiated	Bottom up
HRM practice	Overseas operations are managed by people from home country	Best people worldwide are selected for key positions	Local nationals are in key managerial positions
Evaluation and control	Home standards applied for persons and performances	Combining standards which are universal and local	Determined locally by subsidiary
Identification	Nationality of owner	International company but with national interests	Nationality of host country

Figure 17.8 The linkage between strategy and head office attitude
Source: *Based on Perlmutter (1969) and Cheung and Ebbers (2010)*

In many cases, the need to localise in the Chinese context results in a different type of head office. This switch of the head office attitude is extremely difficult. There are many kinds of barriers to make the move from, for example, an ethnocentric to polycentric (or geocentric) attitude. Think about obstacles such as inexperience of the management team, resistance to share power and fear of losing control. In addition, the formal organisational structure may have to change. In many cases, a (global) division structure does not fit anymore if the strategy moves towards local adaptation. In that case, a regional structure would fit better the new strategy.

An ethnocentric attitude is not per se wrong, but the main challenge is to give enough attention to the Chinese subsidiary. Successful companies, in many cases, have a very senior and accountable sponsor at the global level. For example, at Samsung, the Chinese CEO is one of the three top group executives. The same holds for VW, Sharp electronics, P&G and Amway. There are also numerous companies where the head office restricts China's operations considerably. For example, the first decade of GE in China was not very successful. Up to the early 2000s, GE's local management stated many times that products were needed specifically for the Chinese market. Furthermore, local competitors were growing very fast and they were quickly moving up from the low-end market to the mid-range segment. China management indicated to the head office that adaptation and speed was needed. Yet, GE head office underestimated the need for localisation partly because revenue generated from China was still relatively small (about 4% of total). Only after China became important did the head office's attitude changed.

Of course, a multidomestic strategy should not mean that the head office is totally out of sight. That would be a mistake. Coordinating local activities with the company's head office is important for all localised companies. The main question is how involved should the head office be in local strategic and operational decisions such as portfolio definition, sourcing choices,and budget allocation. The market and the intensity of competition forced western companies to localise, adapt to the customer and reduce costs. This means that the governance structure (and consequently the role of the head office) should change to facilitate this localisation strategy. If this is not happening, there is a disconnection between strategy, head office attitude and governance structure. This change in head office mindset is needed during a period in which the competition battle is specifically on the mass market.

2. *Mass market is needed, operational excellence essential and dual strategy advisable*

The second cluster of success factors relates to the capability to operate on China's mass market. Until recently, the competitive landscape was relatively straightforward. We had the small (but growing) premium segment at the top of the consumer pyramid, mostly served by foreign firms and their brands, sold in high-profile shopping malls. On the other hand, we had at the bottom a large lower-end segment served by local companies. Domestic companies, under their own brand names, mostly sold their products in the Chinese department stores and small family-owned shops. This dichotomy was visible across sectors. For example, in the construction machinery industry, Japan-based Komatsu competed in China with US-based Caterpillar. Both companies profited strongly from the construction boom after 2008 and the strong increase in demand for heavy construction machines. They dominated the hydraulic excavator market which required sophisticated technology. In contrast, Chinese domestic players dominated the wheel loader market which was low-tech and low priced.

Audi, BMW and Mercedes Benz dominated the luxury car segment, while the lower segment was served by local manufactures like BYD, Geely or Chery. The high-quality robot market was dominated by foreign firms, while the Chinese products target mostly middle and low-end users.

Even today, foreign companies are fighting mostly in the premium segment, while the lowest segments are still the battlefield of local Chinese producers. But as indicated, this dichotomy is less strong today due to the evolving middle class and middle segment. Today, the two separated markets are connected through a rapidly expanding new market that Gadiesh and Vestring (2006) called "China's good-enough market". Today, all the parties are active in this segment: Chinese companies moving up the market and large MNEs moving down the market.

For example, we see (new) Chinese competitors in the mid-range construction equipment sector. In 2016, local companies had increased their share to more than 60% on this mass-market with SANY now challenging the western competitors. Also, in the car sales, we witness a growing market share of companies such as Geely and BYD in the middle-class segment, competing with western brands like Renault and Ford. They started at the bottom end of the market, then began to slowly ascend up the price-sophistication ladder and even took the lead in innovation as was the case with the battery car developed by BYD. Robots made by Chinese suppliers still lag behind those made by international companies in terms of quality, technical level and performance parameters. But also in this industry we see some changes.

Multinationals such as P&G, Philips and GE realised that the initial strategy (premium consumer market segment) was running out of growth opportunities. Looking back, not being active in the lower segments of the market left the door open for Chinese competitors to grow unchallenged in this lower-end consumer market, creating economies of scale, connecting to the potential new middles class and building up local name recognition. Galanz, SANY and BYD are typical examples of Chinese firms that were able to grow without western competition in the lower segments of the market. This is the situation today: there is fierce competition on the mass market where both the foreign as well as the domestic firms will compete for the same customer, also in the lower-tier cities. This is demonstrated in Fig. 17.9. It shows that the western multinationals must compete with the fast learning local competitors to attract the attention of the growing middle class.

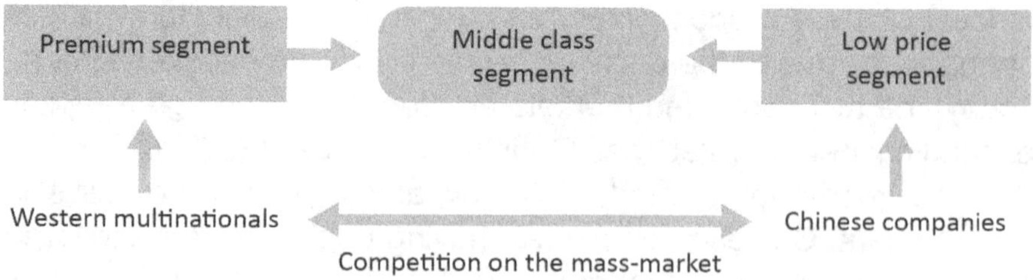

Figure 17.9 Competition on the mass market
Source: *Constructed by author*

This is the real battlefield, and this is where western companies are fighting with local players. One outcome of this intensity of competition is extremely thin profit margins and the need to reduce costs by localising. There are many examples of this increasing competition pressure. In the mid-2000s, GE healthcare was quite successful in China. Together with Siemens healthcare, Philips healthcare and Toshiba Medical systems, it dominated the high-end medical equipment market. After 2006, challenges from local Chinese competitors were growing. For example, Mindray Medical International Ltd. was the market leader for black-and-white scanners and decided to move up the market. In 2006, it launched its first colour ultrasound scanner to target the mid-range market. And the local company became very successful by supplying medical devices to smaller community hospitals and clinics. The competitive pressure from Mindray forced GE to reduce costs, including localising R&D. Another example of increasing competition from local players is the robotics industry. Companies such as Comau (Fiat group) must compete with new Chinese companies such as Siasun. Siasun, founded in 2000, is considered China's largest robot company. It has 1,000 R&D staff and invests about 10% of its annual income on R&D and owns more than hundred patents. A final example of competition in the middle-class segment is the sports industry. Until the mid-2000s, a clear separation existed between foreign brands, such as Nike and Adidas, and local brands in which Li-Ning was dominant. From 2005 onwards, Nike and Adidas already started to expand into the domain of the domestic brands; they went to lower-tier cities by introducing less expensive products. Both put a lot of emphasis on operational efficiency and less expensive sub-brands such as Neo (Adidas) and Converse (Nike) were introduced. The brands became increasingly affordable for the middle segment. The costs were reduced due to local sourcing and more localisation of other operational activities. Domestic brands, meanwhile, started moving up-market in a bid to capture newer consumer segments. For example, China-based Anta acquired Fila from Belle International as a sub-brand for the high-end market.

The need to reduce costs

This intensity of competition and the emphasis on the promising mass market gives pressure for cost reductions. This can be seen in the Chinese smartphone industry. Since 2005, the Chinese market had been growing in two directions: one with extremely low-priced mobile phones (60% of the market) and the other comprised multimedia smartphones with diverse functions such as mobile television. The low-priced cell phones were a competition battle between China-made local brands, like Konka, Kejian and Ningbo Bird. Also, there was stiff competition on the higher-end of the mobile phone segment. Significant players were Apple, Samsung and HTC combined with some Chinese companies with growing (international) name recognition and reputation, such as Xiaomi, Lenovo and TCL. Competition in this segment is based on design and intangible assets.

Xiaomi was founded in April 2010. In April 2014, Xiaomi was the third largest company in China's smartphone market with a market share of 10%. Xiaomi's two phones, the Hongmi Redrice and the Mi3 found themselves on the world's top 10 smartphones list. When they started, it was difficult to convince high quality producers to supply them; Xiaomi had no factory, no record sales and no brand reputation. Finally, in mid-2011, Sharp agreed to supply LCD touchscreens and other suppliers followed. The first smartphone introduced was the Mi-1, and within 30 hours of the announcement, consumers had placed 300,000 pre-orders. The brand became hip and cool. The price is relatively low. The strategy was not to make money on selling phones but to earn money through paid services: subsidising smartphones to make money on paid services, following the business model of Amazon where it sold its Kindle e-reader at cost price and later made money through the content it sold. In a bid to gain the trust of its customers, Xiaomi also disclosed the names of its suppliers for every part and component used in its smartphones. Today, the company has some problems in terms of delivery. Also, one may question the online business model in countries such as India and Indonesia as Internet penetration is low. Despite these challengers, the Xiaomi case makes clear that western MNEs cannot underestimate the branding and quality of Chinese companies any more. They are not just winning on price, sales and distribution, but they are more and more winning on branding.

Local sourcing is the key to reduce costs. Today, KFC sources 98% of its raw materials, including its bread, chicken and vegetables, locally. More than 97% of the ingredients used by McDonald's China (e.g. potatoes, meat, milk, vegetables) originate from within the country. Nearly 95% of Nestlé's products sold in China are manufactured in China (2016). Also, companies in the automotive sector are able to have a very high local content; there are plenty of high-quality suppliers available. However, building a domestic value chain to increase local sourcing is not easy or cheap. Until 1999 (10 years after its first entry), McDonald's was not able to serve French fries made from China-grown potatoes in all its restaurants in the country.

For KFC and McDonald's, local sourcing was difficult due to the structure of the supplier market. For example, poultry farming in China is highly fragmented. Most of the poultry production was run by small-scale, family-owned farms. The nation's top four poultry producers were estimated to make up 10% of the industry revenue in 2015. Sourcing is under these circumstances complicated. How to control hundreds of small suppliers that may use antibiotics and growth hormone? Educating the suppliers is then needed. This was, for example, done by Nestlé. It trained 17,000 Chinese dairy farmers between 2011 and 2016. The same was seen with respect to coffee and coffee farmers. The pressure from local competitors forced Nestlé to source locally and to lower costs of production further.

Although local sourcing is a big challenge for large multinationals, local competition makes it necessary; cost reduction became a must for companies such as KFC, Nestlé, McDonald's and Volkswagen. At the same time, the fragmented market and the difficulty to control suppliers is a risk factor for western MNEs.This was the case in December 2012 when KFC was under attack because a supplier delivered chicken with excessive doses of antibiotics.

The good enough operations of MNEs in China are not good enough anymore due to the increasing local competition on the mass market leading to a need for lower costs at any operational level. Today, operational excellence is the key to succeed on China's mass market. At the same time, western companies still have a competitive advantage in certain premium segments of the market. Consequently, the MNEs must handle the two markets at the same time; they need a dual strategy: a combined strategy to serve the mass market in combination with achieving margins on the premium segment.

Dual strategy

An important strategic choice is between cost leadership and differentiation. In his book, *Competitive Strategy*, Michael Porter (1980) introduced the generic competitive strategies. He concluded that a business (unit) must choose between differentiation and cost leadership or face the risk of being "stuck in the middle" due to confused customers and employees from a blurred corporate strategy and culture. His conclusion was clear: a choice is needed. This sounds logical: a certain type of company needs a certain type of employees. A company that focusses on differentiation strategy needs marketers, while a company that focusses on reducing costs need bookkeepers. Figure 17.10 shows the two strategies. The cost leadership strategy and the differentiation strategy, if executed in the correct way, will result in high profits (or high return on investment as indicated on the vertical axis). If the company is mixing both strategies, it cannot compete with the real cost leaders in the market and, at the same time, it cannot compete against the real

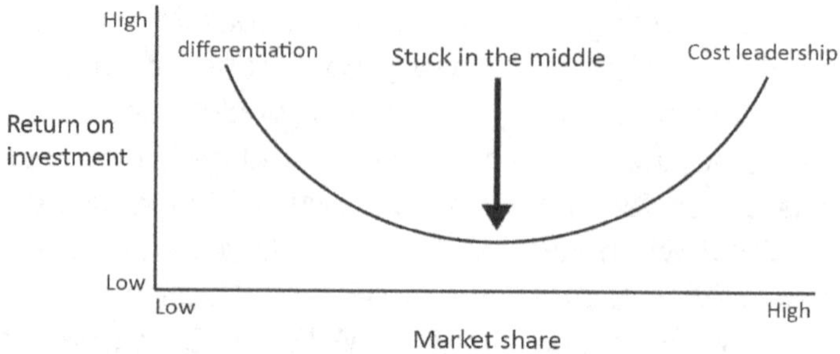

Figure 17.10 Stuck in the middle concept
Source: Based on Porter (1980)

differentiator. Hence, they are stuck in the middle situation which negatively affect profitability.

During the end of the 1980s and the beginning of the 1990s, there was a debate going on regarding the existence of a trade-off. It became clear that, under certain circumstances, both strategies can be implemented together. For example, when cost is strongly determined by market share, large economies of scale can give the company a big enough cost advantage to allow it to spend some of its cost savings on elements to differentiate the products and still achieve cost leadership. The introduction of Japanese cost control methods, such as total quality management and just-in-time, are examples of reducing costs and, at the same time developing a differentiation strategy. Grant (2005) argues, "Common to the success of Japanese companies in consumer goods industries such as cars, motorcycles, consumer electronics, and musical instruments has been the ability to reconcile low cost with high quality and technological progressiveness". Although, difficult to execute, in China, a dual strategy is needed, i.e. a premium segment for margin and the mass market for volume. This is observable across sectors but, in particular, in sectors where economies of scale are important. Some examples make this clear. Coca Cola on one hand and its local brands such as Dongguan-based Taigu beverage group on the other hand. The premium Caterpillar product and, at the same time, the mass market products through its daughter Shangdon SEM Machinery. The acquisition of Mininurse (skin products) by L'Oréal in December 2003 is another example. L'Oréal hoped that the acquisition would give an advantage in the lower segment, and at the same time, creating economies of scale.

Within the differentiation strategy, operational excellence is also needed today. Many MNEs have been running plants in China less efficiently than at home but the good enough execution is not sufficient anymore. Accelerating localisation, changing the head office mindset and reducing costs are all critical success factor. In addition, the role of the government is important.

17.4 The Chinese government as a success factor

Government's involvement in business and, consequently, the government as a success factor in conducting business cannot be underestimated. Government and public relations are very important, surely for larger multinationals. Some of them focus on getting connected with the central government in Beijing, while others concentrate on local governments. For example, PepsiCo concentrates on the central government and less on provincial governments. However, Carrefour had a focus on local governments instead of the central government. Government connection and help are essential. Saying this makes the future of, for example, Uber in China problematic. In September 2015, a group of CEOs shook hands with President Xi Jinping in Seattle. It publicly demonstrated the Chinese government's support for firms that were revolutionising traditional industries with Internet technologies. Microsoft, IBM, Alibaba, Airbnb and Didi-Kuaidi were all present but the CEO of Uber was absent.

Being successful in sectors or regions against government objectives is extremely difficult and the (Chinese) people know it. This can be seen in the outcome of the research conducted by Nyenrode Business University between 2009 and 2015 (Ebbers and Zhang, 2010–2015). During this period, we established a fixed panel of the Chinese middle class and asked them to fill in a quarterly questionnaire. One part of the questionnaire related to the investment opportunities and risks. We asked the panel in which industries they would invest their money and, linked to this, we asked their risk perception in the short and longer term. The outcome has been summarised in Fig. 17.11. In the period between 2010 and 2015, the Chinese government clearly indicated which strategic sectors were important and would receive specific government support in terms of easy licenses, subsidies and lower taxes. It related to the environmental industry, energy sector and new technologies, including alternative-fuel automobiles. Figure 17.11(a)

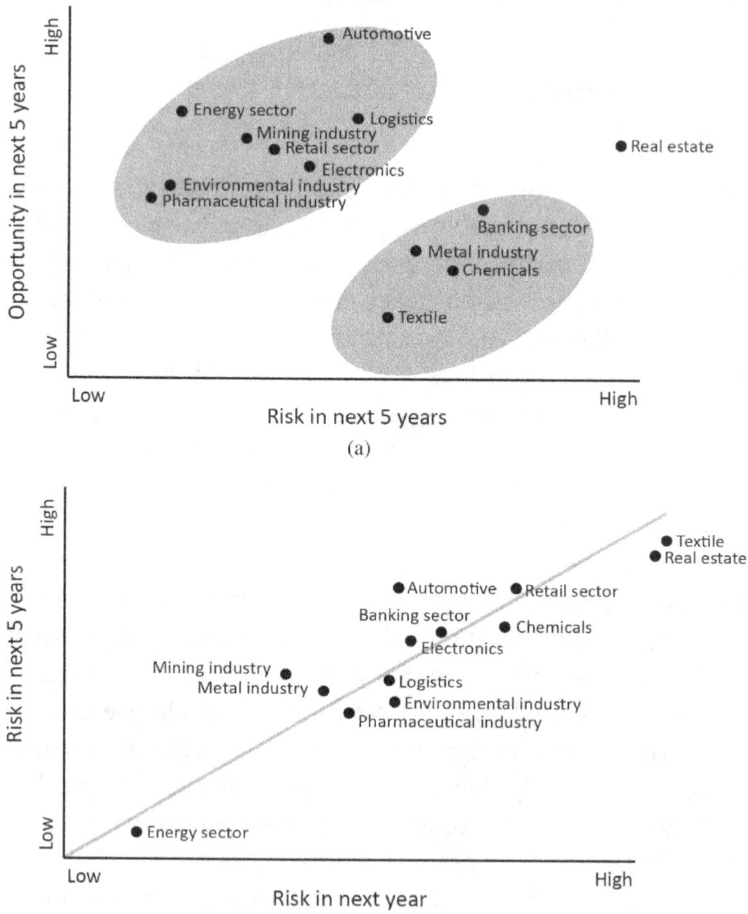

Figure 17.11 Opportunity-risk (a) and short versus longer term risk (b)

Source: *Ebbers and Zhang (2010–2015)*

shows the investment opportunity (vertical axis) and risk perception (horizontal axis) of some industries in the next five years. According to our panelists, we see two main clusters in the matrix. On one hand, there are the industries with low risk and high to medium opportunity. On the other hand, there are industries with high risk and medium to low opportunity. As Fig. 17.11(a) indicates, the energy sector, the environmental industry, logistics, the pharmaceutical industry, retail and electronics are seen as high opportunity and low-risk industries for investment in the next five years. These are the sectors that are labelled as strategic by the government. Chemicals, the metal industry and the banking sector are examples of industries in the high risk-low opportunity segment.

Figure 17.11(b) exhibits the risk perception of next year (horizontal axis) versus the risk perception of the next five years (vertical axis). It is interesting to note that, in general, the industries are scattered along the 45-degree line, the line that equals the risk of next year and the next five years. This implies that, according to our panellists, the risks are quite similar in the short (one year) and long (five years) term. Real estate and textile are identified as high-risk industries, followed by the retail sector and the chemical industry. The Nyenrode panel sees more risk in the automotive, banking and mining sectors in the medium-long term, clearly driven by sentimental factors and articles in the media about overcapacity and government intervention. Low-risk factors are associated with the strategic sectors. The conclusion is clear; according to the middle-class panel, success is hardly possible without a certain degree of government preference related to the sector or product.

The most well-known example of a company being successful thanks to government support is Kodak. In the 1990s, Kodak started its retail store strategy "Kodak Express" and by 1999, it had around 5,500 Kodak Express retail shops in China. But most of the equipment had to be imported. The company realised that to gain economies of scale, it had to start its manufacturing operations in China itself. In 1998, Kodak took over two local manufactures and this deal was supplemented by the guarantee of Kodak to invest a substantial amount of money. As part of the negotiated deal, the

Chinese government promised Kodak that no other foreign company would be allowed to buy local film equipment manufacturing firms till the end of 2002. The government was willing to give this assurance because Kodak's investment would save the loss-making companies and bring advanced technologies. Kodak was also free to expand its operations anywhere in the country. In 2001, Kodak had a market share of 62% in China's roll-film market, leaving Japanese firms such as Fuji far behind. In 2002, Kodak and the Bank of China agreed to provide loans to Chinese investors to establish Kodak retail stores. With this provision of long-term loans by the Bank of China, Kodak Express outlets increased to 7,000 in 700 cities in China in 2002. The case shows that future success is not guaranteed as Kodak missed the digital revolution in its sector. Government interference can also have adverse impact on companies. For example, in May 2015, China's market regulators investigated foreign medical equipment makers such as General Electric, Philips and Siemens over suspicion that they may have paid bribes to hospitals or used illegal strategies to achieve market dominance. This was not the first time. It followed the 2014 investigation and the penalty to GSK of US$500 million for bribing officials to promote its medicine. Not only GSK, but also UCB, AstraZeneca and Astellas Pharma came under the scanner. The government intervention in the medical equipment sector was motivated by its policy of getting lower costs and affordable prices in healthcare. As part of an effort to make medicines more affordable, the National Development and Reform Commission asked 60 drug manufacturers to submit their costs and pricing files for review. The same type of investigation was carried out on dairy producers in 2013 (with some follow-ups in 2016). In the summer of 2013, fines for price fixing were levied on six milk powder companies, including FrieslandCampina, Abbott and Fonterra. Government interventions, like the examples above, are in industries that are closely linked with people's livelihood and in areas where people complain the most about unreasonable prices. The perception is that mostly foreign firms are under attack. This may be the case; foreign firms are more often under investigation than their Chinese competitors.

However, it may be logical because foreign firms dominate many of these industries.

The government also used the brake on western companies that are active in takeovers. Coca Cola wanted to take over Huiyuan Juice Group Ltd. in 2008, but the deal was rejected by the government because the acquisition would curtail market competition. Huiyuan had a 43% share in the 100% fruit juice market. The rejection created a negative sentiment in the market; there was a willing seller and a willing buyer in an industry which has absolutely no economic or national security implications and yet the decision was turned down. Two points should be mentioned in this perspective. Firstly, the objective of the government was to prevent public perception that foreigners are taking over in China. In this sense, the Chinese government is not acting very differently from what we see in western countries. Secondly, Coca Cola underestimated the principle starting point that there should be a win–win situation. Foreign companies can buy non-majority interest in strong, successful Chinese companies, but only if there is some added benefit, such as transfer of technology, advanced management or access to foreign markets. Coca Cola only saw Huiyuan as a non-strategic asset whose takeover would not threaten the Chinese government and its interest. This was a one-sided view and underestimated the importance of a win-win case. In many other sectors, the government intervenes. For example, in July 2013, the Chinese government denied BMW the permission to expand its factory in Shenyang. The Chinese Ministry of Environmental Protection rejected the expansion because of inadequate wastewater analysis. It was the first time that the government had put the expansion plans of automotive manufactures on hold. However, in the majority of cases, foreign companies receive government approval of takeovers in non-strategic sectors. But the approval process can be very slow as was the case of Yum!

Yum! acquired Mongolian Hotpot restaurant operator Little Sheep in 2009. After a long wait (of more than 2 years), Yum! received the final approval from the regulatory authority. By 2008, Little Sheep operated more than 80 company-owned full-service restaurants and 250 franchise restaurants in China. The Little Sheep acquisition would strengthen Yum! in China, but the company also hoped to use Little Sheep to bring the hot pot concept to other international markets. Little Sheep doesn't dominate China's restaurant landscape. It is a big name, but it is still a very small part of the market. So, there was no need to block the deal based on dominant economic position. Still, the government took its time to give approval.

Ever since the melamine-tainted milk scandal in 2008, the Chinese government have laid down strict regulations on food safety. And it reacted strongly on safety scandals at KFC and McDonald's. Trouble for KFC started in November 2012 when a local newspaper accused one of KFC's chicken processing suppliers (Shanxi Suhai Group) of raising chickens in unhygienic conditions and feeding them with toxic growth hormones. The real problem came in December 2012 when CCTV showed that several chicken farms used as many as 18 types of antibiotics and excessive growth hormones. Two chicken processing suppliers, Liuhe Group and Yingtai, were reported to have bought chickens from such farms and sold them to KFC China. KFC China issued a press release on 29 December 2012 in which it stated that the products of the accused suppliers only made up less than 1% of the chicken used in its stores. This explanation annoyed many Chinese and the scandal went out of hand. People expected the American chain to have better quality control than local eateries. Sales went down by 40% year-on-year between December 2012 and February 2013. KFC announced some improvements such as not using small chicken farms anymore as suppliers. With all kind of advertisements and paper placemats in the restaurants, they informed the public that their chickens were bread without antibiotics or hormones. This case was followed by a national outbreak of bird flu in China which again affected the company in early 2013. In March 2013, sales declined by almost 20% from the previous year. Due to the chicken problem, KFC put more emphasis on beef, and in September 2013, they launched a new campaign "Time to Beef Up", promoting its new beef burger. McDonald's also witnessed a safety scandal. Its largest supplier was the OSI Group that supplied beef, fish, pork and chicken. In July 2014, Dragon TV broadcasted an undercover video of the Shanghai Husi operation (owned by OSI). Instructions to use expired meat were written by the management, and the company kept two set of records related to food products, one for the auditors visiting the plant and one for internal use. The documents were written in Chinese, making it difficult for English speaking staff to understand data or operations. Chinese authorities shut down the plant and McDonald's was forced to pull suspect items from their menus. Its share in New York dropped almost 5% following the Shanghai event. All these examples make clear that government intervention (positive and negative) may heavily influence China operations of international operating companies.

17.5 Gradual steps and learning from experience

The so-called Uppsala model (Johanson and Vahlne, 1990) assumes that companies are learning from their internationalisation process, and consequently moving to foreign markets is done in a gradual, step by step approach. This gradualism can be seen from two angles. Firstly, a company starts its internationalisation process with low-risk activities such as export or non-equity based cooperative agreements. Then, slowly, it learns how to operate on foreign markets, and starts to engage in more risky operations such as greenfield investments or takeovers. Secondly, the step by step approach results in entering easy (nearby) markets first, before moving into more difficult markets that are culturally further away from the host country. We can internalise this Uppsala model within the context of China: starting operations in Shanghai before moving into lower-tier cities in the west or starting with a JV when entering China, but after years of learning, the company can do it by themselves and the JV is not needed anymore.

Modes of entry decision

In many cases, the modes of entry decision are a free choice made by the company. Since China entered the WTO in 2001, the government opened up its industries gradually to foreign firms starting with consumer goods, and today, foreign companies are no longer required to partner with local firms in order to invest in most (non-strategic) industries.[1] Nevertheless, western companies may still opt for alliances so as to get access to growing (and newly opened) industries as well as to established customer, supplier and distribution networks in the country through its local partner. KFC chose Beijing (1987) as the first city to open a restaurant. Though a local partner was not required under Chinese law, KFC felt it was necessary. It partnered with Beijing Corporation of Animal Production (a local government-owned chicken company). A third partner, Beijing Tourist Bureau, was in charge of the supervision of all hotels and restaurants in Beijing. KFC had a controlling stake with 60% in the JV whereas the Tourist Bureau and Animal production had 27% and 13%, respectively. In many cases, Chinese partners are keen to cooperate because they can learn modern management concepts, techniques and processes.

Clearly, the mode of entry choice is a key success factor, but there is no standard mix of ingredients that automatically create success. For example, there are many companies (M&S, Volkswagen, Unilever and Walmart) that use not one specific entry mode strategy when internationalising. Instead, they adapted their strategy to each market and we see a broad range of modes of entry; they used franchise concepts, as well as JVs and wholly owned enterprises. Although it may be logical that, after some years, western companies will move away from a JV to get full control, it may be handy to keep the JV construction. A JV is very helpful when dealing with SOEs or government-related entities. This was the driver behind Boon-Edam's choice to continue its JV status although the Chinese JV partner only held 3% of the shares. The status of being a JV helped them to sell the revolving doors and safety lines in China because the Dutch company is seen as a Chinese firm. In general, there is a preference to engage in several JVs at the same time. This approach helps a company avoid becoming overly dependent on one partner. Car producers such as Volkswagen, BMW and GM established many JVs in China.

---

[1]This freedom of ownership is, however, not the case in specific industries. For example, there are requirements in sectors such as automotive and pharmaceuticals to form a joint venture with a local partner.

Even if a mother company is officially in control over a JV, it should be clear that the JV is a separate entity. For this reason, JV-management is complex. Chinese entrepreneurial companies, emphasise quick market response, while MNEs are more concerned with compliance. If MNEs' management systems are imposed upon Chinese JV companies, it may fail to work. There are many illustrations of the large cultural gap between two JV partners. For example, the Nestle-Totole JV. In 2004, Totole spent 10-million-Renminbi on a Rolls-Royce Phantom, which was placed in the lobby of Totole's office building. This was based on the importance of "Face" in Chinese culture. Nestlé was taken by surprise and was not amused about the expenditure. In short, Nestlé had limited control over Totole. But, in principle, this was not a problem as long as Nestlé received a return on its initial investment. In the case of Totole, it did and the JV was a big success (2016).

If a company wants to generate speed and scale, franchising is a logical mode of entry. Franchising is the mode of entry which can be seen a lot in the fast food sector and hotel industry. Examples are fast food operators such as McDonald's, KFC and Burger King, coffee shop brands such as Starbucks, and hotel chains such as Hyatt, Marriott and Hilton. Franchising can be defined as a contractual agreement between two legally independent firms in which one firm, the franchisee, pays the other firm, the franchisor, for the right to sell the franchisor's product and the right to use its trademarks and business format. The biggest benefit for the franchisee is the industry slogan, "be in business for yourself but not by yourself". The franchisee can benefit from the franchisor in terms of brand-name recognition, proven products, marketing systems, technology and know-how. On the other hand, there are also benefits for the franchisor. Reaching a critical level of output, franchisors can spread the fixed costs over a large number of outlets, offering them a competitive cost structure. There are also benefits in terms of increased bargaining power against suppliers.

When looking at the names of the chains above, it will be no surprise that China hosted more than 5,000 franchise systems, foreign and domestic, by the end of 2016 which crossed over 70 industries. The total number of franchised outlets is around 500,000

(Xinhua). It is a popular mode of entry. In May 2016, InterContinental Hotels Group launched its plan for extending its Holiday Inn Express franchise concept. The franchise concept will be more tailored to the Chinese market and in the new concept, the local manager is officially responsible for hotel management. According to the press release of the announcement, it was the only way to increase the speed of new hotels for the mid-scale hotel market: the mass market, driven by the middle class.

It is interesting to note that out of KFC's 5,100 outlets in China (early 2017), 90% were self-owned and 10% franchised. KFC did not use its traditional franchising concept as a means for geographical expansion in China. 90% of the KFC outlets were company owned in contrast to 12% in the US and 10% in the rest of the world. The choice for self-ownership is clear; it wants to keep control over the quality of the food and format of the outlets in China. We see the same with McDonald's. They started in 2004, with franchising, but in a rather slow and cautious approach in order to maintain brand quality and management control. In 2016, only 14% of its restaurants in China were franchised. In early 2017, McDonald's stated that it would almost double the number of stores in Mainland China in the next five years from 2,500 in 2017 to more than 4,500 in 2022. This will be done with the help of two strategic partners: CITIC and Carlyle. The expectation is that this boost of outlets into lower-tier cities is only possible if it substantially uses franchised restaurants and lowering the centralised guidance and control.

Gradualism

The Uppsala model has been associated with gradualism. Companies are going international in a step-by-step approach in which learning points are taken into account when entering another market. This gradualism can also be seen within China. After four years of learning in Shanghai, M&S was ready for further expansion in China. In 2012, it announced it would double the number of stores in China over the next year and the plan was to have 50 stores in 2020. It used the evolutionary step by step approach: an example of internalising the Uppsala model in China. After they learned how to operate in Shanghai, they went to second tier cities such as Wuhan, Ningbo and Changzhou, in many cases, alongside other international retailers such as Zara, H&M and Uniqlo.

Another example of learning by doing and gradualism was Carrefour's entry in China. It gained international experience by conducting business in Belgium, Spain and Latin America before going to Taiwan in 1989. While doing business in Taiwan, Carrefour learned how to adapt and work within the Chinese culture. This gradual approach in terms of modes of entry as well as sequence of markets is shown in Fig. 17.12(a). Carrefour started internationalisation in neighbouring countries Spain and Belgium. The learning experience in Spain has been transmitted to conducting business in Latin America, while experiences in Germany has been used in Central and Eastern Europe. Learning to operate in these markets will help the company to operate successfully in other emerging markets; there is a logical sequence visible. The same holds with respect to modes of entry choice. Carrefour started with strategic alliances and JVs and only after it learned how to operate abroad, there was the choice for a full control entry strategy. Fig. 17.12(b) also shows a summary of the internationalisation process of Carrefour that fits nicely in the gradual approach of the Uppsala model.

Earlier in the chapter, we discussed some features of China's e-commerce sector. In this part, we spend some words on it only to show how the western companies underestimated the speed of

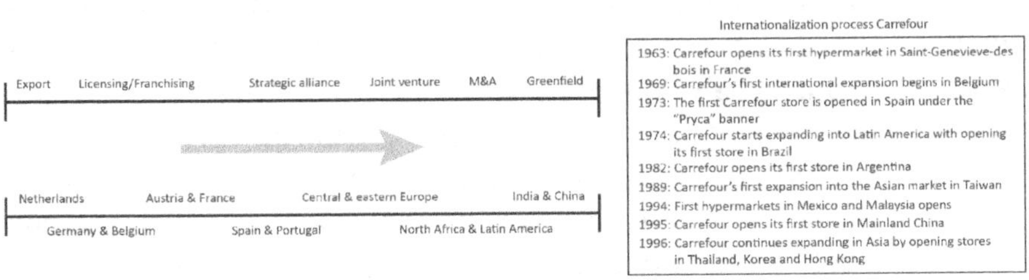

(a) (b)

Figure 17.12 The Uppsala model; (a) stages of modes of entry (upper half) and regional sequence (lower half) and (b) Internationalisation process Carrefour

Source: Based on Ebbers (2016) and Carrefour case (2013)

change of e-commerce in China. Information technology (IT) is the main driver behind e-commerce. However, according to the survey of Booz&Co. with AMCHAM Shanghai that was executed in 2011, this trend was only seen by Chinese companies. Instead of IT, the western companies chose external exposure (increased familiarity with western products) as a leading trend. In addition, more than 40% of the western MNEs said in 2011 that they did not implement an online shopping strategy (referred to as digital strategy in the survey) and don't plan to do so. Whereas 93% of their Chinese competitors said that they are already or will soon be involved in e-commerce. Obviously, digital strategy may have a different meaning depending on the industry. But it is astonishing that in the 2011 survey, this was not seen by MNE-managers in China. In 1993, the concept of e-commerce was introduced in China; firstly, related to B2B but then followed by B2C and C2C. China-based Alibaba (founded in 1999) launched the Taobao website in May 2003. At that time, eBay China dominated the online C2C market, holding 75% of the market share. However, only five years later, in 2008, Taobao held 90% of the market. Growth of e-commerce has been phenomenal. Around 16% of the country's total retail trade was conducted over the Internet in 2016. 11 November is known as Singles' Day in China and it has become a major shopping event for Alibaba. The company brought in US$18 billion in sales just in one day (2016). To put this in context, this sales volume was more than double the sales volume of Thanksgiving, Black Friday and Cyber Monday combined (*Reuters*).

The example of the digital strategy makes clear that underestimation of the Chinese market and Chinese competitors is dangerous, but widely observed when analysing the success and failure factors of western companies in China. In that sense, cultural and institutional factors are not so much the obstacle of being successful. Mostly, it is the attitude of the head office and its disconnection with what is happening in China that result in failures.

Chapter 18

China and the World

Myth 18: China's economic development and its status as global player hurts the multilateral trading system

18.1 Introduction

In 2005, Sara Bongiorni and her family started an interesting adventure, while living in the US. They decided to spend a year without buying anything from China and she summarised this experiment in her book, *A Year Without Made in China* (2007). The rule was straightforward: products with the made in China label had to be avoided. And if it was certain that there was a Chinese component in something, the final product was banned. The experiment absolutely turned the family's daily life upside down. For example, finding sneakers not being made in China was just impossible and only after an extensive search on the Internet (and paying triple the price as the Chinese sneakers) were Italian-made sneakers bought. The same held for finding components of a blender and other consumer products. She made two conclusions. Firstly, she was not aware of already being so close and intensively connected to China and its manufacturing sector. Secondly, she could really appreciate the benefit of having access to low-priced goods from China.

The low price has made shopping more affordable, but has also created adverse effects on western labour and companies. "The China price", screamed a *Business Week* headline in 2004, has become "the three scariest words in US industry (6 December 2004)". As we discussed earlier in the book, the China price is about cheap clothing and electronics filling the shelves at Walmart. For US and EU factory workers, the China price means losing their jobs. To executives, the China price results in fears of a new competitor. To politicians, the term has become shorthand for unfair trading practices. The China price discussion has been renewed by the election of Mr. Trump as the new President of the United States in 2016. Of course, you may question this attitude (as we saw in several previous chapters), but it is understandable if global domination is fading away. This defensive reaction is not new. In the 1960s, a leading French opinion-maker, J.J. Servan-Schreiber, published a book, *The American Challenge* (1968). He concluded that Europe was an unprepared victim to the US capitalist predator with its far superior management, technology and capital. Including its soft power in the field of culture and movies, the US would take over the French economy, culture and society. To stay within the French setting, it was Napoleon that stated, "let China sleep, for when she wakes, the world will tremble" (*The Telegraph*, 2 October 2011).

The learning point of Sara Bongiorni was how connected China and the world already was in the mid-2000s. This integration can be discussed from different angles. Firstly, we have the economic integration through international trade and direct investments. The above examples of the China effect relate to this economic globalisation. Obviously, this development is associated with the rise of China as a new economic power. An interesting observation is that China's interdependency and integration with the global economy today is in many aspects more intense than the US. The high level of integration means that what is happening in China is affecting the world. For example, driven by high economic growth, we witnessed a tremendous pressure on global demand for natural resources. This is good for suppliers of natural resources, but this demand contributed to higher input costs that have hurt many global manufacturers. Besides this direct impact, there are also numerous indirect effects. For example, the success of the domestic fast-speed trains puts so much pressure on Chinese airlines that they are looking for growth opportunities outside China because they cannot compete with the fast-speed trains. The consequence is that these airlines become more active on foreign markets and therefore, airlines such as AF–KLM, Lufthansa and Delta feel the competitive pressure rising.

The same international operating companies also see a new market, driven by the exploding Chinese middle class; a middle class which is larger than the entire population of Japan or the combined population of France and the UK (2016). Western companies are connecting to the Chinese middle class by investing (producing and selling) in China. At the same time, more and more Chinese firms are investing abroad, in many cases with help from the Chinese government. This makes authorities in the US and the EU uncomfortable. Also, there is some discomfort about China's growing influence in Africa that includes buying large assets in minerals, timber, foodstuff and oil. These activities and attitudes are logical in a world that is changing towards emerging markets, away from the traditional mature economies. Until recently, the global economy was dominated by the G7 economies and only lately China has been growing towards economic leadership. It should be kept in mind that China's economic expansion is a relatively new phenomenon. In 2007, China was smaller than the economies of Texas and California combined. The rise of China and other emerging markets resulted in a multipolar world. This is evident by looking at the shift away from the G7 towards the G20. Wolf in 2005 stated, "the economic rise of Asia's giants is the most important story of our age. It will end the more than five centuries of domination by the Europeans and their colonial offshoot" (*Financial Times*, 23 February 2005). This is what actually happened in the previous decade and will continue up to the 2050s when looking at longer-term forecasts.

Besides economic integration, we also will touch upon political integration in this chapter. Political integration refers to involvement in the global institutional framework such as the World Trade

Organisation (WTO), International Monetary Fund (IMF), World Bank (WB) and the United Nations (UN). Obviously, there is a close relationship between economic power and political power. Changes in economic power (such as the shift towards China, India and other emerging markets) must have impact on the multilateral architecture. As a result, governance structures of multilateral organisations must be adapted. The US (and G7) still are dominating the decision-making process within the IMF, while the economic power is shifting to emerging markets. Adjustment in the voting power is needed, but this is a difficult process. Another example of a challenge within the multilateral framework is the role of the IMF in Africa, which is partly substituted by bilateral financial help from China. In particular, infrastructure projects, frequently financed by soft loans, are the centrepiece of Chinese aid, making IMF finance (and its conditionality) less needed.

The third (and final) element of globalisation relates to the social and cultural integration. Social and cultural integration is strongly connected to the concept of "soft-power" (Nye, 2004). This soft power is the influence and attractiveness a nation acquires when others are drawn to its culture and ideas. As we will see in this chapter, China's soft power is growing. Its economic–political model is becoming more attractive to various parts of the world. China's social and cultural globalisation and integration will accelerate in the coming years. Western multinationals are educating the Chinese middle class in fast food, leisure and sustainability issues. Furthermore, the global spread of MBA programmes and students brings greater convergence in business practices. The rapidly growing number of direct flights between China and the world will increase tourism and trade, resulting in closer social (and cultural) integration. This is particularly the case with respect to Africa. It is interesting that this acceleration of direct flights from Africa to China is in strong contradiction with the few direct flights between Africa and the US.

The chapter is organised as follows. In Section 18.2, we start with some observations about China's role in the world. The main aim is to give a feeling how much China is integrated in the globalised world. The increasing role of China in the globalised (and interconnected) world can be measured from different angles, but we are using the KOF Globalisation Index as the starting point. This is followed by Section 18.3 in which the focus is on economic integration through international trade and investments. In Section 18.4, we discuss the political integration. Part of this political integration relates to China's membership in the WTO and the Beijing Consensus. In Section 18.5, we continue with discussing the social and cultural side of globalisation. The emphasis in this part is on China's growing soft power in the world. In the following, we also give a glance towards the future of China's integration.

18.2 Globalisation: A broad perspective

Defined broadly, globalisation is the process of integrating nations and peoples, politically, economically and culturally, into a larger global network. This process is driven by four factors:

- Improvements in technology (especially in communications and transportation)
- Opening up of new markets
- The economic paradigm of more market and less government that resulted in strong deregulation
- Harmonisation of consumer tastes (the young student in Shanghai likes the same Magnum ice cream as the student in Amsterdam)

Essentially, the focus, as the term suggests, is not on nations but on the entire globe. This view was also the starting point of Thomas Friedman's book, *The World is Flat: A Brief History of the Globalized World in the* 21st *Century* (2005). It shows a world in which (individual) connectivity is the norm. Friedman indicates that in today's Globalisation 3.0, individuals are empowered to run global business. They can process information and organise activities with the Internet. This type of globalisation has replaced Globalisation 2.0 which lasted from 1800 to 2000. In this period, MNEs grew and benefited from falling transportation and telecommunication costs. And according to Friedman, before this (1492–1800) we had Globalisation 1.0. The characteristic of this period was that international transactions were organised across and between countries.

The four factors mentioned above are translated by Friedman into 10 flatteners, i.e. drivers that enable individuals from communicating and collaborating on a global scale. We will not go through all the 10 flatteners, but it is clear that the collapse of the Berlin Wall in November 1989 started the opening up of countries in Central and Eastern Europe and allowed people from the other side of the Wall to join the economic mainstream. Also, companies such as Netscape and Google and communities like Wikipedia can be considered as flatteners. They made the Internet (and information) available for people. The technology (think about mobile phones, tablets and other personal devices) created the possibility to make the global supply chain more international through offshoring and outsourcing. Obviously, these flatteners of the world generated the external context to globalise. Through these flatteners, China could connect to the global supply chain activities. This development was complemented by China's adoption of "reform and opening up" in the late 1970s, the paradigm of the market in the 1990s, and its entry in the WTO in 2001. MNEs reacted on this development. It is certainly the case that the initiative of international cooperation and global free trade during the first wave of globalisation was done by governments and that the companies took over the initiative in the Globalisation 2.0 era. It is also true that today an individual can connect with everyone all over the world, but you may question Friedman's notion that this is primarily done by individuals. In today's globalised world, the MNEs are still the key drivers of globalisation. This is why in this book we put so much emphasis in the steps and choices of the MNEs.

Today, China's domestic economic policies matter a great deal to virtually every country in the world. Just think about its impact on resources, the environment (the role of China in the Paris climate agreement after the United States decided to step out in 2017) and its impact on export and import of countries that are very dependent on China. This is quite different from just a decade ago. In January 2007, in the state of the Union, President Bush mentioned Iraq 35 times, Al Queda 25 times and Iran 5 times. China was referred to only once and in a non-economic context (www.archives.gov). This is rather strange because also at that time, the China price created a lot of discontent in the US and this continues (with ups and downs) until today.

The rise of China and the China price is visible everywhere. People in the capital of Spain shoemaking industry, Elche, protested against Chinese competitors who hurt their business. In Italy, employees of the furniture industry demonstrated heavily against Chinese firms. In Scotland, seafood workers and in Mexico, the workers in the maquiladoras protested against Chinese firms. The China price had even undercut Nigerian textile factories. In September 2015 at a press conference, Federal Reserve President Janet Yellen referenced, "heightened concerns about growth in China" as one of the reasons for not raising interest rates. Another example of China's importance to the rest of the world could be seen in August 2015. On 11 August, global financial markets reacted strongly when the Chinese central bank announced (without warning) that the Renminbi would be allowed to find its own market level against the dollar and other major currencies. For the financial markets (and China experts) it was a sign how bad things were getting in China. This was translated into lower expectations of Chinese growth and the American and European stock indices fell by nearly 10% in August 2015. It shows how important China has become for the rest of the world. It also shows the overreaction, associated with a lack of western understanding of China's development and mixing up short-term measures with long-term drivers behind economic development.

KOF Globalisation Index

The broadest way to measure integration is with the help of the KOF Globalisation Index. The Globalisation Index 2017 (Fig. 18.1) shows the most and least integrated countries in the world. The Netherlands, Ireland and Belgium are at the top of the table. This is quite logical as these countries are highly developed, well connected and small.

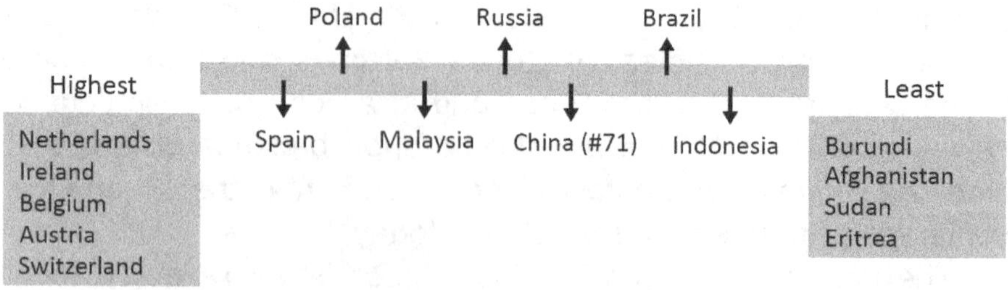

Figure 18.1 Globalisation Index 2017

Note: Not all countries are ranked due to lack and uncertainty of data
Source: KOF Swiss Economic Institute (2017)

Larger high-developed economies such as Spain are in the mid-range. Emerging economies such as Brazil and Indonesia are substantially less globalised. The least globalised countries were Eritrea, Sudan, Afghanistan and Burundi. In the overall index, China is in 71st place.

The overall index is made up of the three sub-indices: economic, social and political globalisation. And these sub-indices are further disaggregated into many variables. Figure 18.2 gives an overview of the most important variables and the weights of the sub-indices. The relatively low rank of China is mainly due to China's low score in the economic globalisation sub-index. This may be surprising given China's role in international trade and FDI. However, as can be seen in Fig. 18.2, most economic variables on the list are adjusted to take into account its GDP. In absolute terms, China is the largest exporter in the world, but export as percentage of GDP is much lower than most (smaller) countries. Furthermore, the low rank is partly determined by government interference in certain sectors and its capital controls.

In many respects, China's globalisation drive is quite similar to that of Japan in the 1980s and South Korea in the 1990s. Export started with low cost and low value-added products, and step by step the transition has been made to exporting higher value-added products and services. Also, the role of the government in helping domestic companies is a common characteristic. In several sectors, the government is visible and intervenes heavily, although more and

Indices and variables	(weight in %)
Economic globalisation	**36%**
- Trade as percentage of GDP	
- Foreign Direct Investment, stock as percentage of GDP	
- Portfolio investments as percentage of GDP	
- Import barriers	
- Tariffs	
- Capital account restrictions	
Social globalisation	**37%**
- International tourism	
- Foreigners in the country	
- Internet users	
- Number of McDonald's restaurants	
- Number of IKEA outlets	
Political globalisation	**27%**
- Number of embassies in the country	
- Membership in international organisations	
- Participation in international treaties	

Figure 18.2 The three main sub-indices of the KOF Globalisation Index
Note: The overview is not a complete list of all variables used
Source: KOF Swiss Economic Institute (2017)

more sectors are opening up. In general, you may label China's policy as free market capitalism and state capitalism at the same time. So, there are large overlaps between China's way of integrating in the global economy and what we saw in other Asian countries. But there are also major differences. The most important one is that China opened the market to foreign competition much earlier than Japan and South Korea. And unlike the Japanese and South Korean carefully orchestrated industrial policies that protected and helped global champions, such as Samsung and Toyota, China does not have an official and central government body driving its globalisation efforts, although SASAC supervises and manages state-owned assets. The specific role and influence of SASAC is somewhat unclear, but on paper it does not interfere with business operations.

In the previous chapters, we discussed the economic, political and social integration in-depth. The aim of the following paragraphs is to summarise the main trends. This overview will help us to better understand the future of China's integration.

18.3 Economic globalisation

Economic development in China after 1978 (and in particular after 2001) was phenomenal. The original Industrial Revolution that emerged in the mid-1700s took two centuries to gain full force. Britain, the revolution's birthplace, required 150 years to double its economic output per person; in the United States, doubling GDP per capita took more than 50 years. After 2001, China doubled its GDP per capita in 10 years. And what is striking is that Britain and the United States began industrialisation with populations of roughly 50 and 100 million, which is so much smaller than when China began its economic take-off, with populations in the market economy of around 800 million. It is clear why China has such a large impact on the world economy, on specific countries, and on companies.

This growth in GDP (and related to this income per capita) resulted in an emerging and fast growing middle class that is willing to spend on western products. The development of income (based on purchasing power parity) has been enormous. In 1980, the start of the reforms, China's per capita GDP (in PPP) was only 2% that in the US. Its living standard was only 3% of that seen in Europe and Japan. Now, its living standard is around 30% of that of the US, Europe and Japan. The development of the middle class is not unique for China and is happening in several emerging markets. However, the speed of change in China is striking. Within a few years China can be labelled as a middle-class society. The shift of the middle class away from the mature OECD economies in Europe and North America to emerging markets in Asia can be seen in Fig. 18.3.

In 2009, 28% of the global middle class was situated in the Asia-Pacific region, while 54% of the global middle class lived in North America and Europe. In 2015, the picture already changed radically with 46% of the global middle class within Asia-Pacific. And this trend is continuing. Expectations are that in 2030, 65% of the global

Region	2009		2015		2020		2025		2030	
	#	%	#	%	#	%	#	%	#	%
North America	338	18	335	11	344	9	350	8	354	7
Europe	664	36	724	24	736	20	738	16	733	14
Central and South America	181	10	285	9	303	8	321	7	335	6
Asia Pacific	525	28	1,380	46	2,023	54	2,784	60	3,492	65
Sub-Saharan Africa	32	2	114	4	132	4	166	4	212	4
Middle East and North Africa	105	6	192	6	228	6	258	6	285	5
World	1,845	100	3,030	100	3,766	100	4,617	100	5,412	100

Figure 18.3 The emerging middle class (millions and % of total)

Source: Based on and adjusted from Kharas (2017)

middle class will be in Asia-Pacific. At that time, the combined share of North America and Europe will only be 21%. Of course, the middle class in these regions are (still) considerably richer than in Asia-Pacific, but as we saw in Chapter 16, the new middle class already have purchasing power to buy branded and premium products. And in many cases purchasing power is higher than what you would expect. I always start the discussion about the middle class in China with a question to my students, “Do you think that there is a market for Sony flat screens in China”? Obviously, the answers relate to income level. Based on the nominal average income per capita (around US$8,000 in 2016), you may question if many people are able to buy such a luxury product. However, this US$8,000 is in nominal terms, but it is obvious that you can do much more with one dollar in China than in the US because of the low price of local products and services. Consequently, in terms of purchasing power this US$8,000 is worth around US$15,000. In addition, buying a flat screen is based on the household income (instead of income per head). If two people are working in the (extended) family, the total household income in purchasing power reaches US$30,000. From this point of view, the market for flat screens is there.

The development of economic integration is summarised in Fig. 18.4. The difference between 1980 and 2016 is striking. In 1980, China’s share in worldwide exports was a tiny 1%, while in 2016 the share increased to almost 15%. The same holds for FDI flows. In 1980, there were no FDI flows to and from China. In 2016, the global share of both inflow and outflow of FDI was around 10%.

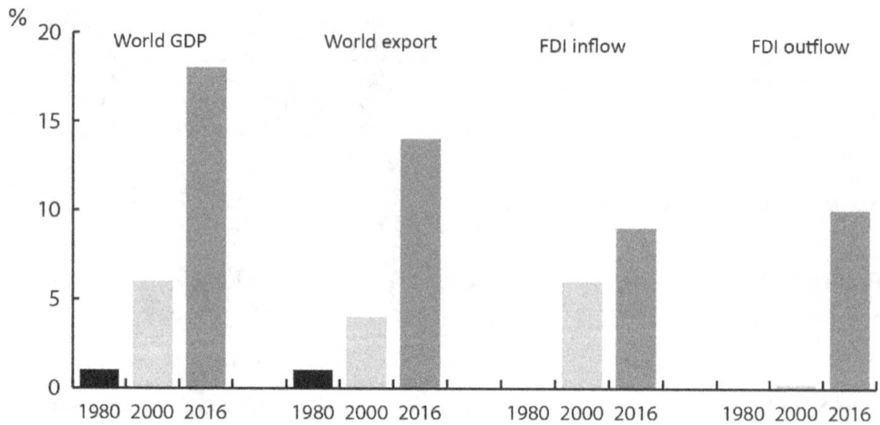

Figure 18.4 China in worldwide GDP, export and investments

Note: GDP based on Purchasing Power Parity (PPP)

Source: Based on WB database

In 2016, China's economy (measures as GDP) was 18% of global production (based on purchasing power parity). These are remarkable changes and gives a feeling how important China is in today's worldwide economic indicators.

International trade

Although China had trade relations with the rest of the world during the period of the first Han emperors in the second century BC, and despite the journeys of Zheng to the coast of Africa (today's Somalia and Kenya) in the early 15th century, until the end of the 1970s China's international trade was negligible. Foreign transactions did not have a great impact on the domestic economy and did not have impact at all on the outside world. As stated in earlier chapters, during the pre-reform trade regime (up to late 1970s), there were a handful of trade corporations owned and controlled by the Ministry of Foreign Trade that were responsible for import and export. But trade was seen as a necessary activity to complement the domestic planning. This changed completely after 1978. Trade began to grow and has been considered as one of the key factors behind China's economic success.

China's development generates pros and cons. What is happening in China may be beneficial to the rest of the world. We already discussed some of these advantages earlier in the book. For example, demand for natural resources helped low-income countries that exports commodities. China, being at the centre of global supply networks, also substantially reduced production costs of many international operating companies (and lowered prices for consumers). The competition from China spurs innovative behaviour and productivity worldwide. And of course, the growing middle class results in a new market for many western companies. Nevertheless, we see some real and often concentrated costs. Think again about the China price that may have a negative impact on wages and jobs in developed countries, although it is difficult to determine this impact. Several studies indicate that competition from China accounted for 10–25% of the decline in the US manufacturing jobs between 1990 and 2015 (Morrison, 2017). Also, less developed countries (LDCs) may feel the negative impact from China's trade domination. The low China price makes it more difficult for them to develop their own manufacturing sectors. Other costs are borne by specific firms in countries both rich and poor, unable to compete.

The growing role in world trade automatically results in more trade tensions and even trade wars. The debate about unfair trade practise accelerated after the mid-2000s when China's current account surplus rose to almost 10% of GDP. At the same time, the US trade deficit exploded. The US merchandise trade deficit with China rose from US$10 billion in 1990 to US$367 billion in 2015 and slightly fell to US$295 billion in early 2017. As stated earlier in the book, there are two views on this China–US trade imbalance. Some analysts argue that the large US merchandise trade deficits with China indicate that the trade relationship is unbalanced, unfair and damaging to the US economy. Others argue that the large US trade deficits with China are a reflection of global shifts in production as well as the emergence of extensive and complex supply chains, where China is often the final point of assembly for export-oriented multinational firms that source goods from multiple countries. The first (more defensive) view can be seen in the steps taken by the US government to fight the trade imbalance (based on Morrison, 2017):

- On 12 January 2017, the US filed a WTO dispute settlement case against China over subsidies given to certain Chinese aluminium producers.
- On 6 January 2017, an advising committee to the president issued a report on the US semiconductor industry, which warned that a "concerted push by China to reshape the market in its favour, using industrial policies backed by over one hundred billion dollars in government-directed funds, threatens the competitiveness of US industry and the national and global benefits it brings".
- On 15 December 2016, the US initiated a WTO dispute settlement case against China over its tariffs-rate quotas for rice, wheat and corn.
- On 13 September 2016, the US initiated a WTO dispute settlement case against China over its use of excessive domestic subsidies for agricultural products.

And this is just a short summary of the US–China commercial tensions. An important discontent of the US is about market access. The Chinese market, despite China's far-reaching WTO accession commitments, remains protected in a number of areas and this create growing frustration by the American companies and government. I would not be surprised if this market access-issue is an important trigger behind future trade-problems. Market access is certainly a problem for several industries. China today still has several types of explicit and implicit market access barriers that disadvantage foreign firms. But be aware that China is a very open economy with respect to trade. China's trade openness is far greater than anything achieved by the US in the post-war period and looks similar to the levels of openness achieved by the UK at the height of its empire. The ratio of trade to GDP for the US rarely exceeded 15% during the 1945–2017 period, compared with China's current ratio of 57% (2017). China is integrated with respect to trade in a way that the US never was.

Foreign Direct Investments

The liberalisation of FDI started in 1979 with the four special economic zones. More regions were opening up in the early 1980s. This was complemented by attractive tax preferences for foreign firms, in particular related to export activities. One important advantage on the supply-side was that because of the influx of foreign companies, it forced the Chinese companies (competitors and suppliers) to increase quality and productivity. After 2000, the outward investments also accelerated. More and more Chinese firms are visible on western markets, and today Chinese firms are very active in global M&A. The year 2015 was the first in Chinese history when its outward FDIs were larger than its incoming FDIs. And this is just the beginning. The world community is merely witnessing the first steps of corporate China's ascent to the international business stage.

The stock of Chinese investments is still low compared to the US and EU countries, but there is a lot of discomfort about China investing abroad. This is partly driven by the non-transparency of many investment projects and the uncertainty about the role of the government or government-related entities in the deals. Chinese diplomacy, soft loans from state-owned banks have complement China's FDI flows in regions such as Africa and Latin America. Examples of these state-owned banks are Exim Bank and China Development Bank. Exim Bank was established in 1994 to promote Chinese exports and FDI specifically in infrastructure such as roads, power plants, pipelines and telecom. Also, the China Development Bank was established in 1994 and has the aim to provide loans to Chinese firms when going abroad. The views of Chinese investments in Africa are in line with the general attitude of Chinese investments worldwide. Chinese investments in, for example, the Democratic Republic of Congo are presented on the one hand as a Marshall Plan, and on the other, as a fresh era of neocolonialism of little benefit to local communities. The positive view on China's investments can mostly be heard in LDCs (that receives investment and aid from China), while the negative view is mostly seen in the western media and politics.

18.4 Political integration: Multilateralism or regionalism

China's investment activities in Africa and Latin America are different from the capital allocated by institutions such as the IMF or western countries. Capital (loans and aid) from the IMF or western countries mostly involved conditionality in the form of specific government measures. For example, the obligation to open up the economy and steps to free capital flows. Frequently, also governance and human right issues are part of the conditionality. In many cases, Chinese capital does not prescribe these market-driven measures. Moreover, there is less interference in domestic political choices. Now, developing countries and upcoming emerging markets have a choice: receiving money from the traditional partners or from China. It is the Beijing versus the Washington Consensus.

Beijing Consensus

Joshua Cooper Ramo introduced the term Beijing Consensus in an article in 2004: "China is marking a path for other nations around the world who are trying to figure out not simply how to develop their countries, but also how to fit into the international order in a way that allows them to be truly independent, to protect their way of life and political choices in a world with a single massively powerful center of gravity. I call this new center and physics of power and development the Beijing Consensus". Others also referred to the Chinese model or infrastructural diplomacy (Ramo 2004). The Beijing Consensus reflects a new approach to development based on China's model for economic growth. Less-developed countries (LDCs) sometimes prefer receiving investments and loans from China instead of the IMF because they are not able (or willing) to accept the IMF conditionalities, based on free market principles. Instead they are looking at China as a country that is growing fast precisely because they do not follow the IMF rules. China's success is an example of economic development that is combining the advantages of free trade under the auspices of the WTO, and at the same time makes clear that sometimes government intervention is needed to smoothen its transition process. This is combined with some discontent by LDCs with failures of structural adjustment policies and "poverty reduction strategies" subscribed by organisations such as the IMF, WB and western donors. From the African perspective, China's success creates an image of a country that has successfully avoided being forced into the neoliberal reforms of the Washington Consensus. The LDCs looked to China as an alternative to western (former colonial) powers. Two African countries: Rwanda and Ethiopia, have adopted explicitly, the policy of imitating the Chinese growth model. A second element of the Beijing Consensus is the political principles of non-interference and self-determination. China does not prescribe a certain government attitude and it does not interfere in domestic issues. In recent years, international organisations and bilateral aid agencies from traditional donors have made their assistance conditional on good governance. China, on the contrary, makes a clear distinction between economics and politics in its interventions in Africa, also supporting undemocratic regimes. This Chinese approach, financial aid without political conditionalities, echoes the humiliations of the "unequal treaties" imposed on China by the west in the 19th century. Of course, self-interest also plays a role. African and Latin-American resources are needed to support domestic growth.

Following China's development path and its choices is tempting, but obviously imitation is not working. China has some special characteristics: the proximity of Hong Kong as a link to the global market, relatively good human development indicators at the start of the growth process and well-functioning government and legal institutions. There is no simple recipe for the "Chinese model" that other countries can copy. But elements of the Chinese growth model can certainly be translated to today's LDCs. This is the essence of the Beijing Consensus: there is an alternative for the strict and fixed one-size-fits-all formula of the IMF and WB. Figure 18.5 shows the difference between the Washington Consensus and the Beijing Consensus (although the Chinese leaders never used this term).

The Washington Consensus introduced by Williamson (1990) describes a set of recommendations and specific economic policies

Washington consensus	Beijing consensus
- Fiscal discipline	- Replacing the market for more government intervention if needed
- Tax reform	- Pragmatic solutions and choices
- Liberalized interest rates	- Trail and error experimentation
- Market driven exchange rate	- Gradual restructuring instead of market driven shock therapy
- Trade liberalization of inward FDI	- Gradual opening up and protecting domestic firms to adjust
- Privatization & deregulation	- Measuring success not only based on GDP
- Strong protection of property rights	

Figure 18.5 Washington versus Beijing Consensus

Source: Author's compilation of features expressed in different sources

which are promoted by the IMF and WB. The Washington Consensus also made clear under which conditions countries in crisis could receive financial aid.

By its name, the Beijing Consensus implies that it is an alternative to the Washington Consensus, but be aware that in many dimensions China follow advices that the IMF recommend. At the same time, China has convincingly demonstrated that deregulation and market-based interest- and exchange rate policy is not the only path to economic growth and successful integration in the global economy. As stated before, governments of developing countries are increasingly following China's growth model. And with China as an example, government intervention and protectionism are seen as essential tools to increase welfare.

The growing importance of the Beijing Consensus has some important implications for the multilateral system. The rise of China (and other Asian miracles) has been achieved precisely by not following the recommendations of IMF, WTO and mainstream economic theories. For example, China had (and still has) limited capital account convertibility, which is against IMF rules. In particular during global currency crises, the capital restrictions proved to be a big advantage. Furthermore, China showed that subsidies and government support are sometimes helpful and needed. State intervention, protecting important industries and gradualism are essential pieces of China's success. It should be noted that every country that has created a successful industrial catch-up has employed some of these factors, including the US and European countries. Obviously, protectionism in itself is bad for longer-term economic development and must be avoided as a structural feature of the economy, but opening up have to be done in a gradual way. There are experts who believe that the central paradigm behind the multilateral trading system may be under attack because of the rise of the Beijing Consensus, including its focus on protectionism and government intervention. However, it should be noted that the Beijing Consensus and its government intervention is from a different dimension; it relates to targeted and focused intervention to reduce the disruption of structural changes in short notice. It is not substituting the market for government intervention. Moreover, a gradual approach to opening up is not the same as protectionism; it is finding a smart and optimum way to open up.

Another consequence of the growing popularity of the Beijing Consensus is that it may affect the global balance of power. China is creating strong economic ties and gaining political power by offering countries beneficial terms of trade, aid and investment. As a result, countries will increasingly look to China for diplomatic support and form alliances with China in the multilateral system. This is one of the reasons why the WTO- Doha Round failed; the change of power from the west to emerging markets makes the discussion about international trade (and investments) difficult. A final consequence of the rising Beijing Consensus is that it may be a threat to the liberal market democracy paradigm. If there is a fundamental choice of people between increasing standard of living or fighting for democracy, people choose welfare above democracy. Of course, people want political leaders they choose, but this is not their first priority. Democratic paradigms are under attack and autocratic regimes (for example, in Russia and Turkey) see in China the proof that economic growth does not have to be associated with increased political freedom or democratisation. China's income per captia has risen at twice the rate of democratic India since 2006. You may say that the IMF and the WB can be criticised for attaching too many conditions to loans. At the same time, China may be underdemanding, which is also worrisome. Think about the capital sent to Venezuela which gave the leaders extra time to ruin the economy.

Political involvement in global governance

There is an important difference between economic and political integration. In economics, the rise of China comes not at the expense (in absolute terms) of the growth in the US or Europe. Clearly, growth in China was and is higher than what we see in the west, but also in the west, there is economic growth. Economic integration is a positive-sum game because the total economic pie becomes larger due to China's development. However, this is not the case when we discuss political integration. The increase in political power of China in the IMF or in specific LDCs automatically means that the power of the US or Europe is falling. Political power is essentially a zero-sum game, i.e. one country's political power inevitably requires a reduction in power somewhere else. This makes the discussion about China's (and other emerging markets) role in the multilateral system complicated. We see this, for example, in the discussion about the voting power in the IMF. The voting power is mostly based on a country's economic power. Despite the enormous increase in China's share in worldwide GDP, its voting power did not change before 2016. China became increasingly frustrated by its limited role in the IMF. Finally, after heavy debates, the allocation of voting power has been adjusted in 2016. The voting power of China increased from 3.8% to 6.2%. Also, the other original BRIC countries received a higher share in the total voting power. However, the (small) increase came at the expense of the group "rest of the world", that includes all the other countries; not at the expense of the US or the OECD countries.

Figure 18.6 makes clear that this adjustment is just a very small reshuffling of voting power. The OECD countries still have their domination, the US still has its veto right with 16.7% of the total votes and China's voting power is still much lower than what you would expect when looking at economic power. It is clear that additional

Countries	Before 2016 (%)	After 2016 reforms (%)
United States	16.7	16.7
Japan	6.2	6.2
Germany	5.8	5.4
France	4.3	4.1
United Kingdom	4.3	4.1
Italy	3.2	3.1
Canada	2.6	2.3
Rest of OECD	20.5	21.3
China	3.8	6.2
India	2.3	2.7
Russian Federation	2.4	2.6
Brazil	1.7	2.3
Rest of the world	26.2	23.2

OECD countries

Figure 18.6 Division of voting power in the IMF, before and after the adjustment in 2016

Source: Based on IMF database and Weisbrot and Johnston (2016)

steps are needed, and it is clear that China (and other emerging economies) must receive a bigger vote in the future.

WTO membership

Looking back, the WTO (and its pre-successor GATT) showed quite some flexibility when it had to react on changes in the external environment. For example, in the 1950s, it was able to incorporate the European integration process in the multilateral system. It pushed strongly to reduce tariffs for countries such as the US, who felt the discriminatory effects of the European integration. This is why tariffs reduced substantially in the 1950s and 1960s. In the early 1970s (Tokyo Round), the GATT had to deal with the impact of the oil crisis and the rise of Japan as a major trading power. The Tokyo Round smoothly absorbed the impact of these two events. The third adjustment came in the 1980s when more and more developing countries were rising in power; LDCs were left out of the GATT process until that time but that was not possible anymore. And again, the GATT was able to absorb the impact in such a way that the multilateral trading system survived. The fourth major adjustment needed was to deal with China's membership. In essence, the WTO accepted China as an LDC, and consequently the country had time to implement WTO rules and legislation in a gradual way. Other WTO countries had to accept this gradual adjustment stage and they did, driven by China's huge potential market and relatively low wages.

Also, China adjusted. A significant portion of the tariff reduction and other trade liberalisation measures that the Chinese government undertook in the 1990s were essentially part of China's WTO accession process. China's entry in the WTO was a clear sign that the government chose the market economy route. The Chinese perspective was that more competition is an essential source of pressure that ultimately results in (additional) structural reforms and increasing productivity. The emphasis in the 1990s was on opening up the manufacturing sector. Only after it became a WTO member did China take large steps with respect to the service sector. Prior to China's membership, the Chinese government severely restricted the service industry. This was in line with what we saw in Japan and South Korea in their development process: the consequence of having a dual economy. On the one hand, there were very competitive export-oriented manufacturing sectors that were forced to contend with the best competitors in the world. On the other hand, the domestically oriented service sectors, in which competition had been muted by government regulations and restrictions on entry, were much less competitive; with low productivity as the result.

Within the context of the WTO, China executed a process of opening up the domestic service industry. It looks like China is quicker in opening up the service sector compared to Japan and South Korea. Having said this, many service sectors are still (partly) closed or restricted. As indicated in Chapter 5, the third plenum of the Communist Party in 2013 can be seen as a breakthrough in opening up the service sector. Industries like elderly care, accounting and auditing, logistics and e-commerce see less and less restrictions. The selection of these industries may mark the beginning of a systematic opening up in the service sector.

Complying to WTO rules is not always easy because WTO rules are not about trade alone anymore. The discussion is not so much on lowering tariffs, but the negotiations are about global rules and regulations that should be implemented by the member states. WTO is essentially more and more about global rules. From this point of view it is logical that countries take time to adjust.

The overview above makes clear that China is able and willing to work within the context of the WTO rules. However, at the same time, subsidies, cheap financing and other preferences helped many SOEs to survive and gave them extra time to adjust. In that sense, some of the policies implemented are in contradiction with the WTO rules. As was mentioned in the introduction of this book, it is the ambiguities feature of China: a relatively loyal member of WTO and at the same time actions that may contradict WTO rules. One example of an initiative that may contradicts with WTO is the growth in bilateral and regional initiatives.

Regional initiatives

Like so many developing countries and countries in transition, China is also frustrated by the negotiations within the WTO-Doha Round. Even after more than 16 years, there is no sight of a final end result. Sixteen years is a long time, and many developments have occurred in this period. The negotiations started at a time when the term BRIC was not even introduced. Furthermore, in the previous 16 years the world changed economically towards the growing Asian countries. In addition, we had the financial and economic crisis that was mostly felt by mature economies. All these events did not make the negotiations easier and there is no new agreement in sight. Consequently, China (as so many other countries) is not waiting for the multilateral deal but is looking for the fast track, i.e. cooperation with countries that are willing to work together. The ASEAN–China Free Trade Agreement is just one example of the 20 Free Trade Agreements it has signed in the previous years. The newest initiative is the One Belt, One Road (OBOR) project: the new silk route, announced by President Xi in

2013 and accelerated in 2015. One Belt refers to what was historically called the Silk Road, stretching from China through Central Asia to Eastern Europe. One Road refers to a maritime road which more or less draws inspiration from the voyages through Southeast Asia to the east coast of Africa by Zheng He in the Ming Dynasty. The new Silk Road starts in Shaanxi province, which is the home province of Xi Jinping. The infrastructural cooperation is broader than a strict regional perspective, but the emphasis is on the neighbouring countries.

Like always, domestic motives drive this initiative. The Silk Road fits in developing the western part of China. It will help the western part of China to develop and therefore fight income inequality between provinces. And it is a way to use the international reserves in a profitable and efficient way. It also may help industries that are burdened by overcapacity problems. The main reasons behind the OBOR initiative are summarised in Fig. 18.7.

The official cornerstone of China's foreign policy is the theory of a Harmonious World. The paradigm, introduced by President Hu Jintao in 2005, revolves around multilateralism, if it is working effectively. Therefore, we see the Chinese actively involving in discussions within

Main motives

- Domestic development
- Reducing income inequality between provinces (eg. Xinjiang region)
- Absorbing lower domestic demand
- Using the RMB internationally
- Reducing overcapacity (as a consequence of the stimulus package)
- Move excess production through FDI outflow
- Connection to mature economies will stimulate innovation and production of higher value added products
- Using the reserves more efficient
- counteracting TTIP and TPP
- Regional integration (instead of only multilateral initiatives through WTO)
- Counteracting IMF fluence (Washington consensus)

Figure 18.7 Motives behind the One Belt One Road initiative

Source: Author's compilation of motives from different sources, 2016–2017

the WTO, IMF and WB. At the same time, the Chinese authorities also stress protection of sovereignty and non-interference in other countries' domestic affairs. In several cases the Chinese voted against UN-missions or IMF-conditionality that interferes with national sovereignty. These principles are rooted strongly in China's era of humiliation in the late 19th and early 20th centuries. Consequently, China is operating (and will continue to operate) both within and outside the existing multilateral institutions. It supports the WB while at the same time greatly expanding the role of the China Development Bank and the Exim Bank. It is supporting the IMF and at the same time, actively promoting the initiative that refers to currency cooperation in Asia.

18.5 Social and cultural integration: Hard and soft power

Often, global politics consists of hard power; countries and international organisations are "asking" other countries (or organisations) to behave in line with their will, either using force or money. Soft power is the ability "to affect others the outcomes one wants through attraction rather than coercion or payment" (Nye, 2004); it is about persuasion instead of intimidating. This soft power is driven by political values, culture and foreign policy. Usually, there is some overlap between hard and soft power. Several developing countries are following China in its views on economic and political development. This is clearly based on China's development, but at the same time it is backed by serious money. For example, it has been calculated that the newest initiatives such as OBOR and the loans from the New Development Bank result in much more financial aid than the costs of the Marshall Plan in today's dollars or the combined financial aid the US and the Soviet Union gave to countries during the Cold War.

For many years, China has been trying to gain soft power, but for authoritarian countries this is difficult. It also not helps if it is investing and giving soft loans to regimes in Venezuela and Zimbabwe. After 2010, China has increased loans to countries that have been ignored (for good reasons) by western countries. But these are exceptions. Most of the financial flow are allocated to LDCs that are eager to build up a stable economic and political environment. These countries accept Chinese help and finance due to China's gain in soft power: as an example country to achieve prosperity. Its soft power increased also because of the problems in democratic countries such as the UK and the US and because questions were raised about the quality of democratic institutions. Gaining soft power accelerated in May 2017 when Mr. Trump announced to step away from the 2015 Paris climate agreement. The political world turned upside down after his announcement. China became visible as global leader in the fight against climate change. In his visit to the EU, China's Premier Li Keqiang, in early 2017, stated that China will follow the Paris agreement and will do what is necessary whatever the circumstances. Of course, this focus on climate change and sustainability is driven by the dramatic environmental situation at home. In the top 25 most polluted cities worldwide, there are seven Chinese cities, including Xingtai, Baoding, Hengshui and Shijiazhuang; all located in the Hebei province (World Health Organisation, 2016).

Economically, China is a great success story, with its rising share in world trade and investments. Politically, China is a flexible authoritarian system whose legitimacy is based on effective governance rather than on democratic elections. The hypothesis that market-driven economic change would force the political system to become more open and pluralistic has proved wrong so far. It is precisely this combination of political centralisation and economic liberalisation that makes China an example for many other countries in transition; they are following the Beijing Consensus as alternative for the IMF and WB advices. At the same time, precisely because of this combination of political centralisation and market forces, there is a limit regarding increasing its soft power. This ceiling to increase soft power also relates to the human right issues and the fact that China is not seen as technological leader. Global influence is not solely based on production or income. History suggests that the key variables behind soft power are not pure economic size but also technological capacity and political positioning. China has undeniably made rapid progress, but there is little concrete evidence to suggest that it is becoming a technological leader. One may look at the structure of exports and see that 30% of its exports are categorised as "high-technology" goods, but at a closer look, nearly half of China's export and around 70% of its high-tech exports are produced by foreign firms. On the international (diplomatic) front, China is fully engaged in the global governance structure. It does not mean that they follow the rules to a tee, but it is clear that China needs the system that is based on rules. it is also understandable that China is looking at the edges of the multilateral rules to find out what is possible and in its best interest.

An introduction to the future

The above overview of China's integration in its many dimensions is short and certainly not complete, but I guess these are important features to start a realistic assessment of China's place in the globalised world. The next (and final) chapter is about the future of China and its role in the world. Forecasting is problematic. In the 1970s, many specialists indicated that the Soviet Union would dominate the Europe–Asia trading route. In the 1980s, the expectation was that the Japanese would dominate the US economically. And in 2012, the conventional wisdom was that Brazil, Russia, India and China (BRIC countries) were set to dominate world trade and the global economy. But today, Brazil is in an economic and political chaos, the Russian growth reduced dramatically due to the geopolitical problems and the low oil price, and China and India are feeling the global crisis. By keeping this in mind, we may start with some remarks about China's future integration in the world (and in a sense the future of multilateral institutions).

The rise of influence will continue. The west will progressively discover, to its discomfort, that the world is no longer western. That counts for institutions, economies, language, currencies as well as values. China will become the largest economy (even in nominal terms) in the next decade. It means the end of the western domination, although the west will stay the richest region for many years to come. But it cannot dominate the rest of the world as it did in the previous decades.

This is in particular difficult for the US. As the single largest economy, they dominated the global governance system. It has held this status since the 1870s, when it surpassed the UK. The US is almost completely unprepared for a life in which it will no longer be globally dominant. Its leaders and citizens only know a world in which the US is dominating and able to set the rules with respect to global governance. The EU is mentally better prepared for the Chinese growth. They already lost their supremacy to the US earlier in history. You may question the precise time frame, but it is clear that China will dominate world economics. The question is not how to reverse this economic shift but how to deal with it. One important historical lesson is that in many cases, the true enemies in the struggle for longer-term welfare are not external competitors, but domestic elites that constantly strive to preserve their own privileges at everyone else's expense. This is also the case in democratic countries.

The reflection above is on economic changes and on GDP, but real leadership also involves elements such as technological leadership and a global moral compass. With respect to China's technological leadership, it is to be expected that China will continue its catching-up process and that we will see more and more Chinese companies as global technological leader. It is logical that certain backwardness is still there. Most of its private companies are less than 20 years old, and it is only a matter of time before they emulate the international success of their Japanese and South Korean peers. China is spending a great deal more money on basic scientific research than most countries. Having said this, technological leadership does not come easy. The main question is how China and its companies will be able to continue its steps in innovation as they are becoming closer to technological leaders.

With respect to China's moral compass worldwide, the pragmatic response from the US and Europe may begin with the recognition that China's system of values differs substantially from that of the west. And that this system of values is not some fragile recent invention but that it is deeply rooted in Chinese traditions of governance. Outsiders can do nothing to change essential aspects of the American system such as the political system, big campaigns, excessive consumption or the constitution regarding rifle-ownership. The same holds with respect to China. China is increasing its soft power (complemented by enormous financial aid and investment programmes) by emphasising how its political and governance structure was able to enhance economic human rights. LDCs are seeing the success and want to copy China's strategy of prioritising material welfare above democracy. However, as long as there is no positive development in the area of human rights, China is unlikely to gain enough soft power to meaningfully influence western countries.

There are ceilings in terms of how much integration a country (and its citizens) are able and willing to have. In the western countries, this ceiling has been approached when looking at events such as the Brexit and the attitude in the US regarding "America first". In that sense, the multilateral structure with its open borders and rule-based system is under attack. Also, China feels discomfort with some elements of the global system. For example, it sees the many dumping cases executed in the WTO context as unfair because it still does not have a market-economy status which may protect against dumping complaints. It also feels some discomfort because the view that protecting certain industries is sometimes needed, is being questioned by the other WTO members, resulting in cases within the WTO dispute settlement body. Also, the attitude regarding the IMF is negative in nature due to the one-size fits all policy. The consequence is the creation, rise and deepening of regional institutions. Examples are the BRICS bank (now called New Development Bank), One Belt, One Road investment fund and the Asian Infrastructure Investment Bank.

But, in essence, the rise of China will not change the global governance structure too much. The many regional initiatives are essentially to complement (not to substitute) the role of the WB and

IMF. It is clear that China's development and its impact on smaller developing countries may contradict now and then with WTO rules, but the multilateral system of global institutions, is much stronger than a country such as China or the US. Of course, China will increase its voting power in IMF and WB, but its ability to transform the deeply rooted principles on which that system rest will be modest. That is also not what the Chinese authorities are aiming for as they know how important the multilateral structure is for their welfare (today and in the future). China seeks to transform some aspects of these institutions while at the same time sponsoring new regional initiatives. But in essence and despite these regional initiatives, the current open, rules-based economic system is safe. We clearly will see some Chinese features in the future global governance system, but not *per se* in a negative way. It is not a transmission of its domestic authoritarian model into the WTO or IMF, but elements which are important for emerging markets, such as China.

Chapter 19

The Future of Globalisation and the Role of China

Myth 19: China will not participate in the globalised world because it does not accept western-based rules

19.1 Introduction

The consensus of conferences on China's development in the early 1990s was that China's growth would vastly reach a ceiling due to inconsistent and non-market-driven policies. The participants referred to predictions that the Soviet Union (and later Japan) would overtake the US and would dominate world economics (and politics); both predictions were clearly not correct. Any kind of long-term projection is subject to a great deal of uncertainty and the further ahead into the future you look, the more uncertain things become. This is why long-term forecasts make use of scenarios. They provide policymakers, strategists and experts with various possible futures; but not forecasting the future.

These scenarios can minimise surprises and broaden the span of thinking about different possibilities. However, scenario building is complex. A deep understanding and knowledge of the field under investigation is absolutely necessary. Data and information from different sources have to be collected and interpreted which makes scenario building very timeconsuming. To reduce the number of possible outcomes, we may focus on black and white scenarios or the most likely scenario.

Also, extrapolation is a method to draw the future picture. This method is quite straightforward. We assume that what is happening today will continue in the future. But in many cases, extrapolation is not accurate. For example, the economic growth today cannot be used to forecast economic development in the future. As countries develop, the forces that increased GDP weaken and growth rates tend to slow. In Japan and Germany, very rapid growth in the 1960s and 1970s gave way to more moderate growth in the 1980s and 1990s. The same can be expected of fast growing emerging markets. Therefore, simple extrapolation gives incorrect answers over long timeframes. Researchers are adjusting for this in their models. For example, in the model of Goldman Sachs (2003), China's GDP growth rate falls to 5% in 2020. By the mid-2040s, growth slows to around 3.5%. Therefore, adjusted extrapolation is needed. Despite the problems related to forecasts, the outcome of most models is the same: China becomes the world's largest economy in the late 2030s. In these models, we assume a reasonable stable context, but it should be clear that, the longer the projection, the more vulnerable the analysis is to "black swans" (Taleb, 2010), unforeseeable surprises with major impacts.

We start Section 19.2 with scenarios on China's future. Most of the scenarios combine the economic and political futures of China, and we will complement this with an assessment of the main risks in the short and long terms. In Section 19.3, we discuss the future world in which China will operate; a world in which globalisation will continue. In Section 19.4, we look at China's perspectives on globalisation and its institutions. It will become clear that changes are needed within the global governance but that these adjustments are modifications within the system instead of changing the whole architecture. This is not in the interest of China either. In the final Section 19.5, we conclude the book with some reflections on the future of globalisation and China's role in it.

19.2 Scenarios

I still remember in one of the conferences I participated, I think it was in 1995, where a dramatic scenario was presented by one of the researchers. According to him, China after Deng Xiaoping would fall into the Yugoslavia scenario after the death of President Tito in 1980. Following the death of Tito, there was a strong shift of power away from the federal government to the republics and autonomous provinces. The consequence was a federal government with little control over economic, cultural and political policy. This loss of central authority gave rise to Serbian ultranationalism which, at the end of the day, resulted in a civil war and falling apart of former Yugoslavia into independent states. This pessimistic scenario was pushed by economic and social differences between the Chinese provinces. The death of Deng Xiaoping would result in political disorder and different fractions not capable of ruling China as a whole. It gives the opportunity for separatist pressure and finally, political independence of these regions. The internal chaos also results in isolation from the global economy and politics. Based on these differences, two Chinas would emerge. On one hand, Tibet, Xinjiang and Manchuria with its specific culture, and on the other hand, mid-China, headed by the coastal areas and its large cities in the east and south.

Of course, there were other scenarios developed in the early 1990s, ranging from economically positive scenarios (successful transition to a market economy and democracy) to scenarios in which the market-led approach of Deng Xiaoping would be stopped, the Reversion to Communism scenario. But, in general, interest in China's future was low. At that time, China's future was only of interest for experts. China's integration in the early 1990s had just started and not many internationally operating companies had plans with China, its labour force or its market. China's domestic policy was only gradually changing towards opening up. This changed considerably after 1992. China's impact on global growth, resource allocation, trade and investment as well as geopolitical balance grew in the 1990s. This is why we saw a revival of China scenarios in the 2000s.

In 2006, the Dutch Ministry of Foreign Affairs (Devillers, 2006) developed a China Scenario 2020 in which the most developed provinces would demand more autonomy in economic, social and political terms. Consequently, China would develop into a federal state in which certain provinces would strongly integrate with the world, while other provinces would integrate with each other. This scenario was named The Gorbachev Files (2006) and later adjusted to The Emperor's Clothes scenario. It is the scenario in which China is a respected international partner, participating harmoniously in the WTO, IMF and WB, as well as in bilateral international relations. However, domestically, the Communist Party and central government are not able to establish economic and political stability. Reforms needed to solve environmental issues, inequality and social security are not being implemented, and there is a growing discomfort in coastal areas about financing the less developed parts of the country.

Another example of scenario building in the 2000s on China is the report published by the World Economic Forum (2006). It built the scenarios based on two core questions:

- Can China implement internal reforms to further strengthen its development?
- How will China's relationship with the rest of the world be?

Based on these questions, three scenarios were developed for the publication: *China and the World in 2025*. The internal side of the scenarios relates to the ability of the authorities to implement needed decisions even if it is against the vested interest. It also connects to the choices regarding market forces and openness, and the way to maintain social stability. A factor on the external side, a factor that is prominently visible again today, is the reaction of China on external decisions such as increasing protectionism from the west. The different paths for China up to 2025 are represented in Fig. 19.1. The internal aspect (horizontal axis) is about the question if there is the willingness to undertake deeper reforms. The international (vertical) axis is about the relationship

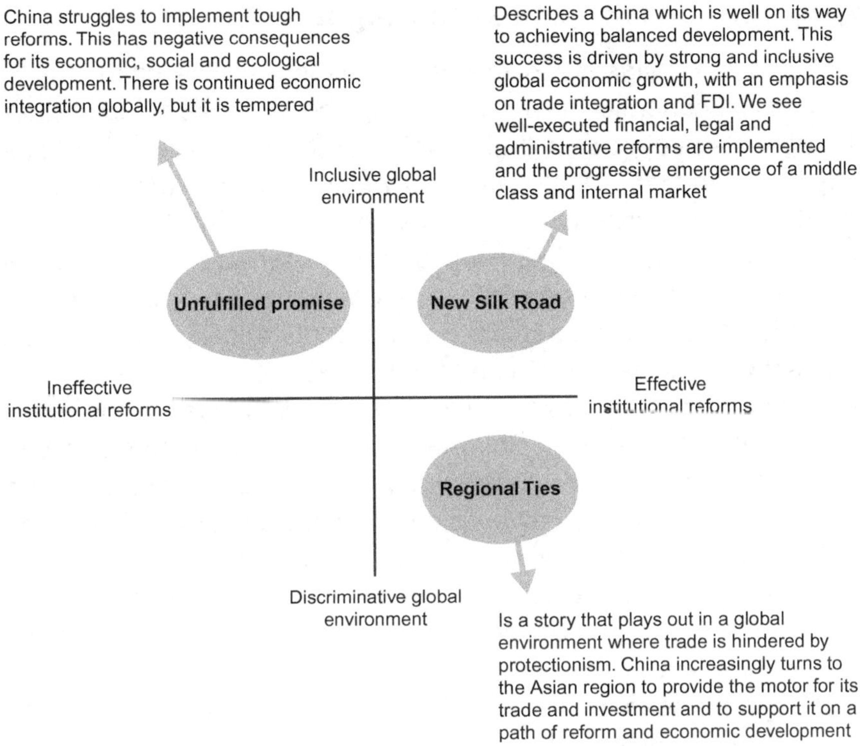

Figure 19.1 China scenarios by the World Economic Forum, 2006

Source: *World Economic Forum (2006)*

between China and the world: more collaborative or increasing protectionism (which will lead to a strong reaction from China's authorities). The general characteristics of the three scenarios are given in the figure above.

In the conclusion of its report, the project team of the World Economic Forum indicated that the scenarios are not scenarios that come true as they stand, but that they can help the reader better understand what could happen: "it gives the boundaries of the plausible"; without taking wild cards (or black swans) into consideration such as a possible Taiwan conflict, social tensions in Hong Kong, natural catastrophes or bank failures.

Nyenrode scenario and assessing future risks

At Nyenrode Business University, we elaborated the scenarios of the World Economic Forum by asking the Chinese middle class (through a survey) about their opinion of the two axes. We established a fixed panel that consisted of the Chinese middle class, situated in four large cities over the period 2010–2015. The first perspective is whether China will demonstrate a continuation of its harmonious domestic economic development or be confronted with domestic chaos, politically as well as economically. The second perspective is whether China will be extroversively driven with emphasis on being a responsible international player in the many multilateral platforms, or if China will choose a much more introversive strategy, looking for confrontation instead of cooperation. We executed the annual survey over a period of six years, but we summarised the outcomes into an average which can be seen in Fig. 19.2. An outcome of minus 1 means internal chaos and inward driven, while the maximum score of 1 means internal harmony and outward oriented.

As can be seen in Fig. 19.2, the Nyenrode panelists are unanimous in their view that China will continue to be open economically and politically in the future. Furthermore, the view regarding the domestic situation is that China will move towards harmony rather than chaos. Our panellist's view was that China is so much integrated in world economics and politics that an outwardly oriented policy and being a responsible player in the multilateral trading

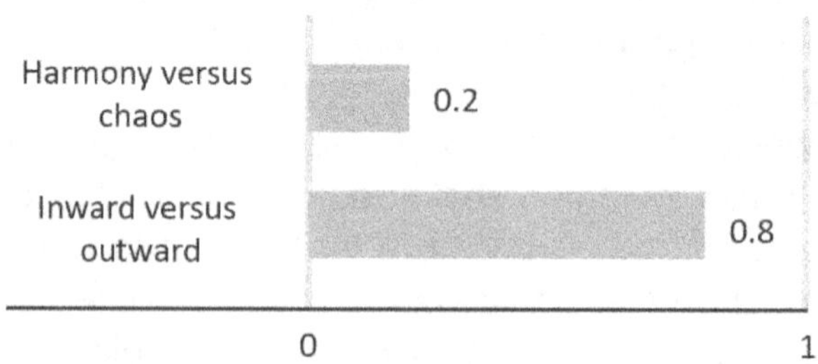

Figure 19.2 Perspectives on the longer-term future

Source: *Ebbers & Zhang (2010–2015)*

system makes sense, is even necessary and, consequently, will continue.

Between 2012 and 2015, we had several round table meetings at Nyenrode Business University to assess China's future risks that were mentioned in several scenarios. Based on the meetings, we developed a risk assessment and divided the risks into three types:

- Internal versus external risk: Internal risk factors connect to the domestic economy. One may think about the risk of a real-estate bubble, the debt problem or the ageing of the population. The external risk factors relate to China's links to the globalised world. An example is protectionism that may hurt China's economy due to its dependency on foreign markets.
- Short- and long-term risk: Long-term risks are challenges in the longer term such as demographic issues and inequality. Short-term risks are related to the next two or three years, for example, the changeover of leadership and the possibility of overinvestments and economic bubbles.
- Low and high risk: Low risk generates some tensions and government measures are needed but the possibility of a strong negative effect on the society is relatively low. High risk refers to a potentially dangerous situation with many spillover effects that may hurt a large part of the economy and society.

The outcome of the round table meetings is summarised in Fig. 19.3. Obviously, the overview shows the basic picture. The real world is much more complex, including many interdependencies between these risk factors. For example, the debt problem may accelerate if the external environment becomes more negative. Or, the ageing problem can easily be transferred towards social cohesion.

External risks involve the increasing tensions in the global governance structure, in particular the IMF and the WTO. The rule-based system is under attack due to regional initiatives and the absence of concrete results of the Doha Round. Another external risk is the rise of protectionism. Exports may also be hurt if important markets such as Europe are slowing down (for example, as a consequence of the Brexit).

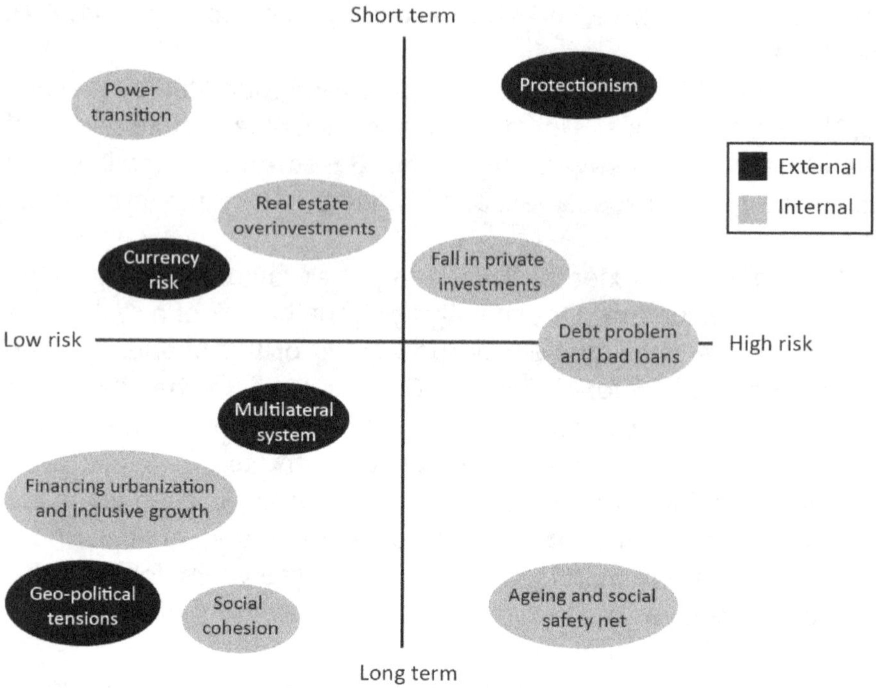

Figure 19.3 Main type of risks in the short and longer term
Source: *Minutes Nyenrode round table meetings (2015)*

Short-term risks involve the next two or three years. One risk is the 19th Congress of the CP in October 2017 that will show the new generation of leaders after President Xi steps down. There are rumours that Xi Jinping would stay in power, despite his two periods of five years. As can be seen in the figure, we labelled this leadership handover as a low risk.[1] The outcome of our round table discussions was that in the longer term, the social cohesion (including inequality in all facets) together with ageing are the key risk factors.

[1]The extension of Xi leadership was approved by the party and government in 2017

A high risk factor is the growing debt problem associated with increasing bank credits and subsidising SOEs. This debt problem which is now mostly in the corporate sector and local governments is a millstone around the neck of the central government. The problem will be even more prominent if the government accelerates its social spending to finance the ageing population, the urbanisation wave and when it increases its social spending on migrant workers. Banks may be in a danger zone due to the increasing bad loans towards the SOEs. The government already reacted by the debt-for-equity-swap plan, restructuring of SOEs and selling some of the SOE assets, but the danger of high debt was still real in 2015 according to the specialists participating in the round tables. And this risk has not been reduced in 2017.

Also in the previous years, we saw scenarios about China's future. One of the latest attempt is the research done by Vanguard (2017). These scenarios are built upon the short- and longer-term economic future. Vanguard (2017) uses two axes to develop four scenarios. The first axis is the short-term macroeconomic policy, resulting in a hard or soft landing. The second axis relates to the longer-term structural reforms being implemented effectively or not. The four scenarios are given in Fig. 19.4.

The scenario-dimensions are interesting because it shows how critical it is for the authorities in China to maintain a subtle balance between the short-term macroeconomic policy (that focus on the demand in the economy) and the longer-term goal to rebalance the economy and implement structural reforms. If the government is stimulating the economy for too long, it may reduce the incentive for reforms which is bad for longer-term development. At the same time, if rebalancing is the only aim, the government is not able (or willing) to stimulate the economy and a hard landing is the result. However, this hard landing may serve as a starting point for longer-term healthy development. These are difficult choices.

Besides scenarios that focus on economics, we also see several scenarios on China that have been focused on the political system. As stated before, in all these political scenarios, the starting point is that China's political structure is unlikely to develop

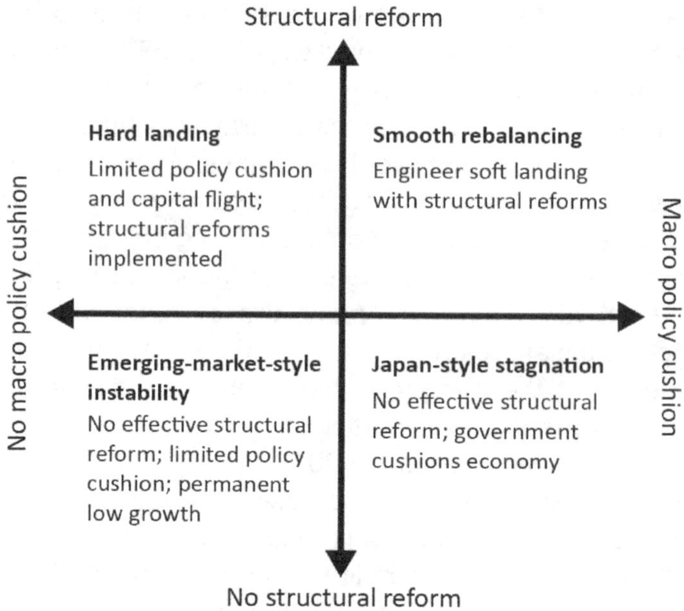

Figure 19.4 China scenarios developed by Vanguard Consultancy
Source: *Vanguard Consultancy (2017)*

along a direct, linear trajectory and therefore,they only indicate the borders of future political landscapes. An example of political scenarios appeared in an essay by Cheng Li (2007). He elaborates on three possible political scenarios for the year 2020.

- The emergence of a democratic China: A wealthier and better-educated middle class, implementing the inclusive growth strategy and a more robust civil society, leading to greater cultural and political pluralism.
- Prolonged chaos: Economic inequality, uncontrolled corruption among the elite, health crises, and environmental degradation trigger intense socio-political and economic crises that undermine the stability of the Communist Party and government.
- A resilient, authoritarian China: Problems among the world's democratic countries make democracy less appealing to the Chinese

people. At the same time, a strong government is necessary to implement the needed reforms and stabilise economic growth. Both factors will further enhance the ruling power of the party.

The first scenario is the Emergence of a Democratic China. Two essential factors contribute to the move towards democracy. Firstly, urbanisation, the middle class and the information revolution. The new urban middle class has access to a large amount of information. Even today, despite efforts by the Chinese government to ban certain information, the Chinese people are, to a certain extent, able to access an enormous amount of information. Also, many non-governmental organisations are active in China and their information reaches many parts of the population. Secondly, the dynamics in the political system itself will shift to more democracy. One should not underestimate the changes that happened in the political system between 1978 and today. Obviously, this is not about diversity of the political structure, but it relates to the trend of incorporating many checks and balances in the (collective) leadership. These checks and balances must create a balance between the two main (informal) groups within the party: the populist and elitist.

The second scenario is the Prolonged Chaos. The changes needed in the political system in this scenario are not enough to guide the economic development. Wrong political choices regarding income inequality, environmental issues and insufficient social spending on healthcare and pensions will intensify socio-political and economic crises and lead to prolonged political chaos. The third scenario, A Resilient, Authoritarian China, is optimistic about the changes inside the political system in such a way that the party together with the government can rule the society, based on its credibility. Indeed, we can see adaptability of the Chinese leadership. China's authoritarian system is not stagnant; it is constantly adjusting and this makes the system more sustainable.

Essentially, the political scenarios refer to the question of how much party and government we will see in the Chinese society. Finding the balance between the visible hand of the bureaucracy and the invisible hand of the market, is extremely difficult. Another balance is associated with the role of the government. Over a longer term, a sustainable party-government bureaucracy must be more predictable, transparent, participatory and inclusive. Otherwise, it will lose its ideological legitimacy. But it is also clear that a strong government (in terms of policy and execution) is needed. It is not possible to solve the environmental damage, income inequality and the welfare burden of an unequal and ageing society with (only) market forces. Li Keqiang stressed the role of the government (again) in his opening speech to the NPC on 6 March 2015. He started his talk stating that pollution is a "blight on people's quality of life and a trouble that weights on their hearts". And he continued with "we need a government that is able to build an effective environmental regime" (Xinhua). It is evident that economic decision-making has been centralised after 2013 when Xi Jinping started his presidency. And, we may even see a further acceleration of this centralisation process in the near future. For example, it is to be expected that the party will be more visible in economic policy and fighting corruption, while the central government will take the lead in the urbanisation process. Also, the government will have a more centralised say in environmental issues and certainly will centralise the building up of a nationwide pension system. One may interpret this centralisation as part of a process towards more government and less market. But you could also argue that this centralisation means rolling back decentralisation where it had unintended outcomes.

19.3 China's future

There are several articles and publications (from western as well as Chinese experts) that are pessimistic about China's rise and its impact on international relations. For example, in 2013, there was an article on the Xinhua website about the rise of China and the six wars China is "sure to fight in the next 50 years". The main driver behind these wars, according to some Chinese groups, is that China is not unified yet and the goal should be full unification. The usual suspects are the unification of Taiwan, taking sovereignty of the Spratly islands, the reconquest of (southern) Tibet, and the fight for the Diaoyu

(Senkaku) and Ryukyo islands. The above issues are well known, but there are also two hidden issues: the unification of outer Mongolia and taking back of regions lost to Russia (claims that are based on the Qing Dynasty). After reading the previous chapters, you know we have a different view on this. We can be quite optimistic about China's development (short and long term) and about the impact China has on the global economy and politics. The analysis below is therefore, a summary of what we discussed before, combining what we see today, what has been seen in history and what we can expect based on the level of integration China needs in the future.

The starting point in the discussion about the future globalised world and China's role in it is to define which global megatrends will continue in the next few decades.

(1) *Globalisation will continue*

In many publications, it is concluded that we reached the globalisation ceiling. Giving away discretional policy is becoming more difficult due to public opinion about democratic deficits. In many cases, the public opinion (as well as policymakers) do not see the advantages of a full connected world. The newest developments in 2016–2017 make this clear. Think about the more protectionist approach in the US under the new president and the Brexit. Also, the problems in the WTO-Doha Round generate a feeling that globalisation is on its return. We do not agree with this view, and it will be explained later in this chapter. In essence, we have our doubts and reservation about hyper-globalisation (a borderless world), but globalisation can go hand in hand with efficient government intervention and under specific circumstances, protectionist behaviour. Within this context, accelerating global integration is possible.

(2) *Governments have less discretionary power*

Governments are losing autonomy in the globalised world. Government policy will be more constrained because of the need to listen and follow public opinion (driven by the middle class and information revolution). At the same time, government policy and autonomy is being more and more constrained by international commitments and treaties. Autonomy will also be attacked by the market. Countries that are integrated in the world economy are not fully free to execute their own nation-driven policy. They must take into consideration the impact its policies will have on the market. Of course, there is need and freedom to act as a sovereign government if government, but the freedom to handle is certainly constrained.

(3) *Asymmetry will stay*

Economic power will shift to emerging markets, mostly in the Asian region. We are moving towards the Asian (emerging market) century. Although the growth in emerging markets may reduce differences between countries, there remains asymmetry in relationships between nation states. This asymmetry in international relations will stay and will continue to impact the multilateral governance structure.

(4) *More political power for China (and other emerging markets)*

The changing world also have consequences on its leadership. Economic dominance can be transformed into political supremacy (and will have its impact on soft power). It is clear that China will be dominant in economic sense. The question, however, is if this will also be translated into a more visible and powerful China in international relations. Looking at China's role in the WTO, its discomfort with the IMF voting power and the One Belt One Road initiative, it looks like China's role and visibility in both the multilateral and bilateral relations are increasing and may increase further in the future. The same can be said with respect to countries such as Brazil, Indonesia and South Africa. Although these new economic powers have some key factors of western democracy, they are also distinctive, sometimes combined with authoritarian modes of rule (Russia, Ukraine and Singapore). This shift in balance of power is permanent; the weakened bargaining position of the west is the new norm.

(5) *Technological shift*

The future role of China also relates to its technological process. Until recently, the perception was that Chinese products and Chinese companies associates with low quality and that it would take some time to change this. Rigid hierarchies within organisations, an educational system that is still focused on repetitive learning rather than debate, and high turnover rates among management makes innovation a challenge in many Chinese companies. In general, changes in the educational system are needed to enhance critical thinking and innovative thinking.

Certainly, the educational system makes out-of-the-box thinking difficult. This is one of the reasons to change the annual college admissions test, the *gaokao*. Before 2014, the emphasis was on English grammar and learning the tricks to pass the *gaokao* (and international tests such as TOEFL or IELTS). The results were high scores in English, but students continued to struggle to communicate in English. Now we see less attention on English. This is not so much a sign of lower importance of English, but it signals a proactive move to change the way English is taught and learnt.

Because China's growth relied mainly on imported technologies, Chinese firms own a tiny fraction of the intellectual property rights of their core technologies. But this is changing. The west is underestimating China, just as it did Japan. Western companies and policy makers woke up in the 1980s to realise that Japan was now making some of the world's highest quality products. Soon, the west will wake up to realise that China is making some of the world's most innovative products. First impressions of this can be seen today. While Switzerland, Sweden, the Netherlands, the US and the UK lead the 2017 rankings in the Global Innovation Index, released by the World Intellectual Property Organisation (WIPO, 2017), Chinese companies are starting to disrupt global competition. Their method is cost-innovation, i.e. the strategy of using Chinese cost advantage in radically new ways to offer more for less. Cost innovation has the following three faces:

- Companies are starting to offer high(er) technology at low cost.
- Companies are presenting customers an almost unmatched choice of products in what used to be considered standardised,

mass-market segments. This strategy results in large variety of products at low cost.
- Companies are using their low cost to offer speciality products at very low prices, turning them into volume business.

China has made indigenous innovation, one of the core elements of its attempt to accelerate the structural shift up the industrial value chain. One of the key measures for this was the obligation to establish a joint venture in China if the western company operates in the high-tech sector. The advantage from the Chinese viewpoint is clear. In the joint venture, the foreign partner will bring in technology and technological knowledge, and this technological development is, therefore, happening in the Chinese partner as well, thus creating higher productivity in the company. Moreover, we may expect many positive spillover effects to other sectors and firms. This process of technology spillover is summarised in Fig. 19.5.

The strategy of using the joint venture construction to increase technological knowledge is not new. It was the cornerstone of opening up in the early 1980s. Looking back, one can say that JVs increased technological knowledge (although research shows mixed results). And even though in many sectors a joint venture is not needed anymore, the central government makes it quite difficult to conduct a high-tech business in China without some elements of technology sharing. To stimulate and accelerate structural transformation, a sort of indigenous innovation policy is understandable,

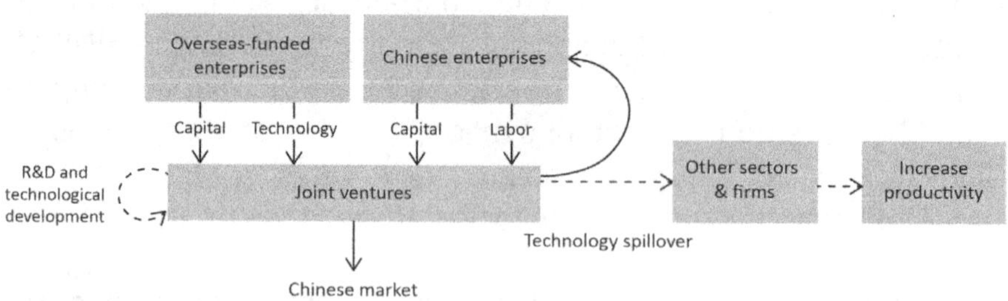

Figure 19.5 Technology spillovers through joint venture constructions

Source: Based on BBVA Research

but recently, this has been complemented by protectionist measures. There have been increasing calls for buy-local stipulations and (other) non-tariff barriers. These measures primarily take the shape of government "local content" mandates and through the preferential treatment given to products officially classified as "national indigenous innovation products".

Obviously, the government is playing a big role in this transformation, but the real innovators are the Chinese companies. It is interesting to quote some elements of the conclusion from Yip and McKern (2016). They observe the impressive transformation that is taking place: "Western CEOs have every reason to pay close attention to what Chinese corporates like Huawei, Haier and Lenovo are doing". The key point is that "Chinese companies are now taking market share from developed economy companies based on innovation and not just low cost. Many Chinese companies, other than Huawei, Haier or Lenovo, have created innovative products, processes and business models. Alibaba, Baidu, Tencent, Mindray, Neusoft and Goodbaby are just some of the better-known examples." The change was not overnight. Innovation has been a key objective of China's five-year plans for at least 15 years. And enormous jumps are made. At the same time, innovation is still low when looking at Intellectual Property Rights (IPRs) and patents. That is why innovation is the top listed focus area in the current 13th plan for 2016–2020.

Looking at the number of patents, it becomes clear that we have to make a division between research on one hand and development on the other hand. We witnessed an enormous growth of domestic patents in China between 2013 and 2016. Although this growth is impressive, we stated earlier in the book that most of these patents can be labelled as small inventive steps rather than new technologies. The number of invention patents is substantially lower than the number of utility patents, which represents incremental adjustments.

In general, the basis for China's transformation from imitator to innovator is relatively thin. The explosion of patents is driven by a small group of companies and a few sectors. And due to the subsidies given to high-tech industries, many of these patents can be labelled as "garbage patents", patents only to achieve high-tech status (and associated government subsidies). China's rise which was based on demographics is changing towards development based on technology. At the same time the other more mature economies are not standing still. They are important innovators, and this will continue. The consequence is a balanced innovation-world in which China is important, but not leading.

19.4 China's perspective on globalisation and its institutions

Obviously, the focus is on China when discussing the future of globalisation and its multilateral institutions in this chapter. However, the attitude of the US is determining partly the future of the global order. If the US is reestablishing itself as a supporter of the global governance system, including cooperation, openness and discussions, this will make the system stronger. But if the US executes protectionist behaviour, it will certainly weaken globalisation and its institutions. The same can be said with respect to the European countries.

A rule-based system is necessary for China

A power transition may generate instability and uncertainty. The consensus view is that China will use its influence to reshape the rules and institutions of the international system to better serve its interest. The US as a declining state will start to see China more and more as a growing economic and security threat. The result of these two trends are tensions, distrust and conflict. This typical feature of a power transition could be seen in a dramatic way in Europe in the late 19th century. The rise of Germany stirred up tension as the UK was the ruling superpower. Germany was dissatisfied with its role internationally and the UK was not willing to give up its dominance, and World War I was the result. But not all power transitions generate war and chaos. The US took over the role of the UK in the first years of the 19th century in a very harmonious way.

And the rise of Japan between 1950 and 1990 did create some tensions and discomfort but, in essence, the shift of power was happening in a relatively harmonious way. There is a clear difference between the two cases: Japan was satisfied with the international system, while Germany was not.

So, the level of dissatisfaction about the global governance structure is an important determinant of the type of power transition. What we will argue below is that China wants to be integrated in the world order. At the same time, it also wants to reshape the rules to its own interest. However, it does not want to change the basic pillars of today's multilateral governance structure. The international order, including its rules, discussions and cooperation is in China's best interest; it needs prosperous and cooperative partners around the world. From the US point of view, a healthy Chinese economy is vital. Economic relations are so intense through global supply chains and investments that the current global order is extremely important for both players. Frictions are there, including cases to fight unfair competition, but it is remarkable that even in the deepest crisis after 2008, trade disputes were kept under control.

The international order, centred around the United Nations, WTO, IMF and World Bank, is under attack. This is logical when looking at the IMF-voting power, the asymmetrical power within the WTO and the Washington consensus as the paradigm behind the choices made by these organisations. Think about their view on capital liberalisation and openness, viewpoints that may contradict with the reality in many new emerging economies. But at the same time, the post-war international order is unique. For example, it absorbed many new members and most of them are satisfied with the system. The international governance structure and its organisations were quite adaptive to changes in the world. For example, the IMF was able to adjust and adapt to many structural developments that occurred in the previous 60 years. The African Independence movements in the 1960s and 1970s resulted in many new IMF members with their own (structural and financial) problems. By 1990, all of Africa's 50 plus countries were members of the IMF. The same holds for the independent countries in Central and Eastern Europe after the collapse of Communism and fall of the Berlin Wall in 1989, and the dissolution of the Soviet Union in 1991. The rise of multiple economic centres (Western Europe, Japan, Newly Industrialising Countries (NICs), and OPEC) in the 1970s and 1980s made currency flexibility necessary. As a result, the IMF changed the rules towards more flexibility in its exchange rate policy. The western order again managed the integration of a new wave of countries, including China from 2001 onwards (Boughton, 2004). Adaptation was also needed during the latest economic crisis in Europe. Until 2009, the focus was on solving crises in developing countries and the advanced economies being the main creditors. Before 2009, most of the Fund's lending went to low- and middle-income countries. But that changed dramatically. Since the world financial crisis and recession, Europe has become the recipient of the majority of IMF loans. Despite protests and distrust, looking back, the IMF as part of the Troika was able to manage the European debt problem.

However, further adjustments are needed. In terms of policy mix and advice, the IMF is seen by LDCs and countries in transition as a rich men club in which the rules are made by the west based on the Washington Consensus. According to a large group of countries, the IMF is an agent of the OECD, G7 or G1 instead of a multilateral body, because it stipulates an uniform prescription independent of cultural differences. In spite of the economic logics, this "One-size-fits-all" policy is, sometimes, in contradiction with reality. Conditions (structural adjustments), including fiscal and monetary policies, are sometimes politically impossible because of domestic opposition. Think about the IMF condition to privatise state assets. There are circumstances that this privatisation is just not possible and in many cases not helpful. Another example is the issue of capital convertibility. Many economists made it clear that this capital convertibility is not always in the best interest of economies in transition, but the IMF has moved only very slowly on the issue of capital account liberalisation. Only after the Asian crisis of 1997 did it change its policy on this. Further changes are needed, such as the voting power issue. The process of adjustment has been slow.

The US and Europe still dominate the IMF (and WB). As we saw in Chapter 18, each international institution has its own challenges. The United Nations must deal with its UN Security Council transformation. The G20 may substitute for the G7 or G8. Also the WTO has its challenges. For example, one cannot explain why the western countries are demanding developing countries and economies in transition to open up more, while they still protect their own agricultural sector. If this is not solved, there could come a situation in which bilateral talks and regional trading agreements will substitute the process in the WTO trading rounds.

But despite the critical points and the need to reform certain elements in the system, the multilateral order can be characterised as non-discriminating, open and based on rules that helped rising countries in their development process. Another characteristic of the international order, as it is today, is its coalition-based character. Of course, there is asymmetrical power in the system, but, in essence, it is an order based on discussions and talks, and it has high levels of cooperation and shared authority over the global system. Both the rising powers and declining powers have the same interest, which is a stable rule-based system.

China is not a system challenger

There is dissatisfaction about the WTO and other institutions, but if they were not there we would be busy in developing them. This is also the viewpoint of Chinese officials. China needs the system, and changes are to be made within the system. Although the media mostly refers to the China–US clash in international trade and FDI relations, China does not face the US; it faces a western-centred system that is open, integrated and rules based with wide political acceptance.

China's policymakers and public see the advantages of being a WTO member and that opening up has been made possible by international institutions such as the WTO. I still remember the media attention at the 15-year anniversary of WTO membership in 2016. It was time to celebrate membership, and it was stressed that

China's development has been accelerated through WTO membership. Despite the trade tensions and the cases handled by the dispute settlement body, China is mostly following WTO rules. An interesting case was related to rare earths. China produces around 90% of global rare earths and has (with 25% of the global reserve) effectively control over supply. China imposed strict quotas in 2010 based on the motivation of reducing the environmental impact of their extraction. Based on the WTO decision that this quota system was against WTO rules, in 2015, China ended its quota system to restrict exports of rare earths. At the end of the day they followed the WTO decision.

There are other examples, and all of them make it clear that China is increasingly working within, rather than outside of the western order. Although some trade tensions happened in the previous years, this is logical with such an intensive trade relationship. China's attitude towards international governance can be seen as risk avoiding, and it is only a moderate reformer rather than system challenger. While it actively pursues its own interest, it sees a stable rule-based order as necessary. The above discussion is about the trading regime, but also with respect to investments; China needs global rules. China's outbound investment has been growing, and this will continue during the next decade(s). It means that a rule-based governance structure is needed. A final argument why we do not see China fighting against a western-centred governance structure relates to ideology.

The ideological battle between China and the US is less intensive than many experts are indicating. China has embraced a market economy and despite the many differences on subjects such as human rights, ideology is not a key obstacle for strategic cooperation between China and the US. Furthermore, the economies are extremely intertwined. Recent setbacks in the relationship are normal because both sides still do not have experience in the new type of relationship between a rising power and the existing one. People may emphasise the distrust between the US and China but essentially, trust is not a precondition for cooperation, even though it is helpful. Cooperation can be purely based on shared interest rather than trust and shared values. At the end of the day, China's growing role in the multilateral system will not change the system fundamentally.

19.5 The future of globalisation and the role of China

The consensus view on globalisation and the global governance structure that guided globalisation in the previous 65 years is that it helped worldwide economic development and that opening up to the global economy is creating economic benefits. Defenders of globalisation have always noted that the richest countries tend to be those most open to trade and investment, driven by the free-market ideology and protected by multilateral institutions. This being correct, we might modify this view; today, as well when looking at the future. Firstly, although globalisation created many benefits, it may be that most of the benefits are being realised today and that further globalisation steps are not helping so much. For example, we already questioned the short-term capital liberalisation, earlier in the book. Secondly, it looks like the countries that did not fully follow the road of globalisation but have adopted parts selectively, have benefited the most. Countries such as China are integrated in the world economy but did not follow the WTO and IMF prescriptions; it is protecting specific industries, there is government support and no capital liberalisation. The irony is that the countries that experienced the greatest growth during the peak of the "Washington Consensus" were Japan, China, South Korea and India, which never embraced this policy mix completely. For years, they had nurtured, protected and subsidised key industries before subjecting them to foreign competition. They had partly controlled the allocation of capital and the international capital flows. And they deliberately manipulated their currency and maintained formal and informal barriers to imports.

Many countries are integrated in the global economy but, at the same time, they switch easily between the market and the government.

Most open countries are also the ones with the biggest governments and, in many cases, the widest social safety nets. The reasons for that is obvious; globalisation, by its very nature, is disruptive. Disruptive events are destabilising and creating two cohorts: winners and losers. Any society, but particularly democratic and fast-changing societies, will tolerate such disruption only if there is confidence that the process is fair and broadly beneficial. This is why governments are needed and why markets and government should be seen as complements. The role of the government therefore is essential to counteract the negative impact of full globalisation, or hyperglobalisation; the term used by Rodrik (2011).

Based on the argument made by Rodrik, we finish the discussion about the future of globalisation with the notion that the combination of full-scale globalisation, political democracy and nation-state sovereignty is not possible. At most, you can have two out of three.

- If we want democracy and hyperglobalisation, decisions must be made and enforced at the global level. You cannot give autonomy to countries for setting their own policies. Consequently, domestic elections are not needed. Essentially, you don't need the nation state in this case. All relevant decisions must be reached within the global platform(s).
- Having both hyperglobalisation and nation-state sovereignty on domestic issues excludes democracy. The government must listen to the global markets (even if the rules are against the choice of its citizens). Setting rules that only fits hyper globalisation result in intensive opposition, but only the global market is leading in political choices.
- Combining political democracy and country sovereignty excludes hyper globalisation. If the national government (eager to listen to to its citizens) is implementing higher minimum wages and higher taxations to pay for a social safety net, it automatically result in capital leaving the country. This should be stopped and capital controls are needed, hence in opposition with hyper globalisation.

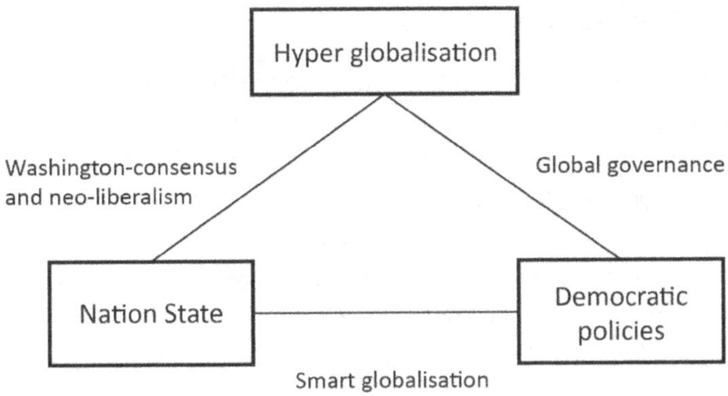

Figure 19.6 The trilemma of world economy

Note: We slightly adjusted the terms, but the trilemma is based on Rodrik
Source: Based on Rodrik (2011)

Figure 19.6 makes it clear that, in the real world, there is a fundamental incompatibility between hyper globalisation on one hand and democracy and national sovereignty on the other. We can combine any two of the three, but never have all three simultaneously. Consequently, we have three possible policy choices: Washington Consensus, global governance and smart globalisation.

Washington Consensus

In this world, the country (and its rules and regulations) is only responsive to the needs of the international economy; domestic objectives are of second importance. Hyper globalisation does not allow nation states to differentiate from the global rule. Government policy is only to serve the market, trade and capital. Every government intervention, being public provision of social insurance, income redistribution or labour protection, will increase costs of (international) firms and its competitiveness. In this world, companies are footloose. The threat of leaving the country constraints national policy autonomy. The result is a small government, deregulation, privatisation and flexible labour contracts. At its most extreme, we see a race-to-the-bottom, resulting in the *de facto* disappearance of nation states as independent sovereign entities.

Global governance

This world is based on multilateral rules which are strong enough, including the power to enforce them. And they are based on democratic forces; citizens can vote on these rules. Democracy is, in this case, not towards the national government, but relates to international organisations. We see global labour standards, convergence of taxation rules, global healthcare and environmental rules. You can label this global governance as global federalism. Of course, nation states will not disappear but national sovereignty will become much lower.

Smart globalisation

Finally, we can downgrade international economic integration. Within this limited version of globalisation, government intervention and industry policy are possible and rules can be fine-tuned towards specific characteristics within countries. This is in line with the situation between 1944 and the early 1990s. The trade regime of the early post-war years (Bretton Woods system) allowed government interventions that were inconsistent with the paradigm of free trade. It permitted democratic states to respond to the demands of the citizens, as long as there was a structural move towards liberalisation and non-discrimination. In essence, it means a lighter version of globalisation, i.e. smart globalisation.

Discomfort with hyper globalisation

The borderless world, the flat world and hyper globalisation are scary words for many people. The momentum in favour of globalisation faded away. In the previous decade, more and more people in societies feel uncomfortable by the fast-changing world and globalisation is associated with this uncertainty. This uneasiness is shown in Fig. 19.7. On the vertical axis the rate of change is indicated, while the time frame is given on the horizontal axis.

Figure 19.7 shows two upward sloping curves. The steepest curve relates to the speed of change due to economic and social globalisation, spurred by technological progress.

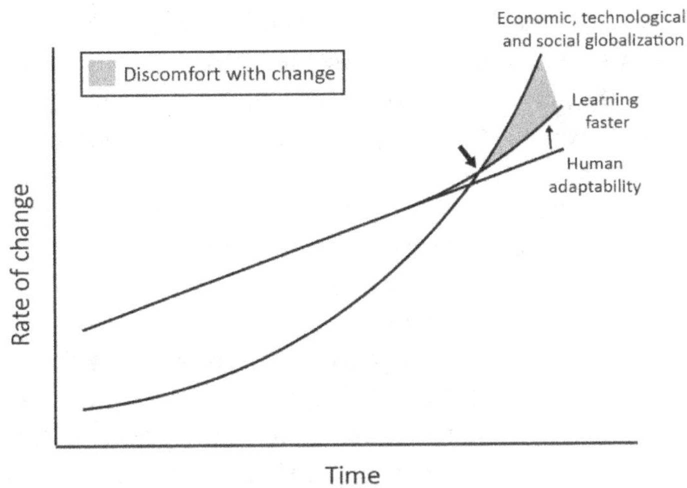

Figure 19.7 Discomfort with hyper globalisation
Source: Adjusted from Friedman (2016)

The pace of change has not only quickened, but is now happening at a global scale including in emerging markets and LDCs. In the year 500 AD, a person could fall asleep and if he woke up in the year 1100 AD, the world in which he lived did not look dramatically different as before his sleep; he would still understand the world and after some adjustment, feel comfortable in his new world. In particular, in the more remote regions disconnected from the economic centres, this would be the case. However, after the Industrial Revolution and, especially, from the start of the 20th century, the speed of change started to accelerate, and the curve in Fig. 19.7 thus becomes steeper. In the previous few decades, the slope of the curve became extremely steep with endlessness connectivity. The consequence is a world that is changing very fast. If a person fell asleep in 1970 and wakes up today, he would not recognise the world in which he lives anymore and is often unable to cope with it.

The second line in Fig. 19.7 is human adaptability. The curve is flat in the beginning. For example, by reading the book of Howard Zinn (2015), it becomes clear how long it took before people accepted the view that slavery was bad and that races are equal.

By following the time-line in the drawing above, we see a steeper curve; people become more flexible, educated, and faster in accepting changes. For example, we adapted relatively smoothly to the mobile revolution. People also adjusted relatively fast to social changes such as the viewpoint about the relationship between employee and employer. So, the human race is adaptable, and we see an acceleration of this adaptability in the previous 30–40 years, thanks to more knowledge and experiences with change; we are learning faster.

As long as the human adaptability curve is above the speed of change in the real world, there is no big uneasiness in the society, but as soon as the lines are crossed, we see a period of discomfort and this is happening today. In this period, people feel disoriented. We cannot adapt to the world as fast as it is changing. We feel out of control and globalisation is an important driver behind this sentiment. We could try to increase our adaptability through education, travel and cultural exchanges but the point is that the human adaptation line will stay relatively flat.

The choice

The global governance world of Fig. 19.6 is not to be expected. The discontent about multilateral institutions is too high in many countries, and the world is too diverse to have this global governance model. The IMF has some image problems and the same holds for the WTO. We are still unable to finish the Doha Round of trade negotiations. Furthermore, bilateral financial flows are substituting for IMF and WB finance. The reality is that most countries are unwilling to give up their sovereignty, their distinctive institutions and their freedom to manage their economies in their own best interests. This holds for China, India and the countries of the EU. It also holds for the US, in particular after President Trump took over. The worst thing we could do right now is to push it any further. In most emerging markets and LDCs, plenty of work still needs to be done to manage the economic integration that has already developed and to ensure that the benefits become more widely shared.

For them, taking the next step in the globalisation drive is not the priority in the next decade.

Also, the Washington Consensus world is not to be expected. It should be noted that Williamson (1999) did not intend the term to imply policies like capital account liberalisation, supply-side economics or a minimal government. This was implemented later by numerous economists. But we still use the term here because, essentially, it is driven by neoliberal views on how the economy operates. This more market and less government paradigm was leading in the 1980s and 1990s, but is under attack after the global crisis in the early 2000s, and its legitimacy has been further constrained by what happened after the financial and economic crisis in 2008.

It means that only one world is left over; a world in which hyper globalisation is being transformed into smart globalisation. This is logical: the nation state is still the core concept in the future and the achievement of democracy will not be given away easily. This lighter version of globalisation means nation-based fiscal and monetary policies, and restrictions on trade and capital, if needed, in such a way that it does not discriminate among trading partners. Furthermore, only temporary protection may be used. It is the smart combination of national policy and globalised rules. The term "smart" essentially refers to flexibility. There must be some flexibility left over for the national policymakers and citizens. This is the world in which China and other emerging markets feel comfortable. And it is the world in which the western order will survive. As stated earlier, we must accept the notion that discussions inside the WTO is not anymore about (only) trade, it is about global rules and therefore, national legislation. Hence, the need to finetune global rules to local circumstances.

This choice of smart globalisation also fit in the view that there is not one way to prosperity. Countries are different in economic structure and cultural dimensions and consequently have the right to implement specific, country-based social arrangements, regulations and institutions. This also counts for non-democratic countries, although discussions are needed on human rights. It is logical that China will make other choices regarding the institutional architecture and democracy in the future than what was done in the west. It looks also very unlikely (looking at its history) that it will replicate western forms of democracy. We will see a more hybrid development with mixed systems. This not only relate to China but to many emerging markets and LDCs. We also see it in developed countries, such as Singapore and Japan.

Final words

In the previous decades, China did not choose for extreme market forces or overwhelming government interference as coordination mechanism. According to the Chinese, smart market and smart government are needed. This means opening-up AND protectionism, market AND government, economy AND environment, high-tech AND commodities, and increasing rules AND reducing unnecessary regulation at the same time, precisely what was elaborated on in the introduction of this book. This ambivalence nature of China will also be seen in the future; with respect to the domestic reform agenda, as well as China's choices regarding globalisation and integration.

Rebalancing the society and finding the optimum integration in the world economic and political systems are the two fundamental topics for the next decade. In 1992, China accelerated its economic reforms towards "a socialist market economy", a system that combined broad state control with market-based allocations of resources. In a 2014 speech, President Xi Jinping described Chinese socialism as willing to incorporate some tenets of capitalism. He spoke of using both the invisible hand of markets and the "visible hand" of state control. He described China's system of market socialism as work in progress (Xi Jinping, 2015). The work is certainly not done yet and important imbalances must be solved. As we explained before, the global system will move from hyper- to smart globalisation; a context in which China feels comfortable. An open, rule-based and transparent global governance structure is in the interest of China, but at the same time, domestic policy autonomy is essential. This include Chinese features such as gradualism, flexibility and prioritising domestic (economic) objectives.

In the Preface and throughout the book, I made clear that the information came mostly from English articles and books, combined with 100-plus company visits and numerous interviews, lectures and discussions on and in China. The reference list does not include Chinese sources. Certainly this creates a problem when so much on China is related to nuances, emotions, feelings and therefore, interpretations. This may be a problem, but I checked my arguments, data and conclusions with Chinese colleagues, students, alumni, managers and politicians. Hopefully, the check and balances were robust enough and the book is seen as a neutral and eclectic piece of work. And, despite all contradictions, interpretation issues, complexities and data reliability issues, is seen as a successful approach of unravelling modern China.

References

Acemoglu, D., Autor, D., Dorn, D., Hanson, G. H. & Price, B. (2016). Import competition and the great US employment sag of the 2000s. *Journal of Labour Economics*, 34(S1), S141–S198.

Aglietta, M. & Bai, G. (2016). China's 13th five-year plan. In: *Pursuit of a Moderately Prosperous Society*, No. 2016–12. CEPII Research Center.

Ahuja, M. A. & Nabar, M. M. (2012). Investment-led growth in China: Global spillovers. *International Monetary Fund*, No. 12–267.

Aizenman, J. & Ito, H. (2011). The 'impossible trinity', the international monetary framework, and the Pacific Rim. Forthcoming In: Kaur and N. Singh (eds.), *Handbook of the Economics of the Pacific Rim*.

Alimi, R. S. (2013). Keynes' Absolute Income Hypothesis and Kuznets Paradox.

Anderson, J. (2007). Is China export-led? *UBS Investment Research Asian Focus*, September 27.

ANZ. (2014). Tapping the Impending Consumption Boom in China, *Special Report on China Consumption*, May 21.

Asian Development Bank. (2003). People's Republic of China: The Development of Private Enterprise.

Atradius, A. (2017). *Country Report China 2017*. January 31.

Atsmon, Y., Magni, M., Li, L. & Liao, W. (2012). Meet the 2020 Chinese consumer. *McKinsey Consumer & Shopper Insights*, March, pp. 1–41.

Aziz, M. J. (2006). Rebalancing China's economy: What does growth theory tell us? *IMF Working Paper*, No. 06–291.

Bai, L. (2014). Economic legacies of the Cultural Revolution. *Job Market Paper*.

Baldwin, R., Ito, T. & Sato, H. (2014). The smile curve: Evolving sources of value added in manufacturing. *Joint Research Program Series, IDE-JETRO.*

Barnett, S., Alla M. & Malhar N. (2012). China must boost household consumption even further to make its growth more inclusive. *Finance & Development*, September.

Bartel, J. & Huang, Y. (2000). Dealing with the bad loans of the Chinese Banks. *APEC Study Centre Discussion Paper Series*, Columbia University.

Barton, D. (2013). The rise of the middle class in China and its impact on the Chinese and world economies. *China–United States Exchange Foundation, US–China Economic Relations in the Next Ten Years: Towards Deeper Engagement and Mutual Benefit*, 1–12.

Barton, D., Chen, Y. & Jin, A. (2013). Mapping China's middle class. *McKinsey Quarterly*, 3, 54–60.

BBVA. (2008–2016). *China Economic Outlook.*

BBVA. (2016). *China Economic Watch*. April 21.

BBVA. (2016). *China Economic Watch*. February 25.

BBVA. (2017). *China Economic Outlook*. Quarter 1 & 2.

Beebe, A., Hew, C., Yueqi, F. & Dailun, S. (2006). *Going Global: Prospects and Challenges for Chinese Companies on the World Stage*. New York: IBM Institute for Business Value-School of Management at Fudan University.

Bertoldi, M. & Melander, A. (2015). China's reforms: Time to walk the talk. *ECFIN-Economic Brief*. Issue 41. April.

Bichler, J. & Schmidkonz, C. (2012). The Chinese indigenous innovation system and its impact on foreign enterprises. *Munich Business School Working Paper*, No. 2012–01.

Bongiorni, S. (2007). *A Year Without "Made in China": One Family's True Life Adventure in the Global Economy*. John Wiley & Sons.

Bonin, J. P. & Huang, Y. (2001). Dealing with the bad loans of the Chinese banks. *Journal of Asian Economics*, 12(2), 197–214.

Bonin, J. P. & Huang, Y. (2002). Foreign entry into Chinese banking: Does WTO membership threaten domestic banks? *World Economy*, 25(8), 1077–1093.

Borders, M. A. (1989). *The Transnational Solution*. Boston, MA: Harvard Business School Press.

Boston Consulting Group. (2006). *The New Global Challengers*. May.

Boston Consulting Group. (2016). *Global Leaders, Challengers, and Champions*. June.

Boughton, M. J. M. (2004). The IMF and the force of history: Ten events and ten ideas that have shaped the institution. *International Monetary Fund Working Paper*, No. 04–75.

Brandt, L., Hsieh, C. & Zhu, X. (2005). China's structural transformation. *Mimeographed*, Berkeley: University of California.

Brandt, L., Ma, D. & Rawski, T. G. (2014). From divergence to convergence: Reevaluating the history behind China's economic boom. *Journal of Economic Literature*, 52(1), 45–123.

Buckley, P. J. & Casson, M. (2016). *The Future of the Multinational Enterprise*. Springer.

Buckley, P. J., Clegg, L. J., Cross, A. R., Liu, X., Voss, H. & Zheng, P. (2007). The determinants of Chinese outward foreign direct investment. *Journal of International Business Studies*, 38(4), 499–518.

Business Confidence Survey. (2012–2017) by European Chamber in China in cooperation with Roland Berger.

Business Week. (2004). *The China Price*. December 6.

Cai, P. (2017). Understanding China's belt and road initiative.

Cai, F. & Du, Y. (eds.). (2009). *The China Population and Labor Yearbook, The Approaching Lewis Turning Point and Its Policy Implications*, Vol. 1. Brill.

Campbell, A. (2015). Defining China's "Civilization State". Where is it heading'. *University of Sydney China Studies Centre Policy Paper*, Sydney.

Casanova, C., Huang, B. & Xia, L. (2015). SOE reforms could unlock the potential of unproductive sectors and boost growth. *BBVA — China Economic Watch*. November 27.

Casanova, C., Huang, B. & Xia, L. (2016). The quest for a structured approach to deleveraging and SOE reform. *BBVA — China Economic Watch*. April 19.

Chamon, M., Liu, K. & Prasad, E. (2013). Income uncertainty and household savings in China. *Journal of Development Economics*, 105, 164–177.

Chan, K. W. (2012). Migration and development in China: Trends, geography and current issues. *Migration and Development*, 1(2), 187–205.

Chan, K. W. (2013). China, internal migration. *The Encyclopedia of Global Human Migration*, 2, 980–995.

Chan, K. W. & Buckingham, W. (2008). Is China abolishing the hukou system? *The China Quarterly*, 195, 582–606.

Chen, Y. (1999). Lost in revolution and reform: The socioeconomic pains of China's red guards generation, 1966–1996. *Journal of Contemporary China*, 8(21), 219–239.

Chenery, H. B. & Moises, S. (1975). *Patterns of Development: 1950–1970.* New York: Oxford University Press for the World Bank.

Cheremukhin, A., Golosov, M., Guriev, S. & Tsyvinski, A. (2015). The economy of People's Republic of China from 1953. *National Bureau of Economic Research Working Papers*, No. 21397.

Cheshmehzangi, A. (2016). China's New-Type Urbanisation Plan (NUP) and the foreseeing challenges for decarbonization of cities: A review. *Energy Procedia*, 104, 146–152.

Chiu, B. & Lewis, M. (2006). *Reforming China's State-owned Enterprises and Banks.* Edward Elgar Publishing.

Chu, C. N. (1991). The Asian mind game: Unlocking the hidden agenda of the business culture — A Westerner's survival manual.

Chua, A. (2011). *Battle Hymn of the Tiger Mother.* Penguin Putnam Inc.

Cieślik, E. (2013). China's shadow banking sector: Recent developments and systemic risk assessment. *Oeconomia*, 13(2), 25–36.

Clark, G. (2005). *The British Industrial Revolution, 1760–1860.* University of California Davis.

Clayton, G. (2003). Economics: Principles & Practices, Chapter 18. In: *Comparative Economic Systems*, Glencoe/McGraw-Hill.

Coase, R. H. (1937). The nature of the firm. *Economica*, 4(16), 387–405.

Cornell University, INSEAD, and WIPO. (2017). The Global Innovation Index 2017: Innovation Feeding the World, Ithaca, Fontainebleau, and Geneva.

Credit Suisse. (2015). *Global Wealth Report 2015.* October 2016.

Dabla-Norris, M. E., Kochhar, M. K., Suphaphiphat, M. N., Ricka, M. F. & Tsounta, E. (2015). Causes and Consequences of income inequality: A Global Perspective. *International Monetary Fund.*

DBS Group Research. (2016). *China: Root Causes and Remedies for Overcapacity.* April 6.

Deng, K. G. (2003). Development and its deadlock in Imperial China, 221 BC–1840 AD. *Economic Development and Cultural Change*, 51(2), 479–522.

Devillers, C. & Schütte, P. (2006). *The Future of China; Four Scenarios The Hague.* September.

Dezan Shira & Associates. (2015). The cost of doing business in ASEAN compared with China. *Asia Briefing.* Issue 16. July–August.

Dimaculangan, P. (2014). The Needham question and the great divergence: Why China fell behind the West and lost the race In: *Ushering the World into the industrial revolution and modernity. Comparative Civilizations Review*, (71), 106.

Dreger, C., Wang, T. & Zhang, Y. (2013). Understanding Chinese consumption: The impact of hukou. *IZA Discussion Paper*, No. 7819. December.

Dreger, C., Wang, T. & Zhang, Y. (2015). Understanding Chinese consumption: The impact of hukou. *Development and Change*, 46(6), 1331–1344.

Ding, L. (2002). Rural–Urban income disparity: Impact of growth, allocative efficiency, and local growth welfare. *China Economic Review*, 13(4), 419–429.

Ding, C. & Zhao, X. (2011). Urbanization in Japan, South Korea, and China: Policy and reality. In: *The Oxford Handbook of Urban Economics and Planning*.

Dong Tao & Weishen Deng (2013). China: Shadow banking — Road to heightened risks. *Credit Suisse Economics Research Paper*. February 22.

Dörrenbächer, C. & Geppert, M., The Integration-Responsiveness framework: A review and application of the concept. *Working Paper*, No. 1. 03/2016. Berlin Institute for International Business Studies (BIIBS).

Dorrucci, E., Pula, G. & Santabárbara, D. (2013). China's economic growth and rebalancing. *ECB Occasional Paper*, No. 142.

Doz, Y. L. & Prahalad, C. K. (1981). Headquarters influence and strategic control in MNCs. *Sloan Management Review (pre-1986)*, 23(1), 15.

Dumbaugh, K. & Martin, M. F. (2009). Understanding China's political system.

Dunning, J. H. (1973). The determinants of international production. *Oxford Economic Papers*, 25(3), 289–336.

Dunning, J. H. (1980). Toward an eclectic theory of international production: Some empirical tests. *Journal of International Business Studies*, 11(1), 9–31.

Dunning, J. H. (1988). The eclectic paradigm of international production: A restatement and some possible extensions. *Journal of International Business Studies*, 19(1), 1–31.

Dunning, J. H. (1998). Location and the multinational enterprise: A neglected factor? *Journal of International Business Studies*, 29(1), 45–66.

Dunning, J. H. & Lundan, S. M. (2008). *Multinational Enterprises and the Global Economy*. Edward Elgar Publishing.

Dunning, J. H. & Narula, R. (1996). The investment development path revisited. *Foreign Direct Investment and Governments: Catalysts for Economic Restructuring*, 1–41.

Ebbers, H. A. (2016). *Internationale bedrijfskunde en globalisering*. Groningen: Noordhoff Uitgevers.

Ebbers, H. A. & Cheung, L. (2010). *Success and Obstacles of Doing Business in China*. Nyenrode-Cap Gemini Research.

Ebbers, H. A. & Zhang, J. (2010–2015). *China Structural Development Monitor*. The Netherlands: Nyenrode University.

Eckart, J. (2016). 8 things you need to know about China's economy. *World Economic Forum*, 23.

Economist Intelligence Unit's (2017). *Democracy Index 2017*.

Elliott, D. J. & Qiao, Y. (2015). *Reforming Shadow Banking in China. Brookings*. May 19.

Elliott, D. J. & Yan, K. (2013). *The Chinese Financial System: An Introduction and Overview*. Brookings Institution.

Elliott, D. J., Kroeber, A. & Qiao, Y. (2015). Shadow banking in China: A primer. *Economic Studies at Brookings*, 3, 1–7.

Elvin, M. (1973). *The Pattern of the Chinese Past: A Social and Economic Interpretation*. Stanford University Press.

Engardio, P. (ed.) (2007). *Chindia; How China and India are Revolutionizing Global Business*. New York: McGraw-Hill.

Esherick, J., Pickowicz, P. & Walder, A. G. (2006). *The Chinese Cultural Revolution as History*.

Eurasia Group. (2011). *China's Great Rebalancing Act*. New York, August.

European Union Chamber of Commerce in China. (2016). *Overcapacity in China: An Impediment to the Party's Reform Agenda*.

EY. (2014). China: Planning for an urban future.

Faber, M. (2009). *The Gloom Boom and Doom Report*.

Fang, C. & Yang, L. (2013). *The End of China's Demographic Dividend: The Perspective of Potential GDP Growth*.

Felipe, J., Abdon, A. & Kumar, U. (2012). Tracking the middle-income trap: What is it, who is in it, and why? *Asian Development Bank Working Paper Series*, No. 306.

Fernandez-Corugedo, E. (2004). *Consumption Theory*. Centre for Central Banking Studies, Bank of England.

Fontagné, L., Gourdon, J. & Jean, S. (2013). Transatlantic trade: Whither partnership, which economic consequences? *CEPII*, *Policy Brief*, 1, September, 12 p.

Frankopan, P. (2015). *The Silk Roads: A New History of the World*. London: Bloomsbury Publishing.

Freedom House (2017). Populists and Autocrats: The Dual Threat to Global Democracy. Freedom in the World Report 2017.

Friedman, T. L. (2005). *The World is Flat: A Brief History of the Twenty-first Century*. Macmillan.

Friedman, T. L. (2017). *Thank You for Being Late: An Optimist's Guide to Thriving in the Age of Accelerations* (Version 2.0, With a New Afterword). Picador/Farrar Straus and Giroux.

Fukumoto, T. & Muto, I. (2012). Rebalancing China's economic growth: Some insights from Japan's experience. *China & World Economy*, 20(1), 62–82. First published in: Fukumoto, T & Muto, I (2011). Rebalancing China's economic growth: Some insights from Japan's experience, No. 11–E5, July. Bank of Japan.

Gan, L. (2013). *Income Inequality and Consumption in China*. Texas A&M University, USA and Southwestern University of Finance and Economics, Chengdu.

Garnaut, R. & Song, L. (2013). *China: A New Model for Growth and Development*. ANU Press.

German Chamber of Commerce in China. (2017). *Labor Market and Salary Report 2015/16.*

Gerschenkron, A. (1952). Economic backwardness in historical perspective. In The Progress of Underdeveloped Areas, ed. B. F. Hoselitz (University of Chicago Press)

Gerschenkron, A. (1962): Economic Backwardness in Historical Perspective. A Book of Essays. Cambridge: Harvard University Press.

Gill, I. S., Kharas, H. J. & Bhattasali, D. (2007). *An East Asian Renaissance: Ideas for Economic Growth*. World Bank Publications.

Goldman Sachs (2003), Dreaming With BRICs: The Path to 2050, Global Economics Paper No: 99, October 1

Goldman Sachs (2013). Global Investment Research. February 26.

Goldman Sachs (2016). Walled In: *China's Great Dilemma*. January.

Grant, R.M. (2005). Contemporary Strategy Analysis. Malden: Blackwell Publishing

Gunnarsson, C. & Ljungberg, J. (2008). China in the global economy: Failure and success. *Thammasat Economic Journal*, 26(4).

Guo, K. & N'Diaye, M. P. (2009). Is China's Export-oriented Growth Sustainable? *International Monetary Fund*, No. 9–172.

Guo, K. & N'Diaye, P. M. B. (2010). Determinants of China's Private Consumption: An International Perspective. *International Monetary Fund*, No. 10–93.

Guo, R. (2012). *Understanding the Chinese Economies*. Academic Press.

Guo, R., Yang, K., Zhao, R. & Hwang, E. G. (2005). How to reform a centrally planned economy: The case of China.

Ha, J. (2006). Understanding household consumption in China: The role of urbanization and other factors. In: *Hong Kong Institute for Monetary Research Conference, 'Urbanisation and the Mainland Economy'*, Vol. 25, Hong Kong.

Harbaugh, R. (2004). China's high savings rates. *The Rise of China Revisited: Perception and Reality*, 18, 12.

Harney, A. (2008). *The China Price: The True Cost of Chinese Competitive Advantage*. Penguin.

Hart, S. & Christensen, C. (2002). The great leap: Driving innovation from the base of the pyramid. *Sloan Management Review*, 44(1): 51–56.

Hawksworth, J., Audino, H. & Clarry, R. (2017). The long view: How will the global economic order change by 2050. Retrieved, 15, 2017.

HBSC (2013). *Macro China Economics: China: Faster Reform, Slower Growth*, June 19.

He, F. (2007). China's economic reform: Success, problems and challenges. *Canberra: East Asian Bureau of Economic Research (EABER) Working Paper Series*, No. 19.

He, W., Goodkind, D. & Kowal, P. (2016). An aging world: 2015. *International Population Reports*, P95/16-1.

Headey, D., Kanbur, R. & Zhang, X. (2008). *China's Growth Strategies*. Routledge.

Hexter, J. & Woetzel, J. (2007). *Operation China: From Strategy to Execution*. Harvard Business Press.

Hofstede, G. (1980). Culture's Consequences: International Differences in Work-Related Values. Beverly Hills CA: Sage

Hofstede, G. (2011). Dimensionalizing cultures: The Hofstede model in context. *Online Readings in Psychology and Culture*, 2(1), 8.

Hollensen, S. (2010). *Internationale Marketing*. Pearson Education.

Holmberg, S. & Rothstein, B. (2014). Correlates of the Level of Democracy. *Working Paper Series*, No. 2014:18, The Quality of Government Institute QoG, University of Gothenburg.

Holz, C. A. (2013). *The Quality of China's GDP Statistics*. Hong Kong University of Science & Technology. November 27.

Holz, C. A. (2014). The quality of China's GDP statistics. *China Economic Review*, 30, 309–338.

Huang, B. & Le, X. (2016). China — The new five-year plan falls short of surprises on the positive side. — *Economic Analysis, BBVA Research*. March.

Huang, Y. (2010). *Reinterpreting China's Success through the New Economic Geography*. Carnegie Endowment for International Peace.

Huang, Y. & Wang, B. (2010). Rebalancing China's economic structure 14. *China: The Next Twenty Years of Reform and Development*, 293.

Hui, X. X. (2009). The Chinese housing reform and the following new urban question. In: *Paper for the 4th International Conference of the International Forum on Urbanism*.

Hutton, W. (2008). *The Writing on the Wall: China and the West in the 21st Century*. UK: Hachette.

Hymer, S. H. (1976). *International Operations of National Firms*. Cambridge: MIT Press.

Iacob, N. K. (2013). The reliability of China's economic data: An analysis of national output. *US–China Economic and Security Review Commission Staff Research Project*. January 28.

Ikenberry, G. J. (2008). The rise of China and the future of the West — Can the liberal system survive. *Foreign Affairs*, 87(1), 23–37.

ING (2015). Speed bumps for Chinese economy. *Business Opportunity Report*. October.

International Monetary Fund — database.

International Labour Organization (2011). A review of global fiscal stimulus. *Joint Discussion Paper Series*, No. 5, EU, and International Institute For Labour Studies. November 16.

Jacques, M. (2009). *When China Rules the World: The Rise of the Middle Kingdom and the End of the Western World*. UK: Penguin.

Jacques, M. (2012). *When China Rules the World: The Rise of the Middle Kingdom and the End of the Western World*. UK: Penguin.

Jacques, M. (2013). How China will change the global political map? *Transatlantic Academy Paper Series*. March 2013.

Jefferson, G. H. & Su, J. (2006). Privatization and restructuring in China: Evidence from shareholding ownership, 1995–2001. *Journal of Comparative Economics*, 34(1), 146–166.

Jefferson, G. H., Jian, S., Yuan, J. & Xinhua, Y. (2003). The impact of ownership reform in Chinese industry, 1995–2001.

Jiang, Y., Lin, T. & Zhuang, J. (2008). Environmental Kuznets Curves in the People's Republic of China: Turning points and regional differences.

Jiang, Y., Lin, T. & Zhuang, J. (2008). Environmental Kuznets Curves in the People's Republic of China: Turning points and regional differences, Asian Development Bank. *Economics Working Paper Series*, No. 141.

Johanson, J. & Vahlne, J. E. (1977). The internationalization process of the firm — A model of knowledge development and increasing foreign market commitments. *Journal of International Business Studies*, 8(1), 23–32.

Johanson, J. & Vahlne, J. E. (1990). The mechanism of internationalisation. *International Marketing Review*, 7(4).

Johansson, Å., Guillemette, Y., Murtin, F., Turner, D., Nicoletti, G., de la Maisonneuve, C. & Spinelli, F. (2012). *Looking to 2060: Long-term Global Growth Prospects: A Going for Growth Report* (No. 3). OECD Publishing.

Jonathan, W. (2009). If you have got it, spend it: Unleashing the Chinese consumer. *McKinsey Global Institute, agosto. La Cina e gli altri.*

Jong, de P., Greeven, M. J. & Ebbers, H. (2017). Getting the numbers right on China's actual overseas investment: The case of the Netherlands. *Journal of Current Chinese Affairs*, 46(1), 187–209.

Kanamori, T. (2004). Fiscal reform in the People's Republic of China — Current issues and future agenda. *ADB Institute Research Paper*, No. 55.

Kang, J. S. & Liao, W. (2016). *Chinese Imports: What's Behind the Slowdown? International Monetary Fund Working Paper*, No. 16–106.

Kang, Y., Shi, L. & Brown, E. D. (2008). *Chinese Corporate Governance: History and institutional Framework*, Vol. 618. Rand Corporation.

Kaufman, A. A. (2010). The "Century of Humiliation," then and now: Chinese perceptions of the international order. *Pacific Focus*, 25(1), 1–33.

Keynes, J. M. (1936). *General Theory of Employment, Interest and Money*. New York: Harcourt, Brace and Co.

Keynes, J. M. (1937). The general theory of employment. *The Quarterly Journal of Economics*, 51(2), 209–223.

Kharas, H. (2017). The unprecedented expansion of the global middle class: An update.

Kindleberger, C. P. (1969). American business abroad. *The International Executive*, 11(2), 11–12.

KKR-Insights. (2012). Global Macro Trends. China's Rebalancing Act, Volume 2.7. July.

Koch-Weser, I. N. (2013). The reliability of China's economic data: An analysis of national output. *US–China Economic and Security Review Commission Staff Research Project*, 4.

KOF Swiss Economic Institute. (2017). *KOF Globalization Index 2017*. Zurich.

Koleski, K. (2017). The 13th five-year plan. *US–China Economic and Security Review*.

Kornai, J. (1980). *Economics of Shortage*. Amsterdam: North Holland.

Kornai, J. (1992). *The Socialist System: The Political Economy of Communism*. Princeton: Princeton University Press.

KPMG. (2012). *The Future for MNCs in China.*

KPMG. (2016). *China Outlook 2016.* March 2.

KPMG. (2016). *The 13th Five-Year Plan — China's Transformation and Integration with the World Economy.* October.

KPMG. (2016). *Mainland China Banking Survey 2016.* September.

Knickerbocker, F. T. (1973). Oligopolistic reaction and multinational enterprise. *The International Executive*, 15(2), 7–9.

Kroeber, A. R. (2016). *China's Economy: What Everyone Needs to Know.* Oxford: Oxford University Press.

Kuznets, S. (1955). Economic growth and income inequality. *The American Economic Review*, 45(1), 1–28.

Kui, N. B. & Thorud, A. (2006). *China's "Triangle of Woes" and Its Impact on Financial Stability in Economic Growth Centre.*

Kuijs, L. & Xu, G. (2008). China's fiscal policy — Moving to center stage. In: *Conference Paper for the Stanford Center for International Development Conference on Social Services, Regulation and Finance.*

Landes, D. S. (1998). *The Wealth and Poverty of Nations: Why Some Are So Rich and Some So Poor.* WWnorton & Company.

Lardy, N. R. (1998). *China's Unfinished Economic Revolution.* Washington: Brookings Institution Press.

Lardy, N. R. (2007). China: Rebalancing economic growth. *The China Balance Sheet in 2007 and Beyond*, 1–24.

Lardy, N. R. (2012). Sustaining China's economic growth after the global financial crisis. *Peterson Institute for International Economics.*

Lardy, N. R. (2014). *Markets Over Mao: The Rise of Private Business in China.* US: Columbia University Press.

Lardy, N. (2016). The changing role of the private sector in China. *Structural Change in China: Implications for Australia World*, 37.

Lardy, N. R. & Borst, N. (2013). A blueprint for rebalancing the Chinese economy. *Policy Brief* (13-02).

Lawrence, S. & Martin, M. F. (2013). Understanding China's political system. Congressional Research Service, *CRS Report for Congress.* March 20.

Lee, J. W. (2014). Will the Renminbi emerge as an international reserve currency? *The World Economy*, 37(1), 42–62.

Leer, V. D. Y. & Yau, J. (2016). China's new silk route: The long and winding road. *Rep. China's New Silk Route the Long and Winding Road.* PWC.

Leonard, M. (2008). What does China think? *Public Affairs.*

Leonard, M., Xinbo, W., Hofman, B., Rediker, D., Economy, E., Levi, M. & Ellis, E. (2016). Geo-economics with Chinese Characteristics: How

China's economic might is reshaping World politics. *World Economic Forum*.

Lewis, W. A. (1954). A model of dualistic economics. *American Economic Review*, 36(1), 46–51.

Lewis, W. A. (1954). *Economic Development with Unlimited Supplies of Labour*. The Manchester School, May 22, 139–192.

Li, C. (2016). The changing face of shadow banking in China. *Asia Focus*. December.

Li, C. (2007). China in the year 2020: Three political scenarios. *Asia Policy*, (4), 17–30.

Lim, J. & Cowling, A. (2016). China's demographic outlook. *RBA Bulletin*, June, 35–42.

Lin, J. Y. (1995). The Needham puzzle: Why the industrial revolution did not originate in China. *Economic Development and Cultural Change*, 43(2), 269–292.

Lin, J. Y. (2004). Lessons of China's transition from a planned economy to a market economy. *Leon Koźmiński Academy of Entrepreneurship and Management*, pp. 1–45.

Lin, J. Y., Tao, R. & Liu, M. (2003). *Decentralization, Deregulation and Economic Transition in China*. London School of Economics, Mimeo.

Lin, S. (2011). China's fiscal policy and fiscal sustainability, In: Ito, T. and F. Parulian (eds.), Assessment on the Impact of Stimulus, Fiscal Transparency and Fiscal Risk. *ERIA Research Project Report* 2010-01, pp. 77–116.

Lombard Odier Investment Managers (2016). *China's Misunderstood Debt Challenges.* October.

Lonner, W. J., Berry, J. W. & Hofstede, G. H. (1980). *Culture's Consequences: International Differences in Work-related Values.*

Lopez-Calva, L. F. & Ortiz-Juarez, E. (2014). A vulnerability approach to the definition of the middle class. *The Journal of Economic Inequality*, 12(1), 23–47.

Lorenz, M. O. (1905). Methods of measuring the concentration of wealth. *Publications of the American Statistical Association*, 9(70), 209–219.

Lu, Y. & Sun, T. (2013). Local Government financing platforms in China: A fortune or misfortune? *International Monetary Fund*, No. 13–243.

Luo, Y. & Tung, R. L. (2007). International expansion of emerging market enterprises: A springboard perspective. 38(4), 481–498.

Ma, G. & Yi, W. (2010). China's high saving rate: Myth and reality. *Economie internationale*, (2), 5–39.

Maddison, A. (1998). *Chinese Economic Performance in the Long Run.* Paris: OECD, Development Centre Studies.

Maddison, A. (2001). *The World Economy: A Millennial Perspective.* Paris: Organization for Economic Cooperation and Development, Development Studies Centre.

Maddison, A. (2003). *The World Economy: Historical Statistics*, Paris: OECD, Development Studies Centre.

Maggu, A. (2012). How should China transition to a consumption driven economy? *CRISIL*, 1.

Magni, M. & Poh, F. (2013). Winning the battle for China's new middle class. *McKinsey Quarterly*, 3, 61–69.

Mahbubani, K. (2008). *The New Asian Hemisphere: The Irresistible Shift of Global Power to the East.* New York: Public Affairs.

Maliszewski, W., Arslanalp, M. S., Caparusso, J., Garrido, J., Guo, M. S., Kang, J. S. & Liao, W. (2016). Resolving China's corporate debt problem. *International Monetary Fund Working Paper.* WP/16/203.

Malthus, T. R. (1798). An essay on the principle of population as it affects the future improvement of society, with remarks on the speculations of Mr. Goodwin, M.

Mathews, J. A. (2006). Dragon multinationals: New players in 21st century globalization. *Asia Pacific Journal of Management*, 23(1), 5–27.

McKinsey Global Institute. (2009). *Preparing for China's Urban Billion.* February.

McKinsey Global Institute. (2016). *China's Choice: Capturing the $5 Trillion Productivity Opportunity.* June.

McKinsey Insights China. (2012). Macroeconomic Model Update, April.

MIREA Asset Global Investments. (2015). *New China: Impact of the Chinese Consumer.* November.

Miesing, P. & Tang, M. (2018). Technology transfer institutions in China: A comparison of value chain and organizational structure perspectives. *World Scientific Book Chapters*, 43–60.

Modigliani, F. & Brumberg, R. (1954). Utility analysis and the consumption function: An interpretation of cross-section data. *Franco Modigliani*, 1, 388–436.

Modigliani, F. & Brumberg, R. (1980). Utility analysis and aggregate consumption functions: An attempt at integration In: A. Abel (ed.), *The Collected Papers of Franco Modigliani.*

Modigliani, F. & Cao, S. L. (2004). The Chinese saving puzzle and the life-cycle hypothesis. *Journal of Economic Literature*, 42(1), 145–170.

Morrison, W. M. (2013). China's economic rise: History, trends, challenges, and implications for the United States. Library of Congress, Congressional Research Service.

Morrison, W. M. (2015). China's economic rise: History, trends, challenges, and implications for the Unites States. *CRS Report.* Washington, DC: Congressional Research Services.

Morrison, W. M. (2017). China–U.S. Trade Issues. Congressional Research Service 7-5700. April 24.

Morrison, W. M. & Labonte, M. (2011). China's currency: An analysis of the economic issues. *Congressional Research Service*, 3.

Moyo, D. (2010). *Dead Aid: Why Aid is Not Working and How There is Another Way for Africa.* Farrar, Straus & Giroux Inc.

Mundell, R. A. (1963). Capital mobility and stabilization policy under fixed and flexible exchange rates. *Canadian Journal of Economics and Political Science/Revue canadienne de economiques et science politique*, 29(4), 475–485.

Muto, I. & Fukumoto, T. (2011). Rebalancing China's economic growth: Some insights from Japan's experience. *Bank of Japan Working Paper Series*, No. 11-E-5. July 2011.

Naisbitt, J. & Naisbitt, D. (2010). *China's Megatrends: The 8 Pillars of a New Society.* Harper Collins.

Naughton, B. J. (2006). *The Chinese Economy: Transitions and Growth.* MIT Press.

Navarro, P. (2006). The Economics of the "China Price". *China Perspectives*, 2006(68), 13–27.

Needham, J. (1969). *The Grand Titration. Science and Society in East and West.* London: George Allen & Unwin.

Needham, J. (2013). *The Grand Titration: Science and Society in East and West*, Vol. 21. Routledge.

Ng, B. K. & Thorud, A. (2006). *China's "Triangle of Woes" and Its Impact on Financial Stability*, No. 0605. Nanyang Technological University, School of Social Sciences, Economic Growth Centre.

Ning-ning, G. U. O. (2007). Causes and solutions of non-performing loan in Chinese commercial banks. *Chinese Business Review*, 6.

Nomura. China Economy. (2011). Global Economics and Strategy-department.

Nye, J. S. (2004). *Soft Power: The Means to Success in World Politics.* New York: Public Affairs.

Nye, J. S. (2011). *The Future of Power.* New York: Public Affairs.

Obstfeld, M., Shambaugh, J. C. & Taylor, A. M. (2005). The trilemma in history: Tradeoffs among exchange rates, monetary policies, and capital mobility. *Review of Economics and Statistics*, 87(3), 423–438.

Penrose, E. T. (2017). Foreign investment and the growth of the firm 1. *International Business*, pp. 33–48. Routledge.

Perlmutter, H. V. (1969). The tortuous evolution of the multinational corporation. *Columbia Journal of World Business*, 4, 9–18.

Plafker, T. (2008). *Doing Business in China: How to Profit in the World's Fastest Growing Market*. US: Time Warner Trade Publishing.

Plasschaert, S. (2011). *Is the Renminbi undervalued? The myths of China's trade surplus and global imbalances* (No. 02/2011). (http://www.ecipe.org/app/uploads/2014/12/WP201201.pdf ?)

Pop, I. I. (2016). *Strengths and Challenges of China's "One Belt, One Road" Initiative*. London: Centre for Geopolitics and Security in Realism Studies.

Porter, M. E. (1980). *Competitive Strategy: Techniques for Analyzing Industries and Competitors*, Vol. 267. New York: Free Press.

Porter, M. E. (1990). The competitive advantage of nations. *Competitive Intelligence Review*, 1(1), 14.

Porter, M. E. (1990). *Competitive Advantage of Nations*. New York: The Free Press.

Porter, M. E. (2011). *Competitive Advantage of Nations: Creating and Sustaining Superior Performance*, Vol. 2. Simon and Schuster.

Prahalad, C. K. & Doz, Y. L. (1987). *The Multinational Mission: Balancing Local Demands and Global Vision*. Simon and Schuster.

PWC. (2015). The World in 2050: Will the Shift in Global Economic Power Continue?

PWC. (2017). The World in 2050. The Long View: How Will the Global Economic Order Change by 2050. February.

Qian, Y. (1999). The institutional foundations of China's market transition. *Working Paper*, Stanford University.

Qian, Y. & Weingast, B. R. (1997). Federalism as a commitment to reserving market incentives. *Journal of Economic Perspectives*, 11(4), 83–92.

Ramo, J. C. (2004). *The Beijing Consensus: Notes on the New Physics of Chinese Power*, London: Foreign Policy Centre.

Rawski, T. G. (2002). *Recent Developments in China's Labor Market*. Report Prepared for the International Policy Group. Geneva: International Labor Office.

Reeves, M., Stalk, G. & Deimler, M. S. (2009). *Business Model Innovation: When the Game Gets Tough, Change the Game.* Boston: Boston Consulting Group.

Retailing, E. (2010). Emerging focus: Rising middle class in emerging markets. *Euromonitor Retailing* [consultado 6 Sep 2013].

Rodrik. D. (2006). Goodbye Washington Consensus, Hello Washington Confusion? A Review of the World Bank's Economic Growth in the 1990s: Learning from a Decade of Reform. *Journal of Economic Literature*, 44, 973–987. .

Rodrik, D. (2011). *The Globalization Paradox: Democracy and the Future of the World Economy.* WW Norton & Company.

Rodrik, D. (2011). *The Globalization Paradox: Why Global Markets, States, and Democracy Can't Coexist.* New York: Oxford University Press.

Roberts, I. & Fang, C. (2015). Potential growth and rebalancing in China. *RBA Bulletin*, 29–38.

Rugman, A. (1981). *Inside the Multinationals: The Economics of Internal Markets.* New York: Columbia University Press.

Rugman, A. M. & Li, J. (2007). Will China's multinationals succeed globally or regionally? *European Management Journal*, 25(5), 333–343.

Sachs, G. (2016*). Walled In: China's Great Dilemma.* Investment Strategy Group, January.

Sachs, J. D. & Woo, W. T. (2001). Understanding China's economic performance. *The Journal of Policy Reform*, 4(1), 1–50.

Sanborn, C. & Chonn, V. (2017). Chinese investment in Peru's mining industry: Blessing or Curse? *China and Sustainable Development in Latin America: The Social and Environmental Dimension*, 183.

Sauer, A. (2016). Humanitarian supply chain performance management: Development and evaluation of a comprehensive performance measurement framework based on the balanced scorecard, *Doctoral Dissertation.* German: Munich Business School.

Scott, R. E. (2011). The benefits of revaluation: Full revaluation of the Chinese yuan would increase US GDP and employment, reduce the federal budget deficit, and help workers in China and other Asian countries. *EPI Briefing Paper*, No. 318. Washington, DC: Economic Policy Institute.

Servan-Schreiber, J. J. (1968). The American challenge. *The International Executive*, 10(4), 13.

Shambaugh, D. L. (2013). *China Goes Global: The Partial Power*, Vol. 111. Oxford: Oxford University Press.

Shambaugh, D. (2016). Contemplating China's future. *The Washington Quarterly*, 39(3), 121–130.

Shen, C., Jin, J. & Zou, H. F. (2006). Fiscal decentralization in China: History, impacts, challenges and next steps. *World Bank Discussion Paper.*

Shen Qing (2014). *Xinhua Insight: The Enigma of China's GDP Statistics*, Xinhua, January 23.

Shenkar, O. (2006). *The Chinese Century: The Rising Chinese Economy and Its Impact on the Global Economy, the Balance of Power, and Your Job*. Pearson Education.

Sheng, A., Edelmann, C., Sheng, C. & Hu, J. (2015). Bringing light upon the shadow: A review of the Chinese shadow banking sector. *Oliver Wyman and Fung Global Institute*, 3.

Shih, S. (1996). *Me-too Is Not My Style: Challenge Difficulties, Break Through Bottlenecks, Create Values.* Taipei: The Acer Foundation.

Shuanglin, L. (2009). The rise and fall of China's government revenue. *EAI Working Paper*, No. 150

Smith, D. (2010). *The Dragon and the Elephant: China, India and the New World Order.* London: Profile Books.

Solow, Robert M. (1994). "Perspectives on Growth Theory," *Journal of Economic Perspectives*, 8(1): 45–54

Stern, D. (2004). The rise and fall of the environmental Kuznets Curve. *World Development*, 32(8), 1419–1439.

Stratford, K. & Cowling, A. (2016). Chinese household income, consumption and savings. *RBA Bulletin*, pp. 31–40. September.

Szamosszegi, A. & Kyle, C. (2011). An analysis of state-owned enterprises and state capitalism in China, Vol. 52, *Capital Trade, Incorporated for US-China Economic and Security Review Commission.*

Thomas, S. C. (2007). China's economic development from 1860 to the present: The roles of sovereignty and the global economy. In: Forum on Public Policy: A Journal of the Oxford Round Table. *Forum on Public Policy.*

Thompson, G. (1998) *Economic Dynamism in the Asia-Pacific: The Growth of Integration and Competitiveness.* Psychology Press

Tisdell, C. (2009). Economic reform and openness in China: China's development policies in the last 30 years. *Economic Analysis and Policy*, 39(2), 271–294.

Tyers, R. (2013). Looking inward for transformative growth in China. *Centre for Applied Macroeconomic Analysis Working Paper*, No. 48/2013.

UBS. (2007). Is China export-led? *Global Economics Research — Publication*. September 27.

United Nations Conference on Trade and Development (UNCTAD). (1992–2017). *World Investment Report*.

United Nations Conference on Trade and Development (UNCTAD). (2013). *World Investment Report*. New York: United Nations.

United Nations Conference on Trade and Development (UNCTAD). (2016). *Trade and Development Report 2016*.

United Nations Development Programme. (2016). National Human Development Report 2016. *Social Innovation for Inclusive Human Development*, August.

United Nations Department of Economic and Social Affairs, Population Division. (2015). *World Population Ageing 2015* (ST/ESA/SER.A/390).

United States Energy Information Administration (2015). *China International Analysis*. May 14.

Viñals, J. & Singh, A. (2011). People's Republic of China: Financial system stability assessment. *IMF Country Report*, No. 11/321.

Wang, D. (2010). *Can Social Security Boost Domestic Consumption in the People's Republic of China?*

Wang, X. S. (2015). *The Chinese Economy in Crisis: State Capacity and Tax Reform*. Routledge.

Wang, Z. & Ma, L. (2014). Fiscal decentralization in China: A literature review. *Annals of Economics & Finance*, 15(2).

Wang, Q., Wu, J. M. & Odenwalder, Z. B. (2017). *Navigating the Transition: China's Future at a Crossroads*. Vanguard Research. March.

Watts, J. S. (2010). *When a Billion Chinese Jump: How China Will Save Mankind — Or Destroy It*. Simon and Schuster.

Weisbrot, M. & Johnston, J. (2016). *Voting Share Reform at the IMF: Will it Make a Difference? Center for Economic and Policy Research (CEPR)*, No. 2016-09.

Wilson, D. & Purushothaman, R. (2003). Dreaming with BRICs: The path to 2050. *Global Economics Paper*, No. 99, 1.

Woetzel, J., Chen, Y., Manyika, J., Roth, E., Seong, J. & Lee, J. (2015). The China effect on global innovation. *McKinsey Quartalsbericht*.

World Bank. (2012). *China 2030: Building a Modern, Harmonious, and Creative Society*. World Bank Publications.

World Bank. (2016). *Live Long and Prosper: Aging in East Asia and Pacific*. World Bank Publications.

Williamson, J. (1990). What Washington means by policy reform. *Latin American Adjustment: How Much Has Happened*, 1, 90–120.

Williamson, J. (1999). What should the World Bank think about the Washington Consensus? Paper prepared as a background to the World Bank's World Development Report 2000. *Institute for International Economics Papers.*

Williamson, J. (2005). The strange history of the Washington Consensus. *Journal of Post Keynesian Economics*, 27(2, Winter, 2004–2005), 195–206.

Willianson, O. E. (1975). *Markets and Hierarchies: Analysis and Antitrust Implications*. New York.

Womack, B. (2014). China's future in a multimodal world order. *Pacific Affairs*, 87(2), June.

World Trade Organization. (2008). Understanding the WTO. *World Trade Organization*.

World Trade Organisation. (2016). *World Trade Statistical Review* 2016.

World Economic Forum. (2016). *Global Gender Gap Report 2016*.

World Bank and Development Research Center of the State Council. (2013). *China 2030 Building a modern, Harmonious, and Creative Society.*

World Economic Forum. (2006). *China and the World: Scenarios to 2025*. Geneva: Switzerland.

Xi, J. (2014). *The Governance of China*. Foreign Languages Press.

Xia, G. (2014). China as a "civilization-state": A historical and comparative interpretation. *Procedia-Social and Behavioral Sciences*, 140, 43–47.

Xing, Y. and Detert, N. How the iPhone widens the United States trade deficit with the People's Republic of China 2010. *ADBI Working Paper*, No. 257. Tokyo: Asian Development Bank Institute.

Xu, C. (2011). The fundamental institutions of China's reforms and development. *Journal of Economic Literature*, 49(4), 1076–1151.

Xu, C. (2015). China's political-economic institutions and development. *Cato Journal.* 35(3), 525–548.

Yan, Q. & Islam, S. (2011). Moving up the value chain: How to make the smiling curve smile*? Case Studies of ICT Firms from an Emerging Economy.*

Yang, D. T., Zhang, J. & Zhou, S. (2012). Why are saving rates so high in China? In *Capitalizing China*, pp. 249–278. University of Chicago Press.

Yanitsky, O. (1986). Urbanization in the USSR: Theory, tendencies and policy. *International Journal of Urban and Regional Research*, 10(2), 265–287.

Yao, Y. (2014). The Chinese Growth Miracle. *Handbook of Economic Growth*, Vol. 2, pp. 943–1031. Elsevier.

Ye, M., Meng, B. & Wei, S. J. (2015). Measuring smile curves in global value chains. *Discussion Paper*, No. 50, Institute of Developing Economies, August 27.

Ying, L., Jiaxu, Z., Dandan, J., Kungui, Z., Qiang, L. & Xuezhang, L. (2015). Estimating Lorenz curve of income in China by cubic spline interpolation. *Journal of Statistics and Mathematical Sciences.* 1(2). December.

Yip, G. S. & McKern, B. (2016). *China's Next Strategic Advantage: From Imitation to Innovation.* MIT Press.

Zeng, Y. & Hesketh, T. (2016). The effects of China's universal two-child policy. *The Lancet*, 388(10054), 1930–1938.

Zhang, K. H. (2006). The role of FDI in China's export performance. *Chinas as the World Factory.*

Zhang, M. L. (2016). *Rebalancing in China — Progress and Prospects. International Monetary Fund.*

Zhang, Y. (2016). Urbanization, inequality, and poverty in the People's Republic of China. *ADBI Working Paper Series*, No. 584. July 2016.

Zhang, J. & Ebbers, H. A. (2015). The effect of price, differentiation and tariff on export performance in an export-driven economy. *Journal of Northeast Asia Development*, 17(December), 36–50.

Zhang, J., Ebbers, H. & Mulder, R. (2012). Competitiveness of Chinese industries — A comparison with the EU. *Review of European Studies*, 4(1), 203.

Zhang, J., Ebbers, H. & van Witteloostuijn, A. (2013). Dynamics of the global competitiveness of Chinese industries. *Post-Communist Economies*, 25(4), 492–511.

Zhang, J., Zhou, C., Witteloostuijn, A. V. & Ebbers, H. (2013). What does the Chinese market need? An empirical study of the determinants of Chinese imports, 1996–2008. *Asia Pacific Business Review*, 19(3), 402–420.

Zhang, Q. & Crooks, R. (2012). *Toward an Environmentally Sustainable Future: Country Environmental Analysis of the People's Republic of China.* Asian Development Bank.

Zhang, X. & Chang, X. (2016). *The Logic of Economic Reform in China.* Berlin, Heidelberg: Springer.

Zheng, S. & Kahn, M. E. (2017). A new era of pollution progress in urban China? *Journal of Economic Perspectives*, 31(1), 71–92.

Zhu, X. (2012). Understanding China's growth: Past, present, and future. *Journal of Economic Perspectives*, 26(4), 103–124.

Zhu, A. & Cai, W. (2012). The Lewis turning point in China and its impacts on the world economy. *AUGUR Working Paper*, No. 1.

Zhuang, J. & Li, S. (2016). Understanding recent trends in income inequality in the People's Republic of China. *ADB Economics Working Paper Series*. No. 489. July.

Zinn, H. & Damon, M. (1998). *A People's History of the United States*. New Press.

Ziying, F. & Wan, G. (2016). The Fiscal Risk of Local Government Revenue in the People's Republic of China. *ADBI Working Paper Series*, No. 567. April.

Websites

http://english.mofcom.gov.cn/article/statistic/

https://www.ecb.europa.eu/home/html/index.en.html

http://www.xinhuanet.com/english/

http://www.xinhuanet.com/english/china/2016-03/17/c_135198880.htm

https://www.ceicdata.com/en

http://www.pbc.gov.cn/english/130437/index.html

http://en.people.cn/

http://www.china.org.cn/china/third_plenary_session/2014-01/15/content_31203056.htm

https://www.economist.com/the-economist-explains/2015/10/26/why-chinas-five-year-plans-are-so-important

https://www.economist.com/china/2015/10/22/command-performance

https://www.thecasecentre.org/main/

https://eia-international.org/tag/china

http://english.cntv.cn/20140123/102682.shtml

https://www.theglobaleconomy.com/China/Trade_balance/

https://www.strategyand.pwc.com/media/file/China_Consumer_Market_Strategies_2011.pdf

https://www.ing.nl/media/ING_EBZ_speed-bumps-for-chinese-economy_tcm162-91647.pdf

https://freedomhouse.org/sites/default/files/Freedom_in_the_World_2017_complete_book.pdf

http://www.roymorgan.com/findings/5593-anz-special-report-on-china-consumption-201405212338

https://www.bloomberg.com/news/articles/2013-11-12/china-is-preparing-to-fine-tune-its-one-child-policy

https://www.economist.com/briefing/2014/09/20/the-deepest-cuts

http://en.people.cn/90882/7629166.html

https://www.dbs.com.sg/iwov-resources/pdf/articles/China%20in%20Transition[lowres].pdf

http://en.ndrc.gov.cn/policyrelease/201612/P020161207645766966662.pdf

http://hdr.undp.org/sites/default/files/reports/2783/undp-ch-_nhdr_2016_en.pdf

https://assets.kpmg.com/content/dam/kpmg/pdf/2012/07/Future-for-MNC-in-China-201206.pdf

http://www.oecd.org/corporate/mne/statistics.htm

https://www.pwc.com.au/government/pwc-the-world-in-2050-full-report-feb-2017.pdf

https://www.miraeasset.com/upload/insights/thought-leadership/Mirae_Asset_New_China_Impact_of_the_Chinese_Consumer_Revisited_201710_Update.pdf

http://www.rroij.com/open-access/estimating-lorenz-curve-of-income-in-china-by-cubic-spline-interpolation-.php?aid=64664

https://www.economist.com/special-report/2014/04/19/ending-apartheid

https://www.ey.com/cn/.../ey-china-planning-for-an-urban-future

http://applied-energy.org/cue2016/index

http://www.chinadaily.com.cn/china/2015-09/17/content_21901190.htm

https://www.bbvaresearch.com/en/public-compuesta/china-economic-outlook-fourth-quarter-2017/

https://www.gloomboomdoom.com/

https://www.archives.gov/

Index

Abbott, 438
absolute income theory, 303
acquisitions, 346
Adidas, 374, 430
administrative decentralisation, 33, 68
administrative structure, 119
AF–KLM, 449
Africa, 461, 470
African Independence movements, 495
after-sales, 406
ageing, 232, 236, 237, 239, 242, 243, 302
agglomeration effects, 201, 203, 323
aggregate data, 17
agriculture, 16
agricultural prices, 179
agricultural sector, 98
Alibaba, 392, 405
Alipay, 392
Amazon, 432
Anta, 431
Apple, 413
appreciation, 278, 280
approval procedures, 258
approval process, 439
ASEAN, 323, 469
Asian crisis, 278, 496
Asian financial crisis, 69
Asian miracles, 464
Asian Tiger, 65, 136
assembly, 105, 339
assembly costs, 287
asset management companies, 267
asset ownership, 172
asymmetry, 490
austerity, 413
authoritarian countries, 471
authoritarian system, 487
autocratic leadership, 368
autonomy, 48, 151

bad debt, 266
bad loans, 91
Baidu, 390, 395, 397
banking sector, 252, 261, 263, 265, 268, 310
bargaining power, 443
Beijing Consensus, 462–464
Beijing Olympic Games, 371
Berlin Wall, 452

Big-Bang, 49
Big-Four, 268
Bilateral investment treaties, 342
binding target, 152, 155, 157, 204
bird flu, 411
black swans, 478
BMW, 419, 423
Boeing, 396
Bolsa Familia, 182
Boon-Edam, 409, 410, 442
borderless world, 489, 502
born globals, 203, 351
Boston Consultancy Group, 353
Boxer Uprising, 28
Bo Xilai, 126
B&Q, 395, 401
brand, 362, 425
Brazil, 241
Bretton Woods system, 502
Brexit, 134
BRIC countries, 466
British Empire, 25
budget deficit, 251
bureaucracy, 124, 366, 375, 389, 487
Bush, 453
business challenges, 383
business cycle, 60, 70
business model, 359, 380, 414
buying habits, 390
buy-local, 493
BYD, 356, 428

C919, 398
Canton system, 24, 26
capital account, 97
capital account convertibility, 283, 464
capital accumulation, 61, 63
capital controls, 285
capital convertibility, 289, 496
capital flows, 284
capital intensive, 272
capital-intensive growth, 81
capital market, 268
capital outflow, 345
capital stock, 64
capitalism, 147, 148
career development, 408
Carrefour, 412, 420, 422, 445
catching up, 31, 33, 65
Caterpillar, 411, 418, 428
CCTV, 440
central bank, 265
central planning, 32, 145
centralisation, 407
centralised decision-making, 424
century of humiliation, 24, 26, 29, 38, 253
cheap credits, 71, 301
ChemChina, 354, 355
Chenery Standard, 80
Chery, 401, 402
Chiang Kai-shek, 31
China Investment Corporation, 340, 349
China price, 209, 212, 448, 453
Chinese Communist Party, 30, 116
Chinese–Japanese war, 28
Chinese merchants, 24
Chinese model, 463
Chinese Revolution, 29
civilisation-state, 38
climate change, 472
Club of Rome, 87
CNOOC, 349
coal, 86, 89

coastal areas, 244
coastal provinces, 334
Coca Cola, 420, 434, 439
collateral, 255
collective leadership, 121, 487
Comau, 430
command economy, 40, 41, 51, 146
command system, 44
committee on foreign investment, 349
communes, 33, 53
Communism, 147, 148, 370
Communist era, 19
Communist Party, 77
Communist Party's Brief, 150
Communist Revolution, 20, 31
community hospitals, 421
comparative advantage, 43, 52, 202, 203, 210, 225
competences, 321
competition, 104, 105, 108, 202, 210, 211, 338, 389, 403
competitive advantage, 202, 326, 359
Confucian culture, 37, 38, 40, 129
Confucianism, 364, 365
Confucius, 39, 365
conglomerates, 62, 356
connectivity, 503
consumer-led growth, 155
consumer loyalty, 409
consumer spending, 298
consumer tastes, 424, 451
consumption, 70, 80, 102, 103, 223, 293
consumption-led growth, 315
consumption ratio, 294, 416
contagious effect, 80
Contractual JV, 399
corporate bonds, 287
corporate debt, 141
corporate savings, 296, 301
corporate tax, 338
corporate Vietnam, 403
corruption, 97, 124, 163, 164, 413, 486
Corruption Perception Index, 163
cost-innovation, 491
cost leadership, 355, 433
cost pressure, 422
counterfeit, 406
country-specific advantages, 326
credit card, 314, 392
credit expansion, 61
credit quotas, 268
crisis manager, 100
cross-contamination, 416
Cultural Revolution, 34, 35, 37, 44, 50, 123, 310
current account, 82, 83, 262, 277, 459
current-income hypothesis, 303
customised products, 419

dairy producers, 438
Dalai Lama, 412
Danone, 400
data-gathering, 4, 9
data quality, 17
debt accumulation, 80
debt burden, 89, 90
debt problem, 91, 112
decentralisation, 41, 122, 126, 128, 254
decentralisation process, 35
decisive role, 77
defaults, 261

deficit countries, 217
deflation, 69
democracy, 128–132, 135, 465, 479, 500, 506
demographic burden, 240
demographic dividend, 98, 239
demographic pyramid, 232, 235
demographic transition, 239
Deng Xiaoping, 31, 42, 55, 58, 72, 121, 159, 378, 479
Denmark, 380
dependency ratio, 97, 193, 239–242, 249
deposit rate, 84, 264, 272
depreciation, 278
deregulation, 47, 464, 501
diamond framework, 202
Diaoyu, 412
Didi Dache, 404
differentiation, 433, 434
digital strategy, 446
discretionary power, 195
Disney, 386, 396
Disneyland, 387
disposable income, 296, 311, 312
disruptive innovation, 361, 403
dissaving, 304
distortions, 62
diversification strategy, 356
Doha Round, 489
Do-It-Yoerself (DIY) concept, 388, 391
dollar, 278, 279
domestic demand, 259
domestic imbalance, 101
downstream activities, 228
dual exchange rate system, 277
dual strategy, 428
dual-track price system, 54, 123, 163
DVD pirates, 396
dynasties, 19

EachNet, 405
early entrance, 409
early-reform period, 45, 57
early reform process, 49
Ease of Doing Business, 364
East Asian development model, 46
East India Company, 25
easy credit, 100
eBay, 405, 407
Eclectic theory, 322
e-commerce, 7, 15, 446
economic globalisation, 456
economic structure, 88, 91, 111
economies of scale, 53, 354, 402
education, 96, 185, 297, 307, 375
efficiency, 65, 80, 131, 147
efficiency phase, 64
efficiency seeking, 324, 325
electronics, 224
elitists, 117
emerging markets, 8, 21, 490
emissions, 86
employees, 382
energy, 88
energy-intensive, 85
energy sector, 436, 437
enterprise autonomy, 47
entrance exam, 190
entrepreneurs, 132
entry strategy, 445
Environmental Kuznets Curve, 87
Equity JV, 399

Ericsson, 415
ethnocentric, 408, 426
EU, 448, 474
European integration, 467
exchange rate, 83, 277, 283
exchange rate system, 277
expats, 408
expenditure approach, 11
export, 209, 215, 218, 221, 226
export dependency, 220, 222, 227
export intensity, 351
export-led growth, 82, 83, 92, 211, 275
export-oriented industry, 66
export strategy, 71, 73
export to GDP ratio, 219
external democracy, 136
external economies of scale, 213
external factors, 389
external risk, 483
external shocks, 283
external view, 23
extrapolation, 478
extraterritorial rule, 26, 27

Face, 365, 371, 372
Facebook, 397
factions, 117
fake products, 405
Falun Gong, 137
family planning, 233, 236
family relationships, 372
fast food, 363
fast-learning, 384
fast-speed train, 449
FDI inflow, 328, 337
FDI outflow, 328, 344
federal reserve, 453
federal state, 480
FedEx, 406
Feng Shui, 370
fertility rate, 232–234, 236
Fila, 431
financial and economic crisis, 59
financial crisis, 288
financial reforms, 315
financial repression, 45, 271
financial sector, 266, 288
firm-specific advantages, 326
first-mover advantage, 408, 410
First Opium War, 25, 26
fiscal policy, 251–253, 255, 257
fiscal stimulus, 90
five-year plan, 32, 77, 145, 149–151, 154, 157, 256
fixed exchange rate, 281
fixed investments, 72
flatteners, 452
flat world, 502
flexibility, 276, 359, 362, 417
floating exchange rate, 276, 281, 283
follow the leader theory, 326
Fonterra, 438
forced savings, 309
forecast, 12, 477
foreign banks, 265, 266
foreign companies, 332
foreign debt, 28
foreign direct investment (FDI), 319, 332, 333, 339, 349, 461
Four Modernisations, 42
Foxconn, 221, 413
fragmentation, 109, 402
franchise systems, 443
franchising, 443
free-market economics, 94
free-market ideology, 499

free trade zones, 159
FrieslandCampina, 438
Fuji, 438

G7, 21, 449, 497
G20, 497
Galanz, 355, 361, 403, 429
gaokao, 190, 369, 491
GATT, 467
GDP targeting, 16
GE, 421, 427
Geely, 350, 428, 429
gender imbalance, 237
gender ratio, 237
geocentric, 426
Germany, 350, 494
ghost cities, 206
Gini coefficient, 170–172, 179
global challengers, 354
global champions, 342
global governance, 466, 483, 502, 504
global governance structure, 473
Global Innovation Index, 491
globalisation, 450, 505
globalisation 1.0, 452
globalisation 2.0, 451, 452
globalisation 3.0, 451
global rules, 469, 505
global strategy, 422
global supply chain, 220, 452
GM, 401, 419
Go Global policy, 342
good enough products, 420
good enough strategy, 359
Google, 397
Gorbachev, 133
Gorbachev Files, 480
governance structure, 113, 114, 120, 123, 124, 129, 428
governance system, 135
government expenditure, 127
government-led growth, 40
government-led industrialisation, 20
government revenues, 127
Government savings, 296, 302
Go-west strategy, 337
gradualism, 123. 165, 19, 39, 55, 68, 78, 97, 444, 464
Great Leap Forward, 9, 33, 41, 123, 231, 310
greenfield investments, 340, 346, 398, 441
gross export, 220
growth model, 59
growth target, 6, 153
GSK, 438
guanxi, 364, 365, 372, 373, 400

Haier, 354, 357, 360
Halo-effect, 3
Han Dynasty, 188
Han emperors, 458
hard-budget constraint, 52
hard landing, 104
hard power, 471
harmonious society, 39, 76, 153, 181
head office, 389, 401, 414, 425, 427
healthcare, 183, 297, 307
heavy industry, 32, 41, 43, 52, 85
Hershey, 411, 418
high-end market, 361
high-skilled labour, 330
holding companies, 348

Home Depot, 388, 391, 394, 401
Honda, 400
Hong Kong, 120, 238, 320, 333, 336, 347, 397
household consumption, 299
household registration system, 187
household responsibility system, 50, 51, 55
household savings, 294, 296, 297
house ownership, 308
housing, 172
housing privatisation, 176, 177
HTC, 431
Huawei, 353, 354
Hu Jintao, 39, 130, 160, 181, 271, 470
hukou, 34, 85, 170, 173, 177, 182, 187, 189, 191, 192, 194, 195, 204, 309
human adaptability, 504
human-centred urbanisation, 196
human development indicator, 47
human resource management, 382
human rights, 137, 475, 505
hump-shaped pattern, 304
hyperglobalisation, 489, 500
hyperinflation, 54

IBM, 355, 367
ideological battle, 498
ideology, 122, 498
IKEA, 392, 394
imbalances, 75, 76, 91, 157
IMF, 136
IMF-conditionality, 462
Imperial China, 20
import, 215, 218, 226
impossible trinity, 284
incentive, 45, 51, 52, 147
inclusive growth, 77, 154, 195, 486
inclusive urbanisation, 206
income distribution, 5, 173
income inequality, 73, 84, 169, 179
income tax, 381
India, 241, 242, 246
indicative targets, 152
indigenous innovation, 229, 492
individualism, 367
indulgence, 368
industrialisation, 32, 67, 200
industrial policy, 75, 330, 334
Industrial Revolution, 20, 21, 94, 136, 456, 503
industrial sector, 81, 98
inequality, 173–175, 185
infant industries, 212, 213
inflation, 10, 11
information revolution, 487, 489
infrastructural investments, 256
infrastructure diplomacy, 324
innovation, 106, 134, 155, 156, 229, 359
innovative behaviour, 129, 459
Institutional reforms, 481
integration, 424, 479
Integration-Responsiveness Grid, 422
intellectual property portfolio, 354
intellectual property rights, 229
InterContinental Hotels, 444
interdependencies, 483
interest margin, 269
interest rate, 252, 264, 267, 271
intermediate control strategies, 399

Internal chaos, 29
internal democracy, 136
internalisation, 321
internalisation advantages, 322
internalising, 399
internal risk, 483
internal view, 23
international currency, 288, 289
International Monetary Fund, 4
international order, 495
Internet penetration, 432
intervention, 276, 280, 282
investment, 12, 70, 103, 223
investment development path, 327, 328
investment-led growth, 72
investment rate, 102
investment share, 79
invisible hand, 147, 165, 487
iPhone, 220, 221, 225, 287
Ireland, 453
iron rice bowl, 39, 52, 80, 307

Japan, 200, 219, 249, 295, 298, 310, 312, 331, 454, 495
Jiangsu province, 238
Jiang Zemin, 58, 116, 159, 341
joint venture, 50, 442, 492
joint venture law, 332
just-in-time, 434

KFC, 363, 378, 404, 412, 418, 420, 423, 432, 440, 444
knowledge-intensive, 325
Kodak, 437, 438
KOF Globalisation Index, 453
Komatsu, 411, 428
Konka, 431
kowtow, 38
Kuaidi Dache, 404
Kuomintang, 30
Kuznets curve, 174

Labour Contract Law, 312
labour costs, 383
labour force, 61, 63, 97, 193, 245
labour law, 184
labour mobility, 189
labour shortage, 243, 244
labour surplus, 66, 193, 196, 245
legal environment, 422
LEGO, 406, 410
lending rate, 84, 272
Lenovo, 353
letters of credit, 288
Lewis turning point, 98, 240, 241, 244
Liaoning province, 8
life-cycle hypothesis, 303
life expectancy, 41, 240
Li Keqiang, 78, 118, 151, 158, 394, 472
Li Keqiang index, 8, 14
Li-Ning, 430
Little Sheep, 440
LLL model, 327
local authorities, 191
local content, 396
local debt, 128, 261
local government, 120, 126, 127, 128, 205, 254, 421, 425
Local Government Financing Vehicles (LGFVs), 260, 263, 270
local initiatives, 49, 68, 122
localisation, 414, 415, 417
local officials, 9, 56

local partner, 442
local responsiveness, 422
local sourcing, 394, 432
location advantages, 323
long-term growth, 99, 100
L'Oréal, 419, 435
Lorenz curve, 170, 171, 182, 183
low-end innovation, 420
low-end market, 403
low-income consumers, 387
low-income countries, 22, 92
low-tech manufacturing, 329

M&A, 340, 346, 357, 398, 461
macroeconomic stability, 68
Made in China, 209, 210
Malthusian catastrophe, 231
managed floating, 279
management skills, 326
managerial capabilities, 322
manager-responsibility, 54
mandarins, 366
mango, 405
man-made data, 7
manufacturing, 73
manufacturing sector, 14, 46, 81, 82
Mao, 33, 34
Maoism, 370
Mao Zedong, 31, 116, 121, 148
marginal propensity to consume, 193
marginal propensity to save, 305, 307
market economy, 91, 147
marketers, 391, 433
market freedom, 142
market seeking, 324, 325
Marks and Spencer, 401
marriage market, 311
Marshall Plan, 461, 471
masculinity, 368
mass-market, 430
mass-market approach, 387
mass middle class, 379
master plan, 49
Maytag, 349
McDonald's, 363, 404, 423, 432, 440, 444
McKinsey, 379
Media Markt, 393, 403, 404
medium-sized enterprises, 262
megacities, 198, 205, 376
melamine scandal, 411
membership, 497
Mercedes Benz, 388, 423
meritocracy, 95, 124, 366
Mexico, 312
middle class, 88, 131–133, 314, 329, 360, 373–375, 457
middle-class society, 456
middle-income, 96
middle-income status, 374
middle-income trap, 92, 93, 161
middle segment, 429
migrants, 197, 199, 309
migrant workers, 173, 181, 187, 188, 193, 306
Mindray, 356, 430
minimum wage, 247, 248, 312
minority holdings, 346
misalignment, 286
mixed economy, 148
mixed ownership, 111, 139, 141
mixed system, 146, 147
mobilisation phase, 65, 66
mode of entry, 389, 399

modernising, 384
mom and pop shops, 394
monetary authorities, 280
monetary policy, 251, 263, 264, 272, 285
money supply, 282
monopolised industries, 180
moral compass, 474
moral hazard, 36
mortgages, 308, 314
M&S, 396, 444
multidomestic strategy, 427
multilateral governance structure, 490, 495
multilateral institutions, 471
multilateralism, 462, 470
multilateral system, 465
multilateral trading system, 447, 482
multinational enterprise (MNE), 319, 324, 386, 397, 451
multi-party system, 119
multiple hats, 113
mutual interest, 373

Nanjing, 30
national census, 7
National Commission for Development and Reform, 150
National People's Congress, 115, 118, 149
nation state, 135
NDRC, 352
Needham puzzle, 22
negative list, 336
neo-colonialism, 461
Nestlé, 432, 443
net export, 46, 70, 71, 222, 223, 227
Netherlands, 367, 453
net outward investment position, 327
New China, 15
new economy, 14
Newly Industrialising Countries (NICs), 496
new normal, 104, 229
New Zealand, 380
Nike, 334, 335, 387, 430
Nissan, 412
non-intervention, 29
non-performing loans, 69, 261, 267
non-state sector, 56
numbers, 370
Nyenrode Business University, 482

Obama, 247
OEM, 361
off-balance activities, 269
off-budget expenditures, 254
off-farm wage, 51
Official Development Aid, 345
official reserves, 289
offshore, 348
oil, 86
Old China, 15
old economy, 14
OLI framework, 321
oligopolistic reaction theory, 326
OLI theory, 322
One Belt One Road, 157, 290, 323, 343, 469
one-child policy, 135, 233–235, 238, 243, 247–249
one country, two systems, 39

one-size-fits-all, 463
onward journeying, 348
open-door policy, 44
opening up, 47, 62, 142, 154, 499
openness, 105, 222, 377
operating model, 414
operational autonomy, 333
operational excellence, 415, 416, 428
Opium, 25
original equipment manufacturer, 355
output method, 11
outward FDI, 347
overcapacity, 108, 111, 141, 157, 383, 402, 470
ownership advantages, 322
ownership freedom, 142
ownership structure, 143

parenting, 369
Paris climate agreement, 452
Paris Treaty, 87
participation rate, 245
Party Congress, 118
party secretaries, 115, 131
party-state bureaucracy, 115
patents, 493, 494
Paternalism, 366
pegged exchange rate, 278
pension, 155, 178, 307
pension system, 488
Peoples Bank of China (PBC), 252, 268, 273
People's Liberation Army, 113
permanent income hypothesis, 303
personal relations, 373
P&G, 410, 418–421, 427
Philips, 335, 424, 429, 430, 438
pilot projects, 55, 68
Piraeus, 350
Pirelli, 355
planned economy, 146, 189
planning system, 31
plenum, 158, 160, 468
Politburo, 16, 117, 121
political choices, 19
political scenarios, 486
political structure, 113
political supremacy, 490
political system, 119, 121
polycentric, 425
population, 235, 379
populists, 117
Porsche, 410
portfolio investment, 319
positive list, 336
positive-sum game, 466
post-reform period, 31
poverty, 35, 172
power distance, 367, 368
power transition, 494, 495
pragmatism, 95, 123
precautionary savings, 305, 308, 314
premium price, 380
premium segment, 433
pre-reform period, 31, 34, 37, 41
price-sensitive, 359
price sensitivity, 393
price system, 57
princeling, 118, 125
private consumption, 303
private firms, 271
private ownership, 32, 177

private sector, 267
privatisation, 63, 104, 176, 501
processing trade, 215, 216, 218, 220, 225
productivity, 51, 61, 65–67, 91, 98, 105, 106, 156, 196, 201, 213, 246, 375
product life cycle, 352
product portfolio, 392, 424
profitability, 301
project finance, 345
promotion process, 152
property rights, 229
property taxes, 208
prosperity, 295
protectionism, 213, 214, 216, 465
provincial GDP, 10
public debt, 251
public housing, 204
public–private partnership, 141
public schools, 194
purchasing power, 174, 288
purchasing power parity, 458

Qing administration, 25
Qing Dynasty, 20, 23

rare earth, 498
rationalisation, 110
R&D, 106, 227, 228, 420
real estate, 437
rebalancing, 59, 75, 78, 84, 96, 97, 100, 101, 107, 152, 154, 156, 206, 226, 228, 259, 274, 506
red tape, 395
red-tapism, 409
reform, 226, 300
reform trinity, 161, 162
regional initiatives, 341, 476
regionalism, 462
regulatory environment, 381
Renault, 409, 411
renminbi, 275, 281, 287, 291
replacement rate, 235
Republic of China, 30
reserve currency, 290
reserve requirement ratio, 273
reserves, 282
residence card, 195, 196
resource seeking, 324, 325
retail deposits, 273
retailers, 422
retail sales, 15, 313
retirement, 304
retirement age, 240, 242
revaluation, 279
risk perception, 437
round-tripping, 5, 320, 333, 338, 348
rule-based, 384, 498
rule-based system, 475
rule by law, 125
rule of law, 95, 125, 126
rural consumers, 360
rural inequality, 178, 179

SAFE, 342, 352
Safe-haven, 290
SAIC, 350, 357
Samsung, 427
SANY, 429
SARS, 411
SASAC, 140, 346, 455
savings, 293
savings rate, 295, 304
savings ratio, 296
scenario, 477
Second Opium War, 27
segmentation, 417

self-made entrepreneurs, 375
self-sufficiently, 109
sensitive sectors, 334
service, 16, 99, 375
service sector, 67, 68, 81, 82, 107, 206, 468
seven pillars, 94, 130
sex ratio, 311
shadow banking, 269
shadow banking system, 261
shadow banks, 270
shadow bank system, 262
Shanghai FTZ, 272, 336
short-term growth, 99
Siemens, 430
silk route, 469
silver, 24
Singapore, 380
skilled labour, 382
small- and medium-sized enterprises (SMEs), 84, 301, 315
smart globalisation, 502
smiling curve, 227, 228
social housing system, 177
socialist harmonious society, 60
socialist market economy, 159, 169
social media, 137, 397
social mobility, 95, 187
social safety net, 307
social security, 183
social security coverage, 308
social security system, 315
social spending, 107, 175, 181, 183, 184, 194, 207, 257, 302
Social unrest, 134
SOE reform, 62, 138–140, 162
SOEs, 107, 108, 254, 258, 297, 301, 341
soft-budget constraint, 36, 37, 40, 50, 53, 138
soft landing, 257
soft loans, 325, 345
soft power, 471, 472, 475
solar panels, 108
Song Dynasty, 188
South Korea, 103, 200, 238, 246, 295, 298, 300, 331, 381, 454
sovereignty, 500, 501
sovereign wealth fund, 340
Special Drawing Rights, 289
special economic zones, 47, 331, 377
speculation, 207, 290
spillover effects, 23, 338
spillovers, 79, 201
springboard perspective, 327
spring festival, 244
Standing Committee, 117, 118
state capitalism, 213, 455
State Council, 114, 118, 120, 150, 158, 192, 205
state-owned banks, 36
state-owned enterprises, 35, 138, 145
State Planning Commission, 148
stimulus package, 70, 109, 217, 245, 253, 256, 258
stimulus plan, 90
stock indices, 453
stock market, 266, 308
strategic asset seeking, 324, 325
strategic sectors, 106
structural changes, 7
structural development, 17
structural reforms, 60, 67, 76, 93, 94, 101, 156, 260, 274, 468
structural shift, 14, 492
structural transformation, 78

stuck in the middle, 433
subsidies, 436
Sun Yat-sen, 29
supply chain, 452
supply-side, 96
surplus countries, 216, 217
surplus of labour, 64
system challenger, 498

3-8-3 plan, 161
Taiwan, 103, 120, 238, 300, 310, 445, 488
take-off, 79, 88, 112, 131, 133
takeovers, 330
Tang Dynasty, 38
Taobao, 405, 407
Taoism, 364, 369
targets, 145, 148, 149
target savers, 264, 309
taxation treaties, 342
tax havens, 320, 348
tax reform, 128, 255, 302, 381
tax structure, 182
tax system, 182
TCL, 355, 361, 431
technology, 349
technology sharing, 492
technology transfer, 213, 340
technological improvement, 88
technological leader, 472
technological progress, 65, 502
technological shift, 490
Tencent, 398
theory of economic backwardness, 47
Tiananmen Square, 46, 57, 69
Tibet, 120, 488
timing, 351
Tito, 479
Tokyo Round, 467
top-down management, 368
total quality management, 434
Totole, 443
townification, 205
township and village enterprises (TVEs), 50, 51, 55, 63, 178
Toyota, 408
trade corporations, 458
trade deficit, 24
trade dependency, 229
trade disequilibrium, 287, 291
trade imbalance, 222, 459
trade liberalisation, 63
trade openness, 460
trade structure, 224
trade surplus, 216, 217, 223, 279
trade tensions, 230
trade union, 358, 412
trading band, 281
traditional growth model, 75
transaction costs, 321
transfer technology, 339
transformation, 331
transition, 463
transnational strategy, 424
transparency, 13, 129
transparent, 384, 488
treasury bills, 286
Treaty of Nanjing, 26
Treaty of Tianjin, 27
Trump, 134, 247, 448, 472
two-child policy, 236, 238

Uber, 390, 392, 395, 404, 435
unbalanced growth, 48
uncertainty, 295, 297, 367
undervaluation, 279, 285
undervalued, 75
unemployment, 140, 153, 181, 189
unequal treaties, 27, 28, 463

unfair competition, 211, 212
United Kingdom, 22, 474, 494
United States, 246, 312, 336, 367, 448, 456, 474, 494
UN Security Council, 497
unskilled labour, 382
upgrading, 225
upper middle class, 379
Uppsala model, 441, 444–445
upstream activities, 228
Urban Development Investment Corporations, 205
urban inequality, 180
urban infrastructure, 207
urbanisation, 102, 157, 187, 197, 200, 203, 205, 310–311
urbanisation rate, 199
US–China disequilibrium, 286
US manufacturing jobs, 459
US trade deficit, 218
utilisation degree, 109, 110

value added, 72, 216, 221, 227, 339, 454
value-added concept, 9
value chain, 415
value proposition, 414
Vanguard, 485
vertical cooperation, 202
vested interest, 56, 111, 123, 165, 194, 480
Volkswagen, 408
Volvo, 350
voting power, 319, 466, 476

Wage, 184, 191, 248, 306, 313
Wahaha, 400
Walmart, 226, 386, 402, 419, 448
Washington Consensus, 68, 462–464, 496, 499, 501, 505
Wealth management products, 270, 271
WeChat, 398
Wen Jiabao, 76, 181, 193
western-centred system, 497
western development strategy, 335
westernising, 363, 384
Whirlpool, 349, 407
wholly foreign-owned enterprise law, 333
working-age population, 239, 241, 246
World Bank, 379
World Economic Forum, 78, 480
WTO, 159, 213, 214, 219, 497
WTO accession process, 468
WTO dispute settlement, 460
WTO dispute settlement body, 475
WTO membership, 467

Xiaomi, 353, 357, 431
Xi Jinping, 118, 122, 196, 435, 470, 484, 488, 506

yen, 284
Yin and Yang, 366, 369, 370
Yin–Yang, 49
Yugoslavia, 479
Yum!, 439

zero-sum game, 466
Zhejiang Province, 55
Zheng, 458
Zhou Enlai, 42
ZTE, 356

CPSIA information can be obtained
at www.ICGtesting.com
Printed in the USA
BVHW041748190319
543081BV00007B/9/P

9 789813 200272